FOREST RESOURCE POLICY

FOREST RESOURCE POLICY

Frederick W. Cubbage
Southeastern Forest Experiment Station
U.S.D.A. Forest Service
Research Triangle Park, North Carolina

Jay O'Laughlin
University of Idaho
College of Forestry, Wildlife and Range Sciences
Moscow, Idaho

Charles S. Bullock III
University of Georgia
Department of Political Science
Athens, Georgia

JOHN WILEY & SONS, INC.
New York Chichester Brisbane Toronto Singapore

ACQUISITIONS EDITOR	Sally Cheney
MARKETING MANAGER	Cathy Faduska
PRODUCTION SUPERVISOR	Marcia Craig
DESIGNER	Lynn Rogan
MANUFACTURING MANAGER	Andrea Price
COPY EDITING SUPERVISOR	Linda Pawelchak
ILLUSTRATION	Jaime Perea

This book was set in ITC Garamond Light by Publication Services and printed and bound by Hamilton Printing Co.

Library of Congress Cataloging in Publication Data

Cubbage, Frederick W.
    Forest resource policy / Frederick W. Cubbage, Jay O'Laughlin,
Charles S. Bullock III.
       p.   cm.
    Includes index.
    ISBN 0–471–62245–1 (cloth : acid-free paper)
    1. Forest policy—United States.   I. O'Laughlin, Jay.
II. Bullock, Charles S., 1942– .   III. Title.
SD565.C83   1993   92-39046
333.75'0973—dc20   CIP

About The Authors

Frederick W. Cubbage is the Research Project Leader of the Economics of Forest Protection and Management Research Work Unit, Southeastern Forest Experiment Station, U.S.D.A. Forest Service, Research Triangle Park, North Carolina. He also holds an appointment as a Professor in the Department of Forestry, North Carolina State University, Raleigh, North Carolina. From 1982 to 1991, Cubbage was an assistant, associate, and full professor at the University of Georgia School of Forest Resources, where he taught and performed research in forest resource policy and forest economics. Fred received his M.S. and Ph.D. degrees at the University of Minnesota College of Forest Resources and a B.S. degree in forestry at Iowa State University. He also worked as a service forester for the state of Kentucky and a research forester with the Southern Forest Experiment Station. He is the author or coauthor of about 200 scientific and professional articles on forest resource policy and economics topics. Cubbage has been recognized in the first Who's Who in Science and Engineering and in Who's Who in the South and Southwest, has served on the Resources for the Future Forest Resource Economics and Policy Advisory Board, has received several research awards, and has served as an officer in the Society of American Foresters and Forest Products Research Society.

Jay O'Laughlin is the Director of the Idaho Forest, Wildlife, and Range Policy Analysis Group at the University of Idaho, a position created by the Idaho legislature in 1989 to provide objective analysis of the impacts of natural resource issues and proposals. He is an Adjunct Professor in the Departments of Forest Resources and Forest Products at the University of Idaho's College of Forestry, Wildlife and Range Sciences. He received his M.S. and Ph.D. degrees in forestry from the University of Minnesota, and has a B.S. in Business Administration from the University of Denver. After service as an artillery officer in Vietnam, he worked in the outdoor recreation products business before enrolling in forestry school. In the 1980s, Jay taught and conducted research in forest policy and economics in the Department of Forest Science at Texas A&M University.

Charles S. Bullock, III is the Richard B. Russell Professor of Political Science at the University of Georgia. He received his Ph.D. from Washington University in St. Louis, and has performed research on Congress, civil rights, and policy implementation. He is the author or coauthor of 11 books and more than 100 articles, including the biennial *Georgia Political Almanac*. He has served as president of the Southern Political Science Association and as an officer in the American Political Science Association. Bullock has been recognized for outstanding teacher by the Department of Political Science and the Honors Program at the University of Georgia, and received the university's Creative Research Award in 1991. He also has received research grants from the National Science Foundation and the National Institute of Education.

Preface

This textbook on forest resource policy culminates many years of work on an increasingly important subject. Most of the issues and problems facing resource professionals today are related to public opinions about and demands for use of forest resources. The state of our biophysical knowledge, skills, and teaching has advanced rapidly in the last two decades. At the same time, the study of forest policy has developed into a separate educational and scientific discipline, drawing upon political science as well as traditional forestry, wildlife, recreation, and range management. This textbook is designed to provide a synthesis of policy analysis frameworks, civics, and forest resource programs to help teach resource professionals about political processes and resource management.

The textbook is intended for classes composed of upper-level undergraduate students or graduate students. It assumes that the students will have had classes in American government, and will vaguely remember the concepts, but not many of the details. The book relies on classic and modern political science literature to discuss the policy process in order to help conceptualize how policy is made, institutional analyses in order to understand how the government and interest groups participate, and case studies of how they seek political advantages in setting policies and controlling resources. The last section of the text discusses the forestry, wildlife, range and recreation programs, and laws that are the result of politics, and integrate political process material discussed earlier with the current status of forest resource programs. This integration of processes, participants, programs, and cases should help re-

source professionals understand how public values and opinions about forests are formed and coalesced, and how they are developed into public programs, affecting both public and private forests. This synthesis should help students understand current programs and politics, and help them anticipate future issues and respond better as resource managers. The book also should serve as a standard reference for information on forest resource laws and programs.

The book is divided into three sections and an appendix. It is meant for use in one quarter or semester course. All or some of the chapters may be used in a course depending on the topical interests of the instructor and the time available.

The first section of the book, consisting of five chapters, examines the political processes that distribute and allocate power and resources in the United States. Chapter 1 introduces two cases illustrating how policy affects resource management, discusses the importance of policy, and reviews forest resources. Chapter 2 outlines the forest policy process based on modern political science approaches. Chapter 3 discusses the historical and modern debates about the use of markets or government to allocate resources—debates that underlie many of our public issues and politics today. Chapter 4 discusses how issues arise, attract a larger audience, and are placed on agendas for consideration. Chapter 5 discusses the criteria used for evaluation and implementation of forest resource programs.

The second section of the textbook covers the participants in the policy process. Chapter

6 discusses the legislature; Chapter 7 the executive branch; Chapter 8 the courts. Chapter 9 discusses the role of interest groups in making forest resource policy. Additionally, due to their increasing importance, Chapter 10 examines environmentalism and professional ethics. Last, Chapter 11 in this section examines the influence of the media in forest resource policy–making.

The final section of the textbook summarizes information on forest resource programs, laws, and policies. Chapter 12 discusses public land ownership and policies; national forest management laws are examined in detail in Chapter 13. Chapter 14 discusses environmental regulation in the United States; Chapter 15 wildlife and fisheries law; and Chapter 16 forest practices regulation. Chapter 17 summarizes the direct and indirect forestry programs designed to assist nonindustrial private forest landowners. The last chapter in the book provides an overview of international forestry issues and programs.

The appendices of the book provide references for the laws affecting forest resources. Appendix A briefly summarizes the principal laws in forestry, wildlife, range, and recreation. Appendix B provides a primer on using and citing legal references, which are necessary for policy study. Appendix C lists the common acronyms in forest resource policy that we could identify.

In total, this book will help one study and teach forest resource policy. We hope it can help instill knowledge and spark interest in the subject that will form the basis for most resource management decisions in the future. No longer can resource professionals use their best scientific knowledge to manage resources without undue public interference, if indeed they ever could. Our success at managing scarce resources in the future will depend on our skill at divining, responding to, and guiding public demands as reflected in the political process. We hope this book will be of significant assistance in that exciting endeavor.

FWC
JOL
CSB

Acknowledgments

Many persons deserve thanks for helping us complete this book. First, we thank our families, who patiently endured the efforts it took over the last few years while writing the book intruded upon our home, as well as professional, life. Second, we would like to thank our colleagues and students who have contributed by providing insights, suggestions, and criticisms that helped improve the contents and presentation of the innumerable drafts of various chapters. Those individuals who helped contribute directly to the completion of the textbook are listed below. To those who are not acknowledged specifically, many thanks also are due for helping us develop this text. Any errors of omission or commission, of course, remain our responsibility.

People who have contributed to this textbook include a few persons who have written small vignettes; many persons who have reviewed all or parts of the textbook; and persons that have helped type, edit, or produce the textbook. A brief draft on the book was written by Fred Cubbage in 1986 with teaching fellowship funding while he was an Eli Lilly Teaching Fellow at the University of Georgia. Charles Bullock served as a Lilly "mentor" at that time. Ron Mulach wrote preliminary drafts of the legal material in Appendices A and B while he was a law student at the University of Georgia, and has critiqued the forest planning chapter since becoming a lawyer with the USDA Office of General Counsel. Chris Deforest, research coordinator at the University of Georgia, wrote and revised the illustration on the Washington State Wilderness Act in Chapter 6, and provided thorough and constructive reviews for every chapter

at one stage. Our interests in forest policy were triggered by Paul Ellefson, who served as an M.S. advisor for Cubbage and a Ph.D. advisor for O'Laughlin at the University of Minnesota. While at the University of Washington, Debra Salazar provided a thorough critique of and added many helpful suggestions to the 1986 version of the Teaching Fellow drafts, and provided many insights about our approach. Several persons provided key background materials for some of the case studies, including Bob Warren at Georgia for the bobcat introduction case in Chapter 1, Debra Salazar for the clear-cutting case in Chapter 2, Richard Hardt and Tom Coffin at Georgia for the national management discussion in Chapter 13, and Mary Elfner at Georgia for the wetlands permit system description in Chapter 14.

Reviewers for the textbook include many anonymous individuals who examined drafts submitted for publication, and many more who reviewed it once it was accepted. The formal reviewers who provided suggestions on part or all of the textbook include Dave Field at the University of Maine, Ben Twight at Pennsylvania State University, Jo Ellen Force at the University of Idaho, Sam Brock at West Virginia University, Harold Wisdom at Virginia Polytechnic Institute and State University, Stephen Daniels at Oregon State University, William Kurtz at the University of Missouri, Steven Bullard at Mississippi State University, and Alan Dyer at Colorado State University. Several other individuals also have used drafts of the book in their classes or read parts of it, and provided verbal feedback. These include David Newman at the University of Georgia, Dennis Le Master at Purdue University, Larry Teeter at Auburn University, and Karen Potter-Witter at Michigan State University.

Many individuals have helped prepare the textbook as well. Laura Edwards at the University of Georgia School of Forest Resources has typed the entire manuscript at least twice, and many chapters more times than that, with great alacrity, skill and tolerance. Other secretaries who helped at Georgia or in North Carolina include Bonnie Fancher, Annelle Nelms, and Judy Talmon. Chris DeForest helped draw graphics for many of the figures. Many research studies also contributed to parts of this text indirectly. The excellent editorial and graphics staff at Wiley and copy editor Linda Pawelchak were perceptive and prompt in making constructive suggestions. Many other persons have contributed to the textbook in some fashion, albeit without mention here. To all who helped this become a reality—thanks!

FWC
JOL
CSB

Brief Contents

PART I   PROCESSES   1

Chapter 1   Forest Resources and
Public Policy   3

Chapter 2   Policy and Political
Processes   23

Chapter 3   Markets, Government,
and Forest Resources   42

Chapter 4   Policy Issues and
Formulation   76

Chapter 5   Policy Analysis,
Evaluation,
and Implementation   98

PART II   PARTICIPANTS   123

Chapter 6   The Legislature   125

Chapter 7   The Executive Branch   153

Chapter 8   The Judiciary and
the Law   176

Chapter 9   Interest Groups   201

Chapter 10   Environmentalism,
Conservation, Ethics,
and Professionalism   226

Chapter 11   Mass Media and
the Forestry Message   253

PART III   PROGRAMS   281

Chapter 12   Public Ownership and
Management of Land   283

Chapter 13   Multiple Use Forestry
and Forest Planning   327

Chapter 14   Federal Environmental
Protection and Regulation   352

Chapter 15   Wildlife Management
and Protection Policy   384

Chapter 16   Regulation of Forest
Practices   420

Chapter 17   Public Assistance for
Private Owners   446

Chapter 18   Forest Resource Policy
in a Global Context   494

APPENDICES   528

Appendix A   Principal Federal Laws
Relating to Forestry, Wildlife and
Fisheries, Range, and Recreation   528

Appendix B   An Introduction to
Legal Research and Citation   540

Appendix C   Forest Resource Policy
Acronymns   547

Contents

PART I   PROCESSES

Chapter 1   Forest Resources and Public Policy   3

Introduction   3
Forestry and Wildlife in the 1990s   4
  Public Opinion and Forestry in
    Texas   5
    Timber Salvage and Replanting
      Efforts   5
    Public Protest and Eventual
      Outcome   6
  Reintroduction of Bobcats on
    Cumberland Island National
    Seashore   6
    NEPA and the Environmental
      Assessment   8
    Public Comments   8
    The Media   9
    Public Meetings   9
    Outcome   9
  The Importance of Public Policy   10
Forest Area and Ownership   10
  Extent of Forests   10
    Closed Forest/Open Forest   11
    Timberland/Woodland   11
    Softwood/Hardwood   13
    Developed Nations/Developing
      Nations   13
    Industrial Wood/Fuelwood   13
  Ownership of Forests   15
    United States of America   15
    Other Nations   15
Forests and Public Policy   16
  Elements of Policy   17
  Instruments of Policy   18
  Definition of Forest Policy   18
  Illustration: Forest Policy
    Statements   19
Plan of the Book   21
Literature Cited   21

Chapter 2   Policy and Political Processes   23

The Study of Forest Policy   23
  Alternative Approaches   23
    Historical   23
    Illustration: Stages of Forestry
      Development   23
    Institutional   23
    Illustration: U.S. Forest Service
      Organization   25
    Process or Analysis   28
  Our Approach   28
Objectives of Forest Policy   28
  Social Objectives   30
  Illustration: Forestry Ends and
    Means Hierarchy   30
  Conflicts among Objectives   30
Analysis of Policy Processes   31
  Policy Process Model   31
  Levels of Politics   33
  Illustration: The Clear-cutting
    Controversy   33
    Clear-cutting Begins in the 1950s   34
    Opposition Mounts in the 1970s   34
    The Monongahela Decision
      of 1975   36
    The National Forest Management
      Act of 1976   36
    Controversy Continues in
      the 1980s   37
  Process Model Applications and
    Limitations   37
Initial Realities about Politics   39
Summary   40
Literature Cited   41

Chapter 3   Markets, Government, and Forest Resources   42

Introduction   42
Forests and American Values   44
  Individualism   44

Community   45
Integration   45
Market and Nonmarket Goods   46
Forest Outputs and Issues   47
  Timber   47
  Wildlife   47
  Range   48
  Water   48
  Recreation   49
  Wilderness   49
  Others   50
Markets and Forest Resources   51
  Neoclassical Economic Theory   51
  Efficient Market Requirements   51
  Public Choice Theory   53
  Illustration: Privatization of the
    New Zealand Forest Service   54
  Market Failure   55
    Property Rights and Privatization   55
    Nonmarket Costs and Benefits   55
    Imperfect Knowledge   57
    Imperfect Competition   58
  Equity   58
    Distribution of Benefits   59
    Justification for Forest Resource
      Programs   59
  Allocation Criteria   60
  Illustration: Historic Forestry Debates   61
    Market Proponents   61
    Government Advocates   64
Government and Forestry   64
  Economic Systems   65
  Conservation and the Land Ethic   67
  Decision Guidelines   68
  Illustration: Modern Forestry Debates   69
    Market Proponents   69
    Government Advocates   70
Summary   72
Literature Cited   72

**Chapter 4   Policy Issues and
  Formulation   76**

Introduction   76
Problems and Issues   76
  Problem Formation   77
  Issue Creation   77
  Issue Types   79
  Illustration: U.S. Forest Service Issue
    Identification   79
Agendas and Issue Expansion   80
  Interest Group Involvement   81
  Issue Expansion   81

Issue Characteristics   83
Symbols and Expansion Strategy   83
Applications   86
Policy Formulation and Adoption   87
  Participants   88
    National   88
    State   89
  Adoption Processes   89
    Rationalism   89
    Incrementalism   90
    Mixed Scanning   93
Alternative Dispute Resolution   93
  Mediation and Negotiation   93
  Illustration: Washington State
    Agreements   94
    Timber/Fish/Wildlife   94
    Sustainable Forestry Roundtable   95
Summary   95
Literature Cited   95

**Chapter 5   Policy Analysis,
  Evaluation, and Implementation   98**

Introduction   98
Analysis and Advocacy   98
Decision and Evaluation Criteria   99
  Ecological   100
    Preserving Options   100
    Biological Diversity   101
  Economic   102
    Efficiency   103
    Sustainability   104
  Social   104
    Freedom   105
    Equity   105
    Decision Processes   106
    Acceptability and Practicality   106
  Political   107
  Integration   107
  Illustration: The Forestry
    Incentives Program   108
    Efficiency   108
    Equity   109
    Capital Substitution and Supply
      Increases   109
Implementation Success   110
  Specific Goals   111
  Quantitative Standards   112
  Program Monitoring   112
  Agency Commitment and Enforcement   113
  Executive and Legislative Commitment   114
  Costs and Benefits   115
  Direct Federal Involvement   115

Program Evaluation   116
  Purposes   116
  Illustration: Bureau of Land
    Management Grazing Policy
    Enforcement   116
      The General Accounting Office   117
      Bureau of Land Management
        Grazing Policies   117
      BLM Trespass Detection Efforts 117
      GAO Recommendations   118
Summary   119
Literature Cited   119

PART II   PARTICIPANTS

Chapter 6   The Legislature   125

Introduction   125
Legislative Powers   125
  Enact Legislation   126
    Constitutional Authority   126
    The Law   126
    Illustration: Washington State
      Wilderness Act of 1984   127
  Raise and Allocate Funds   130
    Raising Revenues   130
    Appropriating Expenditures   134
    Illustration: Funding State Forestry
      Fisheries, and Wildlife Programs 134
    Developing Budgets   136
  Oversight   138
  Limitations   139
    Constitutional   139
    Judicial   139
    Executive   140
Legislative Process   140
Legislative Organization   142
  Types of Committees   143
    Conference Committees   143
    Standing Committees   143
  Functions of Committees   143
    Hearings   144
    Actions   144
    Natural Resources   145
  Congressional Staff   146
    Personal   146
    Committee   146
Individual Legislators   147
  Influential Factors   147
  Issue Selection   148
  Illustration: Pork Barrel and
    National Parks   149
  Representative Philosophy   149

Summary   150
Literature Cited   150

Chapter 7   The Executive Branch   153

The Presidency   153
  Powers   154
    Appointment   154
    Supervision   155
    Legislation   155
    Budget   156
    Foreign Policy   157
  Limitations   158
  Illustration: The Forest Conservation
    Movement under Theodore
    Roosevelt   159
  Congressional Relations   161
  Executive Office of the President   161
    Office of Management and Budget   161
    Council of Economic Advisors   163
    Council on Environmental Quality 163
The Bureaucracy   164
  Policy Formation and
    Implementation   164
  The Iron Triangle   166
  Natural Resource Agencies   167
  Interagency Relationships   169
  Bureaucratic Power   170
  Bureaucratic Problems   171
  Illustration: The Forest Service as
    a Bureaucracy   171
Summary   173
Literature Cited   174

Chapter 8   The Judiciary and
  the Law   176

Introduction   176
Legal Citations   176
Law and Public Policy   178
  Types of Law   178
  Sources of Law   179
  Illustration: The National
    Environmental Policy Act   179
Judicial Powers   182
  Judicial Review   182
  Facts versus Values   182
Judicial Structure   183
  District Courts   184
  Illustration: Wetlands Clearing in
    Louisiana   184
  Appellate Courts   186

Illustration: Timber Harvesting
Practices on the Monongahela
National Forest   187
Supreme Court   188
Standing to Sue   188
Land Use Regulation   189
Special Courts   189
State Courts   189
Illustration: Rural Property Taxes in
Georgia   189
Judicial Actions   191
Decision Processes   191
Remedies   192
Courts and Public Policy   193
Advantages   193
Criticisms   194
Illustration: The Woodpecker and
the Judge   195
National Forest Woodpecker
Management   196
Texas Committee on Natural
Resources and Forest Reform
Network   197
Recent RCW Action   197
Summary   198
Literature Cited   198

Chapter 9   Interest Groups   201

Introduction   201
Models of Group Participation   202
Group Theory   202
Iron Triangles and Specialization   203
Issue Networks   203
Political Parties   205
Types of Interest Groups   206
Citizen Interests Groups   206
Principal Environmental Groups   206
Environmental Group Classifications   209
Trade Associations   212
Professional Associations and Research
Groups   213
Decision Making in Interest Groups   215
Development   215
Structure   216
Process   216
Strategies   217
Tactics   218
Direct Communication   218
Group Member Influence   219
Campaign Contributions and PACs   219
Endorsements and Voting Records   221
Public Relations   221
Problems of Interest Groups   221

Summary   223
Literature Cited   223

Chapter 10   Environmentalism,
Conservation, Ethics, and
Professionalism   226

Introduction   226
Environmentalism and Conservation   226
The Conservation Movement   228
Illustration: The American Forestry
Association and the Creation of
the National Forests   228
Utilitarianism versus Preservation   229
Environmentalists and Conservation   230
Who Is an Environmentalist?   230
The Environmental Movement   231
Critics of Environmentalism   232
Environmental Values and the Needs
Hierarchy   233
Illustration: Environmentalism—
Business Becomes a Believer   234
Conservation Ethics   236
Attitudes toward Nature   237
Deep Ecology   237
Resource Managers   238
Environmental Ethics   238
Leopold's Land Ethic   240
A New Ethic?   241
Old Biases   242
Cooperation and Leadership   242
Professionalism and Ethics   243
Definition of a Profession   243
Code of Ethics   244
Society of American Foresters   244
The Wildlife Society   246
Illustration: Applications of
Professional Ethics   246
Summary   248
Literature Cited   248

Chapter 11   Mass Media and
the Forestry Message   253

Mass Communication   253
Illustration: Herbicide Protests and
the Media   254
Herbicide Hazards   254
Media Involvement   254
Public Relations   255
Media Roles   256
News Reporting and Interpretation   256

Advertisements and Public Relations   258
Education and Entertainment   259
Media Types   260
  Print Media   260
    Newspapers   260
    Magazines   261
    Books   264
  Electronic Broadcasting Media   265
    Radio   265
    Television   266
  Motion Pictures   267
    Forestry and Hollywood   267
    Educational Films and
      Videocassettes   268
The Media and Forest Resources   268
  Advertising   268
  Illustration: The Rio Earth Summit   269
  Public Relations   269
  Illustration: Fernow and Pinchot—Early
    Forestry Promoters   270
  Resource Managers' Public Image   272
  Professionals and the Media   273
    Use of Symbols   273
    Meet the Press   274
Media Effectiveness   275
  Media Power Research   275
  Agenda Setting   275
  Forestry and Wildlife Influences   276
Summary   277
Literature Cited   277

PART III   PROGRAMS

Chapter 12   Public Ownership
  and Management of Land   283

Introduction   283
Early American Land Policy   284
  Expanding the Public
    Domain   285
  Disposing of the Public Lands   287
  Illustration: Looting the Public
    Domain   288
  Retaining Public Lands   289
    Federal Forest Reserves   290
    Roosevelt Expands the
      Reserves   291
    Eastern National Forest
      Purchases   291
Federal Land Management
  Agencies   292
The Department of the Interior   292
  History   292
    Agency Evolution   292
    The 1900s   293

National Park Service   294
  The National Park System   294
  Park Land Types   295
  Current Outdoor Recreation
    Programs   296
Bureau of Reclamation   297
Bureau of Land Management   298
  The Grazing Service   298
  The New BLM   299
  The Federal Land Policy
    and Management Act
    of 1976   300
  Current BLM Practices   300
  Rangeland Issues   300
Fish and Wildlife Service   302
  Early Legislation   302
  A New Agency   303
  Current Programs   303
Bureau of Indian Affairs   303
The USDA Forest Service   304
  Land Areas   304
  Policies and Issues   304
Other Public Lands   307
  The Department of Defense   307
  The Corps of Engineers   307
  State and Local   308
Modern Public Land
  Reservations   309
  Wilderness   309
    Early Efforts   310
    The Wilderness Act of 1964   311
  Wild and Scenic Rivers   312
  National Trails   313
  Alaska National Lands   313
    Statehood and Native Claims   314
    The Tongass National Forest   314
    The Arctic National Wildlife
      Refuge   315
Illustration: Old Growth, Wildlife,
  and Values   316
  Facts and Values   316
  Participants   317
  Continuing Issues   317
Land Acquisitions   319
  Ongoing Purchases   319
  Illustration: The Land and Water
    Conservation Fund   320
    Establishment and
      Structure   320
    Revenue Sources and
      Disbursements   321
    Accomplishments   321
    Ongoing Issues   321
Summary   322
Literature Cited   323

Chapter 13   Multiple Use Forestry and Forest Planning   327

Forest Management Planning Policy   327
Multiple-Use Planning   328
  Public Demands on National Forests   329
  Multiple-Use Sustained-Yield Act (MUSYA) of 1960   330
  Multiple Criticisms   331
Comprehensive Planning   332
  Forest and Rangeland Renewable Resources Planning Act of 1974 (RPA)   332
  National Forest Management Act (NFMA) of 1976   334
    Contents   334
    Implications   336
  The Planning and Appeal Process   337
  Illustration: The Administrative Appeal of the Harper Cliffs Timber Sale   338
    The Process   339
    The Issues   339
    The Outcome   339
  RPA/NFMA Debates   340
    Critics   340
    Advocates   341
  National Forest Planning Today   342
  Forest Planning and Conflict Resolution   344
    Market Approach   344
    Legislative-Judicial Approach   345
    Negotiated Approach   345
  A Retrospective View   341
Summary   347
Literature Cited   347

Chapter 14   Federal Environmental Protection and Regulation   352

Early Forest and Environmental Policy   352
  Colonial America   353
  The United States   354
    Proposed Federal Forestry Regulation   354
    Federal Wildlife Law   354
    Beginning Forest Practice Law   355
    Mid-Century Conservation   356
  The Taking Issue   356
    Early Decisions   357
    Diminution of Value and Public Interest   358
    Modern Regulatory Powers   359
    Recent Court Decisions   360

National Environmental Policy   361
  National Environmental Policy Act   361
  The Environmental Protection Agency   363
Federal Water Pollution Control Act   363
  Section 402—Industrial Point Source Pollution   364
  Section 208 and 319—Nonpoint Source Pollution   364
  Section 404—Wetland Point Source Pollution   366
    Permit Authority   367
    Silvicultural Exemptions   367
    1986 Regulations   368
    Court Cases   369
    Wetlands Definition   370
    Wetlands Area   371
    Wetlands Mitigation   373
    Related Wetlands Legislation   374
      Coastal Zone Management   374
      Farm Bill   374
Clean Air Act   375
  Air Pollutants   375
  Control Methods   375
  Land Use Controls   376
  The 1990 Amendments   377
Other Federal Laws   378
  Coastal Zone Management Act   378
  Federal Environmental Pesticide Control Act   378
Summary   380
Literature Cited   380

Chapter 15   Wildlife Management and Protection Policy   384

Introduction   384
Ownership of Wildlife   385
Wildlife Management Objectives   386
Illustration: Aldo Leopold, Professor of Game Management and Conservationist   387
  A Young Forester   387
  A Game Manager   388
  A Wildlife Ecologist   389
State Wildlife Policy   390
  Controlling the Take   390
  Increasing Populations and Managing Habitat   392
  Nongame Concerns   392
Federal Wildlife Policy   393
  U.S. Fish and Wildlife Service   394
  Principal Laws   394

Lacey Act   394
Migratory Bird Treaty Act   395
Migratory Bird Conservation
    Act and Duck Stamp Act   395
Animal Damage Control Act   396
Fish and
    Wildlife Coordination Act   396
Taylor Grazing Act and Forest
    Wildlife Refuge Act   397
Federal Aid in Wildlife
    Restoration Act   397
Bald Eagle Act   398
Fish Restoration and
    Management Act   398
Sikes Act   398
Land and Water Conservation
    Fund Act   398
Anadromous Fish Conservation
    Act   399
National Wildlife Refuge System
    Administration Act   399
Wild Free-Roaming Horses and
    Burros Protection Act   399
Federal Water Pollution
    Control Laws   400
Marine Mammal Protection Act   400
Endangered Species Act   400
Fishery Conservation and
    Management Act   401
Fish and Wildlife Conservation
    Act   401
Pacific Northwest Power
    Planning and Conservation
    Act   401
Federal Land Management   401
Trends   403
Managing Habitat and Ecosystems   403
Illustration: The Antihunting Issue   404
A History of Conflict   404
Public Sentiment   405
Legal and Institutional Issues   406
The Professional View   407
Protecting Biological Diversity   407
Endangered Species Act   408
    Listing   409
    Critical Habitat   409
    Protection   410
Illustration: The Snail Darter and
    the Dam   412
    Economics and the ESA   413
    The God Committee   413
Social and Political Realities   414
ESA Reauthorization   415
Summary   416
Literature Cited   416

**Chapter 16   Regulation of Forest
    Practices   420**

State Forest Practice Laws   420
Older Laws   421
Modern Laws   423
    Purpose   423
    Administration   424
    Applicability and Exemptions   425
    Violations and Penalities   425
    Regulated Forest Practices   426
Illustration: The Oregon Forest
    Practice Act   426
    The 1971 Law   426
    Implementation and
        1987 Revisions   427
    The 1991 Amendments   428
Local Forestry Regulation   429
Types of Laws   429
    Public Property/Safety
        Protection   429
    Urban/Suburban Environmental
        Protection   430
    General Environmental Protection   431
    Special Feature/Habitat Protection   432
    Forestland Preservation   432
    Penalties for Noncompliance   433
Reasons for Laws   433
    The Northeast   433
    The South   434
    The West   434
Other State Regulations   435
Water Quality   436
Business Practices   436
Policy Responses   437
Alternatives   438
Illustration: Enacting the Maine
    Forest Practice Law   439
    Forestry Issues   439
    Issue Responses   440
    The 1989 Law   440
    Forest Practice Regulations   441
    Policy-Making Implications   441
Current Prospects   442
Summary   443
Literature Cited   443

**Chapter 17   Public Assistance for
    Private Owners   446**

Introduction   446
Taxation   447
Income Taxes   449
    Capital Gains   450

Management Cost Deductions 451
Reforestation Investment Tax
    Incentives 452
Property Taxes 453
    Exemptions and Rebates 455
    Yield Taxes 455
    Modified Property Taxes 455
    Payments in lieu of Taxes 456
Financial Assistance 457
    Agricultural Conservation
        Program 457
    Forestry Incentives Program 457
    Stewardship Incentive Program 460
    State Incentive Programs 461
    Conservation Reserve Programs 462
        Soil Bank 462
        Conservation Reserve 462
        The 1990 Revisions 466
    Sodbuster, Swampbuster, and
        Cross-Compliance 467
    Other Direct Payments 468
    Illustration: Seedling Production
        and Privatization 468
Technical Assistance 469
    Public Programs 469
        Current Status 469
        Illustration: Program Evaluations 470
    Private Assistance 473
    Public and Private Competition 474
    America the Beautiful 475
    Extension Programs 475
    Wildlife Management Assistance 476
Indirect Assistance 477
    Fish and Wildlife Agencies 477
    Publicly Funded Research 477
        Forestry Programs 477
        Research Evaluation 478
        Fish and Wildlife Programs 479
    Forest Protection Programs 479
    Production and Marketing
        Cooperatives 480
Putting it All Together: Total State
    Forest Resource Programs 480
Conclusions 484
    Forestry Goals 484
    Timber Production 486
Summary 487
Literature Cited 488

Chapter 18   Forest Resource
    Policy in a Global Context 494

Introduction 494
Forestry in the Developing World 496

Tropical Deforestation 496
International Development and
    Foreign Aid 497
    Aid Agencies 498
    Aid Policy 499
Social Forestry 499
Sustainable Development 500
Plantation Forestry 501
Illustration: UNCED: The Rumble
    in Rio 503
    Treaties and Politics 503
    Agreements and Outcomes 504
International Trade of Forest
    Products 505
    World Production and Markets 506
        Fuelwood 506
        Industrial Roundwood 506
        Manufactured Wood Products 507
    Trends 508
    Trade Policy 509
    Illustration: U.S. Trade with Canada
        and Japan 510
Comparative Forest Policies in
    the Developed World 512
    Forest Ownership 513
    Regulation 513
    Incentives 516
    Taxation 518
Forests and Global Climate 519
    Contribution of Forests 521
    Evaluation of Forest Policy
        Responses 522
        Market Processes 523
        Public Intervention 523
Summary 524
Literature Cited 525

APPENDICES

Appendix A   Principal Federal
Laws Relating to Forestry, Wildlife
and Fisheries, Range, and
Recreation 528

Appendix B   An Introduction to
Legal Research and Citation 540

Introduction 540
Preliminary Legal Research 540
Primary Legal Research 540
    Judicial Decisions 540
    Statutes 542
        Federal Statutes 542

State Statutes   542
Statute Citators   542
Constitutions   543
   Federal Constitution   543
   State Constitutions   543
Secondary Legal Resources   543
   Legal Periodicals   543
   Legislative History   543
   Administrative and Executive
     Publications   545
   Looseleaf Services   545
   Legal Encyclopedias   545
   Treatises and Restatements   545

Words and Phrases   545
Legal Casebooks and Commercial
   Study Aids   545
References   546

**Appendix C   Forest Resource Policy
  Acronymns**   **547**

Index   **551**

PART I

PROCESSES

Chapter 1

Forest Resources and Public Policy

The penalty good people pay for not being interested in politics is to be governed by people worse than themselves.

—Plato

INTRODUCTION

Forestry, fish and wildlife biology, range science, and outdoor recreation are technical professions. Foresters, fish and wildlife managers, range conservationists, and park rangers apply knowledge from several fields in order to manage forested ecosystems to meet given objectives. Forest resource professionals need to be adept at managing land in order to produce timber, to maintain water quantity and quality, to improve wildlife habitat and livestock forage, and to develop diverse recreational opportunities. But many natural resource professionals bemoan the political context in which they work and are infamous for their preference for the outdoors—whether it be hunting, fishing, backpacking, or observing nature— rather than their aptitude for working with people. This characterization is most certainly exaggerated, particularly for successful natural resource managers. But few people entered the natural resources professions in-

tending to manage people; trees, wildlife, or parks were the lure, not laws, bureaucracies, or legislatures.

The reclusiveness and technical focus of forest resource professionals is intriguing, given the history of forestry in this country. Gifford Pinchot, the first chief of the United States Forest Service, was renowned for his political prowess, not just his technical skills. He was an early leader of the conservation movement, an architect of federal resource policies, and a governor of Pennsylvania. Many of Pinchot's successors as chief also were highly regarded for their political savvy and leadership. Renowned wildlife biologist and forester Aldo Leopold might better characterize the reclusive resource professional, but he was by no means politically inactive. Even John Muir, a great naturalist and advocate for the preservation of national parks and wilderness areas, fought many political battles.

Indeed some of the most successful resource professionals in both the public and private sectors have combined technical skills with an understanding of politics and the ability to work with public policy makers. Modern leaders of wildlife conservation groups have had a tremendous impact on public policy. This combination of technical skills and political abilities has always been important for the leaders in the profession; it now has become increasingly important even for field foresters, wildlife biologists, range scientists, and recreation managers.

Forestry, fish and wildlife biology, range management, outdoor recreation, and resource policy have changed considerably since professional forestry established its roots in the United States during the late nineteenth century. At that time resource professionals spent much of their efforts convincing landowners, the public, and the government that sustained-yield forest management and game protection were both possible and desirable. In the 1920s foresters employed by government agencies designed and implemented forest protection programs to reduce losses from fire and pests. Game management and wilderness preservation were the most prominent resource issues in the 1930s. After World War II private timber companies hired large numbers of foresters in response to increased demands for housing. Wood production increased on both public and private lands. Forestry and wildlife research made tremendous progress. Foresters began to practice a kind of intensive management that the first generation of U.S. foresters could not have anticipated. For a time foresters were able to practice silviculture without much concern for broader political and economic conditions. The same time period saw wildlife professionals evolve from mere enforcers of fish and game laws to wildland habitat managers and public relations experts. Similarly, recreational use of public lands began to increase dramatically after World War II.

Professional autonomy began to dwindle due to the social and political turbulence of the 1960s. The civil rights, antiwar, and environmental movements led to fundamental changes in how Americans viewed their institutions of government. Many people questioned how well government protected their interests. Citizen activism and citizen-based advocacy groups became more prevalent and outspoken.

The environmental movement that began in the late 1960s changed the nature of forest resource management. Many new environmental organizations were established and membership in older conservation groups expanded. Representatives of these groups began to question conventional forestry practices and public land management priorities. They demanded and received a greater role in making natural resource decisions. In response to public concerns, Congress enacted numerous laws regulating environmental quality and public land management. These laws were designed to protect water and air quality, wildlife species and habitat, and other environmental benefits.

Foresters in private industry and private landowners also are affected by public policies. Forest practice acts, best management practices, open burning laws, and many other regulations govern forest practices on industrial and nonindustrial private forest lands. Wildlife and recreation managers, who are employed mostly by public agencies to administer public programs, have always been affected by politics (i.e., taxes, budgets, laws, and bureaucrats). As the impact of public policies affecting private lands increases, so does the demand for public services and scarce resources. Thus our political debates about these concerns have been much more contentious. All resource professionals will be affected by and participate in these forest policy issues in the future.

FORESTRY AND WILDLIFE IN THE 1990s

The surge of interest in the natural environment and the challenge to professional authority have compelled natural resource managers to reconsider their roles. They have had to learn how to respond to society's forest management demands and how to resolve the inevitable conflicts that occur. Although the policy context for resource managers has changed markedly during the last three decades, the next decade may bring even greater changes. The challenges of the 1990s range from local conflicts over land use to global problems related to air pollution, deforestation, and climatic change. Two recent examples of such challenges follow. The events and professional efforts in these two cases help illustrate why public policy is important in forestry and wildlife, and how the political process works in making resource decisions.

Public Opinion and Forestry in Texas

East Texas, an area comparable in size to the state of South Carolina or Maine, has 55 percent of its land in forest cover. One out of every four manufacturing jobs in rural East Texas is in a wood-processing activity (O'Laughlin and Williams 1988, USDA Forest Service 1988). In spite of an extensive forest and a large forest products industry, the general public has a low level of awareness of technical forestry. More than half of the citizens of East Texas who participated in a public opinion survey indicated that they knew little about forest resources and forest practices, and that they had heard little or nothing about the forest products industry. Surprisingly, only 6 percent of the East Texans surveyed realized that timber supports an industry of major importance in the region (American Forest Institute 1985).

The general public may know little about forestry, but beginning in the mid-1970s, groups of concerned citizens from many areas of the state took greater interest in the forests of East Texas. Concerns included timber harvesting methods (particularly clear-cutting), site preparation practices, and air quality (more specifically, the management of smoke from prescribed fire or controlled burning of the forest).

East Texas is within a few hours' drive of three of the nation's ten largest cities. Many Texans use forests for recreation and observe forest management activities firsthand. Their responses to these activities are not always what resource managers expect. An event that occurred in October 1986 illustrates a type of response that has become increasingly common.

Timber Salvage and Replanting Efforts

The scene was the Four Notch area. Site preparation techniques not previously used in Texas's national forests were to be employed there in 1986. Between 1982 and 1984 pine bark beetles had attacked and killed 3500 acres of parklike stands of pine in the area. In 1976 a lawsuit to stop clear-cutting throughout the national forests in Texas led to the classification of Four Notch as a potential addition to the National Wilderness Preservation System, thus halting forest management activities there. When the pine beetle epidemic hit in 1982, an Environmental Assessment (EA) was required under the 1969 National Environmental Policy Act (NEPA) before the control action that professional entomologists felt would limit the spread of the outbreak could be implemented. The regional forester in Atlanta approved the EA in July 1983, but the Sierra Club appealed to the chief to overturn the decision to control the beetles. The appeal was denied. The beetle outbreaks had by then covered 1300 acres and were spreading 50 feet per day along a three-mile front. Hurricane Alicia had complicated matters by soaking the ground, canceling all but one of 18 planned salvage sales. Chainsaw crews from six states arrived to cut a 250-foot buffer strip to slow the spread of the outbreak. In October the Sierra Club appealed again, and the chief again denied the appeal. In December helicopters began removing salvage timber cut in the effort to reduce the spread (Miles 1987).

After the beetle outbreak subsided in July 1984, three-fourths of the timber in the Four Notch area was salvaged, using expensive helicopter logging in order to minimize environmental damage. The Forest Service contracted to have the unsalvaged standing dead timber pushed over and chopped with a Le Tourneau tree crusher so that the wood could be burned efficiently. A prescribed fire would be ignited from the air, and later the area would be planted with pine seedlings. The Sierra Club and the Texas Committee on Natural Resources (TCONR), a Dallas-based environmental activist group, protested this action because it would create a pine monoculture.

Public Protest and Eventual Outcome

In October 1986 *Newsweek* reported that Smokey the Bear had done a turnabout and was napalming East Texas forests (Uehling, Shapiro, and Cohn 1986). The Forest Service was indeed planning to start a circular pattern controlled burn by dripping a jellied mix of gasoline and diesel fuel from a torch suspended from a helicopter. The objective was to reduce the accumulation of dead trees left in the beetles' wake. This unusual method of site preparation elicited action by members of Earth First!, a loosely knit citizens' group. Earth First! members chained themselves to standing dead trees and heavy equipment at the Sam Houston National Forest, east of Huntsville, Texas. Members of the news media were drawn to the scene and treated with photo opportunities that included a large and colorful "Stop the Tree Nazis" banner. The *Houston Chronicle* described a treetop chase scence (Klimko 1986). Forest rangers attempted to apprehend one protester by sawing down the trees that supported his hammock 30 feet off the ground. Six members of the group eventually were arrested.

Temporary injunctions filed by the Texas attorney general on behalf of the Sierra Club and TCONR halted site preparation work, but subsequent federal court actions found no violation of either law or procedure in the Forest Service's planned timber management activities. In the fall of 1987, a prescribed broadcast burn was carried out. Part of it was ignited by helitorch, and because of wet weather, part by traditional ground-based drip torches. Pine seedlings were planted as planned on approximately 60 percent of the Four Notch area. Although the Forest Service eventually did complete its site preparation plans, considerable bad publicity and ill will resulted.

It is unlikely that the Forest Service could have completely avoided this controversy under any circumstances. The Lone Star Chapter of the Sierra Club and TCONR had a history of challenges to national forest management. Extreme environmental groups such as Earth First! would be unlikely to compromise on anything. Such groups question whether timber ever should be harvested. Other groups, such as adjacent landowners or forest industry employees, might question the need for wilderness or the fairness of allowing pest outbreaks on public wilderness land to spread to their private land. Miles (1987) says there were approximately 1000 such episodes. Nevertheless, the issue serves to illustrate that the consequences of land management activities need to be carefully analyzed not only for their technical effectiveness and efficiency, but also for public acceptance. To maintain professional credibility, managers need to include public opinion in their technical assessments of land management alternatives.

The closing paragraph of a *New York Times* article on the Four Notch incident—complete with a photo of one of the "champions of environment" chained to a tree—provides the main lesson (Applebome 1986).

> Both sides agree that the [pine plantation/biodiversity] dispute comes down to a public policy question, and current policies from Washington favor the Forest Service's approach. (p. 8)

REINTRODUCTION OF BOBCATS ON CUMBERLAND ISLAND NATIONAL SEASHORE

Wildlife managers have faced similar problems with public opinion when implementing programs. One example is the reintroduction of bobcats on Cumberland Island, just off the Georgia–Florida coast (Figure 1-1). Warren et al. (1990) described the public policies and political events that influenced two seemingly straightforward management decisions to reintroduce bobcats and led to a public debate.

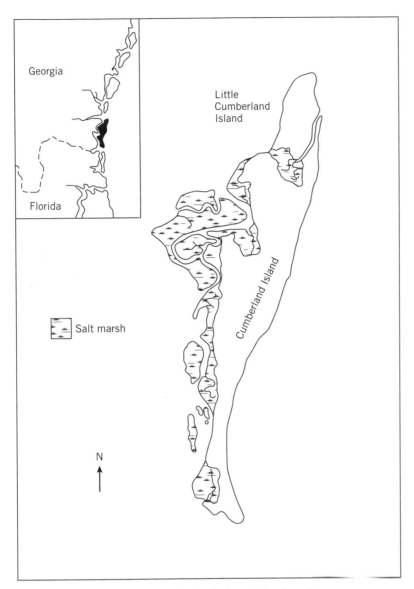

Georgia

Florida

Little
Cumberland
Island

Cumberland Island

Salt marsh

N

Figure 1-1. Location Map of Cumberland Island National Seashore.

With more than 20,000 acres, Cumberland Island is the largest in a series of Atlantic Ocean barrier islands extending from Cape Hatteras, North Carolina, to Talbot Island, Florida. European settlers colonized the island in the sixteenth century and altered the vegetation by farming and by releasing hogs, cattle, and horses. The National Park Foundation began purchasing land on the island in the late 1960s. Congress designated much of the island as the Cumberland Island National Seashore in 1972 (Public Law 92-536)

and reserved much of that area as wilderness in 1982 (Public Law 97-250). The laws directed the National Park Service to manage the seashore in order to provide for outdoor recreation and preserve the related scenic, scientific, and historic values on the island. The laws also allowed hunting, fishing, and trapping to continue on the seashore, because local residents had used the island for centuries.

The National Park Service Resources Management Plan for Cumberland Island National

Seashore specifically addressed the preservation and management of many wildlife species. One specific project under the plan was the documentation of extirpated species and the preparation of Environmental Impact Statements for their reintroduction. As part of the plan, bobcats (last seen on the island in 1907) received the highest priority for reintroduction because they were less likely than other predators to conflict with visitors or island residents. Bobcats characteristically avoid humans and rarely constitute a threat to domestic animals (McCord and Cordoza 1982).

NEPA and the Environmental Assessment

The National Park Service contracted with researchers at the University of Georgia and the U.S. Fish and Wildlife Service to reintroduce the bobcat to Cumberland Island. The researchers planned to conduct various scientific studies in conjunction with the reintroduction. The researchers, on behalf of the Park Service, first had to evaluate the environmental effects of the reintroduction, as required by the 1969 National Environmental Policy Act. NEPA requires environmental impact analysis for any proposed federal actions, including actions that occur with federal funding or on federal lands. An Environmental Assessment (EA) is the initial environmental document used in planning and decision making to determine whether a proposed action might or would have a significant impact on the quality of the human environment. If an action would have such an impact, an Environmental Impact Statement (EIS) must be prepared to ensure NEPA compliance. If the EA indicates that there would be no expected significant impact from the proposed action, an EIS is not required. However, a formal Finding of No Significant Impact (FONSI) must be prepared subsequent to the EA and made available for public review.

The bobcat study team prepared an EA and concluded that no formal (and much more extensive) EIS would be required. Reintroduction was justified because the bobcat would help control native deer and exotic herbivores (feral horses and hogs), as well as help return the island's ecosystem to the balance of nature that prevailed in the eighteenth century. The EA also briefly mentioned the possibility of the bobcats' preying on wild turkeys but discounted its importance. The analysis also had to consider if the reintroduction of the bobcat would jeopardize the potentially endangered Anastasia Island beach mouse, which had been proposed for listing on the federal Endangered Species List. But the EA presented evidence from prior research that the mouse was unlikely to occur on the island.

The EA process required that alternatives to the proposed action be discussed. The study team considered several alternatives, including a less desirable trapping and removal program, as well as the required "no-action" alternative. Each alternative was considered for possible environmental impacts, including its effects on visitors and the retained rights of the remaining residents on the island.

Public Comments

The bobcat study team released the EA document and worked closely with the Cumberland Island National Seashore superintendent and the southeastern regional director of the National Park Service. The National Park Service received 17 written comments on the project from individuals and organizations. One petition with 51 signatures opposed the bobcat reintroduction, as did two individual letters. The 51 persons who signed the petition were hunters who felt that the cats would kill turkeys and scare people. The hunters volunteered to organize hunts to kill deer, hogs, and horses if they were such a problem. The six-member City Council of St. Marys, Georgia, also opposed the reintroduction and voted four to one to send a resolution stating so to the Georgia Department of Natural Resources (DNR). The bobcat study team was never really sure why the council opposed the project but believed that some local hunters had influenced the chairperson of the council to intervene. Given that St. Marys also is host to a new U.S. nuclear submarine base (which probably poses more danger than bobcats), the council's opposition to bobcats off the city's shore was a considerable surprise.

Fourteen letters supported the proposed reintroduction, including ones from the Wilderness Society, the Sierra Club, and one member of the U.S. Congress. Some residents opposed reintroduction because the bobcats might attack pets or children, but another person noted that people would be lucky to even see a bobcat on the island. The Wilderness Society wrote that knowledge of a native predator would enhance the island's wilderness recreational experience, making it seem more wild. The Sierra Club supported the project but questioned the focus of the reintroduction. Was it specifically to reintroduce bobcats, to restore the national seashore to a more natural state, or to be used as the best method of controlling large herbivores on the island?

The Media
The public review and comment stage generated a great deal of controversy. In response to concerns about turkey population declines, the researchers prepared a six-page supporting literature review, which was distributed by the National Park Service. Biologists from the Georgia DNR also helped alleviate concerns about turkeys in their comments to the news media. They stated that bobcats would not wipe out turkeys and might even improve their gene pool as less wary individuals were removed from the population.

The early media coverage of the Environmental Assessment bordered on sensational and focused on the use of bobcats to kill deer and the political controversy that developed involving St. Marys' City Council. Newspaper headlines such as "St. Marys claws at Cumberland bobcat plan" (*Florida Times-Union*, August 24, 1988, p. B1) dramatized the opposition's arguments. An Atlanta TV news broadcast (WSB-TV2) covered the controversy, with interviews of the chairperson of St. Marys' City Council and the superintendent of the national seashore. The newscaster concluded that there would be a "lot of growling" before

the decision was made to release bobcats on the Cumberland Island National Seashore.

Public Meetings
Public meetings were the next step in the EA process. Based on the review comments, the study team realized that the focus on use of bobcats as a deer predator was a mistake and instead stressed in the public meetings that the major justification of the project was to reintroduce a formerly native species in order to restore natural biological diversity and to meet congressional parkland management mandates.

The National Park Service officials and the research study team prepared for the public meetings with trepidation. However, despite the early protests and adverse media coverage, the meetings were uneventful. The biologists presented details on the island, its habitats, wildlife, and the bobcat plans and answered questions. Few people bothered to attend the meeting in St. Marys. A similar meeting in Athens drew a small and supportive audience. Unlike the early news coverage, the biologists had more input and often were interviewed personally at the public hearings; and the resulting newspaper articles were more balanced, deemphasizing the controversial aspects and stressing the broader ecological significance of the project.

Outcome
In the fall of 1988 the Environmental Assessment was approved, and 14 bobcats were trapped on the mainland, evaluated, and equipped with radio transmitters for tracking. As of 1990 most of the bobcats on the island had survived and had at least four litters—indicating preliminary biological success at establishing a viable population on the island. But some political lessons bear noting.

In fall 1989 both an Athens newspaper and the national magazine *Outdoor Life* termed the effort a failure because the 14 bobcats had not reduced the island's deer population, even though the cats had only been there for six months. The study team has since concluded that the focus on predation, rather than biological diversity, was oversold.

Keeping the objectives modest, straightforward, and obtainable could have helped them avoid adverse publicity and opposition. The team also concluded that formal or informal surveys of public concerns should be incorporated early in the planning stages of reintroduction projects. This would lessen public opposition and expedite subsequent plan approval.

THE IMPORTANCE OF PUBLIC POLICY

The management and use of forests can have profound effects on people. Forests provide wood for fuel, paper, furniture, shelter, and artistic uses. Wood can be used for local fuelwood or lumber needs, to supply capital-intensive pulp plants, or to support an export industry. Forests also serve to make our environment habitable and our lives more fulfilling. Forests consume carbon dioxide and produce oxygen; protect watersheds, absorbing rainfall and releasing it slowly into streams; hold soil in place, reducing erosion and the spread of deserts; provide wildlife habitat; and conserve plant and animal gene pools. People also find spiritual renewal in forests and use them to test their skills against nature's challenges and to escape from civilization's burdens.

Forests serve a wide variety of human needs. But not every forest can serve every need. Public policy is a means societies use to decide how forests will be used and who will benefit from their use. Public policies can protect the environment, promote wildlife species, or restrict forest use and management. For example, federal law prohibited federal foresters in East Texas from conducting salvage logging by conventional methods in a potential wilderness area. Public laws helped state and federal resource managers establish bobcats in a designated wilderness area in Georgia. Public policies have different effects on different groups of people. Owners of forest land adjacent to the pine beetle outbreak in the Four Notch area risked losses in their own stands because of the no-control policy; the general public bore no such risk.

Forest policies affect resource management and the people who use forests. Natural resource managers must be concerned about both forests and people. Their work is guided by public policy, and many resource managers participate in the development and implementation of policy. If their participation is to be effective, that is, if forestry, wildlife, and recreation managers are to contribute to the development of accepted public policies, they must understand how policies are formed and what their effects are. Our purpose in writing this book is to help you to gain that understanding.

FOREST AREA AND OWNERSHIP

Forests cover almost one-third of the surface land in the world. The physical and biological diversity of forests, the large number of forests owners with various objectives, and the many uses of forests make the practice of forest resource management and the development of forest resource policy a challenge. What may be a workable forest policy in one region of a country may not, for silvicultural or cultural reasons, work in another region. This book focuses primarily on the United States. But a glimpse at the world forestry situation underscores the need for policies to address social, biological, and geographic conditions. What we make of our forest inheritance is a matter of public and private choice.

EXTENT OF FORESTS

Forest resource policy-making requires basic forest information. Some data on the extent and nature of forests have been collected for almost a century. During the 1980s intensive attempts to compile world natural resource statistics were made. The data are imperfect, and inconsistencies in definitions and methods make it difficult to reconcile numbers obtained by various collection agencies (Peck 1984).

The extent and significance of forests can be classified in many ways. It is not quite enough to say that one-third of the world's land or one-third of the United States is covered by forests, but that is a good starting point. There are several dichotomies that lend some understanding of forests as they relate to people. These two-part classification schemes also are part of the jargon used in discussions about forests and forest policy and are therefore important to understand.

Closed Forest/Open Forest

One worldwide classification scheme separates dense-canopied forests (closed forests), which generally occur in moist or temperate climates, from open-canopied forests found in drier climates. The difference between these two general forest types is that continuous grass cover can grow under open forest canopies; under the closed forest it is too shady for grass to grow. As Figure 1-2 indicates, 22 percent of the world's land area lies

under closed forests. Open forests cover another 10 percent of the earth's land surface.

Shrubland, a separate land classification used only in the developing world, covers another 5 percent of the world's land. Forest fallow occupies another 3 percent and includes areas where tree cover is returning on lands that have been subjected to shifting agricultural practices and abandonment sometime during the past twenty years (World Resources Institute 1986).

Forests cover 32 percent (720 million acres) of the land area in the United States; 21 percent of this is closed forest; and 11 percent is open forest (World Resources Institute 1986). However, federal natural resource agencies in the United States use a different kind of classification scheme.

Timberland/Woodland

In the United States, forest lands are classified by the USDA Forest Service (1982) according to their ability to produce timber. *Timberlands* can produce 20 cubic feet of wood per acre per year and have not been withdrawn from timber production for legal or adminis-

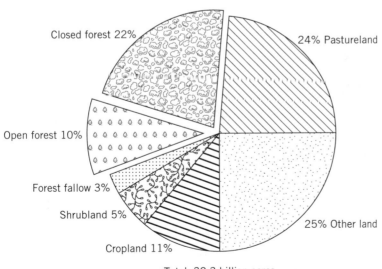

Closed forest 22%

24% Pastureland

Open forest 10%

Forest fallow 3%

Shrubland 5%

Cropland 11%

25% Other land

Total: 32.3 billion acres
(Antarctica excluded)

Figure 1-2. World's Land Use, 1985.
Source: World Resources Institute (1986) from FAO Data

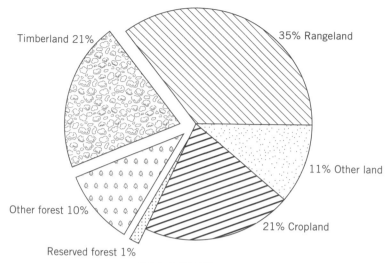

Figure 1-3. U.S. Land Use, 1977.
Source: USDA Forest Service (1982)

trative reasons (such as being designated as a wilderness area). Timberlands cover 21 percent (473 million acres) of the United States and are a subdivision of the 720 million acres of forest lands that are part of the total land base of 2.25 billion acres (Figure 1-3). Forest lands that do not meet this physical productivity criterion because of adverse site conditions cover 10 percent of the United States. These "other forest" lands (USDA Forest Service 1982) are somewhat analogous to open forests. *Woodland,* as defined by the Society of American Foresters (1985), seems to be an acceptable term for these less productive open-canopied forests.[1]

As of 1977 U.S. forest land included 238.8 million acres not considered timberland. These forests covered almost 11 percent of the United States. Timber management on

these forests is limited by physical, biological, and legal constraints. The vast majority (88 percent) of this acreage is in the western states; the remainder (12 percent) is in eastern states. These lands fall into two major categories: "other forest" lands and productive "reserved or deferred" forest lands.

Other forest lands account for 213.1 million acres of lands that are either populated by "noncommercial" species such as post oak or chaparral or do not meet the minimum timber productivity criterion of 20 cubic feet of wood per acre per year. The western United States contains 90 percent of these lands; the East has the other 10 percent. The slow-growing forests of interior Alaska account for 101.7 million acres, or 49 percent, of other forest lands in the West. Chaparral and pinion pine/juniper types account for another 62.8 million acres, or 30 percent, of the western other forest lands. Productive reserved forest lands total 25.7 million acres of productive timberland that is either reserved or deferred from timber production; most is in federal ownership and is in parks, wilderness areas, and wildlife preserves.

---

[1]In common global usage, the term *woodland* is used to describe small areas of trees in clumps, windbreaks, or hedgerows (van Maaren 1984). This is consistent with dictionary definitions (e.g., Random House 1967) that describe a *forest* as a large or extensive land area covered with trees, and a *wood* as a wooded tract smaller than a forest and less wild in character. Indeed, *farm woodlot* is a widely used term in the United States.

Softwood/Hardwood

Another classification scheme distinguishes coniferous tree species (softwoods) from broadleaved tree species (hardwoods). Most softwood species have needlelike leaves that are not shed annually. Most hardwood species have broad leaves that are shed annually. Of the world's closed forest area, 60 percent is hardwood or broadleaved forests, representing 13 percent of total land area. Softwoods or conifers cover approximately 9 percent of the land in the world.

In the United States hardwoods comprise 56 percent (265 million acres) of the timberland area, or 12 percent of all land; softwoods make up the remaining 44 percent (218 million acres) of timberlands, or 9 percent of all U.S. land. Almost two-thirds of the entire U.S. standing timber volume is softwood. Hardwoods dominate the eastern half of the country, with 72 percent of the timberland area. More than 90 percent of the U.S. hardwood timber inventory (wood volume) is in the East. Softwoods dominate the western half of the United States, accounting for 88 percent of western timberland area. More than two-thirds of the United States softwood timber inventory is in the West.

Developed Nations/Developing Nations

World distribution patterns for softwoods and hardwoods are distinctly different and are closely related to the economic development criterion of developed versus developing nations. Most of the developed countries lie outside the Tropics of Capricorn and Cancer. Their temperate forests would be expected to be different from those of the equatorial developing countries. As Figure 1-4 illustrates, the closed forests in the developed world are predominantly softwoods or conifers (71 percent). In the developing world, 94 percent of the closed forests contain hardwoods or broadleaved species. Data on the composition of open forests are not readily available. The developed world category includes North America (Canada and the United States), Europe, the former Soviet Union, and a few other nations (Australia, New Zealand, Japan, Israel, and South Africa). The developing world includes Africa, Latin America, China, and the remainder of Asia (World Resources Institute 1986).

Industrial Wood/Fuelwood

Although forests produce many goods, the importance of wood removals bears special

Developed Countries

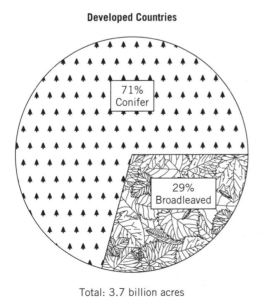

Total: 3.7 billion acres

Developing Countries

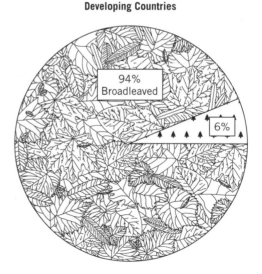

Total: 3.4 billion acres

Figure 1-4.   Closed Forest in Developed/ Developing Countries, 1985.
Source: World Resources Institute (1986) from FAO data

mention because it most directly affects the extent and composition of forests in the world. Timber harvests also cause the most public controversy.

Many countries use trees mostly for solid wood and paper products; many depend on wood to meet basic survival needs. The use of wood, not surprisingly then, follows the division of the developed/developing world classes rather closely. People in developing countries use wood predominantly for fuelwood and charcoal rather than for industrial wood (Figures 1-5a and 1-5b). The need for such fuelwood more than doubled between 1963 and 1983. In contrast, countries in the developed world use wood (termed *industrial roundwood* in Figure 1-5b) primarily to make lumber, panels, and paper products. Wood consumption for industrial uses in the developed world appears to be relatively stable at the present time. Increased energy prices in the developed world have caused a slight increase in industrial and residential fuelwood demand (Figure 1-5a). Both developed and developing countries consume large quantities of wood, and world wood consumption increased 67 percent between 1963 and 1983 (Figure 1-5c).

The most sobering facts regarding wood use and removals in the world are these (Office of Technology Assessment 1984; Food and Agriculture Organization 1985; World Resources Institute 1985, 1986):

1. 80 to 90 percent of the wood removed from tropical forests is used for fuel; 80 percent of this is for cooking food and heating homes.

2. One-and-a-half billion people depend on wood for more than 90 percent of their energy needs.

3. An additional 1 billion people depend on wood for 50 to 90 percent of their energy needs.

4. One-half of the world's population relies on wood as the primary energy source.

5. One-and-a-half billion people are cutting more fuelwood annually than the annual growth rates of forests in their country.

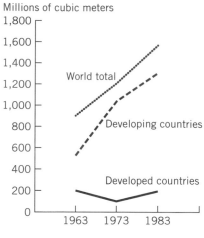

(a) **Fuelwood and Charcoal**

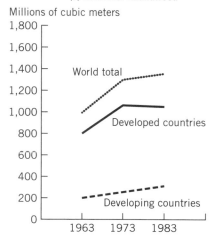

(b) **Industrial Roundwood**

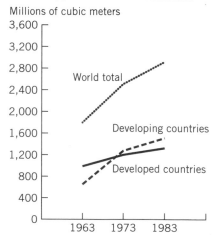

(c) **Total Roundwood Production**

Figure 1-5. World Wood Harvest Trends, 1963–1983.
Source: World Resources Institute (1986) from FAO data.

6. One hundred million people now face an acute scarcity of fuelwood.

7. About 11.3 million hectares or 28 million acres (an area the size of Pennsylvania or Austria) are now being deforested annually.

OWNERSHIP OF FORESTS

Forest ownership is crucial in forest policy. For the most part, owners of forests determine the objectives for the use of forest land and its associated resources. The owner establishes forest management policies and provides the means for accomplishing management goals.

Forests are owned by either public or private entities. There are also useful subdivisions of these two categories. Public ownership vests in government agencies the responsibility for formulating and implementing policies affecting these forests. Private ownership gives management responsibility to individuals or to legal entities such as corporations or trusts. Private ownership is always subject to social purposes and public control (Barlowe 1978). Property arrangements governing forest land and tree ownership vary a great deal among and within nations.

United States of America

In the United States, more forests are privately than publicly owned. Private entities own 55 percent (397 million acres) of all U.S. forest land. When reserved and other forest lands are deducted and only timberlands are considered, the private share increases to 72 percent (Figure 1-6). The vast majority of the other forest lands and productive reserved forests (described earlier) are federally owned. The federal government manages one-third of all land in the United States, 39 percent of the forest land, and 21 percent of the timberland (USDA Forest Service 1982).

The majority of private timberlands are owned by individuals and organizations that do not operate timber-processing facilities and therefore by definition are not considered to be in the forest industry. These nonindustrial private forests (NIPFs) hold the majority of U.S. timberland—58 percent (275 million acres). NIPF owners have been further subdivided by the U.S. Forest Service into farmers and "other private" (doctors, lawyers, professionals, etc.) owners. Corporations and other organizations in the forest industry own 14 percent (66 million acres) of U.S. timberlands (see Figure 1-6).

The largest portion of publicly owned forests in the United States is in the National Forest System, managed by the U.S. Department of Agriculture Forest Service. National forests cover about 190 million acres, an area that is almost twice as large as the state of California. The National Forest System constitutes 18 percent of the nation's timberland area (88 million acres) and contains almost half of the nation's softwood timber inventory. Whether to harvest or preserve these vast old-growth forests is the major forest policy issue in the western states, which contain 76 percent of the national forest acreage. A variety of other federal, state, and local public agencies manage 10 percent (47 million acres) of the timberlands in the country.

Regional timberland ownership patterns vary greatly in the United States (Figure 1-7). Timberlands in the West are predominantly publicly owned, with national forests the largest category. In the North and in the South, nonindustrial private forests are by far the largest category. The Lake States and New England have many state-owned forest lands. More than half of the forest industry timberland is in the South.

Other Nations

Forest property rights vary greatly among nations. Public and private forest ownership statistics are available for most developed countries but not for less developed ones. Probably all countries with forests have placed some of the land in public ownership. Many countries, even those with centrally planned economies, have privately owned forests. For example, 30 percent of the forests of the former country of Yugoslavia were privately owned. In China the

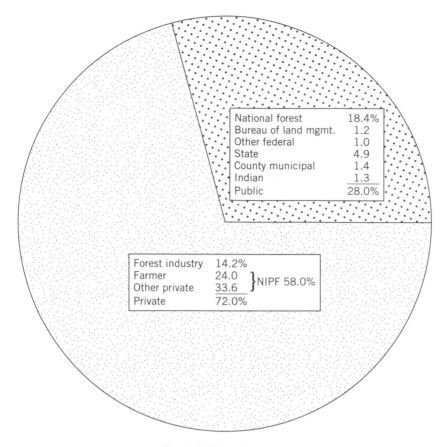

National forest	18.4%
Bureau of land mgmt.	1.2
Other federal	1.0
State	4.9
County municipal	1.4
Indian	1.3
Public	28.0%

Forest industry	14.2%	
Farmer	24.0	}NIPF 58.0%
Other private	33.6	
Private	72.0%	

Total: 482.5 million acres

Figure 1-6. U.S. Timberland Ownership, 1977.
Source: USDA Forest Service (1982).

state owns the forests, but individuals exercise management control and receive forest revenues in some parts of the country. Much of the land in developing countries is held as common property and is managed by the community in social forestry programs.

Public ownership ranges from federal or national to local community ownership. In many European countries there are cooperatively owned forests for which there is no direct U.S. analogy. Churches own a substantial portion of the forests in some European countries (Hummell 1984). Private institutions such as pension funds, insurance companies, and bank-administered trusts own forest lands in industrialized countries, including the United States.

FORESTS AND PUBLIC POLICY

When we speak of forest policy in this book, we are referring to a subset of public policies, those dealing with the use and management of the forests. Thus before going very far in discussing *forest* policies, it is useful to think about what *public* policy is. Political scientists have suggested numerous definitions of public policy; the specific words used are not as important as the concepts that underlie a definition. *Policy* may be defined as a purposive course of action or inaction that an actor or set of actors takes to deal with a problem (Anderson 1984, Heidenheimer, Heclo, and Adams 1983). *Public* policy is made by government officials such as legislators, governors, agency directors, and judges.

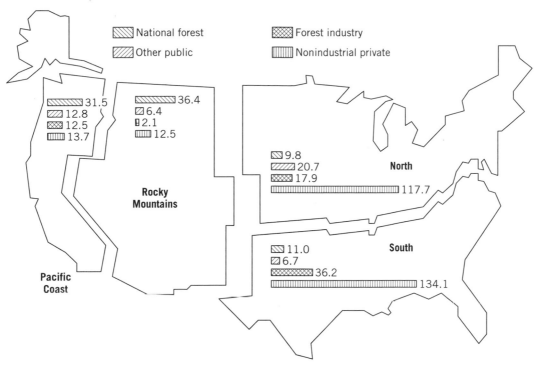

Figure 1-7. U.S. Timberland Ownership by Region, 1977.
Source: USDA Forest Service (1982).

ELEMENTS OF POLICY

Public policy commits the authority of government to a course of action or inaction over time.

Our definition of public policy has five key elements. First, a policy must be *purposive*— it must provide direction. For example, it is the policy of the State of Wisconsin to encourage forest owners to invest in forest management (Stoddard 1988). Thus sustained management of private forests is a goal of public policy in Wisconsin, as it is in many other states.

Second, policy requires patterns of decisions *over time*, not merely discrete, individual decisions such as enactment and implementation of a single law. Thus Wisconsin's policy is expressed in its tax system as well as in its ongoing program of technical assistance for forest owners (Stoddard 1988). The state has taken a series of actions in order to achieve the policy objective. There also are actions that the state has not taken. It has chosen not to purchase all private forests and have the state forestry agency manage them. Policies reflect public choices to pursue some courses of action and to refrain from pursuing others.

A third element of the definition is that policy is followed by an *individual actor or set of actors (a group)*—those who have the authority to make the policy and those who must comply with it. Wisconsin's policy guides the actions of state forestry and tax officials. It also provides opportunities for owners of nonindustrial private forests to use programs that will increase timberland investment returns or favor production of certain goods.

Fourth, a policy is made to deal with some *problem or matter of concern*. Sometimes a problem may be caused by the different values and objectives of different groups. At other times groups may not agree on the means to achieve a given objective. States' attempts to promote investment in the management of private forests reflect a concern that there is insufficient private forestry activity. The policy is intended to increase tree planting, timber stand improvement, or wildlife management practices.

Finally, public policy reflects *social choices* made through governmental institutions. Governments have various instruments at their disposal to achieve public policy goals. All of these policy instruments or tools are used to promote some kinds of behaviors and to discourage others. Policymakers decide which instrument, if any, to use in particular situations.

INSTRUMENTS OF POLICY

One instrument the government uses to enforce policy is coercion, or the use of the legal system to regulate behavior. Governments may demand that people engage in particular activities (e.g., some states require landowners to reforest after harvesting timber) and refrain from engaging in others (e.g., states prohibit hunting during much of the year). The law also is used to regulate relations between citizens. Thus the courts and police enforce landowners' rights to prohibit trespassing.

A second policy instrument is the provision of services. State governments routinely offer numerous services to owners of forest land. States provide fire control, technical assistance in land management, and market information. The federal government provides funds for forestry research, much of which produces valuable information for landowners, forestry agencies, and wood products manufacturing firms.

Governments also use money or financial incentives as a tool to achieve policy objectives. The federal government, through the Conservation Reserve Program, has paid money to farmers to plant trees on erodible sites. States offer property tax incentives to landowners to maintain their land in forest cover. Some states also offer cost sharing and low-interest loans to promote investment in

forest management. Taxes also are used to discourage some behavior. Cigarette and alcohol sales are taxed to raise revenue and discourage consumption. Developed land is taxed at higher rates than undeveloped land in most states, in hopes of preserving rural land.

Government management of publicly owned land is another important policy tool. The federal government manages numerous public land systems including wildlife refuges, national forests, and national parks. State and local governments also manage public lands for a variety of purposes. When policymakers believe that public goals cannot be met on private lands, public ownership is an option to be considered.

Policymakers have a variety of instruments available to them. Political, economic, physical, and biological conditions will affect the relative effectiveness of each type of tool. Often several policy instruments are used together. For example, wildlife policy employs public ownership of refuges, public research, regulation of hunting on all lands, and tax incentives for private owners in order to protect and manage wildlife populations and to provide recreational opportunities for citizens.

DEFINITION OF FOREST POLICY

We can use the preceding analysis to construct a definition of forest policy. *Forest policy* may be considered a purposive course of action or inaction followed by an individual or group in dealing with a matter of concern regarding the use of forest resources. Forest policies guide how forests will be used, usually to achieve some stated or implicit objective. Policies also determine who will benefit from forest use and who will bear costs associated with forest management and use. Wisconsin's policy promotes retention of land in forest cover. It also offers benefits to landowners (presumably in order to benefit society) and imposes costs on other taxpayers.

FORESTS AND PUBLIC POLICY

ILLUSTRATION: FOREST POLICY STATEMENTS

In order to clarify the meaning of forest policy, selected policy statements are presented. As the examples indicate, many forest policies are vague. Such lack of specificity often is intentional because policymakers usually must appeal to a variety of groups with dissimilar views and values. More specific policies with well-defined objectives quite often are divisive because they clearly identify winners and losers. To avoid disagreement, policymakers retreat to ambiguity and leave specifics to implementing agencies. Moreover, the technical nature of many resource issues and the variability in forest conditions make it impractical to construct policies that are too specific. In many cases, specificity would require lengthy statements or prescriptions. Ambiguity in policies provides flexibility for resource managers to use their professional training and experience in resolving issues.

Although policy ambiguity is often a political necessity and is even technically desirable in many circumstances, it does have drawbacks. Vague policies make it difficult to set priorities and identify exactly what is to be accomplished. For example, a forester who must make land use decisions on the basis of "multiple use" does not have a well-defined set of decision rules or criteria for guidance (Davis and Johnson 1987). Vague policies also make it difficult to evaluate program success or failure. Finally, ambiguity invites conflict and managers who must implement vague policies often find themselves in the middle of heated arguments.

U.S. FEDERAL LANDS

Forest Reserve Organic Administration Act (1897), as amended.

No national forest shall be established, except to improve and protect the forest within the boundaries, or for the purpose of securing favorable conditions of water flows, and to furnish a continuous supply of timber for the use and necessities of the citizens of the United States.

Transfer Act (1905)

The following famous forest policy statement is from a letter sent to the chief of the Forest Service (Gifford Pinchot) by the secretary of agriculture (James Wilson) on February 1, 1905, the date the Transfer Act was approved by Pres. Theodore Roosevelt. Pinchot wrote the letter for Wilson's signature.

In the management of each reserve local questions will be decided upon local grounds;...and where conflicting interests must be reconciled, the question will always be decided from the standpoint of the greatest good of the greatest number in the long run.

National Park Service Act (1916)

[The purpose of a national park is] to conserve the scenery and the natural and historic objects and the wild life therein and to provide for the enjoyment of the same in such manner and by such means as will leave them unimpaired for the enjoyment of future generations.

Multiple-Use Sustained-Yield Act (1960)

[I]t is the policy of the Congress that the national forests are established and shall be administered for outdoor recreation, range, timber, watershed, and wildlife and fish purposes.

"Multiple use" means the management of all the various renewable surface resources of the national forests so they are utilized in the combination that will best meet the needs of the American people; making the most judicious use of the land for some or all of these resources or related services over areas large enough to provide sufficient latitude for periodic adjustments in use to conform to changing needs and conditions; that some land will be used for less than all of the resources; and harmonious and coordinated management of the various resources, each with the other, without impairment of the productivity of the land, with consideration being given to the relative values of the various resources and not necessarily the combination of uses that will give the greatest dollar return or the greatest unit output.

"Sustained yield of the several products and services" means the achievement and maintenance in perpetuity of a high-level annual or regular periodic output of the various renewable resources of the national forests without impairment of the productivity of the land.

Wilderness Act (1964)

[I]t is hereby declared to be the policy of the Congress to secure for the American people of present and future generations the benefits of an enduring resource of wilderness.

National Forest Management Act (1976)

It is the policy of the Congress that all forested lands in the National Forest System shall be maintained in appropriate forest cover with species of trees, degree of stocking, rate of growth, and conditions of stand designed to secure the maximum benefits of multiple use sustained yield management in accordance with land management plans.

[T]he Secretary, by regulation, shall establish procedures, including public hearings where appropriate, to give the Federal, State, and local governments and the public adequate notice and an opportunity to comment upon the formulation of standards, criteria, and guidelines applicable to Forest Service programs.

STATE FOREST POLICIES

Arkansas Forestry Commission (Best Management Practices Guidelines for Silviculture)

When possible, stream crossing should take place during periods of dry weather when stream flow is low and the threat of erosion is minimized.

California's Forests and Rangelands (Assessment 1988)

[The state should] encourage California's resource-based industries to aggressively market and promote products here and overseas, through the use of marketing boards, trading companies, information clearing houses, and other methods.

INTEREST GROUPS

Wilderness Society (from Wilderness, 51(181):3; 1988.)

The Wilderness Society is working to restore funding for stewardship and public-use programs and to reduce funding for logging and road construction.

National Wildlife Federation (in Hair 1988)

We need a National Wetlands Protection Policy that explicitly protects wetlands. At the very least, such

a policy should halt the further destruction and degradation of the nation's wetlands. It should require degraded and destroyed wetlands to be restored. And it should encourage the creation of man-made wetlands to increase the nation's resource base.

American Forestry Association (Priorities for 1988, from Annual Report 1987)

Conduct a national campaign to increase funding for National Forest recreation facility expansion, improvement and operation through expanded fees, taxes and appropriation.

FOREST PRODUCTS COMPANIES

International Paper Company (Annual Report 1984)

The objective of our land and timber strategy is to manage our extensive assets to bring the highest economic return for our share owners. We cultivate and harvest trees, develop real estate holdings, explore for oil, gas, and minerals and conduct farming operations. We are deeply committed to protecting and enhancing wildlife, watersheds and recreational areas, and we also have programs that make lands available to the public for hunting, fishing and other recreational activities.

Champion International, Inc. (Annual Report 1986)

Champion is committed to making the most efficient use of its 6.5 million acres of owned and controlled domestic timberlands that make the company one of the largest private landowners in the country. Our long-term objective is to ensure an adequate supply of fiber to our pulp and paper mills at a favorable cost, and to maximize the value of the timber we harvest.

FOREST POLICIES IN OTHER COUNTRIES

The Forestry Act of Sweden (1980)

There shall be a forestry plan for every holding with guidelines for forest management on that holding...in accordance with [government] regulations.

[F]orest owners are obliged...to notify the County Forestry Board of cutting to be carried out on their land.

If a forest stand is over-aged, and the timber-producing capacity of an area is exploited to only a minor extent, the County Forestry Board may decide to force clear cutting and the establishment of a new stand.

Peru's Forest and Wildlife Law (1975)

[F]orest and wildlife resources are public domain and no private person may acquire rights thereto.

Tanzania Forest Ordinance (1982, from Schmithusen 1986)

Any person who without a license or other lawful authority fells, cuts, damages, or removes any national Tree [*sic*] in any state controlled forest, lease hold or free hold land, shall be guilty of an offense against this Ordinance.

The Indian Forest Act (1927)

[T]he State Government may...regulate or prohibit in any forest or wasteland the breaking up or clearing of land for cultivation; the pasturing of cattle; or the firing or clearing of the vegetation.

PLAN OF THE BOOK

This book begins with an examination of how and why forest resource policies are made and discusses the policy process. It then reviews the principal players in making forest policy and concludes with chapters that summarize current forest resource public programs. The text is written for use in forest resource policy classes, which in our experience include students of forestry, outdoor recreation, fisheries and wildlife, range, and resource conservation. Thus the text focuses primarily on forests and their management by these allied professions, and our examples will draw on policy issues in each field of study at various times.

Chapter 2 summarizes the general *process* by which policy issues arise, are considered by governments, and are resolved. Chapter 3 offers insights regarding why governments make particular policy decisions by comparing how markets and governments function in free societies. Chapters 4 and 5 examine how policy-making processes work and how policy decisions are made and evaluated.

Chapters 6 through 11 discuss participants in policy-making and explore why they behave in particular ways and how they influence policy. Participants include government officials and institutions—legislatures, courts, executives, and administrative agencies. They also include unofficial participants such as interest groups, the media, and natural resource professionals.

Chapters 12 through 17 describe *programs* associated with forest policies in the United States—public ownership of forest land, federal forest resource planning, environmental protection, wildlife management, government regulation of forest practices on private lands, and government assistance to owners of nonindustrial private forests. We describe how these policies developed and examine their effects. Finally, Chapter 18 examines forest policies in an international context.

LITERATURE CITED

American Forest Institute. 1985. The forest industry in perspective: Public opinion and the forest products industry—the outlook in 1985. American Forest Institute, Washington, DC.

Anderson, James E. 1984. Public Policy-Making, 3rd ed. Holt, Rinehart & Winston. New York. 179 pp.

Applebome, Peter. 1986. Beetle infestation a bitter environmental harvest. *New York Times,* November 29, 1986, p. 8.

Barlowe, Raleigh. 1978. Land Resource Economics, 3rd ed. Prentice Hall. Englewood Cliffs, NJ. 653 p.

Davis, Lawrence S. and K. Norman Johnson. 1987. Forest Management, 3rd Edition. McGraw-Hill. New York, NY. 790 p.

Food and Agriculture Organization. 1985. Tropical Forestry Action Plan. Food and Agriculture Organization of the United Nations. Rome, Italy. 159 pp.

Hair, Jay D. 1988. Wanted: A national wetlands policy. Pp. 17–19 in: Proceedings, Conference on Increasing Our Wetland Resources. National Wildlife Federation. Washington, DC.

Heidenheimer, Arnold J., Hugo Heclo, and Carolyn Teich Adams. 1983. Comparative Public Policy: The Politics of Social Choice in Europe and America, 2nd ed. St. Martins Press. New York. 367 pp.

Hummel, Fred C. 1984. Institutions and administration. Pp. 213–257 in F. C. Hummel (ed.), Forest Policy: A Contribution to Resource Development. Martinus Nijhoff/Dr W. Junk Publishers. The Hague, Netherlands. 310 pp.

Klimko, Frank. 1986. Six arrested in protest against tree burning. *Houston Chronicle*, October 22, 1986, pp. 1, 10.

McCord, C. M., and J. E. Cardoza. 1982. Bobcat and lynx. Pp. 728–768 in J. A. Chapman and G. E. Feldhamer (eds.), Wild Mammals of North America: Biology, Management, and Economics. Johns Hopkins University Press. Baltimore, MD.

Miles, Bruce R. 1987. Tragedy of the Four Notch: Should we "protect" wilderness by allowing insects to run rampant in its timber? *American Forests* 93(3,4):26–29, 76–79.

Office of Technology Assessment. 1984. Technologies to sustain tropical forest resources. U.S. Congress Office of Technology Assessment, OTA-F-214, Washington, DC. 344 pp.

O'Laughlin, Jay, and Richard A. Williams. 1988. Forests and the Texas economy. Texas Agricultural Experiment Station B-1596, College Station, TX. 65 pp.

Peck, Tim J. 1984. The world perspective. Pp. 21–66 in F. C. Hummel (ed.), Forest Policy: A Contribution to Resource Development. Martinus Nijhoff/Dr W. Junk Publishers, The Hague, Netherlands. 310 pp.

Random House. 1967. American College Dictionary. New York. 1444 pp.

Schmithusen, F. 1986. Forest legislation in selected African countries. FAO Forestry Paper 65. Food and Agricultural Organization of the United Nations. Rome, Italy. 345 pp.

Society of American Foresters. 1983. Terminology of Forest Science, Technology, Practice and Products. Bethesda, MD. 370 pp.

Society of American Foresters. 1985. Defining commercial timberland. SAF 85-06. Position Statement of the SAF and Report by the SAF Task Force. Bethesda, MD. 29 pp.

Stoddard, Glenn M. 1988. Integrated resource management and private forestry: One state's approach. *Journal of Forestry* 86(2):38–40.

Uehling, Mark D., Daniel Shapiro, and Bob Cohn. 1986. Napalming American forests: Smokey the Bear gives and takes some heavy heat. *Newsweek*, October 20, 1986, p. 36.

USDA Forest Service. 1982. An Assessment of the Timber Situation in the United States, 1952–2030. Forest Resource Report No. 23. Washington, DC. 499 pp.

USDA Forest Service. 1988. The South's Fourth Forest: Alternatives for the Future. Forest Resource Report No. 24. Washington, DC. 512 pp.

van Maaren, Adriaan. 1984. Forests and forestry in national life. Pp. 1–19 in F. C. Hummel (ed.), Forest Policy: A Contribution to Resource Development. Martinus Nijhoff/Dr W. Junk Publishers. The Hague, Netherlands. 310 pp.

Warren, Robert J., Michael J. Conroy, William E. James, Leslie A. Baker, and Duane R. Diefenbach. 1990. Reintroduction of bobcats on Cumberland Island, Georgia: A biopolitical lesson. *Transactions of the 55th North American Wildlife and Natural Resources Conference* 55:580–589.

World Resources Institute. 1985. Tropical forests: A call for action. Part I—The plan. International Task Force Report, World Resources Institute. Washington, DC. 49 pp.

World Resources Institute. 1986. World Resources, 1986: An Assessment of the Resource Base That Supports the Global Economy. Basic Books. New York. 353 pp.

Chapter 2

Policy and Political Processes

Those who cannot remember the past are condemned to repeat it.

—*George Santayana 1905*

...there is no one "grand unified theory of public policy." We can make a useful start toward understanding American public policy by considering matters such as these: Who is involved in policy formation, and on what kinds of issues, under what conditions, and to what effect? Just how do policy problems develop?

—*James Anderson et al. 1984*

THE STUDY OF FOREST POLICY

The first chapter in this text presented a definition of forest policy and reasons for its study. This chapter discusses several approaches for studying forest policy. Some policy analysts examine the *historical* development of a policy. Others *compare* policies and institutions in different counties or states or divide the *policy-making process* into stages and analyze events at each stage. Still others focus on the *institutions* responsible for the development of policy. Finally, some students of public policy attempt to *evaluate* policies. These various approaches help explain why and how existing policies have evolved, develop models that allow us to determine when a policy is good or bad, and aid us in predicting how policies might change

in the future. Each approach makes a unique contribution and we will use all in this book. Some chapters emphasize one approach more than others, but our intent is to integrate them in order to better understand why, how, and with what consequences governments make forest resource policies.

ALTERNATIVE APPROACHES

Historical

Historical approaches review past events and laws in order to describe the evolution of forest resource policy. This approach is best exemplified by Dana (1956) and Dana and Fairfax (1980). History is important. It helps to know how past problems arose, what alternatives were considered, and the reasons for making a policy choice. Past events shape not only current policies, but also the alternatives to be considered in the future. As Santayana noted, one who forgets the past is doomed to repeat it.

A variant of the historical approach is the preparation and discussion of case studies. Case studies provide information on the genesis, development, and perhaps resolution of resource policy issues. They form the basis for discussions of objectives, policy alternatives, interest group activities, and policy outcomes. Well-prepared cases are helpful in prompting analysis and interchange about specific forest policy issues. Historical case studies often are interesting and revealing.

Despite its merits, the study of history alone has drawbacks. Students may find history dull, and certainly less appealing than it is to their professors, who experienced "history" as current events in the halcyon days of their youth. History also requires some framework of analysis to interpret the lessons of the past and to apply them to new events. Such frameworks, when integrated with historical study, may reveal insights that allow us to generalize to other contexts.

Illustration: Stages of Forestry Development

An historical approach to forest policy reveals that many places in the world have followed similar patterns in the use and development of forest resources. Marty (1986) describes three stages of forestry development that commonly occur—settlement, protective custody, and management (Table 2-1). The development of American forestry and forest policy can fit within this analytical construct. Doing so not only increases understanding of the historical development of American forest policy, but it also sheds light on tropical deforestation and the fuelwood crisis. These issues can be better understood when we realize that at one time the United States was not a developed nation, but a developing country. We have been through stages of forest resource development that other nations are only beginning. And some countries, such as Germany and Japan, are much more advanced than the United States in their forest management efforts.

Marty (1986) states that the settlement stage involves using timber resources to create lumber and other wood products that help a society develop and expand its frontiers—that is, fulfill its "Manifest Destiny." Jobs and income are created, and land is cleared for agriculture. But all too often this stage is characterized by destructive logging practices, uncontrolled fires, and indiscriminate conversion of some unsuitable areas from forest to croplands. The United States went through this stage during the eighteenth and nineteenth centuries and, on some lands, this stage persisted through the first half of the twentieth century. Many countries in the developing world are still within or just emerging from the settlement stage.

The custodial stage commonly follows settlement and is a constructive response to previous destruction. It recognizes that forests are a limited resource, and that it is possible to conserve forests by controlling logging practices and fire and by regenerating them. In this stage, forest-based industry declines as readily accessible timber supplies are exhausted. Forest land is placed under professional management, and the rebuilding of the forest is usually initiated. Some developing countries have established schools of forestry, forestry agencies, and national forests. These countries are attempting to practice long-term management of their forest resources. This is a difficult task in countries where people still urgently need food and shelter.

The management stage evolves from the custodial stage, and forests once again become capable of supporting forest-based industry. Management includes planned or natural reforestation, timber stand improvement, timber harvest scheduling, and forest environmental protection. Noncommercial uses of the forest such as recreation also are developed to benefit broader segments of society.

The management stage may be broken into various phases. In the United States public land policies led to cooperative public/private protection programs, then to recognition of multiple uses, and finally to the "fully planned" stage of management. The inclusion of the Reforestation Tax Incentives program of 1980 as the last entry in Table 2-1 says more about how American forest policies are pushed through the policy process than it does about historical development, and will be discussed in Chapter 17.

This historical model may oversimplify stages of development. Countries may be in more than one stage at a time, or even regress. Historical cycles have reoccurred. But the model does illustrate that countries or communities go through different stages in the exploitation of their forest resources. These stages also reflect broader economic conditions in a country. When people are well housed and well fed, they are more willing to conserve resources for the future. Economic development often occurs before forest conservation does. Utilization of the forest is often necessary to promote economic development, or even to help promote sustainable resource use.

Institutional

A second approach to the study of forest resource policy may be termed institutional (Behan 1984, Clawson 1984). This approach focuses on the institutions and organizations that make forest policy. Institutions are the official policy-making branches of government and the administrative and regulatory agencies involved in public policy. Government institutions represent structured patterns of individual behavior. Organizations and institutions persist over time and affect public policy by giving advantages to certain groups in society. They control resources or provide services that interest particular groups. Some groups will have greater access and power under one structure than another.

By examining institutional and organizational structure, duties, and functions, one can discover how power is distributed and how particular circumstances yield particular policy outcomes. Institutional studies often examine laws and programs—the outputs of institutions and organizations. Institutional studies also may be made to compare forestry organizations and conditions in different countries and to recommend appropriate organizations for them. This is sometimes termed the *comparative approach* to the study of forest policies (Hummell 1984). This approach to studying policy, however, still lacks the power to explain the political process.

Illustration: U.S. Forest Service Organization

A common way to depict the organizational arrangement of an institution is with an organization chart, with positions of authority arranged in hierarchical fashion and reflecting the allocation of resources and power that has developed over time. For example, for the Forest Service, the top level of the hierarchy is the president, who appoints the secretary of the Department of Agriculture as a cabinet member.

The secretary of agriculture is assisted by the assistant secretary for Natural Resources and the Environment, who in turn governs the operations of the Forest Service and the Soil Conservation Service. The secretary of agriculture seldom has had forest resource training or experience, but the assistant secretary often has. Note that the Forest Service is part of the Department of Agriculture, not the Department of the Interior, which controls most other federal lands. This placement, coupled with the fact that the secretary often does not have much knowledge of or interest in forestry, has historically given the Forest Service more independence than land management agencies in the Department of the Interior.

One indicator of this independence is that the chief of the Forest Service has always been a professional (usually a forester) promoted up through the ranks of the organization, not a political appointee as in Interior. The chief directs the Forest Service to achieve its legislative mandates, including the provision of sufficient supplies of timber, water, recreation, and other forest resources. Beneath the chief are six staff deputy chiefs and officials of the three principal programmatic branches of the Forest Service—the

TABLE 2-1. Historical Approach to U.S. Forest Policy

| Path of Resource of Development | | | | | | | |
| (1) | (2) | (3) Management | | | | | |
Settlement (1)	Custodial (2)	Public Land (3a)	Private Land (3b)	Multiple Use (3c)	Fully-Planned (3d)	Date	Description of Policy
x						pre 1872	Laissez-faire; disposal of public lands
	x					1872	Yellowstone National Park established
	x					1876	First of 200 bills to create forest reserves
	x					1889	American Forestry Association-(AFA) and American Association for the Advancement of Science-(AAAS) petition Congress for reserves
	x					1891	Creative Act established Forest Reserves
		x				1897	Organic Act for Forest Reserves established management authority
		x				1905	Transfer Act transferred reserves from Dept. Interior to Dept. Agriculture
	x					1911	Weeks Act purchased established national forest lands in the East
	x	x	x			1924	Clarke-McNary Act established forest fire protection on private lands
		x	x			1928	McSweeney-McNary Act established Forest Experiment Stations
		x				1930	Knutson-Vandenberg Act established funds for regeneration on national forests

TABLE 2-1. *(Continued)*

Path of Resource of Development

(1)	(2)	(3) *Management*					
Settlement (1)	Custodial (2)	Public Land (3a)	Private Land (3b)	Multiple Use (3c)	Fully-Planned (3d)	Date	Description of Policy
			x			1930s	Tree planting in southern United States
			x			1940s	Tree planting in northern United States
		x				1944	Sustained Yield Forest Management Act
		x		x		1960	Multiple Use–Sustained Yield Act
				x		1964	Wilderness Act
	x	x	x	x		1970	National Environmental Policy Act
		x				1973	Courts petitioned to review Forest Service compliance with Organic Act of 1897
			x			1973	Forestry Incentives Program (FIP)—tree planting and timber stand improvement
					x	1974	Forest and Rangeland Renewable Resources Planning Act (RPA)
				x		1975	Eastern Wilderness Act
					x	1976	National Forest Management Act (NFMA ammendments to RPA)
			x			1980	Recreational Boating Safety and Facilities Act (Title III–Reforestation Tax Incentives)

Source: Adapted from Marty 1986.

National Forest System, the Forest Research, and State and Private Forestry. In 1991 a fourth branch—International Forestry—was created (Figure 2-1).

The three original branches of the Forest Service reflect the historical needs the agency was created to address and the strength of their modern constituencies. The National Forest System (NFS) is by far the largest branch of the Forest Service and includes programs in timber, fisheries and wildlife, recreation, range, and water, spread through the nation. These programs appeal to a broad range of constituents, helping create strong congressional support for national forest programs. The Forest Experiment Stations perform research on many problems, but they have much smaller budgets and staffing levels than the NFS. Forest Service research has focused on public and private forest management in the past, and it is becoming more environmentally oriented now. State and Private Forestry—designed to help nonindustrial private forest owners—has the smallest staff and budget of the three programmatic branches. This is partially because states have developed their own forestry programs to assist private owners and achieve other forest-based objectives. The addition of International Forestry as a fourth program branch indicates the increasing importance of world affairs and issues such as tropical deforestation. The program had less than fifty employees in 1992, but was increasing in importance rapidly. The distribution of budgets and personnel among Forest Service programs reflects the "institutionalized" priorities determined by the policy process.

Process or Analysis

A third approach that may be used to study forest policy examines the process of policy formation. This approach has been termed a *procedural* or *analytical* approach (Behan 1984, Dunn 1981, Worrell 1970). The process approach relies on models of political decision-making processes and applies them to forestry issues. A general framework is used to examine how issues arise; how political decisions are made; how legislative, exec-

utive, or judicial systems operate; and how interest groups influence policy. This approach provides a foundation for analyzing and dealing with new issues, which is lacking in the other approaches. It is, however, somewhat abstract, which may be less appealing to practically oriented forestry and wildlife students. The process approach also may be used to *evaluate* how policies were developed or their effectiveness.

Our Approach

In this textbook, we rely to some degree on all the preceding approaches. Forest policy encompasses history, institutions, processes, and current events, and all elements of policy research can be useful. History tells us where we have been and why current policies exist. Current events illustrate the overriding importance of understanding policy and its impacts on forest, wildlife, range, and recreation management. The study of institutions tells us about formal public organizations, laws, and participants in the policy process. Analysis of the process itself helps us understand how issues arise and are resolved.

We present a process model in the remainder of this chapter and use it in Chapter 4 to describe how issues arise, are placed on policy agendas, and are resolved. This model provides an initial framework for analyzing a variety of events and issues, facilitates wider generalizations, and is flexible enough to be applied to new resource management situations as they arise.

OBJECTIVES OF FOREST POLICY

Forest resource policy, or any other policy, tries to assure that actions will contribute to some ends, objectives, or goals that are deemed desirable by society. Many policy objectives or ends are desirable only because they are means toward the achievement of other ends. Therefore, forest policy objectives must be closely related to the general objectives, attitudes, and values of society itself.

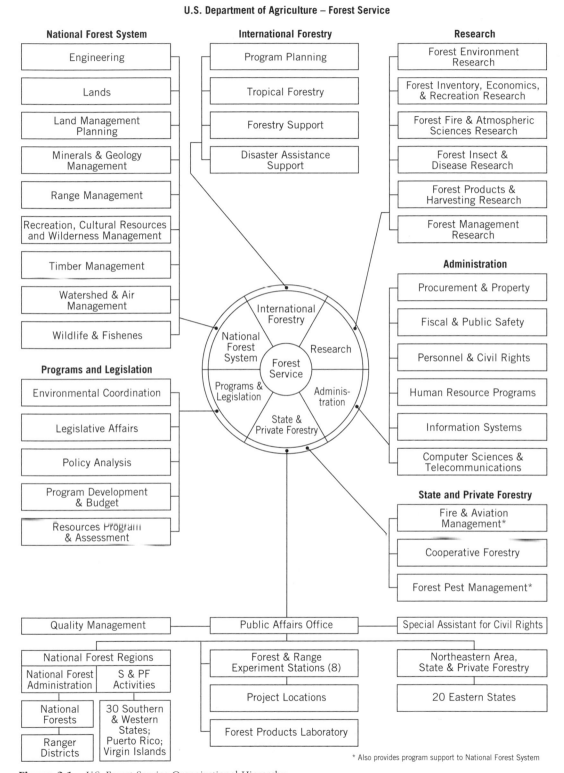

Figure 2-1. U.S. Forest Service Organizational Hierarchy.
Source: USDA Forest Service

SOCIAL OBJECTIVES

In general, people want to obtain direct benefits from forest resources, such as wood, water, wildlife, fish, forage, recreation, and a variety of environmental amenities. The attainment of these benefits serves broad social purposes. The difficulty in forest resource policy is agreeing on and attaining a balanced mix of purposes and benefits.

A primal objective of society is survival; all societies strive to be self-perpetuating. Almost all other social objectives relate to this ultimate end. These subordinate, fundamental social objectives include providing food, shelter, and clothing; providing full employment; maintaining stable economic growth; and protecting the environment. In the United States, other broad social objectives include promoting an equitable distribution of wealth, maintaining democratic political systems, providing freedom of choice, and maintaining the health and welfare of the population. These social goals and others are embodied in the U.S. Constitution, the Bill of Rights, federal and state laws, and other public policy documents.

ILLUSTRATION: FORESTRY ENDS AND MEANS HIERARCHY

Policies come in an interrelated hierarchical series of means and ends (Duerr 1982, Worrell 1970). Consider a traditional forestry job—a forester or a technician is perched in a lookout tower, scanning the horizon in every direction for a plume of smoke, the sign of a forest fire. What the lookout is doing seems straightforward and simple—spotting a fire and reporting its location. The practice of regularly and systematically checking for smoke is a policy in itself. The immediate objective is to minimize the number of acres burned. But at another level, the lookout is helping to ensure that there will be adequate supplies of timber to maintain economic stability, and ultimately help society prosper. Indeed, there

- Survival of society
- Economic stability
- Adequate wood supplies
- Growth of timber
- Reduce occurrence and severity of wild forest fires
- Keep forest fire damage to a minimum
- Immediately supress all wildfires
- Discover all wildfires as soon as possible
- Staff all lookout posts (towers or airplanes when burning index reaches a certain level)

Figure 2-2. The Fire Lookout's Hierarchy of Ends and Means.

is a chain of interrelated policies, or ends and means in this example, as illustrated in Figure 2-2.

This hierarchy of interrelated means, ends, and policies illustrates that the nature of an objective or a policy depends on the vantage point from which it is viewed in the hierarchy. An end is almost always a means to some other end. Forest policies need to serve society's needs. The lookout's search for a plume of smoke may be the reason for the existence of that particular job, but it serves a larger purpose of forest protection, which is a matter of public forest policy. Most resource management activities are tied to broader social objectives.

CONFLICTS AMONG OBJECTIVES

The importance of objectives is somewhat obviated by the realities of politics. Participants in policy-making often have conflicting objectives. We may not be able to eliminate conflict, but it is useful to understand how conflicting social objectives may produce policies that are internally inconsistent. According to Worrell (1970), there are at least four classes of conflicts among forest policy objectives:

1. **Physical Impossibility** One objective prevents or interferes with the attainment of another. For example, forest road building may temporarily reduce water quality.

2. **Economic Conflict** The total amount of funds available for resource management are limited. For example, federal and state natural resource budgets are small and must be allocated among competing resource programs; in addition, they compete with defense and social programs.

3. **Value Conflicts** Different groups may have conflicting values about resource use and preservation. For example, local lumber mill workers prefer timber harvests for primary or secondary forest products manufacture so they can keep their jobs; wilderness advocates prefer to preserve forests for less tangible benefits to society.

4. **Time Perspectives** Individuals are often considered to have short planning horizons in natural resource use and management as compared to a longer time horizon that society may prefer for resource conservation. For example, poor people in less developed countries are deforesting their environment more rapidly than world opinion generally deems prudent, perhaps to the detriment of future generations in their countries or to the world as a whole.

These possible conflicts in objectives are a principal source of forest resource issues. It is not physically possible to manage for all uses on all forest stands. Even if it were, scarce budgets or personnel would present problems. Additionally, many people do not agree on the objectives for which forests should be used, either in the present or for future benefits.

ANALYSIS OF POLICY PROCESSES

Forest resource policy is one form of public policy. Thus, policy process models can apply to forest resource issues, as they do to other social issues. These models aid in understanding the process, help individuals work within the system to implement policies, or help change policy outcomes to those favored by the participants. Many theories of public policy exist; none is universally accepted. In this text, we will base analysis of forest policy issues on models developed by Anderson (1979) and Jones (1970). One characteristic of these models is that explicit deliberation over appropriate objectives for policy does not occur. Instead, the policy process seeks to solve immediate problems via the "best" method possible. This does not obviate the importance of policy objectives, but it recognizes that disagreement regarding appropriate objectives may itself be a problem.

POLICY PROCESS MODEL

Anderson et al. (1984) describe six steps in the policy process—problem formation, policy agenda, policy formulation, policy adoption, policy implementation, and policy evaluation (Figure 2-3). The first step involves identification of a problem. A problem means that someone or some group is not satisfied with the current policy (status quo) regarding some matter. Different individuals define problems differently. During the mid-1980s in Florida, several serious highway accidents were attributed to reduced visibility caused by smoke from prescribed burns. Most people saw these accidents as a problem, but they identified different causes and solutions. Most saw an air pollution problem and called for more regulation of burning. But one observer suggested that the situation could be defined as a traffic problem and that it could be solved by regulating traffic during burns. The way in which a problem is defined constrains the set of solutions (or policy changes) that will be considered.

Public policy involves deciding which problems to address and what methods to use. In order to change an existing policy, the first step is to get government officials recognize the problem. Problems become public when large numbers of people are involved and organize to seek relief from a governmental institution or agency. The people who perceive the problem demand action from the people who have authority to

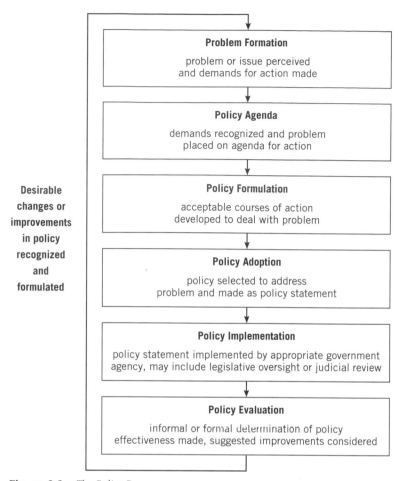

Figure 2-3. The Policy Process.
Source: Adapted from Anderson et al. (1984)

change the policy, such as legislators, judges, agency heads, or local government officials.

People demand government action for thousands of problems. However, only a fraction receive serious attention. Those that do comprise the policy agenda. (Agenda-setting theory, the study of why some problems receive government attention and others do not, will be discussed in Chapter 4.) Once problems or issues reach agenda status, policy formulation begins. Acceptable courses of action must be developed to deal with public problems. Seldom will these courses involve radical changes, and policymakers often choose not to act.

Policy adoption occurs when the policymakers accept a particular solution to a problem. New policies may be adopted by government agencies operating within their legislative mandates or may require specific legislative or judicial action. Policy adoption implies that the government intends to follow a new course of action regarding the problem or issue. Frequently, adoption also implies that funds must be appropriated to execute the new policy.

Once the policy statement (law, rule, or order) is adopted, government must implement the policy. The content and effect of public policy may change greatly during implementation. Policy is usually carried out by administrative agencies, but Congress and the courts also may be involved in natural resource issues. Congress may circumscribe administrative discretion by passing detailed legislation, through oversight, or by selectively funding individual line items in agency budgets. During the mid-1980s Congress reduced appropriations for Forest Service road building to limit timber harvests in areas that were then roadless. State legislation is generally much more specific and prescriptive than is federal law. Courts do not enact legislation, but they often are asked to interpret the meaning of the sometimes vague laws enacted by Congress. Overall, though, administrative agencies are the most important actors in implementing (or altering) policy.

Once implemented, policies are sometimes evaluated. Did the policy work? Did the Forestry Incentives Program, which provides federal cost-share payments to landowners, get more trees planted? Did state programs of technical forestry assistance to private forest landowners increase timber supplies? What were the costs and returns from the programs? Systematic evaluation of policies and programs seeks to quantify the social impact of policies and the extent to which stated objectives have been met. In the past formal evaluation was infrequent, but it is increasing given current state and federal budget austerity. Attempts to evaluate program costs and benefits before enacting legislation also have increased in recent years. Implementation and evaluation are discussed in Chapter 5.

Anderson's policy model traces a policy from the problem formation stage to its evaluation stage. Adding a loop to the process (Figure 2-3) shows that policy making is an iterative process. Seldom do problems or issues merely appear from nowhere in the formation stage. Rather, they are based on some prior policy. Perhaps the opinions or values of a group or society changed, or natural events triggered concern about existing policies—for some reason the current policy is now perceived as a problem by some people. The process then begins anew and ends with a new policy—problem resolution—and perhaps policy evaluation. Informal feedback or formal evaluation of the new policy may produce minor or major changes in formal policy statements or administrative implementation.

LEVELS OF POLITICS

The general model that Anderson presents may apply to different levels of politics. Three broad levels exist—micropolitics, subsystem politics, and macro- or national interest politics (Anderson 1979, 1984). *Micropolitics* refers to an individual's or firm's seeking a favorable ruling from an administrative agency or passage of a special bill that in the legislature. Such rulings and laws are designed to distribute government funds or modify regulations in order to aid the individual or firm. *Subsystem politics* involve a small segment of national politics, such as an interest group (or groups), a public agency, or a congressional committee. National politics involve a broad variety of interest groups, politicians, and public institutions.

Anderson's model also can be applied to administrative politics and policy-making—that is, how agencies make decisions about their programs and policies. For example, the adoption of clear-cutting as the dominant silvicultural method used by the Forest Service resulted from an administrative process. Opposition to this policy, however, eventually moved the process to a subsystem or even national level of politics, as the following illustration shows.

ILLUSTRATION: THE CLEAR-CUTTING CONTROVERSY

The ongoing clear-cutting controversy illustrates how Anderson's policy formation model can be applied to analyze issues. The Forest Reserve Act (Creative Act) of 1891 established a national policy of keeping some forested land in federal ownership. One objective for creating the forest reserves (later the national forests) was to protect remaining uncut forests from the perceived problem of destructive logging practices and catastrophic fires that had characterized lumbering in the Northeast, Midwest, and Southeast. The Organic Act of 1897 provided management direction for the forest reserves, including provisions allowing the harvest of timber. However, little timber was harvested from national forests for decades.

Clear-cutting Begins in the 1950s

Before World War II not much of the nation's wood supply came from national forests. After World War II the public needed more timber and other resources from the national forests. Housing construction and recreational use increased. In order to respond to the perceived need for building materials, national forests increased harvest levels and began the widespread use of clear-cutting during the 1950s and 1960s. This action was the result of Forest Service problem formation (step 1 in Anderson's model), but the agency only superficially went through the policy agenda and policy formulation stages (steps 2 and 3). Instead, it summarily developed, adopted, and implemented the administrative policy of clear-cutting, probably without much concern for nontimber client groups (steps 4 and 5). The clear-cutting policy was helpful, though, in providing more timber from national forests.

Many people began to oppose Forest Service clear-cutting as early as the late 1940s and continuing through the 1950s and 1960s. Critics of clear-cutting argued that it destroyed wildlife habitat and caused erosion that damaged fisheries and that clear-cuts were too large and often located on fragile and inappropriate sites. These complaints essentially began anew the problem formation stage of policy-making (step 1).

Federal foresters responded to criticism by claiming that the selection of harvest methods was a technical decision that should be left to professionals. They contended that clear-cutting was an economically efficient means to remove overmature and unproductive stands and to regenerate desirable species, thereby increasing forest productivity and usefulness. Mounting opposition led to an agency "information and education" program in 1965, designed to explain to the public that harvesting practices on the national forests were good for wood production and

environmental quality. Thus, although some citizens believed clear-cutting was the problem, Forest Service officials believed that misinformed citizens were the problem.

Opposition Mounts in the 1970s

At about the same time, a group of citizens from West Virginia organized to oppose clear-cutting on the Monongahela National Forest (Figure 2-4), demanding changes in agency administrative policy. The citizens believed that clear-cutting destroyed habitat for small game and fish. Nevertheless, Forest Service officials refused to abandon the program. Citizens complained to state legislators and to members of Congress, who all lodged complaints of some type about clear-cutting with the Forest Service. However, the state legislature could not direct the federal Forest Service to change practices, and the state's congressional representatives could not get the agency to change, either. Thus the attempts by opponents to have the clear-cutting issue placed on the Forest Service agenda for change were initially unsuccessful.

Similar, intense local opposition to clear-cutting and terracing on the Bitterroot National Forest in Montana also developed (Figure 2-5). Sen. Lee Metcalf of Montana asked Dean Arnold Bolle of the University of Montana, School of Forestry to conduct a study of Forest Service practices. The Bolle Report, issued in 1970, roundly criticized the agency. The report concluded that clear-cut units were too large, clear-cuts were used where other methods would have been more appropriate, and the costs of reforestation (including building terraces to help collect water for seedlings) far exceeded the returns one could expect from such poor sites. The problems on the Bitterroot attracted national media coverage, including articles in the *New York Times* and *Washington Post*.

In 1971, the Sierra Club published *Clearcut: The Deforestation of America* (Wood 1971), which discussed Monongahela and called for a new forest policy. In the same year Sen. Frank Church of Idaho conducted hearings on Forest Service harvesting practices. Senator Church's committee heard

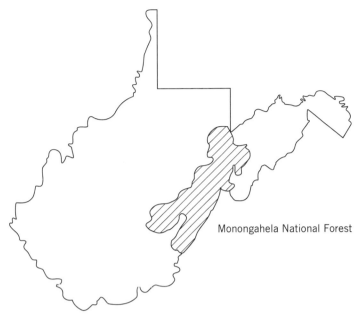

Figure 2-4.   Location of the Monongahela National Forest in West Virginia.

testimony from a variety of concerned citizens, agency officials, and forest scientists. The committee decided that no new legislation was necessary but that care should be taken in the planning and implementation of clear-cut harvests. The committee issued non-binding guidelines. The Forest Service agreed to abide by the Church guidelines.

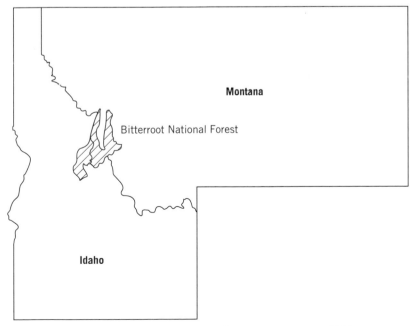

Figure 2-5.   Location of the Bitterroot National Forest in Montana and Idaho.

The Monongahela Decision of 1975

Although national press coverage of the issue abated, local opposition continued. Some groups that were unable to change Forest Service policies tried another approach to get on the policy agenda and reduce clear-cutting. In May 1973 the Izaak Walton League, the West Virginia Highlands Conservancy, and others filed suit against the secretary of agriculture to enjoin the Forest Service from conducting several planned clear-cuts on the Monongahela National Forest. The suit claimed that clear-cutting, as practiced, violated the language in the Organic Act of 1897 that allowed the harvest of "dead, matured or large-growth" trees and required the marking of individual trees before removal. On behalf of the Forest Service, government attorneys argued that the requirements of the Organic Act were outdated and infeasible and that the language should not be taken literally. The court ruled in favor of the plaintiffs, stating that current Forest Service practices were inconsistent with a literal reading of the the statute. The judges wrote that if the requirements were indeed outdated, then Congress should change the law (Barlow 1978).

The U.S. Department of Agriculture filed an appeal in the Fourth Circuit Court of Appeals. The appeals court upheld the trial court decision in August 1975 (*West Virginia Division of the Izaak Walton League of America, Inc.* v. *Butz,* 367 F. Supp. 422 [1973], 522 F.2d 945 [1975]). The appeals court ruling applied the injunction to stop Forest Service clear-cutting in all states in the Fourth Circuit (West Virginia, Virginia, North Carolina, and South Carolina). The Forest Service complied by halting all timber sale offerings scheduled in the four states. A district court ruling in Alaska used the Monongahela reasoning to halt a clear-cutting operation there. Forest Service officials predicted that if the decision were implemented nationwide, a 50 percent reduction in timber availability from the national forests would result. They also contended that the costs of administering timber sales would increase by more than 100 percent if the agency were required to comply with a lit-eral interpretation of the Organic Act (Fairfax and Achterman 1977).

The National Forest Management Act of 1976

The results of the Monongahela decision again placed clear-cutting and national forest management on Congress's agenda, and many different bills to deal with the problem were considered. Sen. Jennings Randolph of West Virginia introduced a bill that would have limited Forest Service management discretion. Groups supporting the Randolph bill argued that Forest Service decision-making was biased toward the production of timber and that other resource values were being ignored. They wanted Congress to rein in the agency and force it to practice multiple use management.

Sen. Hubert Humphrey of Minnesota sponsored a bill that was supported by members of the wood products industry. The bill would have repealed the section of the Organic Act that was the basis for the Monongahela decision. It contained no specific direction regarding harvesting methods or environmental issues and would have preserved the Forest Service's discretion in forest management. Supporters of the bill argued that forest management was a technical enterprise and that Congress could not legislate good silviculture.

Congress eventually enacted the National Forest Management Act of 1976 (NFMA), an amended version of the Humphrey bill. The NFMA contained a provision that defined criteria for clear-cuts similar to the Church guidelines, but the provision contained no absolute requirements. NFMA also addressed other environmental issues raised in the Randolph bill (species diversity, rotation age, marginal lands, nondeclining even flow), but again it mandated no firm requirements. Much of the law dealt with national forest planning. Congress required the secretary of agriculture to develop regulations to guide planning. Interdisciplinary teams were to play a major role in the planning process. Similarly, procedures were to be developed to facilitate public participation in national forest planning. Thus Congress did adopt a policy (NFMA) that was supposed to solve the problem of clear-cutting on national forests.

Controversy Continues in the 1980s

Despite NFMA the Forest Service continued to use clear-cutting for most timber harvests in the 1980s (as its policy implementation). The Forest Service and its foresters seemed to be wedded to even-age management regimes of clear-cut and plant, and public opposition grew more virulent. Public opposition and lawsuits were initiated to stop any cutting of the old-growth (or ancient) forests in the Pacific Northwest in order to protect spotted owls, a species threatened with extinction. Similar opposition developed in the South to oppose harvests near red-cockaded woodpeckers, another endangered species. By 1990 many foresters within the agency voiced opposition to clear-cutting as well, and scientists suggested the Forest Service look at new approaches to forest management. These actions revived the issue of appropriate timber harvest methods. By 1990, the agency developed a "New Perspectives" program to implement alternative silvicultural and harvesting systems. In June 1992, the chief of the Forest Service announced that the agency would stop the use of clear-cutting whenever possible.

The continual issue of clear-cutting on national forest land illustrates how the policy process occurs. Problems are identified, placed on agendas for action (often with some difficulty), and alternative policies are considered. New policies may be adopted and implemented, and sometimes accepted. Formal evaluation of policies may be performed by agencies or other branches of government (e.g., Congress). Informal feedback—such as the public dissatisfaction with clear-cutting—also provides a means of evaluating the success or acceptability of a policy.

The clear-cutting controversy illustrates that the policy process operates in a political and social environment that includes demands and support for agency policies. The Forest Service adopted the policy of clear-cutting to respond to public demands for housing and forest industry demands for timber. But the agency's failure to develop support from all groups led to pervasive opposition. This caused the issue to expand from local concerns to sub-system and then national levels of politics over the last four decades.

PROCESS MODEL APPLICATIONS AND LIMITATIONS

Other natural resource issues also aptly illustrate the elements of the policy process. Problem formation requires that some members of society perceive that a forestry problem exists—that is, the current policies are unsatisfactory. For example, in the 1970s water pollution from forestry activities was identified as a problem. Air pollution, herbicide and pesticide usage, and solid waste disposal also were perceived as resource problems. Once sufficient public interest and support were generated, the issues were placed on federal and state government agendas. Demands by conservation groups and individual citizens forced legislators, bureaucrats, and judges to address these environmental issues.

The three branches of the federal government adopted numerous policies in order to solve environmental problems in the form of laws, administrative regulations, and court rulings. Congress enacted new laws such as the National Environmental Policy Act of 1969 and the Federal Environmental Pesticide Control Act of 1972, and made substantial revisions to existing statutes, such as the Federal Water Pollution Control Act Amendments of 1972, 1977, and 1987, the Clean Air Act Amendments of 1970 and 1977, and the National Forest Management Act of 1976. It also created the Environmental Protection Agency to help protect the environment and administer the new laws. Administrative rules were developed to control forestry pollution under the federal water quality laws; public input guidelines were formulated as administrative policies under the National Forest Management Act (NFMA). These policies have undergone periodic reviews to examine their effectiveness in achieving the original policy objectives. The laws and administrative rules also have been challenged in court, such as the Monongahela clear-cutting decision that led to the NFMA. Policymakers have also revised some of the goals, with substantial interest group involvement. Implementation problems are corrected, additional problems perceived, and new policies formulated and implemented; the process continues.

The process model applies equally well to discrete, smaller problems addressed at the state, local, or agency level. The steps are the same; only the number of people and groups involved in the process differ.

A few additional generalizations can be made about policy process models. First, they tend to oversimplify the process. Events that lead to any forest resource policy are detailed and complex. Models of the policy process capture the spirit, but not the guts, of a policy decision. In fact, making policy is quite messy (Jones 1984). The "policy process" sounds sterile, especially compared with the flesh and blood bargaining, logrolling, threats, firings, and power struggles that actually are involved. Losing a job in a power struggle is much more personal than the term *policy process* might imply.

The sequence of events in policy process models need not be followed in order, and steps may be omitted in some cases, as the clear-cutting illustration shows. Also some activities may occur simultaneously. There are no clear criteria for judging when a policy action is complete. Additionally, the government agenda is created not only by the private sector, but also by the government itself, either as a consequence of the effects of existing policies and programs or as a result of specific issues. The activities need not be limited to a single institution. Policy implementation is not performed solely by bureaucrats, nor is legislation developed only by legislators. Different institutions and organizations may perform different activities for different issues.

However, any model or theory serves only to describe the abstract workings of an event; policy models are no different. A statement that a timber stand averages 5000 board feet of pine sawtimber per acre sounds trivial, but it conceals the hard work, hot weather, rain, bugs, briars, or snakes that may have been encountered in the stand volume cruise. Even so, abstractions or summaries are still useful.

A process model helps one view forest policies as the result of a series of political events. To perceive and solve a problem implies that one group is satisfied and another is not. Policy-making clearly involves political choices among competing claims, and the models help depict this. They help identify the rules of the game of making political decisions.

Public policy models could also be applied on a micro level—to the politics and processes in individual public agencies or private organizations. The perception of a problem, demands for action, placement on the agenda, and adoption and implementation of new policies occur in the workplace as well as in government. This is not the focus of this text, but the parallel can prove useful in dealing within organizations and institutions as well as in making public policy. When they are not satisfied with their employer's policies, people may seek to change them through the "system" or policy-making process. If unsuccessful, they may vote with their feet and leave.

The model we have adopted here contributes to an understanding of political decision-making. Models are helpful if they simplify and order political life, yet conform to reality. A model should identify the significant variables in decision-making—the issues, agendas, actors, and outputs. A model must also communicate something meaningful about the political system and how it operates. Additionally, a model can help direct inquiry and research; it can help in formulating and testing hypotheses and in analyzing policies.

Our policy process model helps explain the process by which resource policies—purposive courses of action followed over time—are initiated, proposed, deliberated, and resolved. As such, it can help natural resource managers to be more effective participants in making and implementing policy decisions that affect their jobs.

INITIAL REALITIES ABOUT POLITICS

In addition to presenting a general model of policy-making, we should note that public policies are a result of *politics*. Natural resource managers often decry the problems of politics in general and bemoan specific policies as well. They often feel that the political process is the problem, not the solution to problems. Politicians, the courts, interest groups, the media, and others are castigated for creating new problems and worsening old ones. The political process itself is suspect and not to be trusted with decisions better left to trained professionals. This pessimistic view of government is inappropriate; government has limits and failings, but so do businesses and people.

Jones (1984) discusses some "initial realities" that might temper some of the idealism of resource managers and place the role of government policy in perspective (Table 2-2). The first class of realities discusses the differing perceptions of problems and the degree of action required by government. The

TABLE 2-2. Initial Realities About Political Processes

About Problems
1. Events in society are interpreted in different ways by different people at different times.
2. Many problems may result from the same event.
3. Not all public problems are acted on in government.
4. Many private problems are acted on in government.
5. Many private problems are acted on in government as though they were public problems.
6. Most problems are not solved by government, though many are acted on there.
7. Policymakers are not faced with a given problem.
8. Most people do not maintain interest in other people's problems.
9. Public problems may lack a supporting public among those directly affected.

About Decision-Making
1. Many policy actors proceed as if goals were unambiguous.
2. Most decision-making is based on little information and poor communication.
3. Problems and demands are constantly being defined and redefined in the policy process.
4. Policymakers sometimes define problems for people who have not defined problems for themselves.
5. Most people do not prefer large change.
6. Most people cannot identify a public policy.
7. All policy systems have a bias.
8. No ideal policy system exists apart from the preferences of the architect of that system.
9. Most decision-making is incremental in nature.
10. People have varying degrees of access to the policy process in government.

About Programs
1. Programs requiring intergovernmental and public participation invite variable interpretations of purpose.
2. Inconsistent interpretations of program purposes are often not resolved.
3. Programs may be implemented without provisions for learning about failure.
4. Programs often reflect an attainable consensus rather than a substantive conviction.
5. Many programs are developed and implemented without the problems ever having been clearly defined [sic].

Source: From *An Introduction to the Study of Public Policy,* 3rd ed., by Charles O. Jones, p. 34. Copyright ©1984, 1977, 1970 by Wadsworth, Inc. Reprinted by permission of Brooks/Cole Publishing Co., Pacific Grove, CA 939540.

second group discusses the unclear nature of public policy problems, the incremental nature of the decision-making process, and the inherent biases in any political system. The third group points out the inconsistencies of government programs, their lack of formal evaluation, and their often unclear or only partially agreed-upon purposes.

Jones (1984, p. 35) writes that

Taken together, these propositions suggest a highly relative and pluralistic decision-making system characterized by compromise, incrementalism, and continual adjustment, yet subject to biases in one direction or the other. Over time this system may be self-correcting with regard to the many social and economic interests that make up the policy; in the short run it tends to favor those groups with enough resources to make a lot of noise.

Overall, Jones's observations on the political process provide a useful introduction to more detailed study of forest resources policy. Obviously, the U.S. policy-making process is not ideal. But these realities would apply to any political system. Using criteria such as duration, individual freedom, access to government, or acceptance of policy, the U.S. government must certainly be considered more successful than most.

Jones's initial realities illustrate the complexity and disorderliness of the policy-making process. It really is much more than six boxes tied together with a feedback loop. Most national forestry legislation has gone through a complex process before enactment, including, at least, passage by the legislature and signing by the president. Enactment of some laws, such as the National Forest Management Act of 1976, was prompted by a court ruling that the law was being administered incorrectly. Policies are not the product of one governing mind, but rather a conglomeration of ideas and compromises among many people and institutions.

Jones's initial realities indicate that forest policies would develop incrementally. Drastic changes in forest (or other) policies are the exception rather than the rule. Apparently small changes have, however, had some substantial long-term consequences. Authorizing the reservation of the national forests rather than disposing of the land to individuals was a significant policy change in the late nineteenth century. Similarly, purchasing back forest lands from private owners in the East to create national forests, as provided in the Weeks Law of 1911, proved not to be an incremental decision. Both of these changes occurred after considerable debate, proposed legislation, and compromise and were not perhaps seen as radical at the time. But the authorized change in directions did lead to substantial policy changes in the long run.

However, unsuccessful proposals made in the 1980s to dispose of some public land confirm the preference for small changes. These proposals were viewed as radical and received so little support that the Reagan administration could not even find Congress members willing to sponsor such legislation. The same could be said of unsuccessful efforts in the 1930s to greatly expand the national forest system and regulate all private forest landowners.

Jones also intimates that fragmented and inconsistent policies are common. Given the diversity of the process and groups seeking governmental action, it is not surprising that some policies may be contradictory. Tobacco subsidies, taxes on cigarette sales, and cancer warning labels on cigarette packages do not represent consistent policy. Nevertheless, both the tobacco industry and antismoking groups can claim success in their lobbying for governmental action. Another characteristic of policy is that diverse criteria are used to judge policies and goals. Economic criteria may be important but are by no means dominant. Innumerable other political and social criteria, explicitly or implicitly stated, are used to make policy decisions. These points are revisited throughout this book.

SUMMARY

Forest resource policy may be studied in many ways. History describes past events that led to present policies. Institutional studies describe the workings of the official and un-official organizations that make or influence policy. Process or analytical approaches develop models to explain how issues arise, are placed on agendas, and are resolved. Case studies rely on past or current events to illustrate the policy process.

In theory, forest policies are designed to meet an explicit social objective. In practice, policies often are proposed and selected to resolve an immediate problem, without explicit definition of objectives. We presented a simple six-step process model for the study of forest resource issues. Problems are perceived, and demands are made to place those problems on a specific agenda for action. New policies are then formulated to deal with the problem, and a specific policy is selected to address the problem. That policy statement is then implemented and subsequently evaluated for its effectiveness. Based on the evaluations and continual public feedback, improvements in the selected policy are considered and perhaps adopted. Last, we noted that policy problems are often ill-defined; all policy systems have a bias; policy changes usually are incremental; and public programs often are inconsistent, reflecting obtainable consensus, not substantive convictions.

LITERATURE CITED

Anderson, James E. 1979. Public Policy-Making, 2nd ed. Holt, Rinehart & Winston. New York. 200 pp.

Anderson, James E. 1984. Public Policy-Making, 3rd ed. Holt, Rinehart & Winston. New York. 179 pp.

Anderson, James E., David W. Brady, Charles S. Bullock III, and Joseph Stewart, Jr. 1984. Public Policy and Politics in America, 2nd ed. Brooks/Cole Publishing Co. Monterey, CA. 422 pp.

Barlow, Tom. 1978. Evolution of the National Forest Management Act of 1976. *Environmental Law* 8(2):539–547.

Behan, R. W. 1984. What is and what should be taught in university forest policy courses? Pp. 42–52 in Proceedings, Workshop on Forest Policy Education. Resources for the Future. Washington, DC.

Clawson, Marion. 1984. An overview of forest policy education. Pp. 78–103 in Proceedings, Workshop on Forest Policy Education. Resources for the Future. Washington, DC.

Dana, Samuel T. 1956. Forest and Range Policy. McGraw-Hill. New York. 455 pp.

Dana, Samuel T., and Sally K. Fairfax. 1980. Forest and Range Policy, 2nd ed. McGraw-Hill. New York. 458 pp.

Duerr, William A. 1982. Criteria for forest management. Pp. 57–66 in William A. Duerr et al. (eds.), Forest Resource Management: Decision-Making Principles and Cases. O.S.U. Bookstores. Corvallis, OR.

Dunn, B. Allen. 1981. Forest policy instruction in the forestry curriculum—conference proceedings. Clemson University, Department of Forestry. Clemson, SC. 21 pp.

Fairfax, Sally K., and Gail L. Achterman. 1977. The Monongahela controversy and the political process. *Journal of Forestry*, 75(8):485–487.

Hummel, F. C. (ed.). 1984. Forest Policy—A Contribution to Resource Development. Martinus Nijhoff/Dr W. Junk Publishers. The Hague. 310 pp.

Jones, Charles O. 1970. An Introduction to the Study of Public Policy. Wadsworth Publishing Co. Belmont, CA. 170 pp.

Jones, Charles O. 1984. An Introduction to the Study of Public Policy, 3rd ed. Brooks/Cole Publishing Co. Monterey, CA. 276 pp.

Marty, Robert J. 1986. The economics of forestry—forestry and economic development. Pp. 409–410 in G. W. Sharpe et al. (eds.), McGraw-Hill. New York.

Santayana, George. 1905. The Life of Reason. Scribner. New York. (reprinted 1954)

Wood, Nancy. 1971. Clearcut: The Deforestation of America. Sierra Club. San Francisco, CA. 151 pp.

Worrell, Albert C. 1970. Principles of Forest Policy. McGraw-Hill. New York. 243 pp.

Chapter 3

Markets, Government, and Forest Resources

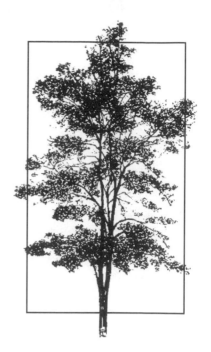

Government, even in its best state, is but a necessary evil; in its worst state, an intolerable one.

—Thomas Paine, Common Sense, Chapter 1

Why has government been instituted at all? Because the passions of men will not conform to the dictates of reason and justice without constraint.

—Alexander Hamilton, Federalist Paper No. 15

INTRODUCTION

Many debates in resource policy relate to whether decisions regarding production of forest outputs are more appropriately made by the private or the public sector. Are there situations in which public ownership and government management are more socially desirable than private ownership and management? To what extent should government intervene in the management decisions of private owners? Many economists argue that resource decisions are best made by private owners because governments are coercive while market exchange is voluntary. Others counter with the argument that government decision-making provides opportunity for the expression of civic values that are not considered in market transactions.

People have always had a "love–hate" relationship with governing. When a few people are put together in virtually any situation, they naturally organize themselves in some fashion to deal with shared goals and purposes. Once people have designed institutions to achieve those purposes, they spend a remarkable amount of time and energy complaining about what they have created. That is human nature and also fundamentally why some people favor certain institutional means of accomplishing objectives that others perceive as foolish.

In almost all countries—except those with extremely strong ideological commitments to centrally planned economies, such as the former Soviet Union and the current People's Republic of China—the public and private economic sectors work together to provide the goods that citizens want. Even communist countries have some private markets; all market countries have a large amount of government control. As Figure 3–1 illustrates, the private and public sectors take different routes to achieving the desired end of satisfying human wants by providing goods and services. The private sector relies on the mechanism of prices determined in markets. The public sector, or government, relies mostly on the policy-making process whereby decisions regarding programs and budgets are politically determined, although market prices and costs of goods are considered in decisions.

This chapter reviews the ideas that underlie historic and current debates regarding the relative effectiveness of markets versus governments in the efficient allocation and distribution of natural resources. Resource allocation refers to decisions about how all resources—including natural resources—will

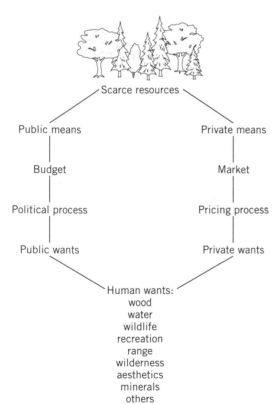

Figure 3–1 The interplay of public and private economies.

be used. Distribution focuses on who receives the benefits and who bears the costs of resource allocation decisions.

Public policies may take several approaches to determining resource allocation and distribution: (1) unregulated markets, (2) government education or assistance for landowners in order to promote public goals, (3) government regulation of resource management on private lands, and (4) public ownership and government management of forest land. These approaches define roles for government and for markets in the allocation and distribution of forest resources. All four approaches are used as forest resource policies in the United States.

Historically, in the United States as in virtually all other countries, the public and private sectors have worked together to achieve socially desired forest outputs in what may be termed a "mixed economy." Several observers, such as Duerr and Duerr (1982), have referred to the American blend of market and socialistic approaches to forest resource management and policy. The pattern of ownership of timberland (see Figure 1–6) is but one piece of evidence of the operation of a mixed economy in the U.S. forestry sector.

American citizens, public policy makers, policy analysts, and resource managers have debated the relative merits of government and markets since colonial times. This debate remains crucial for natural resource management today. Public budgeting problems ensure that all government spending will be scrutinized closely. Many forest resources are not traded in markets, so government must be involved in their production or protection. Additionally, even some market goods, such as timber or recreation, may not be optimally produced under private market systems and may require government intervention.

This chapter begins by examining the influence of American social values on forest resource policy and continues with a discussion of the theory of markets in regulating the production and consumption of forest outputs. An examination of government roles in resource management policy follows. Several illustrations of forestry debates regarding the appropriate roles of markets and government also are presented. The themes underlying these government/market debates are quite likely to shape discussions about forest policy in the 1990s and beyond. The debate may be summarized in a single question: What is the appropriate mix of government and market processes that will produce the natural resource outputs people in society want? The answer is a matter of public policy.

FORESTS AND AMERICAN VALUES

Much of America's public policy rests on a value system developed throughout our history. Everyone agrees that public policies should be good, just, and proper. But the meaning of these terms varies from one group to another. Most industrial foresters do not share the same values regarding land use as do members of the Wilderness Society. Both might agree that some type of land ethic is appropriate. But industry professionals are apt to translate this idea into land use for commodity production, Wilderness Society members would favor intentionally leaving land in its natural state. Quite clearly, their different value orientations lead to different conclusions as to what is the appropriate objective for forest use and management.

Values vary over time and by country. For example, in the 1500s Martin Luther disapproved of monopoly control of resources and the use of supply and demand to set prices (Kapp and Kapp 1949). Luther believed that resources should cost only their "true" worth. These beliefs reflect concern about maintaining community morals. Those who hold such beliefs are willing to restrict private activity in order to protect the communal order. In the United States communal values have been challenged by a more individualistic orientation.

American values form the basis for all our public and forest resource policies. Americans have always favored individualism and usually favored private property rights. *Life, liberty, and the pursuit of happiness* were the watchwords of the American revolution against England; the Bill of Rights codifies the many constitutional provisions that protect individual freedom and prevent the unlawful seizure of private property by the government. This heritage of individual freedom is balanced by strong pressures to conform to community morals. For example, the Puritan belief system, the Protestant work ethic, and the Catholic emphasis on family and community all temper unbridled individualism.

Another broad theme underlying U.S. public policy has been a tension between government and markets regarding the regulation of commerce. Most settlers came to America for greater personal opportunity and individual freedom; during the American revolution they rebelled against oppressive government. In place of an oppressive English monarch, the colonists formed a very weak government, embodied in the Articles of Confederation. The Articles were clearly inadequate, however, leading to thirteen petty fiefdoms, not a United States. Thus the U.S. Constitution was drafted, allowing the formation of a strong federal government that could control trade, commerce, and freedom. The *Federalist Papers*, which embodied a role for government as well as for markets in determining U.S. policies, were a powerful and determining force leading to the ratification of the Constitution. Even so, the laissez-faire approach favored by many original settlers and by some modern economists still remains important.

INDIVIDUALISM

American values can be summarized into a few principal goals of society that have endured until today. First, the United States continues to try to ensure individual, market, and political freedom, including preservation of law and order. Second, the public wants to ensure equal opportunity, if not equal outcomes, as well as fairness and community stability. The American nation also remains committed to improving living standards of its citizens by encouraging economic growth and by providing essential social services for the needy. Last, although it may be a newer public goal, substantial efforts to protect the environment and natural resources from pollution or other harm are clearly favored.

The American value of individualism may be translated into direct preferences for allowing people the freedom to satisfy their desires and individual rights of liberty so long as their actions do not endanger or infringe on the rights of others. These rights include the right to take risks, such as using wilderness areas for rock climbing, as long as others are not endangered. Freedom also implies that individuals should have the choice among as many alternatives as possible, and that forest resource uses should not be restricted unnecessarily.

Individualism also favors entrepreneurship and the work ethic. America is often viewed as the land of opportunity, where any individual (e.g., as in the Horatio Alger stories) with ability and perseverance can make his or her fortune. To some extent, individualism and entrepreneurship imply that government control should be limited so that individuals can pursue their goals. Friedman (1962) suggests that political freedom and market freedom (capitalism) are inextricably linked. But somehow the rights of others need to be protected too.

COMMUNITY

The norms of community and equity have been long-standing American traditions. The first settlers in America came and lived as families in towns—not as individuals taming the West. In recent years the goal of preserving the family served the Reagan political campaigns well; Jimmy Carter became well-known by attending local caucus meetings in Iowa and town meetings in New Hampshire. Preserving communities has been part of forest policy since the national forests were created, and community stability remains crucial in debates about old-growth forests. Community and democracy are long-held traditions influencing public decisions. The principles of federalism support the role of a strong

democratic government in making decisions for the community and society. These principles have been expanded greatly in the last two centuries. Democracy also requires trust and honesty among citizens and the elected and appointed government officials.

The related concepts of fairness, justice, and equity also influence the selection of public policies. Provision of a social safety net may favor preserving local communities dependent on public timber, or seeking alternative means for generating local income and employment. Equity implies that policies should be fair among classes of people. Those who gain from policies should pay for them. It even implies that policies should favor disadvantaged groups. Equity considerations may favor small landowners, small mills, or minority groups in developing recreation programs. Equity also will favor equal opportunity for different users of the forest. Equity over time will favor protecting and improving the U.S. forest resource base now, so that future generations may enjoy its benefits as well.

INTEGRATION

Alexis de Tocqueville, a French aristocrat who toured the United States in the early 1800s, was one of the first observers to note the tension between American commitments to the ideals of individualism and to equality and community. Belief in individualism implied limited government with minimal restrictions on private activities. Unfortunately, he noted, individualism also tended to break down the community ties that supported the family, the church, and democratic government (de Tocqueville 1848).

In response to the belief that the nation, church, and community should take precedence over the individual, social scientist Amitai Etzioni (1989, p. 14) suggests that Americans need both individual market freedoms and shared community values: "Individuals and community are both completely essential, and hence have the same fundamental standing" (p. 14). Individuals are not free actors, devoid of the influences of class, power, or social structure, acting only as participants in economic decisions. Nor is the state omnipotent and social conformity required. Instead, people must evaluate social values and market signals in making personal decisions.

Recent political and economic reforms in Eastern Europe and the former Soviet Union reflect these same tensions. The eastern European communist countries rushed toward greater individual and economic freedom in 1989, and the USSR followed and broke apart in 1991. But neither the politicians nor the citizens themselves were eager to abandon the social safety net that ensured employment, food, and shelter. They sought greater political and economic freedom common in capitalistic countries, but they still wanted to avoid the extreme individual risk, especially unemployment, common in market systems.

Individualism, community, and equity are persistent underlying themes in current policy debates regarding the respective roles of government and markets in many facets of American life, including natural resource management and policy.

MARKET AND NONMARKET GOODS

Forests produce what have been termed both *market* and *nonmarket goods*. That is, forests produce goods such as timber that can be sold by landowners and bought by loggers and goods such as clean water that have no direct market value. This distinction between the types of forest outputs may be carried further, depending upon the amount of exclusion possible of a good and the degree to which a good may be used by more than one person (termed *joint consumption*).

Savas (1982) defines these different types of goods as (1) pure individually consumed goods with feasibility for complete exclusion (private goods), (2) pure jointly consumed goods with feasibility for complete exclusion (toll goods), (3) pure individually consumed goods where complete exclusion is infeasible (common-pool goods), and (4) pure jointly

consumed goods where complete exclusion is infeasible (collective goods).

Classifying goods in this manner helps describe the conditions necessary for the goods to be produced. Private goods (such as timber) are owned by individuals and usually only consumed by individuals after a payment is made. Common-pool goods, such as air, open range, groundwater aquifers, or fish in the sea, are consumed by individuals, but it is difficult or impossible to make people pay for their use. Toll goods, such as movies, water supplies, and national parks and forests, do have exclusive properties or potentials, so users could be excluded unless they pay. Collective goods, such as national defense, police protection, picturesque scenery, and air and water pollution control, are consumed by many and owned by none, thus making direct payments for such benefits impossible.

The distinctions among these types of goods vary depending on the nature of each good and the property rights legally assigned to each. Generally, however, goods with exclusive rights can be traded satisfactorily in market transactions. Goods characterized by joint consumption are less likely to be satisfactorily allocated by market processes alone, because there are no appropriable property rights and thus no "market" price. Thus, government intervention may be deemed appropriate for making and enforcing decisions about collective or common-pool goods—which ones to provide, how to finance them by taxes or other means, how to allocate their costs, and how to allocate the goods themselves if some control can be exercised over consumption (Savas 1982).

This is not to say that governments themselves need to provide collective goods or services. They could instead work with private firms to provide such services. Contracts, franchises, grants, vouchers, private markets, or other means could be used to provide for and allocate collective and common-pool goods. Depending on the type of resources produced, various governmental, contractual, private market, or other arrangements for providing services might be used. These are discussed in the remainder of this chapter, and indeed in the rest of the text as well.

FOREST OUTPUTS AND ISSUES

Forests produce a variety of goods, with varying degrees of joint consumption and excludability. Additionally, forests are unique in their degree of joint production—one forest may produce timber, recreation, water, wildlife, fish, forage, scenic amenities, and oxygen, among other outputs. The extent to which forest outputs are considered commodities that have market prices also varies. These characteristics of noncommodity and commodity value, joint production, joint consumption, and excludability have contributed to the development of numerous resource management and policy issues.

TIMBER

Timber is the forest output most often sold in markets. Not all forest lands will grow commercially desirable timber within a time frame that makes timber production financially attractive. Many forested lands are reserved from timber production for wilderness areas, parks, wildlife refuges, and even suburban developments. Nevertheless, timber is still the principal market good provided by forests.

The intensity of timber management varies widely. On most of the radiata pine plantations in New Zealand, intensive forest management practices occur throughout the life of a stand, including planting, applying herbicides, thinning, pruning, burning, fertilizing, and merchandising the final harvests. Forest industry managers in the United States usually employ intensive site preparation, planting, and competition control in southern pine and Douglas-fir stands. Management of natural hardwood stands in the Northeast or in the Lake States often is much less intensive and usually is confined to modest efforts at timber stand improvement or perhaps some type of planned silvicultural harvest methods.

Timber management of natural stands often is less intensive in less developed countries, although intensively managed plantations are becoming more common.

Timber management issues are diverse and will be discussed throughout this text. They include questions about whether we will have adequate timber (at reasonable prices) in the future; the trade-offs between intensive management (monocultures, herbicides, prescribed fires) and environmental protection (biological diversity and naturalness); and whether economic (e.g., net present value), biological (e.g., mean annual increment), or social (e.g., sustained yield–even flow) criteria should determine timber management practices. Timber production issues also arise from competition and conflicts with other forest resources, such as wilderness, recreation, fish, and wildlife. Appropriate management and harvest policies for timber on national forest and private lands are debated often.

WILDLIFE

Wild animals are common-pool goods that are seldom controlled exclusively by one forest owner. The individual ranges for some species of wildlife and fish may be contained within one forest ownership, but most are not. Landowners need to fence, post, and patrol their lands to exclude others from harvesting animals. Even if owners can eliminate trespassing, they cannot avoid the effects of other people's land use practices on wildlife populations. Management practices of many owners over a large land area will determine the effective stocking levels on any individual's land.

These characteristics of wildlife have motivated some governments to claim public ownership of wild animals and fish. Very large forest estates can be managed to encourage greater wildlife populations in their environments and to regulate the take of some, but not all, wildlife species on their property. Generally, however, our state and federal wildlife, fishery, or natural resource agencies are authorized to manage wildlife populations via hunting and fishing regulations on public and private land. These agencies also own and manage forest, wetland, and prairie areas as wildlife refuges. U.S. public ownership of wildlife and fish traces back to British wildlife law. Despite common-pool characteristics, private ownership of wildlife does occur in some other countries and in the United States on large private hunting estates.

Wildlife management issues such as the degree of effort and expense spent on managing game and nongame species, federal versus state control of wildlife resources, appropriate population levels and hunting regulations, and protection of endangered species are continual concerns. Public attention recently has focused on protection of wildlife habitat from destruction by farming, timber harvesting, and urban development. Wildlife interest groups lobby for protection from herbicides, pesticides, or water pollution; public policies related to these concerns affect forest management to a considerable extent.

RANGE

Range resource management deals with pasture, prairie, and open forest lands. Many public agencies such as the Forest Service and the Bureau of Land Management have jurisdiction over forest and range lands. Range management issues have been among the most vitriolic and violent in U.S. history, and many remain unresolved. Settling the West, fencing the open range, federal retention of range lands, and federal range lease policies have all been hotly contested, beginning with gunfights in the nineteenth century and continuing with personal threats to public land managers today. In 1991 "cattle-free by '93" was a rallying cry for environmentalists in the West, who described cattle as "hooved locusts."

Open range is often cited as a classic case of a common-pool good—one that any individual (or cow) could use, although none had exclusive rights. The classical argument (Hardin 1968) against an open range is that

it leads to overgrazing and destruction of the range. Cattle owners seek to maximize their own herd's grass consumption. This short-sighted behavior occurs because no one has exclusive property rights, and thus no incentive to conserve forage for their own future use—because someone else will beat them to it.

Open range in the United States today has aspects of an exclusive resource. The U.S. Forest Service and the Bureau of Land Management lease most of the range lands under their jurisdiction to individual permittees. Through various political maneuvers, however, associations of permittees generally have managed to keep grazing lease payments for federal lands well below those for similar private lands, raising the issue of a public subsidy. Land management practices on federal range lands are the subject of frequent debate. Feral horses and burros are protected by public policy, even as they adversely impact range resources. Practices such as draglining native vegetation (tearing up shrubs with bulldozers and chains) are common and controversial. The overall condition of public rangelands could be greatly improved. Cattle conflict with wildlife, water quality, and recreation; yet cattle ranching is part of America's romantic heritage.

WATER

Water quantity and quality are valuable outputs of forested lands and are affected by forest management practices. In the western United States, water yield from forest lands has been a public concern for decades. In the East, excessive water yields from cutover, denuded forest lands were used as the principal justification for the Weeks Law, which authorized purchasing and managing national forest lands in the Appalachian Mountains during the early part of the century. The Johnstown flood killed at least 2000 people in Pennsylvania in 1889. Part of the devastation was attributed to deforested hillsides in the watershed, much as flooding and human misery in Bangladesh and Thailand today are partly attributed to deforestation of mountainous areas. In the 1980s concern about forest water yields in the East heightened again, as the growing population placed increasing demands on limited supplies.

Water quality became a paramount public policy topic in the 1970s. The 1972 Federal Water Pollution Control Act (FWPCA) Amendments, and later amendments as well, have mandated that our nation's waters be restored to fishable, swimmable, and drinkable conditions and that no further degradation of water quality in existing streams and lakes can occur. This has led to efforts to control industrial point source pollution (e.g., manufacturing plants such as pulp mills) and nonpoint source (broad area) pollution (e.g., from forest and agricultural lands). It also led to federal regulations designed to protect wetlands from point and nonpoint source pollution. President Bush declared there would be no net loss of wetlands, thus limiting losses from indiscriminate conversion to other uses.

Water quality and quantity policies can have direct impacts on forest management practices and, obviously, on fish and wildlife populations. The 1972 FWPCA spurred the development of *best management practices* (BMPs) to control forestry-related pollution and protect designated uses of water, including fish spawning and rearing requirements. Many western states have statutory forest practice acts that require BMPs; most eastern states rely on voluntary compliance with BMPs.

Water quantity also is affected by forestry practices. Timber harvesting generally increases water yields in a particular watershed. But to have much effect on regional water supplies, harvesting would have to occur on a massive scale and would likely disrupt other forestry or wildlife management objectives and outputs. Wetlands are an important component in preserving long-term stable water flows because they act as storage buffers and water quality filters. Thus many states have enacted or are considering enacting wetlands protection laws, in part to protect limited domestic water supplies and in part to protect wildlife habitat and provide other environmental benefits.

RECREATION

Forest recreation in the United States has increased in importance throughout this century. Prior to World War II, there was little recreation on the national forests and national parks because of their distance from most population centers. After the war, the affluence, leisure time, and mobility of Americans increased. National parks and national forests became popular recreation destinations. At the same time, national forests began increasing their timber harvests to meet needs for new home construction.

The increasing pressures from people using forests for recreation and timber production have led to numerous public land debates. National forest management plans are often criticized by recreational and environmental groups for paying inadequate attention to outdoor recreation or wildlife concerns. Different outdoor recreation groups prefer different and sometimes incompatible uses. Some favor dispersed forms of recreation such as backpacking, bird watching, and cross-country skiing. Others advocate intensive recreation development to support downhill skiing, off-road vehicle travel, and recreational vehicle camping.

In the national parks, enduring issues include policies for lodging and concession facilities, the maintenance of existing parks, land acquisition for park expansion, and control of development blight adjacent to parks. The need for user fees for public land recreation is hotly debated. Competition between public and private camping facilities has been an issue. The regulation of forested areas to ensure scenic views now occurs, much to the pleasure of some landowners, and the displeasure of others. As pressures for both intensive and dispersed outdoor recreation facilities increase, so will debates over national, state, and local outdoor recreation policy.

WILDERNESS

Public forest land may be reserved as a wilderness area. Private forest land may be taken by eminent domain powers of the government and included as public wilderness or other reserves. Criteria for reserving wilderness lands in the United States have been rather fluid, ranging from no evidence of human habitation or alteration of the environment (i.e., no stumps or roads) to little evidence of recent human activity in an area. The amount of forest land that we could and should set aside for wilderness lands is an enduring issue for public policy debate. Wilderness advocates assert that we need more natural forest land to provide biological diversity, support viable wildlife populations, prevent extinction of endangered species, and protect many other benefits. People who oppose expansion of wilderness areas suggest that we need forest products, oil, minerals, or even developed recreation areas more than we need additional areas that will be allowed to revert to natural conditions. Some say we have enough wilderness; others disagree. As the outbreak of pine beetles in Texas described in Chapter 1 illustrated, wilderness management practices (or lack thereof) on public lands may also adversely affect adjacent forest properties—a vital issue to those neighbors. The massive wildfires that occurred in Yellowstone in 1988 could not be confined to wilderness and focused national attention on the plight of public land neighbors.

OTHERS

Forests produce many other outputs. Minerals, gas, and oil lie beneath forest lands. Local roads may be built to remove timber or allow for forest recreation; state and federal highways may pass through forests. Hiking trails, scenic rivers and streams, and lakes are all apt to be located in forested lands. Perhaps most important, people like to live in forested areas and have built residences and vacation homes on forest land at an increasing rate.

This greater focus on the amenity values of forests has led to a plethora of public policy issues. Protecting scenic rivers and trails may preclude timber harvests on adjacent forest lands. Suburban sprawl has led to increasing disputes about timber harvesting, log transport, smoke, and chemical applications in formerly rural areas. Many homeowners now appreciate forests for their contribution to a pleasant rural atmosphere, rather than for timber production. Development sites are usually worth more with trees than without, which also militates against timber harvesting, or at least against clear-cutting.

As more people move to forested areas, problems with wildlife may increase. People generate garbage, attracting unwanted raccoons, rats, mice, or other pests. By the late 1980s residents throughout the United States became alarmed about Lyme disease, which is spread by tiny ticks that thrive on deer. The disease can cause permanent arthritis-like symptoms and impair heart function. Many suburban residents have called for a complete eradication of deer, an ironic twist for people who moved out of town to enjoy the rural quality of life.

Forests provide fuelwood for heating and cooking, thereby releasing carbon dioxide and methane gases. Growing forests produce oxygen and convert atmospheric carbon dioxide to stored carbon compounds, thus ameliorating the "greenhouse effect" of global warming. In developing countries, slash and burn agricultural practices contribute to the loss of millions of acres of forests each year, perhaps contributing to increased global warming.

Last, we should mention that there are illegal forest outputs as well. Most notably, marijuana is reputed to be the second largest cash crop (after timber) grown on U.S. national forests. This is a private good that is grown on public land and sold in a (black) market. There are many reports of threats to foresters who discover the weed and of booby traps on national forest land. Control of such illicit activities is an important public policy.

These problems are not unique to the United States. Managing forest lands, preventing timber theft, and protecting natural resources are extremely difficult in some developing countries, where poverty, unequal distribution of land, and fuelwood use prevail. The cultivation of hemp, coca, and opium and the processing of hashish, cocaine, and heroin in forests are lucrative and prevalent. Forests serve to harbor guerrillas and as places for battle; many such forests are destroyed by warfare.

MARKETS AND FOREST RESOURCES

The preceding section described the value system that underlies public policy in the United States, outlined the types of goods that forests provide, and highlighted some current policy issues regarding the use of forests. This section examines the extent to which a private-market, free-enterprise economic system can provide efficient and equitable resource allocations. We pay particular attention to the characteristics of markets and the goods that are traded in them. Generally, a *market* may be defined as the place, time, persons, and circumstances involved in the exchanges of a good for a price (Duerr 1960).

NEOCLASSICAL ECONOMIC THEORY

Classical political economists generally believed that goods had value because people found them useful in satisfying needs for food, shelter, or clothing. This theory of value failed to explain why water, which was very useful, had a low market price, and diamonds, which had very little use, had high market prices. Neoclassical economists, most notably Adam Smith, developed a theory of value based not only on practical usefulness, but also on psychological value and the costs of production.

Smith and other economists in the eighteenth and nineteenth centuries developed the concept that market prices are determined by the equilibrium of supply (production costs) and demand (utility). In 1776 Smith championed the effectiveness of profits and markets to allocate resources and improve society:

> But it is only for the sake of profit that any man employs his capital in the support of industry; and

he will always, therefore, endeavor to employ it in the support of value, or to exchange for the greatest quantity of either money or other goods.... He is in this, as in many other cases, led by an invisible hand to promote an end which is not part of his intention. Nor is it always the worse for society that it was no part of it. By pursuing his own interest he frequently promotes that of the society more effectually than when he really intends to promote it. (1776/1976, p. 477)

At the end of the nineteenth century, Alfred Marshall formalized the principles that Smith had enunciated. Using mathematics and many basic assumptions, neoclassical economists have proven in theory that a price system generates a completely efficient organization of a pure free-enterprise, private-market economic system (Randall 1981). This terminology often is shortened to the more common term *free-market economy*.

The value premises and theoretical assumptions that underlie the neoclassical analysis of pure free-enterprise market economies raise crucial issues. Neoclassical market superiority is based on the value position that the personal wants of individuals should govern the use of resources and that *efficiency* should be the sole criterion for allocating goods and services. Personal desires and efficiency are consistent with the individualistic, entrepreneurial strain of the American character. They are not always consistent with American commitments to equity, equality, and community—which also form important bases for public policies.

EFFICIENT MARKET REQUIREMENTS

Economists enumerate several requirements for the efficient operation of market economies, which are the basic assumption of neoclassical theory. Efficiency generally implies producing the greatest value of market goods with a given set of inputs, or producing a given output at the lowest possible cost. Although the neoclassical model of a market economy identifies a set of four conditions necessary to achieve efficiency, these conditions often do not hold in practice. A brief description of these conditions follows:

1. The first requirement is the establishment of *property rights*—all goods must be owned and property rights must be well defined, exclusive, enforceable, and transferable (Gwartney and Stroup 1982, Randall 1981). When property rights are well defined, it is clear where one person's rights end and another's rights begin. Exclusivity implies that anyone wishing to use a resource must have permission from the owner; that is, the owner has the right to exclude other potential users. Enforcement ensures that owners can exercise their rights. When property rights are not enforceable, problems of overexploitation and inadequate provision emerge (see previous discussion of types of goods). When property rights are well defined, exclusive, and enforced, the owner's efforts will be rewarded directly, and costs will not be imposed on others without their consent. Transferability makes market transactions possible and ensures that those who value a good the most will be able to purchase it. All of these conditions regarding property rights ensure that owners have the incentive and the means to allocate resources efficiently.

2. Both buyers and sellers must be *well-informed* regarding the qualitative and quantitative characteristics of goods and services and the terms of any exchange (Gwartney and Stroup 1982, Kneese, Ayres, and d'Arge 1970). A forest landowner who underestimates the value of stumpage on the property may choose to withhold timber from the market or may sell it for less than it is actually worth. Similarly, an owner who is uninformed regarding logging practices may allow an unscrupulous or unskilled logger to degrade the productive capacity of the land.

3. Competition among buyers and sellers must exist to ensure efficient resource allocation. No individual firm should be able to affect any market price significantly by decreasing or increasing the supply of goods and services offered or purchased. Thus all assets must be individually owned and managed and participants in any exchange must be small units. This is commonly referred to as *atomistic competition* (Kneese et al. 1970). Imperfect competition may exist in many timber markets where there may be only a few or, in some cases, only one buyer or seller.

4. A final neoclassical assumption for the efficient operation of markets is that transaction costs must equal zero (Musgrave and Musgrave 1984, Pejovich 1984). Transaction costs may be defined as any costs incurred in negotiation, contracting, or monitoring the terms of an exchange (De Alessi 1980). In reality, there are always some transaction costs; large ones lead to market inefficiency. Thus whenever a forest owner incurs costs in preparing, negotiating, and monitoring a timber sale contract, transaction costs are greater than zero.

If property rights to all resources are established, all participants in the market are well informed, the market is competitive, and transaction costs are zero, then economic theory implies that voluntary exchange of privately owned assets is the most efficient way to allocate scarce resources. The parties to any market exchange (buyer and seller) determine the value. Prices serve as the incentive for production of goods and services, ration consumption, and signal changes in supply and demand by reflecting scarcity. Interest rates reflect the price of capital, allocating resource use over time. The price mechanism allows individuals to serve the common good while pursuing their own interests. An implication of this analysis is that the role of government should be limited to deciding questions of income distribution and defining and enforcing the rules of property and exchange.

PUBLIC CHOICE THEORY

In addition to demonstrating and advocating that free markets are most efficient at allocating resources, many economists have advocated that economic principles affect government management (and mismanagement) as well. Modern advocates for greater reliance on free markets to allocate resources have relied on public choice theory and suggest that many publicly-owned resources should be privatized (see Anderson 1983, Deacon and Johnson 1985, Dowdle 1984, Hanke 1984, Stroup and Baden 1983, Wolf 1988).

The first and foremost contention of privatization is that private, transferable ownership rights are necessary to prevent resource abuse (Stroup and Baden 1983). Lack of private ownership provides no incentive for wise use, defined as use that produces the highest measure of economic efficiency. Freely transferable private ownership of resources, it is argued, would allow the market to ration scarce resources in an equitable and efficient manner. Bid and asked prices would provide owners with information and incentives. Prices would simultaneously inform consumers of the values that others place on a particular resource. Privatizers contend that private ownership and resource allocation by the market price mechanism promote efficiency, adaptiveness, and individual freedom. By contrast, privatizers conclude that government programs promote inefficiency, rigidity, and coercion. Of course, these claims have been widely challenged.

Public choice theory has been used in support of privatization. The theory suggests that failures of government agencies and programs are worse than market failures and imperfections. Governmental failings are generally attributed to perverse economic incentives in government agencies and the involvement of specialized interest groups seeking preferential treatment at the expense of the general public or other groups (Buchanan and Tullock 1972, Niskansen 1971, Stigler 1971).

Public choice theory states that five factors tend to undermine the accountability of public decision makers or bureaucrats (Stroup and Baden 1973, 1983):

1. No citizen has the time, resources, or desire to analyze every policy issue.

2. Some individuals and interest groups do try to influence specific policies in which they have a pronounced interest. These actors tend to dominate a particular policy arena because others with more diffuse interests do not care enough to participate.

3. Political representation limits the accountability of policy makers because individual legislators represent many citizens with varying preferences and beliefs. Representatives elected by citizens are not compelled to vote in a manner consistent with any individual preference system. This differs substantially from market processes, where each purchase by an individual is a "vote" in favor of a specific good or outcome.

4. Elected officials prefer to provide benefits (resources) to constituents now, rather than preserve them or defer consumption to the future.

5. Governments have no internal control on efficiency or no incentive to reduce costs. In fact, bureaucratic incentives favor growth, not stasis; the bigger the budget, the better. O'Toole (1988) criticizes the U.S. Forest Service on this point, contending the agency's primary goal is to maximize its budget.

Wolf (1988) calls these problems with government involvement "nonmarket failure." Just as markets may fail to perfectly allocate goods and services, so might government, the nonmarket sector. Characteristics of nonmarket goods and services produce four conditions that lead to problems in efficiency and equity: (1) With public goods, such as national defense, law enforcement, education, and research, outputs are difficult to define and measure. The quality of the product is particularly hard to maintain. (2) Government often has a monopoly; consumers have no other choices. (3) Government production technology is uncertain. (4) The connection between program costs and benefits is tenuous. As a result, there is little incentive to reduce costs or terminate an unnecessary program. Thus program expenses increase without respect to benefits.

The nature of government services leads to abuses. All agencies try to expand their clientele, personnel, and budgets. They also try to develop territories and control information, to the detriment of the public. Political processes may produce large inequities based on the distribution of power and privilege. Public policies place authority in the hands of some to be exercised over others. Such power may be applied with scruple, compassion, and competence. But it may not be; opportunities for corruption and abuse arise, resulting in social inequity.

The shortcomings of government programs have been evident in natural resource management. Stroup and Baden (1983) cite several examples, including clear-cutting on environmentally fragile forest soils, below-cost U.S. Forest Service timber sales that cost more to administer than the revenue produced; overgrazing on Bureau of Land Management range lands, public water projects that benefit a few heavily subsidized interest groups, and costly removal of vegetation by dragging chains between two bulldozers to uproot pinyon pine-juniper grazing lands for little or even negative benefits in terms of wildlife protection or grazing habitat. Zaslowsky (1989) paints an extremely bleak picture of how cattle grazing on public lands is turning the American West into a new desert, while private lands remain reasonably well managed.

ILLUSTRATION: PRIVATIZATION OF THE NEW ZEALAND FOREST SERVICE

One solution to the problems posited by public choice incentives is to simply privatize public lands. Debates over public (govern-ment) versus private (market) provision of goods and services have not been confined to the United States. In the 1980s several countries made significant shifts in public policies. Great Britain, France, Portugal, Australia, and New Zealand altered public policies to favor market processes rather than government ownership or control. The most significant of these changes in the forestry sector was the reorganization of the New Zealand Forest Service. The reorganization has been described as privatization or corporatization (Hemphill 1988).

During this century, New Zealand developed extensive social controls and state ownership of industries such as banking, hotels, transportation, mining, and forestry. The New Zealand Forest Service had functions akin to those of the U.S. Forest Service: research, landowner assistance, policy development, pest control, and the management of publicly owned forest land. In most of the areas, the N.Z. Forest Service performed in a manner comparable to the U.S. Forest Service. However, public forest land management in New Zealand was much different.

The N.Z. Forest Service operated most of its land on a commercial basis. Many old-growth forests were cut and left and often did not regenerate. (This did not foster good relations with environmental groups.) The N.Z. Forest Service was successful in establishing vast plantations of exotic Douglas-fir and Monterey pine before World War II. The agency acquired land, managed plantations, and sold timber for many products. However, the operations consistently lost money because they tried to fulfill political objectives at the expense of business objectives (Hemphill 1988).

In 1983 New Zealand citizens elected a new prime minister from the Labour Party. His minister of finance promptly set about dismantling the entanglement of the state in industry. One result was that the Forest Service was broken up into several entities.

A new Ministry of Forests took over the research, landowner assistance, pest control, and policy development roles. A new Ministry of Environment was created and given control of the remaining native forests, most of which were reserved as national parks. Industry had few objections to this, because by this stage these parks contained relatively little merchantable timber volume. The plantation forests and sawmills were placed into a public New Zealand Forestry Corporation, which was put up for sale to private investors.

The results of the reorganization were dramatic and traumatic. First, privatization led the N.Z. Forestry Corporation to realize its first profit in years. Second, during the formation of the corporation, all employees of the old N.Z. Forest Service were laid off and had to reapply and compete for jobs in the new organization. After the change, employment was reduced by 60 percent. In August 1989 the N.Z. Forestry Corporation did offer its forest lands for sale, even advertising in the *Wall Street Journal*. Subsequent land claims by the native Maori people, however, forced most of the sale offerings to be changed from "forest land" to "current timber on forest land plus certain growing rights."

Hemphill (1988) notes that many people doubt that such privatization could occur in the United States. However, New Zealand is far more socialized than the United States, and still took such actions. As this chapter has indicated, there are many reasons and proposals for increased privatization or corporatization of U.S. public forests. These have included outright sale, long-term leasing of productive forest lands to industry for management and harvest rights, short-term granting of concession rights to the land, and cost-sharing arrangements between public and private organizations.

Problems with public range management in the western United States have prompted similar calls for privatization. The argument is that privatization might help eliminate overgrazing and encourage wildlife habitat renovation, which could be largely paid for by hunting on these lands. These issues of public or private resource ownership and management will form the basis for many U.S. natural resource policy deliberations in the 1990s.

MARKET FAILURE

Markets often fail to meet the previously described requirements or conditions for efficient operation that are the basic neoclassical assumptions of market superiority. When market failure is severe, analysts and interest groups often call for some form of government action (Cubbage and Haynes 1988, Wolf 1979). The following sections examine the causes and consequences of market failures in the allocation of forest resources.

Property Rights

Property rights to a resource confer control of that resource. Such rights are most valuable when ownership is outright and exclusive and the property can be easily exchanged for other goods and services. Market failure may occur when property rights are inadequately defined, not exclusive, or poorly enforced. These types of market failure occur with collective and common-pool goods.

Unregulated market allocation could result in overexploitation of common-pool goods and inadequate provision of collective goods. Difficulties in excluding potential users from these types of goods make establishment of property rights costly, and thus unlikely. Public policy responses to these problems may take several approaches. The most common response is government management of a resource in the form of public ownership. Another response is government regulation of private owners. Despite the arguments of privatizers, large-scale transfer of public lands to private owners is unlikely in the United States. Private management of public lands, such as hotel, restaurant, gift shop, and tour guide concessions in national parks, is more common and is likely to increase.

Nonmarket Costs and Benefits

Another area of market failure occurs when the costs and benefits associated with a good are not reflected in market prices. Economists refer to nonmarket costs or benefits as *externalities*, or secondary effects. These occur when the activities of one person affect the welfare of other persons who have no direct means of control over those activities, whether it be in production, consumption, or exchange (Hirshleifer 1984). Externalities may occur among individuals and firms at one point in time or over periods of time. In forestry, external or secondary outputs are pervasive, both among current forest landowners and among present and future generations. Soil erosion, loss of site productivity, and pollution are examples of external costs (Griffin and Stoll 1984).

Polluted air and water are not counted in the cost of production for the individual firm; instead, society bears the cost. Governmental intervention in the market may force firms to internalize such external costs, either through taxes, regulations, redefinition of property rights, or other means. External benefits may occur when producers fail to capture all the value of a product through the price of a market exchange. This seems to promise a bonus, but in practice it does not. Producers will make less of the good than would be socially desirable (Lindblom 1977). An example of external benefits is leaving soil erosion buffer zones or windbreaks on agricultural lands. These provide excellent wildlife habitat, but landowners generally have no mechanism to capture such secondary benefits.

Water and air pollution may result from timber management activities, such as site preparation, harvesting, or road building. Applications of chemicals such as fertilizers, pesticides, or fire retardants to forest and range lands have the potential for external effects, as do prescribed burns. Forest and range managers also produce positive externalities. By performing prescribed burns for timber or range management, they are likely to increase habitat for some wildlife. But private forest and range owners, like farmers, are unlikely to receive the full value of increased wildlife production, as they are seldom paid for their habitat improvements.

America's forests were heavily harvested in the 1800s. Some timberland was cleared and became productive farms; other forests were cut, burned, and left idle for decades (this is sometimes referred to as timber *mining*). Cut-over timberlands may not have represented a significant cost to former owners or timber cutters who harvested and abandoned the lands, but they were a cost to society. These denuded lands contributed to flooding and soil erosion, property damage, and loss of life. Abandoned cut-over forest lands created conditions for horrendous fires that were common near the turn of the century. Wisconsin's Peshtigo fire, on the same day as the Chicago fire in 1871, claimed 1200 lives, or about 1 percent of the entire population of Wisconsin at the time. Such devastation helped stir the first conservation movement, eventually leading to the establishment of national forest reserves that, in total, were larger than the state of California by the end of Theodore Roosevelt's term as president. The national forests were established to provide goods that were slighted by market forces—specifically, watershed protection and future supplies of timber. Similar concerns with failures of markets in conserving tropical forests continue today.

With natural resources, the time dimension of market externalities is particularly important. Because the independent decisions that generate prices are made by individuals whose life spans and forest land tenures are relatively brief, there is no assurance that prices will provide adequate guides for decisions with far-reaching consequences (Randall 1981). Pigou, a political economist in the early twentieth century, believed that money is an unacceptable measure of satisfaction when resource consumption decisions have effects in the distant future. He believed that the time preference of individuals would generally be short, leading them to consume more resources (particularly nature's exhaustible resources) than would be consistent with the general interests and welfare. Thus, society's time horizon would be longer than that of individuals. Based on this premise, Pigou argued that there was a general presumption in favor of government action to conserve natural resources (Alston 1983). The newly developing field of ecological economics also has questioned whether interest rates adequately allocate resources over time.

Forest resources are obviously a long-term investment. Timber rotations usually exceed 20 years, even in the South, and are 50 to 100 or more years in the North and West. Expecting private timberland owners to make investments from which they will never see returns is optimistic, no matter how financially or socially desirable such investments may be. Thus, the market mechanism may not entice as much timber production as may be desirable. Or at the least, markets may not lead to production of enough desirable species of appropriate age classes. Instead, default management will occur, yielding less desirable or even noncommercial forest species that benefit neither the current owner, heirs to the property, nor society.

These concerns with intertemporal allocation reflect differences in private (high) and social (low) discount interest rates. Landowners may discount future income considerably, but society may not, even though both pay the same interest rate on borrowed capital. As a society, we generally recognize an obligation to leave future generations with a relatively intact resource base. Therefore, preserving the productive capacity of the land becomes a social objective even when it may not be an objective for a private owner. If wise and ethical land management practices are not profitable, individual incentives may lead to destructive practices, overuse, or noninvestment.

Privatizers disagree with arguments that markets will not protect the interests of future generations. Stroup and Baden (1983) suggest that landowners would speculate and hoard resources such as timber in anticipation of potentially high market profits. Increasing real (inflation-adjusted) prices will reward landowners and prompt more forest management than would government programs. Wolf (1988) contends that markets have a longer view than government because politicians are always trying to solve problems quickly in order to curry political support be-

fore the next election rolls around. Privatizers feel that pressure for immediate action translates into hastily developed and executed government programs that make corporate product development, marketing, and capital investment decisions seem almost leisurely by comparison.

Nevertheless, public policy generally reflects the view that government is better able to protect long-term social interests than is the market. Many forestry laws are designed to ensure adequate production of timber and other forest outputs for the future, as well as to protect against harmful side effects of logging and other forest practices (Cubbage and Siegel 1985).

Imperfect Knowledge

Perfect knowledge is perhaps the most heroic of the four assumptions of neoclassical economic theory. Achieving an optimum allocation of goods and services is not possible when persons are unaware of their own preferences or of the quality of goods and services they buy. No consumer is omniscient. The problem of inadequate knowledge exists in all forms of organization (Lindblom 1977). For any individual or organization, information is costly (Randall 1981). The benefits of obtaining perfect, or even adequate, information must be weighed against its opportunity costs. Information costs money to acquire and analyze. Excessive deliberation or too much information penalize indecisive buyers and sellers.

In forestry, the problem of imperfect knowledge lies more in production than in consumption. Timber or wildlife producers are apt to be largely unaware of the value of the goods they are producing. First, landowners may not realize that forestry investments can be financially attractive, so they fail to grow timber or manage for wildlife habitat. Second, some producers—particularly nonindustrial private forest landowners—may know very little about the quantities, qualities, or market prices of the timber they grow. Third, there may be only limited or no private markets for wildlife for owners of small forest tracts, although hunting leases are an active market in some regions of the United States.

Public forestry technical assistance and education programs are provided to nonindustrial private forestland owners to help correct disparities in knowledge and information and help ensure that all firms compete under the same rules. Such public programs may help owners realize that growing timber and managing for wildlife can be profitable. They also may help owners better estimate volumes and values so that they do not sell timber or price hunting leases for less than they could.

Imperfect Competition

The price mechanism works best when buyers and sellers are many in number and small in size and cannot individually affect prices, conditions commonly referred to as perfect competition. However, modern production processes generally occur on a large scale, and firms have obvious opportunities to influence prices (Randall 1981). In fact economists today refer to the U.S. economy as one of monopolistic competition, where producers may influence product prices because of differences in products—such as cars, houses, etc., (Schumpeter 1949). Firms are not faced with a given market price (a flat demand curve). Instead each firm has a downward sloping demand curve, indicating that it can influence the quantities consumed by changing prices. Lower prices will prompt more people to buy, and vice versa.

Public and private timber sellers may face another problem of imperfect competition—oligopsony. In any given market area, such as a papermill timbershed, there may be thousands of forest landowners (timber producers), but only a few to perhaps at most a dozen buyers. The fewer the buyers, the lower the competition. Illegal collusive practices such as price-fixing, bid rigging, and dividing markets are more likely with fewer buyers. If buyers collude, private owners could receive less for stumpage, perceive growing timber as undesirable, and fail to reinvest in growing timber. Timber would

be underproduced from a social perspective. State foresters and private forestry consultants may help landowners improve competition by assisting in making timber sales and by recommending that they obtain several bids for sales rather than taking the first offer (see Vardaman 1989).

EQUITY

Markets and governments are both less than perfect; markets sometimes generate inefficient resource allocations and government efforts to correct market failures sometimes produce no improvement. Securing the greatest amount of outputs in relation to inputs (efficiency) is desirable, but it is not enough. Equity—who benefits from resource utilization, and who pays the costs—is also important (Clawson 1975). The question of how natural resources will be distributed to segments of society in a fair and equitable manner casts some doubt on market solutions to questions of resource allocation.

Given many assumptions about economic rationality, economists have shown mathematically that free markets are most efficient. Any government involvement or interference with a perfect market would then, of course, reduce efficiency. This loss of efficiency is used by critics to seek government elimination from the marketplace. But they miss the point that some groups prefer to use other criteria in addition to efficiency in allocating resources.

Efficiency usually can be measured, although the evaluation of nonmarket benefits is sometimes difficult and produces dubious results. Costs are easier to determine than are benefits, but external costs such as pollution are difficult to value. Analysts measure the relationship between the benefits and costs associated with resource allocation decisions and weigh various alternatives with their calculations. Equity considerations cannot be tested in the same manner. Gains and losses in economic welfare are elusive, and a "balance" between gain and loss is difficult to define (Clawson 1975).

Who will receive the benefits and/or bear the costs of particular resource allocations and, when resources are scarce, how will supplies be rationed? If a private forest owner is required to protect habitat for endangered wildlife, who should pay the costs in opportunities foregone? If a wilderness area cannot accommodate all the hikers or canoeists who would like to use it, how should permits be rationed? Should the government use the price mechanism, a lottery, a queue, or some other means to distribute wilderness use privileges? How will the resulting distribution of resources be measured? These questions defy neat answers. Analysts can attempt to describe the inequality that exists or results from a particular resource allocation alternative, thus sharpening issues and defining choices that society must make about the degree of inequality it will tolerate. But even this descriptive process will tax analytical capability.

Distribution of Benefits

People earn income by working or using their capital and resources. Rich people usually earn more of their income through investment than do poor people, and they are rewarded for their managerial skills rather than for manual labor. It is important for society to reward capital investment and resource development because these processes generate economic growth and improved standards of living. But many who are not wealthy, and earn most of their income by physical labor, believe the unequal distribution of wealth is unfair (Randall 1981).

In fact, Karl Marx (1875), coauthor of the *Communist Manifesto*, suggested that goods should be distributed to individuals based on their needs, while individuals should also produce according to their abilities. As the collapse of communism in Eastern Europe suggests, this doctrine sounds better in principle than it performs in practice. The government alone did not prove particularly equitable at determining what individual needs were, nor was it adept at coercing production based on altruism for the social good. The gap between the wealthy and the poor

is a continuing public policy concern in most countries, including the United States.

Equitable distribution of wealth and equal opportunity for advancement historically have been important American political values. The question remains how far one should go in sacrificing efficiency (the pure-enterprise market criterion) in order to achieve equity and equality (Hirshleifer 1984). Excessive government efforts to guarantee equal results can effectively destroy incentives to innovate, change, and grow. Modern economists realize that Adam Smith's invisible hand has limits in allocating resources. But they have little faith that government intervention will improve matters.

Others tend to support the role of government in resource allocation. Leman (1984, p. 127) writes that

> Equity is not only an inescapable question in theory; it also has long been a, perhaps the, central concern in politics. As Jacob Viner (1960) has pointed out, the 19th century doctrine of laissez-faire fell into disfavor precisely because of concern about inequities in the resulting distribution of wealth and income. Jonathan Hughes (1977) points out that it was at the turn of century, during the period of the American economy's greatest growth, that the most ideas emerged on extending nonmarket control over economic life.

In the case of land resources, Brubaker (1983) asserts that equity is the main issue presented by public intervention. All social actions create gainers and losers, but constitutional questions regarding ownership compound concern with land. Should owners bear costs not asked of other citizens? Who should reap the gains of intervention if land values increase? Pay if they decrease? Traditional economic efficiency criteria that measure the relationship of costs and benefits have not been nearly as influential in such decisions as have legal doctrines or political processes.

Justification for Forest Resource Programs

Equity considerations often have been used to justify government involvement in producing and allocating forest, wildlife, and recreation resources. Even timber markets may have side effects that are not deemed fair or equitable by everyone. For example, timber supply does not respond well to price changes. Thus prices fluctuate up and down, but the amount of wood available for sale does not change much. The fears of a timber *famine* have been publicized by foresters since Pinchot first popularized the term in the 1900s. These fears were used to argue for setting aside national forests and for developing a host of public forestry programs that exist today. The "problem" of a timber shortage has now been supplanted by arguments that instead of a timber famine, timber prices will increase rapidly, which is deemed undesirable by advocates for public forestry programs (Hair 1978, Manthy 1978). These arguments contend that high prices for timber will translate into high prices of homes for all Americans.

Equity, not efficiency, is a major justification for public parks, wildlife reserves, and the associated public resource management agencies. From the time of John Muir at the turn of the twentieth century, conservationists believed that government should set aside national parks to protect their beauty and spiritual value for all Americans. Allowing private firms to own and exploit areas such as Yellowstone and Yosemite was deemed inequitable. Some would benefit at the expense of many. Wildlife policies can also be traced partly to equity concerns—namely that all people should receive benefits from fish and game—not just the few rich enough to exploit them first, as in the European tradition.

Natural resource investments are significant because they usually occur in poor regions and counties. Although some rural landowners may be affluent, the local economies of resource-dependent regions usually are not. Community stability, income for poor people, maintenance of a business infrastructure, and the effect of forest income being multiplied through the local economy have all been cited as reasons to support natural resource programs. Similar arguments are made regarding the benefits derived from

timber, minerals, or hunting income, especially in the American West, and for rural recreation facilities and economic contributions. Natural resource exports also may help a country's balance of trade. So do foreign tourists who visit state and federal parks.

Inequality in gains and costs is perhaps inevitable for any public or private program. The complexity of our economy, differences in natural ability and inherited wealth, and simple chance all produce inequities in gains, costs, and benefit–cost relations (Clawson 1975). Impersonal market allocations based on price mechanisms may have difficulty dealing with complex and sensitive concerns in distributional issues that involve economic equity and welfare.

ALLOCATION CRITERIA

A useful summary of the strength (efficiency) and weakness (equity) of the market comes from an article on the history of the wood dealer system in Mississippi (Flick 1985).

> The two great merits of capitalism are the impersonal character of the constraints it places on people and its unrivaled flexibility (Scitovsky 1980). Individuals are free to enter, exit, buy, sell, produce, and adapt as they see fit. There is little mercy, however, for those landowners, dealers, or producers who make mistakes. In the aggregate, the system is flexible in that it can move rapidly from nonadapters to innovators, always keeping its center of gravity near the most efficient and productive.
>
> Its great faults tend to be its fragmentation, and consequent lack of provision for the future, and its unsatisfying distributive consequences.... The pressure of competition forces each player to seek his maximum advantage. The least advantaged players, usually landowners, producers, and laborers, are traditionally ill-equipped to negotiate profitable contracts.... (p. 138)

In assessing the appropriateness of markets in the allocation of forest resources and the distribution of wealth derived from these resources, we need to consider three classes of factors.

1. The nature of the relevant goods and services needs to be examined in the light of associated market conditions. How does the existing market and the attributes of the desired goods affect the likelihood and extent of market failure? Is production of a particular good or development of a resource likely to be plagued by inadequate property rights or externalities? Are markets for a particular good in a specific region characterized by poorly informed buyers or sellers or by imperfect competition? Is the presence of large transaction costs likely to distort market allocations? These factors relate to the extent to which markets can efficiently allocate particular resources.

2. The social distribution of goods needs to be considered. Is the nature of a particular forest output such that market price is an inappropriate mechanism that excludes certain segments of society from obtaining that good? Will market price transactions increase inequality in the distribution of wealth to a level that is socially unacceptable? Will drastic changes in price levels create instability that unfairly burdens particular regions or groups of people? These factors reflect American society's concerns with equity and social equality.

3. Is the market for a particular output effective for producing goods relative to other social institutions? If markets are imperfect, can other institutions improve social outcomes? In the next section the focus is directed at how government, at times an alternative to the market, performs in allocating resources and distributing wealth.

ILLUSTRATION: HISTORIC FORESTRY DEBATES

The debate over public and private processes for providing and allocating goods and services is intense, particularly in the field of natural resources—and forestry is no exception. This illustration reviews some of the historical arguments for and against government involvement in the management of forest resources. Most of these arguments persist today.

Market Proponents

Perhaps the classic statement of the benefits of free markets was made by Wilson Compton in 1919 during a national debate over federal regulation of private timber cutting and forest management. Compton was secretary-manager of the National Lumber Manufacturers' Association from 1918 until 1944, when he left to become the president of Washington State University in Pullman. He is credited with lessening competitive rivalry in the lumber industry, which resulted in a strong industry trade association that was able to focus national attention on forest policy (Robbins 1983).

Compton soundly criticized Gifford Pinchot and other foresters of the early era of American forestry who advocated public regulation of private forests. Compton stated that government foresters did not represent public opinion and devised their own self-serving interpretation of the "public interest." Furthermore, in his view foresters lacked a fundamental understanding of forest industry economics. Compton (1919) observed that

> Whether or not it is good forestry to have forests for the sake of having trees, it is not good economics. Forestry cannot safely construct its own kind of economics without considering the nation's needs for the products of all other industries, which are taken from the same land which might otherwise grow trees, and which are made by the same labor which might otherwise make wood products—and then assert that a program of forest renewal based thereon is a correct interpretation of the public interest. (p. 1337)

Compton (1919) discussed the economic implications of forestry in fourteen points, summarized as follows (p. 1337–1339).

1. Cheap and plentiful timber is not necessarily a sign of national wealth.

    The great forests of original timber added greatly to national wealth. A policy to perpetuate stands of the same quality would be a national waste. It would be a national waste to employ soil, capital, and labor for a less profitable use when a more profitable use was available. Low prices for forest products traded for high prices for other commodities is unwise public economy.

2. Removal of the original American forests without provision for forest renewal on most of the land thus cleared is not necessarily a national misfortune.

> Some lands are better suited for tree growth and some are better suited for agricultural or industrial development. There is neither reason nor truth in the slogan that: Where a tree is cut another tree should be grown. Such a policy, pursued throughout this land, would entail great waste in the use of the nation's resources. It is the thoughtless cry of those who believe that nature left unaided and undisturbed should be the universal regulator of the economic life of mankind.

3. That old trees are being cut down faster than new trees are growing up does not of itself signify a public loss.

4. The virtual disappearance of certain species of timber is not necessarily detrimental to public welfare.

> For commercial purposes many species are readily interchangeable. The same things now made from a hundred commercial species could be made without the loss of utility from a dozen different species well selected for permanent growth, with no impairment of public wealth.

5. It is probably not true that all the lands in the United States better suited for growing trees than for growing anything else should be used for growing trees.

> Land's greatest productive use should not dictate its use or the occupation of its people. Demands for other products and other land use are equally important. Otherwise, the United States would have a vast oversupply of timber.

6. The disappearance of forest industries in certain regions because of exhaustion of nearby timber supplies is not necessarily either a local or national misfortune.

> Clearing forest land frequently paved the way for industrial and agricultural expansion that produced greater wealth than the forest industries in their prime. Surely, there is no public economy in making a wasteful use of capital and human effort.

7. Economically the original timber in the United States is in large part a "mine" and not a "crop."

> The business of lumber manufacture is to make boards out of trees, not grow trees. By making boards well, lumber manufacturers serve the public best. Even ownership of forestland places the owner under no obligation—moral, social, or legal—to undertake the growing of trees when to do so would be unprofitable, any more than the ownership of potential farm land obliges the owner to raise farm crops when he could do so only at a loss.
>
> If the growing of timber is an appropriate private enterprise, which I doubt, the interest of the public (provided it is well informed) in the maintenance of permanent timber supplies will find expression in some form which will result in economic conditions making profitable private enterprise in growing timber. If it is not an appropriate private enterprise the sooner adequate provision is made for doing it as a public enterprise the better. Public agencies would, under such conditions, experience no difficulty in acquiring from present owners the lands appropriate for use in reforestation.
>
> Public indifference and inactivity cannot, however, encumber the private owner of timber lands with the responsibility for, or expense of, doing something the public should do, but does not.

8. Local shrinkage of employment for labor, caused by vanishing forest industries in certain regions, has been by no means an unmixed evil for labor.

> Employment at higher wages has usually been secured by removal to similar industries in other regions, or to other industries in the same region, the higher prices for the products resulting from increasing scarcity of raw material, making the payment of higher wages possible. Temporary dislocation of labor has always accompanied at some stage the industrial use of exhaustible natural resources.

9. The idleness of some cut-over timber lands is the inevitable temporary result of clearing the forests from lands upon which maintenance of permanent forest growth would be poor public economy. Agriculture, stockraising or other purposes will eventually absorb these lands.

10. The idleness of other cut-over timber lands is the inevitable result of clearing the forest from lands upon which re-growing of a new forest would be poor private economy.

> If the public needs these lands to be reforested before the time when enlightened self-interest—which is the essential driving force of all business and industry—induces the private owner to engage in timber growing, the public should itself engage in reforestation of lands appropriate therefore.

11. Private owners of timberland are under no different or greater obligation to use land permanently to grow timber than the owner of agricultural land is to use the land to grow crops if the growing of crops is unprofitable. The public need for food is at least no less than the need for lumber.

12. The obligation of landowners to use land as to do no damage to another's property and to do no public injury, does not include an additional obligation to use land to benefit the public at large at individual loss to the landowner.

Failure to reforest cut-over lands is not to do a public injury. On the contrary, private reforestation enterprises today on most of the cut-over land would, on the whole, be a public loss because it would involve a relative wasteful use of the nation's resources of labor and capital.

13. If the public is interested in any use of timberlands or of cut-over lands different from that which the enlightened self-interest of the owner may dictate, the public which is the beneficiary should pay the additional cost.

> A single class of private property may not be singled out to sustain a burden, in behalf of the public as a whole, which is not imposed upon other classes of private property.

14. The maintenance in idleness of cut-over land is not always wasteful.

> Idleness is not always wasteful. Timber and forest economies cannot be dissociated from the intricate and everchanging economic relations of all industry. To ensure future supplies: A uniform national policy of forest protection and of public acquisition of cut-over lands appropriate for permanent forestation should be adequate and practicable. But the duty of the public should not be confused with the public obligation of private industry. The specific public obligation of the lumber industry is to do well its task of making and selling boards. Along with all others in the nation it shares in the obligation to provide adequate forest for future industry. But this is an obligation common to all and not exclusive upon the lumber industry or upon present owners of its raw material. Being so, the burden of provision for the future should be borne by the public which will profit therefrom, and not by a single industry; lest thereby it undermine the very industry whose future it seeks to safeguard. Economic forces which rule all productive activities will overwhelm a forest policy set up in defiance of them.

Compton's fourteen points cogently express the virtue of markets in allocating resources. He does, however, imply that a government role in fire protection or perhaps even growing of timber might be appropriate. Needless to say, his points were controversial then, as they are today. Most of them remain relevant in discussions of the regulation of private forestry and the maintenance of timber-dependent communities.

Government Advocates

Many early foresters supported extensive roles for the government, as evidenced by their successful drives to establish the national forests. In promoting federal regulation of private forestry, a group of foresters called the Committee for the Application of Forestry (1919a, b) rebutted Compton's ideas on a point-by-point basis. They conceded that clearing of the forests for agricultural and industrial development was a sound economic premise. However, they disagreed that clearing of virgin forests was often followed by settlement, pointing out that much cut-over land was left as unproductive wasteland. They also disputed that one species could economically substitute for another, citing the irreplaceable losses society would incur if all the longleaf pine, hickory, yellow poplar, and black walnut were harvested. History, however, does support Compton's belief in species substitutions.

The committee (1919b) also believed that a loss of local forest industries was indeed a significant problem, especially when mills were not replaced by other industry. Continual migratory lumbering was not socially desirable, especially because the overall work force in timber industries seemed to be shrinking. They also contended that timber should not be mined, and that it was appropriate to grow trees as a crop. The invisible hand of Adam Smith was specifically dismissed. The committee said that after a century of unrestrained industrialism, most people recognized that "Public welfare, increase in human progress and happiness, can be secured only by subordinating the self-interest of a few to the common good of the many" (p. 961). The committee noted that Compton, in his fourteenth point, hedgingly admitted that it may be wasteful to maintain cut-over lands in idleness—contradicting many of his earlier points.

In summary, the committee (1919b) reported that:

We have attempted to answer specifically each of Dr. Compton's points. As a matter of fact, his entire argument, stripped of its "pseudo-economic sophistries," simmers down to two points:

1. The past and present treatment of the forests by the lumber industry is fully compatible with the public welfare; even the admitted large stretches of idle land, the virtual disappearance of many of our most important kinds of timber, the decline in lumber and wood-using industries, are not only not evils, but actually promote the national welfare.

2. The lumber industry, although it retains ownership of the bulk of our best forest land, is under no moral, social, or legal obligation to so handle the forests of the country as to provide for the future needs of the people unless such treatment can be shown to be highly profitable to the individual owner. (p. 964)

The committee concluded by stating "that if these two points represent the true opinion of the leaders of the lumber industry, we are willing to join issues with them and go to the people for a verdict." (p. 964)

GOVERNMENT AND FORESTRY

In the abstract world of economic theory, individuals will voluntarily exchange goods and services in the marketplace, prices will equilibrate supply and demand, and social welfare will axiomatically be maximized. Markets will be characterized by atomistic competition with many producers and consumers, perfect knowledge by both groups, complete and exclusive property rights (no unpriced values or externalities), and no transaction costs. Equity would not be a concern, because the market would reward individual consumers and producers according to their talents and efforts, and the altruism of the wealthy would provide food, shelter, and clothing for the less fortunate.

In the real world, this fantasy degenerates—perhaps to a greater extent in the forest resources sector than in other manufacturing or service sectors. In fact, criticizing neoclassical economics in forestry is attacking a straw man. Nevertheless, critics of government programs charge that they are even less efficient than imperfect markets. Critics propose dismantling public programs and allowing markets to allocate resources. Because such arguments will always provide a forum for policy debate, the reasons for public intervention bear further discussion.

ECONOMIC SYSTEMS

Societies face two choices in designing institutions to coordinate the production and distribution of goods and services. In capitalistic societies, markets and prices are used to allocate resources and distribute goods and services, with a good bit of government regulation. Prices and markets are efficient, but they are impersonal and disorderly. Massive unemployment can occur, regions can endure sustained poverty, or some groups may suffer systematic discrimination.

Some societies have chosen to avoid the imperfections of the price system by relying on central planning to coordinate their economies. Planners allocate resources to industries, select production processes, establish quotas for individual production units, and set wages. The purposes of central coordination are to promote equality in the distribution of income and wealth, minimize production externalities, and implement a long-term view in decisions regarding resource allocation (Randall 1981). But central planning has its problems. The most funda-

mental have to do with information and motivation. Central planners require enormous amounts of information to perform their coordination function. When their information is inadequate or incorrect, shortages or surpluses result. The huge bureaucracies necessary to develop and implement plans often are rigid and slow to correct errors. In contrast, enterprise economies rely on price as a means to equilibrate supply and demand. Although markets and prices sometimes fail to allocate resources well, they require much less effort than central planning and they tend to be self-correcting.

Motivation or incentive problems also can be addressed by prices. In centrally planned economies, where reward tends not to be linked to performance, workers have little motivation to produce or excel. In contrast, prices in the markets for labor, goods, and capital offer a powerful incentive to workers and investors. Inefficient firms will go out of business; efficient ones will produce more, for the benefit of the firm and society.

These problems with central planning as a coordination mechanism are reflected in the relative economic performances of different countries. Communist countries with centrally planned economies have performed very poorly. But when such countries have decreased central planning, their economies have often improved, although they still lag behind countries with freer market and political systems.

The second economic choice that societies face relates to ownership of the means of production. Ownership can be monopolized by the state, as in a socialist economy, or distributed via markets and prices in the private sector, as in a capitalist economy. Some socialist economies rely on public ownership with market prices rather than only central planning. Indeed more and more socialist countries are making greater use of prices and entrepreneurship in their economic systems.

Although a pure enterprise economy (private ownership of means of production, price as coordinating mechanism) and a centrally planned communist economy represent the polar extremes, few actual economies conform to either ideal. Rather, most countries have a mix of economic institutions. Communist countries in Eastern Europe and Asia came closest to complete government domination of economic decisions. But some communist countries, such as the former Yugoslavia, have long used the price system to help guide the activities of state enterprises (Lindblom 1977). More recently, the former Soviet Union and China have tried to integrate market prices into their economies in order to promote economic growth, albeit with mixed results. Introducing market mechanisms into the Soviet Union probably helped destabilize the communist society. Raising prices to "market" levels in the newly formed Commonwealth of Independent States in 1991 and 1992 led to massive public protests and riots. It remains to be seen whether these countries can effectively make the transition from a mostly centrally-planned economy to more of a market economy.

In democratic countries in western Europe, there is extensive government ownership in major industries and government planning to guide industrial production. Japan, Korea, and Taiwan also have operated successfully with a large degree of central control. East Germany was often considered a model for the efficiency of centralized planning (Thurow 1985), but the iron-handed economic and political control led to massive protests, emigration, and the collapse of the communist government in 1989. The United States often is viewed as being among the countries with the least government intervention in the economy; but even here, federal, state, and local governments use a variety of policy tools to moderate and guide the workings of the price system. These tools include government ownership, taxes, subsidies, trade restrictions, and regulations (Randall 1981). All have been used in the forest sector as well as others, with varying effects.

In reality, all countries operate with a mixed economy, not pure capitalism or pure communism. Companies may mistreat workers, cheat consumers, or ruin the environment. Government regulations attempt to prevent this. Similarly government welfare programs try to cushion the harshest effects of markets: joblessness, poverty, homelessness, illness, and so on. In fact, government is the biggest industry in most advanced nations. In 1987 government spending comprised 37 percent of the gross national product (GNP) in the United States, 33 percent in Japan, and 47 percent in (then) West Germany. Much of that spending was transfer payments—shifts of income between different groups. Government employment was 16 percent of the total in the United States and West Germany, and 6 percent in Japan (Samuelson 1989).

Leading modern forest economists, including Duerr (1960) and Gregory (1972), have tended to reject laissez-faire as an acceptable doctrine. Duerr, recognized by Alston (1983) as the father of modern American forestry economics, clearly felt that the invisible hand might well not lead individuals to serve society's aims. Economic systems should not only seek "freedom for the individual from superfluous state control, but more pointedly, from unbridled private initiative." Duerr argued that society worked through established political, social, educational, and government institutions to establish common values. He rejected a belief in atomistic competition and felt that a pluralistic society had greater importance. Gregory conceded that profit-maximizing models of neoclassical microeconomics were useful but did not represent the activities of large firms in the forest industry. Such firms seek security and growth, not maximum profits. Above all, Gregory was a pragmatist willing to accept second-best economic solutions that society deemed legitimate. Once society determined goals, then efficiency analysis should guide forest management. Economists should operate within this constraint and spell out the opportunity costs involved, but not reject all goals except efficiency (Alston 1983).

Modern economists widely accept a positive role for the state, particularly with regard to natural resources. *The Economics of the Coming Spaceship Earth*, Boulding (1966) epitomized economic concern for the environment. He argued that the closed earth of the future requires economic principles different from those of the open earth of the past. The open "cowboy" economy of the romantic past was characterized by limitless resources and reckless, exploitive, and violent behavior. The closed "spacetraveler" economy of the present arose because the earth no longer has unlimited reserves of anything, either for extraction or pollution abatement. In the cowboy economy, production and consumption are regarded favorably; a spaceman economy should minimize both. Cowboy economies live for the day and ignore tomorrow. Spaceman economies must conserve resources for future generations. Unfettered markets clearly resemble cowboy economic systems.

CONSERVATION AND THE LAND ETHIC

In *Small Is Beautiful*, radical economist E. F. Schumacher (1975) rejected economic efficiency as the only relevant criterion for decisions.

I am asking what it means, what sort of meaning the method of economics actually produces. And the answer to this question cannot be in doubt: Something is uneconomic when it fails to earn an adequate profit in terms of money. The method of economics does not, and cannot, produce any other meaning. Numerous attempts have been made to obscure this fact, and they have caused a very great deal of confusion; but the fact remains. Society, or a group of individuals within society, may decide to hang on to an activity or asset for non-economic reasons—social, aesthetic, moral, or political—but this does in no way alter its uneconomic character. The judgment of economics, in other words, is an extremely fragmentary judgment; out of the large number of aspects which in real life have to be seen and judged together before a decision can be taken, economics supplies only one—whether a thing yields a money profit to those who undertake it or not. (p. 42)

Environmentalists are even less enamored with laissez-faire economic efficiency criteria (profit) than are radical economists. Michael McCloskey (1981), former executive director of the Sierra Club, invoked stewardship, not merely profits, as the criterion that should guide private landowners. He urged landowners to take a long view toward the land and said they should strive to ensure that no appreciable decline in its fertility occurred. Even though national forests were to be managed for multiple use, McCloskey warned against managing private lands as "national sacrifice" areas. Multiple use and amenity values are to be protected, and environmental values safeguarded, on private as well as public lands.

McCloskey (1981) echoed Aldo Leopold's (1949) call for a land ethic. Leopold, a professional forester and wildlife biologist who spent part of his career with the Forest Service, criticized the strength of the profit motive in land use decisions in his posthumously published classic, *A Sand County Almanac*.

Considering the prodigious achievements of the profit motive in wrecking land, one hesitates to reject it as a vehicle for restoring land. I incline to believe we have overestimated the scope of the profit motive. Is it profitable for the individual to build a beautiful home? To give his children a higher education? No, it is seldom profitable, yet we do both. These are, in fact, ethical and aesthetic premises which underlie the economic system. Once accepted, economic forces tend to align the smaller details of social organization into harmony with them.... (p. 201)

In some instances, the assumed lack of profit in these "waste" areas has proved to be wrong, but only after most of them had been done away with.... (p. 249)

Leopold continually advocated governmental conservation, yet he also recognized its limits.

Government ownership, operation, subsidy, or regulation is now widely prevalent in forestry, range management, soil and watershed management, park and wilderness conservation, fisheries management, and migratory bird management, with more to come. Most of this growth in governmental conservation is proper and logical, some of it is inevitable. That I imply no disapproval of it is implicit in the fact that I have spent most of my life working for it. Nevertheless, the question arises: What is the ultimate magnitude of the enterprise? Will the tax base carry its eventual ramifications? At what point will governmental conservation, like the mastodon, become handicapped by its own dimensions? The answer, if there is any, seems to be in a land ethic, or some other force which assigns more obligation to the private landowner. (p. 250)

Leopold went on to describe such a land ethic.

To sum up: a system of conservation based solely on economic self-interest is hopelessly lopsided. It tends to ignore, and thus eventually to eliminate, many elements in the land community that lack commercial value, but that are (as far as we know) essential to its healthy functioning. It assumes, falsely, I think, that the economic parts of the biotic clock will function without the uneconomic parts. It tends to relegate to government many functions eventually too large, too complex, or too widely dispersed to be performed by government.... (p. 251)

Leopold's proposal stimulated foresters, environmentalists, policy makers, and philosophers to reexamine conservation problems and their solutions. Although disagreement continues about the exact nature of the roles of government and markets, there is consensus that individual responsibility and a land ethic are essential elements of resource conservation. Development and perpetuation of that ethic will require the contributions of schools, families, communities, and clubs, as well as government.

DECISION GUIDELINES

This chapter has presented a considerable amount of material regarding the merits of markets and governments in managing natural resources. Laissez-faire market policies

were crucial in shaping the early U.S. economy. In the 1900s the United States steadily shifted to more government involvement in resource protection and management. Today national forests, national parks, federal wildlife refuges, range lands, and state forest lands are owned and managed by the government. Many environmental and public land laws authorize federal and state agencies to protect wildlife, assist private forest landowners, prevent water and air pollution, ensure efficient operations of markets, and serve many other public purposes.

Despite the increases in government laws and agencies, not all people are satisfied with existing government solutions. Government bureaucracies tend to grow due to interest group pressure, legislative support, and managerial ambition, but the market problems agencies were designed to correct seldom improve. Furthermore, tighter government budgets have forced reductions in the size of many agencies. Many European countries have even made substantial progress toward privatizing formerly state-owned industries.

Faced with the choice between imperfect markets and imperfect governments, what is the best way to manage and allocate forest resources? Wolf (1988) suggests several guidelines for choice. Generally, he concludes that markets do a better job than government in terms of efficiently producing the maximum amount of goods with the minimum amount of inputs (costs). Additionally, markets usually are better at sustaining a high rate of growth over time, and they lead to more innovation and rapid change. Although market failures may exist, the deviation of market prices from socially optimal prices is outweighed by the nonpricing efficiencies generated by market incentives and competition. Wolf does note that whether the characteristics associated with dynamic efficiency—rapid growth, innovation, change, and flexibility—are viewed as desirable goals or as unsettling risks depends on the eyes, hearts, and minds of the beholders.

Both market and nonmarket systems have flaws in terms of equity. Markets' relatively objective and impersonal processes do provide opportunities for fairness. But inequities arise because of very different starting points, including familial wealth and influence and individual talents. Inequities occur in the business world as well: Big firms may have economic advantages; firms may discriminate in hiring and promotion; and superiors may use their power over employees in unscrupulous ways. Government systems can be unfair, too. Arbitrariness, pettiness, favoritism, rigidity, and bureaucratic delays may characterize government institutions more than private organizations.

Social and political criteria may favor government in a pluralistic democracy over a pure market regime. Citizens can organize, vote, and lobby to influence political decision making. Governments also have budget and oversight capabilities that can be used to ensure fairness in program implementation. Special interests still may become more important than public interests in the government process, however.

This debate between the balance of market processes and government involvement in resource management will continue. The choices made will depend on the values of the public and of policymakers, the political strength of the interest groups involved, the nature of the resources themselves, and the budgets available for government programs. Individuals and groups favoring economic efficiency, growth, and change are apt to favor market processes for management and allocation of resources. Individuals favoring public involvement, equity, and accountability surely will favor government solutions. Many believe that markets offer the best opportunities for economic freedom and advancement; but others contend that government should play a greater role in ensuring equal opportunity, or even equal outcomes. Natural resources have many common-pool and collective good characteristics that seem to favor government involvement. Environmental groups are increasing in number and influence, so we can expect increasing demands for public programs to protect the environment. All of these beliefs and trends will be tempered by our ability to tax and pay for any programs deemed necessary.

ILLUSTRATION: MODERN FORESTRY DEBATES

Market Proponents

Despite, or perhaps as a result of, the history of socialized forestry in the United States, there are forestry professionals who advocate strong support of free market approaches to forestry problems (e.g., Dowdle 1984, Vardaman 1970, Wishart 1984). Seventy years after Wilson Compton's carefully considered support for market forces in forestry, modern forestry advocates of laissez-faire appear even less hopeful about the government role than Compton was. Critiques of government intervention in forestry were common in the early 1980s.

Consulting forester James Vardaman (1970, 1978, 1989) suggests that nonindustrial private forest lands are not poorly managed or underproductive, as many people believe, or that the government should spend public funds for increased timber production. He declares that nonindustrial private forests will grow whatever timber this country needs as long as it makes money for the owners. If the owners cannot make money, then the country does not need the timber as much as some people say it does.

Two employees of Georgia-Pacific have criticized government involvement in forestry. Wishart (1984) considered most government intervention to be unnecessary—little more than a subsidy for special interests. Moshofsky (1981) roundly criticized government regulation and ownership as a means to allocate any resources except air and public waters. He asserted that a healthy property rights system is essential to the functioning of the marketplace, which is best able to assure the most efficient and productive use of land for the benefit of everyone. He stated that by assuring property rights and minimizing regulations, the landowner's self-interest can determine the use of land resources. This, he believes, is the key to good stewardship, because in the process of serving their own interest, landowners end up "serving the interest of everyone else—providing food, fiber, minerals, building space, recreation, creating jobs and generating tax revenues.... This is what the marketplace is all about—millions of consumers and producers interacting with their choices—and their dollars—every day." (p. 104)

Moshofsky continues, "Sure, the market and decisions of private property owners aren't perfect—but it's time everyone realizes no system is perfect and that the market system ranks head and shoulders above any known alternative—particularly government. In the marketplace, people vote with their dollars—many times a day. In the government arena, they get to vote once every two years for members of Congress, once every six years for senators—and every four years for president. They never get to vote on the many decisions made in government. In a real sense, the marketplace is far more democratic, responsive, and just than the political system." (p. 105)

Many who have examined the role of markets and the government in forestry have concluded that markets are preferable (e.g. Allen 1984, Dowdle and Hanke 1985, Hanke 1984, Pejovich 1984). In general, they simply believe that markets allocate scarce resources better than the government. Additionally, they believe that markets are much better at avoiding gross inefficiencies or maldistribution of resources than are governments.

The debate between markets and government in forestry abated after the early 1980s but was renewed with vigor at the end of the decade and in the early 1990s. The debate over protecting spotted owls by reserving old-growth stands in the West prompted extensive criticisms of government control. National timber interest groups attacked regulations to protect endangered species and preserve wetlands as being excessive. And in 1991 the Society of American Foresters elected a vice-president (who rotated in as president in 1992) who campaigned on the platform that we needed fewer regulations, that we needed to grow and cut more tim-

ber, and that we should let the free enterprise system work. In 1992 many southern state forestry organizations began campaigning against government regulations and the "taking" of private land without compensation. Clearly, the debate over the role of government will continue.

Government Advocates

Lekachman (1984) discussed a number of current market imperfections that led him to believe that natural resources are best protected by the *public* marketplace—the political process. He recounted a number of severe problems with the idealized world of laissez-faire and noted that even in the supposedly conservative 1980s, the public continued to record an undiminished concern for the environment and advocacy for political protection. He observed the U.S. marketplace:

> Far from the preferred model of many enterprises vigorously engaged in price and quality competition, American reality is a corporate landscape planted with market imperfections. In several markets, among them steel and automobiles, major producers have habitually avoided price competition and, when threatened by Japanese or European rivals, have responded by exerting political pressure for protection.... The imperfections of market organization notorious in the American economy result—according to their degree—in misallocations of resources, higher prices, and diminished consumer gratifications.... (p. 78)

Lekachman also doubted that corporate decisions are necessarily made in the interest of private individuals. The separation of management and ownership has been a cliché of corporate literature. Managers may not represent stockholders nearly so much as themselves. They also have a bias in favor of immediate results, reinforced by security analysts' emphasis on short-term earnings. According to Lekachman, "Quite often balance sheets and income statements can be improved most readily not by improvements in efficiency, devotion of additional resources to research and development, astute management of natural resources, or improved quality but by complex financial maneuvers, manipulation of the tax code, and strategic acquisitions." (p. 80). Also, corporate politics may be no less venal than public politics and may do nothing to increase profits.

Modern corporations bear little resemblance to the neoclassical ideal of many small producers operating in a free market. Corporations are large and attempt to influence prices through monopoly powers and by seeking governmental policies that favor their industry or firm. Their belief in free markets often ceases at the point where greater profits can be gleaned through governmental involvement (Lekachman 1984). Corporations are not beyond betraying the common trust or breaching ethics to make a profit. Violations of law such as knowingly dumping toxic chemicals in New York's "Love Canal" in the 1970s, securities fraud and insider trading on Wall Street in 1988, or the spilling of crude oil in Alaska in 1989 indicate that unbridled capitalistic pursuit of profits may prompt perverse behavior.

Lekachman also debunked the problems of government bureaucracies compared to the lean efficiency of profit maximizers: "Daily experience with banks, credit card issuers, auto dealers, department stores, and utilities should by now have made Max Weber's message clear: bureaucracy is not a function of ownership, it is a consequence of size, specialization, and division of labor." (p. 81). Actual choices in forestlands lie between public and corporate bureaucracies. Lekachman preferred the first. Salazar and Lee (1990) found that private organizations were no more efficient than public ones. Despite significant imperfections, the political process acts as a check on the operations of public bureaucrats. Unsatisfactory public bureaucrats are refused appointment or removed from office (e.g., during the Reagan administration, Anne Burford was removed as head of EPA, as was James Watt, secretary of the interior) and replaced with those more acceptable. In practice, shareholders have little opportunity to do the same with unpopular corporate managers.

There are actually two kinds of markets— a political market and a private market. Each has advantages and disadvantages, but the political market is more accountable. The choice is between two imperfect institutions— market institutions *as they actually operate* or political institutions *as they actually operate*. In disputed territory such as natural resources, Lekachman (1984) would choose the latter.

The continual expansion of the role of government regulations in the 1990s also indicates that the free market advocates of the 1980s had not convinced a majority of Americans or policymakers of pure free market superiority. Most people believed the environment needed protecting from market pressures, including development, commercialization of parks, and unbridled timber harvests. When the Society of American Foresters' president called for an end to government interference and increased timber production in 1992, a slew of letters to the editor in the *Journal of Forestry* lambasted the message as being regressive and inappropriate for the forestry profession. A positive role for government and a broader view of forest resource management were advocated by many.

When one analyzes markets in forestry, virtually every neoclassical economic assumption that underlies the superiority of a pure market system is violated to some degree. All the identifiable problems with market distribution of goods and services occur in natural resources. Wildlife and pollution have common-pool characteristics, timber markets are dominated by a few buyers, producers lack complete information, and current and future externalities abound. The fairness of profits for large forestry corporations based on marginal returns to forest owners is moot, and the social safety net for forestry-dependent communities remains important.

The actual or perceived shortcomings of markets, combined with political incentives to adopt public programs, have led to extensive government involvement in forest resource allocation and distribution. Governments do protect public goods and provide services unlikely to be provided by markets. Disagreements over the relative amount of government intervention and its costs and benefits will persist. Debate on these issues is healthy, as long as it does not degenerate into ideological warfare. Constructive discourse constantly challenges the way policies are designed and carried out with new alternative approaches to providing what we want and need from our forests.

SUMMARY

Forest resources may be grown, managed, and used for a variety of outputs. These include timber, wildlife, range, water, fish, recreation, wilderness, and others. Types of forest resources may range from goods that are traded by private individuals in private markets, such as timber, or public, collective goods that are not traded in markets, such as water and air quality. There is much debate over the efficiency, equity, and democracy of market versus government processes in general and in forestry in particular. Markets are often characterized as being more efficient than government. However, the theoretical assumptions underlying market superiority often do not hold with natural resources. Many natural resources are public goods that are not traded in private markets, imperfect knowledge of even market products is common, and competition is often weak.

Arguments in favor of more equitable distributions of goods have generally been used to support government programs, but government allocation also has drawbacks, including rigidity, high costs, bureaucratic red tape, and impersonal, unresponsive officials. Public participation in making decisions is also cited to favor government involvement in resource decisions. In the sense of voting or lobbying, this is true; in terms of purchasing specific goods, markets may offer more individual freedom. These debates will continue to dominate forest resource policy in the future, much as they have in the past, and as they do today. The illustrations of historic and current forestry debates in this chapter present the gist of the issues that will likely remain a feature of American forest resource policy deliberations for as long as individualism, equity, and community endure as American values.

LITERATURE CITED

Allen, William R. 1984. Managing timberlands for the community's benefit. Pp. 63–75 in Selling the Federal Forests. Contribution No. 50. University of Washington, College of Forest Resources. Seattle.

Alston, Richard M. 1983. The Individual vs. the Public Interest. Westview Press. Boulder, CO. 250 pp.

Anderson, Terry L. 1983. Water Crisis: Ending the Policy Drought. The Johns Hopkins University Press. Baltimore, MD. 121 pp.

Boulding, Kenneth E. 1966. The economics of the coming spaceship earth. Pp. 3–14 in Environmental Quality in a Growing Economy. Essays from the sixth RFF Forum. Resources for the Future/Johns Hopkins Press. Baltimore, MD.

Brubaker, Sterling. 1983. Land use concepts. Pp. 95–114 in Governmental Interventions, Social Needs, and the Management of U.S. Forests. Resources for the Future. Washington, DC.

Buchanan, James, and Gordon Tullock. 1962. The Calculus of Consent. University of Michigan Press. Ann Arbor. 361 pp.

Clawson, Marion. 1975. Forests for Whom and for What. Resources for the Future/Johns Hopkins Press. Baltimore, MD. 175 pp.

Committee for the Application of Forestry. 1919a. Forest devastation: A national danger and a plan to meet it. *Journal of Forestry* 17(8):911–945.

Committee for the Application of Forestry. 1919b. An answer to Dr. Compton's fourteen points. *Journal of Forestry* 17(8): 946–964.

Compton, Wilson. 1919. Forest economics: Some thoughts on an old subject. *American Forests* 25(309):1337–1339.

Cubbage, Frederick W., and Richard W. Haynes. 1988. Forest resources, free markets, and public policy. *Forum for Applied Research and Public Policy* 3(1):39–46.

Cubbage, Frederick W., and William C. Siegel. 1985. The law regulating private forest practices. *Journal of Forestry* 83(9): 538–545.

Deacon, Robert T., and M. Bruce Johnson. 1985. Forest Lands: Public and Private. Pacific Institute for Public Policy Research. San Francisco. 332 pp.

De Alessi, Louis. 1980. The economics of property rights: A review of the evidence. *Research in Law and Economics* 2:1–47.

de Tocqueville, Alexis. 1848. Democracy in America. Doubleday. Garden City, NY. 778 pp. (Reprinted 1969)

Dowdle, Barney, 1984. The case for selling federal timberlands. Pp. 16–21 in Selling the Federal Forests. Contribution No. 50. University of Washington College of Forest Resources. Seattle.

Dowdle, Barney, and Steven H. Hanke. 1985. Public timber policy and the wood-products industry. Pp. 77–102 in Forestlands: Public and Private. Pacific Institute for Public Policy Research. San Francisco.

Duerr, William A. 1960. Fundamentals of Forestry Economics. McGraw-Hill. New York. 579 pp.

Duerr, William A., and Jean B. Duerr. 1982. Social values and policies. Pp. 319–338 in William A. Duerr, Dennis E. Teeguarden, Neils B. Christiansen, and Sam Guttenberg (eds.), Forest Resource Management: Decision-Making Principles and Cases. O.S.U. Bookstores, Inc. Corvallis, OR.

Etzioni, Amitai. 1989. Choosing social science paradigms: Merging disciplines. *National Forum* 69(2):12–14.

Flick, Warren. 1985. The wood dealer system in Mississippi: An essay on regional economics and culture. *Journal of Forest History* 29(3):131–138.

Friedman, Milton. 1962. Capitalism and Freedom. University of Chicago Press. Chicago. 202 pp.

Gregory, G. Robinson. 1972. Forest Resource Economics. Ronald Press. New York. 548 pp.

Griffin, Ronald C., and John R. Stoll. 1984. Evolutionary processes in soil conservation policy. *Land Economics* 60(1):30–39.

Gwartney, James D., and Richard Stroup. 1982. Microeconomics: Private and Public Choice, 3rd ed. Academic Press. New York. 447 pp.

Hair, Dwight. 1978. Does the U.S. face a shortfall of timber? *Journal of Forestry* 76(5):276–278.

Hanke, Steve H. 1984. On privatization. Pp. 84–92 in Proceedings, Symposium on Selling the Federal Forests. Institute of Forest Resources Contribution No. 50. University of Washington, College of Forest Resources. Seattle.

Hardin, Garrett. 1968. The tragedy of the commons. *Science* 162(3859):1243–1248.

Hays, Samuel P. 1959. Conservation and the Gospel of Efficiency. Harvard University Press. Cambridge, MA. 297 pp.

Hemphill, Dallas C. 1988. The corporatization of public forestry—or—Is America ready for free enterprise? *The Consultant* 33(3):52–54.

Hirshleifer, Jack. 1984. Price Theory and Applications, 3rd ed. Prentice Hall. Englewood Cliffs, NJ. 574 pp.

Hughes, Jonathon R. T. 1977. The Governmental Habit: Economic Controls from Colonial Times to the Present. Basic Books. New York. 260 pp.

Kapp, K. William, and Lore L. Kapp (eds.). 1949. Readings in Economics. Barnes & Noble. New York. 444 pp.

Kneese, Allen V., Robert U. Ayres, and Ralph C. d'Arge. 1970. Economics and the Environment. Resources for the Future/Johns Hopkins Press. Baltimore, MD. 132 pp.

Lekachman, Robert. 1984. Public timber and the public interest. Pp. 76–92 in Selling the Federal Forests. Contribution No. 50. University of Washington, College of Forest Resources. Seattle.

Leman, Christopher K. 1984. The revolution of the saints: The ideology of privatization and its consequences for the public lands. Pp. 93–162 in Selling the Federal Forests. Contribution No. 50. University of Washington College of Forest Resources. Seattle.

Leopold, Aldo. 1949. A Sand County Almanac. Oxford University Press. New York. 226 pp. (reprinted 1966)

Lindblom, Charles E. 1977. Politics and Markets. Basic Books. New York. 403 pp.

Manthy, Robert S. 1978. Will timber be scarce? *Journal of Forestry* 76(5):278–280.

Marx, Karl. 1875. Critique of the Gotha Program. In Eugene Kamenka (ed.), 1983. The Portable Karl Marx. Penguin Books. New York. 606 pp.

McCloskey, Michael. 1981. The responsibility of the private owner for forest land stewardship. Pp. 99–100 in Land-Use Allocation: Processes, People, Politics, Professionals. Proceedings of the 1980 Convention of the Society of American Foresters. Bethesda, MD.

Moshofsky, William J. 1981. Influence of the market on private and public land-use allocation. Pp. 102–105 in Land-Use Allocation: Processes, People, Politics, Professionals. Proceedings of the 1980 Convention of the Society of American Foresters. Bethesda, MD.

Musgrave, Richard A., and Peggy B. Musgrave. 1984. Public Finance in Theory and Practice, 4th ed. McGraw-Hill. New York. 824 pp.

Niskanen, William A. 1971. Bureaucracy and Representative Government. Aldine-Atherton. Chicago. 241 pp.

Ostrom, Vincent, and Elinor Ostrom. 1977. Pp. 7–49, Public Goods and Public Choices. In E.S. Savas (ed.), Alternatives for Delivering Public Services. Westview Press. Boulder, CO. 178 pp.

O'Toole, Randall. 1988. Reforming the Forest Service. Island Press. Washington, DC. 247 pp.

Pejovich, Steve. 1984. Origins and consequences of alternative property rights. Pp. 163–175 in Selling the Federal Forests. Contribution No. 50. University of Washington, College of Forest Resources. Seattle.

Randall, Alan. 1981. Resource Economics. Grid Publishing. Columbus, OH. 415 pp.

Robbins, William G. 1983. Compton, Wilson Martindale (1890–1967). Pp. 96–97 in Richard C. Davis (ed.), Encyclopedia of American Forest and Conservation History, Vol. I. MacMillan. New York. 400 pp.

Salazar, Debra J., and Robert G. Lee. 1990. Natural Resource Policy Analysis and Rational Choice Theory: A Strategy for Empirical Research. *Natural Resources Journal* 30:(283–300).

Samuelson, Robert J. 1989. Economics made easy. *Newsweek* 114(22):64, November 27.

Savas, E. S. 1982. Privatizing the Public Sector. Chatham House. Chatham, NJ. 164 pp.

Sax, Joseph L. 1984. The claim for retention of the public lands. In Sterling Brubaker (ed.), Rethinking the Federal Lands. Resources of the Future. Washington, DC. 306 pp.

Schumacher, E. F. 1975. Small Is Beautiful. Harper & Row. New York. 290 pp.

Schumpeter, Joseph A. 1949. Imperfect competition. Pp. 349–358 in Readings in Economics. Barnes & Noble. New York.

Scitovsky, Tibor. 1980. Can capitalism survive?—An old question in a new setting. *American Economic Review* 70:1–9.

Smith, Adam. 1776. The Wealth of Nations, Book IV. Reprinted by University of Chicago Press, Chicago, 1976. 524 p. in Book IV.

Stigler, George. 1971. The theory of economic regulation. *Bell Journal of Economics and Management Science* 2(1):3–21.

Stroup, Richard L., and John A. Baden. 1973. Externality, property rights, and the management of our national forests. *The Journal of Law and Economics* 16(2):303–312.

Stroup, Richard L., and John A. Baden. 1983. Natural Resources: Bureaucratic Myths and Environmental Management. Pacific

Institute for Public Policy Research/Ballinger Publishing Company. Cambridge, MA. 148 pp.

Thurow, Lester C. 1985. The other deficit. *Resources* 80(Spring):5–9.

Vardaman, James M. 1970. The smartest fellow around. *American Forests* 76(11):8, 61–63.

Vardaman, James M. 1978. Attitude of foresters toward the small, private landowner: A consulting forester's opinion. *Journal of Forestry* 76(6):368–369, 387.

Vardaman, James M. 1989. How to make money growing trees. Wiley. New York. 296 pp.

Walzer, Michael. 1983. Spheres of Justice. Basic Books. New York. 345 pp.

Wishart, John. 1984. FIP: Special-interest subsidy or tool for tomorrow. *American Forests* 90(7):11, 52–54.

Wolf, Charles, Jr. 1979. A theory of nonmarket failure: Framework for implementation analysis. *Journal of Law and Economics* 22(1):107–140.

Wolf, Charles, Jr. 1988. Markets or Government: Choosing between Imperfect Alternatives. MIT Press. Cambridge, MA. 220 pp.

Zaslowsky, Dyan. 1989. A public beef: Are grazing cattle turning the American West into a new desert? *Harrowsmith* (January/February): 39–47.

Chapter 4

Policy Issues and Formulation

The outcome of every conflict is determined by the extent to which the audience becomes involved in it. That is, the outcome of all conflict is determined by the scope of its contagion.

—*E. E. Schattschneider 1960*

The subactivities associated with formulation are thus summarized as research, review, projection, and selection. They may occur very systematically—almost scientifically—or in quite haphazard fashion. Sometimes the process is reconstructed as having been rational and scientific, when in fact the decision itself was made quite haphazardly. And the time frame for formulation may be measured in minutes or years.

—*Charles Jones 1984*

INTRODUCTION

The first step in the policy process consists of problem recognition and formation, followed by demands to place the problem on the policy-making agenda. Jones (1984) defines this initial activity as problem perception and definition. This component of the policy process is crucial in determining whether problems are acted on or ignored by government.

Once issues reach agenda status, the people seeking a change or the decision makers considering the change must formulate new policies. As Jones (1984) suggested, formulation consists of research, review, projection, and selection. The decision makers must investigate the problem, interpret the results, consider the feasibility of alternative proposals, and select an appropriate policy intended to resolve the issue. In this chapter, problem identification, agenda setting, and the policy formulation and adoption processes will be discussed. These are the first four steps in the policy process model depicted in Figure 2-3.

PROBLEMS AND ISSUES

The policy process begins with the recognition of a problem or issue. These two terms are often used interchangeably, although they differ slightly in meaning. Definitions for *problem* from *Webster's Third International Dictionary* include

A question raised for inquiry, consideration or solution.
An intricate unsettled question.

Similarly, definitions of *issue* include

A matter that is in dispute between two or more parties: a point of debate or controversy.
The point at which an unsettled matter is ready for a decision.

Problem connotes an unsatisfactory situation, need, or want in a neutral tone; *issue* implies more of a debate or controversy regarding the situation. There are thousands of natural resource problems; only a few become important issues.

Forest resource problems occur at the global, national, state, local, or institutional level. The U.S. Congress enacted the National Forest Management Act of 1976 in response to problems in managing the national forests. Many states have adopted regulations governing private forest management in order to solve perceived problems of destructive timber cutting or water pollution. Many local municipalities have enacted statutes restricting or banning logging within their boundaries. Forestry institutions, such as the Forest Service, state departments of natural resources, or even forestry and wildlife schools, continually change policies, develop new programs, or reorganize in order to better address some problem or need. Thus, definitions of problems and issues generally apply to a broad range of institutions but will be used primarily in a national or state context in this text. Furthermore, we will define an issue as existing only when two or more parties debate a problem.

PROBLEM FORMATION

Underlying the list of initial realities about politics (See Table 2-2) is Jones's (1984) definition of a problem as a condition or situation that produces needs or dissatisfactions for which relief or change is sought. He observes that many private problems are acted on in government (such as businesses seeking special favors) but not all public problems are acted on in government, nor do most people (the general public), maintain an interest in other people's problems. Also, public problems may lack a supporting constituency, even among people directly affected. Thus, policymakers often define problems and implement programs with only limited public scrutiny or feedback.

In an analysis of congressional legislation, Dodd and Schott (1979) found that most bills are enacted without opposition or conflict among interest groups. This suggests that the problems perceived by an interest group are often ignored by others, making such legislation easy to pass. Major disagreements among interest groups give rise to the wider-based issues that are more commonly cited and examined in policy studies. Issues are therefore problems characterized by significant disagreement.

ISSUE CREATION

Occasionally, perceived problems with existing policies receive the attention of a large number of people. Issues also may be considered problems that are widely recognized and debated by the public and result from a combination of events and interest group actions (Figure 4-1).

Cobb and Elder (1972) suggest that an issue may be created or triggered by four means. First, issues may be initiated by one or more groups who perceive an unfavorable bias toward their views in the existing distribution of positions or resources. For example, creation of the national forests in the East stemmed from perceptions that private owners had mismanaged their forest land. Timber harvesting had led to hazardous flood conditions, and there seemed to be little prospect for forest regeneration under private ownership.

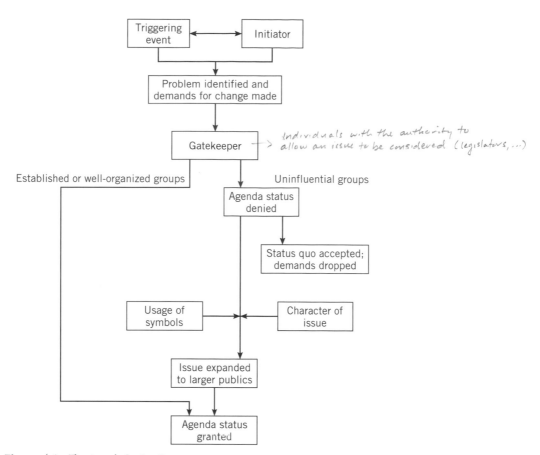

Figure 4-1 The Agenda-Setting Process
Source: Adapted from Cobb and Elder (1972), Jones (1984), and Schattschneider (1960).

Second, persons or groups may initiate and exploit issues for their own gain. Government agencies, and sometimes scientists, have been accused of exaggerating or even creating problems that can be solved by new programs, enlarged budgets, or extensive research. Without problems or issues, agencies are unnecessary. Most applied research and a considerable amount of basic research responds to current issues. Enthusiasm for enhanced research funding has been suggested to color some scientists' beliefs about public problems, such as global climate change. Interest groups also may create issues to obtain favorable natural resource policies and expand their organizations. Without animals, forests, and lands to protect, most conservation groups would have little reason to exist.

Third, issues may be created by unanticipated events. The Exxon Valdez oil spill in Alaska's Prince William Sound in 1989 prompted calls for prohibition of new oil drilling in the Alaska National Wildlife Refuge. Nuclear accidents at Three-Mile Island in the United States and Chernobyl in the former Soviet Union buttressed the already pervasive public sentiments against the proliferation of nuclear power generation facilities. The 1988 Yellowstone fires focused public attention on resource management and fire policy in the national parks.

Fourth, issues can be initiated by people or groups who do not stand to reap any direct benefits. These people obtain satisfaction from acting in what they perceive to be the public interest. Members of environmental interest groups usually claim, either explicitly or implicitly, to be altruists interested only in conserving or preserving natural resources for the benefit of society. Forest conservation groups formed at the turn of the century and soil, water, and wildlife groups formed in the

1930s were responding to perceived resource conservation problems. These forest exploitation and soil erosion issues did not need to be created, but merely amplified, in order to prompt action.

Issue Types

Issues may be placed into three legislative categories: distribution, regulation, and redistribution (Lowi 1964). Every government policy falls within one of these mutually exclusive categories. *Distributive* issues involve short-run high-priority "pork barrel" problems regarding the appropriation of funds for individual projects. Such legislation is usually assembled in piecemeal fashion, and conflicts are uncommon. Indeed, issues regarding such projects are resolved without much publicity and are seldom heard of by the general public. Providing funding for new parks, bridges and highways, or other public facilities are typical of distributive legislation.

Regulatory issues are specific and individual in effect, but they can be aggregated to indicate an overall policy direction. The accumulated effects of many bodies of polluted water led to a national issue of how to clean up water everywhere. Regulatory issues occur partially because administrators are unable to resolve conflicts, causing issues to revert to the legislature or the judiciary (Cobb and Elder 1972). *Redistributive* issues—taking revenues from some groups and distributing them to others—usually involve large numbers of people and deal with equitable distribution of resources. Accordingly, they are likely to gain quick access to a formal policy-making agenda.

Illustration: U.S. Forest Service Issue Identification

This illustration draws upon descriptions and definitions of issues developed by the U.S. Forest Service for use in forest planning (Wagstaff et al. 1980). The rangers managing the U.S. national forests rely on two types of networks to identify public forest resource management issues. The *formal* network includes organized interest groups or institutions—for example, a recreational vehicle club or a city council. *Informal* networks consist of casual discussions or complaints aired between resource managers and citizens regarding the citizens' interests, attitudes, and opinions.

The Forest Service recognizes three types of public resource management issues: (1) An *emerging* issue concerns a problem that may evolve into a specific request for the distribution, regulation, or redistribution of forest resources; (2) An *existing* issue is a direct request by the public for the distribution, regulation, or redistribution of forest resources; and (3) a *disruptive* issue is a direct request by the public that is beyond the control of the resource manager at that given administrative level. A disruptive issue can develop into a crisis situation and therefore requires immediate attention and action. Managers need to respond to emerging and existing issues as quickly and efficiently as possible to avoid their developing into disruptive ones.

The Forest Service developed some guidelines for issue identification as part of the forest planning process (Wagstaff et al. 1980). Accordingly, an issue should

- Have potential conflicts or ongoing conflicts,
- Have potential for a change in management plans.
- Have an effect on the allocation of resources.
- Deal with the here and now.
- Require a Forest Service role in resolution.
- Be capable of being written as a question.
- Be verifiable through public involvement.
- Be composed of subissues that are resolvable; otherwise, there is no point in dealing with the issue in a particular forest plan.

Issues that meet the preceding criteria are to be addressed in the national forest planning process. Other issues may exist as well, but they are either dealt with at the regional or national level or are overlooked.

AGENDAS AND ISSUE EXPANSION

Before an issue can be resolved, it must be placed on the agenda of a decision maker. The many issues that exist must be brought to the attention of government before policy changes can be considered. People must aggregate, organize, and contact government representatives in order to get their issue placed on the agenda (Jones 1984). Sometimes politicians take the lead in developing policy agendas. For example, Senators Leahy (D-VT) and Wirth (D-CO) were leaders in developing federal policies on global climate change in the early 1990s.

Cobb and Elder (1972) identify two types of policy agendas. The *general*, or *systemic*, agenda consists of all the issues that the public thinks deserve attention—a general, vague group of problems that should be addressed. The systemic agenda is essentially a discussion (rather than action) agenda of important issues, such as water pollution, wilderness preservation, crime, or equitable taxation. Such agendas exist nationally, locally, or even within institutions. General agenda items form the basis for specific action agenda items.

Formal agendas consist of explicit issues that are up for active and serious consideration by some public or private organization that has authority over the issue. Several elements of this definition are useful in understanding forest resource policies. Explicitness requires that issues be defined clearly enough to allow action on a specific policy alternative: Can the annual allowable cut of timber be increased? Can buffer strips protect streams from sedimentation caused by soil erosion? Can Forest Service and Bureau of Land Management lands be exchanged in Oregon and California? Should there be more wilderness areas in Idaho and Montana? Policymakers can consider and act on these explicit issues.

Formal agenda items include issues on the dockets of decision-making bodies such as legislatures, courts, regulatory agencies, private firms, interest groups, commissions and committees, and governors and presidents. Viable legislative bills represent issues on the formal agenda. For instance, in 1984 the Georgia legislature considered and then passed a bill requiring that any new state government building be built only with lumber manufactured in Georgia—doubtless a policy reaction to the issue of Canadian lumber imports. However, the governor vetoed the bill, negating the proposed policy change. Court cases involving forestry, such as the Monongahela clear-cutting issue, nonpoint source water pollution, and wetlands dredge and fill regulations, have been placed on court agendas for resolution. Decisions to invest (or disinvest) in timberlands were on the agenda of corporate forestry decision makers in the 1980s. Specific proposals to improve public education in the face of shrinking budgets were on the agenda of almost every state in the 1980s and early 1990s.

Formal agendas may consist of old items that have their action alternatives fairly well delineated, or new items without well-defined action alternatives. Some items come up for regular review, such as the federal and state agency requests for budget appropriations. Other items, such as tax reform or government reorganization, occur frequently but irregularly. New agenda items may arise as a result of the action of a key decision maker in a specific situation, through mobilization of mass support, or by activation of public interest groups and the media, such as the antiwar movement in the 1960s or the many issues dealing with the clear-cutting controversy in national forest management.

People or groups that want an issue resolved first try to get recognition, and then to achieve agenda status. They strive to have their concerns placed on agendas, presuming that policies will change in their favor. Favorable action is not guaranteed; problems may be ignored, or even exacerbated. In 1978 President Carter tried to eliminate preferential tax treatment of capital gains income which included timber sale income, but Congress instead reduced the effective capital gains rate from 49 to 28 percent. Despite possible setbacks, groups continually seek to gain agenda status.

What determines if issues will reach formal agenda status? Gatekeepers—the individuals with authority to allow the issue to be considered (i.e., legislators, congressional staff, judges, district foresters)—are the first hurdle governing agenda status. The issue itself, the way it develops, the characteristics and strategies of the groups involved, and the issue characteristics also affect the likelihood of an issue's passing the gatekeeper and being placed on the agenda (see Figure 4-1).

INTEREST GROUP INVOLVEMENT

Four factors affect whether an issue will reach agenda status (Jones 1984). One is the reaction to the issue itself: How many people are affected? How do different groups perceive the problem? How intense are their feelings? Second, group organization, size, structure, and leadership are important. A third set of determinants relates to group representation. Are the people affected by a problem well represented? Do policymakers empathize with their concerns? Can the affected groups muster support? Last, the policy process itself is important. The relationship between affected groups and policymakers, the previous responsiveness of the policymakers, and the policy-making and interest group leaders' characteristics all affect issue outcomes.

Jones (1984) identifies four groups that seek agenda status.

1. A well-organized group with established access to policymakers (e.g., the American Medical Association, the American Petroleum Institute).

2. A well-organized group without established access (e.g., environmental groups for many issues).

3. A poorly organized group with established access (e.g., the coal industry, farmers, or others with definite advantages in access but limited capacity for coalescing or defining their interests).

4. The poorly organized group without established access (e.g., many of the socially and economically disadvantaged groups in the society, such as the homeless; or native populations in tropical rain forests).

Different groups use different strategies in trying to gain agenda status (i.e., to get past the gatekeeper). Well-organized groups already having access will simply contact key policymakers to secure desirable policy changes. In fact, they will affect policies with as little publicity as possible in order to avoid alerting others whose reactions might complicate matters. Well-organized groups without established access can also secure access if they deem it necessary. Such groups will have obvious potential political power, and elected decision makers, in particular, will respond to their demands. Many national environmental groups, particularly the National Wildlife Federation or the Sierra Club, have probably reached this organizational status. At the state level, forest industry lobbyists and groups may gain direct access more easily than environmental groups, at least in the South.

ISSUE EXPANSION

The fourth group—outsiders in the political system—are likely to try to expand issues and involve other interest groups in order to gain agenda status. Issues are of concern to groups that are directly affected, and to their audiences—other people who may have some interest. If one group in a conflict believes itself to be at a disadvantage, it will attempt to draw more people and other groups into the fight. Expanding the scope of a conflict often is the weaker party's only hope (Schattschneider 1960).

Politicians and bureaucrats try to keep information and power to themselves, thus controlling policy in Washington, DC. However, those who lose out in behind-the-scenes policy debates and struggles try to widen the circle by spreading information to summon political allies within the administration or Congress or to rally public opinion (Smith 1988). The attempts of uninfluential players to involve more groups are the basis of the issue expansion process. Environmental groups have learned this lesson well and frequently attempt to expand issues beyond administrative agencies to other interest groups with better access to gatekeepers, and to legislative committees that dominate much policy-making.

Generally, the greater the size of the audience to which an issue can be enlarged, the greater the likelihood that it can attain access to a formal agenda. Issue expansion implies that members of a particular public are aware of an issue and have opinions regarding its resolution. Four classes of publics may become involved in an issue, ranging from the initial participants to the general populace (Cobb and Elder 1972).

Initial disputants first seek support from *identification groups* that share their interests. Identification groups generally assume that issues involving their peers are important. When the Forest Service became involved in the clear-cutting controversy, the Society of American Foresters immediately became involved based on their common interests.

The second round of conflict expansion involves *attention groups*—those concerned with related issues. In the clear-cutting controversy, the National Association of Home Builders and the AFL-CIO became involved in the issue because they believed that changes in national forest harvesting policy could raise lumber prices, thus adversely affecting members of their organizations. In 1984 the Society of American Foresters adopted an official policy of supporting zero population growth. This was an attention group response, because population growth was deemed to have adverse effects on resource conservation.

Identification groups and attention groups consist of identifiable organizations. As such, they are specific publics. The mass public—individuals not formally affiliated with such groups—may also become involved in issues. The *attentive public* consists of those who are generally interested in and informed about policy issues. These individuals are generally the better-educated and higher-income members of society. They may express their opinions to their elected and appointed officials, write to legislators or newspapers, or speak at public hearings. The attentive public became involved in much of the environmental legislation enacted during the 1970s and is ubiquitous in local issues such as zoning or plant siting. Forest management issues may involve members of the attentive public at the national level, such as hearings stemming from the clear-cutting controversy or from the impact of wetlands protection on forestry and agriculture. In the late 1980s and early 1990s, debates over timber harvests and spotted owls, tropical deforestation, and global climate change gained the attention of large groups of the public.

The *general public* consists of people who are uninterested, uninformed, and inactive on most issues. They are the last group to become involved in an issue and require that issues be very general. Their involvement is usually unorganized and short-lived. For example, only about one-half of those registered actually vote in presidential elections; local election turnouts are much lower. At the national level, forestry issues probably never attracted the general public until climate change and spotted owls became important. Even the general public has probably heard these issues and formed opinions, although appropriate personal responses are elusive.

For groups lacking access to a gatekeeper, issues confined to identification groups will have difficulty in reaching formal agenda status. Involving attention groups increases the chance of getting a hearing; most issues involving the attentive public will be placed on the agenda. Items that expand to the general public will certainly be placed on the national policy agenda (Cobb and Elder 1972).

ISSUE CHARACTERISTICS

The characteristics of an issue determine how much publicity it will receive and how broad its appeal to public groups will be, leading to placement on a formal agenda. Ambiguously defined issues are more likely to expand to a wider audience because more people may feel that they could be affected. Narrow, precisely defined issues will appeal only to identification or possibly attention groups that understand the problem. In the 1950s Sen. Joe McCarthy made many of his charges regarding communist conspiracies as ambiguous as possible to involve as many people as possible. Although ambiguity helps issue expansion, eventually groups must make specific demands for an issue to receive formal consideration. Otherwise decision makers may claim to be unable to respond to the problem.

Defining problems as being socially significant—affecting the basic welfare of a segment of the population—also helps expansion. Interest groups continually attempt to link their problems to universal issues such as national security, hunger, housing, jobs, health, or equity. Basic human needs will embrace a large constituency. The forest industry invariably tries to link issues such as clear-cutting or herbicide use to the basic need for affordable housing. Sustained-yield timber harvests and below-cost timber sales on national forests have been justified by the need to maintain jobs and community stability in the West. Forest recreation and wilderness use advocates have argued that their preferred programs are necessary because people have a psychological need to "get away from it all." Most of the environmental legislation enacted in the 1970s was related to protecting the health of people, animals, or plants.

Technical terms limit issue expansion. Scientists, lobbyists for the coal industry, and even midwestern congressional representatives continually refer to acid precipitation in technical, scientific terms. Environmental groups focus more on pollution, dead trees, and dead fish. More people understand nontechnical language, and it naturally attracts a larger audience. Foresters have usually couched their problems in scientific terms (except for Pinchot and the early conservation crusaders), environmentalists in more approachable jargon. Colorful language promotes expansion.

The lack of a clear precedent for solving an issue also may attract attention; however, novelty may impede placement of an issue on a formal agenda. Policymakers avoid overly controversial issues or solutions. Few politicians advocate legalizing drugs, despite rampant drug-related crime. Politicians will, however, seek to promote less controversial new programs that they then can be remembered for.

The greater the long-term consequences of an issue, the greater is the likelihood that the issue will expand. Foresters argue that investments in forest regeneration will provide long-term benefits to our heirs. Environmental protection, wilderness, and wildlife groups plead similar arguments for their resource concerns. This may attract attention, but all groups still face difficulty in convincing individual landowners to act for the benefit of future generations.

Naturally, the preceding techniques may be used simultaneously to expand an issue. Additionally, the reverse of any of them could be used to contain or suppress an issue.

SYMBOLS AND EXPANSION STRATEGY

Advocates or opponents of a policy use symbolic representations to define an issue in terms favorable to their point of view. Language, pictures, and the mass media are instrumental in getting issues on an agenda. Interest groups use symbols for effect or impact; reality and accuracy are secondary concerns. The connotations of a story, advertisement, or film clip are the key to defining an issue and provoking a response. Once on a formal agenda, more specific, substantive suggestions for policy changes can be made.

Symbols often are overlooked by resource professionals, who are more concerned with technical practice than its public image. For example, in 1983 and 1984 the Society of American Foresters (SAF) ran a large national and local public relations effort with Ralph Waite (former star of the "Waltons" television show) talking in general terms about the benefits of forests. Yet some local SAF chapters voiced dissatisfaction with the advertisements because they were scientifically debatable: Foresters questioned whether trees really clean water, as Ralph Waite claimed. Although accuracy is desirable, imagery is far more important than science in delivering messages to the attentive public. Political image makers recognized these benefits long ago. The Sierra Club has run ads on Music Television (MTV) that show pristine forest scenes and contain pleas to join the group. Wildlife groups use beautiful scenery and furry animals to help advocate their policies. The American Forest Council has been successful at promoting its Tree Farm Program with video and print publicity campaigns starring Tree Farm members Jimmy and Rosalyn Carter. The forest industry realized these benefits and began a national ad campaign promoting wise use in 1989, relying on excellent pictures of managed forests and simple captions. Use of the media is discussed in detail in Chapter 11.

The combination of symbols, group actions, and the media focuses attention on problems. Provocative words can attract instant attention; neutral language can dull the senses. Bureaucracies can obfuscate issues. James Watt, President Reagan's first secretary of the interior, was a master of colorful phrases, as was Nixon's vice-president, Spiro Agnew, a decade earlier, albeit not necessarily with favorable results. Table 4-1 lists a few examples of colorful and neutral ways to describe the same items. Obviously, some will elicit a greater response than others. Radical activists in the 1960s often could provoke attack by calling police officers "pigs." However, symbolic language should be used judiciously. It can create a backlash instead of a positive response. Watt resigned before Reagan's term expired after causing too much controversy.

In addition to the broadcast media and written word, pictures in the print media also can be effective. Conservation magazines generally rely on photographs and brief articles. Smokey the Bear, charred forests, and cuddly animals have provided effective forestry publicity for decades. Cartoons have also been used for centuries to lampoon policies and politicians and to promote new programs. In the 1920s and 1930s, J. N. "Ding" Darling's conservation cartoons and personal activism regarding soil conservation helped prompt establishment of the federal Soil Erosion Service (now the Soil Conservation Service) and the National Wildlife Federation (Figure 4-2). James Watt hoped that by reversing the direction that the buffalo on the seal of the Department of the Interior faced from left (liberal) to right (conservative), he could similarly change the agency's ideology.

Interest groups may select various strategies to expand the appeal of their issue to larger audiences. They may try to arouse latent support from the public, primarily via media coverage, or they may try to provoke action, such as the demonstrators at the Democratic national convention did in Chicago in 1968 or as Ghandi did in India to win independence from England. Preservationists who climb trees or lie down in front of skidders try to provoke responses and gain media coverage. Symbols may be used to discourage or dissuade the other side from active opposition to the issue. The anti-abortion movement has been adept at using pictures of unborn fetuses or phrases such as "baby killers" to muffle opposition to its cause; pro-choice groups have responded by carrying coat hangers covered with blood in their demonstrations.

Interest groups may try to demonstrate their strength by various means, such as marches, protests, or rallies. Loggers have circled their trucks around the statehouse in Sacramento, California, during some of the public debates on forest regulation; farmers have plowed up the Mall in Washington, DC., with their tractors; civil rights activists marched from Selma to Montgomery, Al-

TABLE 4-1. Alternative Phrases Used to Describe Selected Public Policy Features

Neutral or Technical Words (possible users)	Colorful or Descriptive Words (possible users)
economic scarcity (economists)	timber famine (Gifford Pinchot)
media critics of government policies	nattering nabobs of negativism (Spiro Agnew)
police officers	pigs (hippies)
revenue enhancements (politicians)	more taxes (taxpayers)
asset management (Reagan)	land giveaway (environmentalists)
privatization (conservative economists)	
incentive (government officials)	subsidy (economists)
benefits of wilderness experience (wilderness advocates)	subsidizing of rich elitists (mining industry)
fish and wildlife biologists	prairie fairies and tree huggers (James Watt)
public assistance (government officials)	welfare, government control (conservatives)
environmentalists	extremists (forest industry)
public works project (politicians)	pork-barrel project (citizens)
old-growth forests (foresters)	ancient forests (preservation groups)
low pH precipitation (scientists)	acid rain (citizens)
riparian area (ecologists)	streambank (citizens)
cattle (most people)	hooved locusts (environmentalists)
harvest level (wildlife biologists)	hunter kill (citizens)
shifting agriculture (agriculturalists)	slash and burn agriculture (citizens)
wise use movement (development interests)	brown movement (environmentalists)

abama. Groups also try to revitalize their membership by stressing symbolic concepts such as solidarity—"in unions, there is strength" in the United States or "solidarnosc" in Poland.

Issue expansion to gain agenda status is the exception, not the rule, however, in American politics (Jones 1984). Schattschneider (1960) notes that democratic politics may help resolve issues, but biases still exist. Nationalization of politics may help break up local power monopolies. Nevertheless, a tremendous amount of the conflict is controlled by making it so private that it is virtually in-

visible. In the end, it is the loser of the behind-the-scenes struggles who calls for outside help. Smith (1988), describing Washington politics, suggests this principle has not changed in decades. Issue expansion may sometimes be a helpful agenda-setting strategy, but it usually represents a last resort for uninfluential groups.

Issue expansion may help gain attention, but specific demands and possible solutions are needed once an issue is placed on the formal agenda. Also, issue expansion and symbolic representations can get out of control, backfire, or produce undesirable results. The

AS LAND GOES, SO GOES MAN

Figure 4-2 Ding's Half Century: "Although the United States has readily available resources greater than that of any other nation or group of nations, the resources were not unlimited, and cartoons such as this were drawn to emphasize that fact."
Source: Darling 1962.

intensity of belief is important, too, not just the number of people involved. A kamikaze truck bomber in Beirut triggered a U.S. withdrawal from the area faster than did a year of issue expansion, interest group activity, and media criticism.

APPLICATIONS

Issues may expand and reach a formal policy agenda as previously described. Groups also may strive to prevent an issue from reaching an agenda. They may try to define an issue in terms that are dull, narrow, or technical. They may try to discredit other interest group leaders or appeal to members of groups rather than deal with the leaders themselves. For example, President Reagan successfully appealed to blue-collar union members in the elections of 1980 and 1984, despite official union endorsements for Carter and Mondale. Agenda status also may be denied or at least defused by taking limited actions, such as establishing a commission or panel to study the matter, or token hiring of minorities and women.

Another method to keep issues off policy agendas is simply to anticipate and respond to problems as they arise. This seems almost trite, but a significant number of major issues probably could be avoided by listening to citizens who perceive a problem, talking with them about the problem and alternative policies, and amending or adapting the existing policy to improve the status quo. In the Monongahela issue in West Virginia, the Forest Service received complaints from citizens, interest groups, and the entire West Virginia congressional delegation about clear-cutting. The agency's intransigence certainly helped lead to the eventual court action that stopped timber sales in the entire region and eventually led to the National Forest Management Act of 1976.

A similar harvesting controversy on state forest lands in Michigan remained localized when the state Department of Natural Resources responded quickly to the concerns of citizens, communicated departmental goals, brought in appropriate outside experts, and modified some of the policies causing the problems (Hacker 1983). An example drawn from the South also illustrates the importance of responsiveness. A forester had a policy of shooting all stray dogs that wandered onto company forest lands. Needless to say, local residents who lost their treasured pets and hunting dogs were less than pleased and complained vocally. Both the forester and his company ignored their pleas, but soon mysterious fires burned several thousand acres of young pine plantations. A timely policy change would have been prudent in this case.

Reasonable demands can and often should be handled at the local level by listening and responding to citizens. Voluntary local policy changes require flexibility and a willingness to work with those who complain. But such changes probably are quicker, less aggravating, and more tailored to local conditions than state or national legislation could be.

POLICY FORMULATION AND ADOPTION

After an issue has reached formal agenda status, formulation—the next step in the policy process—occurs as policymakers design specific proposals. This is eventually followed by adoption of a proposed solution to a particular problem. Formulation includes not only creating proposals and plans, but also choosing the criteria for selecting among alternatives. In this chapter, we discuss the participants and processes of formulating alternatives; evaluative criteria will be discussed in Chapter 5.

Adoption consists of selecting a policy to try to resolve an issue and then implementing it. Several models of public policy formulation and adoption have been proposed by political scientists. Two of the most important—rationalism and incrementalism—are presented later in this chapter. So are some newer approaches for resolving environmental and natural resource issues.

Anderson et al. (1984, p. 7) define formulation as "the development of pertinent and acceptable proposed courses of action for dealing with a public problem." The course of action may result in a proposed law, executive order, or administrative rule, but policymakers often decide that no government action will be taken. Simply put, agenda status need not yield a policy change. If problems that achieve agenda status are perceived as too minor, or perhaps as too difficult to solve, the status quo will be preserved. Or if existing policies are deemed adequate, policymakers will "stay the course" and dismiss the issue.

Some additional insights regarding formulation are provided by Jones (1984). First, formulation need not be limited to one set of actors; two or more groups may produce competing (or complementary) proposals. Formulation may occur without a clear problem definition or much contact with the affected groups. Formulation and reformulation may occur continually without achieving sufficient support for any one proposal. People who lose in one part of the formulation process may appeal in other parts.

PARTICIPANTS

Who formulates policy proposals? At the national level, the president, members of Congress, judges, and government agency personnel (bureaucrats) are obvious formulators. Congressional staff and interest group representatives also participate in formulation. Equivalent officeholders at the state level suggest proposals. Constituents may suggest goals, but they rarely develop specific proposals and plans for reaching them.

National

In the twentieth century, the president and his chief aides and advisors in the Executive Office have been the major source of initiatives in the development of policy recommendations, including provision of draft bills (Anderson 1979). Naturally, Congress rarely accepts the president's proposals without modifying them, but the proposals do provide a starting point for further deliberations. Many proposals are developed by career and appointed officials in administrative departments and agencies. These proposals deal with problems familiar to the agency. Lower-level policy changes may be made by agencies if they already have statutory authority; new laws must be enacted by Congress.

Presidents and Congress sometimes create special study groups or commissions to examine issues and develop policy proposals. The first U.S. Outdoor Recreation Resources Review Committee (1962) was established by Congress in 1958 to examine the nation's outdoor recreation resources and programs. It took four years of hearings and deliberations, but the committee's report formed the basis for subsequent legislation and state planning efforts. It also led to the establishment of the Bureau of Outdoor Recreation as a federal planning and funding organization (Dana and Fairfax 1980). A second such committee, the President's Commission on Outdoor Recreation in America, was authorized in 1984. It recommended government programs and funding of more than $1 billion in its 1987 report, much to President Reagan's chagrin. As of 1991 none of the recommendations had been implemented, but they will provide bases for future public debate. The Public Land Law Review Commission, chartered in 1964, issued its final report in 1970 and made proposals for legislation affecting public forest resources. However, its commodity-production bias caused it to be virtually ignored as the environmental movement awakened (Dana and Fairfax 1980).

Federal legislators also formulate policy. Personal or committee staff may be involved, or the legislators may act on the basis of their own interests, information from hearings, or requests from interest groups or constituents. Legislative support units, such as the Congressional Research Service, Office of Technology Assessment, and General Accounting Office, also contribute ideas and expertise for developing policy proposals.

Interest groups often offer specific legislative proposals through supportive members of Congress. In the natural resources area, all the major citizen conservation groups have numerous lobbyists who work directly with Congress members and congressional staff. Forestry, range, and mining trade associations also participate in congressional deliberations specific to their interests or in wider issues such as clean air, clean water, or labor relations law. Conservation groups and trade associations often participate in policymaking through issues that challenge laws or through agency implementation of laws that are brought to the courts.

There are many additional sources of policy proposals, including the Ford, Rockefeller, and Carnegie foundations. Private nonprofit research "think tanks" such as the liberal Brookings Institution and the conservative American Enterprise Institute are influential. Natural resource policymakers have depended for several decades on the ideas, analyses, conferences, and books from Resources for the Future and the Conservation Foundation. World Resources Institute, Worldwatch, the World Wildlife Fund, and other global nonprofit organizations proposed many new policies in the late 1980s. So did the conservative Pacific Institute for Policy Studies, which advocated the benefits of markets rather than governments in allocating natural resources. The academic community also has participated in formulation by analyzing problems and evaluating alternative solutions, as well as by seeking government research funding.

State

At the state level, ideas for policy proposals may come from model acts developed by the National Conference of Commissioners on Uniform State Laws, the Council of State Governments, the American Law Institute, or numerous other organizations. It is much easier to revise a borrowed bill than to start drafting one from scratch (Davies 1975). In forestry, the National Conference of State Legislatures has been active in investigating and publicizing forest resource issues and development opportunities (Meeks 1982, Morandi, Meeks, and Sacarto 1984), although it has not developed specific model bills. The Council of State Planning Agencies has studied appropriate policies for development of state natural resources (Nothdurft 1984).

Lobbyists often try to protect the status quo in state legislatures but propose legislation when appropriate. Elected officials campaign by making promises to take action on general issues. If elected, subsequent initiatives become a principal source of new legislative ideas and administrative policies as officials try to make good on their promises. State agencies and appointed officials in state gov-

ernment may be expected to submit ideas for legislation and administrative policies. Legislative staff also contribute, but less so than at the national level because of the small staff size. Although ideas for bills often come from individuals or legislators, it usually takes the efforts of many to turn an idea into a bill.

ADOPTION PROCESSES

Several political models have been developed to describe how policy formulation and adoption occur. At one end of the spectrum, models based on *rationalism* assume that policies are selected after a thorough analysis of all alternatives and chosen on the basis of clear criteria. At the other end, the *incremental* model suggests that policy is formulated only as a small variation from past policies, with little analysis of program alternatives or impacts.

Rationalism

Rationalism, or the rational-comprehensive approach to decision making, assumes that policies are selected in order to maximize the net value to society or to most effectively achieve a given end. The salient assumptions of rationalism are as follows (Anderson 1979, pp. 9–10):

1. The decision maker is confronted with a given problem that can be separated from other problems or at least considered meaningfully in comparison with them.

2. The goals, values, or objectives that guide the decision maker are clarified and ranked according to their importance.

3. The various alternatives for dealing with the problem are examined.

4. The consequences (costs and benefits) that would follow from the selection of each alternative are investigated.

5. Each alternative, and its attendant consequences, can be compared with the other alternatives.

6. The decision maker will choose that alternative, and its consequences, that max-

imizes the attainment of his or her goals, values, or objectives.

Rational decision making involves reasoned choices about the desirability of adopting different courses of action to resolve issues (Dunn 1981). Professionals in public administration generally are trained in the rational approach to executing public policy. Federal government planning, programming, and budgeting (PPB) procedures initiated in the 1960s were designed to institute rational-comprehensive policy analysis and decision making (Schick 1966, Schultze 1968).

The 1974 Forest and Rangeland Renewable Resources Planning Act (RPA), as amended by the National Forest Management Act (NFMA) of 1976, is an attempt to institute rational-comprehensive planning for national forests. These planning efforts include an assessment of all forest resources in the United States, both public and private. Current data on and projections for outdoor recreation, range, timber, water, and wildlife and fish resource supplies and demands for the next fifty years must be summarized. Based on this assessment, which is to occur every ten years, the Forest Service must develop and examine alternative means to meet the nation's forest resource needs and estimate the costs and benefits of the alternatives. The agency must then present its suggested program to the president, who considers it and sends it to Congress along with budget recommendations (Shands 1981).

Whether these massive Forest Service planning efforts have been worth the cost is subject to considerable debate, as discussed in Chapter 13. Schweitzer, Cortner, and Vann (1984) listed many reasons that rational-comprehensive forest planning may be worth it (Table 4-2) and discussed whether the benefits had been realized. In the final analysis, they concluded that the benefits of planning are difficult to quantify and depend largely on judgments regarding the value of the possible improvements and the success in achieving them. Schweitzer et al. (1984) concluded that:

Thus there is no completely objective means of weighing the benefits against the costs of RPA/NFMA planning. Determining if the benefits are sufficient to justify the expenditure of tax-payer's dollars requires use of political, rather than objective, criteria (p. 407).

Although the rational-comprehensive approach seems laudable, its assumptions are unrealistic. Decision makers are seldom faced with clear objectives or concrete problems (Lindblom 1968). Thus they have to define problems and goals as well as consider alternatives. The assumption that values are known, agreed-upon, and unchanging also is a problem, as the RPA/NFMA experience illustrates. Achieving efficient policy is possible if there are known objectives and values; unknown or conflicting values stymie rational decision making. Facts and values cannot always be separated, let alone quantified.

Rationalism also makes unrealistic demands on the decision maker. It requires information on the alternatives for dealing with the problem, knowledge of the effects of various policy alternatives, and economic measures of those effects. In most situations, lack of time and data, poorly quantified input/output relationships, unknown future effects, and the complexity of calculations undermine these assumptions (Wildavsky 1969). If one has to clarify all objectives, consider all alternatives, quantify their effects, and calculate the benefit–cost relationships, the decision-making process will be interminable. Rationalism also ignores sunk (previously spent) costs. Theoretically, the policy alternative that meets the goals most efficiently will be selected. In practice, previous decisions and commitments or investments in existing policies and programs may preclude many new policy alternatives from consideration (Anderson 1979).

Incrementalism

Lindblom (1959) proposed successive limited comparisons, or incrementalism, as a model of the policy-making process that fits the real world better than rationalism. Incrementalism, or the science of "muddling through,"

TABLE 4-2.   Expected Benefits of Natural Resource Planning

- Improve public access to information
- Improve dialogue among interest groups
- Give better information to managers
- Make explicit things never made explicit before
- Give a better idea of land suitability and capability
- Provide a mechanism for consistent agency data systems
- Require the forester to consider national needs
- Require setting out a fuller range of alternatives
- Force cost analyses of decisions
- Delay decisions
- Increase control by the agency's chief
- Increase control by Congress
- Strengthen the district ranger's authority
- Reduce resistance to change
- Lead to greater timber harvests
- Make land more productive
- Lead to better land management
- Lead to larger total budgets
- Provide a means for reducing budgets
- Improve the balance among budgets for various uses
- Save money
- Improve the balance of budgets among forests
- Return more revenues than the original costs of planning
- Improve the coordination of federal–state planning
- Reduce litigation
- Increase professionalism

Source: Schweitzer et al. (1984). Reprinted by permission of the *Journal of Forestry*, Society of American Foresters.

offers a distinct contrast to the rational-comprehensive model. Lindblom stated that rationalism is impossible for complex problems. It could only be practiced for relatively simple problems, and then only in a somewhat modified form. In practice, public agencies and administrators restrict their attention to relatively few policy alternatives among the countless number imaginable. As such, they practice what Lindblom labeled "successive limited comparisons," a policy-making method that continually builds from the current situation. This has been widely referred to as incrementalism—policy as a variation of the past.

Table 4-3 summarizes the differences between the rational-comprehensive (beginning with a new root) and incremental (branching from past policy) methods of policy-making. Several components of muddling through are important. First, the goals and values and the analysis of needed actions are intertwined as inseparable means and ends. Second, consensus is usually the criterion for good policy. If most of the actors in the process can agree, the policy is deemed successful. Third, incrementalism greatly reduces analysis. Only the most apparent values, outcomes, and alternatives are considered; other important ones may be neglected. Fourth, the successive lim-

TABLE 4-3. Rational-Comprehensive versus Successive Limited Comparisons (Incrementalism) in Policy-Making

Rational-Comprehensive (Root)	Successive Limited Comparisons (Branch)
1a. Clarification of values or objectives distinct from and usually prerequisite to empirical analysis of alternative policies.	1b. Selection of value goals and empirical analysis of the needed action are not distinct from one another but are closely intertwined.
2a. Policy formulation is therefore approached through means-end analysis: First the ends are isolated, then the means to achieve them are sought.	2b. Since means and ends are not distinct, means-end analysis is often inappropriate or limited.
3a. The test of a "good" policy is that it can be shown to be the most appropriate means to desired ends.	3b. The test of a "good" policy is typically that various analysts find themselves directly agreeing on a policy (without their agreeing that it is the most appropriate means to agreed objective).
4a. Analysis is comprehensive; every important relevant factor is taken into account.	4b. Analysis is drastically limited: (i) Important possible outcomes are neglected. (ii) Important alternative potential policies are neglected. (iii) Important affected values are neglected.
5a. Theory is often heavily relied upon.	5b. A succession of comparisons greatly reduces or eliminates reliance on theory.

Source: Lindblom 1959

ited comparisons tend to produce policies that differ only slightly from existing policies. Such small changes in existing policy tend to make major policy shifts difficult to consider.

Forest resource policymakers often muddle through. Vague policy goals (e.g., multiple use) call for gradual policy change from the status quo. Precise policy objectives tend to prevent agreement on policies; vague goal statements often prove less divisive. Most environmental organizations and forest industry associations support "multiple use management" of the nation's public forests. This is an imprecise objective that allows members of each group to read their own interests into it in the balance that they believe is appropriate. Environmentalists use the goal of multiple use to argue that timber harvesting and livestock grazing should not interfere with wildlife habitat, recreation, and scenery. Timber interests often contend that multiple use means that most national forest land should be available for timber management and eventual harvest that only disrupts the forest scene for a relatively short period of time and may even enhance some other uses as timber roads bring in hunters, fishers, and birdwatchers.

Policymakers rarely have the time and money to investigate the full range of policy choices, so incrementalism presents a realistic alternative to rationalism. It also protects policymakers from the uncertainty associated with markedly new or different policies (Boulding 1981). The ability to foresee the full consequences of a major policy change is very limited. This is not wholly unintended since, as President Lyndon Johnson observed, "If the full implications of any bill were known before its enactment, it would never get passed" (Kearns 1976). Thus, supporting and retreating from policies that are only slightly different from existing policies is usually less costly financially and politically. Additionally, many policy decisions rest on large prior investments in current programs. Abandoning these sunk costs and starting anew would be excessively expensive. Last but not least, it is simply easier to continue existing programs than to continually perform rational-comprehensive analyses of new alternatives. Most forestry programs are variations of the past, not new untested approaches.

Mixed Scanning

Obviously, incrementalism has a strong appeal and is followed to some degree by most policymakers. But muddling through has its shortcomings. Incrementalism favors the most powerful and organized interests in society as well as the status quo. Short-run, incremental changes do not lead to social innovation or great changes (Etzioni 1967). Creating the national forests, declaring "war" on poverty, integrating schools, and implementing the National Environmental Policy Act (NEPA) were not incremental decisions. Though infrequent, such bold and fundamental policy shifts are highly significant and provide the basis for many subsequent incremental decisions. Every public natural resource policy since 1969 has built upon the NEPA cornerstone that requires analysis of environmental impact of federal projects and public participation in project plans.

Etzioni (1967) developed mixed scanning as a decision-making model that allows for both fundamental and incremental decisions, depending on the situation. Incrementalism is probably adequate for many decisions. For others, a more comprehensive, rational process may be required. In Congress, incrementalism seems rampant. Perhaps at the agency level or in individual project decisions, opportunities for rational decision making increase. The two approaches may also be combined when only a few serious alternatives are considered (incrementalism), but the costs, benefits, and decision criteria for each are carefully evaluated (rationalism) before the decision is made. NEPA requires rationalism by requiring the consideration of alternatives on major projects.

ALTERNATIVE DISPUTE RESOLUTION

In subsequent chapters, we will look at policy-making in a variety of institutional settings, including courts, legislatures, and administrative agencies. In recent years, some new alternatives for resolving natural resource and environmental issues have been developed, which bear discussion. These techniques are loosely termed *alternative dispute resolution* and rely on personal meetings rather than legislatures and courts.

MEDIATION AND NEGOTIATION

Environmental mediation is one form of alternative dispute resolution. In this approach, persons and groups with different interests are brought together in formal, structured meetings in order to agree on resource policies. A mediator or facilitator tries to help participants identify problems, suggest solutions, establish decision criteria, and move toward a policy consensus acceptable to most interests. Individuals involved in mediated disputes usually agree to participate voluntarily, meet as a group, try to reach an acceptable compromise, and abide by the decision. Well over 100 environmental disputes have been mediated since 1973 (Bingham 1986).

Principled negotiation is another form of dispute resolution. Fisher and Ury (1981) popularized the approach, which was widely promoted in the 1980s. The first step is to separate personal differences from the problem, in order to avoid emotional debates. The second is to focus on interests, not positions. This implies an examination of what people want, not of the specific programs or means of achieving those wants. Third, there should be many proposed alternatives in the search for agreement. Last, objective criteria must be agreed on for decision making.

Mediation is an attempt to reconcile differences among parties by the use of an intermediary. It is a promising means of resolving environmental disputes, but all the necessary conditions cannot be met in all instances. When people have fundamentally different values, mediation is unlikely to work. Members of some radical environmental groups refuse to participate in mediated approaches because they reject the premise that our governmental system is acceptable. Animal rights groups are unlikely to ever accept the wearing of furs. Industrial timber "beasts" or rapacious land developers may never yield their belief that private property rights are inviolable and unlimited.

If mediation does not work, then the issue goes back to the policy process for resolution through legislation and/or judicial review. Some issues on national forests have been successfully mediated. Several examples are provided in Chapter 13, which focuses on national forest planning.

Idaho's approach to forestry nonpoint source water pollution control is a negotiated Antidegradation Agreement signed by representatives of forestry, mining, and agricultural industry associations; Indian tribes; and citizen conservation groups (Turner and O'Laughlin 1991). There are likely to be more negotiated approaches to natural resources issues in the future. Interested parties seem to recognize that legislatures and courts cannot solve all their problems.

ILLUSTRATION: WASHINGTON STATE AGREEMENTS

Two agreements forged in the state of Washington in the late 1980s illustrate how mediation may help solve resource conflicts. The Timber/Fish/Wildlife (TFW) agreement, which was initiated in 1986 and continued through the early 1990s, brought several opposing interest groups together to negotiate a consensual agreement regarding forest practices in riparian zones on state and private lands (Dick 1987). The Washington Sustainable Forestry Roundtable, which was formed after TFW, expanded forest practice discussion to all state and private lands in Washington.

Timber/Fish/Wildlife

The Washington Forest Practice Board was considering state forest practice rule revisions to deal with riparian management and cumulative watershed effects. Members of the wood products industry sought stable regulations; Native Indians wanted better protection of fish habitat; and state agencies wanted less conflict (Salazar and Cubbage 1990).

The TFW agreement involved three elements. As Salazar and Cubbage (1990) explained,

The first element was regulatory changes in riparian management rules, the application review process, and standards for road construction and abandonment. The second involved cooperative efforts to coordinate harvest and road planning and wildlife habitat protection. Landowners and other TFW participants agreed to support an inventory of abandoned roads and to cooperate on road construction and closure plans as well as access management (Waldo 1987). Landowners agreed to establish upland management areas to protect wildlife habitat. Landowners also may submit management plans as an alternative to complying with the prescriptive requirements of forest practice rules. The Department of Natural Resources (DNR) was authorized to assist landowners with such plans.

The third component of the TFW agreement was the use of adaptive management (a system of reforms designed and implemented as experiments) to resolve technical disputes. Research agendas address gaps in knowledge of timber/fisheries/wildlife interactions, and participants review the TFW program annually to evaluate its effectiveness in timber management and public resource protection. Finally, the DNR would establish lists of priority issues to guide field review of forest practice applications. Where priority issues are involved, local regulators may call in additional experts and engage in a more lengthy review process. Priority issues, annual reviews, and research and monitoring are all designed to generate agreement regarding technical questions.

TFW participants chose to delay consideration of several issues that involved conflicts of basic values. Two such issues are harvest of old-growth timber on state lands and compensation for landowners who are required to leave merchantable timber in riparian zones (p. 18).

The TFW agreement was heralded as an excellent approach to resolve resource conflicts without costly legal and political battles and has remained in effect through the early 1990s.

Sustainable Forestry Roundtable

The success of the TFW agreement was one factor that helped lead to the creation of the Washington Sustainable Forestry Roundtable, which expanded the negotiation process among the different forest resource interests in the state (Gray 1991). The forty-member panel was convened in November 1989 by Washington Public Lands Commissioner Brian Boyle. The panel included representatives from environmental groups, the forest products industry, Indian tribes, county governments, and state agencies. The roundtable goal was to achieve sustainable forest practices—those that maintain "biological ecological integrity while producing forest products forever."

The roundtable reached final agreement on recommended forest practices on October 10, 1990. The practice guidelines included a limit on annual timber harvests of no more than 4 percent of an owner's forest land in a watershed area, a requirement to manage 10 percent of an owner's forest land to protect fish and wildlife habitat, and a restriction to prevent large contiguous clear-cuts. If approved, the proposals were to remain in effect for 10 years to provide forest landowners wth a sense of stability and to encourage forest land investment (Gray 1991).

The proposals were hailed as a landmark agreement to resolve conflicts between timber and environmental groups. However, when the participating environmental groups took the proposals back to their constituencies for ratification, the proposals were accepted only with conditions, including opposition to the 10-year life of the agreement and support for greater wildlife habitat set-asides in timber zones. The conditions essentially scuttled the roundtable agreement and process. In 1991 Commissioner Boyle attempted to salvage the best features of the proposals and sought to implement them via legislation instead of consensual agreement (Gray 1991).

The evolving process of TFW and roundtable negotiations in Washington offer promise as a model for diverse interest groups working together. The TFW reached agreement on many issues. But the roundtable's ultimate failure to reach agreement, and the need to resort to legislative proposals instead, indicates that negotiation is by no means a panacea for resolving all natural resource issues.

SUMMARY

Issues are disagreements between two or more groups over existing policies regarding the distribution of power or resources. Influential or well-organized groups usually are able to get their issues on agendas for change. Groups unable to get their problems considered by policymakers may try to expand the issue to wider audiences, which may force policymakers to consider the issue. The use of symbols and the media help more people become aware of an issue, thus enhancing its potential for being placed on a specific policy agenda.

Policy formulation and adoption consist of developing and choosing among alternatives to resolve policy issues. Elected officials, professional legislative staff, bureaucrats, interest group members, and other people help formulate and select policies. Two prominent models of formulation and adoption are rationalism and incrementalism. Rational models suggest that policy is formed by thorough, comprehensive analyses designed to maximize social benefits. Incrementalism suggests that new policy is formed by making small changes from existing policies, with consensus being the principal criterion for success. Mixed scanning is a synthesis of both, suggesting that small changes dominate policy choices but that some major policy shifts do occur periodically. Environmental mediation and negotiation techniques have emerged as new means to resolve natural resource conflicts without government legislation.

LITERATURE CITED

Anderson, James E. 1979. Public Policy-Making, 2nd ed. Holt, Rinehart & Winston. New York. 200 pp.

Anderson, James E., David W. Brady, Charles S. Bullock III, and Joseph Stewart, Jr. 1984.

Public Policy and Politics in America, 2nd ed. Brooks/Cole Publishing Co. Monterey, CA. 422 pp.

Bingham, Gail. 1986. Resolving Environmental Disputes: A Decade of Experience. The Conservation Foundation. Washington, DC. 284 pp.

Boulding, Kenneth E. 1981. On the virtues of muddling through. *Technology Review* 83(4):6.

Cobb, Roger W., and Charles D. Elder. 1972. Participation in American Politics: The Dynamics of Agenda-Building. Johns Hopkins University Press. Baltimore, MD. 182 pp.

Dana, Samuel T., and Sally K. Fairfax. 1980. Forest and Range Policy, 2nd ed. McGraw-Hill. New York. 458 pp.

Darling, Jay N. 1962. Ding's Half Century, John M. Henry (ed.). Duell, Sloan, and Pearce. New York. 180 pp.

Davies, Jack. 1975. Legislative Law and Process. West Publishing Co. St. Paul, MN. 279 pp.

Dick, Malcolm R. 1987. Washington state pioneers new management approach. *Journal of Forestry* 85(8):5–9.

Dodd, Lawrence C., and Richard L. Schott. 1979. Congress and the Administrative State. Wiley. New York. 363 pp.

Dunn, William N. 1981. Public Policy Analysis: An Introduction. Prentice Hall. Englewood Cliffs, NJ. 388 pp.

Etzioni, Amitai. 1967. Mixed-scanning: A "third" approach to decision-making. *Public Administration Review* 27(5):385–392.

Fisher, Roger, and William Ury. 1981. Getting to Yes. Penguin Books. New York. 161 pp.

Gray, Gerald J. 1991. Washington's sustainable forestry roundtable process falters. *Resource Hotline* 7(1):1–2.

Hacker, Jan J. 1983. How Michigan prevented another Monongahela. *Journal of Forestry* 81(10):665–668.

Jones, Charles O. 1970. An Introduction to the Study of Public Policy. Wadsworth. Belmont, CA. 170 pp.

Jones, Charles O. 1984. An Introduction to the Study of Public Policy, 3rd ed. Brooks/Cole Publishing Co. Monterey, CA. 276 pp.

Kearns, Doris. 1976. Lyndon Johnson and the American Dream. Harper & Row. New York. 432 pp.

Lindblom, Charles E. 1959. The science of "muddling through." *Public Administration Review* 19(2):79–88.

Lindblom, Charles E. 1968. The Policy-Making Process. Prentice Hall. Englewood Cliffs, NJ. 122 pp.

Lowi, Theodore. 1964. American business, public policy, case studies and political theory. *World Politics* 16(4):677–715.

Meeks, Gordon, Jr. 1982. A Legislator's Guide to Forest Resource Management. National Conference of State Legislatures. Denver, CO. 98 pp.

Morandi, Larry, Gordon Meeks, Jr., and Douglas M. Sacarto. 1984. Renewing Resources: A Critique of the Issues. National Conference of State Legislatures. Denver, CO. 133 pp.

Nothdurft, William E. 1984. Renewing America. Council of State Planning Agencies. Washington, DC. 198 pp.

Salazar, Debra J., and Frederick W. Cubbage. 1990. Regulating private forestry in the West and the South. *Journal of Forestry* 88(1):14–19.

Schattschneider, E. E. 1960. The Semisovereign People. Holt, Rinehart & Winston. New York. 147 pp.

Schick, Allen. 1966. The road to PPB: The stages of budget reform. *Public Administration Review* 26(4):243–258.

Schultze, Charles L. 1968. The Politics and Economics of Public Spending. The Brookings Institution, H. Rowan Gaither Lectures in Systems Science. Washington, DC. 143 pp.

Schweitzer, Dennis L., Hanna J. Cortner, and Barbara H. Vann. 1984. Is planning worth it? *Journal of Forestry* 82(7):404–407.

Shands, William E. 1981. Forest and Rangeland Renewable Resources Planning. Pp. 1–20 in A Citizen's Guide to the Forest and Rangeland Renewable Resources Planning Act. Publication FS-365. USDA Forest Service. Washington, DC.

Smith, Hedrick. 1988. The Power Game: How Washington Works. Random House. New York. 793 pp.

Society of American Foresters. 1984. Position statement on the establishment of a national population policy and office of population policy. *Journal of Forestry* 82(9):569.

Turner, Allen C., and Jay O'Laughlin. 1991. State agency roles in Idaho water quality policy: Idaho Forest, Wildlife and Range Policy Analysis Group Report No. 5. University of Idaho, Moscow. 212 pp.

U.S. Outdoor Recreation Resources Review Commission. 1962. Outdoor Recreation for America. A Report to the President and to the Congress by the ORRRC. U.S. Government Printing Office. Washington, DC. 245 pp.

Wagstaff, Fred J., James Hagemeier, James Kent, and Jo Anne Tremaine. 1980. Issue identification and resolution. Pp. 17–22 in User Guide to Sociology and Economics—Mining and Reclamation in the West. USDA Forest Service General Technical Report INT-73. Intermountain Forest and Range Experiment Station, Ogden, UT.

Waldo, J. 1987. Timber/Fish/Wildlife, a Better Future in Our Woodlands and Streams. Northwest Renewable Resources Center. Seattle. 54 pp.

Wildavsky, Aaron. 1969. Rescuing policy analysis from PPBS. *Public Administration Review* 29:189–202.

Chapter 5

Policy Analysis, Evaluation and Implementation

INTRODUCTION

The preceding chapters discussed the policy process through the policy formulation stage. This chapter reviews specific criteria that have been used in resource decision-making to choose among alternatives and to evaluate public policies. Then an analytical framework is presented for evaluating the success of public programs designed to resolve issues over resource use or allocation.

Practicing politicians and those who study politics have devoted much more attention to the structure of government and the development of public policy than to the aftermath of program initiation. Traditionally, it was expected that once a decision-making body had formulated a policy statement, the program would be self-executing. This seldom occurs and implementation often leads to disappointment. Analysis of policy alternatives and the evaluation of a program after it has been implemented provide a means to compare actual program performance to expectations.

ANALYSIS AND ADVOCACY

One part of both the policy adoption and evaluation stages in the policy process is the analysis of alternative policies. Another aspect is policy advocacy, by the chief executive or governor, public agencies, citizens and interest groups, or legislators themselves. The distinction between analysis and advocacy is often murky, leading to considerable confusion. Clarification of these two different approaches to policy is important before we discuss policy evaluation.

When they consider a problem, policy analysts, planners, foresters, and other technical specialists generally analyze the issue in a rational-comprehensive fashion. In theory, analysts objectively and fairly examine a problem through the use of some model. Analysis involves examining an issue or policy to explain its causes, alternatives, participants, and outcomes in an unbiased manner. Policy advocacy is obviously quite different. It involves individuals or groups who are trying to prescribe appropriate policies. Advocacy does not imply a detailed study of an issue and its alternatives, but rather the use of rhetoric, persuasion, and organization of presented written or verbal arguments to influence policy outcomes. People advocate policies as part of the political process; they analyze policies as part of their roles as resource professionals.

Again in theory, professionals and planners are involved only in analysis, and citizens advocate solutions to public issues. In practice, personal beliefs and values can affect professional judgments. Therefore, decision makers must account for their own biases as well as those in the information they receive from other people. Good analysis is free of value judgments, but a dilemma arises because determining the absence of values in an analysis requires some judgment. The problem is similar to that expressed by Supreme Court Justice Potter Stewart when he said he could not define pornography, but he knew it when he saw it.

Despite personal and professional biases, analysis of natural resource issues should proceed in a neutral fashion, and much effort should focus on developing an understanding of opposing views. Clearly identifying the problem or disagreement at issue is a first step. Identifying possible alternatives to resolve the issue, their relative merits, and the interest groups favoring them is also helpful. Last, stating explicit criteria that can be used to choose among alternative courses of action makes decisions easier to render. This framework for analyzing alternatives sounds like the rational-comprehensive model. However, the analyses for a particular issue need not be totally comprehensive, but rather they can vary in scope according to the detail requested by decision makers and the time available to conduct the analysis. By providing such information to policymakers, the formulation of policy choices remains analytical, even when values are involved.

DECISION AND EVALUATION CRITERIA

Various criteria may be used in the analysis of alternative forest resource policies in order to select a policy choice. The same criteria also are used to evaluate existing programs and policies.

Criteria are needed to provide some measure of the opportunity cost or trade-offs involved in following one public policy alternative versus another. There are a huge number of public policies and programs that may be socially desirable, but we surely cannot afford the time, expense, and taxes to implement them all. Given that we have scarce resources—land, forests, water, wildlife, labor, capital, and so on—criteria are needed to help select among competing alternatives and to evaluate ongoing policies.

Criteria may be defined as standards of comparison used in making judgments or decisions about alternative policies. Criteria may combine facts with value judgments, but they usually are normative (value oriented) in nature. Even apparently neutral criteria such as economic internal rate of return imply that financial returns on investment capital, not biological or social benefits, are to be maximized. Policymakers always use criteria of some sort, either explicitly or implicitly, to make decisions. For purposes of policy analysis, explicit criteria are obviously superior. Policymakers often consider various standards when selecting appropriate courses of action, including ecological, economic, social, and political criteria.

ECOLOGICAL

Probably the first question that should be asked of any policy is a factual one: Is the particular policy physically possible? or is it biologically feasible? Considering a policy that cannot be implemented is senseless. Can an endangered plant or animal species be saved from extinction? Can cut-over forest lands in the South be naturally regenerated with pine? Such questions need to be answered on their technical merits before any policy alternatives can be considered further.

Clawson (1975) notes that the social scientist or the policymaker should expect to find controversy regarding the facts of some physical and biological relationships. Is acid rain damaging forests and fish? Is the global climate changing? Experts disagree on these and many other issues. Nevertheless, decisions must be made. There is seldom complete consensus within the scientific community. Thus policymakers must frequently act without complete information and universally agreed-upon goals and problems, as suggested by Jones's (1984) initial realities presented in Table 2-2.

Even when experts are reasonably sure of the facts, risk and uncertainty are still significant factors. Biological and social programs are prone to natural and human disasters. Trees burn, insects attack, banks fail, and economies collapse. Policymakers must act on the best available information.

Natural resource managers often have relied on a prevalent biological criterion—maximizing biological productivity. For timber, this implies setting rotations at the age of greatest mean annual increment of growth. For fish or wildlife populations, it implies maximizing the annual population harvest. Maximizing total volume produced (yield) may be another biological criterion. Maximizing physical yields may not maximize economic returns, but to managers trained in the subculture of traditional fish and wildlife ecology or silviculture, such criteria have been accepted as a tenet of faith. Sustained yield of wood, fish, or game is a similar physical criterion. When managers are faced with an unknown future, competing demands

from resource users, and a cacophony of speculative economic recommendations, the biological tenets of faith provide reassurance. Even these tenets are not without complications, however. For instance, does maximum sustained yield of deer refer to maximum number of animals, maximum total weight of harvest, or maximum number of trophy bucks?

Sustained yield has become an important criterion for international forestry. *Sustainable agriculture* and *agroforestry* are popular terms or goals for resource use in developing countries. Although the criteria are nebulous, their general intent is that continuous cropping and harvesting of market and nonmarket products is preferred to slash and burn practices of shifting agriculture that are a cause of deforestation and may outpace the capacity of land to recover. Using such vague criteria as sustainability for decision making may not be very helpful, however. In forestry and agriculture, sustained biological yield has evolved into a preferred policy of sustainable economic development, which implies that interlocking ecological and human economic systems must be sustained together over time (MacNeill 1989).

Preserving Options

Worrell (1970) suggests that the notion of a *critical zone*—a condition where site productivity or species viability is threatened—be used to evaluate resource policies. According to Ciriacy-Wantrup (1963), resource policies that do not disturb ecosystems situated in a critical zone or force ecosystems into it are preferred. For example, Satterlund (1972) discusses the concept of a *critical point* in watershed management. Erosion will deteriorate a site at an increasing rate unless the process is reversed. When erosion progresses beyond the critical point, the soil mantle will continue to erode until it is completely removed, and little can be done to prevent it.

Criteria used to select policies that do not force ecosystems into the critical zone have become much more important since the advent of the environmental movement. The principal tenet behind the Endangered Species Act of 1973 (ESA) is that as a nation the United States should strive to prevent the loss of any plants or animals—that is, keep them out of the threatened and endangered zones that will ultimately lead to their extinction. The ESA codifies this biological criterion for resource management and requires that the federal government protect endangered species in all its projects and further extends this protection against any harmful activities on all lands in the nation. This ecological criterion for resource management is based on social values—namely, that a majority of Americans believe that the preservation of all wildlife and plants is intrinsically "good." This social value is reflected in the law passed by Congress as a national policy.

The biological criterion of preserving all species that is embodied in ESA has become a rallying cry for preservation interests. We often are warned that we are losing hundreds or perhaps thousands of plant and animal species each year, some of which may be valuable to humans. Seemingly worthless species often have proven to possess significant applications. Wild corn in Mexico has helped infuse blight resistance in domestic crop varieties; rare plant extracts provide successful treatments for Hodgkin's disease and childhood leukemia (Sawhill 1990); and a pokeweed extract has been shown to slow AIDS (Nesmith 1990). Taxol, a chemical extracted from the bark of the Pacific Yew, has been shown to be effective in treating forms of ovarian cancer. We never know which species may have important commercial values. Nor do we know which ones are the keystone species in an ecosystem, whose loss may cause collapse of the system. Thus we should try to preserve as many species and as much critical habitat as possible. And it is now the law of the land.

Preventing irreversible environmental damage is also relevant to global issues. Tropical deforestation, which may be caused by excessive slash and burn agriculture, is often considered unwise, at least by those who do not do it, because it destroys the productivity of the land for future generations. Furthermore, such deforestation may contribute to global warming, which could have truly irreversible, adverse effects on existing terrestrial ecosystems.

A related, broader criterion that economists use in judging policies is called *option value*. Option value goes further than just suggesting that ecosystems should be kept out of the critical zone. It suggests that policies should be chosen that do not preclude other future uses. Similarly, any actions that will have irreversible environmental effects should be avoided. Preventing extinction preserves options and avoids irreversible consequences. Converting forest lands from less developed to more developed uses also may foreclose other uses and conflict with option value. Permanent, resource-altering, single-use policies and practices would be avoided using this criterion.

Biological Diversity

Biological diversity has become perhaps the most widely debated criterion in natural resource allocation decisions in recent years. In 1988 a bill supporting protection of biological diversity of federal lands was introduced into Congress, and hearings on the proposal were held in 1989. This issue was partially triggered by a thorough and well-publicized Wilderness Society study on protecting biological diversity in national forests (Wilcove 1988). In general, the biological diversity criterion is based on the premise that more diverse ecosystems are more stable and preferable to less diverse ecosystems. More diverse ecosystems are more likely to maintain themselves over time and provide ecological and social benefits (Norse et al. 1986). Diversity also is related to avoiding forcing plants or animals into the critical zone. As mentioned before, because we are unlikely to know which plant or animal is the crucial link in an ecosystem, protecting diversity per se is considered desirable.

Questions often arise as to just what biological diversity is. Wilcove (1988, p. 3) clearly summarizes the concept.

Biological diversity in its broadest sense is simply diversity of life, but as a subject for study, it can be divided into three levels (Office of Technology Assessment 1987, Norse et al. 1986). The most obvious of these levels is *species diversity*, reflecting the richness and variety of plants, animals, fungi, and bacteria that inhabit the globe. Less obvious, but no less important, is the *genetic diversity* that exists within any species, reflecting the differences in genetic makeup among individuals and between populations of a given species. Finally, there is a higher level of biological diversity, termed *ecosystem* or *community diversity*, that encompasses the distinctive assemblages of species occurring in different physical settings (emphasis in original).

Interest groups, including the Wilderness Society and the National Wildlife Federation, have begun to use the concept of biological diversity to argue for changes in management practices on national forest and other public, and even private, lands. In brief, the argument is that the Forest Service has relied on even-aged management and harvested many intermittent small tracts in order to maximize timber growth and favor game species in a forest. The conservation/preservation interest groups feel that maximizing game and timber species alone is not a desirable objective. These groups do not define diversity as simply the greatest number of plant and animal species on each site, but rather as a broad variety of ecosystems—community diversity. These should include old-growth, natural forests, and avoid fragmented habitat so that interior as well as edge species are allowed to prosper and move among forests.

Heavy timber harvesting and site preparation equipment tend to destroy most sensitive plants and ecosystems—such as the old-growth longleaf pine/wiregrass association in Florida—and replace them with less fragile ecosystems such as longleaf plantations and broomsedge. Although forest plantations may produce as many kinds of species as natural stands, management that relies exclusively on plantation management will reduce ecosystem and community diversity. Similar cases can be made for favoring large areas of old-growth stands in order to favor species such as the threatened northern spotted owl in the Pacific Northwest, rather than common open-country species such as dark-eyed juncos and brown-headed cowbirds.

Many forest management practices affect biological diversity. These include forest type conversions, forest monocultures, pesticide use, and habitat fragmentation, among others. Although they are not opposed to all such practices, conservation groups such as the Wilderness Society are opposed to most current national forest management plans, which they believe rely too heavily on these practices, thus reducing biological diversity. Conservation groups also use the diversity argument to favor wetland protection and protection of nongame and invertebrate animals and obscure plant species as well as of better-known species. This expansion of protection for more species will surely place more restrictions on commercial forest uses. Protecting biodiversity also is a paramount concern in the tropics, where very complex ecosystems may depend on just a few keystone species (Wilson 1989).

The forest industry and developers oppose any further national legislation to protect biological diversity on federal and private lands. They fear that at the very least, it would further reduce timber growing and harvesting on national forest lands. At worst, it might be used as a backdoor entree to land use planning on private forest lands as well. They assert that further regulation of private lands to protect biodiversity would be unwise, unjust, and unconstitutional.

ECONOMIC

Ecological criteria may help narrow the policy choices and are being used more often to select or dictate desirable management practices. These criteria can and have been used to determine timber rotations and deer-carrying capacity for deer and other wildlife. Until 1991 the controversy over spotted owl protection in the Pacific Northwest relied solely on ecological criteria. Ecological criteria are, however, clearly nonmarket in nature. They will not necessarily help private forest landowners and firms maximize profits, or government agencies allocate budget dollars between game and nongame programs.

Economic criteria are more helpful in making these types of decisions.

Efficiency

Economic efficiency criteria are concerned with the best way to allocate scarce resources among competing demands, usually using private market (financial) or social (economic) measures. These criteria assume that efficiency is superior to equity when allocating resources, as discussed in Chapter 3. Discounted cash flow criteria (i.e., internal rate of return, net present value, benefit–cost ratio, and other variants) are generally preferable to nondiscounted measures (i.e., accounting rate of return, payback period) because they account for the time value of money—cash incomes or outflows in the future are worth less than those today. Economic criteria have different meanings in the public and private sectors. Private firms are generally interested in maximizing their financial returns, and in their analysis all costs and returns are valued at market prices. Public enterprises are generally charged with maximizing their economic (social) returns—where costs and benefits are valued at their social opportunity costs—and secondary benefits and costs also are included in the analysis (Gregersen and Contreras 1979).

Many applications of economic criteria could be listed. Worrell (1970) includes the following:

- Forest policies that make at least one person better off and no one worse off (Pareto optimality) are preferred (a welfare economics criterion).
- Forest policies that result in the greatest possible output with a given input (or achieve a given output with the least input) are preferred (technical efficiency).
- Forest policies that result in total discounted benefits exceeding total discounted costs (exceed the hurdle rate or alternative rate of return) are preferred (a benefit–cost ratio greater than 1.0).
- Forest policies that result in the greatest positive difference between total benefits and total costs are preferred. This is profit

maximization in private firms or maximum net benefit for public projects.

Economic efficiency criteria are used by most private firms and government agencies in analyzing project or program investment decisions. Efficiency in resource use is often difficult to determine in practice. For public agencies, this criterion of maximizing output with a given set of budgetary resources is a worthwhile goal. Private firms cannot exist without producing profits, but that does not necessarily mean they always try to maximize profit by trading off other worthy goals and objectives.

Most economic analyses rely on discounted cash flow measures. For decisions to accept or reject an individual project, all discounted cash flow criteria usually provide acceptable results. For mutually exclusive project decisions, net present value is considered theoretically superior to internal rate of return or the benefit–cost ratio (Brealey and Myers 1984, Clutter et al. 1983), but it is often favored less than internal rate of return for practical applications (Cubbage and Redmond 1985, Foster 1984, Leuschner 1984). For social project analyses, the benefit–cost ratio is usually used (Gregersen and Contreras 1979).

Economic efficiency has obvious merits, but it is seldom the sole determining criterion because it does have limitations. It is difficult to identify all the benefits and costs associated with a project. What are the benefits from public expenditures for higher education? What is the value of forestry extension workshops to private forest landowners? Even if the factors can be identified, the input–output relationships (production functions) affected by a program often are difficult or impossible to quantify. Even if all costs and benefits can be identified, they are difficult to measure in comparable units. The Forest Service has been mandated to value recreation, water, wildlife, range, and timber in dollars as part of the RPA/NFMA planning process. But critics of that approach say that values affixed to nonmarket outputs such as fish and game are too small, biasing the forest plans toward production of market commodities, namely timber (Williamson 1985).

Subjective considerations are another problem with economic criteria. Not all decisions or decision processes can be quantified. Even in private firms, qualitative factors such as strategic planning, market share, wood supply, or environmental protection may be as important as economic criteria in investment decisions (Cleaves and O'Laughlin 1986, Cubbage and Redmond 1985, Duerr 1982). Although budget scrutiny and economic criteria are increasing in importance at the state and federal level, to conclude that they should be or are the sole decision criterion would be foolish. Pork barrel projects and subsystem politics ensure that many decisions will continue to be made on the basis of satisfying constituents or interest groups, not on economic efficiency criteria.

Sustainability

Sustainable economic development has become a modern-day criterion for judging the acceptability of development policies. As discussed in Chapter 3, steady economic growth is a worthy social objective because it raises the standard of living of many people. Although some redistribution of wealth may help eliminate poverty, economic growth usually is thought of as a more important goal. A five- to tenfold increase in economic activity would be required over the next 50 years in order to meet the needs and aspirations of a burgeoning world population, as well as to begin to reduce mass poverty. Reducing poverty is necessary to stop the accelerating decline in the planet's stock of basic capital: its forests, soils, species, fisheries, waters, and atmosphere (MacNeill 1989).

Based on these premises, the World United Nations Commission on Environment and Development defined *sustainable development* as new paths of economic and social development that "meet the needs of the present without compromising the ability of future generations to meet their own needs."(cited in MacNeill 1989, p. 157.) The broad goal of sustainability will entail lower-level goals of

stabilizing the earth's population; reducing pollution; discouraging deforestation, desertification, and species destruction; and reducing per capita energy consumption, among other actions. Environment and economics ought to be merged in decision making (MacNeill 1989). Achieving sustainable economic development will be a challenging goal for resource policy-making.

Social

Another loose grouping of decision rules may be defined as social criteria. It may be physically possible to undertake an alternative and it may be the most economically efficient, yet that alternative may fail to be selected on the basis of other criteria. For example, in Oklahoma and Arkansas, Weyerhaeuser acquired the locally owned Dierks lumber company in the 1970s. Dierks had generally managed its property with selective cutting practices and allowed local people open access to use the land for hunting, fishing, and recreation. On the basis of economic efficiency criteria, Weyerhaeuser began to convert all the selectively managed pine-hardwood stands into pine plantations by clear-cutting and replanting in blocks of 700 acres or more. Local residents complained and eventually enlisted assistance from the National Wildlife Federation, which held shares of the company's stock. The conservation group instigated a stockholders' initiative against the company, and Weyerhaeuser agreed to have its practices examined by a blue-ribbon panel. Eventually, based upon the recomendation of the panel, the company reduced the size of its clear-cuts and improved wildlife habitat protection measures. Essentially, the company's original policy met economic efficiency criteria but failed on other grounds—it did not meet with social or cultural acceptance—a criterion suggested by Clawson (1975). By adding social criteria to its decision making process, Weyerhauser reduced its profits in order to increase its social acceptance.

Freedom

Borrowing from Dahl and Lindblom (1953), Worrell (1970) suggests four important social criteria for making decisions: freedom, democracy, subjective equality, and appropriate inclusion. *Freedom* may be defined as the absence of obstacles to the realization of a person's desires. Thus, people should have as much freedom as possible to fulfill their wants or desires with forest resources. This criterion is important in the debates about the right to take risks in the wilderness. The Forest Service and National Park Service have policies allowing personal risk for wilderness users. Many users feel that they should be completely self-sufficient in wilderness areas and receive no external assistance—not even being rescued when they are in danger (Irland 1979, McAvoy and Dustin 1983). The regulation of mountain climbers and hang gliders, who face greater risks and hazards of fatal accidents, also falls under this criterion. Legislators may have the right to regulate private land, or even make motorcyclists wear helmets, but many people feel that there should be no constraints to physical challenges in the woods (although arson or timber theft still should be proscribed). Allowing freedom to satisfy one's desires is based on the long-standing American value of individual freedom. Freedom is particularly important in forests—some of the last "wild" lands left.

A related criterion, freedom of choice, suggests that individuals should have as wide a range of activities to perform as possible. More choices are preferred to fewer; thus, forest policies designed for multiple use would be preferable to single-use policies.

Equity

The needs for subjective equality described by Worrel (1970) are a component of equity criteria. *Equity* refers to the distribution of benefits and costs associated with a program (Clawson 1975). Who gains and who pays? Subjective equality stems from America's acceptance of an egalitarian society, with fair opportunities and benefits for all, or perhaps even preferential opportunities for small en-trepreneurs or underprivileged classes. Thus, equitable forest policies should distribute benefits and costs fairly, and perhaps even give advantages to the poor or disadvantaged members of society.

The graduated personal income tax is based on equity considerations. In theory, low-income people are taxed at small marginal tax rates and high-income people at higher rates. This approach is based on a preference for vertical equity, that is, that public programs should treat individuals in different income classes according to their ability to pay or their needs. Horizontal equity suggests that individuals in similar situations with similar incomes should be treated the same (Musgrave and Musgrave 1984). Suggestions for relief from "excessive" property taxes in many states have run aground due to horizontal equity considerations. Local services depend heavily on property taxes. Owners of agricultural and forest land have suggested alternatives such as increased income taxes or sales taxes at the state level, with funds redistributed to the counties. However, urban constituents and legislators observe that this merely shifts the tax burden for rural services to urban residents, and they object to such proposals.

In many developing countries, some income redistribution is attempted through project selection that favors income earned by the poor more than income earned by the rich. The World Bank forestry project selection guidelines specifically state that a portion of the income created by a project must be directly received by the lower-income members of society. The "trickle-down" theory (income for rich people will trickle down to the poor) is not widely accepted. One might suggest instead that direct handouts be given to the poor. But this is not generally politically feasible in the United States or elsewhere, so project selection has been a good alternative tool in effecting income redistribution.

Equity criteria in forestry have been construed to imply that policies serving a greater number of people are preferred to policies serving only a few. This idea formed the basis of Gifford Pinchot's oft-quoted phrase that the national forests should provide "the greatest good for the greatest number in the long run." To some degree, this reflects a variant of the sustained-yield concept and certainly rests on Pinchot's utilitarian goals for American forests. Subsequent national forest legislation, including the Multiple-Use Sustained-Yield Act of 1960 and RPA/NFMA, rests upon these principles. These equity criteria also provide a powerful symbol for those who oppose wilderness because they believe it is a "playground for the rich." Western wilderness areas generally are inaccessible to those without the time and money to fly in to remote airstrips, pack in on horseback, and raft down wild rivers or without the skill and equipment to backpack through arduous terrain. However, recreation is only one of many purposes of wilderness. Equity criteria also are used in arguments to support local rural communities, which often depend on timber harvests for income.

Decision Processes

A number of other criteria focus on how decisions are made, not on the substantive merits of the outcome (Worrell 1970). Political equality or democracy may be used as a criterion to ensure that no one citizen's preferences carry more weight than those of any other; all should be equally important. Given that all policy systems have a bias, this is probably unrealistic, but it can serve as a goal in the decision process. In the extensive public participation requirements of RPA/NFMA for developing national forest plans and meeting NEPA requirements, the Forest Service attempts to weigh all comments equally and then use them to help select the "best" management alternative. Seldom is the preferred alternative the one that produces maximum social benefits, as economic efficiency would require.

The appropriate inclusion (or public involvement) criterion suggests that everyone should be given an opportunity to express his or her opinion on an issue, particularly those who are affected most by the policy (Worrell 1970). NEPA and NFMA embody this criterion.

As another example, the Society of American Foresters (1983) stated that landowners, timber operators, and forestry professionals should be consulted when establishing a state forest practices act.

Also, forest policies should be developed by due process, a process that is understood and agreed upon by the participants. This criterion helps eliminate arbitrary selection of alternatives (Worrell 1970). Due process requirements have been codified in some major forestry and environmental legislation. NFMA requires that detailed procedures be followed in developing forest plans. Federal and state environmental impact statements also involve rigorous procedures that must be followed. Failure to follow these processes can lead to disapproval of the plans or provide the basis for court action.

Acceptability and Practicality

Policies should be socially and culturally acceptable and operationally practical (Clawson 1975). Social and cultural attitudes always affect public policies. Forest managers who neglect these attitudes do so at their peril. Programs that are physically and biologically sound may founder on public attitudes. For example, the use of 2,4,5-T and other herbicides in forest management met most other criteria but ran aground because of public attitudes.

The degree of public acceptance of the regulation of forest practices differs significantly among regions of the country. People on the West Coast have accepted some state regulations governing cutting practices since the 1940s and still accept much stricter regulations than the few states in the East that have forest-cutting regulations. Landowners in the South adamantly opposed forest practice acts when they were proposed by the Environmental Protection Agency in the 1970s, and no southern state has a forest practice act yet. Perhaps the pervasive influence of the large proportion of public land in the West, coupled with the potential for more environmental problems on steep slopes, made regulation more culturally acceptable there than in the South.

Cultural attitudes are crucial in developing natural resource policies in other countries. Europeans generally accept far more state control of forest resources than do U.S. citizens, including open access for all citizens for recreation on private forest land. In order to develop forest resource programs in developing countries, one first must learn what is culturally acceptable, including land and tree tenure policies, commercial rights, the variety of useful forest products, and even spiritual values related to trees or forest areas. Subsequent policies must be based on these social mores first, and anything else second.

Policies must also be operationally and administratively practical to be successful, whether they are implemented by public agencies or private firms. Clawson (1975) illustrated this problem with regulation of timber cutting on private lands. Could harvest operations in the East be inspected as much as in the West? The plethora of small tracts and the much greater number of private landowners in the East are probably the main reasons that few states believe that forest practice acts are reasonable. Limited budgets and personnel ceilings also constrain programs. Public agencies can support only the programs that have adequate budgets and personnel. With fixed or often dwindling budget appropriations, agencies must weigh the benefits of new policy initiatives against the costs of reducing other programs. Private firms, too, usually face capital rationing or personnel limits imposed by corporate policies.

POLITICAL

Political factors usually influence policy selection (Anderson 1979). These are not evaluation criteria per se, but factors that influence public policy decisions. First, the decision maker's values are probably the most direct and pervasive influence on personal decisions. Political party affiliation is another important factor that determines how legislators vote on issues. Environmental issues have been particularly subject to partisan division. Democrats in Congress have tended to support restrictive measures to protect the environment, while Republicans generally have opposed such legislation.

Constituency interests obviously affect how legislators vote, and probably how bureaucrats implement and administer programs. Where constituent demands are clear, legislators often vote accordingly. Public opinion is unlikely to provide guidance on individual policy decisions, but it probably shapes the general boundaries and direction of public policy. These political factors affecting the decisions of legislators are discussed in more detail in Chapter 6.

Policymakers who are unfamiliar with a problem often decide by deferring to the judgment of others. Committees and subcommittees in Congress specialize in individual subject areas, so most members follow their recommendations. Judges often make decisions by deferring to the legislative intent, if it can be determined (Salisbury 1973). The intent of ambiguous phrases in a law can often be discerned by examination of congressional debate on the bill, thereby making floor debates significant in establishing the record. The judicial practice of *stare decisis* (let the precedents stand) is also, in effect, deference to prior decisions and other jurisdictions. Executives, administrators, and legislators also frequently make decisions on the basis of precedents—a bias toward the status quo. However, Anderson (1979, p. 77) observed that "Those adversely affected by existing precedents are likely to find them lacking in virtue and utility."

The few generally incremental alternatives that meet the other criteria may be rather similar; it will be the political criteria that ultimately determine which policy is selected and implemented. Politicians must authorize programs and appropriate funds, or even alternatives that meet all other criteria will not be implemented.

INTEGRATION

Naturally, all criteria interact in policy formulation, adoption, and evaluation. Often they may be considered in sequential fashion in order to eliminate alternatives that are unreasonable and to narrow the field to a few acceptable policy choices, as suggested by Etzioni's (1967) mixed-scanning approach. Ecological criteria certainly will be used as a first screen to see if it is technically feasible to adopt and implement a resource policy successfully. These criteria alone are becoming much more important in selecting and evaluating public programs for forest lands. Certainly today, most successful policies must take care to protect the environment—including forestry and wildlife programs, farm programs, and urban programs. Indeed, environmental criteria may become the overriding factor in determining public land policies.

Economic criteria are used by private firms to make project decisions and to help maximize returns to shareholders. They also are used by public agencies to perform benefit–cost analyses of existing or proposed programs. Grossly inefficient alternatives usually are eliminated by economic criteria, although some infamous boondoggles do slip through. The U.S. Army somehow spent $7000 on a coffee pot and $500 on a hammer. Former Sen. William Proxmire from Wisconsin had little problem finding recipients for his monthly Golden Fleece award—given for the most flagrant waste of taxpayers' dollars. Social and equity criteria are considered in all major public issues, as are acceptability and practicality. Political factors also obviously influence policy selection.

ILLUSTRATION: THE FORESTRY INCENTIVES PROGRAM

Analyses of the Forestry Incentives Program (FIP) made in the mid-1970s and an evaluation in 1981 provide good examples of how decision/evaluation criteria are used in making public policy. Based on fears of future timber shortages, rising relative prices, and presumed underproductivity on the part of nonindustrial private forest (NIPF) landowners, several cost-share programs have been enacted by Congress and by individual states to aid NIPF owners in producing more timber. The Forestry Incentives Program was enacted by Congress in 1973 to help increase wood fiber production on NIPF lands (Mills 1976). FIP is based on the premise that the social benefits of producing more wood exceed the private returns. Therefore the government subsidizes private owners to make their returns more closely approximate the social returns (Gregersen 1977). The federal government pays from 50 to 75 percent of the cost of the planting or timber stand improvement, not to exceed specified limits per acre. The forest landowner pays the remainder.

Researchers in the Forest Service evaluated the Forestry Incentives Program in 1974 and 1975, immediately after the program was implemented. The analysis was designed to evaluate the initial social and administrative efficiency of the program. In 1981 the State and Private Forestry branch of the Forest Service evaluated FIP after the Reagan administration had proposed eliminating funding for the program and after five years of program implementation (1974–1979).

Efficiency

The 1974 analysis of FIP found that program efficiency varied depending on the stand treatment, the species, the site quality, and the tract size (Mills 1976, Mills and Cain 1978). Most investments had satisfactory returns, with an average financial return of 10.2 percent, but some areas were better than others. Timber stand improvement usually had higher rates of return than tree planting, due to the shorter discounting period before returns are realized. Fast-growing species usually had higher rates of return because the present value of their future harvests was greater than that of slow-growing species. Similarly, good sites that would yield more timber in less time had higher returns. Only in rare instances would the effect of discounting future returns, which favors fast growth and early harvests, be outweighed by higher stumpage values for some slow-growing trees. Although harvest costs per se were not included in the financial analyses, it is unlikely that tracts of less than ten acres would be economical to harvest.

FIP allocations in 1974 did favor the better sites, particularly those on private lands in the South, indicating economic efficiency. However, some low-return sites did receive funding, particularly oak–hickory timber stand improvement in the central states and most work in the Rocky Mountains and central plains (Mills and Cain 1978). Based on this 1974 review, Forest Service program administrators tried to place greater focus on activities with greater returns. Some funds were still allocated elsewhere, however, in order to ensure that some constituents in all states could receive some federal funds.

The 1979 national update of the 1974 study found that program efficiency had improved (Risbrudt and Ellefson 1983, Risbrudt, Kaiser, and Ellefson 1983a). Average treatment size increased substantially from the initial years and practices on lower quality lands had been curtailed. The study found that the FIP payments would eventually result in an additional 1.3 billion cubic feet of timber over the first rotation compared to that generated by current management practices; 93 percent of the acreage established in trees under FIP was retained after the first five years (Risbrudt et al. 1983b).

Subsequent budget discussions between the Forest Service and the Office of Management and Budget (OMB) in the early 1980s relied heavily on the evaluation of the 1979 FIP program. Although the OMB budget examiner generally felt that FIP was an unwarranted subsidy to landowners, he was at least partially convinced that the returns to the government were reasonable when measured with efficiency criteria. Similar State and Private Forestry presentations before congressional subcommittees proved to be even more persuasive. Congressional funding for the program was never cut during the 1980s, and even increased slightly. But at $12.5 million per year, FIP is almost inconsequential in a trillion-dollar budget.

Two other issues regarding FIP were also relevant in these analyses. Equity of the program was one concern, and substitution of federal funds for private capital another.

Equity

FIP was not enacted nor intended to improve equity or income distribution, but rather to produce more wood fiber. However, FIP has equity implications, because it is likely to benefit richer forest owners more than poorer forest owners because the former can receive more cost-share funds on large land parcels. Also, because the program is relatively small and unpublicized, some persons suggest that more funds are received by better educated and informed persons who are generally wealthier. In fact, the program actually excludes landowners with more than 500 acres (initially) or 1000 acres (as of 1980) of eligible forest land. Also, the program does distribute most payments to owners of land in poor rural areas, if not to poor persons. At least the dollars spent under FIP will boost the personal income of forest laborers and help local economies.

One administrative rule regarding FIP allows a higher cost-share rate of up to 90 percent for those people whose incomes are below the poverty level. However, this has seldom been used even by the persons who qualify, so it has not had much effect on vertical equity.

FIP allocates funds to the states on the basis of the amount of NIPF land in the state, the potential biological and financial productivity of the forest land in the state, and the state's expenditures in previous years (Mills, Hart, and McKnight 1974). Therefore it would appear that it promotes horizontal inequity by transferring federal revenues from the West (with a majority of public lands) and the North (with low site productivity) to the South. This is not totally accurate. Private landowners with similar site class lands in all regions of the country are treated quite similarly by the program; it just happens that the most productive NIPF forest lands favored by the program are in the South.

Capital Substitution and Supply Increases

According to the policy analyses, it seems that the FIP program was efficient—its social (and private) benefits exceeded its social costs. But was it necessary? Might landowners plant trees or perform timber stand improvement without public assistance? Does FIP increase timber supplies and harvests—its ultimate goal as a production incentives program? Several additional policy analyses addressed these questions.

Essentially, the question of whether landowners would plant trees without FIP is one of substituting public funds for private capital. Two contradictory econometric studies were performed in the early 1980s on capital substitution. De Steiguer (1983, 1984) used a single model to test if public funds had substituted for private dollars for tree planting for selected southern states. His analysis found that FIP contributed incremental funds beyond those that would be invested by private landowners. Cohen (1983) used a variety of models, all of which led her to conclude that considerable capital substitution had occurred. On the average, she estimated that public funds had supplanted about 40 to 50 percent of the capital that would have been spent by private landowners, with a range from 20 to 100 percent depending on the model formulation. More recently, Lee, Kaiser, and Alig (1992) developed a plantation market model to estimate the effects of four federal cost-share programs on other tree planting in the South. Bases on their models, they could find no evidence that capital substitution had occurred.

In a study examining the supply issue, Wallace and Silver (1983) could find no statistically significant evidence that FIP had increased or decreased timber supplies in southeastern Georgia, despite large public FIP expenditures in the region. This suggests capital substitution. However, they noted that it would be difficult to measure volume increases from only seven to eight years of tree growth under the program. Another interpretation of the study might suggest that FIP did not prompt shorter rotations and reductions in growing stock.

Some consulting and state foresters believe that FIP is counterproductive because owners may delay or fail to perform tree planting in hopes of getting government cost-share funds. Because FIP funds are inade-

quate to cover all requests, the harvest sites grow brush instead for several years and become more of a problem than if landowners initiated their own planting. Additionally, government-subsidized tree planting may reduce the value of stumpage grown by other private landowners at their own expense. One other study by Boyd (1983) did find that FIP was apt to increase the likelihood that owners would plant trees, but it did not increase the likelihood of timber harvest.

Overall, these studies of capital substitution and supply effects could be used to argue for different policies. Most studies ultimately found that FIP was efficient and that it did not substitute government capital for private capital. However, concerns about its delaying private investments are hard to test, and it has not been empirically proven to actually increase total timber supplies in a region. This mixed bag of evaluative information and unknown impacts provides the fodder for ongoing program appropriations, along with interest group input. Proponents and opponents of FIP, like other government programs, are apt to use the available information that supports the policy they favor most.

IMPLEMENTATION SUCCESS

In most cases, programs will not live up to their advanced billing because sponsors oversell the program in order to secure its enactment. To attract support within the legislature, advocates may promise more for the program than it can deliver or boast that the innovation will reach a broader segment of the population than is feasible given the likely level of funding. Thus a program that might succeed if it were focused will be spread so thinly that it fails to have much impact on the participants. On the other hand, some notable programs have achieved more than anticipated—such as the Marshall Plan to help Europe recover from World War II, the Interstate Highway System, or even the Wilderness Act.

Evaluation and review are particularly important for public programs because there is less preimplementation testing than in the private sector. Before a company invests billions of dollars in a new product, it conducts widespread testing to determine the effectiveness of the product or its likely acceptance in the marketplace. However, this market research does not guarantee success, as is illustrated by adverse public reactions to the "new Coke" and Ford's Edsel. Political pressures prevent the government from performing marketing research or restricting programs to a few groups, because once enacted, the benefits of new programs are sought by all legislators. Even programs that are designed to help certain segments of society, such as students from impoverished backgrounds, have eligibility standards set so that virtually every congressional district will derive some benefits (Edwards 1977). Similarly, the Conservation Reserve Program (CRP) of the late 1980s, which was intended to establish permanent grass or tree cover on highly erodible lands, managed to channel funds to almost every state in the country, despite much greater costs in some regions than in others.

People who have studied program implementation have identified a number of factors that may be associated with success. Cynics contend that all programs are doomed to fail or fall short, regardless of the intentions of their creators. Indicative of this perspective is the best-selling book *Implementation: How Great Expectations in Washington are Dashed in Oakland, Or, Why It's Amazing that Federal Programs Work at All...* (Pressman and Wildavsky 1973). Although no program may satisfy everyone's great expectations, one need not look very far to discover programs that have produced results. Thus, even though racial isolation remains a problem in some school systems, the total segregation that existed in about a third of the country prior to the *Brown* v. *Board of Education* antidiscrimination ruling in 1954 is a thing of the past. Air and water quality in the United States is not as pristine as when the first settlers arrived, but there clearly have been improvements during the last generation due to federal laws. Once we accept that some programs are more successful than others, it then makes sense

to search for those conditions associated with success. A number of more important factors are described in the following sections.

SPECIFIC GOALS

It would seem obvious that for a program to succeed its goals and objectives must be clearly stated. Without such specifics, a program's results may well be disappointing. In fact, even the use of the terms *goals*, *ends*, *objectives*, and *purposes* can cause confusion. We generally will use these four terms interchangeably to signify the policy to be implemented or achieved. As suggested in Chapter 2, ends and means may be interchangeable depending on where one is in the means–ends hierarchy. In the forest planning literature, goals usually denote more general statements of purpose, and objectives are more specific and often measurable, (e.g., criteria for decision making). Some corporate planning literature reverses these same definitions.

Most programs include a statement of purpose, but if the goals are vague, for example, "to carry out regulation in the public interest" or "to improve air quality," then one can never know whether the program is living up to its potential. Is it successful if air quality is improved only 2 percent or 10 percent or 20 percent? Or should there be a statement that a certain share of the pollutants are to be removed? Similarly, the Federal Water Pollution Control Act Amendments of 1972 mandated that our nation's waters be restored to or maintained in a fishable and swimmable state. Although this clearly suggested that substantial improvements would be needed in the water quality prevailing at that time, it was not an overly specific standard. Setting "fishable and swimmable" criteria was left to subsequent federal agency rule making.

Although the advantages of a clear statement of purpose are obvious, most statutes leave critical issues to be resolved later. It is easier to gain agenda status with vague issues than with specific proposals. In drafting legislation, legislators often find it advantageous not to be overly specific. Uncertainty fostered by imprecision may be necessary to put together the coalition needed to pass the legislation. Some decision makers will support the proposal because they interpret the goals and outcomes differently. For example, before Congress will approve the creation of a new national seashore, the Interior Committees from both houses must assure themselves that there is no opposition from the local community that would be most directly affected. When the Cumberland Island National Seashore in Georgia was created, a number of local leaders thought that the Park Service would build a bridge to the island that would facilitate development, so they supported the program. In actuality, there was never an intent to build a bridge, and access to the island continues to be limited to a few ferry crossings per day. Thus the designation of the national seashore has not created the tourist mecca that local officials expected.

QUANTITATIVE STANDARDS

The standards used to measure the success of programs represent another area in which specific, clear benchmarks are desirable. Automobile emission legislation, for example, stipulated that 90 percent of the carbon monoxide being emitted in 1970 was to be removed from emissions by 1975.

Sometimes it may take years before precise standards are defined. Water quality laws offer an example. In order to protect water quality, the Environmental Protection Agency (EPA) has developed specific, numeric criteria or water quality standards (WQS) that must be met in all streams. Development of these WQSs took years, however, and they are still a topic of debate in the 1990s. Even natural variability of runoff from forested watersheds could cause WQS violations. Timber harvesting or other land management practices also could cause unavoidable problems. Implementation of forestry best management practices (BMPs) has been suggested as one means of substituting for strict enforcement of WQSs, but this issue is still a subject of

debate among the EPA, public and private forest landowners, concerned citizens, and state natural resource agencies. The evolution of water quality standards demonstrates that quantitative standards are difficult to devise for some activities. Thus some programs will be inherently more difficult to evaluate than others.

PROGRAM MONITORING

Monitoring means tracking program success over time. Are things improving? If so, the policy is probably working. If not, the policy may need modification. Successful programs need clear objectives, quantitative standards to measure success, and an agency to implement and monitor the results. Even with clear goals and precise standards, compliance may lag in the absence of an agency responsible for monitoring performance. Although the creation of a monitor is important, there are conditions that may enhance the effectiveness of the monitor. Creation of a new agency to handle a new program can focus greater attention on a program than if the new task is assigned to an existing agency that has other responsibilities. Agency staff levels also can be a factor. If responsibilities far exceed staff capabilities, there will be little effective monitoring. The monitor may become involved only in the aftermath of a crisis resulting from inadequate attention. For wetlands protection and enforcement, the U.S. Department of the Army Corps of Engineers and the EPA have extremely small staffs, which limits their regulatory effectiveness.

To be effective, the monitor must have data on the program. If those subject to regulation must file periodic reports, the job of the monitor will be easier than if the monitoring agency must go out and gather the data itself. With a new program, training may be necessary to ensure that the reports being filed have been done accurately and provide information on successes and failures.

Monitoring should be a part of all public programs, regulatory and nonregulatory alike. Wildlife game managers must monitor population levels, age structure, fecundity, hunter success ratios, and other factors in order to set sound hunting seasons and bag limits. Recreation managers must monitor park usage to evaluate park protection measures needed and program effectiveness. State foresters must evaluate their fire prevention and suppression efforts on private lands in order to optimize the use of their firefighting equipment and personnel, or even to request greater agency funding levels.

A related important factor in the success of natural resource management programs is the amount of funding provided for operation and maintenance versus new land acquisitions or building programs. Many of the recreational facilities of the National Park System were built by the Civilian Conservation Corps (CCC) during the depression in the 1930s. These facilities include lodges, campgrounds, trails, picnic grounds, shelters, and much more. The National Park System expanded by acquisitions throughout much of the 1970s, but the funding for maintenance and repair did not increase proportionately. Thus the National Park System faces severe problems with aging and unsafe facilities and deteriorating assets (General Accounting Office 1988). Similar problems have occurred in many states, which have closed parks permanently or part-time because they do not have large enough operating budgets to pay personnel. Some of these problems truly are political in nature—officials get much more publicity and credit for creating parks (or building dams, highways, bridges, and buildings) than they do for appropriating funds to operate and repair existing facilities.

AGENCY COMMITMENT AND ENFORCEMENT

Although data collection and program monitoring are important, they alone are not sufficient to guarantee program success. Forestry and wildlife management assistance and public land management, among other programs, require vigorous implementation by dedicated agencies to foster success. Game and fire protection programs and campground management require agencies to enforce regulations and prosecute violators, as do environmental protection laws.

The critical importance of enforcement helps explain why a policy adopted by a legislature may be more successful than one articulated by the court. Legislatures can, and often do, create agencies to carry out their mandates or add the new program to an existing agency. Courts have no such power. In the absence of an enforcement mechanism, court decisions rely heavily on voluntary compliance. Pres. Andrew Jackson once angrily responded to an adverse court decision by saying that Chief Justice John Marshall had made his decision; now let him try to enforce it.

Program success is a function of the degree of agency commitment. An agency weakly committed to implementing a program may be little better than no agency at all. Although it would be unusual for an agency charged with program implementation to intentionally sabotage the effort, the agency's enthusiasm may be reduced because of competing responsibilities. An agency's commitment will be greater to those programs with which it has had a longer relationship, so that new responsibilities are assigned lower priorities (Orfield 1969). Therefore, when the creator of a new program wants to enhance the probability of active enforcement, a new agency will be created to handle the program rather than its being assigned to an existing bureau.

The Corps of Engineers' administration of the federal wetlands regulation program illustrates these problems. The corps was traditionally in charge of dredging and filling operations for the nation's canals and harbors. Under the 1972 Federal Water Pollution Control Act Amendments, the corps was given a new responsibility for regulating dredge and fill operations for environmental protection purposes. The corps also had an expanded definition of the nation's waterways, which included wetlands, foisted upon it. Compared to its traditional focus on building dams and controlling navigation, wetlands protection remained one of the corps' least favorite and least aggressively implemented programs.

The most aggressive implementation strategy is to create a new agency and have it report directly to a chief administrative official. This was clearly the logic that accompanied the consolidation of federal environmental programs in 1970. William Ruckelshaus was named to head a new agency, the Environmental Protection Agency. The EPA was given authority for pollution control programs that had previously resided in numerous departments. The new agency's identity was tied to these programs and implementation became much more aggressive.

Despite the general pattern whereby agencies accord little attention to new responsibilities, there are conditions under which an existing agency may move swiftly to meet new challenges. An agency whose previous responsibilities have become politically unpopular or less significant will gladly adopt new programs. Provision of new budgets with new programs, rather than sacrifice of existing funds, also will increase an agency's enthusiasm for implementation. Competition among agencies may prompt vigorous program implementation. The Forest Service became much more interested in developing recreation programs after the National Park Service was established. Similarly, the Corps of Engineers has moved more aggressively to implement wetlands regulation after the EPA created its own Office of Wetlands in 1986. Even black sheep look more attractive when courted by another suitor.

The level of interest in the program among key agency personnel is another factor in the degree of commitment. If new or existing staff members already have an interest in the problem, they will relish the opportunity to pursue it. If they do not, they will not; bureaucrats often avoid expanded job responsibilities (Rodgers and Bullock 1976). When the Environmental Protection Agency was created, most staff members brought with them a missionary zeal for protecting the environment and were eager to implement such programs. On the other hand, the original National Wilderness Preservation System carved a large share of its acreage out of the National Forest System; foresters were much less enthusiastic about the new preserve areas, and some have continued to oppose expansion of the Wilderness System.

EXECUTIVE AND LEGISLATIVE COMMITMENT

Enforcement agencies are ultimately responsible to both the legislative and executive branches. Congress assigns responsibilities and provides the financial support for program execution. Thus declining congressional commitment can result in lower budgets and a decreased capacity to implement a program. Similarly, a president may use the appointment and supervision powers to deemphasize a program. President Reagan tried to reorient environmental policy in this way.

Although no program is created without strong initial support in some quarters, that support may quickly erode. Costs may be greater than were forecast, or enforcement may prove more onerous or widespread than had been foreseen. Opponents may unite to curb implementation or to modify or even repeal the legislation. Congress has repeatedly modified pollution control standards rather than pursue enforcement at what would be unacceptable costs for the consumer or for particular industries required to implement those controls. In 1991 many Congress members began efforts to reduce the amount of land subject to wetlands regulation, in response to a generous 1989 definition agreed to by the EPA, Army Corps of Engineers, Soil Conservation Service, and U.S. Fish and Wildlife Service.

Support for programs can also decline due to changes in public support and interest. Programs do not remain in the public eye for an extended period (Kingdon 1984). As previously mentioned, similar problems occur with maintenance of public facilities compared to creating or building them. Commitment of the executive branch to an enforcement program may change with a new administration. At the state level, each governor hopes to become identified in the public mind and in the history books with a particular set of innovations. As a result of this orientation, a new governor will not be particularly enthusiastic about supporting, much less extending, programs identified with his or her predecessor. Instead the new chief executive will seek to shift attention and momentum to new programs. For example, governors often focus on new education reform packages. Other topics have included protection of the environment and prosecution of criminals. Shifts at the national level may be less pronounced, but a new party in the White House has led to marked changes in commitment to natural resource programs.

Costs and Benefits

Following the rational-comprehensive model of policy adoption, implementation should succeed when the benefits of a program are greater than the costs of noncompliance. Costs include items already discussed, as well as political embarrassment, lack of public support, and a rebuke from one's superiors. Positive inducements may come in the form of praise from superiors, increased support for an agency's programs, or personal satisfaction in a job well done.

There is truth in the old adage that one can draw more flies with a teaspoon of honey than with a gallon of vinegar. Inducements for program compliance, therefore, tend to be more effective than sanctions for noncompliance. Nonetheless, if programmatic goals are sufficiently unpopular, compliance may be achieved only through coercion. In development of public policy related to private forests, we do not yet know the relative efficiency of technical assistance (inducement) and landowner regulation (sanction). It is likely that some combination of the two policy instruments will be most appropriate.

Problems of enforcement due to inadequate penalties also exist in the area of environmental protection. For example, most states in the United States now have developed voluntary best management practices (BMPs) to control nonpoint source pollution

resulting from forestry activities. However, without some mechanism to enforce compliance, voluntary BMPs are unlikely to be adequate by themselves. Thus some states enforce voluntary BMP programs by prosecuting blatant violators under existing water quality protection laws.

West Virginia and Massachusetts use this principle to enforce BMPs for logging. West Virginia loggers who are registered and notify the state before harvests usually are advised in informal conferences to take corrective action if their logging operations cause violations of state water quality standards. Loggers who do not register usually are prosecuted if violations occur. Massachusetts requires loggers to be licensed. Those who repeatedly violate BMPs may have their licenses revoked.

Some economists have argued that compliance is greater when fines are stiffer—few rational individuals wish to accept the possibility of a severe punishment. Similarly, in some criminal trials when the penalty is perceived to be disproportionate to the misdeed, juries will acquit even though they believe the defendant to be guilty. Thus there must be a balance between severity and what is seen as reasonable or acceptable. Street crime might go down if convicted robbers had their hands cut off—or convictions for robbery might drop to near zero.

Direct Federal Involvement

Implementation may be more successful when the federal government is directly involved in program execution. Federal resources greatly outstrip those of private individuals and of state and local governments. Therefore, active federal participation means that distributive or enforcement programs, including litigation, can be more extensive than if left up to private efforts. In the case of criminal activities, the resources of the FBI exceed those of nonfederal government entities.

Federal involvement also is advantageous when a proscribed activity enjoys widespread support in some areas of the country. Until recently, states made little effort to control pollution resulting from farm, forestry, and development activities until federal laws mandated such planning. In the past, state-level wetlands protection was less rigorous than the federal efforts. But now several states are implementing rigorous wetlands programs, including Maryland, Massachusetts, and Maine.

When sufficient authority exists, federal officials may supplant state or local authorities. By doing so, not only are the specifically involved communities brought into compliance, but neighboring communities will correct their ways to forestall a similar federal takeover (Rodgers and Bullock 1976). Even if the federal involvement or regulation is not forthcoming, the threat of such involvement may prompt state action. Based on persistent federal efforts to regulate private forestry, 13 states enacted forest practice legislation in the 1940s. This helped forestall further federal action.

An advantage of federal involvement is the potential for uniform standards nationwide. When that occurs, the possibility for achieving a competitive advantage by having weaker standards is removed. If all communities must live up to the same standards for air or water quality, then no state has an incentive to maintain lower standards in order to attract industry from other states. It also is cheaper for firms to comply with uniform standards.

The notion of uniform standards has not, however, been uniformly pursued in clean air programs. The strategy instead has been to allow some additional pollution in communities that have relatively clean air while enforcing higher standards on areas such as Los Angeles where the air quality has deteriorated to seriously low levels. Although federal law stipulates this sort of unequal enforcement, it plays into the hands of those in the areas facing more stringent regulation as they plead for additional time.

PROGRAM EVALUATION

The preceding sections on analytical criteria and program implementation provide the basis for a discussion of policy evaluation, the last step of the policy process model presented in Chapter 2. Public programs may be evaluated by the relevant agencies themselves, by interest groups concerned with program implementation, by academic researchers or consultants, or by legislative oversight committees.

PURPOSES

Program evaluations may be made to determine if agencies and regulations are accomplishing their legislatively mandated missions. They also may be made to reevaluate objectives and provide feedback for development of new policies. In making evaluations, officials will often use criteria such as efficiency and equity to assess success. Efficiency may include social efficiency—whether society as a whole benefits from such programs. It also may evaluate administrative efficiency—whether the program is being managed in a cost-efficient manner. Equity evaluation criteria are used to assess distributive costs and benefits of public programs. The Forestry Incentives Program case presented earlier in this chapter illustrates the use of economic efficiency and equity criteria in program evaluation and demonstrates how program evaluations occur on an ongoing basis over time.

Program evaluations may be performed using the decision criteria and the factors influencing program success discussed earlier. Rather than elaborate on more theories of program evaluation, we will illustrate its use with another case study—the Bureau of Land Management's enforcement of grazing policy.

ILLUSTRATION: BUREAU OF LAND MANAGEMENT GRAZING POLICY ENFORCEMENT

One example of program evaluation is provided by a U.S. General Accounting Office (GAO) review of the Bureau of Land Management (BLM) grazing policies. GAO is a branch of Congress that was established in 1921 to oversee the expenditures of the executive branch. In 1950 Congress turned routine audits over to other agencies and gave GAO responsibility for investigations and analyses of policies as well as programs.

The General Accounting Office

GAO serves as the "watchdog" for Congress, evaluating programs to make sure they are being implemented well. Many of the approximately 5000 employees of GAO have advanced degrees in a variety of disciplines, including accounting, law, public administration, social and physical sciences, and economics.

About 80 percent of GAO's investigations come in response to requests from Congress members. The rest are initiated by GAO itself. In 1989 GAO published 881 reports in response to 1100 requests. Employees of the agency also testified 217 times before congressional committees and issued more than 3800 legal opinions to assist in the drafting of legislation (Shepard 1990).

A 1990 GAO report evaluated the BLM and its control of illegal grazing on public lands. The review was prompted by concerns that illegal grazing could cause harm to rangelands that were already in poor shape, and that poor enforcement was costing the federal government substantial revenues.

Bureau of Land Management Grazing Policies

Before 1934 livestock grazing on public lands was not controlled, and the lands were damaged by decades of overgrazing. The Taylor Grazing Act of 1934 (43 U.S.C. 315 *et seq.*) authorized regulation of grazing, but the Bureau of Land Management exerted only nominal control over public rangeland. Faced with continued rangeland deterioration, Congress passed the Federal Land Policy and Management Act (FLPMA) of 1976 (43 U.S.C. 1701 *et seq.*). The act established a federal commitment to (1) retain ownership of public lands, (2) improve deteriorated lands, and (3) manage the lands so as to ensure their productive capacity in perpetuity. The Public Rangelands Improvement Act (PRIA) of 1978 (43 U.S.C. 1901 *et seq.*) reaffirmed the national policy to manage, maintain, and improve the condition of public rangelands.

The Bureau of Land Management manages public rangeland under FLPMA, including 162 million acres of rangelands in 16 western states. BLM rangelands are managed through renewable permits and leases to about 19,600 livestock operators. The permits and leases specify the number and type of livestock allowed on the allotments, the time and duration of use for grazing, and special conditions or use restrictions. BLM issues permits for up to 10 years but may alter, suspend, or cancel them if range conditions are being degraded or permit conditions violated. In 1989 BLM charged operators $1.81 per animal unit month (AUM). An AUM is the forage required to support a 1000 pound cow, a horse, or five sheep for one month. Comparable commercial values for forage were $8.49 per AUM in 1989 (General Accounting Office 1990).

In order to protect public range, BLM is authorized to prosecute grazing trespassers. The BLM grazing regulations (43 C.F.R. 4100) established three levels of grazing trespass—nonwillful, willful, and repeated willful—with progressively harsher penalties for each level. Nonwillful trespass convictions require the offender to pay the commercial value of the forage consumed. For willful trespass, that penalty doubles, and the violator also pays charges for damages to the land and BLM expenses incurred to detect, investigate, and resolve the violation. For repeated willful trespass, the required penalty is three times the commercial value of forage consumed, plus compensation of BLM expenses. For any type of trespass, BLM may suspend or cancel all or portions of the grazing permit.

BLM Trespass Detection Efforts

Despite the clearly stated policies to protect the public rangelands, the GAO evaluation found that the trespass detection efforts made by BLM were minimal. The GAO investigation found that grazing trespass clearly was occurring, and that BLM detection efforts were not even sufficient to identify the extent of the problem. GAO found that BLM administration had not developed a systematic method for detecting violations.

The BLM identified staffing shortfalls as a major obstacle to a serious trespass protection program. Between 1981 and 1990, BLM range staff decreased by 25 percent, from 551 to 443 persons. In 1990 each range staff member was, on average, responsible for 47 permits and 392,000 acres of public rangelands. At least 26 were responsible for more than 1 million acres each, an area about the size of Delaware.

The GAO study conceded that more staff certainly would help detect and prosecute trespass, but it observed that significant staff or budget increases were unlikely given federal budget limitations. However, the GAO said that BLM efforts even given current staff levels were still inadequate. About 319 BLM range staff had direct responsibility for detecting trespass, and about 119 of them did not visit half or more of their grazing allotments during fiscal year 1989. The BLM handbook states that trespass detection should be a top priority. The BLM, however, had not established trespass detection as a work-load measure of performance, and detection results were not categorized as reportable accomplishments.

The GAO review also found that the penalties applied by BLM were seldom as severe as required by law. In fiscal year (FY)1989, BLM closed 345 formal trespass cases with penalties—259 nonwillful, 77 willful, and 9 repeated willful. GAO estimated that an additional 1300 to 1900 additional trespass cases occurred in FY 1989. These cases were considered nonwillful and were handled informally by a telephone call or visit to the violator. Although BLM regulations do not allow it, many range staff used this approach in hopes of maintaining good agency–operator working relationships and to avoid unnecessary conflicts. In addition to informally resolving most trespass incidents, BLM did not assess required penalties for the more serious violations that were formally processed. BLM detection and prosecution costs were not collected in 71 of the 86 willful and repeated willful cases in FY 1989. Additionally, BLM

did not penalize any of the 77 willful trespassers. Only one of the nine willful offenders even had a permit partially suspended, and none was canceled. BLM staff members defended the lax prosecution by saying that they thought penalties were optional or discretionary, rather than mandatory.

GAO Recommendations

Given BLM's desultory enforcement efforts, GAO recommended that greater congressional oversight was needed for the trespass enforcement program. GAO concluded that grazing permittees and leasees, and ranchers adjacent to federal lands, operate essentially on an honor system with little threat of compliance checks by BLM. Additionally, BLM record-keeping procedures and management information systems were judged inadequate.

To correct these problems, GAO recommended that trespass detection should be a reportable, measurable work-load standard; random checks on selected allotments should be made to promote compliance; and livestock operators with repeated violations should receive follow-up visits. Furthermore, GAO recommended either better enforcement of nonwillful violations or amendment of the law to formally allow local resolution of these violations. GAO said that complete case records should be kept and that the required penalties should be implemented for willful and repeated willful grazing trespass. The comments from the Department of the Interior simply stated that they agreed with GAO's recommendations for improving unauthorized grazing detection and deterrent efforts (General Accounting Office 1990).

The evaluation of BLM range enforcement actions demonstrates how GAO assesses federal agency implementation of laws passed by Congress. GAO reviewed the pertinent laws and their intent and obtained data to assess the effectiveness of the agency effort. GAO asked BLM supervisors for data on grazing trespass cases and sent questionnaires to about one-half of the range staff. GAO interviewed officials at BLM headquarters and visited BLM area offices in four states.

Using the criterion of administrative effectiveness in implementing the relevant laws, or of protecting public rangelands, the results of the GAO evaluation certainly were disappointing. BLM simply did not seem to be protecting rangelands as well as it should, even with limited staff. A briefer review of Forest Service monitoring of grazing allotments in 1991 found the agency's efforts to be somewhat better, but still inadequate (General Accounting Office 1991). These problems could be traced to historical subsystem politics. Ranchers help elect and support Congress members. Congress members impede strict enforcement of range laws so ranchers benefit, and the general public pays. These relationships are discussed in detail in Chapters 7 and 9. These and other ongoing problems of public range management have been pervasive since the West was settled and are a habitual congressional agenda item.

SUMMARY

Analysis of policy alternatives needs to be done as objectively as possible to provide information to policymakers. When evaluating the effectiveness of a proposed or existing program, many decision criteria can and should be used; any or all may influence policy decisions. Ecological criteria can determine whether a policy can be implemented, its effect on the environment, or even appropriate management regimes. Economic efficiency criteria measure costs and returns in either private financial terms or with social welfare or benefit–cost measures. Social criteria such as freedom of choice, equitable distribution of costs and benefits, due process, and practicality also influence policy selection and success of implementation. Politics, of course, is eventually a crucial factor in decisions about public policies and programs.

Many factors can influence the success or failure of public programs. Specific goals, quantitative standards, and ongoing program monitoring will help lead to success. Programs are more likely to be successful if created with new departmental or agency

responsibilities than if assigned to existing agencies or bureaus. Aggressive agencies will lead to greater program success. Continuing commitment on the part of the legislature and the executive also are important. Finally, program costs and benefits and the degree of federal involvement also influence success.

LITERATURE CITED

Anderson, James E. 1979. Public Policy-Making, 2nd ed. Holt, Rinehart & Winston. New York. 200 pp.

Boyd, Roy. 1983. The effects of FIP and forester assistance on nonindustrial private forests. Pp. 198–203 in Nonindustrial Private Forests: A Review of Economic and Policy Studies. Duke University School of Forestry and Environmental Studies. Durham, NC.

Brealey, Richard, and Stewart Myers. 1984. Principles of Corporate Finance, 2nd ed. McGraw-Hill. New York. 847 pp.

Ciriacy-Wantrup, S. V. 1963. Resource Conservation Economics and Policies. University of California Press. Berkeley.

Clawson, Marion. 1975. Forests for Whom and for What? Johns Hopkins University Press/Resources for the Future. Baltimore, MD. 175 pp.

Cleaves, David A., and Jay O'Laughlin. 1986. Analyzing structure in wood-based industry. *Forest Products Journal* 36(4):9–14, 36(5):11–17.

Clutter, Jerome L., James C. Fortson, Leon V. Pienaar, Graham H. Brister, and Robert L. Bailey. 1983. Timber Management: A Quantitative Approach. Wiley. New York. 333 pp.

Cohen, Melinda A. 1983. Public cost-share programs and private investment in forestry in the South. Pp. 181–188 in Nonindustrial Private Forests: A Review of Economic and Policy Studies. Duke University, School of Forestry and Environmental Studies. Durham, NC.

Cubbage, Frederick W., and Clair H. Redmond. 1985. Capital budgeting practices in the forest products industry. *Forest Products Journal* 35(9):55–60.

Dahl, Robert A., and Charles E. Lindblom. 1953. Politics, Economics and Welfare. Harper and Brothers. New York. 556 pp.

de Steiguer, J. E. 1983. The influence of incentive programs on nonindustrial private forestry investment. Pp. 157–163 in Nonindustrial Private Forests: A Review of Economic and Policy Studies. Duke University, School of Forestry and Environmental Studies. Durham, NC.

de Steiguer, J. E. 1984. Impact of cost-share programs on private reforestation investment. *Forest Science* 39(3):697–704.

Duerr, William A. 1982. Criteria for forest management. Pp. 57–66 in William A. Duerr, Dennis E. Teeguarden, Neils B. Christiansen, and Sam Guttenberg. (eds.), O.S.U. Forest Resource Management: Decision-Making Principles and Cases. O.S.U. Bookstores. Corvallis, OR.

Edwards, George C., III. 1977. Congressional responsiveness to public opinion: A policy perspective. *Policy Studies Journal* 5(Summer):485–491.

Etzioni, Amitai. 1967. Mixed-scanning: A "third" approach to decision-making. *Public Administration Review* 27(5):385–392.

Foster, Bennett B. 1984. A Service Forester's guide to investment terminologies—which ones are most easily understood by landowners? *Southern Journal of Applied Forestry* 8(3):115–119.

General Accounting Office. 1988. Park Service managers report shortfalls in maintenance funding. Report No. GAO1RECD-88-918R. U.S. Government Printing Office. Washington, DC. 88 pp.

General Accounting Office. 1990. BLM efforts to prevent unauthorized livestock grazing need strengthening. Report No. GAO/RECD-90-17. U.S. Government Printing Office. Washington, DC. 16 pp.

General Accounting Office. 1991. Rangeland management: Forest Service not performing needed monitoring of grazing allotments. Report No. GAO1RECD-91-148. U.S. Government Printing Office. Washington, DC. 8 pp.

Gregersen, Hans M. 1977. Can we afford small woodland subsidies—it depends. Pp. 62–68 in Proceedings, 1976 SAF National Convention, Society of American Foresters. New Orleans.

Gregersen, Hans M., and Arnoldo H. Contreras. 1979. Economic Analysis of Forestry Projects. FAO Forestry Paper 17. Food and Agriculture Organization of the United Nations. Rome. 193 pp.

Irland, Lloyd C. 1979. Wilderness Economics and Policy. Lexington Press. Lexington, MA. 225 pp.

Jones, Charles O. 1984. An Introduction to the Study of Public Policy, 3rd ed. Brooks/Cole Publishing Company. Monterey, CA. 276 pp.

Kearns, Doris. 1976. Lyndon Johnson and the American Dream. Harper & Row. New York. 432 pp.

Kingdon, John W. 1984. Agendas, Alternatives, and Public Policies. Little, Brown. Boston. 240 pp.

Lee, Karen J., H. Fred Kaiser, and Ralph J. Alig. 1992. Substitution of public for private funding in planting southern pine. *Southern Journal of Applied Forestry.* In press.

Leuschner, William A. 1984. Introduction to Forest Resource Management. Wiley. New York. 298 pp.

MacNeill, Jim. 1989. Strategies for sustainable economic development. *Scientific American* 261(3):155–165.

McAvoy, Leo H., and Daniel L. Dustin. 1983. In search of balance: A no-rescue wilderness proposal. *Western Wildlands* 9(2):2–5.

Mills, Thomas J., Thomas P. Hart, and J. S. McKnight. 1974. Forestry incentives: How funds were apportioned to the states in 1974. *Journal of Forestry.* 72(8):478–482.

Mills, Thomas J. 1976. Cost effectiveness of the 1974 Forestry Incentives Program (FIP). Research Paper RM-175. USDA Forest Service, Rocky Mountain Forest and Range Experiment Station. Fort Collins, CO. 23 pp.

Mills, Thomas J., and Daria Cain. 1978. Timber yield and financial return performance of the 1974 Forestry Incentives Program. Research Paper RM-204. USDA Forest Service, Rocky Mountain Forest and Range Experiment Station. Fort Collins, CO. 56 pp.

Musgrave, Richard A., and Peggy B. Musgrave. 1984. Public Finance in Theory and Practice, 4th ed. McGraw-Hill. New York. 824 pp.

Nesmith, Jeff. 1990. Pokeweed plant can slow AIDS. *Atlanta Journal/Atlanta Constitution,* September 11, p. C-6.

Norse, E., K. Rosenbaum, D. Wilcove, B. Wilcox, W. Romme, D. Johnston, and M. Stout. 1986. Conserving biological diversity in our national forests. The Wilderness Society. Washington, DC.

Office of Technology Assessment. 1987. Technologies to maintain biological diversity. OTA-F-330. U.S. Government Printing Office. Washington, DC.

Orfield, Gary. 1969. The Reconstruction of Southern Education. Wiley. New York. 376 pp.

Pressman, Jeffrey L., and Aaron Wildavsky. 1973. Implementation: How Great Expectations in Washington Are Dashed in Oakland; or Why It's Amazing That Federal Programs Work at All, This Being a Saga of the Economic Development Administration as Told by Two Sympathetic Observers Who Seek to Build Morals on a Foundation of Ruined Hopes. University of California Press. Berkeley. 182 pp.

Risbrudt, Christopher D., and Paul V. Ellefson. 1983. An economic evaluation of the 1979 Forestry Incentives Program. Station Bulletin 550-1983. University of Minnesota Agricultural Experiment Station. St. Paul. 55 pp.

Risbrudt, Christopher D., H. Fred Kaiser, and Paul V. Ellefson. 1983a. Cost-effectiveness of the 1979 Forestry Incentives Program. *Journal of Forestry* 81(5):298–301.

Risbrudt, Christopher D., Mark H. Goforth, Andrew Wheatcraft, and Paul V. Ellefson. 1983b. 1974 Forestry Incentives Program investments: Retention as of 1981. Station Bulletin 552-1983. University of Minnesota Agricultural Experiment Station. St. Paul. 33 pp.

Rodgers, Harrell R., Jr., and Charles S. Bullock III. 1976. Coercion to Compliance. Lexington Books. Lexington, MA. 189 pp.

Salisbury, Robert H. 1973. Governing America: Public Choice and Political Action. Appleton-Century-Crofts. New York. 368 pp.

Satterlund, Donald R. 1972. Wildland Watershed Management. Ronald Press. New York. 370 pp.

Sawhill, John C. 1990. Can a species be worthless? *Nature Conservancy* 49(4):3.

Shephard, Scott. 1990. Watchdog agency of Congress "lets chips fall where they may." *Atlanta Journal/Atlanta Constitution.* July 1, p. A-7.

Society of American Foresters. 1983. SAF forest policies and positions 1983. Washington, DC. 50 pp.

Wallace, T. Dudley, and J. Lew Silver. 1983. Public cost-sharing and production in nonindustrial private forests: The case of FIP in Georgia. Pp. 165–180 in Nonindustrial Private Forests—A Review of Economic and Policy Studies. Duke University, School of Forestry and Environmental Studies. Durham, NC.

Wilcove, David S. 1988. National Forests: Policies for the future, Volume 2—Protecting biological diversity. The Wilderness Society. Washington, DC. 50 pp.

Williamson, Lonnie. 1985. Forest Service voodoo. *Outdoor Life* 175(3):54–56.

Wilson, Edward V. 1989. Threats to biodiversity. *Scientific American* 261(3):108–116.

Worrell, Albert C. 1970. Principles of Forest Policy. McGraw-Hill. New York. 243 pp.

PART II

PARTICIPANTS

Chapter 6

The Legislature

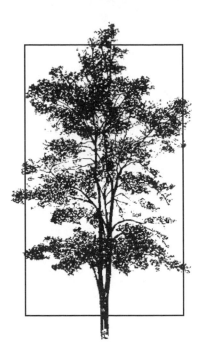

The law is the last result of human wisdom acting upon human experience for the benefit of the public.

—Samuel Johnson, circa 1750

The Congress shall have Power To lay and collect Taxes, Duties, Imports and Excises, to pay The Debts and provide for the common Defence and general Welfare of the United States …

—Constitution of the United States, 1787

INTRODUCTION

The first five chapters of this book illustrated that forest resource policy is a product of political processes. The chapters in this section focus on the official and unofficial participants in those processes that result in forest resource policy. Official policymakers include those given constitutional or statutory authority to make laws and implement policies—legislatures, the executive, and courts. Unofficial participants—including interest groups and the media—do not have authority to make policy, but do influence official policymakers.

According to the representative model of decision making, people perceive problems or issues; problems are brought to the atten-

tion of elected officials; laws are enacted by legislatures and implemented by administrative agencies; and disputes over laws are resolved by the judicial system. The legislative process that makes forest policy is presented in this chapter. The legislative system and processes are described primarily from the perspective of the federal government. Most state systems are quite similar.

LEGISLATIVE POWERS

The U.S. Constitution and the state constitutions grant specific powers to the legislature. The principal powers include enacting laws, raising and allocating funds, and overseeing the implementation of laws. The U.S. Constitution is simple and short. Most state constitutions are not as brief or elegant, but they authorize and delegate similar legislative powers.

Enact Legislation

Constitutional Authority

Article I of the U.S. Constitution, which comprises almost half of the document, sets forth the powers granted to Congress. It establishes two houses or bodies: a House of Representatives and a Senate. The composition of the House, which is currently at 435 members, is based on state population. Each state sends two senators to the Senate. Section VII of Article I authorizes Congress to pass bills that become law if approved by the president. Section VIII authorizes Congress "to lay and collect taxes, duties, imports, and excises, to pay the debts and provide for the common defence and general welfare of the United States..." and then enumerates specific powers falling under this authority. The specific powers granted in Section VIII of the Constitution include borrowing money, controlling naturalization of citizens; granting patents; establishing courts inferior to the U.S. Supreme Court; and raising, supporting, and calling forth armies and navies.

One of the most significant powers granted Congress is "to regulate commerce with foreign nations and among the several states, and with Indian tribes." This "commerce clause" has been the basis for a host of federal laws dealing with such areas as trucking, crime, and minimum wage laws that affect all states. Virtually all federal environmental laws relating to natural resources are at least partially based on the commerce clause. For example, the Clean Water Act grants authority to the U.S. Army Corps of Engineers to regulate wetlands dredge and fill operations in order to protect such resources from damage or destruction during development or silvicultural operations. Wetlands fall under federal jurisdiction because waterfowl may fly across state boundaries and land in ponds or wetlands. In fact, one judicial determination of whether the Army Corps of Engineers has jurisdiction in regulating a wetland involves whether a "reasonable bird" would land there.

Section VIII also allows Congress to make all laws that shall be necessary and proper for "carrying into execution the foregoing powers." The Constitution does, however, place limits on congressional authority. The "reserved powers" clause—the Tenth Amendment—states that "The powers not delegated to the United States by the Constitution, nor prohibited by it to the States, are reserved to the States respectively, or to the people." Thus all powers not specifically delegated to Congress are reserved for the states. The police power—the authority to secure the comfort, safety, and prosperity of citizens—is one of the most significant reserved powers. The police power provides the basis for government regulation of land use. Local zoning laws, state fish and game laws, and forest practice acts exemplify state exercise of police powers.

The Law

Laws enacted by legislatures are generally termed *acts* or *statutes*. Statutes are bills passed by a legislature and signed into law by the executive (governor or president). The Constitution, statutes, and common law—in which decisions of individual judges establish precedents independent of statutory law—form the basis of the legal system (Hoban and Brooks 1987, Siegel 1982).

Laws may be enacted for many reasons and their objectives may be stated with great precision or in very general terms. Laws generally attempt to create, maintain, or restore order, stability, and justice (Anderson and Kumpf 1972). Laws are enacted to achieve many objectives, which are summarized in the following paragraphs along with a few illustrative applications to natural resources.

Laws may be enacted to protect the state, such as those designed to provide for a national defense or to raise taxes. Laws for establishing and managing the national forests, parks, and wildlife refuges are intended to benefit the general public. Some laws are designed to protect the public health, safety, and morals. Most environmental laws—such as the Clean Water Act, the Clean Air Act, and the Federal Insecticide, Fungicide, and Rodenticide Act (FIFRA)—have public health and safety objectives. Occupational safety and wage laws, which affect forest products firms, promote public health and safety by protecting individuals from harmful working conditions. They also govern who is eligible for employment and employment benefits and may affect wages received.

Antitrust laws are designed to promote free market competition. Among other things, they prevent businesses from colluding to restrain trade—by "fixing" prices of raw or processed forest products, by dividing up market territories, or by other means. Violations of these laws in the 1970s cost forest industry companies $750 million in penalties. It is no wonder, then, that most meetings of industrial forestry associations are opened with a statement avowing that antitrust laws will be observed.

Laws may protect people from discrimination or crime and public or private property from damage. Laws that authorize prosecution of individuals who damage others' property are crucial for natural resources protection. For example, individuals who trespass to hunt on others' property or steal timber from private lands may be prosecuted in state criminal courts. Those who illegally kill game or violate state water quality laws during timber harvests also may be prosecuted as criminal offenders.

Criminal laws regulate relationships between individuals and society. Civil laws regulate relationships among citizens or businesses. Many civil laws are designed to facilitate, restrain, or promote business practices. They deal with contract enforcement, fraud protection, banking regulation, creditor protection, debtor rehabilitation, and practical expediency. When someone violates civil law, he or she may be sued by other persons, firms, or the government in order to stop such violations or to recover monetary damages.

The preceding discussion of the purposes for laws is not all-encompassing; other rea-

sons certainly exist. In addition, these various objectives may conflict. When this occurs, lawmakers use social, economic, or physical criteria to determine which objectives take priority. As society's values change, so will the laws that are deemed desirable or undesirable. As technology and trade evolve, new laws arise and others become obsolete.

A wide variety of federal laws affect forest and other natural resources. These include laws that established the national forest, national park, and national wildlife refuge systems and provided for their management. For example, based on the Wilderness Act of 1964, new wilderness areas are established by individual laws. Laws also provide for federal research and technology transfer regarding forest and wildlife resources, protect the environment from pollution, and authorize many other important programs. Appendix A summarizes many of the important federal laws affecting natural resources.

States often have similar legislation affecting forest resources within their borders. In fact, many state forestry, wildlife, and environmental laws were prompted by initial federal legislative action. States also have enacted legislation specifically to qualify for forestry and wildlife assistance from the federal government.

Illustration: Washington State Wilderness Act of 1984

In 1984 Congress approved 20 wilderness bills, designating more than 8.3 million acres of public lands as part of the National Wilderness Preservation System. One of these bills established more than 1 million acres of new wilderness in the state of Washington. This case study follows the Washington State Wilderness Act from its origin as a skeletal bill to enactment as Public Law 98-339. The case illustrates the legislative role in making natural resource policy, as well as the many different players involved in enacting legislation.

The Wilderness Act of 1964 set the stage for evaluating and designating public lands as wilderness areas. Wilderness is legally defined in the act as follows (16 U.S.C.A. 1132 [b]):

A wilderness, in contrast with those areas where man and his own works dominate the landscape, is hereby recognized as an area where the earth and its community of life are untrammeled by man, where man himself is a visitor who does not remain. An area of wilderness is further defined to mean in this chapter an area of undeveloped Federal land retaining its primeval character and influence, without permanent improvements or human habitation, which is protected and managed so as to preserve its natural conditions and which (1) generally appears to have been affected primarily by the forces of nature, with the imprint of man's work substantially unnoticeable; (2) has outstanding opportunities for solitude or a primitive and unconfined type of recreation; (3) has at least five thousand acres of land or is of sufficient size as to make practicable its preservation and use in an unimpaired condition; and (4) may also contain ecological, geological, or other features of scientific, educational, scenic, or historical value.

In the late 1970s the Forest Service conducted its second major modern review of potential national forest wilderness areas. The study was called the Roadless Area Review and Evaluation, commonly called RARE II. Of the 2.5 million acres evaluated in Washington, the Carter administration recommended 363,000 acres for wilderness status. However, court cases in the early 1980s (*State of California* v. *Bergland*, 483 F.Supp. 465 [1980]; *State of California* v. *Block*, F.2d 653 [1982]) cast doubt on the validity of the RARE II process, prompting Congress to proceed one state at a time in designating new wilderness areas. Thus it fell to the Washington congressional delegation to decide on how much wilderness—and which areas—to carve from the roadless national forest lands in the state of Washington.

Sen. Slade Gorton and Henry Jackson introduced a bill in Congress (Senate Bill 837, or S. 837) on March 17, 1983, to enact the Carter administration's RARE II recommendations as wilderness. Senator Gorton said:

It is vitally important to protect and preserve those areas in the State which have outstanding natural characteristics and high value as wilderness. Those areas should be preserved for the benefit of future generations. At the same time, we realize the value and importance of the timber resources in our State and the concerns of the forest products industry on the uncertainty that has resulted from the RARE II process. For this reason, it is advisable to move expeditiously to release lands not appropriate for wilderness designation for other uses. (*Congressional Record*, March 17, 1983, p. S3285)

Both senators emphasized that S. 837 was a legislative vehicle, a starting point for working toward an actual wilderness bill so that all interested parties could express their views on the size and location of new wilderness areas. Another simmering issue concerned *release/sufficiency language*, a technical term referring to how roadless public lands *not* designated as wilderness would be managed in the future.

Senate Bill 837 was referred to the Senate Committee on Energy and Natural Resources, chaired by Sen. James McClure of Idaho. At Gorton's and Jackson's request, McClure instructed the committee staff to schedule hearings on the bill. Field hearings were scheduled in Seattle and Spokane for June 2 and 3, 1983. On those two days the senators, accompanied by their key legislative aides, heard testimony from more than 200 witnesses. Those statements became part of a voluminous hearing record, which also incorporated an additional 692 letters and statements.

Senator Jackson died on September 1, 1983, and Dan Evans, formerly governor of the state of Washington, was appointed, then elected, to replace him. Senator Evans was appointed, at his request, to a seat on the Senate subcommittee with jurisdiction over wilderness bills. The subcommittee held a hearing in Washington, DC on September 30, 1983. A number of "back-home" groups testified at the hearing, as did several national interest groups, such as the Wilderness Society and forest industry organizations. On September 29 the committee heard comments on S. 837 from John Block, secretary of the U.S. Department of Agriculture. Block stated that the Reagan administration would only support S. 837 if the Senate deleted certain areas from the RARE II recommendation, dropping the proposed wilderness acreage from 363,000 acres to 229,000.

The Washington State congressional delegation (the eight members of the House of Representatives and the two senators) had agreed informally to let the Senate take the lead on wilderness legislation. Thus there was no omnibus House wilderness bill paralleling S. 837, and there was little activity in the House until the Senate bill came to it for approval in June 1984. Two minor bills, H.R. 663 and H.R. 4537, were introduced but were never acted upon. Instead, the eight representatives were kept apprised of the progress of the Senate legislation and were actively involved in determining the wilderness boundaries within their own congressional districts. They also had a hand in determining the scope of the overall bill and in setting the policies to be incorporated in the bill for identifying the wilderness lands and releasing the nonwilderness areas.

Nothing of record happened from September 30, 1983, until March 6, 1984, when the entire Washington delegation unveiled a new 1 million acre proposal. Yet during those five months, a great deal had transpired at the staff level. Each representative had a key legislative staffer who, among other legislative duties, was responsible for tracking S. 837, filtering and responding to letters about it, and lobbying on the subject. The House and Senate staffers, both on personal staff and committee staff, had been busy meeting with interest groups and agencies, spending hours on the telephone and preparing maps. Gorton's small conference room was dubbed the "Wilderness War Room" and was strewn with letters, maps, and other documents.

On January 26, 1984, the 10-member congressional delegation met for the first time since Senator Jackson's death. They gave themselves five weeks to develop a proposal to flesh out S. 837. On February 6 the two senators released "discussion-only" maps delineating some 877,000 acres of wilderness, then they went back to Washington State to absorb comments and criticisms during the 12-day congressional recess beginning February 10. The senators and representatives then held two private negotiating sessions on February 29 and March 6 to settle the unresolved boundary and area disputes, while lobbyists, reporters, and staff hovered outside the "War Room" office in the Capitol building. In the words of one participant, "It truly was an extraordinary effort, when you consider that eight House Members and two Senators met for nearly 10 hours of uninterrupted time, poring over maps, trying to understand the timber values and the wilderness values involved" (Rep. Don Bonker, *Congressional Record*, June 18, 1984, at H5974). At 8 P.M. on March 6, "after well over four hours, members paraded into the hallway sporting relieved grins" (Anderson 1984, p. A-21). They had reached consensus on the Washington State Wilderness Act.

The March 6 compromise was a remarkable document for what it contained and how it was created. The delegation ignored Secretary Block's entreaties to keep the bill at 229,000 acres. It rejected interest group demands that all 2.5 million roadless acres become wilderness. The wilderness release provisions proved to be a major stumbling block, but Senator McClure, who chaired the Energy and Natural Resources Committee, and his House counterpart, Rep. John Seiberling of Ohio, hammered out a compromise agreement that all sides from Washington could live with.

After the delegation had agreed on the million acre compromise, subsequent approval by the Senate committee, then by the full Senate and the House, was anticlimactic. Seiberling and McClure respected the prevailing congressional doctrine of concurring with whatever wilderness proposal a state's delegation could agree on and moved to report the affected bill out of their respective committees. There was a hue and cry from interest groups and the administration. John Crowell, the USDA assistant secretary in charge of the national forests, denounced the delegation's plan for its "outrageously excessive acreage" (Connelly and Torvik 1984). Sawmill owners labeled it catastrophic; environmentalists pronounced it grossly inadequate. Rep. Thomas Foley later noted that, "...no single member of our delegation—and more importantly, no particular interest group—is completely satisfied with the provisions of the legislation" (*Congressional Record*, June 18, 1984, at H5976).

On May 2, 1984, the Senate Energy Committee approved the revision of the original S. 837 and sent it to the full Senate for consideration. The committee also generated a report to accompany the revised bill (Senate Report 98-461). On May 24 the full Senate gave the nod to the Washington State Wilderness Act by voice vote and sent it to the House of Representatives.

The bill breezed through the House committee and subcommittee that had jurisdiction. On June 7, 1984, Representative Seiberling's Public Lands subcommittee held a short hearing on S. 837. The eight Washington State representatives sat shoulder to shoulder before the subcommittee and lauded the bill. The subcommittee speedily approved S. 837 without any changes, as did the full House Interior Committee on June 13. On June 18 the full House took up S. 837 directly under a special rule, and a parade of representatives embraced the bill. Every member of the Washington delegation trumpeted praise for the bill, for how it was assembled, and for the spirit of compromise: "...everyone lost a little, but gained a lot. And that was our goal." (Anderson 1984, p. A-21).

Members hailed S. 837 as "an excellent example of how good environmental policy and good economic policy go hand in hand" (Rep. Nick Lowry at H5973) and "a fair and balanced proposal that strikes a delicate compromise between the widely divergent views held by both the public and the delegation on this issue" (Rep. Al Swift at H5975).

President Reagan signed S. 837 into law without ceremony on July 3, 1984. The Washington State Wilderness Act expanded four existing wilderness areas and created 18 new ones, for a total of 1.03 million acres of new wilderness. It also created a new Mount Baker National Recreation Area, designated a North Cascades Scenic Highway area, and effected some miscellaneous land exchanges and other public lands housekeeping measures.

This Washington wilderness example shows how different official and unofficial policymakers helped shape and pass the act. The U.S. Forest Service, in the executive branch of the federal government, tried to identify wilderness areas nationally through the RARE II process. The state of California successfully challenged this process in court, so Congress had to designate new state wilderness areas state by state. The Washington congressional delegation worked for more than a year on the state wilderness bill, with input from constituents, lobbyists, loggers, and environmentalists. The personal congressional staff resolved many of the earlier issues. Then the two senators and eight representatives (five Republicans, five Democrats, ranging from conservative to liberal) met in a closed room without staff to set the final wilderness boundaries. The bill then zipped through both congressional resource committees and both houses. At least in this case, the political process worked quite well, although *both* forest products and environmental interest groups called the result "unacceptable" and "a catastrophe." So perhaps it really was a reasonable legislative compromise.

RAISE AND ALLOCATE FUNDS

Raising Revenues

Legislatures raise and allocate money. Government revenues may come from personal and corporate income taxes, use taxes, excise taxes, debt financing (borrowing), the sale of assets such as land and timber, and other sources. The largest source of federal revenue—the personal income tax—was not authorized until 1913 by the Sixteenth Amendment to the Constitution. Corporate income taxes are levied on the profits of business enterprises that range from large integrated forest products firms to small boating marinas. Social insurance taxes fund the social security and worker's compensation programs. Federal surcharges on hunting and fishing equipment, most of which are then divided among the states, are examples of excise taxes. Sales of lands and buildings represent a small share of federal income today, but they were important in the early years of the United States and were targeted by President Reagan as a possible means of generating additional revenue. U.S. Treasury bills (T-bills) and U.S. savings bonds are the best-known federal borrowing mechanisms, but there are many others. In fiscal year 1990 the total federal budget outlays were $1252 billion. Receipts were $1032 billion, leaving a deficit of $220 billion. For the total budget, 37 percent of federal revenues came from individual income taxes, 8 percent from corporate income taxes, 30 percent from social insurance taxes, 3 percent from excise taxes, 18 percent from borrowing, and 4 percent from other sources (Internal Revenue Service 1990).

Annual budget expenditures for the U.S. Forest Service during the 1980s averaged about $2 billion. Most revenue came from general congressional appropriations, but the Forest Service averaged about $1 billion in income from timber sales, grazing leases, royalties from mining and oil leases, user fees, concessionaire payments, and the like; most of this money was returned to the U.S. Treasury (Figure 6-1). Other natural resource agencies, such as the National Park Service and the Fish and Wildlife Service, also generate some funds from user fees and concessionaires, who provide lodging, meals, and other services on federal lands.

All federal agencies, including the Forest Service, rely primarily on congressional appropriations for ongoing program support. This policy of Congress's appropriating funds and agencies' returning revenues to the general treasury seems inconsistent. But it may prevent public agencies from focusing excessively on obtaining revenues from market commodities, at the expense of other services. For example, the Knutson-Vandenburg Act of 1930 requires timber purchasers to pay a share of the sale costs into a fund that is used directly for regeneration and

may be used for wildlife and recreation management and national forest administration. O'Toole (1988) charges that the direct payment of K-V funds to the Forest Service has distorted agency policies, leading to below-cost sales and support of timber harvests even by such unlikely groups as wildlife specialists and recreation managers, who stand to receive a share of the sale amount. This perceived problem is consistent with the general public choice literature discussed in Chapter 3.

States obtain revenue from personal and corporate income taxes, sales taxes, gambling and lottery shares, and property taxes. State or local governments also may receive transfer payments from the federal government. Property taxes and sales taxes generally are the largest revenue sources for county and local governments and are used to provide schools, roads, water, and other public services. In counties with large proportions of forest land and few people, therefore, forest landowners will bear much of the local tax burden, although fewer services are likely to be required. Counties with national forest lands in them receive 25 percent of the proceeds from the sale of national forest timber. These are termed *payments in-lieu-of-tax* and are meant to replace the property taxes that the federal government does not have to pay. For counties in which timber sales are infrequent, there is a formula whereby in-lieu-of-tax transfer payments are made. These transfer payments are major points of contention in national forest timber sale policies.

Some states have large personal and corporate income taxes, particularly some northeastern and midwestern states. Others, including Connecticut, New Hampshire, Florida, Texas, and Washington have little or no personal income taxes. Many states have recently begun to rely on gambling or lottery sales to generate revenue that may be targeted for special programs such as education or fish and wildlife. Sales taxes on consumer goods are important in most states, and some states have options for local governments to add their own sales tax, which may be targeted to pay for specific projects.

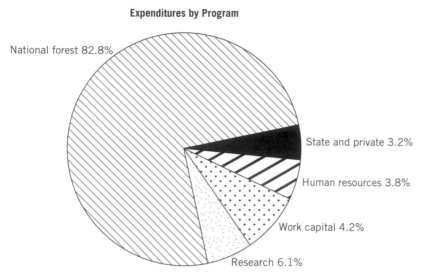

Expenditures by Program

National forest 82.8%

State and private 3.2%

Human resources 3.8%

Work capital 4.2%

Research 6.1%

Total expenditures: $2,078 million

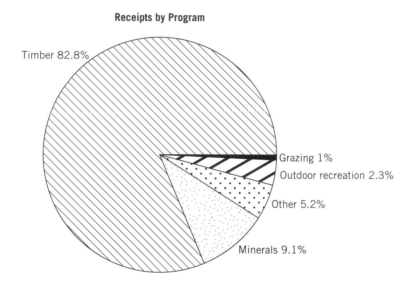

Receipts by Program

Timber 82.8%

Grazing 1%

Outdoor recreation 2.3%

Other 5.2%

Minerals 9.1%

Total receipts: $1,320 million

Figure 6-1. U.S. Forest Service Expenditures and Receipts, 1986
Source: USDA Forest Service 1987

Federal agencies rely principally on congressional appropriations for expenditures. Funding for state forestry programs, however, comes from a variety of sources (Figure 6-2). In 1987 state appropriations comprised 69 percent of total funding for state forestry programs. Revenue from timber, seedling, and other sales comprised about 9.5 percent of state revenue sources. Other governments, mostly counties, provided 3.5 percent of the revenue, mostly from assessments for fire protection. Federal cost-shares to the states comprised about 4 percent of state forestry programs. Expenditures for state programs included fire control (61 percent), state forest management (11 percent), cooperative

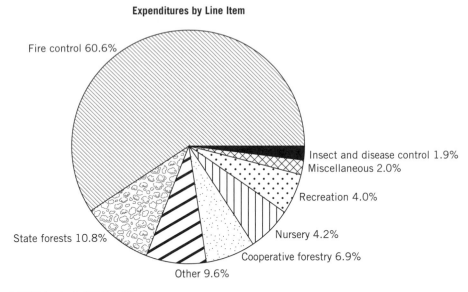

Total 1987 budget: $853 million

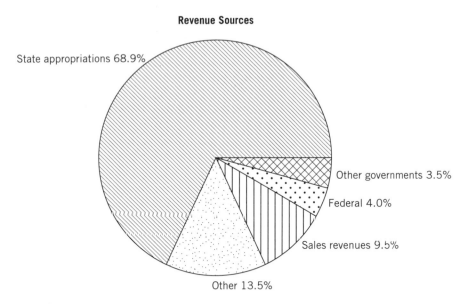

Total: $808 million

Figure 6-2. Total of All 50 State Forestry Program Expenditures and Revenue Sources, 1987
Source: Cubbage and Lickwar 1988

forestry (7 percent), nurseries and recreation (4 percent each), and insect and disease control (2 percent) (Cubbage and Lickwar 1988).

Taxation spawns a host of issues regarding revenue generation at all levels of government. Issues relevant to forest resources are discussed in more detail in subsequent chap-

ters. Put simply, most of the taxation issues concern whether particular kinds of taxes are effective at raising revenue, reasonably easy to administer and collect, and equitable for most taxpayers. Innumerable books and articles have been written on the effectiveness, incidence, and equity of taxes, as well as other means of generating revenue. Among others, texts by Musgrave and Musgrave (1984), Simons (1938), and Singer (1976) are standard references.

Appropriating Expenditures

Most public programs first must be authorized by a law, and then funded by an appropriation of revenue. Congress and state legislatures generally authorize an ongoing level of expenditures for a public program in its enabling legislation. In a separate action, legislatures must actually appropriate the funds for such programs. In fiscal year 1990, 20 percent of the $1.25 trillion appropriated federal budget was spent on social security payments; 24 percent on national defense; 15 percent on interest on debt; 12 percent on low-income assistance programs (unemployment, food stamps, housing assistance); 8 percent on Medicare; 5 percent on other health programs; 3 percent on education and social services; 5 percent on commerce and housing; and 8 percent on other programs (Internal Revenue Service 1990).

The distinction between authorization and appropriation is significant. For example, when Congress established the National Park Service in 1916, the authorizing legislation stated the purposes of national park management and directed the secretary of the Department of the Interior to achieve those purposes. Each year Park Service officials must request appropriations from Congress in order to manage the national parks.

In the enabling legislation, Congress generally authorizes a maximum amount of funds or calls for such funds as necessary to operate the program. However, an authorization of expenditures does not require that funds actually be appropriated. Most programs are authorized at levels far exceeding the eventual appropriations Congress gives them. Authorizing a program through legislation is only the first step in enacting favorable public policies; achieving adequate, stable funding (appropriations) is equally important and often more difficult.

With most federal natural resource programs, the appropriations process is a continual concern. In fiscal year 1990 pollution con-

trol programs, water resources development, and public lands management accounted for only $17 billion, or 1.36 percent of the total federal budget (Internal Revenue Service 1990).

In the early 1980s and early 1990s, natural resource agencies were threatened with significant budget reductions, for several reasons. First, increasing federal deficits prompted close scrutiny of all appropriations. Second, the annual appropriations bills must be approved by the president. The Reagan and Bush administrations did not place high priorities on natural resource programs. Third, and perhaps most significant, a large share of the natural resource agency budgets is relatively easy to cut in the budget process. Payments for social security, interest on the national debt, and the costs of social programs are impossible to change without new enabling legislation. The bulk of the budgets for natural resource agencies may be reduced without new legislation. Le Master (1982, 1984) stated that 71% of the Forest Service budget was controllable in the early 1980s, making it a prime target for the president's Office of Management and Budget federal budget reductions. The National Park Service, Fish and Wildlife Service, Soil Conservation Service, and Environmental Protection Agency have been equally beleaguered by budget cutting. So have state natural resource programs. Even when natural resource budgets are not reduced, they seem to have increased less than those of defense and social programs.

Illustration: Funding State Forestry, Fisheries, and Wildlife Programs

State forestry, fisheries, and wildlife programs are funded by several sources. State forestry programs are funded mostly by state appropriations, federal cost-shares, timber and seedling sales revenue, and other sources. Fish and wildlife programs receive most of their funding from hunting and fishing license revenues, and a lesser amount from state appropriations. Distribution to the states from federal excise taxes on hunting and fishing equipment provides funds for wildlife programs. Nongame programs often are supported in part by state income tax checkoff programs.

In order to determine whether state and federal budgetary problems have adversely impacted state natural resource programs, several studies have been conducted. For state forestry programs, Cubbage and Lick- war (1988) found that total state forestry budgets increased substantially in nominal dollar terms from 1978 to 1987. But taking out the effect of inflation, forestry budgets appear only to have been stable, at best (Figure 6-3). Significant regional differences were masked by national averages. Forestry bud-

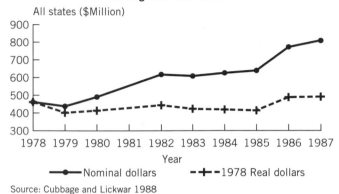

**State Forestry Program Budgets
funding from 1978 to 1987**

All states ($Million)

Source: Cubbage and Lickwar 1988

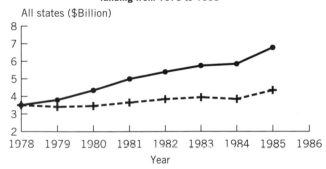

**State Natural Resource Budgets
funding from 1978 to 1985**

All states ($Billion)

Source: Cubbage and Lickwar 1988

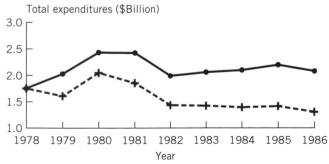

**U.S. Forest Service Budgets
funding from 1978 to 1986**

Total expenditures ($Billion)

Source: USDA Forest Service 1981–1986

Figure 6-3. Budget Trends for Selected Natural Resource Program Areas

gets increased the most in the South, with only Louisiana reporting funding declines in budgets over the time period. Both Oregon and Washington had declining budgets in the 10-year period. In the Northeast, Maine and Massachusetts experienced budget declines from 1978 to 1987.

Total forestry program budgets constituted a shrinking portion of total natural resource and total state budgets from 1978 to 1986. However, they fared better than did the Forest Service in the federal appropriations process from 1978 to 1986 (see Figure 6-3).

A report by the Wildlife Conservation Fund of America analyzed revenues received by state agencies for fish and wildlife programs from 1979 to 1986 (Williamson 1987). During that period, state fish and wildlife program revenues increased 88%, from $612 million to $1,152 billion. As shown in Figure 6-3, total state forestry funding during this period increased 76%, from $439 million to $808 million. Thus it appears that total fish and wildlife funding increased at a slightly greater rate than forestry programs.

Differences in funding sources between wildlife and forestry programs are interesting. Hunting and fishing license fees were $615 million in 1986; state forestry sales revenues, private contributions, and other non-appropriated income totaled only $202 million. State appropriations for fish and wildlife programs increased substantially from 1979 to 1986, from $57 million to $162 million. So did forestry program appropriations, increasing from $289 million to $517 million from 1978 to 1987. Total state forestry program appropriations still were more than three times greater than state fish and wildlife program appropriations.

Federal wildlife payments to the states— financed largely by excise taxes on hunting and fishing equipment—increased to $797 million in 1986; forestry federal cost-share funding dropped to only about $33 million by 1986. State wildlife agencies also benefited from state income tax checkoff programs, which rose from $89 million in 1979 to $155 million in 1986. On the other hand, revenues for state forestry agencies from other governments (mostly counties) dropped from $54 million to $26 million. In general, these trends suggest that funding increases for general natural resource and for specific wildlife programs have outpaced those for forestry, perhaps due to, among other reasons, a broader base of creative funding mechanisms, more telling interest group support, and greater perceived needs.

Developing Budgets

A review of the congressional budget process sheds some light on the particular problems faced by natural resource agencies as their budgets are impacted in the continual effort to reduce federal budget deficits. The federal budget begins with the president's budget message to Congress each January, published as the Economic Report of the president. The president's budget is based on program requests from each federal agency, which are revised (usually downward) by the president's Office of Management and Budget. The president's budget is then sent to Congress and parceled out to the 13 subcommittees of the Appropriations Committees in the House and Senate for extensive hearings and close scrutiny.

The modern congressional budget process was established by the Congressional Budget and Impoundment Control Act of 1974. The act was intended to facilitate completion of the annual budget by the beginning of the federal fiscal year on October 1, to further congressional budget research expertise, and to prevent the president from impounding (refusing to spend) appropriated funds, as president Nixon had done in the early 1970s. The schedule of actions required by the 1974 act is summarized in Table 6-1 (Lee and Johnson 1983). Congress develops the budget through a series of actions required by both houses, with final budget approval by September 25. After some success in the mid 1970s, trying to reconcile the revenues and expenses in both houses by that deadline has proven unattainable, so Congress often passes continuing resolutions after October 1 that allow the federal government to operate (with no increases in funding) until a budget bill finally is enacted.

TABLE 6-1.   1974 Congressional Budget and Impoundment Control Act Budget Process Timetable

On or before	Action to be completed
November 10	President submits current services budget
Fourteenth day after Congress convenes in January	President submits budget
March 15	Committees and joint committees submit reports to budget committees
April 1	Congressional Budget Office submits report to budget committees
April 15	Budget committees report first concurrent resolution on the budget to their houses
May 15	Committees report bills and resolutions authorizing new budget authority
May 15	Congress completes action on first concurrent resolution on the budget
Seventh day after Labor Day	Congress completes action on bills and resolutions providing new budget authority and new spending authority
September 15	Congress completes action on second required concurrent resolution on the budget
September 25	Congress completes action on reconciliation bill or resolution, or both, implementing second required concurrent resolution
October 1	Fiscal year begins

Source: Lee and Johnson 1983

Federal budget deficits increased throughout the 1980s and early 1990s. Deficits had long been a matter of general concern (a systemic agenda item), but their large increases led to specific agenda proposals in the early 1980s and again in 1992 to balance the budget, such as a constitutional amendment or giving the President an item veto. Many analysts feared that massive federal deficits would cause inflation, create excessive federal borrowing demands that would crowd out corporate borrowing for investments, and lead to other problems with the U.S. economy. Deficits averaged more than $200 billion each year, and the total U.S. debt reached about $3.4 trillion by 1991. Additionally, the United States began relying more heavily on foreign countries to finance the debt. In 1981 the U.S. was the world's largest creditor nation, owning net foreign assets of almost $150 billion. By 1989 it had borrowed so much to finance the deficit that it was the largest debtor na-

tion, owing more than $650 billion to other countries.

These problems in the early 1980s led to passage of the Balanced Budget and Emergency Deficit Control Act of 1985, commonly known as Gramm-Rudman-Hollings, or Gramm-Rudman, after its sponsors. Gramm-Rudman was designed to gradually reduce the additions to the federal budget deficit to zero by fiscal year 1991. Maximum allowable annual deficits were initially to be $171.9 billion in fiscal year 1986, $144 billion in 1987, $108 billion in 1988, $72 billion in 1989, $36 billion in 1990, and zero in 1991. Congressional amendments adopted in 1987 set more lenient targets, delaying the date for achieving a balanced budget until 1993, and allowing a fiscal year 1990 deficit of $110 billion, and a 1991 deficit of $64 billion.

Deficit reduction under Gramm-Rudman is complex. The budget authority is changed. If deficit goals are not met, the General Accounting Office (GAO)—a part of Congress—was to make across-the-board cuts, called *sequestrations*, in all eligible programs. However, only about one-third of the federal budget, including almost all natural resource programs, is subject to cuts. Much of the defense budget, interest payments, social security payments, poverty programs, state unemployment, and other expenditures are exempt.

In 1986 the Supreme Court ruled that congressional delegation of the across-the-board cuts to GAO was unconstitutional because it violated the separation of powers between the legislative and executive branches—but Congress was still bound by the yearly deficit targets, albeit voluntarily. In September 1987 Congress passed new legislation as a rider to the debt ceiling bill; this act delegated responsibility for the across-the-board cuts to the president's Office of Management and Budget, which was deemed constitutional.

As of fiscal year 1990, the Gramm-Rudman targets were met in passing the budget, albeit with difficulty and some creative accounting. However, the actual deficits usually were much greater than those forecast in the budget process, and some large expenditures such as the savings and loan bailout and the war with Iraq were not counted. Gramm-Rudman was amended in 1990, and separate deficit targets were set for domestic, defense, and international budget expenditures. Despite many changes, Gramm-Rudman theoretically was still binding as of 1991, but Congress never met the targets—deficits exceeded $350 billion by fiscal year 1992.

The vulnerability of federal natural resource programs to large budget cuts under Gramm-Rudman has caused considerable concern to forestry and environmental interest groups, and they have lobbied continually to preserve federal appropriations for conservation programs. Seven environmental interest groups—Environmental Safety, Defenders of Wildlife, National Parks and Conservation Association, National Wildlife Federation, Sierra Club, the Wilderness Society, and the U.S. Public

Interest Research Group—responded to proposed Gramm–Rudman cuts with an issue paper on "The Environmental Solution to the Deficit Dilemma." They proposed eliminating unnecessary natural resource expenses, including national forest road construction, uranium enrichment programs, and Army Corps of Engineers water projects. They also proposed closing environmentally destructive tax loopholes, taxing pollution, and encouraging conservation (Environmental Safety et al. 1986).

The 1990 amendments to Gramm-Rudman required that spending increases be directly offset by spending decreases. Thus natural resource budget raisers will need nonresource budget offsets, and vice versa. This explicit competition has led some to begin referring to the search for offsets as "the shark tank" (Hill and Rockwell 1991). This debate over budget deficits is sure to dominate federal natural resource policy, and affect state policy, for years.

States have budgeting problems too. Most state constitutions forbid deficit financing, so a budget deficit is illegal. This leads to difficulty in finding funding for ongoing and new programs when projected state revenues fall. Periodic national recessions in the 1980s and early 1990s and curtailment of many federal spending programs created great problems for states, including significant reductions in natural resource program budgets, hiring freezes, and closing of some park facilities.

OVERSIGHT

In addition to enacting laws, raising revenues, and appropriating funds, legislatures also possess oversight powers. *Oversight* is the power of review, and implies the ability to ensure that policies and programs are carried out correctly. Legislatures enact laws; executive agencies implement them. Congress frequently holds oversight hearings to review programs or policies, to gather information for future use, or to elicit action by the executive branch. Oversight hearing can be distinguished from many other legislative hearings, which usually are held to solicit comments to be used in preparing a specific bill (Tarnapol 1986), although they too may be used for oversight. Oversight hearings may lead to changes in the enabling legislation or in the administrative rules that often are enacted subsequent to broad congressional legislation. Oversight also occurs at the state and local level.

Natural resources agencies sometimes participate in oversight hearings and investigations in Washington. Hearings have occurred on the nation's forest management and research needs, log export and clear-cutting policies, Department of the Interior mineral and oil leases, and Environmental Protection Agency programs, to mention a few. Special bipartisan commissions have held oversight hearings on social security, public lands, outdoor recreation, and timber resources in the last three decades. Each of these has eventually led to new policies and legislation by Congress.

The General Accounting Office, which audits federal agencies and analyzes program cost-effectiveness, serves as one of the principal oversight branches of Congress and continually prepares evaluations and presents reports on the implementation of natural resource programs. The Congressional Research Service, which provides analysis and evaluation of legislation, as well as bibliographic, research, and speech writing services, can play a role in oversight hearings. The Office of Technology Assessment helps with legislation and oversight functions, and in the 1980s it prepared reports on the competitiveness of the forest products industry, tropical deforestation, and biological diversity.

LIMITATIONS

The legislative branch obviously has significant powers. However, as with the other branches of government, its actions are checked by its two partners in the policy process—the executive and judicial branches—and by specific provisions in the U.S. Constitution.

Constitutional

The Constitution expressly prohibits Congress from many actions. Article I states that Congress must not suspend the right of *habeas corpus* (protection against imprisonment without a just cause or a trial), nor pass an *ex post facto* law (one that would make something illegal retroactively). Exports from one state to another cannot be taxed by the federal government nor can states tax imports from other states.

The Bill of Rights—the first 10 amendments to the Constitution—places significant limits on congressional authority and is crucial in natural resources law. These 10 amendments guarantee freedom of speech, of the press, and of people to assemble. These fundamental principles have allowed massive public involvement in American politics. Based on the need for a well-regulated militia, the Second Amendment grants the right to keep and bear arms—leading to continual issues about gun control that affect wildlife management and public safety. The Bill of Rights also prohibits quartering soldiers in homes, unreasonable searches, requiring testimony against oneself, and cruel and unusual punishment.

The Fifth Amendment may affect natural resources legislation more than any other. It states that no person shall "be deprived of life, liberty, or property, without due process of law; nor shall private property be taken for public use without due compensation." This is referred to as the "taking clause" and is the crux of the issue of how far states can go in regulating private landowners' actions for public benefits. The Fifth Amendment also is applied to the states through the Fourteenth Amendment, which declares that states cannot deprive any person of life, liberty, or property without due process of law. The natural resource applications of these regulatory limits are discussed in detail in Chapter 14.

Judicial

Congress and the state legislatures are limited by court rulings on the constitutionality of the laws they enact. Under the doctrine of judicial review, federal courts may review legislation enacted by Congress to determine whether it complies with the strictures of the U.S. Constitution. State courts perform a similar function with state laws and constitutions. State laws also may be reviewed by federal courts if they conflict with federal constitutional provisions. Such cases must be brought to court by plaintiffs before courts can rule on their constitutionality. Many laws governing natural resource use have been subjected to judicial review, including state forest practice acts and local land use zoning laws.

Courts limit legislatures and influence policy by their interpretation of laws and agency implementation. Congress, in particular, tends to enact broad enabling legislation that allows various interpretations of intent. Incrementalism and consensus-building approaches to policy promote abstract legislative language that produces less conflict than specific rules written as law. Once enabling legislation is enacted, writing the specific rules and administrative statutes is usually delegated to administrative agencies. For example, Congress adopted general enabling language in the National Forest Management Act of 1976 and left the development of specific rules to the Forest Service. Groups dissatisfied with administrative action and rule making often bring suit; it is up to the courts to determine if the agency's actions are consistent with legislative intent based on the wording of the law, congressional debates, and public testimony in the legislative record.

Executive

Executive veto, or more commonly the threat of veto, also may limit legislative action. The president can veto any bill, but only the entire bill. This often has led Congress to attach riders (unrelated statutes) to major legislation that already meets with presidential approval or would be embarrassing for the president to veto. For example, the Forestry Incentives Act was attached as an amendment (Title 10) to the general farm bill—the Agriculture and Consumer Protection Act of 1973. Catch-all omnibus spending bills, which appropriate funds for a huge number of programs, have become the norm in recent (Democratic-controlled) congressional sessions, making it more difficult for the (Republican) president to use the veto.

Many state governors have authority to use a line-item veto, which allows them to delete any line or portion of a bill, including appropriations. This makes a governor's powers to prevent undesirable legislation or funding much greater than the president's. A line-item presidential veto has been proposed, but many people fear that it would upset the balance of power between the executive and legislative branches. Furthermore, the enactment of such legislation by a Democratic Congress with a Republican president is politically unlikely, beacuse it might be used to eliminate individual legislator's pork barrel projects.

The desire of the relevant executive agency to carry out the law is another limit on legislative action. If an agency is adverse to, or even mildly dilatory in, implementing a law, legislative intent may be stymied. Recall that policy constitutes a course of action over time. If Congress enacts a law that the president opposes, implementation is apt to be uninspired. But if a law is consistent with the interests and policy goals of an agency, implementation will be aggressive. Although unenthusiastic agencies may impede implementation, such intransigence has limits, because the legislature can use its oversight and budget powers to force implementation. Interest groups have effectively brought suits to force agency compliance with laws. Examples include the implementation of the Endangered Species Act by the U.S. Fish and Wildlife Service in the case of the northern spotted owl and the National Marine Fisheries Service in the case of salmon in the Columbia and Snake rivers.

LEGISLATIVE PROCESS

The steps in the legislative process—how a bill becomes a law—are described in most introductory political science textbooks. It is useful to review them briefly before discussing legislative organization. The process at the national level is illustrated in Figure

6-4. A senator, representative, or group of Congress members first introduces a similar bill into the Senate, the House, or both. To reach this stage, a problem must have gained the attention of the legislators, through efforts of either constituents or interest groups, or through the issue expansion process.

Upon being introduced in one or both houses, the bill is referred to one or more standing committees. The committee may refer the bill to a subcommittee, especially in the House of Representatives. If the bill is taken seriously, the subcommittee will review it, probably hold hearings, and report the original or an amended version of the bill back to the full committee. If passed by the full committee, possibly with more changes, the bill will be reported out for floor action by the entire House or Senate. House bills must go to the Rules Committee, which sets the conditions for floor debate (e.g., length of time for debate and whether amendments can be offered).

The American Pulpwood Association (1981) provided its members with an overview of the legislative process, which is an indication of its importance in forestry. The association's handbook clearly describes what happens when a bill is reported out of committee (p. 25–26).

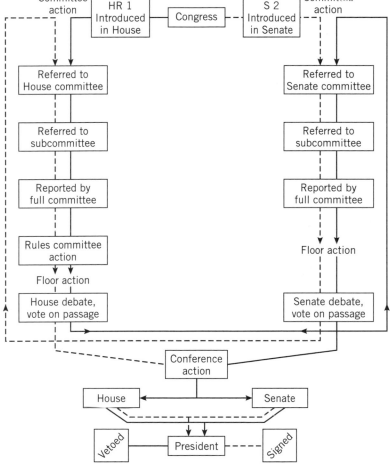

Figure 6-4. The Legislative Process
Source: Congressional Quarterly Almanac, 1984.

A committee report usually sets forth the problem which is to be met by the proposed legislation. It then gives an explanation of the various sections of the bill and any amendments, together with their relation to existing law. Highlights of testimony and reasons for adoption of the bill may or may not be stated. A Minority Report of arguments against part or all of the bill may be presented when the committee report is given to the House or to the Senate. The Bill and its Committee Report is then processed and given a number, and copies are made available to Members of Congress and to the public.

Bills reported to the Senate automatically go to the Senate Calendar of Business. They may be called up for action out of order by unanimous consent. Large numbers of non-controversial bills are also disposed of on call of the Calendar. On these bills, Senators may be recognized for no more than five minutes. No roll call votes are taken and such bills are passed "without objection."

In the House the much larger volume of bills handled requires a complicated system of Calendars. All House reported bills go first to one of three Calendars: Union (tax or expense bills); House (public bills) or Private (personal claims for aid). Non-controversial House or Union bills may also be placed on the Unanimous Consent Calendar for fast action. A bill gets on the Discharge Calendar only when a majority of the House petitions to take it away from a committee that is not giving it due consideration.

A motion to consider a bill is the procedure most used to bring important legislation to the floor for debate. Senators may speak for hours against it, a device sometimes used to delay or prevent action (filibuster). If there is agreement, the bill becomes pending business and debate starts. Senators may speak as long and as often as they please, but not more than twice on the same subject in a single legislative day. Currently it takes a vote of 60 Senators to stop a filibuster.

The rules under which the House operates do not permit extended debate. When debate is finally permitted, the opening statement is usually made by the member in charge of the bill. Thereafter any committee amendments are considered first and then amendments from the floor may be presented and debated.

Each house may pass or defeat the bill on the floor, again after revising the legislation as it deems best. Either a roll call or a voice vote is adequate; a simple majority of voting members will pass the bill. If the versions of the bill passed by the two houses are not identical, a conference committee will be convened to try to resolve the differences. The conference committee is composed of key members of the standing committees or subcommittees that initially considered the legislation. Again, the American Pulpwood Association (1981) summarized the remainder of the process (p. 26).

The number of conferees from each house may vary from three to any larger number and there does not need to be the same number from each house, since they do not vote as a body, but as separate units trying to reach a compromise. If they fail to agree, the legislation may die in conference committee or a new set of conferees may be appointed. If they agree, each group takes the conference report back to its own house. If both houses approve, then the leaders of both houses sign and the act is sent to the President.

From the time the President receives an act he has ten days to sign or veto it. If he fails to act within ten days, the act becomes law automatically unless Congress has adjourned before the ten days are up. In that case, it does not pass and the procedure is known as a pocket veto. When the President actually vetoes an act, it is returned with a message of explanation to the house where it originated. A two-thirds vote of both houses is necessary to override the President's veto.

State legislation generally follows a similar process, although specifics vary considerably. Committees and subcommittees are less numerous in some states. In some northeastern states, joint committees composed of members from both houses meet to consider legislation. The sessions are generally much shorter in the states, and only eight states are considered to have professional full-time legislatures. Legislatures in some states—Texas is one example—enact budgets for two years at a time and only meet every other year. Other peculiarities exist from state to state.

LEGISLATIVE ORGANIZATION

Congress is divided into the Senate, with two senators elected at-large from each state, and the House of Representatives, which presently has 435 members. Representation in the House is apportioned according to state population, with each state having at least one representative. Senators are elected every six years, so only one-third run for reelection every two years. Representatives serve two-year terms, so they must run for reelection accordingly. Neither senators nor representatives have limits on the number of terms they may serve, although this was considered and defeated in several state referendums in 1991. Congressional term limits are likely to remain a general agenda item in the 1990s, reflecting a national perception that de facto life-long tenure for Congress members has created problems in government.

The creation of a bicameral (composed of two bodies) Congress reflects a compromise made at the Constitutional Convention in 1787 designed to prevent Congress from being dominated by the most populous states. Each House district has approximately the same number of constituents, averaging about 550,000 people during the 1990s. All state legislatures except Nebraska also have both a Senate and House with the state's Senate districts being larger than those of the House. Since the 1960s one-person one-vote court rulings have mandated that all districts within each legislative body must have representation proportional to population, except for the U.S. Senate.

Most work in Congress is performed by its standing committees and subcommittees (Smith and Deering 1984, Wilson 1885). Most analysis, oversight, and shaping of legislation occurs in committees or subcommittees, where legislators are assisted by personal and committee staff. State legislatures also rely heavily on committees to develop legislation, but in most states, work is performed by individual legislators rather than by full-time committee or personal staff, although the availability of staff varies widely among states.

TYPES OF COMMITTEES

There are four general types of legislative committees. The first, *select committees*, are appointed on an ad hoc basis for special assignments. *Joint standing committees* con-

sider specific recurring issues that are of concern to both houses. For example, Congress has a Joint Committee on Taxation and a Joint Economic Committee. *Conference* and *standing committees*, the other two types of committees, are described in the following sections.

Conference Committees

Often Senate and House bills differ significantly, in terms of both policies established and funding authorized. A separate conference committee is appointed for each bill on which House and Senate versions differ. Conference committee members must develop compromises satisfactory to both houses. Occasionally, the bills differ so markedly that agreement cannot be reached, and the bill dies in conference.

Congressional conference committee decisions have had a significant impact on natural resources. Nominally, all legislation approved in conference must have been included in either the House or Senate version. However, the section of the 1891 general land laws that authorized presidential creation of forest reserves was actually inserted in the conference committee (Dana and Fairfax 1980). Authorization of the reserves eventually led to the establishment of almost 150 million acres of national forests in the West between 1891 and 1907. More recently, conference committee deliberations have played a role in determining whether strict or moderate versions of environmental regulations are enacted and in authorizing funding levels for wildlife and forestry programs.

Standing Committees

Standing committees serve on a continuous basis in each house of the Congress and in most states. Almost all bills are assigned to one or more of the standing committees for review. Standing committees are the workhorses of the legislature; they are crucial in shaping legislation.

FUNCTIONS OF COMMITTEES

Bills sent to a committee usually are referred to a subcommittee for further deliberation and refinement. The subcommittee may hold hearings, a practice customary for most major bills, at which testimony is given by either invited or subpoenaed witnesses. Committees and subcommittees occasionally hold closed hearings, but most are open to the public.

Hearings

Congressional hearings serve many purposes. Their principal purpose is to provide information to members of the legislature or to staff personnel. Hearings are held on most major laws that are considered in Congress, as well as on annual appropriations bills. Committees may hold hearings to exercise legislative oversight over agencies to see if they are administering the law as the legislature intended. Hearings can be held by a full committee, by a subcommittee, or by joint committees of both houses. Sometimes there are simultaneous hearings on the same topic by more than one committee of the House and Senate.

Consistent with the incremental (muddling through) model of politics presented in Chapter 4, vocal advocates are needed to inform decision makers of the consequences of proposed policy changes. Hearings provide an opportunity for those affected by legislation to support or oppose its passage or suggest changes. Hearings convey to legislators technical information about the scientific and physical effects of proposed policies as well as political information—feedback on constituents' or groups' support or opposition. Hearings have been common in forestry issues and legislation. In 1989 Congress held hearings on forest fire policy, management of the Tongass National Forest, old-growth forest reservation, sustained yield, below-cost timber sales, Forest Service road building, the National Forest Management Act, global climate change, and many other forest resource topics.

Hearings also may serve as a propaganda channel through which the committee can reach larger audiences. By holding national or regional hearings, legislators can publicize and promote bills they advocate, expand issues to a larger audience, and gain the support of additional constituents and groups. During consideration of the Wilderness Act, the National Trails Act, and the Wild and Scenic Rivers Act, several national and regional hearings were held to build support for the legislation. In 1984 regional hearings were held to evaluate support for a conservation reserve and agricultural forestation (soil bank) program. Strong support was expressed, and these provisions became part of the Food Security Act of 1985, generally called the farm bill.

Hearings may serve as a safety valve for persons and interest groups. Even if their views are not a determining factor, the opportunity to go on record regarding an issue placates people somewhat because they were involved in the process. The chance to be heard by a legislative committee, coupled with the American tradition of majority rule, encourages losers to comply with the eventual decisions. Hearings also help inform and sensitize people to the views of opposing groups, leading to more informed discussion among advocates of different policies.

Although useful, hearings do have drawbacks. Inaccurate or misleading information is sometimes presented. Hearings are advocacy forums where witnesses present limited information that supports only their side of an issue. Hearings also may convey unrepresentative opinions, reflect committee bias, or represent stagings by the staff, all depending on who is scheduled to testify. Even when attempts to achieve balanced testimony are made, accurate information about the technical consequences of proposed legislation and the desires of the American public are difficult to ascertain. The hearings themselves as well as the voluminous records they produce are expensive as well.

Actions

Legislative committees and subcommittees have several options. They may disregard or pigeonhole bills assigned to their committee. With more than 5000 bills introduced in Congress each year, many share this fate. Only a few hundred become law, and most of these are commemoratives that require no further action or implementation—such as bills proclaiming national days for teachers, farmers, or other groups. Committees may hold hearings but choose not to present the bill to the full body, or they may vote to defeat a bill. Only on rare occasions does a committee accept a bill as written and report it for action on the floor unamended.

Usually, after gathering suggestions and information through hearings, subcommittees meet to consider or "mark-up" the pending legislation. During mark-up, changes and additions are made to the bill's original text through amendments that may be proposed by any member of the subcommittee. Next, the bill goes to the full committee where further revisions may occur. The full committee may approve or "report" the bill and recommend passage, or it may not take any action at all, thus letting the bill die in committee.

Natural Resources

Several House and Senate committees deal with natural resource issues. The National Wildlife Federation (1990, 1991) annually summarizes information on the activities, congressional chairperson, and chief of staff for each.

The Committee on Agriculture in the House and the Committee on Agriculture, Nutrition, and Forestry in the Senate are responsible for general forestry programs, except those dealing with public lands. Cooperative forest management and protection, forestry research, farm programs, and soil conservation legislation all fall under the aegis of the agriculture committees and the Forestry (Senate) and Forest (House) subcommittees.

Forest resource programs directly related to public lands, such as the national forests, national parks, Bureau of Land Management, and Bureau of Indian Affairs, usually are considered by the Committee on Energy and Natural Resources (Senate) and the Committee on Interior and Insular Affairs (House). Important House subcommittees include Public Lands, Mines and Mining, Environmental Pollution, and others. The Committee on Environment and Public Works (Senate) and the

Committee on Public Works and Transportation (House) deal with flood control, water power, federal buildings, and roads. Environmental Pollution, Water Resources, Toxic Substances and Environmental Oversight are important subcommittees. These committees have been responsible for most of the air and water pollution control laws that have affected forest resources.

The House Committees on Education and Labor and on Energy and Commerce influence public and private forestry organizations, as do similar Senate Committees on Labor and Human Services and on Commerce, Science, and Transportation. Business and labor regulations and relations, consumer protection, energy programs, and education all affect the operation of forest products firms in the course of their business. The American Pulpwood Association's (1981) lobbying activities focus more on these committees than on any others.

Both the House and Senate have committees on appropriations, which are crucial in budgeting. The relevant subcommittees hold hearings on budgets for most federal agencies. In recent years the House and Senate Appropriations Committees usually have appropriated more funds for natural resource agencies and programs than recommended by the president's Office of Management and Budget.

The House Ways and Means Committee is responsible for initiating all taxation bills. The capital gains treatment of timber income, reforestation tax credits, and other tax legislation affecting forestry are considered by Ways and Means. Finance is the parallel committee in the Senate, but the Constitution requires that tax bills originate in the House.

Each of these committees deals with significant conservation and forestry legislation. The effectiveness and impact of each committee depends on the importance of particular issues, the strength of constituency and interest group support for legislation, the partisan support for specific bills, the makeup of the committee, and the strength of the committee and subcommittee leaders (Le Master 1984).

CONGRESSIONAL STAFF

Faced with an overwhelming work load and the need for information and specialized expertise in many subjects, Congress members rely heavily on staff support. Malbin (1980) stated that Congress could not function without its large staff and called them "unelected representatives." There are two types of staffs. In general, personal staff are a conduit for constituent interests. Committee staff have the major responsibility for shaping legislation.

Until the 1946 Legislative Reorganization Act, staff positions on standing committees were primarily patronage positions—filled by congressional appointees. The 1946 act authorized the establishment of permanent professional positions for committees and allowed the creation of temporary investigative staff as needed. Employing temporary and permanent committee staff for these positions still depends on a Congress Members' discretion, but the positions themselves are permanent. Many committee staff are retained even when Congress members change. Individual staffers, however, have no permanent job security; they may be fired at will by their Congress member. By the 1970s, the distinction between permanent and temporary committee staff was fuzzy. In addition to majority party leaders, even members of the minority party in Congress were authorized to hire their own committee staff. Between 1973 to 1985 congressional staff jumped from 11,500 to 24,000 (Smith 1988).

The 1946 legislation also prompted the growth of members' personal staffs. Since 1947 total House staff increased over 400 percent, and Senate staff increased almost 600 percent (Malbin 1980). The Congressional Staff Directory and the Advance Locator publish names of congressional staff yearly (Brownson 1985a, 1985b).

Personal

Personal staff are appointed by individual representatives and senators. The size of senators' personal staff varies according to their state's population. In 1989 senators from the least populous states were allocated an annual staff budget of $754,800; California senators were allocated $1,612,773. Each senator from Virginia had about 35 personal staff members, some in Washington, DC, and some in Virginia. Budgets for U.S. representatives' personal staff vary less, because their districts are of similar sizes. In 1989 personnel budgets for House members could not exceed $431,000. As in the Senate, House staff are typically divided between Washington and their home districts. In many state legislatures, elected officials, except for a few legislative leaders, usually do not have permanent paid personal staff. In some states, each legislator may be authorized to have one staffer or may share a secretary with another legislator.

Personal staff perform several functions. Some assist in committee meetings, interact with lobbyists and interest groups, write speeches, and draft bills. Some perform primarily clerical tasks, including constituency services and correspondence. Staff members may visit with constituents who journey to Washington and help resolve constituents' problems (casework) with government agencies; much of this casework is now handled by staffers in the legislator's home district. Correspondence tasks include responding to pressure and opinion mail, requests for information, and opinion ballots, as well as sending letters of congratulation or condolence. A third type of personal staff includes political experts, who are primarily concerned with campaigns and strategies for reelection and are often involved with education and publicity on behalf of the legislator.

These staff positions are strictly patronage positions. Legislative assistants and administrative assistants often have substantial influence on which issues will be addressed by legislators, on the information that they receive, and on how they will vote. As such, staff members are important gatekeepers in setting the legislator's agenda.

Committee

Committee staff are very important in congressional deliberations, perhaps to the point of usurping some authority of elected officials (Malbin 1980). Committee staff positions are partisan, with most appointments made by the majority but some by the minority members of each committee. If the political balance of the house changes or a new committee chair is chosen, committee staff are subject to sudden dismissal. However, such shifts in power are rare, and even committee staff appointed by departing individual legislators often are retained by either their successors or others on the committee. Some committees' staff are less partisan than others. For example, the Joint Committee on Taxation, due to the technical nature of its topic, has a nonpartisan staff that provides credible, reliable information to all its members.

The committee staff perform many important functions. They research topics relevant to the committee or the particular party or legislator they represent, becoming experts in a particular subject area. They organize committee hearings, prepare committee reports, and draft bills and amendments. They help prepare and write conference committee reports. Staff also serve as the committee's principal liaison with both the executive branch and interest groups. Several of the functions staff perform give them great influence in agenda setting as gatekeepers. Many Washington, DC, lobbyists consider committee staff to be the most important legislative contact. Le Master (1984) suggests that staff can function in place of legislators and exert some control over congressional decisions.

Despite their influence, committee staff operate under distinct limitations. Although they are appointed, they must refrain from overt partisan activities, including campaigning for particular delegates or parties. Despite charges of excessive influence, committee staff do represent the committee members and are employed primarily as analysts. As such, they must at least avoid advocating policies and proposals not supported by the committee member to whom they report. Although they may be well known on Capitol Hill, they are expected to be anonymous in their contributions to legislation so that the representatives and senators receive the credit.

INDIVIDUAL LEGISLATORS

The structure of Congress and its committees is crucial in determining the outcomes of legislation. But like all institutions, the activities, styles, and personalities of individual members also are important in determining the policies considered and adopted. Many studies have analyzed the factors that influence legislators' decisions.

INFLUENTIAL FACTORS

Legislators may be influenced by many pressures. External influential factors include elections, interest groups, constituents, the chief executive, and the bureaucracy. Also relevant are forces inside the legislature, including committees, party leadership, and personal and committee staff. After receiving information from all these sources, legislators must exercise their own judgment to arrive at the decision they deem best.

Kingdon (1981) concluded that of the factors influencing legislators, recommendations made by trusted colleagues and constituents have the greatest influence. Because legislators rely most heavily on these sources for voting guidance, other actors in the system, such as lobbyists and administration policymakers, tend to work through these two gatekeeper groups. Kingdon stated that all influences are considered, and often legislators seem to have an informal checklist of forces they consult before arriving at a decision.

Constituent interests are important influences in decision making and voting, but legislators do have considerable latitude. Legislators try to build trust with people in their district, and they oppose constituent preferences only when the issue is particularly important to them or not particularly important to the constituents. Legislators occasionally may vote against the consensus of their constituents without adverse effects. However, a string of roll call votes unpopular with constituents may lead to distrust and loss of support at election time.

Fenno (1978) observed 18 members of the House of Representatives as they visited their home districts to determine how their time was spent with and influenced by constituents. He portrayed constituent relations as a series of concentric circles. A representative's spouse, personal friends, and campaign contributors had the most influence. Next were voters who provided support in the primary election, followed by those in the district from whom support could be expected in a general election. The outer circle encompassed the entire constituency, friend and foe alike. As might be expected, representatives were influenced most by inner circles, and hardly at all by the outer circle of constituents.

ISSUE SELECTION

More than 5000 bills are introduced in Congress each year. No member can possibly become involved in all issues. Committee and subcommittee specialization and congressional staff help individual legislators deal with the vast array of issues. Legislators vie for appointment to committees that are important in Congress, are relevant to their constituents' interests, and deal with timely topics. With seniority comes the opportunity to serve on more influential committees and, for members of the majority party, election to subcommittee and committee chairs.

Like all interest groups, forestry and wildlife interests have been supported by influential legislators. Many of these supporters sponsored legislation that still bears their name. These include the Lacey Act of 1900, which protects fish and wildlife from exploitation; the Weeks Law of 1911, which authorized national forest purchases in the East; the Clarke-McNary (fire prevention) and McNary-McSweeney (forestry research) acts in the 1920s; the McIntire-Stennis Act of 1962, which provides forestry research funds to universities; and the "Packwood Amendment" of 1980, which authorizes tax credits for reforestation. Sen. Charles McNary of Oregon was instrumental in setting the direction for federal policy related to private forests. Sens. John

Stennis, from Mississippi, and Robert Packwood, from Oregon, supported forestry interests throughout the 1980s. Minnesota Sen. Hubert Humphrey consistently supported forestry legislation and appropriations and sponsored the Forest and Rangeland Renewable Resources Planning Act of 1974. State legislators may be even more closely aligned with particular interest groups and often exert considerable influence on legislation and appropriations.

Within the forest policy arena, some legislators have consistently supported legislation favoring timber production, while others support wilderness and parks bills. Rep. Phil Burton from California and Sen. Frank Church from Idaho strongly supported wilderness allocations. Sens. James McClure from Idaho and Packwood from Oregon and Rep. Wayne Aspinall from Colorado consistently supported timber resource and forest products industry development legislation.

Legislators may adopt various strategies in issue selection and may seek to become leaders in controversial areas. Sen. Henry Jackson (environmental laws, foreign policy) from Washington and Rep. Morris Udall (land use, mining) from Arizona epitomized this strategy in the 1970s. Other legislators prefer to avoid controversial issues. They may select low-key issues, try to vote with the majority, and never buck the wishes of their constituents. Such legislators are apt to be less sure of reelection, so try they to work on "safe" issues.

Many legislators seek publicity and prestige through involvement in congressional oversight. Sen. Joseph McCarthy's hearings in the 1950s on communist activities typify such an approach. Sen. Church led hearings on clear-cutting in the 1970s. More recently, in the 1980s and 1990s, Rep. John Dingell from Michigan chaired the Commerce Committee's Oversight and Investigations Subcommittee and gained considerable notoriety for vigorous investigations and criticisms of exorbitant defense contracts and research funding and ethics. He also led investigations into mismanagement of the Environmental Protection Agency, which eventually led to Administrator Anne Burford's being cited for contempt of Congress and resigning from office. Oversight is clearly necessary, and the opportunity to receive national exposure in congressional hearings is alluring to aspirants for reelection or higher office.

Other legislators seem less interested in publicity than in providing services to their constituents and local communities. Southern members of Congress are renowned for their quiet pursuit of federal largesse, such as defense facilities, but they are not unique; westerners are equally adept at lining up water development projects in their districts. Pork barrel politics—bringing home the bacon to local constituents—are pervasive throughout the federal and state legislatures.

ILLUSTRATION: PORK BARREL AND NATIONAL PARKS

The creation of national parks in the 1980s provides a graphic illustration of how the political process creates new policies and how Congress members employ pork barrel projects to the advantage of their home districts. As part of their ideology of privatization (as discussed in Chapter 3) Pres. Ronald Reagan and his first secretary of the interior, James Watt, established an official policy of not creating any new national parks. They believed this would help solve the problem of what they considered to be excessive federal government, and Secretary Watt acted unilaterally to implement lower-lever policies to stop purchases of land for national parks.

Until Reagan became president, nominations for battlefield sites, monuments, seashores, and the 13 other types of units within the purview of the National Park Service (NPS) had to be formally reviewed by an NPS panel that included historians, scientists, and other scholars. Congressional committees overseeing the U.S. Department of the Interior (USDI) have the power to authorize new sites and appropriate money to run them. Congress took the NPS panel evaluation seriously. Reagan, Watt, and Watt's successors as interior secretary opposed spending money to open new sites. So they disbanded the evaluation committee and the NPS did

not recommended a new site for more than a decade. As a result, national park designations were left entirely to Congress (Begley and Hager 1990).

As a result of this policy change, Congress itself authorized and funded about 20 sites, some of rather dubious national significance. These include the Keith-Albee Movie Theater in Huntington, West Virginia, which received $4.5 million with the help of Senator Byrd; and Steamtown, a national historic site in Scranton, Pennsylvania, sponsored by Rep. Joseph McDade. Steamtown was authorized to become a visitors center to display an old-style railroad in 1986, and Congress appropriated $43 million for its restoration in 1990. Congress members provided funds for local constituents to establish the parks and hoped that they would attract tourists and generate more income in these areas. However, even interest groups (such as the National Parks and Conservation Association) who generally support the NPS in general oppose many of these congressional pork barrel projects (Begley and Hager 1990).

Creating new parks of little merit has costs for existing parks. Maintenance and operating funds for truly significant parks have dwindled greatly, and some established facilities have been forced to close, as mentioned in Chapter 5. Additionally, NPS salaries have gotten so low that many park ranger positions go unfilled, and many NPS employees have quit to join state park systems. Perhaps negative publicity will force reform, and pork barrel parks will be a thing of the past, thus enhancing funds for existing facilities. One step in this direction was made in 1991, when the federal government considered a new civil service job series for professional recreation managers for all federal agencies, with reasonable salary grade levels for the employees.

REPRESENTATIVE PHILOSOPHY

When elected to office in the 1700s, British statesman Edmund Burke said, "You choose a member indeed, but not a member of Bristol, but of Parliament." Elected representatives today face the same dilemma—should they support legislation desirable for their constituents, or should they act as they deem best for the broader interests of their state or country when constituent demands and larger interests clash?

A dichotomy between trustees and delegates made by Wahlke et al. (1962) outlines the different philosophies. Trustees follow the course of action they think is right or just and exercise independent judgment. Instead of slavishly following the wishes of their constituents, they may seek to lead their constituents and hope to convince the constituents to agree with them. On the other hand, delegates always follow the course of action dictated by constituents. A problem with acting as a delegate is determining constituents' desires. Few constituents have opinion on many issues, but those few may be extremely vocal and at odds with the silent majority. On other issues, the district may be so heterogeneous and people's opinions may be so mixed that consensus is unattainable. Strength of opinions also is important to the delegate, as is the significance of the group supporting or opposing a program.

Elected officials who act as delegates may be less sure of reelection, and may want to avoid offending constituents. First-year legislators also are more likely to act like delegates than are senior legislators. Senators may act more like delegates near the end of their term as they face reelection than they do shortly after election. Congress members from "safe" districts, who are always elected by wide margins, may be more inclined to act as trustees. Most legislators probably combine the two philosophies, depending on their opinion, the salience of the issue, and the mood of the electorate at the time.

SUMMARY

The legislative branch of the federal government is granted specific, but limited, powers by the U.S. Constitution. Congress generally enacts laws to create or maintain order and safety; to establish frameworks for individual and business interactions; to protect individuals, natural resources, and the public welfare; to ensure equal opportunity for citizens; to provide basic social services for individuals; and for many other purposes. Congress collects revenues through such mechanisms as personal and corporate income taxes, social insurance taxes, excise taxes, and borrowing. Members of Congress appropriate funds for individual programs and agencies. Congress is responsible for administrative oversight to ensure that laws are implemented correctly. Limits on the power of Congress include executive implementation or veto, judicial rulings, and specific constitutional protections contained in the Bill of Rights.

Bills become federal law after first being introduced into and then passed by both houses—the Senate and the House of Representatives. After introduction, bills are referred to a standing committee for further deliberation, hearings, and action, and from there they usually go to a subcommittee. Bills receiving favorable action in committee are reported out for consideration by the entire House or Senate. Differences between House and Senate bills must be resolved by a joint conference committee before being sent to the president for signature or veto.

Individual legislators are aided by personal staff, who assist with legislation, respond to constituent requests, and help Congress members get reelected. Standing committee staff are experts on particular subject matters. They perform research, organize committee meetings, prepare committee reports, draft bills and amendments, and serve as liaisons with interest groups and executive agencies. Legislators are influenced most by trusted colleagues and constituents, and perhaps to some extent, by congressional staff. Lobbyists and administration policymakers tend to work through these sources to achieve their policy goals.

LITERATURE CITED

American Pulpwood Association. 1981. APA Legislative Handbook. Paper 81–A-2. Washington, DC. 46 pp.

Anderson, Ronald A. and Walter A. Kumpf. 1972. Business Law, 9th ed. South-Western Publishing Co. Cincinnati. 918 pp. + appen.

Anderson, Ross. 1984. The Washington wilderness bill. *Seattle Times*, April 15, pp. A-20, A-21.

Begley, Sharon, and Mary Hager. 1990. Pork-barrel politics. *Newsweek* 116(22):60–62, November 26.

Brownson, Charles B. (ed.) 1985a. Congressional Staff Directory Advance Locater. Congressional Staff Directory. Mount Vernon, VA. 443 pp.

Brownson, Charles B. (ed.) 1985b. The Congressional Staff Directory. Mount Vernon, VA. 1201 pp.

Congressional Quarterly. 1984. Congressional Quarterly Almanac. 98th Congress, 2nd session.

Connelly, Joel, and Solveig Torvik. 1984. Reagan signs our wilderness bill. *Seattle Post-Intelligence*, July 4, pp. A-1, A-5.

Cubbage, Frederick W., and Peter M. Lickwar. 1988. Trends in funding state forestry programs. *Journal of Forestry* 86(12):19–25.

Dana, Samuel T., and Sally K. Fairfax. 1980. Forest and Range Policy, 2nd ed. McGraw-Hill. New York. 458 pp.

Environmental Safety, Defenders of Wildlife, National Wildlife Federation, Sierra Club, The Wilderness Society, U.S. Public Interest Research Group. 1986. The environmental solution to the deficit dilemma. mimeo 6 p.

Fenno, Richard R., Jr. 1978. Home Style. Little, Brown. Boston. 304 pp.

Hill, Lawrence W., and H. William Rockwell, Jr. 1991. Policy update—budget balance. *Journal of Forestry* 89(4):7.

Hoban, Thomas M., and Richard O. Brooks. 1987. Green Justice: The Environment and the Courts. Westview Press. Boulder, Co. 250 pp.

Internal Revenue Service. 1990. Your federal income tax for individuals. Publication 17. Department of the Treasury. U.S. Government Printing Office. Washington, DC. 226 pp.

Kingdon, John W. 1981. Congressmen's Voting Decisions, 2nd ed. Harper & Row. New York. 346 pp.

Le Master, Dennis C. 1982. Forest Service funding under RPA. *Journal of Forestry* 80(3):161–163.

Le Master, Dennis C. 1984. Decade of Change. Greenwood Press. Westport, CT. 290 pp.

Lee, Robert D., Jr., and Ronald W. Johnson. 1983. Public Budgeting Systems, 3rd ed. University Park Press. Baltimore, MD. 372 pp.

Malbin, Michael J. 1980. Unelected Representatives: Congressional Staff and the Future of Representative Government. Basic Books. New York. 279 pp.

Musgrave, Richard A., and Peggy B. Musgrave. 1984. Public Finance in Theory and Practice, 4th ed. McGraw-Hill. New York. 824 pp.

National Wildlife Federation. 1990. Conservation Directory 1990. Washington, DC. 343 pp.

National Wildlife Foundation. 1991. Conservation Directory, 36th ed. Washington DC. 380 pp.

O'Toole, Randal. 1988. Reforming the Forest Service. Island Press. Covelo, CA. 247 pp.

Senate Report 98-461. 1984. 98th Congress, 2d Session. Report to accompany S. 837, from the Committee on Energy and Natural Resources. 29 pp.

Siegel, William C. 1982. Forest management and the law. Pp. 339–362 in William A. Duerr et al. (eds.), Forest Resource Management: Decision-Making Principles and Cases. rev. ed. OSU Book Stores. Corvallis, OR. 612 pp.

Simons, Henry C. 1938. Personal Income Taxation—The Definition of Income as a Problem of Fiscal Policy. University of Chicago Press. Chicago. 238 pp.

Singer, Neil M. 1976. Public Microeconomics, 2nd ed. Little, Brown. Boston. 447 pp.

Smith, Hedrick. 1988. The Power Game: How Washington Works. Random House. New York. 793 pp.

Smith, Steven S., and Christopher J. Deering. 1984. Committees in Congress. Congressional Quarterly Press. Washington, DC. 291 pp.

Tarnapol, Paula J. 1986. SAF takes part in oversight hearing. *Journal of Forestry* 84(11) 5–6.

USDA Forest Service. 1982–1987. Report of the Forest Service, Fiscal Years 1981–1986. Washington, DC. U.S. Government Printing Office.

Wahlke, John C., Heinz Eulau, William Buchannan, and Leroy C. Ferguson. 1962. The Legislative System. Wiley. New York. 517 pp.

Williamson, Lonnie L. 1987. State wildlife revenues increase. *Outdoor News Bulletin* 41(20):2–3, October 2. Wildlife Management Institute. Washington, DC.

Wilson, Woodrow. 1885. Congressional Government: A Study in American Politics, 2nd ed. Houghton Mifflin. Boston. 333 pp.

Chapter 7

The Executive Branch

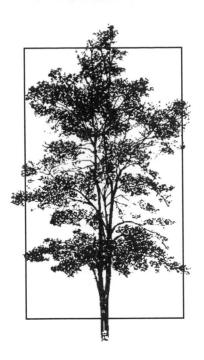

Far better it is to dare mighty things, to win glorious triumphs, even though checkered by failure, than to take rank with those poor spirits who neither enjoy much or suffer much, because they live in the gray twilight that knows not victory or defeat.

—Theodore Roosevelt 1899

THE PRESIDENCY

The executive branch includes the president or governor, executive advisors, and the government agencies that implement laws enacted by Congress or state legislatures. This chapter focuses on the executive branch of the national government. Although the details of executive authority and practice differ among the states, the general principles are similar. Article II of the U.S. Constitution states that "The executive Power shall be vested in a President of the United States of America." The power and influence of presidents has varied greatly among them, as well as within the tenure of individual presidents. Some, including taciturn Calvin Coolidge and muddling Ulysses S. Grant, have shunned expansion of presidential power and influence. Others have sought such power and influence, and some have achieved many of their political objectives. Theodore Roosevelt (TR) dared to make forestry and conservation a centerpiece of his administration, thus chang-

ing the course of U.S. natural resource policy. Franklin D. Roosevelt (FDR) put depression-era unemployed people to work in the national forests and national parks. Richard Nixon unwillingly presided over the greatest expansion of environmental protection and conservation laws since TR. Dwight Eisenhower and Ronald Reagan favored development and use of natural resources.

The strength of the president is probably the principal factor affecting most legislative initiatives during this century. In 1913, Theodore Roosevelt, an activist president and the successful proponent of a host of conservation laws, wrote

My belief was that it was not only his [the President's] right but his duty to do anything that the needs of the Nation demanded unless such action was forbidden by the Constitution or by the laws (p. 357).

Most of TR's successors have agreed with this broad interpretation of the chief executive's authority. Franklin Roosevelt, who was elected president for an unprecedented four terms, reshaped the role of the federal government. His success, and fears that a president could, in fact, become dictatorial, prompted Congress to limit presidents to serve only two terms. Escapades such as Watergate and the Iran-Contra affair reveal that some modern administrations have overlooked even those limitations recognized by TR.

The actual power wielded by a president depends on personality, political skills, economic and social conditions, the distribution of power in Congress, and the president's electoral "mandate" from the people. Presidential policy preferences and interpretation of the appropriate role of government also affect the pursuit and use of power.

POWERS

The Constitution directs the president to "take Care that the Laws be faithfully executed." This implicitly charges the president with administering the laws through a government bureaucracy. Presidents were granted many specific powers for implementing laws and have assumed others.

Appointment

The president appoints cabinet members as well as their top policy-making deputies, ambassadors, consuls, Supreme Court justices, lower federal court judges, and all other officers of the United States whose appointments are not otherwise provided for in the Constitution or by statute. Approximately 7000 federal jobs are subject to presidential appointment. The president may remove as well as appoint most agency heads and ambassadors.

Federal judges are appointed, subject to Senate confirmation, for life terms. Presidents use judicial appointments to pay political debts and to pursue their own policy goals. Careful appointment of judges can lengthen the period of a president's influence on policy. The federal judiciary consisted of 846 members in 1991; 265 Carter appointees remained on the bench—most of whom were liberal Democrats. President Reagan appointed four Supreme Court justices and almost 400 federal judges in the lower courts. By 1991 President Bush had appointed two Supreme Court justices and 94 lower court judges and had 142 vacant positions to fill (Mullins 1991). These appointments will influence public policy long after Reagan's and Bush's terms of office, casting the shadow of their presidencies into the next century. The appointment of conservative jurists by Reagan and Bush has affected environmental law and regulation by suggesting that there definitely are some limits in how much private landowners can be regulated.

Cabinet officers also must be confirmed by the Senate, but thereafter they serve at the pleasure of the president. The appointment of agency heads and their subordinates provides a more direct means for presidents to influence natural resource policy. A comparison between Carter's and Reagan's appointments is revealing. Carter appointed Cecil Andrus as secretary of the interior; Douglas Costle as administrator of the Environmental Protection Agency (EPA); Bob Berglund as secretary of agriculture; and Rupert Cutler as the assistant secretary of agriculture for natural resources and environment, the overseer of the Forest Service and the Soil Conservation Service. All were strong supporters of environmental protection. Under Cutler, a former Wilderness Society official and Michigan State University professor, one of the principal administration initiatives was an unsuccessful attempt to resolve the wilderness issue on national forests through the Roadless Area Review and Evaluation (RARE II) process.

Reagan initially appointed James Watt as secretary of the interior, Anne Gorsuch (who married and became Anne Burford) as head of the EPA, John Block, an Illinois farmer, as secretary of agriculture, and John Crowell as assistant agriculture secretary for natural resources and environment. Watt's principal goal was to increase private businesses' access to federal resources. Burford proved to be a poor enforcer of EPA regulations and was eventually charged with contempt of Congress for failure to carry out EPA programs. Crowell, former legal counsel with Louisiana-Pacific Corporation, encouraged increases in timber harvests on national forests in the West. This shift in agency heads led to a greater focus on commodity programs and more favorable attitudes toward business under Reagan than under Carter.

President Bush campaigned as an environmentalist, and some, but not all, of his departmental appointments reflected this claim. He appointed William Reilly—president of World Wildlife Fund and the Conservation Foundation and a highly respected conservationist—as head of EPA. Clayton Yeutter, a free trade/market advocate and Reagan-era holdover, was retained as secretary of agriculture and then replaced by U.S. Rep. James Madigan, a Republican farmer from Illinois. James Cason, a former real estate developer and business advocate from the Department of the Interior, was nominated as assistant secretary of agriculture for natural resources and the environment. Faced with majority opposition in the Senate, however, he was forced to withdraw. James Moseley, a Missouri farmer, was eventually named and confirmed instead. Manuel Lujan, Jr., a former Congressman from New Mexico with an uneven record of support for environmental programs, became secretary of the interior.

Supervision

As the head of the executive branch, the president is charged with seeing that the laws are faithfully executed. As discussed later in this chapter, many administrative agencies carry out legislative directives. Whenever scandal erupts, presidential critics are quick to charge the president and the chief lieutenants with dereliction and, perhaps, even malfeasance. In reality it is not practicable for the president to be acquainted with or able to control all the actions of the bureaucracy. The federal bureaucracy is vast and only a few of federal officials are appointed by the pres-

ident. Most federal workers are Civil Service employees, or civil servants. The president's ability to supervise these employees is constrained by the terms under which they serve. Moreover, some agencies have such strongly ingrained professional norms—the Forest Service, in particular—that presidential direction contrary to agency values and objectives is resisted. Nevertheless, the extended tenure of any president can effect substantial change in government agencies.

Legislation

Presidents participate in most major legislation. The president presents an annual State of the Union address that includes a status report on the administration and a call for new programs and reforms of existing ones. Members of the president's party introduce legislation in each house embodying proposals from the State of the Union address. Presidents also use special messages to Congress and press conferences to launch programs. Governors usually exert more influence in their state legislatures than the president can in Congress. Many state legislatures also have governor's floor leaders—not to be confused with the majority and minority party floor leaders—who bear chief responsibility for enacting the governor's proposals.

The chief executive may veto (or threaten to veto) legislation by returning a bill unsigned with an attached list of objections. Overturning a presidential veto requires that two-thirds of the members of both houses of Congress vote to do so. The president also may use a pocket veto by merely retaining unsigned any bill that is sent to the White House within 10 days of congressional adjournment. Occasionally pocket vetos have been used to punish intransigent agencies that resist presidential programs. Most governors have item vetos, which help prevent the attachment of riders to important omnibus bills. Item vetos allow governors to strike funding for specific programs from appropriations bills, facilitating budget balancing and removal of pork barrel projects opposed by the governor. The president cannot delete funds for individual projects or agencies but must accept or reject legislation in its entirety. A presidential line-item veto has been suggested as a tool to help curb the federal deficit.

The use or threat of a veto is a significant executive power to prevent undesirable legislation or to change its content before passage. Presidents Nixon and Ford vetoed 109 bills and were overridden only 17 times. Carter vetoed 31 bills, 2 were overridden; Reagan vetoed 78 with 9 overrides; and as of late 1992, Bush had vetoed 33 and none was overridden. FDR vetoed 635 bills during his tenure; Truman 250; and Eisenhower 181 (Puente 1992). Tommy Thompson, who served as governor of Wisconsin from 1986 through 1991, used the line-item veto more than 1000 times (Taylor 1991). In North Carolina, on the other hand, the governor has neither an item veto nor a "bill" veto and therefore little ability to shape legislation.

The president is the leader of a political party and as such is often its chief lobbyist. President Reagan's numerous telephone calls to legislators were widely credited with producing House support for his economic reform proposals. Presidents, such as Jimmy Carter, who find lobbying distasteful generally have less successful relations with Congress. Presidents also may call on the more than 1000 federal agency congressional liaisons, who nominally support presidential initiatives. The White House also has an Office of Congressional Relations to help lobby Congress.

Presidential opportunities to influence public opinion and gain support for programs through the media are significant. Theodore Roosevelt and his confederate Gifford Pinchot waged highly publicized campaigns for conservation causes. Roosevelt convened the first national Governor's Conference and made conservation one of its principal program thrusts. Presidential power depends greatly on the popular support that can be mustered through public speeches, radio, TV, press releases, and the like. President Reagan, frequently referred to as the "Great Communicator," mastered the use of prime-time television; one TV press conference generated a deluge of mail urging members of Congress to support economic reforms and tax cuts in 1981.

Budget

One of the executive's most significant powers is control over the budget. Before the Budget and Accounting Act of 1921, executive departments submitted their requests for appropriations directly to Congress. The Budget Act authorized presidents to present a single executive budget and created a new agency, the Bureau of the Budget, to assist them. The president's annual budget message provides the basis for most subsequent budget deliberations and sets the tone of debate in Congress and the media. President Reagan's budgets, however, were largely ignored by the Democratic Congress.

The budget process underwent a major modification in 1974 when the Congressional Budget and Impoundment Control Act was passed. Congress moved to reform the budget process because of persistent failure to enact appropriations bills by the start of the fiscal year, President Nixon's refusal to spend appropriated funds for items such as water pollution control, and large deficits. All of these indicated that the budgeting process was out of control. This act took away presidential authority to impound funds unilaterally and enhanced Congress's budgetary role, as described in the previous chapter.

The president's budget procedure involves the individual agencies, the Office of Management and Budget (OMB, formerly the Bureau of the Budget) and White House policymakers (Le Master 1984). Every March, as shown in Figure 7-1, OMB provides agencies with guidelines for developing their budget requests. OMB evaluates agency requests and projected revenues. Working with the White House, OMB sets general guidelines and ceilings for agencies. Bargaining between OMB and individual agencies may ensue, and after another round of presidential and agency review, numbers are finalized in the president's budget message. In January the president transmits the budget to Congress, which then begins its own deliberations. The pro-

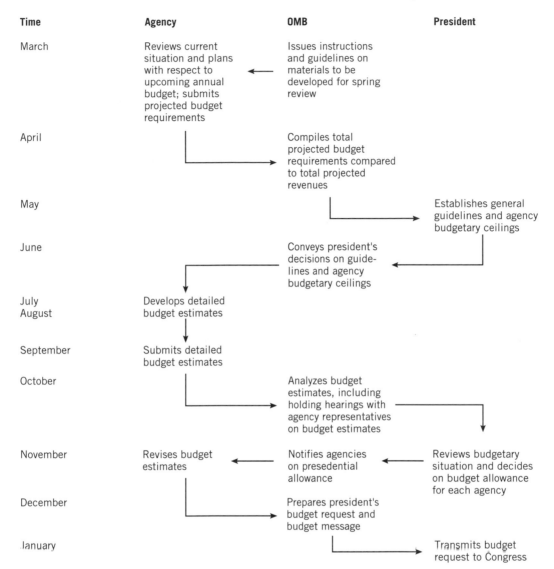

Time	Agency	OMB	President
March	Reviews current situation and plans with respect to upcoming annual budget; submits projected budget requirements	Issues instructions and guidelines on materials to be developed for spring review	
April		Compiles total projected budget requirements compared to total projected revenues	
May			Establishes general guidelines and agency budgetary ceilings
June		Conveys president's decisions on guidelines and agency budgetary ceilings	
July August	Develops detailed budget estimates		
September	Submits detailed budget estimates		
October		Analyzes budget estimates, including holding hearings with agency representatives on budget estimates	
November	Revises budget estimates	Notifies agencies on presedential allowance	Reviews budgetary situation and decides on budget allowance for each agency
December		Prepares president's budget request and budget message	
January			Transmits budget request to Congress

Figure 7-1 Formulation of the Executive Budget
Source: Le Master 1984.

cess, despite the Congressional Budget Act, is dominated by the president and OMB. A presidential item veto would further enhance the budgetary authority of the executive and therefore has been opposed by congressional leaders.

Foreign Policy

Although less relevant to natural resources, foreign policy issues are dominated by the president. Access to State Department expertise, responsibility for negotiations with other nations, and a much greater congressional concern for domestic policies that directly affect their constituents provide the president an advantage in setting foreign policy (Wildavsky 1966). Presidents have used foreign policy powers in natural resources issues, including wildlife protection, the export of Canadian lumber to the United States, and the 1992 Earth Summit in Rio de Janiero. As global environmental issues become more pressing, presidential foreign policy becomes more important in natural resource policy.

For example, the international Montreal Protocol in 1988 was developed by the president's executive office; it is designed to limit the emissions of ozone-destroying chloro-fluoro-carbons (CFCs) into the atmosphere. President Bush focused some of his environmental initiatives on tropical forestry issues.

LIMITATIONS

Despite the executive branch's impressive powers, executives face significant limitations. The framers of the Constitution wanted a strong presidency to promote federalism but were equally concerned that the president's powers be substantially weaker than those of King George III of England. As a result, the president does indeed lead the nation, but Congress must enact the actual legislation. If the president's program is only moderately popular, if the executive is inept at dealing with Congress, if public opinion polls show the president to have little popular support or if Congress simply opposes presidential initiatives, the president's powers, especially to set new directions, can be illusory (Neustadt 1980). Weak presidents, or those faced with hostile majorities in Congress, may try to lead but may find few followers.

Congress may restrain the power of the president in numerous ways. The Budget Reform Act of 1974 created the Congressional Budget Office and freed Congress from exclusive reliance on budget figures from the executive office. Congress has developed budgets that differ significantly from those proposed by the president. In 1989, for example, the House of Representatives substantially increased President Bush's proposed environmental and natural resource program budget. Congress added $539 million to the executive budget for the EPA. Similarly, the National Park Service received $168 million more than the president desired, the Fish and Wildlife Service $71 million more, and other major wildlife habitat programs $103 million more.

Congress may bury special presidential projects in committees, deny presidential initiatives in foreign affairs, or hold oversight hearings on execution of the laws. The Senate must advise and consent to the presidential appointees and has been known to refuse, delay, or embarrass those at odds with the majority of the Senate, especially if there is a hint of scandal associated with the nominee. In 1987 the Senate rejected Robert Bork, President Reagan's appointee to the Supreme Court, on ideological grounds, and the nomination of a second candidate was withdrawn when it was revealed that he had used marijuana in his college days and as a professor. President Bush's first choice to head the Defense Department, former Texas Senator John Tower, was rejected by the Senate. In the 1973 War Powers Resolution, Congress limited presidential power to involve the United States in undeclared wars. But as is often the case in foreign policy, questions remain about Congress's authority to limit the president's ability to dispatch military troops to trouble spots such as Grenada, Panama, or Saudi Arabia.

The courts also limit the executive branch's powers, albeit somewhat less vigorously than Congress does. Courts have generally given the president wide discretionary authority in domestic and, particularly, foreign affairs. The courts can, however, declare laws enacted at the president's behest to be unconstitutional. A series of rulings invalidating key components of the depression-era New Deal program prompted FDR's unsuccessful attempt to pack the Supreme Court with judges who agreed with his philosophies and policies. The Court sealed Richard Nixon's fate by ordering him to give the incriminating Watergate tapes to Congress.

The intransigence of the bureaucracy presents another obstacle to the policies of the president (McConnell 1976, Neustadt 1980). Even a dynamic president is apt to have greater success in nudging Congress than in steering administrative agencies. Although appointing agency heads and controlling budgets provide a large measure of influence, rank and file bureaucrats are slow to change direction, especially if they have strong allies in Congress. If bureaucrats do not support administration policies, implementation will be hit and miss (Aberbach and Rockman 1978).

Presidents come and go; bureaucracies and their supporting interest groups seem to live forever. Decentralized agencies with strong local support, such as the National Park Service, are particularly difficult to redirect. This may not always be undesirable; a slow-moving but expert body of permanent Civil Service workers may prevent presidents and cabinet officers from making drastic and perhaps unwise changes. However, a decade or more ago of one party in control of the presidency—such as the FDR/Truman years and Reagan/Bush years—can even affect the hearts, souls, and actions of bureaucrats.

Illustration: The Forest Conservation Movement under Theodore Roosevelt

Without a doubt, Teddy Roosevelt (TR) made the most significant contributions of any president to forest conservation by exercising his presidential powers. TR, along with his ally Gifford Pinchot, made forest and natural resources conservation one of the priorities of his presidential tenure from 1901 to 1909. When TR assumed the office in 1901, after President McKinley was assassinated, he sought advice from Pinchot, of the Bureau of Forestry (the predecessor to the U.S. Forest Service), and F. H. Newell, who became director of the Reclamation Service—the agency charged with the development of water resources in the West. Pinchot and Newell drafted several pages of text stressing the importance of forestry that Roosevelt used in his first message to Congress on December 2, 1901 (Pinchot 1947, p. 190).

The fundamental idea of forestry is the perpetuation of forests by use. Forest protection is not an end in itself; it is a means to increase and sustain the resources of our country and the industries which depend on them. The preservation of our forests is an imperative business necessity. We have come to see clearly that whatever destroys the forest, except to make way for agriculture, threatens our well-being.

The practical usefulness of the national forest reserves to the mining, grazing, irrigation, and other interests of the regions in which the reserves lie, T.R. continued, has led to a widespread demand by the people of the West for their protection and extension. The forest reserves will inevitably be of still greater use in the future than in the past. Additions should be made to them whenever practicable, and their usefulness should be increased by a thoroughly businesslike management.

...these various functions...should be united in the Bureau of Forestry, to which they properly belong. The present diffusion of responsibility is bad from every standpoint. It prevents that effective cooperation between Government and the men who utilize the resources of the reserves, without which the interests of both must suffer.

TR's first congressional address set the agenda for action throughout his presidency. He expanded the forest reserves, as they were then called, and had their administration transferred from the General Land Office in the Department of the Interior to the Bureau of Forestry in the Department of Agriculture. In these efforts, he was advised and aided by Gifford Pinchot, who had been the head of the Bureau of Forestry in Agriculture since 1898. Roosevelt had a great deal of respect for Pinchot. TR (1913, p. 394) states in his autobiography that

Gifford Pinchot is the man to whom the nation owes most for what has been accomplished as regards the preservation of natural resources in the country. He led, and indeed during most of its vital period embodied, the fight for preservation through use of the forests....He was the foremost leader in the great struggle to coordinate all our social and governmental forces in the effort to secure the adoption of a rational and farseeing policy for securing the conservation of all our national resources....Taking into account the varied nature of the work he did, its vital importance to the nation and the fact that as regards much of it he was practically breaking new ground, and taking into account also his tireless energy and activity, his fearlessness, his complete disinterestedness, his single-minded devotion to the interests of the plain people, and his extraordinary efficiency, I believe it is but just to say that among the many, many public officials who under my administration rendered literally invaluable service to the people of the United States, he, on the whole, stood first.

The team of Roosevelt and Pinchot achieved most of the goals set forth in the 1901 congressional address. When TR became president in 1901, he inherited a forest reserve system of almost 40 million acres. After the first forest reserves were authorized in 1891, President Harrison created a total of 13 million acres of reserves in the West by the end of his term in March 1893. By the end of 1893, President Cleveland set aside another 4.5 million acres, but thereafter he took no action due to lack of provisions for protections or administration of the reserves. However, in February 1897, Cleveland created 13 new reserves, totalling 21.3 million acres, as one of his last acts before leaving office.

The forest reserve system was administered by the General Land Office in the Department of the Interior. The Bureau of Forestry, in the Department of Agriculture, had the principal tasks of collecting data, advising private landowners about the practice of forestry, and publicizing forest management. Pinchot lobbied tirelessly to transfer the administration of the forest reserves from the Land Office (where they were managed by political appointees) to the Bureau of Forestry (where they would be managed by foresters). In 1905 Congress authorized the transfer of the reserves through passage of the Transfer Act.

In 1905 Secretary of Agriculture Jim Wilson signed a letter of instructions for Pinchot, written by Pinchot himself, stating the principles to be followed in the management of the reserves (Pinchot 1947). The instructions stressed that the forests were to be used for the good of all people, not the temporary benefit of individuals or companies, and that all the resources of these lands were for *use* and were to be administered in an efficient and businesslike manner. The letter also authorized the agency to regulate use of the reserves and to favor local input and considerations in making resource decisions. And, "…where conflicting interests must be reconciled the question will always be decided from the standpoint of the greatest good of the greatest number in the long run." (Pinchot 1947, p. 261).

Throughout the TR/Pinchot campaign to transfer administration of the forest reserves, Roosevelt also was active in declaring and setting aside new forest reserves. In his seven years as president, TR added roughly 100 million acres to the reserves.

The creation of forest reserves was opposed by some western interests. In 1907 Congress tacked a rider onto the agriculture appropriations bill that rescinded presidential authority to reserve any more lands in the six northwestern states. But Roosevelt and Pinchot had planned to add 16 million additional acres in these states, and they acted quickly to add them to the reserve system before TR signed the appropriations bill. To quote Roosevelt (1913, p. 404–405) regarding the last reserves:

I signed the last proclamation a couple of days before, by my signature, the [agriculture] bill became law; and when the friends of the special interests in the Senate got their amendment through and woke up, they discovered that sixteen million acres of timberland had been saved for the people by putting them in the National Forests before the land grabbers could get them. The opponents of the Forest Service turned handsprings in their wrath; and dire were their threats against the executive; but the threats could not be carried out, and were really only a tribute to the efficiency of our action.

Roosevelt's final proclamations did indeed hold up, and his activism has led to the large National Forest System we enjoy today. The 1907 bill, incidentally, changed the name from the Forest Reserves to the National Forests.

Roosevelt's activism was not confined to forestry. He promoted the use and development of water resources for drinking water, navigation, and power, particularly in the West. An avid hunter and sportsman, Roosevelt used his presidential powers of reservation to establish national parks and the first wildlife refuges in the United States. Again, to quote from his 1913 autobiography:

During the seven and a half years closing on March 4, 1909, more was accomplished for the protection of wildlife in the United States than during all previous years, excepting only the creation of Yellowstone National Park. The record includes the creation of five National Parks—Crater Lake, Oregon; Wind Cave, South Dakota; Platt, Oklahoma; Sully Hill, North Dakota; and Mesa Verde, Colorado; four big game refuges in Oklahoma, Arizona, Montana, and Washington; fifty-one bird reservations; and the enactment of laws for the protection of wildlife in Alaska, the District of Columbia, and on the National Bird reserves.

The impressive accomplishments of Roosevelt and his agency appointees permanently changed the direction of natural resource policy in the United States. The public agenda shifted from one favoring disposal of public lands to one favoring protection of public rights and retention of land in government ownership. This was accompanied by TR's focus on helping the "small person"—farmer, business owner, landowner, or consumer—overcome the greed and monopoly of big business and vested interests. President Taft declined to continue Roosevelt's activist role for government and indeed fired Pinchot and many other members of TR's conservationist cabinet. But the principles of government involvement in natural resources retention and active management had been established.

During what is now called the progressive conservation movement that climaxed in TR's presidency, three enduring values of resource management became established. The first was the belief that the public's natural resources should be managed to provide multiple benefits. The second was opposition to the special interests, including the "timber or cattle barons" of the old West. The third belief was that expert, political management of natural resources by public agencies would rectify errors from past abuse (Culhane 1981).

CONGRESSIONAL RELATIONS

In addition to presidential leadership and vigor, several other factors influence the outcome of executive initiatives. Presidents in control of their own political parties who enjoy a congressional majority will be more successful (Jones 1970, Ripley 1969). Usually, however, the president needs to develop bipartisan support in Congress. Obviously, when the congressional majority party is not in the White House, presidents must make overtures beyond their own party if any initiatives are to be enacted. In only 12 of the 37 years between 1955 and 1992 has the president had the "luxury" of friendly majorities in both houses of Congress. Although the greatest bursts of policy innovation have occurred when ambitious presidents such as FDR and Lyndon Johnson enjoyed large Democratic majorities in both houses, most presidents have been able to achieve some of their goals even when their partisans are outnumbered in Congress.

Even when one party has both congressional majorities and the White House, the president can be repeatedly thwarted. President Carter made several efforts to redirect natural resource policy. He tried to stop construction of federal irrigation dams in the West, noting that they constituted a waste of public funds. He floated proposals to create a federal Department of Natural Resources. In both cases Democratic members of Congress led the opposition. This kind of intraparty split can occur because of the structure of American government. In parliamentary systems, common in Western Europe, party members select their leader. The leader of the majority party becomes the prime minister and he or she then has more influence over parliament than the president does over Congress.

EXECUTIVE OFFICE OF THE PRESIDENT

Office of Management and Budget

The Executive Office of the President includes many distinct agencies, including the Office of Management and Budget (OMB), Council of Economic Advisors, Council on Environmental Quality, and the National Security Council. Of these, the OMB has the greatest immediate impact on natural resource policies, primarily through its budgeting powers.

OMB has three major powers and some lesser ones that influence forest policy (Edwards 1977, Sample 1989). First, OMB obviously affects the allocation of resources among government programs. Recently OMB has played a crucial role in balancing federal spending priorities, while keeping the grand total within accepted deficit limits. OMB acts as an examiner of individual agency budgets. If OMB is convinced of their merits, it becomes an agency proponent to White House officials. As an examiner, OMB must assess demands for a program, the need for federal involvement, and the cost-effectiveness of a program. Such justifications form the basis for programs in the overall executive budget process (Sample 1989).

Second, OMB serves as an intermediary between agencies and Congress. Prior to the appearance of an agency representative before a congressional committee, testimony must be approved by OMB. Proposed legislation is routinely referred by Congress to the agency that would be responsible for implementation. If the proposal would cost money, OMB will help shape the agency's response by deciding whether the proposal is at variance with the president's budget priorities. Since OMB opposition may foretell a veto should Congress pass the legislation, legislators often choose not to pursue bills that OMB opposes. However, if there is strong support in Congress, as can occur with popular constituency legislation, it may enact bills disapproved by OMB. The Forest and Rangeland Renewable Resources Planning Act of 1974 (RPA) was enacted despite opposition from the presidential budget office.

Third, the president relies on OMB for analysis and speech preparation, most notably the State of the Union and budget addresses delivered to Congress in January. OMB also makes recommendations to the president on bills passed by Congress. When OMB approves of a bill, it is signed into law by the president 95 percent of the time, even if the department that would implement the program objects (Wayne, Cole, and Hyde 1979).

OMB has lesser powers as well. It must approve all government statistical forms and questionnaires, a process that usually takes months. OMB also oversees computer purchase forms and purchases and must approve government publication procedures. These powers significantly impact the day-to-day operations of most government agencies. OMB freezes on questionnaires, computer purchases, and publications occur periodically, and besides controlling waste, they may irritate agency personnel or handicap agency accomplishments.

The Paperwork Reduction Act gave OMB authority to approve forms and eliminate those deemed duplicative. President Reagan also issued an executive order requiring agencies to perform benefit-cost analyses of any proposed regulations, and submit these to OMB. Critics charge that these powers have enabled OMB to usurp the regulatory authority that Congress delegates to some 100 agencies. Under the Reagan administration, OMB delayed or halted promulgation of scores of regulations designed to protect workers, consumers, and the environment, on the premise that they required too much paperwork or were too expensive. For instance, OMB held up for five years an EPA proposal to ban asbestos, reasoning that future cancer deaths should be discounted and valued at as little as $22,000 per person. OMB's ability to continue to use these powers to impede agency regulations was ruled illegal by a federal appeals court and was being appealed to the U.S. Supreme Court in 1989 (Karr 1989). The requirements for benefit-cost analyses were implemented aggressively by the Bush administration in the 1990s to impede the proliferation of agency regulations.

A final power of OMB is that of dictating the form and substance of the budget allocation procedures. The Forest Service is required to perform extensive planning under RPA, but OMB will not accept the RPA format or results in its deliberations. This forces the Forest Service into considerable duplication of effort.

Despite its authority, OMB is not omnipotent. The agency is relatively small, with about

500 professional staff, and had an annual budget of less than $100 million during the 1980s. There are generally just one or two budget examiners per agency. They simply cannot know the details of every budget item and must depend on the agencies for information. As mentioned, OMB disapproval will not guarantee congressional defeat nor will its approval guarantee passage. OMB has steadfastly opposed water projects, and Congress has consistently ignored its recommendations if they were popular constituency items (Davis 1977). The relationship of the agencies and their supporting interest groups also are important in determining the fate of OMB suggestions.

If nothing else, OMB at least practices what it preaches. It has not only said no to innumerable congressional and agency projects, it has declined opportunities to increase its own size. Most notably, OMB happily ceded authority to administer the Environmental Impact Statement process to the Council on Environmental Quality in 1970. It also has tried to minimize the collection of unneeded data (Popovich 1977).

In forestry, OMB predilections favoring economy and efficiency have caused it to support particular forest policies and oppose others (Sample 1989). OMB is unlikely to support larger budgets and greater reliance on federal lands to meet the demand for forest resources. On private lands, OMB takes a dim view of public investment for private gain (e.g., the capital substitution question discussed in Chapter 5). Thus OMB continues to oppose forestry cost-sharing and incentives programs, and it is only slightly less critical of indirect federal assistance through such actions as favorable tax treatments. OMB strongly favors increased efforts to educate private landowners about existing economic opportunities. OMB also tends to favor research that may reduce costs, as long as the benefits of that research do not accrue only to large firms.

Council of Economic Advisors

The Employment Act of 1946 directed that the Council of Economic Advisors (CEA) be cre-

ated to provide the president with interpretations of economic events, forecasts of the economic future, and explanations of complex economic matters. Along with advising and educating the president, the CEA is directed to set targets for unemployment rates and productivity. The CEA has no specific responsibilities but is the president's tutor in the "dismal science" of economics. The head of the CEA usually is a respected academic economist.

The role played by the CEA has varied from president to president, and probably reached its peak during the Kennedy and Johnson administrations of the 1960s (Hargrove and Nelson 1984, Kessel 1984). President Kennedy heeded CEA advice to cut tax rates to stimulate the economy. President Johnson's CEA chair, Walter Heller (1966), described his role as that of educator of the president, responsible for explaining why particular economic events occurred and what consequences would likely flow from them. Beginning in the early 1960s, the CEA worked closely with the secretary of the treasury and the director of OMB, a potentially powerful trio on economic issues.

During the Nixon and Reagan administrations, there were frequent conflicts between the head of CEA and the Treasury Secretary, as the latter disparaged the CEA for its academic and impractical perspectives. Other presidents have paid closer attention to CEA recommendations. According to Kessel (1984), Charles Schultze, CEA chair under President Carter, explained that as economic data were released, he would

give the President advance indication of what they are, almost always accompanied by some interpretations. In other words, a running commentary on the state of the economy goes from me to him. These do not normally have policy suggestions but are fairly obviously policy-oriented. And I meet with the President one-on-one about every two weeks for a general session without a fixed agenda.

Council on Environmental Quality

The Council on Environmental Quality (CEQ) was created by the National Environmental

Policy Act of 1970 as environmental protection rose toward the top of the national policy agenda. This three-member body is responsible for recommending environmental policy to the president and monitoring the implementation of such policies. The CEQ makes annual reports on U.S. environmental quality, which are useful reference works. President Reagan disbanded the CEQ, but President Bush revived the organization soon after taking office.

THE BUREAUCRACY

The writers of the Constitution provided for the president to have assistants, but the bureaucracy has grown far beyond their expectations. Departments and a multitude of independent offices have been added as Congress deemed necessary. Figure 7-2 depicts the government of the United States and the executive departments. Not shown in Figure 7-2 are the many agencies that make up the departments. Table 7-1 lists the independent offices and establishments in the federal government. A listing of all federal agencies is contained in annual United States Government manuals.

Units have been added to the bureaucracy to deal with newly recognized national responsibilities. The Environmental Protection Agency was created as an independent office by the National Environmental Policy Act of 1969 when the federal government became concerned about such issues as water and air pollution. Interest groups and members of Congress proposed elevating EPA to department-level status in 1989 and 1990, so it would have better access to the chief executive, but President Bush opposed this proposal. Other agencies, such as the Securities and Exchange Commission, were chartered to correct problems that Congress recognized were beyond the scope of state or local regulation.

The president is the head of the administration for all government agencies. However, presidential power over administrative organizations is limited. Most agencies are strongly supported by their individual constituent groups and members of Congress. Presidents who seek to force new directions on agencies often have been frustrated. Individuals chosen by the president to implement directives from the White House have often "gone native," becoming advocates for their agency in policy debates with presidential advisors. The ability to ignore presidential preferences is promoted by the professional status of most agency staff members who are protected from arbitrary and capricious removal by Civil Service regulations. Even removal for cause is exceedingly difficult.

POLICY FORMULATION AND IMPLEMENTATION

When rules and regulations are drafted by an agency to implement unpopular laws, the agencies, not Congress, get criticized. The Forest Service is a classic example. Congress requires the agency to manage the National Forest System for multiple uses and for a sustained yield of resource outputs over time. Sustained-yield timber harvest policies draw unending fire from some forest industry firms, many forest economists, and environmentalists. Release of uncut and unroaded lands for multiple use (including timber harvest) engenders harsh criticism from wilderness advocates. The Forest Service struggles valiantly to develop forest plans by implementing the procedural and technical strictures of the muddled RPA/NFMA legislation, but it is rewarded with administrative appeals or lawsuits challenging almost every plan and timber sale.

Agencies often are criticized for excessive zeal or patent lethargy in implementing laws. The bureaucracy and endless paperwork and red tape have become almost synonymous. However, most of these actions or inactions are attempts by agencies to implement sometimes overlapping or conflicting policies designed by Congress. The paperwork multiplies in an attempt to control abuses and to

Figure 7-2 The Government of the United States
Source: Dye, Greene, and Parthemos 1980

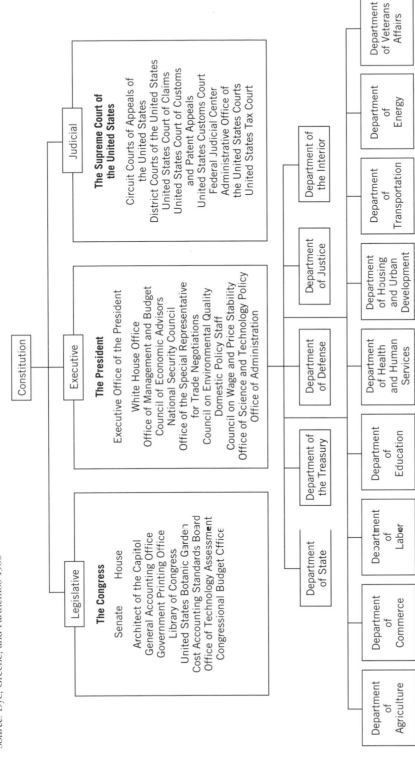

TABLE 7-1. List of Independent Federal Offices and Establishments, 1988

ACTION

Administrative Conference of the United States	Inter-American Foundation
American Battle Monuments Commission	International Communication Agency
Appalachian Regional Commission	Interstate Commerce Commission
Board for International Broadcasting	National Aeronautics and Space Administration
Canal Zone Government	National Credit Union Administration
Civil Aeronautics Board	National Foundation on the Arts and the Humanities
Commission on Civil Rights	National Labor Relations Board
Commission of Fine Arts	National Mediation Board
Commodity Futures Trading Commission	National Transportation Safety Board
Community Services Administration	Nuclear Regulatory Commission
Consumer Product Safety Commission	Occupational Safety and Health Review Commission
Environmental Protection Agency	Overseas Private Investment Corporation
Equal Employment Opportunity Commission	Panama Canal Company
Export-Import Bank of the United States	Pennsylvania Avenue Development Corporation
Farm Credit Administration	Pension Benefit Guaranty Corp.
Federal Communications Commission	Postal Rate Commission
Federal Deposit Insurance Corporation	Railroad Retirement Board
Federal Election Commission	Renegotiation Board
Federal Home Loan Bank Board	Securities and Exchange Commission
Federal Maritime Commission	Selective Service System
Federal Mediation and Conciliation Service	Small Business Administration
Federal Reserve System, Board of Governors of the	Tennessee Valley Authority
Federal Trade Commission	U.S. Arms Control and Disarmament Agency
Foreign Claims Settlement Commission of the United States	U.S. Civil Service commission
General Services Administration	U.S. International Trade Commission
Indian Claims Commission	U.S. Postal Service

Source: Adapted from Dye, Greene, and Parthemos 1980

prevent arbitrary actions. The difficult task is to maintain balance and control without becoming inundated with rules and paperwork.

Agencies play a necessary role in policy formulation. Agency personnel prepare preliminary regulations that are submitted for public comment through publication in the *Federal Register*, and they hold hearings and review written comments to shape the final regulations. Planned activities may be formally presented to congressional committees or subcommittees or discussed informally with key legislators and their staffs.

Because agencies are populated by personnel specialists and a variety of professional civil servants—in contrast to the generalized and amateur standing of cabinet officers and members of Congress—shrewdness and persistence are necessary if Congress is to control the expert bureaucrats.

THE IRON TRIANGLE

Although government agencies and bureaucrats generally serve the public, they are not selfless. Bureaucrats, like most individuals, are utility-maximizers. Because government agencies are not motivated by profits, maximizing returns is not relevant. Instead, maximizing individual power and influence, agency size and budget, and job stability are the utility measures bureaucrats use. Climbing the agency ladder supplants climbing the corporate ladder. These factors tend to reward agencies and individuals that spend the most, not the least (Niskanen 1971). Because most bureaus or agencies administer programs that benefit a certain sector of society, the individuals and interest groups that are advantaged often help bureaucrats expand their agencies and protect their turf (Buchanan and Tullock 1962). Interest groups help agencies by lobbying Congress directly for programs and appropriations or indirectly by generating constituent interest. Bureaus reciprocate by favoring the interest groups when formulating regulations. Only the president, the OMB budget balancers, and the taxpayers lose in the process.

This relationship among agencies, interest groups, and individual committees and subcommittees in Congress is often referred to as the *iron triangle*, and it is promoted by the congressional norms of reciprocity and specialization. Congressional committees authorize and appropriate, the bureaucracies administer, and interest groups seek to promote their policy goals. Le Master (1984) illustrates the iron triangle for forestry (Figure 7-3) and suggests that the process may not be as strong in forestry as in other arenas because commodity-production interest groups usually have views that differ from those of conservation and environmental interest groups. Thus, some stalemates result because the congressional committees face a divided forestry clientele. A similar split has developed in the Interior Committee, which once was dominated by user-oriented westerners but now has some eastern environmentalists on it (Fenno 1973). These splits are atypical of what is to be expected in an iron triangle.

Each bureau has some interest group supporters, and there may be supporters for specific programs. For example, the State and Private Forestry (S&PF) branch of the U.S. Forest Service is supported largely by groups such as the National Association of State Foresters and the Forest Farmers Association. President Reagan's OMB consistently recommended deleting all funds for S&PF—compared to annual funding levels under the Carter administration of about $75 million per year. However, the interest groups supporting S&PF prevailed in Congress, to the extent that annual budgets by 1990 increased to $104 million. This illustrates the difficulty the president faces in overcoming effective iron triangle relationships.

The role of interest groups notwithstanding, close relationships between agencies and congressional committees present some advantages. First, if the agencies are to implement laws well, they need to be able to confer with members of Congress and their staffs about legislative intent. Second, agencies often must implement controversial policies. When constituents respond with complaints to legislators, good relations help prevent misunderstandings or negative congressional reactions such as budget cuts. Close relationships are likely to promote trust in the bureaucracy with the benefit of increasing appropriations (Clawson 1977).

Iron triangles tend to provide power and funding for all participants, often to the detriment of the president, the budget, and the public at large (Browne 1986). Agencies, subcommittee members, and interest groups try to confine policy deliberations to themselves. These subsystems function behind the scenes unless issues are expanded.

NATURAL RESOURCE AGENCIES

Many federal and state agencies are responsible for implementing natural resource programs. These programs range from research to enforcement of standards in the marketplace. No single rule describes the distribution of resource programs among agencies. Some agencies' mandates are defined by a particular function, others by a resource

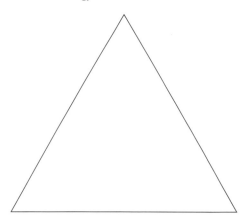

House Committees

Agriculture
Appropriations
Interior and Related Agencies

Senate Committees

Agriculture
Appropriations
Energy and Natural Resources

Forest Service

Commodity-Production Interest Groups

(e.g., the Industrial Forestry
Association, the National Forest
Products Association, the Southern
Forest Products Association, and the
Western Timber Industry)

Conservation Interest Groups

(e.g., the American Forestry
Association, the Izaak Walton
League, the National Audubon
Society, the National Wildlife
Federation, and the Sierra Club)

Figure 7-3 The Iron Triangle for Forestry
Source: Le Master 1984.

or set of resources. For example, the Occupational Health and Safety Administration (OSHA) has a functional mandate. OSHA regulates workplace conditions in all types of industries, from pulp mills to the manufacture of hunting rifles. In contrast, the responsibilities of the National Park Service include a variety of functions related to a particular set of resources. The Park Service conducts research, educates park visitors, and manipulates ecosystems. In the following paragraphs, five functions or types of programs relevant to natural resource management are described, adapted from a classification by Clawson (1977).

First, many government agencies conduct and support research. Federal research in natural resources is performed in or administered by the Research branch of the U.S. Forest Service, the National Park Service, the Agricultural Research Service, the Fish and Wildlife Service, the Environmental Protection Agency, and the National Science Foundation (NSF), to mention a few. The research supported by these agencies ranges from exploration of basic questions in science (NSF) to answering practical resource management questions (Forest Service).

A second type of natural resource program is the management of public lands and projects. The federal government "owns" or holds about one-third of the nation's land and has a variety of agencies that manage these land areas. States, counties, and municipalities also own and manage about 100 million acres of land, including 30 million acres of timberland. Public lands are managed for commercial wood production, as parks and preserves, and to protect municipal water supplies. Most of these agencies exercise considerable discretion in the development of management programs. Chapters 12 and 13 discuss public land management.

A third arena of government involvement is the regulation of land and resource use. The Environmental Protection Agency is charged with protecting the nation's air and water from pollution. The Fish and Wildlife Service and state game and fish departments regulate the taking of game populations and the protection of nongame species. State coastal zone agencies limit development to maintain coastal ecosystems. In general, state and federal governments regulate pollution; state and local governments are responsible for regulation of private land use; and the federal government controls the exploitation of resources on federal lands and waters. Chapters 14 through 16 discuss government regulation.

Fourth, government also helps provide education and subsidies in order to induce private persons or local governments to undertake socially desirable resource-use activities. A variety of tax, subsidy (cost-share), and education programs and agencies are involved in forest resources. The Agricultural Extension Service provides information to rural and urban citizens; the Soil Conservation Service assists in developing farm and woodlot plans; and state forestry agencies provide on-the-ground technical advice to forest landowners. Chapter 17 discusses these programs in detail.

A fifth set of programs regulates business and labor, thus influencing resource-dependent industries. Bargaining relations between firms and employers, federal employment standards and minimum wage laws, trucking regulations, occupational safety, and workers' compensation laws are crucial for the forest products industry. The Department of Labor, OSHA, and the Interstate Commerce Commission are some of the federal agencies responsible for these programs. Federal and state tax laws and agencies also determine accounting rules, influence investment patterns, and even affect employment patterns.

INTERAGENCY RELATIONSHIPS

Figure 7-2 diagrammed the relationships among the three branches of government, the Executive Office of the President, and the various departments. Generally, executive policy stemming from the president and executive advisors is directed to the respective secretaries of each department. Each department also has several assistant secretaries who supervise at least one bureau chief who, in turn, directs activities within his or her particular agency.

Each department and agency also has to deal with other executive agencies either formally or informally. The National Environmental Policy Act requires coordination among federal agencies in planning and taking actions that will significantly affect the environment. Another example is the consultation between agencies required under Section 7 of the Endangered Species Act.

Bureaus develop relationships, which may be cordial or hostile, with other bureaus. Dislike among agencies is endemic because they often compete for the same dollars and programs. Particularly in recent years, any gain achieved by one agency is apt to be realized at the expense of another.

Relationships among related forestry agencies have been particularly cool. Transfer of the forest reserves from Interior to Agriculture initiated ill will between the two departments. Then, in 1910, Pinchot, as chief of the Forest Service, complained to President Taft that Secretary of the Interior Ballinger had mismanaged coal claims on lands in Alaska. Actually, the charges stemmed from conservationists' frustration over lack of access to Taft's White House. Taft was unsympathetic, so Pinchot raised a public outcry about Ballinger to discredit him. Taft promptly fired Pinchot for insubordination (Dana and Fairfax 1980). Interior has repeatedly attempted to regain control of the Forest Service, most recently under Carter's reorganization plan for federal natural resource agencies (Andrus 1977), but with no success.

The Forest Service continued cool relationships with the National Park Service, an agency in the Department of the Interior, for many years. Although the Forest Service relied on presidential reservations of land from the public domain for the creation of national forests, the national parks had to be carved out of existing agency ownerships. Thus much of the National Park System came at the expense of the National Forest System. Like all good bureaucrats, Forest Service employees were displeased by the loss of land, programs, funds, and jobs.

BUREAUCRATIC POWER

Bureaucracies may be effective and powerful for various reasons. The iron triangle concept suggests that agencies' power and influence rest on their relationships with Congress and their ability to provide services for interest group clientele. In fact, clientele and other external support are only some of the factors that lead to a powerful agency. Also important are its internal strengths, such as the general expertise, knowledge, and information that an agency has at its disposal and can use in advocating particular policies and programs (Rourke 1984).

Natural resource agencies develop strong support for a number of reasons, including affiliation with large and influential constituencies, strong linkages to economic concerns (i.e., income and employment), a service-oriented mission, and congressional or presidential support. The nature of the agency mission, agency professionalism, leadership astuteness, and esprit de corps also are important in developing strong agencies (Clarke and McCool 1985). Utilitarian, expandable agency missions authorized by organic acts (such as the Forest Service) have favored agency power; narrow or preservationist missions created by executive order (such as

the National Park Service) have not. Scientific and military agencies have enjoyed more power than interdisciplinary agencies. A strong agency founder and recruitment from within favor agency influence; political appointments of agency heads do not. A coherent public image and agency character lead to power; servility and a tenuous management approach do not (Clarke and McCool, 1985).

Clarke and McCool (1985) analyzed the clout of seven principal natural resource agencies in the United States. The Army Corps of Engineers (COE) and the U.S. Forest Service were classed as bureaucratic superstars, aided by their professional and scientific expertise, clear but expandable missions, production- or commodity-oriented objectives, and high esprit de corps. By contrast, the National Park Service (NPS), the U.S. Fish and Wildlife Service (FWS), and the Soil Conservation Service (SCS) were classed as agencies that merely muddle through. Both the NPS and FWS were initially saddled with the conflicting missions of preservation (of parks or wildlife) and development (of outdoor recreation or hunting), which were difficult to reconcile. These ambiguous and contradictory goals hampered agency coalescence and interest group influence. The SCS mission was clear, but narrow, which has led to stable funding levels at best. Finally, the Bureau of Reclamation (BuRec) and the Bureau of Land Management (BLM) were designated as organizational shooting stars. The agencies' fortunes seem to rise and fall rapidly with presidential preferences, external events, or interest group whims, but they do not seem tied to long-run positive determinants of power.

Agency budgets, personnel, and status rankings support the preceding observations. From 1950 to 1980 the Corps of Engineers had by far the greatest increase in agency annual budgets, followed by the Forest Service. In fact, the COE's budget increased about fivefold, from $600 million to $2.9 billion; the Forest Service's budget increased over tenfold, from less than $200 million to $2 billion. During this same time period, the Bureau of Reclamation's budget increased only slightly, the BLM budget moderately, and the NPS, SCS, and FWS budgets rose only modestly. Work forces for all agencies except the Bureau of Reclamation increased moderately from 1950 on, but the Forest Service and the Corps of Engineers added the greatest number of permanent positions.

BUREAUCRATIC PROBLEMS

Clawson (1977) discussed several problems that may occur in the administration of government bureaus. Agencies tend to ossify—they become so rigid over time that they cannot adapt or change and even perform poorly on traditional tasks. Kaufman (1967) dissected the culture and ideology within the Forest Service and concluded that it engendered conformity. Twight and Lyden (1988) suggested that conformity and rigidity still prevail in the Forest Service. Public agencies are not unique in this respect. Private bureaucracies also become ossified. General Motors, Ford, IBM, and a host of other companies have faced similar problems in recent decades.

Entropy—the tendency toward inefficiency—is a related problem. Infamous red tape and paperwork spawned by government agencies or large corporations are a symptom of entropy. Some of these problems have been addressed by creating new agencies, such as the Bureau of Land Management, to develop fresh approaches to problems.

Agency capture by its clientele is another common problem, especially for regulatory agencies (Niskanen 1971, Stigler 1971). Rather than protecting users, the Interstate Commerce Commission helped prevent competition in the trucking industry, and it took congressional deregulation to open trucking up to competition. Many people believe that the Bureau of Land Management has been captured by ranchers, causing lease prices for public rangelands to be far less than those on private lands. In fact, agency critics refer to BLM as the Bureau of Livestock and Mining. Others believe the U.S. Forest Service has been captured by the timber industry. Capture

is associated with iron triangle relationships. Such entrenchment makes the agencies uncontrollable by the department secretary or the president. In the short-run, agencies may benefit. But in the long-run, they may face virulent public or administration opposition, which could eliminate or hobble their programs.

In brief, the fundamental problem of a bureaucracy is how its power is controlled. One approach is to enact very prescriptive laws that leave agencies little room for interpretation or entrepreneurial empire building. State laws requiring the leaving of seed trees, such as in Virginia and Maryland, or the old forest practice laws in California, Oregon, and Washington, exemplify prescriptive legislation. Another approach is the enactment of broader laws that require massive public participation in agency decision making, such as NEPA and NFMA. Legislators must choose among a spectrum of such options in order to control agencies and effectively implement public policies.

ILLUSTRATION: THE FOREST SERVICE AS A BUREAUCRACY

The U.S. Forest Service provides a fascinating example of the advantages and perils of ideology and public service in a federal agency. As stated in this chapter, the forest reserves initially were administered by the General Land Office in the Department of the Interior. Field administrators were political appointees who were not trained foresters, seldom visited the forests under their charge, and often were considered less than ethical (Pinchot 1947). Gifford Pinchot and President Theodore Roosevelt campaigned to transfer the reserves from Interior to the Department of Agriculture in order to escape from the rampant politicism of the General Land Office, to provide for their professional management by foresters in the Forest Service, and probably to increase their own personal influence over forestry practices and budgets as well.

Pinchot's concept of a businesslike management of the national forests for the public good was instilled into the foresters of that time and has become institutionalized since. Pinchot's (1947, p. 64) statement about the merits of forestry as a career is telling.

Most of these youngsters I discouraged on the ground that if a boy had the stuff in him to make a good forester he would keep at it anyhow. I told them Forestry meant hardship and hard work, much responsibility, and small pay, which was the cold fact.

Kaufman (1967) analyzed the many factors, carried forward from Pinchot's time, that led to a very uniform ideology among Forest Service employees. Pinchot's quote about hard work and low pay is referred to often, helping self-select individuals who will make personal sacrifices for the profession and organization. Training people through internal courses and lateral transfers, using symbols such as uniforms and equipment, and selecting dedicated foresters have encouraged conformity. Additionally, the Forest Service has internal forms, policies, and budget procedures that are common nationwide. The agency requires detailed reporting, maintenance of official diaries, periodic inspections, and sanctions for noncompliance with administrative policies.

On the other hand, Kaufman (1967) noted that some factors might tend to promote independence and disunity in the organization. Agency governance is very decentralized. Field officers, most notably district rangers, appear to have great autonomy in their districts and might be subject to capture by local populations. Their personal preferences may subsume agency policies. And indeed, they have been directed to be sensitive and responsive to local interests since Pinchot's era.

Kaufman found, however, that these tendencies toward independence were completely overcome by factors favoring conformity. Professionals working for the Forest Service shared common personal backgrounds, usually were trained as foresters, were willing to make personal sacrifices for the organization, and held similar professional tenets of faith. The self-selection of applicants, internal socialization, frequent transfer of professionals among districts, and promotion exclusively from within the service encourage high esprit de corps and high acceptance of agency beliefs and actions.

Early Forest Service management principles included a decentralized administration; the practice of forestry in a rather narrow silvicultural sense, mostly for commercial timber uses; and a commitment to the economic stability of surrounding communities (Dana and Fairfax 1980). Throughout the early decades of the Forest Service, this ideology and commitment to the organization served the agency well. Forest fires were controlled; forests were harvested, replanted, and managed; grazing and other developed uses were regulated; and commodity users and employees were generally satisfied with the agency. Indeed, even as late as 1979 the Forest Service won recognition for being one of the 10 best-managed public or private organizations in the United States (Clarke and McCool 1985).

The rigid ideology of the agency, however, has served it and the public less well since the modern environmental movement began in the 1960s. Silvicultural practices that were common and accepted in the West, most notably clear-cutting, proved extremely unpopular when exported to the eastern national forests and now face intense opposition in the West as well. Pressures for increased recreational use, wildlife management, and multiresource planning have challenged the traditional fire control and silvicultural orientation of the Forest Service. Even worse, wilderness preservation strikes at the heart of Pinchot's traditional wisdom of forest use, and bans on timber harvests to protect the northern spotted owl and red-cockaded woodpecker have challenged conventional management wisdom. Traditional forest industry commodity interests are often outnumbered and out-lobbied by environmentalists in efforts to shape Forest Service policy.

One might hope that with its multiple-use mandates, the traditional Forest Service ideologies would change to encompass this broader charter. At least two analysts— Culhane (1981) and Leman (1981)—believe that the Forest Service has become more flexible and responsive to these demands. Culhane (1981) argues that the strong socialization of the Forest Service helped it respond adequately to the environmental movement. First, it escaped capture from any one sector in the 1950s and 1960s, thus giving the service credibility as an independent, professional resource management agency. Second, its multiple-use laws, responsibilities, and clientele have led to broad-based political support and professional pride. The analysis of power, budgets, and personnel by Clarke and McCool (1985) tends to support the contention that the Forest Service's mission, ideology, professionalism, promotion practices, and constituency support have served it well compared to other natural resource agencies.

Twight and Lyden (1988), however, in a 1980 analysis of district rangers' opinions, found no statistical evidence of more flexibility of rangers' opinions, suggesting that multiple-use goals were not completely incorporated into the Forest Service ideology. Rangers continued to conform strongly to a single agency perspective, favoring a single timber constituency, not one made up of many groups.

The agency's response to challenges to forest plans prepared in the 1980s supports the view that the Forest Service still held traditional beliefs. Many plans were appealed to the chief on the basis of inadequate wildlife protection or wilderness preservation. Regional foresters, forest supervisors, and forest planners often did not respond to these appeals with pleasure, tending instead to favor traditional silvicultural policies. There still may be hope, however. Dale Robertson, promoted to chief of the Forest Service in 1987, placed special emphasis on recreational and wildlife uses of the national forests and promoted the development of the "New Perspectives" management program for the national forests in the 1990s. Many new foresters in the agency seem to favor a broader set of resource management objectives; some have

formed and joined an organization called the Association of Forest Service Employees for Environmental Ethics. The chief and top management seem to be trying to change service policies quickly. A 1990 follow-up survey to Twight and Lyden's found that Forest Service employees were more environmentally aware than in 1980, and that the agency's ideology was changing from within (Brown and Harris 1991).

The Forest Service illustrates the problems facing public agencies. The agency expanded after World War II in order to manage the public forests for use by predominantly commercial clients. In so doing, its personnel developed a strong commitment and conformity with the initial organizational goals. In the last two decades, public awareness, changing values, and legislated policy goals have changed perceptibly from those prevalent in the days of Theodore Roosevelt and Gifford Pinchot. The agency may have had difficulty shifting its organizational beliefs and responses from predominantly single use to multiple objectives, but it has capitalized on its enlarged constituency by increasing clients, agency power, budget, and size. However, this has not been achieved without increasing confrontation, administrative and legal challenges, and declining agency morale. Adapting to new public values and attendant desires for the national forests while maintaining agency power and influence will continue to challenge the Forest Service for years to come.

SUMMARY

Chief executives—the president of the United States or governors in each state—have many constitutional powers. They appoint agency heads, judges, and, in the case of the president, diplomatic ambassadors to foreign countries. Chief executives supervise the administrative agencies that implement laws and make policy. Executives also promote legislation, which is actually submitted by members of their party elected to the legislature. The president develops and submits the annual budget request to Congress; governors have even greater budget control in the states. Legislative opposition, judicial interpretation, or bureaucratic intransigence may restrain the chief executive's policy initiatives.

The bureaucracy is part of the executive branch, nominally serving at the chief executive's behest. Agencies inevitably develop close relationships with the clients they serve and with individual congressional or legislative subcommittees, thus promoting their programs without executive approval or direction. Factors such as professionalism, constituency support, a flexible but not contradictory mission, and commodity-oriented programs have helped form strong agencies. Executives and legislators may control bureaucracies by promoting prescriptive legislation or by requiring substantial public input into agency decision making.

LITERATURE CITED

Aberbach, Joel D., and Bert A. Rockman. 1978. Bureaucrats and clientele groups: A view from Capitol Hill. *American Political Science Review* 22 (December):818–832.

Andrus, Cecil D. 1977. Interior's forest policy interests. Pp. 55–59 in Centers of Influence and U.S. Forest Policy. Duke University, School of Forestry and Environmental Studies. Durham, NC.

Brown, Greg, and Charles C. Harris. 1991. A summary of three papers on change in the U.S. Forest Service. Presented at the Society of American Foresters, National Convention, Economics, Policy, and Law Working Group. August 4–7. San Francisco.

Browne, William P. 1986. Policy and interests: Instability and change in a classic issue subsystem. Pp. 183–201 in Alan J. Cigler and Burdett A. Loomis (eds), Interest Group Politics, 2nd ed. Congressional Quarterly. Washington, DC.

Buchanan, James M., and Gordon Tullock. 1962. The Calculus of Consent. University of Michigan Press. Ann Arbor. 361 pp.

Clarke, Jeanne Nienaber, and Daniel McCool. 1985. Staking Out the Terrain: Power Differentials among Natural Resource Management Agencies. State University of New York Press. Albany. 198 pp.

Clawson, Marion. 1977. Maximizing options and advantages in the federal bureaucracy: The natural resource agencies. Pp. 75–87 in Centers of Influence and U.S. Forest Policy. Duke University, School of Forestry and Environmental Studies. Durham. NC.

Culhane, Paul F. 1981. Public Land Politics: Interest Group Influence in the Forest Service and Bureau of Land Management. Johns Hopkins Press. Baltimore, MD. 398 pp.

Dana, Samuel T., and Sally K. Fairfax. 1980. Forest and Range Policy, 2nd ed. McGraw-Hill. New York. 455 pp.

Davis, Robert K. 1977. The White House and OMB as Centers of Influence in Forest Policy. Pp. 52–54 in Centers of Influence and U.S. Forest Policy. Duke University, School of Forestry and Environmental Studies. Durham, NC.

Dye, Thomas R., Lee S. Greene, and George S. Parthemos. 1980. Governing the American Democracy. St. Martin's Press. New York. 624 pp. + appen.

Edwards, James O. 1977. U.S. forest policy: The role of the Office of Management and Budget. Pp. 37–47 in Centers of Influence and U.S. Forest Policy. Duke University, School of Forestry and Environmental Studies. Durham. NC.

Fenno, Richard F. 1973. Congressmen in Committees. Little, Brown. Boston. 303 pp.

Hargrove, Erwin C., and Michael Nelson. 1984. Presidents, Politics, and Policy. Knopf. New York. 288 pp.

Heller, Walter W. 1966. New Dimensions of Political Economy. Harvard University Press. Cambridge, MA. 203 pp.

Hurley, Patricia A., David W. Brady, and Joseph Cooper. 1977. Measuring legislative potential for policy change. *Legislative Studies Quarterly* 1(August):385–398.

Jones, Charles O. 1970. The Minority Party in Congress. Little, Brown. Boston. 204 pp.

Karr, Albert R. 1989. Critics say White House budget office has usurped authority from agencies. *Wall Street Journal*, September 1, 1989, p. B48.

Kaufman, Herbert. 1967. The Forest Ranger. Resources for the Future. Johns Hopkins Press. Baltimore, MD. 259 pp.

Kessel, John H. 1984. Presidential Parties. Dorsey Press. Homewood, IL. 645 pp.

Leman, Christopher K. 1981. The forest ranger revisited: Administrative behavior in the U.S. Forest Service in the 1980s. Paper presented at the 1981 Annual Meeting of the American Political Science Association. New York.

Le Master, Dennis C. 1984. Decade of Change. Greenwood Press. Westport, Connecticut. 290 pp.

McConnell, Grant. 1976. The Modern Presidency, 2nd ed. St. Martin's Press. New York. 133 pp.

Mullins, March E. 1991. Presidential bench mark. *USA Today*, September 10, p. 1.

Neustadt, Richard E. 1980. Presidential Power: The Politics of Leadership. Wiley. New York. 286 pp.

Niskanen, William A. 1971. Bureaucracy and Representative Government. Aldine-Atherton. Chicago. 241 pp.

Pinchot, Gifford. 1947. Breaking New Ground. Harcourt, Brace, and Company. New York. 522 pp. Reprinted by Island Press. Covela, California.

Popovich, Luke. 1977. The scrooges downtown. Pp. 48–51 in Centers of Influence and U.S. Forest Policy. Duke University, School of Forestry and Environmental Studies. Durham, NC.

Puente, Maria. 1992. Unblemished veto record may haunt Bush. *USA Today*, June 22, p. 4A.

Ripley, Randall. 1969. Majority Party Leadership in Congress. Little, Brown. Boston. 194 pp.

Roosevelt, Theodore. 1899. Speech before the Hamilton Club, Chicago. April 10, 1899. Pp. 317 in Theodore Roosevelt. by Charles E. Banks and Leroy Armstrong. Copyright 1901 by E. R. Dumont. 413 pp.

Roosevelt, Theodore. 1913. An Autobiography. Macmillan. New York. 615 pp.

Rourke, Francis E. 1984. Bureaucracy, Politics, and Public Policy, 3rd ed. Little, Brown. Boston. 244 pp.

Sample, V. Alaric. 1989. National forest, policy-making and program planning: The role of the president's Office of Management and Budget. *Journal of Forestry* 87(1):17–25.

Stigler, George J. 1971. The theory of economic regulation. *Bell Journal of Economics* 2(1):3–21.

Taylor, Elizabeth. 1991. Toughlove from Dr. No. *Time* 138(7):19. August 19.

Twight, Ben W., and Fremont J. Lyden. 1988. Multiple use vs. organizational commitment. *Forest Science* 34(2):474–486.

United States Government Manual 1984/1985. 1984. Office of the Federal Register, National Archives and Records Service, General Services Administration. U.S. Government Printing Office. Washington, DC.

Wayne, Stephen, Richard Cole, and James Hyde. 1979. Advising the president on enrolled legislation. *Political Science Quarterly* 94(Summer):303–317.

Wildavsky, Aaron. 1966. The two presidencies. *Trans-Action* 4(December):7–14.

Chapter 8

The Judiciary and The Law

The administration of justice is the firmest pillar of government.

—George Washington 1789

Within these limits the power vested in the American courts of justice of pronouncing a statute to be unconstitutional forms one of the most powerful barriers that have ever been devised against the tyranny of political assemblies.

—Alexis de Tocqueville 1835

INTRODUCTION

Courts have played an increasingly important role in shaping forest resource policies. As the third branch of government, courts always have been significant in natural resource policy, determining penalties for violations and ruling on the constitutionality of federal and state laws. For example, early in this century a federal district court held the Migratory Bird Law (Weeks-McClean Act of 1915) to be unconstitutional, leading Congress to enact as a substitute the Migratory Bird Treaty Act of 1918. In the first law, Congress attempted to regulate hunting of migratory birds. The 1918 court ruled that Congress lacked the constitutional authority to do this. The Treaty Act passed by the Senate was an agreement with Canada. Because the federal government has the authority to establish treaties with other nations, federal regulation of hunting as part of a treaty was deemed to be legal.

This chapter discusses the law and judicial systems. Chapter 6 briefly reviewed types of laws and why the legislature enacts them. This chapter classifies laws further, as they provide the basis for all subsequent judicial enforcement. It then outlines the structure and powers of courts, with applications to natural resource issues.

LEGAL CITATIONS

Many legal citations are referenced in this chapter. Although the legal citation form seems intimidating, it is easy and necessary to grasp its basics in order to understand public policy decisions. Table 8-1 provides a few example citations of laws and court decisions.

TABLE 8-1. Common Citation Forms

Law citations	
76 Stat. 806; 16 U.S.C. 582a-582a-7(1962) (McIntire Stennis Act)	
- Volume 76 - United States Statutes at Large - Page 806	- -Title 16 - United States Code - Section 582a…to 582a-7
P.L. 92-500 ***(Federal Water Pollution Control Act Amendments of 1972)***	
- Public Law - 92nd Congress	- 500th Law
26 U.S.C. 631 (Capital Gains Treatment of Timber)	
- Title 26 - Section 631	- United States Code
Court cases	
Avoyelles Sportsmen's League v. Alexander 473 F. Supp. 525[1979]	
- Volume 473 - Page 525 - Avoyelles Sportsmen's League - plaintiff - Alexander - respondent	- Federal Supplements - 1979-date of decision
Penn. v. Mahon 260 U.S. 393[1922]	
- Volume 260 - Page 393 - Pennsylvania Coal - plaintiff (in appeal) - Mahon - respondent	- U.S. Reports - 1922

Appendix B summarizes legal research and citation formats in some detail. Law citations generally are composed of a volume number, the title or code name, and a page or statute number.

Many court case citations are similar—they include the names of the litigants, the volume number, the name of the abstracting document, a page number, and the date, in that order. The corporation or individuals against whom a civil suit is brought are referred to as respondents of defendants. Legal citations always list the plaintiffs first and the respondents second. Criminal cases involve a prosecutor (usually the government) and a defendant (the person charged with a crime).

Once a bill is passed by both houses of Congress, it is referred to as an act and printed in its final version as a separate "slip law." If signed by the president, the bill becomes law and is placed in the U.S. Statutes at Large. The statutes are numbered according to the congressional session and the chrono-

logical order in which the bill was passed. For example, P.L. 92-500 (The Federal Water Pollution Control Act Amendments of 1972) means Public Law, 92nd Congress, 500th act passed. Individual federal and state bills are codified periodically—that is, they are incorporated into the U.S. Code or state codes. The codes consist of many volumes that contain all the laws enacted, divided into subject areas. Most states have a conservation and natural resources code. Most federal conservation, forestry, and wildlife laws are contained in volume 16 of the U.S. Code (cited as 16 U.S.C.).

Agency regulations to implement congressional laws also may be issued. These are written by the department or agency, and after a review period, they become administrative law. The Code of Federal Regulations (C.F.R.) maintains a current compilation of all these laws. Court cases stem from suits regarding these administrative laws. The citation form for these laws is somewhat uniform.

LAW AND PUBLIC POLICY

Public policy has been defined as a purposive course of action adopted by government to address a problem. Because governments use a variety of means to address problems, public policy may take many forms. Governments may provide services to citizens. States provide fire protection for privately owned forest lands. Governments also may use money to address problems. The U.S. Congress appropriates funds to manage public lands in the West. Similarly, the federal government may partially reimburse owners of nonindustrial forest lands directly with cost-share payments or indirectly with income tax credits for their reforestation expenditures.

Another way that governments implement public policies is through the legal system. Lawyers and litigation are a pervasive part of society. Many definitions for law and the legal system are available. We will define *law* as a system of rules that order social life (Hart 1961, Nonet and Selznick 1978). Law is made up of three elements: (1) formulated legislation, including constitutions, statutes, treaties, ordinances, and codes; (2) rules of law determined by the courts in deciding cases; and (3) the system of legal concepts and techniques that forms the basis of judicial action. Law may be viewed as a means of social control, or as a means of seeking justice. The rule of law governs how individuals, firms, and public agencies may act (Corley, Reed, and Shedd 1990).

TYPES OF LAW

There are many different types and sources of law. One distinction is between public and private laws. Public law includes constitutional law, administrative law, and criminal law. In public law, society or "the people" are involved and are represented by a government agency, officer, or official. Private law deals with legal relationships between individuals or firms and includes the law of contracts, law of torts (or injuries), and the law of property.

Another distinction is between substantive and procedural law. Substantive law defines the legal relationship between one person and others, or between persons and the state. Procedural law deals with the methods and means by which substantive law is made and administered. Substantive laws define rights and duties; procedural laws provide a means to enforce those rights and duties. The prohibition on "taking" or harming an endangered species is substantive law; rules requiring preparation of an Environmental Assessment are procedural law.

A third distinction is whether laws are enforced by civil or criminal sanctions (Blackburn, Klayman, and Malin 1988). Civil suits involve litigation between private or public parties, that is, individuals, corporations, or government agencies. Disagreement may stem from an injury (referred to as a tort) or a violation of a contract or commercial agreement. The courts also may protect individuals from irreparable harm.

Civil suits regarding forest resource laws are more common than criminal proceedings. Civil actions may involve landowners or corporations that violate state or federal laws or disputes among individuals or corporations regarding personal and business dealings. Challenges to clear-cutting on the Monongahela National Forest in the early 1970s came in the form of civil proceedings in federal courts. Enforcement of most public regulations of the actions of private landowners falls in this class. Water, recreation, and rangeland uses usually are governed by civil laws, as are employer–employee relations.

Criminal sanctions enforce citizens' duties to society. The purpose of criminal law is to punish wrongdoers. Punishment may involve a fine (payable to the state) or a jail sentence. Criminal actions may include violations of constitutional, legislative, or administrative law. Constitutional violations are rare in forestry. Legislative law violations are more common at the state level where the acts usually are more specific. Most violations occur at the administrative law level. A common type of criminal violation in natural resources involves the illegal taking of wildlife. Arson also is a crime, for forests as well as for buildings. Several state forest practice regulations have criminal penalties for blatant violations of the law. Violators of some environmental protection measures, such as toxic waste disposal, may face criminal prosecution. Land trespass and timber theft are crimes.

SOURCES OF LAW

The rules that constitute our legal system are derived from the United States Constitution, state constitutions, legislatures, administrative agencies, and courts (Siegel 1982). The U.S. Constitution is the supreme law of our land. The Constitution creates a governmental structure, allocates authority among various branches and levels of government, restricts government authority in specific instances, and lists several rights of citizens. All other laws must be consistent with the Constitution to be valid. State constitutions perform similar functions; in addition, they must be consistent with the provisions of the U.S. Constitution.

Legislative or statutory laws are enacted by the U.S. Congress and by state and local legislative bodies, and the rules are enacted by federal or state agencies to implement those laws. The primary function of legislatures is to make laws. Much of the resource and environmental law is in the form of statutes, such as the National Environmental Policy Act, the Endangered Species Act, the National Forest Management Act, state laws that regulate coastal development, and local zoning ordinances. Acts of Congress must not violate the Constitution, and under the Constitution's supremacy clause, acts of state legislatures must also conform to the supreme law of the land.

Statutory laws (statutes) often authorize administrative agencies to make rules, which are referred to as administrative law. The federal Clean Water Act authorizes the Environmental Protection Agency to promulgate and enforce rules to protect water quality. Rules defining effluent standards have the force of law. Maine's Shoreland Areas Act authorizes municipal governments to promulgate rules to regulate development along designated shorelines. State and federal agencies now issue reams of regulations that govern the actions of private citizens and corporations (Gellhorn and Boyer 1981, Siegel 1982).

Courts are another source of law. Courts rule on disputes between citizens. The body of law that has developed as a result of these decisions is called common law or case law. Common law has developed in English-speaking countries and is applied in all states in the United States except Louisiana, where the Napoleonic Code is the basis for law (Siegel 1982).

Courts also contribute to the development of the legal system by interpreting constitutional, statutory, and administrative law. When citizens bring cases to a court, judges must determine whether a government action is contrary to the Constitution, an administrative action is consistent with relevant statutes, or an agency's actions are consistent with its own administrative rules.

Law is an instrument of public policy. It is not the only instrument but it is used widely. People often complain that we have too many laws, lawsuits, and lawyers. But we have taken little action to reduce our reliance on law. The proliferation of rules (through legislatures, administrative agencies, and courts) and lawsuits reflects the growing complexity of our society, as well as our continuing belief in, or even fascination with, the value of law. This belief in law is not new; when he was helping develop the Constitution, Samuel Adams stated that the Constitution made the United States a nation of laws, not men.

ILLUSTRATION: THE NATIONAL ENVIRONMENTAL POLICY ACT

The conservation movement in the United States in the late nineteenth and early twentieth centuries was a response to unbridled resource exploitation by private interests. The conservationists felt that government scientists and administrators could help the country prevent waste and avoid monopolization of natural resources. The environmental movement that began in the 1960s, however, was more skeptical than hopeful concerning the role of government in natural resources conservation. Large federal bureaucracies had developed close ties to the interests that stood to benefit from their decisions, and many groups were left out of agency decision-making processes (Schoenbaum 1982). As one response to these problems, Congress passed the National Environmental Policy Act (NEPA) of 1969, which went into effect on January 1, 1970.

NEPA mandated that all federal agencies evaluate the environmental effects of their programs, especially on federal lands. NEPA was designed to reform the federal decision-making process by defining new substantive goals and procedural rules that federal agencies had to follow. The procedural rules in NEPA explained the steps required for analysis of environmental impacts. The courts have been instrumental in determining when NEPA has been obeyed by federal agencies. As of 1982 more than a thousand court cases had been filed under NEPA to try to stop agency actions (Schoenbaum 1982).

The first section of the National Environmental Policy Act states that the federal government, in cooperation with the states and other public and private organizations, should

Use all practicable means and measures, including financial and technical assistance, in a manner calculated to foster and promote the general welfare, to create and maintain conditions under which man and nature can exist in productive harmony, and fulfill the social, economic, and other requirements of present and future generations of Americans.

Furthermore, the act mandated that the federal government use all possible means to

1. Fulfill the responsibilities of each generation as a trustee of the environment for succeeding generations.

2. Assure for all Americans safe, healthful, productive, and esthetically and culturally pleasing surroundings.

3. Attain the widest range of beneficial uses of the environment without degradation, risk to health or safety, or other undesirable or unintended consequences.

4. Preserve important historic, cultural, and natural aspects of our national heritage and maintain, wherever possible, an environment that supports diversity, and variety of individual choice.

5. Achieve a balance between population and resource use that will permit high standards of living and a wide sharing of life's amenities.

6. Enhance the quality of renewable resources and approach the maximum attainable recycling of depletable resources.

In order to accomplish these lofty objectives, Section 1 of NEPA set forth detailed, systematic, and interdisciplinary procedures that incorporate the natural, social, and environmental sciences in the planning of actions that impact the environment. These procedures must be followed by all federal agencies. Agencies were also required to identify and develop procedures to quantify environmental amenities and values to be used in decision making. For every major federal action significantly affecting the quality of the environment, agencies were required to prepare a detailed statement that included the environmental impact of the action, any adverse environmental impacts that should be avoided, alternatives to the proposed action, relationships between short-term use and long-term productivity, and any irreversible or irretrievable commitments of resources that might occur. In making this detailed environmental impact statement, federal agencies had to seek comments from other agencies with legal jurisdiction or technical expertise regarding the environmental impact. The statement also must be reviewed by the president, the Council on Environmental Quality, and the public.

These broad mandates of the original NEPA bill required federal agencies to prepare a detailed Environmental Impact Statement (EIS) for major federal actions. The Council on Environmental Quality, which was created by the act, issued procedural regulations for conducting an impact analysis and writing an EIS (40 C.F.R. 1500 et seq. [1981]). The CFR rules first required "scoping"—an early and open process outlining the scope of issues to be addressed. An EIS is intended to force action to ensure that the policies and goals defined in NEPA are infused into the ongoing policy actions of the federal government. Every EIS has many sections including a summary, a statement of purpose and need, alternatives including the proposed action, environmental consequences, cost–benefit analyses, invitations for comments, and a schedule for agency actions.

It is not always necessary for an agency to complete a full-blown EIS. In some situations the less-detailed Environmental Assessment (EA) document may be adequate to determine if a proposed action can significantly impact the human environment. If not, then the agency can file a finding of no significant impact (FONSI), and the NEPA process essentially ends. If so, the EA facilitates the preparation of an EIS. The EA must include a brief discussion of the need for the proposed action, alternative actions, and their environmental impacts. The EA also must list agencies and persons consulted during its preparation (Daniels and Kelly 1990, Yost and Rubin 1990).

NEPA and its subsequent regulations have been used extensively to achieve the broad environmental goals stated in the act. Through its procedural rules, the law has allowed a variety of citizen and other interest groups extensive involvement in the federal decision-making process.

In addition to increasing citizen input in decisions, NEPA also provided the basis for litigation in federal courts. Most cases were brought to court by citizen and environmental groups seeking to halt government agency action. In most cases, the basis of the complaint was either (1) that

the agency violated NEPA by not preparing an EIS or (2) that the EIS prepared was inadequate. The groups bringing these civil suits usually sought to stop the federal project or action. The courts' disposition of these cases has varied from complete dismissal of the suits, to requiring an agency to prepare or revise an EIS, to issuing temporary or permanent injunctions (Schoenbaum 1982).

Perhaps the most important element of NEPA is its use of a procedural rule, the requirement of assessing environmental impact, to ensure a substantive goal, protection of the environment. Many federal officials and private businesspersons complain that environmentalists' NEPA lawsuits sidestep the substantive attributes of federal projects and, instead, fasten onto technicalities. Indeed, technicalities or procedural rules are the only legal tools NEPA gives to potential litigants. For example, environmentalists cannot go to court to challenge a federal law only on the basis that it will have an adverse effect on fish habitat. Instead they can use NEPA and challenge the procedures used to decide what will be done and the degree of environmental protection afforded fish. Thus procedural rules may divert attention away from the substantive issues of a natural resources conflict. This is important because much of American law is composed of procedural rules. Usually when we complain about red tape and technicalities, we are criticizing procedural requirements. The courts play a major role in interpreting these requirements.

Another important issue that has developed regarding the EIS process is the level of detail required and the management authority granted by an approved statement. For example, does the preparation of an EIS for all the national forests in a region, or even for a particular national forest, grant authority to spray herbicides on a particular tract? By the early 1990s it appeared that site-specific actions would require an environmental assessment or environmental notification in addition to the comprehensive Environmental Impact Statements for entire programs or projects.

JUDICIAL POWERS

Article III of the U.S. Constitution authorized a Supreme Court and such inferior courts as Congress shall establish. Judges were authorized to hold their offices "during good Behavior"—essentially a lifetime appointment. Section 2 of Article III states that "The Judicial power shall extend to all Cases, in Law and Equity, arising under this Constitution, the Laws of the United States, and Treaties made, or which shall be made." Furthermore, Section 2 authorized federal courts to try a wide variety of cases. These include cases involving federal employees; cases in which the United States is a party; and controversies between two or more states, between citizens of different states, and between foreign citizens and states. This brief authority granted in Article III has led to the creation of an extensive federal court system that tries cases involving interpretation or violation of constitutional, legislative, and administrative law.

Federal and state courts settle legal disputes between individuals, firms, or governments. In order for a civil suit to be considered, someone who is dissatisfied (a plaintiff) must bring a suit to court. Courts can only decide on disputes between litigants and on laws that are challenged in court. Laws that are unpopular but not challenged will remain in effect. Most suits that are filed do not come to trial and are settled out of court.

JUDICIAL REVIEW

It is less than apparent from the phrasing of Article III of the Constitution that the judiciary could rule on the constitutionality of laws enacted by Congress and signed by the president. However, it was commonly believed that the such judicial review was intended by the authors of the Constitution, based on discussions and writing at that time, including the Federalist Papers (1788). Judicial review also had been used by state courts.

Whatever the intent of the framers may have been, in 1803 the Supreme Court clearly established the principle of judicial review in the famous case of *Marbury* v. *Madison* (1 Cranch 137 [1803]). The relatively weak Supreme Court of the time, under the guidance of Chief Justice John Marshall, declared a provision of the Judiciary Act of 1789 unconstitutional. This power, however, was not exercised again by the Supreme Court until the Dred Scott case in 1857 (*Dred Scott* v. *Sandford,* 19 Howard 393 [1857]). The Supreme Court began to review congressional legislation, particularly social legislation, more frequently after the Civil War. In modern times judicial review has become an integral component of the system of checks and balances. As illustrated in the case of migratory birds cited in the chapter introduction, judicial review has been applied in natural resources law; its application to federal timber sales is now one of the key issues in resolving the controversy surrounding old-growth forests and spotted owls in the Pacific Northwest. According to Yost and Rubin (1990), it is judicial review that has given NEPA its significance.

In the absence of an enforcement mechanism, court decisions rely heavily upon voluntary compliance. Sometimes if a judge has reason to doubt whether good faith compliance will be forthcoming on the part of those being regulated, the court may retain jurisdiction over the case. Judges who have ordered improvements in local jails often have required periodic reports from cities and counties responsible for operating the facilities. If there is little indication of compliance, the judge can quickly step in and write a more precise decision or punish the noncompliant for being in contempt of the court order. However, even if a judge retains control of the case, lack of an enforcement agency will impede judicial policy execution, as mentioned in Chapter 5.

FACTS VERSUS VALUES

The courts rule on matters of fact to determine if a law has been violated. Although courts often have to decipher legislative intent, they less frequently rule on the constitutionality of a law. In jury trials, the jury decides the issues of fact while the judge rules on points of law. In nonjury trials, the judge decides issues of both fact and law. Courts are supposed to enforce legislative decisions equitably, so long as they do not violate any constitutional mandates. The personal values of the judge are not supposed to influence the outcome, although there are many instances in which judges have been captives of their values or slaves to ambition. Legislators, on the other hand, are expected to enact legislation based on people's values—their own or their constituents.

A number of interesting state forestry decisions illustrate the roles and limits of the judiciary. In a controversy regarding the legality of a Cook County (Chicago area), Illinois, ordinance that authorized establishment and purchase of forest preserves, the court distinguished between the legislative and judicial roles (*Perkins* v. *Board of Commissioners,* 271 Ill. 449, 111 N.E. 580 [1916]). The justices wrote that: "criticisms against the wisdom of a policy, or applicability of a statute are subjects for legislative consideration, and not for the court in determining the constitutionality of the act." The court ruled that establishment of the preserves was legal but specifically avoided judging if it was wise.

In a decision regarding states' use of the police power to regulate private individuals, the Washington State Supreme Court lucidly described the differences between legislative and judicial powers (77 Wash. 2d 130, 459 P.2d 789 [1969]). The opinion says that

Highlighting the issue here is the marked difference between the decision making processes of the judiciary and those of the legislative branch of the government under our constitutions. Whereas the judges must determine the facts from the evidence, avoiding personal predilections and opinions, come to a conclusion of ultimate fact from the proof presented, and apply the law thereto regardless of personal animus, bias or feelings, the legislative branch of government under our constitution is free of such strictures. Legislators may well have been

selected by the people not in spite of but because of openly declared opinions, prejudices and predilections. Unlike the judges, legislators need not base their decisions upon the weight of evidence, but may vote against the preponderance of it or vote upon a proposition without hearing any evidence whatever. In prescribing the police power, all that is constitutionally required of the legislature is that a state of facts can reasonably be conceived to exist which would justify the legislation. If the courts can reasonably conceive of such a state of facts, they must presume that such facts actually did exist and that the statute being tested was passed with reference to them. . . .

It is not the court's function to decide whether the statute is sound or unsound, wise or unwise, effectual or ineffectual—but only whether it is within the legislature's constitutional power to enact it. This comports with the general democratic principle that powers of self-government have been largely reserved by the people to be exercised through their legislatures and not their courts.

The judges in the Washington case upheld a law requiring the wearing of motorcycle helmets, but much of the court's reasoning was based on an earlier decision regarding the constitutionality of a state forest practice law regulating private forest landowners' actions. A number of federal forestry cases, which will be considered in the next section, also demonstrate the importance of questions of facts and laws in judicial decisions.

JUDICIAL STRUCTURE

The federal and most state court systems have a three-tier system for civil and criminal cases. The lowest level consists of district trial courts, the intermediate level of appellate courts, and the highest level of a supreme court. Various special courts, such as tax court and claims court, exist but do not deal with natural resources issues as often. Federal jurisdiction in legal controversies requires that the case concern an interpretation of the U.S. Constitution or federal laws, that the United States be a litigant, or that the case involve a controversy between states, or between citizens of different states. State jurisdiction obviously involves cases dealing with state law, between citizens in a state, or between a state and its own citizens or corporations. The structure of the federal court system is shown in Figure 8-1; most state systems closely replicate this system.

DISTRICT COURTS

District courts, at both the federal and the state levels, are the courts of original jurisdiction for a case. District courts—often termed *trial courts*—consider questions of facts and law. Legal questions may arise concerning the meaning of a law and its application to a particular circumstance. District courts may examine purely factual questions regarding whether a violation of a law has indeed occurred. When the legal application of a law is clear, district courts must then examine the factual evidence presented by the litigants to determine if a violation has occurred and, if so, to impose an appropriate penalty or corrective action. District courts also may consider questions of constitutionality, but facts are the principal concern.

ILLUSTRATION: WETLANDS CLEARING IN LOUISIANA

The case of *Avoyelles Sportsmen's League* v. *Alexander* (473 F. Supp. 525 [1979]) illustrates the detail of the factual matter considered by federal district courts. In *Avoyelles,* a Louisiana forest landowner in the Mississippi River delta (a codefendant) was clearing a bottomland hardwood forest in order to plant soybeans. Local hunting clubs (the plaintiffs) were angry because the lands they had leased for hunting were being cleared. The clubs, in conjunction with the Environmental Defense Fund and the National Wildlife Federation, claimed that the land-operations violated various laws and were being performed without a permit. At issue was the applicability of the Federal Water Pollution Control Act Amendments of 1972, specifically Section 404, regulating dredge and fill operations. The plaintiffs sued Clifford Alexander, the secretary of the army (the Corps of Engineers is charged with administering Section 404), Douglas Costle, the administrator of the U.S. Environmental Protection Agency, and the landowner.

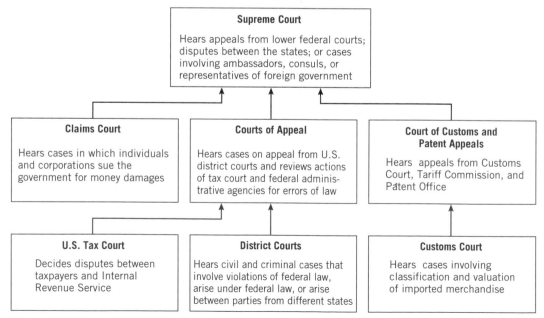

Figure 8-1. The Federal Court System
Source: Dye, Greene, and Pasthemos 1980.

The decision illustrates the significance and the detail of the factual matter considered. The court had to determine if the land-clearing operations were point sources of pollution, as defined by Section 404 of the Federal Water Pollution Control Act Amendments of 1972 and 1977, and thus whether the landowner could be denied permission to convert the wetland from bottomland hardwoods to soybeans. The district court determined that

More than half of the tract, i.e., everything at or below 45.8 feet MSL [mean sea level], is subject to the average annual flood. Virtually all of the tract, i.e., everything at or below 49.6 feet MSL is subject to the average bi-annual flood.

The clearing of the Lake Long Tract began in June of 1978. Sometime prior to that loggers had harvested much of the commercially valuable hardwoods with chainsaws. Thereafter, the private defendants took various steps to remove all the remaining trees and vegetation from the tract so that it could be put to agricultural use and specifically into soybean production.

Initially, bulldozers outfitted with shearing blades cut the timber and vegetation at or just above ground level. The shearing blades were v-shaped, had a serrated edge and flat bottom and were approximately 18-20 feet in length. The blades were adjusted to be free floating so that they would ride along the top surface of the ground. Occasionally, however, the blades would gouge the surface of the ground. Although the blades were adjusted to ride on the ground's surface, they did scrape the leaf litter and humus that overlaid the soil as they moved from tree to tree.

After the shearing was completed in a section, bulldozers outfitted with rake blades pushed the felled trees into windrows. The upper portion of the raking blade was solid whereas the lower portion had tines that permitted soil to pass through the openings. The raking blades were also outfitted so that they generally operated on top of the soil. However, in the process of windrowing the trees and debris, soil and leaf litter was also scraped into the windrows. It is not clear whether the blades themselves or the broom-like action of the trees and brush that they were pushing actually scraped the soil and the overlying leaf litter. In any event the photographic evidence clearly demonstrated that soil and leaf litter was piled up during the windrowing process—this movement filled in low

areas and along with the discing which followed, had a levelling effect on the surface of the land.

From these facts, the court concluded that

We determine that defendants' land-clearing equipment (bulldozers fitted with V-blades, bulldozers fitted with raking blades, and the tractor-pulled rakes), ditch excavation equipment (the backhoe used to excavate the three-quarter mile drainage ditch as well as any equipment used to excavate the proposed drainage ditches) and discing equipment (unless used in connection with "normal farming"), are point sources. The general definition of point source and the illustrative examples connote that a point source is an isolate, identifiable activity that conveys a pollutant, dredged or fill material. The operation of defendants' equipment was certainly an identifiable and isolate activity. It also conveyed dredged or fill material since it collected, gathered and transported the sheared trees and vegetation, leaf litter and soil across the wetland which, for reasons set out below, we determine to be dredged material. It is clear beyond cavil that any machinery used in ditch excavation is a point source since such machinery excavates the wetland soil and when so doing discharges this soil back into the wetland.

The court stated that a wetland, as classified under Section 404, constituted anything that was "inundated or saturated by surface or ground water at a frequency and duration sufficient to support, and that under normal circumstances do support, *a prevalence of vegetation typically adopted [sic] for life in saturated soil conditions....* The above quoted definition makes it clear that wetlands include the vegetation that grows thereon".

The court ruled that the clear-cutting and clearing of bottomland hardwoods did not constitute normal farming or silviculture operations and would not be exempt from the Section 404 permit program. The gist of this decision was that clear-cutting bottomland hardwoods in order to convert land use required a permit from the Corps of Engineers under Section 404. Also of significance, the meaning of wetlands was construed quite broadly. Subsequently, the court of appeals affirmed the decision of the district court, although it defined wetlands slightly less liberally (511 F. Supp. 278 [1981], 715 F.2d 897 [1983]).

The *Avoyelles* decision illustrates the detailed legal and factual questions that a district court may have to consider. The court had to determine at least one crucial question of law—namely, did the Section 404 permit requirements of the Federal Water Pollution Control Act apply to clear-cutting bottomland hardwoods for conversion to soybean fields, or was this a normal farming or silviculture operation? The court also had to determine at least two equally important questions of fact: (1) Did clearing the forest, root-raking, piling, burning, and discing constitute a dredge and fill operation—that is, were wetlands filled, and (2) was the area indeed a wetland? In this case, the court decided that (1) land conversion was not exempt from the permit requirements, (2) soil movement during clearing was a fill operation, and (3) the bottomland hardwoods were indeed wetlands. It thus concluded that clear-cutting hardwoods and then clearing the land would require a permit from the Corps of Engineers, which could deny such permits for many reasons related to its assigned responsibilities under the Federal Water Pollution Control Act.

APPELLATE COURTS

State and federal courts of appeal hear cases in which one of the litigants is dissatisfied with the trial court ruling and appeals. Appeals focus only on questions of law and constitutionality. They generally assume that the facts of a case have been settled in the district court decision.

Currently, the United States has 11 regional federal circuit courts of appeal, and another appelate court in the District of Columbia that can decide cases with national authority. The appellate districts, or "circuits," are divided according to state lines. The 12 circuit courts hear appeals from the 94 district courts and from the U.S. Tax Court as well. Appeals to the circuit court may be made only by the losing party in a district court case. Circuit court decisions apply in all the states in that circuit. Different circuits are not legally bound to follow the mandates of a decision in another circuit unless a similar district court decision is rendered in both circuits. However, many agencies or citizens will voluntarily follow the decisions of another circuit in order to avoid further litigation or expense that might be fruitless. There are instances, however, when similar factual situations will result in conflicting decisions between two circuits. Such differences can be resolved by the U.S. Supreme Court. A Supreme Court decision, of course, applies to all U.S. federal courts, federal laws, and federal agencies.

The circuit courts concentrate on whether the law was correctly applied by the trial court. It is rare for circuit courts to reverse district court findings of fact. The circuit courts have been very important in natural resource policy. Most of the significant federal public land management laws and environmental protection laws have been challenged and affected by eventual circuit court decisions. As illustrated, the *Avoyelles* case regarding clear-cutting in and conversion of wetlands was upheld by the federal circuit court in New Orleans.

Another significant environmental protection case stemmed from the 1972 Federal Water Pollution Control Act Amendments. The amendments brought nonpoint source pollution, including that from forestry activities, under the federal act regulating water pollution. Section 208 required areawide regional planning for nonpoint pollution. Initial interpretations of the act suggested that such planning and control would be required only for urban areas. However, a challenge to the law was heard by the District of Columbia Court of Appeals. The judges ruled that areawide planning should apply throughout the United States, although it could be less comprehensive in rural areas (*Natural Resources Defense Council* v. *Train*, 396 F.Supp. 1386 [1975]; *Natural Resources Defense Council* v. *Costle*, 564 F.2d 1369 [1977]). Thus, forestry activities must take into consideration means to avoid nonpoint source pollution (Anderson, Mandelker, and Tarlock 1984).

ILLUSTRATION: TIMBER HARVESTING PRACTICES ON THE MONONGAHELA NATIONAL FOREST

Without a doubt, the most significant case affecting public forest land management was *Izaak Walton League* v. *Butz* (367 F.Supp. 422 [1973], 522 F.2d 945 [1975]). The Forest Service Organic Act of 1897, as amended, provided that the Secretary of Agriculture could manage the national forests and had the authority to harvest timber. Specifically, the law authorized the secretary of agriculture to designate for sale "the dead, matured or large growth of trees found upon national forests." Additionally, the law stated that the timber "before being sold, shall be marked and designated."

As the clear-cutting controversy discussion in Chapter 2 indicated, many people were dissatisfied with Forest Service management practices. Because they were unable to change agency practices, they sought judicial relief (Hacker 1983). The West Virginia Division of the Izaak Walton League and others who opposed pervasive clear-cutting by the Forest Service sued Earl Butz, the secretary of agriculture, and the Forest Service. The plaintiffs charged that the Forest Service cutting policies violated the 1897 Organic Act. The federal district and appellate courts agreed.

The appellate judges said that "matured," as defined by Congress, undoubtedly referred to the physiological maturity of trees, not the economic maturity on which the Forest Service based its argument. However, the court ruled that the law did not specify an economic basis for harvesting.

Since Congress used the word [maturity] in its physiological sense at the time of the passage of the Organic Act, we know of no canon of statutory construction which would justify or require that its meaning be changed merely because during the intervening years the timber industry has developed the commercial concept of economic or management maturity.

The court found that the language requiring timber to be marked clearly applied to individual trees, not stands.

We find the statutory language to be simple and unambiguous. The term "marked" in the context of forestry is well defined and means "selection and indication by a blaze, paint or marking hammer on the stem of trees to be felled or retained." "Designate," on the other hand, is a much broader term and merely means to "indicate." The two words are not synonymous or interchangeable and in using them conjunctively it is evident that Congress intended that the Forest Service designate the area from which the timber was to be sold and, additionally, placed upon the Service the obligation to mark each individual tree which was authorized to be cut.

The Forest Service argued against the literal interpretation of the law, saying that forest science had progressed greatly since the 1897 legislation was written. The court recognized the change but stated that its task was to adjudicate disputes about laws as they were written, not as they were affected by social norms or technology. Though acknowledging the possible consequences, the judges wrote that courts should not alter legislation, a responsibility assigned Congress.

The appellants urge that this change of policy was in the public interest and that the courts should not permit a literal reading of the 1897 Act to frustrate the modern science of silviculture and forest management presently practiced by the Forest Service to meet the nation's current timber demands. Economic exigencies, however, do not grant the courts a license to rewrite a statute no matter how desirable the purpose or result might be. If the words of the statute are clear, the court should not add to or alter them to accomplish a purpose that does not appear on the face of the statute or from its legislative history.

The 1975 appellate court ruling invalidated the Forest Service sales procedures throughout the Fourth Circuit Court region. Faced with the prospects of similar suits and defeats in other districts, the Forest Service sought new organic legislation, as suggested by the court. These efforts eventually led to the National Forest Management Act of 1976, which repealed the Organic Act of 1897 and currently provides the basis for national forest planning and management.

SUPREME COURT

The United States Supreme Court, consisting of nine justices, hears appeals from lower federal courts and has original jurisdiction in disputes between the states, as well as cases involving emissaries from other governments. The Supreme Court examines questions of law and the constitutionality of congressional acts. When considering an appeal, the Supreme Court may take one of three courses of action. Because it hears fewer than 200 cases a year, its most frequent response is to decline to hear the appeal—termed *certiorari denied*. In choosing which of the many cases to hear, the Court operates on the "rule of four," meaning that after a review by their law clerks, if four of the justices think a case raises significant questions, briefs will be requested and the case will be scheduled for oral argument.

Refusal to hear an appeal need not mean that the Supreme Court agrees with the decision of the lower court. The Supreme Court receives many appeals; it only accepts those it deems most significant for constitutional questions, its interests, or the case's impact. Whatever the reason, the decision of the appellate court stands and applies throughout that circuit. It is not binding in other circuits, but it may influence court decisions regarding similar cases. When the Supreme Court hears a case, it may affirm the appellate court decision, in which case the decision applies nationwide. Alternatively, it may reverse the court of appeals decision, negating any lower court rulings and setting forth guidelines to be followed in future similar litigation. Affirmation or reversal may apply to the entire case under consideration, or perhaps to only a portion of the case and law in question.

Standing to Sue

Several significant environmental law challenges have reached the U.S. Supreme Court. The case of *Sierra Club* v. *Morton* (423 F.2d 24 [1970], 405 U.S. 727 [1972]) provides an interesting example of court deliberations regarding the legal rights of natural objects. The case involved a proposed ski resort in California's Mineral King Valley. The Sierra Club opposed the development and sued Rodgers Morton, the secretary of the interior. Traditionally, plaintiffs in such suits were required to demonstrate that they would suffer personal injury or loss because of the proposed action. They would then have "standing" to sue to prevent execution of (enjoin) the project. The Sierra Club sued but was denied standing because it failed to prove personal injury or loss. The case was appealed to the Supreme Court. In a split decision, the Supreme Court narrowly rejected the appeal.

Justice William O. Douglas, an ardent environmentalist, wrote a vigorous dissent, perhaps in hopes that the Court would one day reverse its opinion. In his dissenting opinion, Douglas suggested that because trees and other inanimate objects cannot bring suit, groups should be allowed to sue on their behalf, without demonstrating personal injury (Douglas 1960, 1965). Stone (1974) lays out the legal and philosophical arguments in favor of legal rights for inanimate objects.

Two more recent cases have involved standing to bring suit. In a case in Hawaii in the 1980s—*Palila* v. *Hawaii Department of Land and Natural Resources*—the Sierra Club and Audubon Society filed a successful suit to protect a rare Hawaiian bird species and were granted standing as interest groups. The use of the name of the palila bird, listed as the first plaintiff, is merely symbolic. In a 1990 decision, the U.S. Supreme Court reversed the U.S. Court of Appeals for the District of Columbia and held that the National Wildlife Federation did not have standing to bring a nationwide challenge to numerous (more than 1250) revocation decisions of public land withdrawals and classifications by the Bureau of Land Management (*Lujan* v. *National Wildlife Federation*, 110 S.Ct. 3177, 3189, [1990]).

The *Lujan* decision said that plaintiffs must (1) demonstrate a specific injury, (2) demonstrate that the injury is imminent, and (3) cite a concrete action before attacking generic regulations. This decision has had some impact on restricting standing in federal courts, according to a National Wildlife Federation attorney (Coffin 1990). The ruling may require a group to demonstrate a specific harm to its interests and may allow suits to be filed only on imminent, not proposed, actions. Furthermore, generic lawsuits against an agency may fail to be granted standing; instead, groups may have to file site-by-site lawsuits (Coffin 1990). The more restrictive interpretation of standing, which was decided on a narrow 5–4 margin, was written by Anton Scalia, a Reagan appointee to the bench. This Court decision illustrates the importance of the president in nominating members of the judiciary.

Land Use Regulation

The Supreme Court has heard many cases involving land use regulation and zoning laws. In these decisions, the Court has helped define the conditions under which the government may use its police powers to regulate the actions of private forest landowners with state forest practices acts. Cubbage and Siegel (1985) review many of these cases, which are discussed in Chapter 14.

One case illustrates the interaction between state and federal supreme courts. Under the Washington State forest practice law, landowners are required to get a permit before harvesting timber. This is the one law specifically regulating forestry practices that was appealed to both the state and federal supreme courts. A Washington landowner claimed that this limitation on use constituted a taking of private property without due compensation, in violation of the Fifth Amendment due process clause of the U.S. Constitution and similar state provisions. The Washington State Supreme Court denied the landowner's assertion. Because the U.S. Constitution was involved, the landowner appealed the case to the U.S. Supreme Court, which affirmed the state court decision without comment (*State v. Dexter,* 32 Wash.2d 551, 202 P.2d 906, 70 S.Ct. 147 [1947]).

SPECIAL COURTS

Special federal courts include the Claims Court, the Court of Customs and Patent Appeals, the Customs Court, and the U.S. Tax Court. They are generally less important in natural resource issues, with a few exceptions. Tax court rulings may significantly affect forest landowners, particularly regarding IRS interpretations and rulings on capital gains treatment of timber and expensing of reforestation and forest management costs. In claims courts, individuals and corporations may sue the government for money damages. In the controversial Redwood National Park expansion, plaintiffs attempted to recover monetary damages for loss of use of their adjacent lands through inverse condemnation proceedings (Iadarola 1979). In these proceedings, individuals may claim that their land use is so restricted that any productive uses are removed, so they should be compensated. Such suits are common with federal projects such as highways and dams, because they divide and isolate land parcels. They occur to a much lesser degree with parks.

STATE COURTS

Each state has a judicial system similar to the federal system, as do most local municipalities. In 1980, 25 million civil and criminal cases were heard by more than 18,000 state and local courts. In that same year there were 206,000 federal cases. State courts prosecute many more criminal cases than do federal courts and affect general business practices more. Interactions of the state judiciaries with the federal judiciary are fairly infrequent, but federal courts may review state court decisions in some instances, for example, when constitutional questions arise (Goldman and Jahnige 1985). As with federal courts, state district courts usually rule on questions of fact and law, appellate courts mostly on questions of law.

ILLUSTRATION: RURAL PROPERTY TAXES IN GEORGIA

The similarity between state and federal court procedures and the detailed factual and legal questions courts deal with can be illustrated by decisions from the Georgia state courts. Rural land taxation was a continuing controversy in Georgia throughout the 1980s as the state's urban areas grew, most notably around Atlanta. This caused sale prices of urban fringe farm and forest lands to increase far beyond the prices received for similar land in purely rural regions of the state. Greater metropolitan area sale prices led tax assessors in the suburban fringe areas to appraise other agricultural land and forest land at values well in excess of their productive capacity for crop or timber production. Higher assessed values mean higher annual property taxes and tend to make traditional rural farming and timber practices unprofitable, thus encouraging conversion to more developed land uses.

Most other states in the nation recognized this problem and enacted current-use assessment laws that allow qualifying landowners to register their lands and receive reduced assessments and taxes based on the productive use of the land. In exchange, the owners usually must enter a contract that requires them to pay back taxes, or perhaps a penalty and interest if they withdraw their land from the favored rural uses. Georgia, however, resisted enacting a current-use law. Dissatisfied landowners in several counties, who did not want to sell their land or pay exorbitant urban taxes on agricultural or forest lands, sought judicial relief.

The cases revolved around the statutory law in the Georgia Code (OCGA 48-5-1) that property should be assessed "at its fair market value," which was defined as "the amount a knowledgeable buyer would pay for the property and a willing seller would accept for the property at an arms length, bona fide sale." To determine the fair market value of real property tax, assessors must consider four criteria: "(i) Existing zoning of property; (ii) Existing use of property; (iii) Existing covenants or restrictions in deed dedicating the property to a particular use; and (iv) Any other factors deemed pertinent in arriving at fair market value."

In Georgia, property owners preferred that criterion (ii) "existing use" be weighted most heavily to determine fair market value. Tax assessors, however, preferred and generally used the concept of "highest and best use" of real property in making their assessments, which fell under criterion (iv) "any other factors deemed pertinent." Strict application of the highest and best use criterion could have two socially undesirable results. First, it could force rural land into more developed uses, even if owners did not want to sell. Many landowners deemed forced conversion to other uses inequitable. Second, it could lead to confiscation of the land for failure to pay taxes. Highest and best use taxation also could make landowners pay more taxes that would reduce or eliminate farm and forestry profits.

Two cases in counties surrounding Atlanta challenged the highest and best use assessments. In *Dotson v. Henry County* (155 Ga. App. 557, 271 S.E.2d 691 [1981]), the landowners contended that highest and best use should not be the only factor in determining fair market value, contrary to the practice of the tax assessors. Expert witnesses testified that land in the county would be worth no more than $200 to $700 per acre for agricultural purposes, and that an income capitalization approach (discounted cash flow of revenues and costs) should be considered in determining value, as suggested in part (ii) of the relevant Georgia Code, because it was a standard method of arriving at value. The trial court concurred with *Dotson* et al.; so did the appellate court after Henry County appealed.

A similar case, *Sibley v. Cobb County Board of Tax Assessors*, also tested the county's right to appraise rural land at its highest and best use, and was appealed through several levels of state courts (244 Ga. 404, 260 S.E. 2d 313 [1979]; 248 Ga. 383, 283 S.E.2d 452 [1981]; 171 Ga. App. 65 [1984]). The plaintiffs in the case, including a judge named Sibley, brought suit contending that the county tax assessors raised appraised values drastically by considering only highest and best use, which was inequitable and violated the complete definition of "fair market value." Furthermore, the plaintiffs claimed that the assessor's consideration of "existing use" was insufficient and alleged that "the entire rural land digest remains void and illegal for failure of the Defendants to lawfully assess such rural land solely according to its present zoning, existing uses, and other restrictions." The district trial court, however, held for the Cobb county tax assessors.

Sibley et al. appealed the decision. The appellate court noted that Sibley had owned his land since the 1930s, plaintiff Hill for 65 years, and plaintiff McAfee for 32 years. Furthermore, plaintiff Power owned 80 acres of timberland that had been held by his family since 1840. The court found that none of these taxpayers wanted to sell his property. After noting these and other facts, the appellate court found two errors that caused it to reverse the trial court and require reassessments. The first error was that tax assessors inappropriately considered prices for sales of rural land in surrounding counties by not excluding sales for "special" or "speculative" purposes. The second error was that the Cobb County assessors did not give sufficient weight to existing agricultural and timberland use.

The *Dotson* and *Sibley* decisions again illustrate the detailed questions of fact and law that trial and appellate courts must consider. The courts had to determine legislative intent inherent in the phrase "fair market value" of land and whether the assessors in the counties had correctly implemented this intent, and later (in a subsequent case) whether the assessors reassessed the plaintiffs' land adequately. Other related cases were concurrently being tried or considered for litigation.

Eventually, the controversies over rural land appraisals and subsequent taxation throughout the state prompted statewide legislative hearings on property tax reform in 1989 and a flurry of bills for property tax revision in the 1990 legislative session. The legislature authorized a constitutional amendment to allow current-use assessments for property taxation and to exempt timber from annual taxation. The amendment was approved by the voters in November 1990, after considerable negative media coverage in the Atlanta papers and on television. A law to implement the change in property tax appraisal was enacted in 1991, and many ongoing administrative debates regarding the implementation of the new timber tax system continued throughout 1992.

JUDICIAL ACTIONS

Traditional jurisprudence processes may consist of pretrial, trial, and appeal stages. Criminal trials may result in innocent, guilty, or "no contest" verdicts and various penalties. Civil litigants usually seek monetary compensation or other actions.

DECISION PROCESSES

The idealized case of traditional jurisprudence goes through three stages: pretrial, trial, and appeal. Trial and appeal are often considered the most important parts of this process, highlighting the adversarial nature of the judicial system. In practice, however, adversarial proceedings are much less common than negotiated out-of-court settlements. In federal district courts, more than 90% of civil cases are settled out of court prior to the trial or before its conclusion, and more than 60% of criminal defendants avoid a trial judgment by a plea of guilty or *nolo contendere* (no contest). The prosecution reduces or drops the charges for more than half the remaining criminal defendants. Thus, only about one in six defendants goes through a complete trial (Goldman and Jahnige 1985).

A typical trial involves a judge, two parties or litigants (plaintiff and respondent in a civil suit; prosecutor and defendant in a criminal case), their lawyers, witnesses, and a jury. Juries are supposed to decide what has happened based on questions of fact. In many civil suits, juries also set damages by deciding how much the case is worth to the plaintiff. The standard of proof in a civil case is which side "a preponderance of the evidence favors." In a criminal case, a jury decides whether the defendant is guilty "beyond a reasonable doubt" (Goldman and Jahnige 1985).

REMEDIES

Litigation is based on a charge that a statute, regulation, or accepted code of behavior has been breached. Violations may take various forms. A law may be violated by an individual, corporation, or government agency. Companies may dump waste illegally in a river; individual landowners may cut timber without the requisite permit; or prior to 1976 the Forest Service may have cut trees incorrectly by not marking each one.

Depending on the type of violation, courts may take several actions. They may declare laws to be unconstitutional, but this is rare. In criminal proceedings courts may find defendants guilty and levy fines or imprisonments accordingly, or they may render a not guilty verdict. Civil suits are more relevant than criminal cases in natural resource management. In civil cases, plaintiffs must prove that the respondent has violated a civil law. If the respondent is found guilty, monetary damages may be assessed or the respondent may be ordered to remedy the problem or injury. These issues may be heard by a judge alone or by a judge and jury. If there is a jury, it decides questions of fact (e.g., whether the respondent performed a specific action), whereas the judge decides issues of law. The judge instructs the jury on the relevant provisions of law and provides guidance.

The equity remedy is often used in environmental cases. Under this approach, judges can act, without a jury, to prevent a pending or proposed activity while the legal challenge is considered. Cases in equity seek to have an action enjoined or prevented, whereas cases in law ask damages to compensate for wrongful acts. In equity cases, judges can first issue a temporary restraining order, without notice of the proceedings being given to the respondent. Such orders are designed to preserve the status quo while the court makes a more complete examination of the facts and are issued for a period of 10 days or less.

Following the temporary restraining order, judges may issue a preliminary injunction for the period of time they deem best, after arguments by both the plaintiff and the respondent are heard. The hearing consists of traditional adversarial procedures including arguments and supporting materials. Again the intent of a preliminary injunction is to prevent harm from occurring or continuing. After a complete trial, a permanent injunction on the respondent's action may be issued if the plaintiff's allegations are proven. This implies that the respondent's proposed actions were illegal under federal or state law.

Citizens Against Toxic Sprays v. *Bergland* (428 F. Supp. 908 [1977]) is an example of the equity model. In this case a citizens' group, as plaintiff, asked a federal district court in Oregon to prevent the Forest Service from using phenoxy herbicides on the Siuslaw National Forest. The court ruled that the vegetation management EIS prepared by the Forest Service did an inadequate job of analyzing the health hazards associated with herbicides. Because the EIS did not comply with NEPA, the court enjoined the agency from further use of 2,4,5-T and silvex on the Siuslaw National Forest.

Courts also may respond with an equity remedy for procedural failings—failure to follow the due process requirements mandated in a law. The National Forest Management Act of 1976 requires detailed procedures for public input in the forest planning process. Failure of a national forest to meet the requirements may prompt appeals to the chief of the Forest Service or provide bases for court challenges. NEPA, with its requirements for the preparation of an EIS, can provide grounds for court action on the basis of a procedural failing. Many states also require EIS reports for private corporations and plants, such as pulp and paper mills. Because of the required detail, agencies or corporations can inadvertently omit part of the detailed procedures, thus giving the courts cause to invalidate their action. If due process is not followed, courts will typically send the plan back or halt the project until corrective actions are taken and the EIS meets all requirements.

The president's Council on Environmental Quality examined 114 NEPA procedural-based Environmental Impact Statement lawsuits filed in 1981. The Defense and Transportation departments were the most frequent targets of lawsuits, followed by Interior and Agriculture. Sixty-five percent of the cases involving NEPA were brought against these four departments. The most frequent plaintiffs were environmental groups, followed by individuals and citizen groups, local governments, business groups, and property owners. Of the 114 cases, 52 were brought because of an agency's failure to prepare an EIS; 58 suits claimed inadequate statements (Hall 1983).

Courts also may respond to arbitrary and capricious actions by government agencies. Such actions imply that the agency has failed to act on the basis of fact or good logic or judgment. In response to a lawsuit filed by citizen groups, federal district Judge Thomas Zilly ruled in 1988 that the U.S. Fish and Wildlife Service had acted in an arbitrary and capricious manner by choosing not to list the northern spotted owl under the Endangered Species Act. Subsequent to that ruling, the agency listed the owl as a threatened species in 1990.

COURTS AND PUBLIC POLICY

The judiciary has become increasingly important in forestry matters, as in most other fields. The merits of pervasive court involvement are debatable, particularly in the opinion of professional forest resource managers. However, the involvement of the judiciary offers advantages as well as disadvantages.

ADVANTAGES

Depending on one's viewpoint, appeals to the judiciary are either an opportunity or a problem. Environmental groups commonly perceive the option of judicial action as desirable, particularly when they have been unsuccessful at changing agency practices. The courts also provide access to a decision-making arena for those with unpopular causes and modest resources. Although attorney fees and court costs are not inexpensive, they are less expensive than developing a massive public relations campaign to expand an issue and change policy.

Courts provide a forum for individuals who may have just claims, based on law, but do not have policy-making authority. The Forest Service (and the forestry profession) has often been criticized for excessive reliance on clear-cutting. Without frequent court challenges, the agency might practice clear-cutting almost exclusively. When policymakers discriminate against certain classes of people, such as in the Georgia property tax cases illustrated earlier, courts offer an opportunity to protect individual rights. Courts also enforce civil and contractual responsibilities and adjudicate criminal violations. These roles are all indispensable in guaranteeing property rights and fair exchange (required for the market system to work) and to ensure personal freedom (required for democracy to work).

The courts offer the opportunity to secure fairly rapid consideration of an issue, especially when a temporary injunction is being sought. Trials that fully explore the issues may take considerably longer, but at least agenda status is achieved sooner. The possibility of court action also helps groups obtain credibility quickly and provides considerable bargaining leverage for other negotiated compromises to change agency policies or to settle personal disagreements.

Once on the court docket, vague issues or problems must be reduced to concrete matters of substance. Judges can consider only specific violations of law. If specificity is lacking, the case will be dismissed readily. In the federal judiciary, there usually is extensive pretrial contact between the opposing attorneys and with the judge. Prior to trial, the issues will be narrowed as the litigants agree on facts that are uncontested.

The judiciary offers an opportunity for relatively independent action on issues. Federal judges hold their offices essentially for life. State judges usually hold de facto lifetime tenure. Although states provide for periodic review of their jurists through elections or challenges from candidates who would replace them, judges' tenure tends to be very secure. Judicial tenure makes judges relatively immune to political pressure, as clearly demonstrated in school desegregation decisions. That is not to say that judges do not feel or respond to public opinion. They do. But the pressure is less than that put on executives or legislators.

Judges deal with a variety of issues and are by nature generalists, except on matters of law. Theoretically, their personal opinions are not supposed to determine how they rule on an issue. Some significant exceptions exist, particularly on issues highly salient to the judge. As previously mentioned, Supreme Court Justice William O. Douglas was a well-known environmentalist, and Judge Miles Lord in Minnesota was a well-known environmental activist. Current Supreme Court Justices William Rehnquist and Anton Scalia are developing reputations as ardent conservatives. Interest groups are aware of a judge's personal biases from prior trials. When initiating a test case on a particular law, they will attempt to bring suit in the most favorable jurisdiction.

CRITICISMS

Several criticisms have been made of judicial involvement. Anderson (1977) examines some of these misconceptions and largely dismisses the problems. One issue is the role of the courts in determining forest resource policies. Critics charge that the courts are the least democratic branch of government, representing fewer interests than legislatures. By definition, judicial decisions are based on adversarial proceedings that consider two principal alternatives. Compromise often is

difficult in court, although it is relatively easy and common at the pretrial stage. Because court decisions may affect many people, such decisions should fall under the legislative aegis instead; but the legislature can always change the law—judges can only interpret it. These criticisms have merit, but the judiciary is generally only performing its role as defined by the Constitution and the evolving roles of the judiciary in our society.

Legislatures often are careful to avoid specificity in their laws, as noted before, so courts must interpret their intent. The vagueness of the Georgia property tax laws illustrates this function of the courts. The laws listed four criteria for determining land value but gave no instructions regarding the relative weights of each criterion. Thus disagreements about assessments in some counties had to be settled by the courts. In fact, the owners of timberland were glad to be able to seek favorable court action.

Courts have been criticized for their role in deciding technical forestry issues. Some resource managers feel their professional skills and expertise should preclude judicial interference. They find it presumptuous that judges should tell foresters how to manage resources, probably incorrectly at that. Sampson (1985, p.4) expresses the prevalent view: "How can we change the system so that decisions are made out in the forest, with foresters, biologists, and pest managers making their case to the affected public; instead of in Washington, D.C., with lawyers arguing in front of a judge?"

Anderson (1977) rebuts such beliefs, noting that the courts often handle highly technical issues. In court, public agencies, environmental interest groups, private corporations, individuals, or other litigants all have opportunities to state their case using technical information. Medical malpractice, industrial accidents, voting districts, antitrust actions, and tax questions, to mention a few, are all complex issues. Courts may obtain technical information from legal arguments and briefs, expert witnesses, or *amicus curiae* (friend of the court) testimony submitted by technical groups such as professional societies. Basing their decision on extensive evidence, the judges decide who has presented the most persuasive arguments. The wording in the *Izaak Walton League* and *Avoyelles* cases presented earlier indicates the highly technical detail considered by the courts.

Standing to sue, which was discussed earlier, is another significant issue in natural resources litigation. Environmental groups often seek broad standing in order to protect the environment; agencies and development interests often prefer narrow standing strictures. When private property rights are impaired, individuals have traditionally had authority to bring suit. This also applies to corporations, which are considered persons under common law. More recently, when public property rights have been impaired, groups have had standing if they can prove that they were affected by a public policy decision. Groups may initiate class action suits, in which they litigate on behalf of many people in a similar situation. Although trees do not specifically have standing to date, that does not imply they never will. The strategy most groups use when suing public agencies is to not only show that their group is affected, but also to enlist the cooperation of disgruntled local landowners affected by the policy in question.

Another concern with judicial intervention is the proliferation of litigation. The majority of the national forest plans mandated under the National Forest Management Act will be subject to administrative appeals to the chief of the Forest Service, and many will be brought to court. Despite the merits of public involvement and due process, employees of the Forest Service consider this excessive. In 1992 changes to restrict or eliminate the agency appeal process were proposed.

Forestry is not unique in the number of lawsuits it has generated. But again, environmental groups, and even industry groups, welcome the opportunity to challenge agency plans in the courts. In the early 1980s the United States had about 600,000 lawyers and about 25 million lawsuits per year. This immense caseload prompts judges to try to lessen the number of cases they hear. Courts may refuse to hear a case because it lacks merit; the U.S. Supreme Court hears only a fraction of the cases appealed to it. Judges may also encourage out-of-court settlements.

The glut of cases in the judiciary at the federal level and in many states has prompted some litigants to seek a private market solution. A small but growing number of parties have agreed to be bound by the decisions of privately hired judges or arbitrators. These judges, who are frequently retired from the bench, are paid jointly by the two parties. Standard rules of evidence apply and at the conclusion of the hearing, the judge renders a verdict. An advantage is that a court date will come much sooner, and this will help minimize sky-rocketing fees for attorneys, as well as settle the issue more quickly.

ILLUSTRATION: THE WOODPECKER AND THE JUDGE

The role of the courts in deciding technical wildlife and forestry issues is well illustrated by a Texas case about management of national forests to protect red-cockaded woodpecker habitat. The red-cockaded woodpecker (RCW) was listed as an endangered species in 1970. At 7¼" the RCW is small next to better-known endangered birds such as the bald eagle, whooping crane, and California condor; but the impact of the RCW on forest management is large. To date, only the northern spotted owl has affected public forest land management more than the RCW.

The RCW inhabits southern pine forests, of which there is certainly no shortage. However, the RCW has peculiar habitat requirements. Unlike other woodpeckers, the RCW chooses to chisel out its den cavity in live pine trees, a laborious task that may take as long as four years. The RCW prefers mature pines that have been infected with redheart fungus, which tends to weaken the heartwood and make the birds' excavation chores somewhat easier. Most trees with nest cavities are more than 70 years old; the youngest tree that a nest cavity has been discovered in is 63 years old. Furthermore, the RCW prefers open parklike stands containing little understory and forages for insects on trees that are at least 30 years old. In much of the vast southern pinery, hardwoods form a substantial component of the forest, to the detriment of the RCW.

National Forest Woodpecker Management

Only 10 percent of the timberlands in the South are publicly owned. Most of these lands are national forests, where pines are typically managed on 60- to 80-year even-aged rotations. Few private landowners now have trees more than 60 years old, precluding viable RCW populations on almost all private lands. For all practical purposes, the future of the RCW depends on southern national forests, which are estimated to contain 70 percent of the known woodpecker colonies in Texas (Wolf 1991).

In 1988 Judge Robert M. Parker, a federal judge in the Eastern District of Texas, ruled that the U.S. Forest Service "jeopardized" the existence of the RCW under Section 7 of the Endangered Species Act of 1973 (ESA). Furthermore, Forest Service management practices represented a "taking" of the RCW under Section 9 of the ESA. The judge's ruling enjoined the Forest Service from clear-cutting within three-quarters of a mile of an active RCW colony site and spelled out specific silvicultural prescriptions that the Forest Service must employ to protect the RCW (*Sierra Club v. Lyng*, Civ. No. L-85-69-CA, E.D. Texas, June 17, 1988).

A radius of three-quarters of a mile, or 1200 meters, encompasses an area totaling 1117 acres. When the 1200 meters is cir-

cumscribed around each RCW colony, a total of 200,000 acres, approximately one-third of the National Forests in Texas, fell under Judge Parker's mandate. The judge allowed the Forest Service 60 days to develop a "comprehensive plan" for management within the 1200-meter radius that would meet his approval. On October 20, 1988, the judge once again refused to allow clear-cutting and ordered the implementation of his prescription for the RCW.

On what basis did a federal district judge decide to take silvicultural matters into his own hands? Table 8-2 documents undisputed declines in the RCW population in the national forests in Texas. The judge said, "The entire population of red-cockaded woodpeckers in the Texas national forests will be extinct by 1995 if no changes are made in the present practices of the Forest Service." (*Sierra Club v. Lyng*). Table 8-3 summarizes Judge Parker's findings of fact regarding the cause of RCW population decline.

The environmental groups that brought suit were pleased that the judge agreed on stricter measures to protect the woodpecker, based on the ESA and the facts of the case. Professional foresters were annoyed with Judge Parker's findings and his silvicultural prescription that overrode their own professional training and judgment. However, the population declines were irrefutable, and it appeared (see Table 8-2) that the Forest Service was not adequately protecting the RCW's welfare, even though 8100 acres of national forests were being managed for the RCW in the proposed NFMA forest management plan. Judge Parker felt that the Forest Service plan

TABLE 8-2. Active Red-Cockaded Woodpecker Colonies on National Forests in Texas

Forest	Period	Decline (percent)	Number of Colonies
Sabine	1978–1987	76	25–7
Davy Crockett	1983–1987	41	46–27
Angelina	1983–1987	42	38–22

Notes: Sam Houston National Forest: 105 active colonies, 6/13/89; 107 active colonies, 9/11/89.

Sources: All but Sam Houston N.F.: Findings of Fact in Civil Action No. L-85-69-CA; Sam Houston National Forest: District ranger.

TABLE 8-3. Findings of Fact—Causes of Red-Cockaded Woodpecker Decline

* Habitat fragmentation due to clear-cutting
* Clear-cutting within foraging area
* Clear-cutting within 200 feet of colony sites
* Failure to control hardwood mid-story
* Failure to employ prescribed fire
* Failure to provide appropriate basal area
* Lack of cavity trees
* Damage to trees from roads and equipment

Source: Civil Action No. L-85-69-CA

for the RCW did not provide adequate protection from extinction.

In his ruling, the judge offered his opinion as to why the Forest Service used clear-cutting.

The sole reason for the Forest Service's adoption of even-age or clear-cutting as the management method of choice is the fact that it is preferred by the timber companies...[because] the greatest market for government employees in private industry is with the large timber companies. This fact provides an incentive for agency personnel to accommodate industry desires—thus, that explains the high level of influence the timber companies have over policies and practices of the Forest Service.

Again, environmental groups applauded these sentiments; foresters did not.

Texas Committee on Natural Resources and Forest Reform Network

Some background on the plaintiffs and their legal strategy in this case is interesting. The RCW case was really a legal challenge to the way the Forest Service conducts its business; in particular, the reliance upon even-age management, including but not limited to clear-cutting, as the preferred forest management method. One of the plaintiffs was the Texas Committee on Natural Resources (TCONR), a group with a history of challenging the Forest Service on this same issue (Fritz 1983, Kaufman 1984, Wolf 1991). The other plaintiffs were the Sierra Club and the Wilderness Society.

In 1976 TCONR's leader, Edward C. Fritz, an attorney living in the Dallas area, filed suit against the clear-cutting practices of the Forest Service in Texas (Spurr 1977, 1981). As Luke Popovich (1977, p.273) colorfully put it, TCONR "accused the agency of violating every law except gravity." That suit (*Texas Committee on Natural Resources* v. *Bergland*, 433 F. Supp. 1235 [E.D. Tex. 1977]) alleged that the Forest Service had violated the Organic Act (1897), the Wilderness Act (1964), NEPA (1969), ESA (1973), and NFMA (1976). Judge William Wayne Justice, a federal judge in the Eastern District of Texas, found merit only in the NEPA allegation and ruled that the agency had violated the EIS process with its even-aged management practices in Texas. Judge Justice enjoined the Forest Service from any type of even-aged management. The agency appealed, and the district court decision was reversed by the circuit court of appeals in New Orleans (*Texas Committee on Natural Resources* v. *Bergland*, 573 F. 2d 201 [5th Cir. 1978]).

Fritz has continued his campaign against clear-cutting on the national forests, as well as his legal tactics. However, he recognized that lawsuits and national forest plan appeals alone would be inadequate to halt clear-cutting in the East. So he formed the Forest Reform Network, which consists of local groups around the country that aim to halt Forest Service clear-cutting via new legislation (Wolf 1991). Members of the group are young, committed, and energetic lobbyists and have prompted the Forest Biodiversity and Clearcutting Prohibition Act to be introduced into Congress in 1991. Hearings on the bill were held in June of 1992. The Forest Reform Network promises to increase in national importance.

Recent RCW Action

TCONR also was the plaintiff in a series of legal actions against the Forest Service that began in 1985, roughly coinciding with the release of the proposed Forest and Land Management Plan for the National Forests in Texas. These challenges dealt primarily with southern pine beetle suppression efforts and RCW protection, which were a precursor to the RCW case, and will foster more legal action in the future. As Judge Parker put it in his June 17, 1988, ruling, "The continuing battle over the overall management of the national forests (as distinguished from the management involving the red-cockaded woodpecker colonies) is not yet over, and the remaining shots by the various opposing parties have yet to be fired."

The "blanket" lawsuit strategy employed in *TCONR v. Bergland* in 1976 was to throw a handful of stuff against the wall and see what stuck. That time NEPA stuck, but only temporarily. The same strategy was used beginning in 1985 by the same plaintiff. This time, with a different judge in the same court, ESA stuck. Judge Parker decided to rule on an NFMA allegation, but he ruled out the Wilderness Act and NEPA allegations.

As Judge Parker mentioned in his October 20, 1988, ruling on Forest Service silvicultural alternatives, the case is "now ripe for appeal." In fact, the case has been appealed to circuit court in New Orleans. A decision has not been reached as of this writing. However, the U.S. Fish and Wildlife Service is on record as stating that the judge's orders are not in the long-term best interests of the RCW. So is Dr. Richard Connor, the U.S. Forest Service biologist whom the judge relied on for the findings of fact presented in Tables 8-2 and 8-3.

Nonetheless, in March 1989, the Forest Service adopted the judicial silvicultural prescription for the RCW throughout the South uniformly in national forest districts with less than 250 active RCW colonies. As a result, timber purchasers in the South filed an administrative appeal with the Forest Service, protesting the management plan. This appeal was denied in October 1989. In response, the Region 8 Forest Service Timber Purchasers Council filed a citizen's suit against the Forest Service, alleging that the service adopted the policy without public comment or consultation with the U.S. Fish and Wildlife Service.

The 1989 forest industry challenge (*Region 8 Forest Service Timber Purchasers Council v. Alcock*, Civil No. 89-2741 [N.D.Ga.]) met with mixed results. The judge recognized the industry's standing to challenge the Forest Service for failure to comply with the Endangered Species Act. She further stated that the Forest Service could not avoid judicial review of its 1989 policy by announcing another policy in 1990. Ultimately, however, she did grant the government's motion to dismiss the industry challenge that the Forest Service failed to prepare adequate environmental analyses (American Forest Resource Alliance 1990). New plans to protect the woodpecker were being developed in the early 1990s.

SUMMARY

Courts have played an increasing role in shaping forest resource policy. They hear cases regarding public laws—the general rules that govern social life. Laws may be classified in many ways. They may originate in the Constitution, be enacted by legislatures, or be developed by administrative agencies. They also may involve civil actions between private citizens or corporations, or criminal sanctions to protect society from wrongdoers. Courts help protect property rights and individual freedom.

Courts have the authority to settle controversies between individuals who bring suit and those who respond or defend themselves. They also may review legislative acts to determine if they are constitutional. The federal and most state courts have a three-tier system for civil and criminal cases. The lowest level consists of district courts, the intermediate level of appellate courts, and the highest of a supreme court. In civil cases, judges may issue temporary or permanent stop work orders (injunctions), order corrective action, or assess fines. Criminal sanctions may include fines or imprisonment. Courts have had a substantial role in implementing resource policy for wildlife and for forestry, as the illustrations involving wetlands, national forest management, and property taxes illustrate.

LITERATURE CITED

American Forest Resource Alliance. 1990. National Update. May 2, 1990. Washington, DC. 2 p.

Anderson, Frederick R. 1977. A judicious look at shibboleths about the judiciary. Pp. 68–72, in Centers of Influence and U.S. Forest Policy. Duke University, School of Forestry and Environmental Studies. Durham, NC.

Anderson, Frederick R., Daniel R. Mandelker, and A. Dan Tarlock. 1984. Environmental Protection: Law and Policy. Little, Brown. Boston. 978 pp.

Blackburn, John D., Elliot I. Klayman, and Martin H. Malin. 1988. The Legal Environment of Business, 3rd ed. Irwin. Homewood, IL. 666 pp.

Coffin, James B. 1990. Top court standing decision is pinching enviros a little. *Public Lands News* 15(24):6–7, December 6.

Corley, Robert N., O. Lee Reed, and Peter J. Shedd. 1990. The Legal Environment of Business, 8th ed. McGraw-Hill. New York. 903 pp.

Cubbage, Frederick W., and William C. Siegel. 1985. The law regulating private forestry. *Journal of Forestry* 83(9):538–545.

Daniels, Steven E., and Christine M. Kelly. 1990. Deciding between an EA and an EIS may be a question of mitigation. *Western Journal of Applied Forestry* 5(4):111–116.

Douglas, William O. 1960. My Wilderness: The Pacific West. Doubleday. Garden City, NY. 206 pp.

Douglas, William O. 1965. A Wilderness Bill of Rights. Little, Brown. Boston. 192 pp.

Dye, Thomas R., Lee Seifert Greene, and George S. Parthemos. 1980. Governing the American Democracy. St. Martin's Press. New York. 624 pp. + appen.

Federalist Papers. 1788. New American Library of World Literature. New York. 560 pp. (reprinted 1961)

Fritz, Edward C. 1983. Sterile Forest: The Case Against Clear-Cutting. Eakin Press. Austin, TX. 271 pp.

Gellhorn, Ernest, and Barry B. Boyer. 1981. Administrative Law and Process in a Nutshell, 2nd ed. West Publishing Company. St. Paul, MN. 445 pp.

Goldman, Sheldon, and Thomas P. Jahnige. 1985. The Federal Courts as a Political System, 3rd ed. Harper & Row. New York. 263 pp.

Hacker, Jan J. 1983. How Michigan prevented another Monongahela. *Journal of Forestry* 81(10): 665–668.

Hall, Bob. 1983. National highlights. *Journal of Forestry* 81(11): 712–713.

Hart, H. L. A. 1961. The Concept of Law. Oxford University Press. Oxford, England. 263 pp.

Iadarola, Angelo A. 1979. Federal condemnation of private forestlands—the search for "just compensation." Monograph presented to the Society of American Foresters 1979 National Convention, Economics and Policy Working Group Technical Session. Wilkinson, Gragun, and Barker Law Offices. Washington, DC. 103 pp.

Kaufman, Wallace. 1984. Reading about resources. *American Forests* 90(6): 57.

Nonet, Philippe, and Philip Selznick. 1978. Law and Society in Transition: Toward Responsive Law. Harper & Row. New York. 122 pp.

Popovich, Luke. 1977. The multiple abuse law—Justice on the Fritz in Texas. *Journal of Forestry* 75(5): 273–275.

Sampson, Neil. 1985. On the fireline....*AFA's Resource Hotline* 1(15): 4, August 6.

Schoenbaum, Thomas J. 1982. Environmental Policy Law: Cases, Readings, and Text. The Foundation Press. Mineola, NY. 1065 pp.

Siegel, William ljC. 1982. Forest management and the law. Pp. 339–362 in William A. Duerr, Dennis E. Teeguarden, Niels B. Christiansen, and Sam Guttenberg (eds.), Forest Resource Management: Decision-Making Principles and Cases, rev. ed. OSU Book Stoves. Corvallis, OR. 612 pp.

Spurr, Stephen H. 1977. Use of professional competence by the judiciary. *Journal of Forestry* 75(4): 198–200.

Spurr, Stephen H. 1981. Clear cutting on national forests. *Natural Resources Journal* 21(2): 223–243.

Stone, Christopher D. 1974. Should trees have standing? Toward legal rights for natural objects. Kaufman. Los Altos, CA. 102 pp.

Turner, Allen C., and Jay O'Laughlin. 1991. State agency roles in Idaho water quality policy. Report No. 5, Idaho Forest, Wildlife and Range Policy Analysis Group, University of Idaho, Moscow. 212 pp.

Yost, Nicholas C., and James W. Rubin. 1990. The National Environmental Policy Act. In Sheldon C. Novick et al. (eds.), Law of Environmental Protection. Clark Boardman. New York. (Looseleaf)

Wolf, Tom. 1991. Fritz vs. the Feds. *American Forests* 97(11/12): 52–53, 65–67.

Chapter 9

Interest Groups

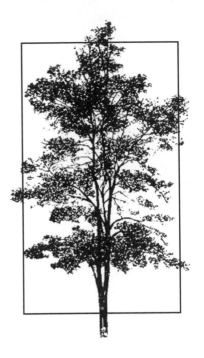

Contrary to tradition, against the public morals, and hostile to good government, the lobby has reached such a position of power that it threatens government itself. Its size, its power, its capacity for evil, its greed, trickery, deception and fraud condemn it to the death it deserves.

—Hugo L. Black 1935

Issue networks are not discreetly different arrangements from iron triangles, but are iron triangles with greatly increased group population, with a further disaggregation of power, with less predictable participants, with reduced cohesion and homogeneity caused by the mobilization of value-changing groups, which in turn leads to the reduced capacity to "close" on a decision... the twin ideas of issue network and iron triangle remain useful starting points.

—A. Grant Jordan 1981

INTRODUCTION

Thus far we have discussed models of policy processes and the official sectors of government that have authority to make public policy. In addition to official policymakers, many other groups and individuals strongly influence forest resource policy. Chapters 6 through 8 indicated that legislatures, the courts, and the executive branch all respond to input from constituents, litigants, and interest groups in making policy. In fact, interest groups often are perceived as crucial in making public policy. This chapter discusses their role in determining resource policy.

An *interest group* may be defined as an organization of individuals sharing one or more interests who try to influence decisions of government agencies, political representatives, or other policymakers. If a group of individuals gets together, organizes a rod-and-gun club, pools their resources, and purchases some land for a fish and game preserve where they can fish and hunt, they would not be considered an interest group. But if they attempt to persuade the state fish and game department to stock trout in the lake on their preserve, they become an interest group (Montsma 1969).

A *lobbyist* works for an interest group and represents the cause of that group in the political system (Montsma 1969). The quote at the beginning of the chapter from Sen. Hugo Black (who later became a Supreme Court justice) reflects a still prevalent attitude about the malevolence of "the lobby" (interest groups). Interest groups have become even more important in recent decades.

Interest groups and lobbyists have proliferated since the 1960s. In 1961 there were only 365 registered lobbyists for Congress; in 1987 there were more than 23,000—more than 43 lobbyists for each member of the House and Senate. The District of Columbia Bar Association, most of whose members are lobbyists, listed 12,564 members in 1961 and 46,000 in 1987. Also, many groups and businesses have located their headquarters in Washington, DC. In 1968 only 100 trade associations and corporations had offices in the national capital. By 1986 there were 3500 such offices in Washington, DC. Changes in campaign finance laws in 1971 and 1974 prompted the growth of political action committees (PACs)—groups created to provide campaign support and political funding to politicians. In 1974 there were 608 PACs; by 1987 there were more than 4100 (Smith 1988).

Groups have tended to focus on single issues as the number of groups has increased. The use of computers has helped groups develop more sophisticated, timely, and specialized grass-roots lobbying campaigns. Institutions—corporations, universities, state and local governments, and foreign interests—have increased their lobbying efforts. The creation of government programs—such as social security, Medicare, environmental protection—from the 1930s through the 1970s created new constituencies and led to a greater number of interest groups (Loomis and Cigler 1986).

MODELS OF GROUP PARTICIPATION

Interest groups may participate in policy-making in various ways. In the broadest sense, political parties are interest groups that represent large numbers of people. The primary distinction between American political parties and interest groups is that parties offer candidates for election, while interest groups attempt to influence public officials. Interest groups may help determine legislation and policy implementation by working with Congress and public agencies (iron triangles) or through more diverse group interactions (issue networks), as suggested in the quote by Jordan at the beginning of the chapter.

GROUP THEORY

Interest group theorists have traditionally viewed group activity as a desirable way for individuals to exert influence in the policy process. They assume that no clearly defined and agreed-upon conception of the public interest exists on most issues. Rather, the public interest emerges from the input and struggle among many self-interested groups. The eventual consensus and compromises among these groups are enacted by legislatures and then implemented by government agencies (Hayes 1986).

A classic description of group theory suggests that laws reflect a balance of power between different interest groups (Latham 1952, p. 390).

The legislature referees the group struggle, ratifies the victories of the successful coalitions, and records the terms of the surrenders, compromises, and conquests in terms of statutes. Every statute tends to represent compromise because the process of accommodating conflicts of group interest is one of deliberation and consent. The legislative vote on any issue tends to represent the composition of strength, i.e. the balance of power, among the contending groups at the moment of voting. What may be called public policy is the equilibrium reached in this struggle at any given moment, and it represents a balance which the contending factions of groups constantly strive to weight in their favor.

The group theory model suggests that the legislature acts as a passive arbitrator of group disputes, merely enacting the agreed-upon compromises of different groups into law. In practice, legislators obviously also are very active participants in the process, helping not only to enact compromises, but also to define problems, select alternatives, and implement programs (Schattschneider 1960).

IRON TRIANGLES AND SPECIALIZATION

Group theory helps explain how specialized interests may influence policy. But it is not very helpful in explaining the enactment of specific policies and the development of policy subsystems. In the federal government, and in state governments as well, interest groups tend to cooperate with congressional subcommittees and government agencies in a narrow, specialized policy area. A prevalent model of these relationships is referred to as the iron triangle (see Chapter 7). This model is based on the tendency in Washington, DC, for larger organizations (i.e., the Senate or U.S. Department of Agriculture) to defer to their smaller, more specialized subunits (i.e., the Senate Subcommittee on Conservation and Forestry or the Forest Service) at both the legislative and bureaucratic levels. Although the ultimate decision concerning an issue is made by the larger unit, the opinions of the smaller units usually are the basis for those decisions.

Congressional deference to specialized smaller units can be explained by two observations: (1) specialization is the quickest means of making an impact in Washington; and (2) selecting areas of specialization relevant to a Congress member's constituency allows the representative to provide benefits to his or her voters. Within a bureaucracy, specialization and technical skills are the bases for bureaucratic power. Interest groups, by definition, tend to represent specialized interests that interact with Congress members and government bureaucrats to obtain desired policies and funding for programs they support and to oppose some programs they do not. This specialization and cooperation among the three sectors (Congress, agencies,

and interest groups) is referred to as the iron triangle.

ISSUE NETWORKS

The proliferation of interest groups in the last two decades has led to many more players in the policymaking process. The traditional iron triangle concept, although useful, perhaps has become outdated because of the many, diverse groups whose policy interests overlap. For example, traditional agricultural interests are no longer the only participants in making farm policy and enacting federal farm bills. The 1985 and 1990 Food Security Acts (farm bill) contained the customary price support and production control features that have characterized U.S. farm policy for decades. But they also authorized a new Conservation Reserve Program—to plant erodible areas with permanent grass, wildlife plants, or tree cover. The 1985 farm bill developed new programs designed to discourage farmers from draining wetlands ("swampbuster") or tilling marginal lands ("sodbuster"). The 1990 farm bill continued these provisions. The swampbuster, sodbuster, and conservation reserve provisions of the farm bill, which were proposed and supported by environmental groups, clearly indicate that the agricultural iron triangle has been expanded beyond the traditional farm commodity production interest groups, the Department of Agriculture, and the agricultural committees in Congress.

Involvement of more groups in the policymaking process has led to the creation of *issue networks* (Heclo 1978). This concept suggests that clearly identifiable, stable "triangle" groups are becoming less common, and groups are becoming involved in issues more on the basis of evaluations of individual problems and their impact on their membership. Participants in an issue network also seek policy outcomes that are self-serving. However, networks involve so many different policymakers and interests that the effect on policy-making is unpredictable. Network decisions involve more conflict and confrontation than do iron triangle consensual agreements. The many groups involved are competing for policy leadership, member satisfaction, and political advantages. Thus decisions often will not meet the needs of many of those attempting to exert influence (Browne 1986).

Browne (1986) illustrates the issue network that was involved in getting the 1985 farm bill passed (Figure 9-1). As the diagram indicates, this is far more than an iron triangle. Many groups were involved, and all interacted in some way. Although the groups may be acquainted with each other, stable, continuous interaction as suggested in the iron triangle concept is missing.

The issue network model suggests a trend toward a more fluid political system, which offers advantages and disadvantages. Issue networks help policy-making as the nation shifts from a two-party power-based system to an issue-based political system. They permit the executive to work with the legislature better as the party loyalty of Congress members appears to be waning. Issue networks allow for more integrated and holistic policies and laws that consider broad impacts across narrow interests.

The development of issue networks, however, does have drawbacks. Participation by many groups tends to impede compromise, making it more difficult to reach consensus. More groups increase rather than reduce complexity, which impedes policy solutions. If unable to gain success, groups often will try to block a compromise and prevent closure, leaving issues unresolved. The complexity and multiple interactions also make it

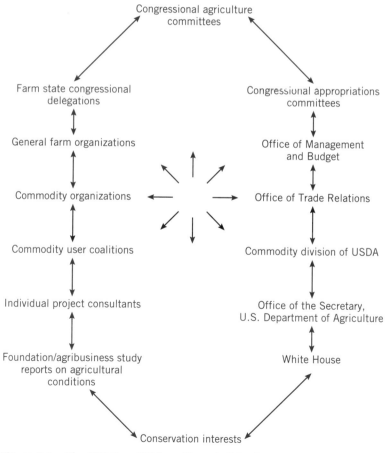

Figure 9-1. The 1985 Farm Bill Issue Network: Price Supports

difficult to credit or blame individual politicians or groups for success or failure in making policy, thus undermining the public's confidence in their abilities and the process (Heclo 1978).

POLITICAL PARTIES

Although not often classed as interest groups per se, political parties are obviously crucial in their representation of broad interests in electing politicians and making policy. American political parties are loose coalitions of individuals and groups formed to attract sufficient votes to gain control of the government. American political parties must have a broad-based appeal to attract millions of voters from diverse ethnic, economic, and social backgrounds. Indeed many critics contend that little difference exists between the parties. However, the Democratic and Republican parties can be clearly differentiated by (1) their opinions and policy positions, (2) the types of voters supporting their candidates, and (3) differences in congressional voting records (Dye, Greener, and Parthemos 1980).

Most ethnic groups, except blacks, have split their votes between the parties in presidential elections. However, through the 1970s the Democratic party received disproportionate support from Catholics, nonwhites, lower educational groups, younger people, manual laborers, and union members. The Republican party received greater support from Protestants, whites, higher educational groups, older people, professionals and businesspeople, and white-collar workers. Union members and young people, however, made up a much larger share of Republican voters in the three presidential elections during the 1980s than in previous elections.

Dye, Greene, and Parthemos (1980, p. 246) further distinguish between traditional Democratic and Republican beliefs.

Democratic leaders have faith in the wisdom of government and expect to be able to use its power effectively to redistribute wealth, mitigate misfor-

tune, and provide services. They wish to improve the lot of the uneducated, the deprived minorities, and the poor. They believe in social security, immigration, integration of the races, minimum wages, and public education. Republican chiefs, although willing to accept some of these goals, are more inclined to rely on individual initiative, hard work, frugality, and self-denial. They place somewhat less faith in the capacity of government than do their Democratic counterparts.

These different supporting constituencies and values are reflected in congressional voting records and presidential policies. Republicans tend to favor less government regulation and taxation, Democrats more. Democrats sponsor more labor legislation and tend to support education and welfare programs. Of course, many individual exceptions exist. For example, in the 1980s and 1990s, Republicans sought active government involvement to oppose abortion and control pornography; Democrats favored more personal choice.

Democrats more often have been associated with environmental protection laws and Republicans with favoring development. However, President Bush campaigned in 1988 as an environmentalist, not as one who favored development, and proposed many environmental laws and policies. After the defeat of their presidential candidate in 1988, many Democrats formally stated that they see less need for government intervention in the economy and people's lives. Thus the differences between the parties seem to be less distinct than in the past.

Political parties and political ideology also affect interest groups. Peterson and Walker (1986) compared the Carter and the Reagan administrations in 1980 and 1985, respectively, and found that substantial shifts occurred in interest group perceptions of government agencies. In 1980, 75 percent of the business-oriented, for-profit interest groups felt that agency cooperation with their conservative interests was unfavorable under the Carter administration. On the other hand, 81 percent of the nonprofit and citizen groups felt that agencies were more cooperative to their liberal agenda under Carter than under

Reagan. In 1985, cooperation from the federal agencies in the Reagan administration was viewed favorably by 69 percent of the business interest groups and unfavorably by 87 percent of the nonprofit and citizen groups.

These tremendous differences in interest group views and access under the two administrations underscore the continuing importance of political parties. The broad ideological shifts from Carter (Democrat) to Reagan and Bush (Republicans), coupled with continuing budget constraints, drastically altered the traditional iron triangle relationships. Many previously safe or secure programs became subject to scrutiny and threat of reduction or elimination. Many groups with narrow commercial, occupational, or professional interests found themselves drawn into alliances with both the major political parties, whether they liked it or not (Peterson and Walker 1986).

Although political party ideology has affected the relationships of agencies and interest groups, it has not necessarily reduced the number or size of groups. The unpopular environmental policies proposed by President Reagan and his outspoken Secretary of the Interior James Watt were adeptly used by environmental interest groups to attract new members. In the late 1980s proposals for more environmental regulation did not cause business interest groups to atrophy, but rather enhanced their ability to extract more dues from members in order to expand efforts to limit the spread of regulation.

In sum, political parties do matter, but their method of influence is changing. The traditional divisions among political parties have eroded considerably in the 1980s, particularly in presidential elections. Minority groups have become more important in the United States, and the South has voted Republican in most recent presidential elections, but Democrats continue to maintain majorities in Congress. These trends have led to a shift away from politics of regional, religious, and ethnic blocs toward the new politics of the 1980s and 1990s, carried out through the mass media and dominated by ideology. As both political parties have built national staffs

of media consultants, direct mail specialists, and fund-raisers to engage in this new form of political mobilization, they begin to resemble the staffs of some of the larger citizen interest groups (Peterson and Walker 1986).

TYPES OF INTEREST GROUPS

Interest groups may be divided into three categories—citizen interest groups, trade associations, and professional associations. These types of groups differ in their policy objectives and their strategies for lobbying.

CITIZEN INTEREST GROUPS

Citizen interest groups are comprised of individuals who share a general interest in some particular policy arena. Citizen groups concerned with the environment and conservation have been among the strongest and most effective national lobbying forces in the last two decades. A few of these interest groups were formed during the first forestry conservation movement in the last quarter of the nineteenth century, a few in the 1920s and 1930s, and many in the 1960s and 1970s.

Principal Environmental Groups
Tables 9-1 and 9-2 summarize information on many of the largest conservation groups in the United States. The best known environmentalist citizen groups are listed in Table 9-1. In the 1980s they joined together as a coalition called the "Environmental Leadership Conference" (Peterson 1982), sometimes called the "Gang of Ten" (Walsh 1985), and published an "Environmental Strategy for the Future" (Cahn 1985). The consensus view of these groups called for a legislative and litigative strategy targeted at natural resource institutions.

The National Wildlife Federation, National Audubon Society, and Sierra Club are probably the three best known environmental groups. The National Wildlife Federation lists 5.8 million "members and supporters" (Table 9-1), of which almost 1 million are

TABLE 9-1. Prominent Environmental Citizen Interest Groups

The "Group of Ten" (Peterson 1982)	Founded	Members	Publications
Environmental Defense Fund	1967	200,000	EDF Letter
Multidisciplinary teams of lawyers, scientists, and economists develop economically viable solutions to environmental problems.			
Friends of the Earth	1969	50,000	Friends of the Earth Newsmagazine; other newsletters
Global advocacy organization with affiliates in 37 countries revitalized in 1990 by merger with Environmental Policy Institute and the Oceanic Society.			
Izaak Walton League of America	1922	50,000	Outdoor America; Splash; Outdoor Ethics Newsletter
Public education to promote conservation, enjoyment, and wholesome utilization of natural resources.			
Natural Resources Defense Council	1970	125,000	Amicus Journal; NRDC Newsline
Interdisciplinary legal and scientific approach to monitor government agencies, bring legal action, and disseminate information.			
National Audubon Society	1905	550,000	Audubon; American Birds; others
Science, policy research, forceful lobbying, litigation, and citizen action to protect air, water, land, and habitat critical to human and planetary health.			
National Parks and Conservation Association	1919	285,000[a]	National Parks Magazine
Preservation, promotion, and improvement of national park system.			
National Wildlife Federation	1936	5,500,000[b]	National Wildlife; International Wildlife; Ranger Rick Magazine
Education for wise use and proper management of earth's resources; litigates environmental disputes.			
Sierra Club	1892	650,000	Sierra; National News Report; various newsletters
Protect wild places; promote responsible use of earth's resources; legislation, litigation, public information, publishing, outings, conferences.			
The Wilderness Society	1935	375,000	Wilderness
Preserve wilderness and wildlife; protect forests, parks, rivers, shorelands; foster an American land ethic.			

[a] Includes contributors as well as members.
[b] Includes 970,000 "members" receiving one of the two wildlife magazines. The other "supporters" include subscribers to Ranger Rick magazine and purchasers of federation "nature" products such as T-shirts and mugs (Lancaster 1991)
Source: National Wildlife Federation 1992

dues-paying members. The Sierra Club and National Audubon Society each have about a half-million members. The National Rifle Association boasts a membership of 3 million (Table 9-2). All groups in Table 9-1 have grown remarkably during the 1980s, except Friends of the Earth, which lost half its membership, but then it was rejuvenated in 1990 by its merger with two other groups, including the tenth member of the "gang"—the Environmental Policy Institute.

The American Forestry Association (1875) and the Sierra Club (1892) are the oldest citizen conservation groups. In the early twen-

TABLE 9-2. Other Conservation or Environmental Citizen Interest Groups

Groups	Founded	Members	Publications
American Farm Bureau Federation	1919	3,900,000	AFB Official Newsletter
Promote national well-being by formulating action for educational improvement and economical opportunity; has a Natural Resources and Environmental Resources Division; local, statewide, national, international scope.			
American Forests	1975	unlisted[a]	American Forests; Resource Hotline; others
"Intelligent" management and use of forest resources and public appreciation. New name as of 1992; formerly American Forestry Association.			
Cousteau Society	1973	250,000	Calypso Log; Dolphin Log
Environmental education.			
Defenders of Wildlife	1947	82,000	Defenders
Education and advocacy; abundance and diversity of wildlife.			
Earth First!	1981	10,000	Earth First!; Ecodefense
Loosely organized groups of activists; forest management is one of their concerns; tactics run from demonstrations to tree-spiking and other forms of "ecotage."			
Environmental Action	1970	unlisted[b]	Environmental Action
Lobbyists for most environmental issues; research and education in EA Foundataion.			
Friends of Animals	1957	120,000	Act'ion Line
Animal protection; eliminate human brutality to animals.			
Fund for Animals	1967	250,000	None listed
Advocacy group for animal protection.			
Greenpeace USA	1970	2,500,000[c]	Greenpeace magazine
Preserving the earth and its life; marine mammals; no nukes.			
National Geographic Society	1888	9,700,000	National Geographic magazine
Increase and diffusion of geographic knowledge.			
National Rifle Association	1871	3,000,000	American Rifleman; American Hunter
Gun ownership; hunter safety.			

tieth century, the American Forestry Association was the preeminent national organization in the drive to create and expand western national forests, purchase eastern national forests, and promote federal and state cooperation in preventing forest fires and destructive forest cutting practices. The Sierra Club expanded from its western base during the 1960s and has become a leading national conservation group.

The Izaak Walton League, originally an angler's organization formed in 1922, focuses on broad water resource and public lands issues. In 1935 conservationist and political cartoonist Jay N. "Ding" Darling helped found and served as the first president of the National Wildlife Federation so that conservation interests could exert greater political influence. The group has now grown to be the largest and probably the most influential environmental group in Washington.

The Natural Resources Defense Council, Environmental Defense Fund, and Friends of the Earth were formed in the 1960s

TABLE 9-2. continued

Groups	Founded	Members	Publications
Trout Unlimited	1959	65,000	Trout Magazine
Protect clean water; enhance trout and salmon fishery resources.			
Wildlife Conservation/ Legislative Fund of America	1978	1,000,000	Update Newsletter; others
Protect hunting, fishing, trapping heritage, and scientific wildlife management practice; WCFA is legal defense, information, public education, and research arm; WLFA is legislative and political arm.			
World Wildlife Fund	1961	670,000	FOCUS
Protect endangered wildlife and wildlands, especially in tropics; affiliated with Conservation Foundation (see Table 9-3)			

Citizen Groups that Manage Land	Founded	Members	Publications
Ducks Unlimited	1937	550,000	Ducks Unlimited Magazine
Conservation, restoration, and management of waterfowl habitat.			
Nature Conservancy	1951	590,000	Nature Conservancy Magazine
Preserve biological diversity; management of 1100 nature sanctuaries; protection of about 3,500,000 acres of natural areas.			

Coalitions of Organizations	Founded	Members	Publications
Global Tomorrow Coalition	1981	126 Organizations	Interaction; many others
Publicize global trends in population, resources, environment, development; more than 10 million members overall.			
Natural Resources Council of America	1946	71 organizations	none listed
Political information to members; facilitate communications; not an action organization.			

[a]Estimate: 80,000
[b]Estimate: 25,000
[c]"Active supporters"
Source: National Wildlife Federation 1992, except Earth First! (Russell 1987)

and 1970s. The first two focus on legal action to promote environmental issues. Friends of the Earth, Greenpeace, and Earth First! have probably been the most radical of the interest groups listed. They favor direct action and confrontation to oppose activities such as building nuclear power plants, whaling, and timber harvesting.

Many other conservation organizations exist. The Nature Conservancy solicits contributions of land and cash from individuals and corporations in order to acquire and protect natural habitats. By 1991 it had protected almost 3.5 million acres of land in the United States. The National Rifle Association is a powerful interest group often involved in conservation, as well as gun control, issues. The Wildlife Management Institute and the Sport Fishing Institute, funded by hunting and rifle equipment and fishing tackle manufacturers, support their members' interests. State-level conservation organizations are legion—some of them are affiliated with national organizations; many are not.

Environmental Group Classifications

The conservationist, environmentalist, or preservationist interest groups may be categorized in various ways. They are made up of different types of individuals, have different value orientations, use different tactics, and vary in size and scope.

Environmental groups may be classed by demographics. After reviewing many demographic studies of environmentalists, Milbrath (1984) concluded that young people are more environmentally oriented than their elders, females are more environmentally oriented than males, and whites are more environmentally oriented than blacks. People employed in service industries are more environmentally oriented than those who produce and sell material goods. According to Milbrath (1984), empirical research does not seem to support the conjecture of some, for example, Tucker (1982) or a congressional report (NFPA 1982), that environmentalism is an upper-class movement.

Environmentalists also have been classified according to the underlying attitudes, beliefs, and values that are manifested in many environmental issues. A useful dichotomy for making a general distinction among environmental interest groups is that of norm-oriented and value-oriented environmentalists. Devall (1980) suggested that one of the two great streams of modern environmentalism is reformist or norm-oriented. Reformist goals include attempting to regulate air and water pollution and to control some remaining pieces of wild lands as designated wilderness areas. The other great stream of environmentalism is revolutionary or value-oriented. Followers of this stream support many reformist goals, but they are seeking a new relationship between people and nature that Devall (1980) called "deep ecology," which is discussed in Chapter 10.

Michael McCloskey of the Sierra Club found the norm- and value-oriented dichotomy useful. He believes the distinction depends on whether people believe it is wise to work within the context of the basic social, political, and economic institutions to achieve incremental progress, or whether most energy must attempt to change institutions. Value-oriented environmentalists want to change the relationship of individuals to society and the ways in which society works. The norm-oriented are reformers but do not quarrel with the basic ways in which society

operates. According to McCloskey, most of today's major national environmental organizations are norm-oriented (Borelli 1987).

Having studied environmentalists in the United States, England, and Germany, Milbrath (1984) observed that the majority of environmentalists reject the ideology of market capitalism. They lack a commitment to material and economic goals. They protest their alienation from decision-making processes and the usurpation of policy decisions by experts with dominant economic values. The emotional and spiritual components of the environmental movement are very important.

Another classification of citizen conservation groups is the continuum or "spectrum" drawn by Arnold (1982). This classification scheme has two dimensions (Figure 9-2). At the top of the spectrum are the preferred tactics (or norm-orientation) of various groups. At the bottom are the political (or value) orientations of the groups. The continuum runs from tactics of information, education, and research by "conservative" groups represented by the American Forestry Association, through political and legal tactics of more "liberal" groups, to "radical" and "revolutionary" groups espousing civil disobedience, such as Earth First! and Greenpeace.

Many of the large national organizations in the Group of Ten (see Table 9-1) have begun to take a more global view of environmental issues, which by their very nature preclude direct involvement. By doing so, the groups have left the domestic environmental agenda unfinished at a time when there is a resurgence of interest in traditional national conservation issues such as forest practices and wildlife protection.

Forest practice issues have become a special focus of militant "monkeywrenchers"— persons who use tools (wrenches) to damage equipment—inspired by their originator, Edward Abbey. Abbey is a famous western philosopher and author. Earth First! and other monkeywrenchers employ, among other tactics, tree spiking, woods burning, and the sabotaging of heavy equipment (Boerner 1987, Foreman and Haywood 1987, Franklin and

Proposed Spectrum of Environmental Organizations

The social impact of this structure tends toward the right-hand side of the chart; groups placed farther to the right-hand side provide those on the left-hand side with the appearance of moderation while furthering the movement's goals.

Preferred Tactics (cumulative from left to right; each set of tactics may include those listed to its left on this chart)

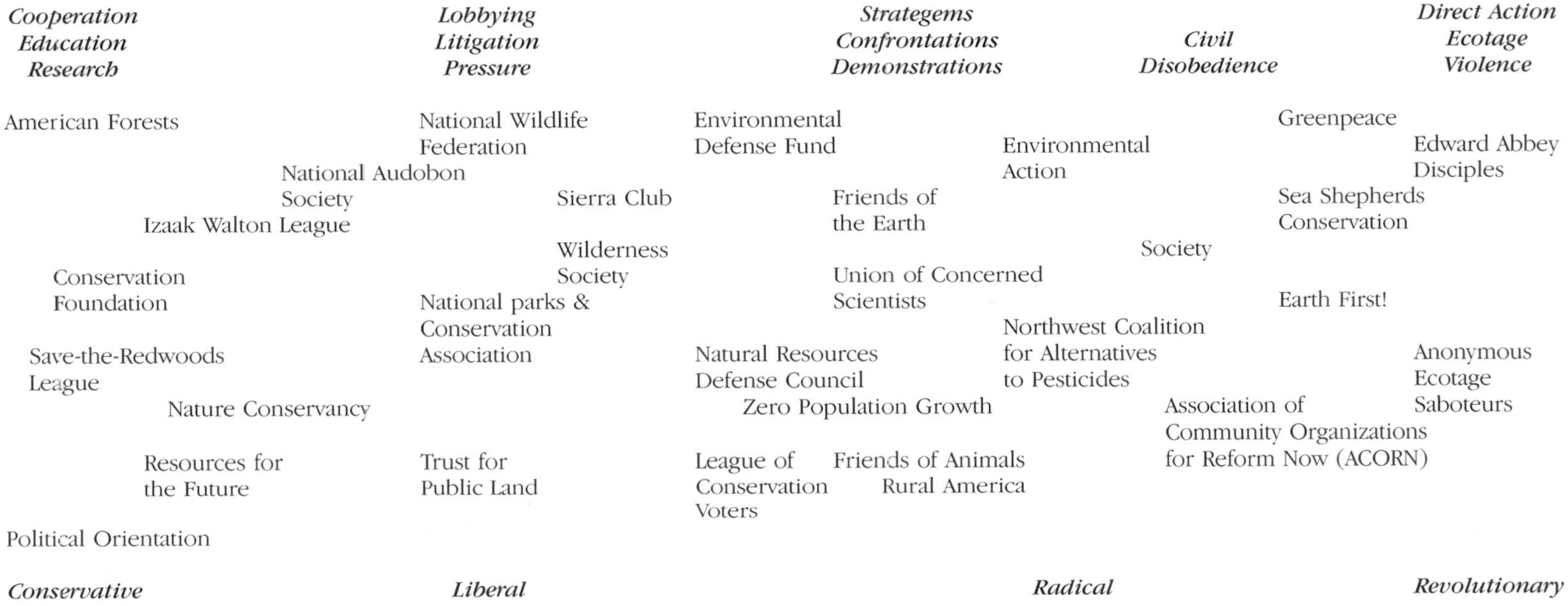

Cooperation / Education / Research	*Lobbying / Litigation / Pressure*	*Strategems / Confrontations / Demonstrations*	*Civil Disobedience*	*Direct Action / Ecotage / Violence*
				Edward Abbey Disciples
			Greenpeace	
				Sea Shepherds Conservation
			Society	
		Environmental Action		
			Earth First!	
American Forests	National Wildlife Federation	Environmental Defense Fund		
National Audobon Society	Sierra Club			
Izaak Walton League		Friends of the Earth		
	Wilderness Society			
		Union of Concerned Scientists		
Conservation Foundation	National parks & Conservation Association		Northwest Coalition for Alternatives to Pesticides	Anonymous Ecotage Saboteurs
Save-the-Redwoods League		Natural Resources Defense Council		
Nature Conservancy		Zero Population Growth	Association of Community Organizations for Reform Now (ACORN)	
	Trust for Public Land	League of Conservation Voters	Friends of Animals Rural America	
Resources for the Future				

Political Orientation

Conservative	*Liberal*	*Radical*	*Revolutionary*

A proposed spectrum of selected environmental organizations, located according to their major actions as reported in newspaper articles since 1965, and according to their own descriptions from brochures and newsletters. Each group may perform single actions in other areas of the spectrum. Relative placements judged by the author upon the evidence described.

Figure 9-2. Classifying Environmental Organizations on a Continuum of Preferred Tactics and a Continuum of Political Orientations.
Source: Arnold 1982.

Sowell 1987, and Walt 1986). At least one sawmill worker was almost killed when a log spiked with a nail was cut, and the saw teeth flew out and cut the man's throat. Rewards for information on tree spikers have been offered (AFA 1987). Tree spiking is now a federal crime (TFA 1988). The Sea Shepherds Conservation Society, concerned with the protection of marine mammals, has sunk two whaling ships. "Ecophilosopher" groups are emerging to focus on toxic issues, bioregionalism, and "Green" politics. All of these groups desire radical social change and are characterized by an intense personal involvement that the big national groups cannot always offer (Borelli 1987, Russell 1987).

A new wave of concern regarding environmental issues began in the mid-1980s. Previously, issues were generally national in scope, such as acid rain and wasteful national forest management policies. Now the emphasis is both expanding to a global perspective and contracting to a grass-roots local level. Environmental problems affecting the entire planet became the focus of cover stories in *National Geographic* (Grosvenor 1988) and *Time* (Miller 1989). The United Nations Conference on Environment and Development in 1992 solidified the international status of environmental concerns. Rose (1988) described an upsurge of citizen interest in community quality-of-life issues, and environmentalists became involved in a broad array of issues (Lancaster 1991).

TRADE ASSOCIATIONS

Natural resource interest groups oriented toward the production of commodities are the second type of interest group. These organizations are generally termed *trade associations* and are comprised of companies or firms concerned with the impact of government on their business, the promotion of their products, and the image of their industry. The term *lobbyist* conjures up the image of the trade association representative. These organizations provide information and services to their members and channel their members' concerns to government officials. Many large companies employ professional lobbyists or maintain Washington offices, in addition to belonging to trade associations. Most small firms belong to and rely on a trade association to represent their interests in Washington and keep them apprised of policy changes that may affect them.

In the early 1980s the principal coordinating body for the forest products trade associations was the Forest Industries Advisory Council. The group had no formal structure but consisted of approximately 120 participating members who met once a year. In 1985 the advisory council stopped holding annual meetings due to the excessive cost and delegated its policy-making authority to the Forest Industries Council (FIC).

The individual trade associations serve their members' needs and also have helped execute tasks judged important by the FIC. Their names indicate their areas of interest— American Plywood Association (plywood production), American Pulpwood Association (pulpwood procurement), and American Paper Institute (paper manufacturing). The American Forest Council functions as the public relations and long-term image-building arm of the industry and manages the Tree Farm program, which is designed to recognize private owners who grow trees and promote timber growing. The National Forest Products Association represents the solid wood products sector, including both large and small firms and a number of smaller regional trade associations. Many regional associations also exist, such as the Western Wood Products Association, the Intermountain Forest Industries Association, and the Southeastern Lumber Manufacturers Association.

Faced with a great number of issues, forest products firms formed a new organization named the American Forest Resource Alliance (AFRA) in 1989. The alliance included forestry trade associations and individual firms. AFRA's principal goals were to develop a comprehensive program to achieve full, predictable, sustained utilization of forest resources. AFRA pursued five program areas to foster a favorable business environment for forestry firms—litigation, legislative affairs, communications, technical support, and coalition and grass-roots lobbying. The alliance prospectus indicates that such an ambitious program is not inexpensive, entailing an expense of more than $5 million per year (AFRA 1989). It notes, however, that the 10 largest environmental groups had combined budgets of $156 million, much of which is spent directly or indirectly on lobbying. In 1992 AFRA was folded back into the National Forest Products Association, and its efforts continued.

A number of trade associations function at the state level. Some states have several forestry trade associations and conservation groups. Most southern states have only one trade association representing both industrial and independent private forest landowners, or other citizens generally interested in forestry. Although these southern trade associations nominally represent both industrial and nonindustrial sectors, most of their income is derived from assessments on forest products firms. Thus, they tend to focus on industrial land management or wood procurement issues. The Forest Farmers Association, also a southern trade and conservation association, represents forest landowners principally. Some states in the West, Northeast, and the Midwest have separate forest landowner and industrial forestry associations.

Many issues faced by state forestry associations parallel those at the national level. Throughout the 1980s and 1990s, these organizations have dealt with state proposals for wetlands laws, regulatory best management practices, and property tax reforms. Most western states already have state forest practice acts; several eastern states are reluctantly discussing similar legislation. Massachusetts enacted a Cutting Practices Act in 1982, and Maine and Connecticut enacted forest practice acts in 1989 and 1991, respectively (see Chapter 16). Regulations of log trucking, local logging ordinances, and forest landowner liability for injury to trespassers or for illegal garbage dumps have also been common issues for state forestry associations.

National laws and policies also affect states and are monitored by forestry trade associations. Water pollution controls, air quality laws that affect prescribed burning, and income tax treatment of timber have all attracted comment from trade association representatives. So have labor laws and proposals to strictly regulate herbicide applications to protect endangered plants.

PROFESSIONAL ASSOCIATIONS AND RESEARCH GROUPS

Professional associations and societies are composed of professionals who are employed in natural resources. Membership in professional organizations is independent of employment. Government, academic, and business professionals all may belong to the same society. As a result these groups often are less cohesive than other groups when considering, adopting, or acting on policy issues.

Examples of natural resource societies (Table 9-3) include the Society of American Foresters, Ecological Society of America, Forest Products Research Society, Wildlife Society, Society for Range Management, and American Fisheries Society. Support in these societies ranges from a few thousand to more than 20,000 members. Large organizations, such as the American Bar Association, American Medical Association, and the American Society of Agricultural Engineers have substantially greater memberships and budgets.

A number of the groups listed in Table 9-3 provide information related to natural resources and environmental policy issues by conducting research and disseminating results to citizens, trade associations, professionals, government officials, and policymakers. These groups do not openly solicit membership. Some, such as Resources for the Future and the World Resources Institute, depend on philanthropic institutions such as the Rockefeller Foundation for financial support. These groups—often referred to as "think tanks" (Smith 1991)—have been influential in explicating policy alternatives, performing policy analyses, and making policy recommendations.

TABLE 9-3. Professional and Research Interest Groups

Professional Organizations	Founded	Members	Publications
American Fisheries Society	1870	8,500	Fisheries; Transactions of AFS; other
Ecological Society of America	1915	6,200	Ecology; Bulletin of ESA; Ecological Monographs
Forest Products Research Society	1937	3,000	Forest Products Journal; Wood Science
Society of American Foresters	1900	18,000	Journal of Forestry; Forest Science; Southern, Northern, Western Journal of Applied Forestry
Society of Range Management	1948	5,000	Journal of Range Management; Rangelands
The Wildlife Society	1937	8,200	Journal of Wildlife Management; Wildlife Society Bulletin; others

Information and Research Groups	Founded	Members	Publications
American Association for the Advancement of Science	1870	132,000	Science
Further the work of scientists.			
Conservation Foundation	1948	n.a.	Conservation Foundation letter; Resolve
Research and publications on variety of issues; technical assistance in land use and dispute resolution; affiliated with World Wildlife Fund (see Table 9-2).			
Environmental Law Institute	1969	n.a.	Resources; study reports and books
Research and education in development, conservation, use of natural resources; environmental quality; design of new institutional arrangements for environmental policy.			

Nonprofit professional associations usually represent individuals for technical or professional reasons. Often their organizational efforts focus on information and scientific exchange, professional employment and advancement, educational standards, or registration and licensing. Some nonprofit professional associations, such as the American Medical Association or the American Bar Association, also are very effective as a lobbying force. Most of the professional resource associations seem to be less effective at establishing and promoting policy positions. The Society of American Foresters (SAF) is composed of foresters from industry, state and federal agencies, universities, and private consultants, as well as wildlife managers, wilderness advocates, recreation managers, hydrologists, biologists, and accountants. This diversity inhibits consensus on issues such as wilderness set-asides, endangered species, and industrial and nonindustrial timber tax policies, among others. In fact, one former executive director of the SAF purposefully avoided any policy involvement for fear of antagonizing the membership. Nonetheless, the SAF has adopted an ongoing set of broad policy statements and more focused position statements that address specific current issues (Society of American Foresters 1990).

TABLE 9-3. continued

Information and Research Groups	Founded	Members	Publications
Soil and Water Conservation Society	1945	12,000	Journal of Soil and Water Conservation
Advance science and art of good land and water use; multidisciplinary forums to recommend land and water management policies.			
Sport Fishing Institute	1949	n.a.	SFI Bulletin
Research, education, scientific advisory to help ensure aquatic ecosystem productivity and fishing opportunities; funded by fishing tackle manufacturers.			
Wildlife Management Institute	unlisted	n.a.	Outdoor News Bulletin; others
Science and education promoting professional management of natural resources; supported by industries (including sporting arms), groups, and individuals.			
World Resources Institute	1982	n.a.	World Resources Report; Policy series
Policy research center; disseminate information.			
WorldWatch Institute	1974	n.a.	WorldWatch Magazine; State of the World; series; others
Identify and analyze global problems and trends; disseminate information.			

Coalition of Organizations	Founded	Members	Publications
Renewable Natural Resources Foundation	1972	16 organizations	Renewable Resources Journal
Interdisciplinary cooperation among member organizations; most are professional societies.			

n.a.—not applicable

Source: National Wildlife Federation 1992, except for the Forest Products Research Society.

DECISION MAKING IN INTEREST GROUPS

Like all organizations, interest groups must consider a variety of issues, decide how to allocate their resources and time, and adopt strategies to achieve their objectives. The policies and approaches they use generally are similar because they have similar structures, but some groups are better organized than others.

DEVELOPMENT

Interest groups originate and evolve to address problems or policies that affect people with similar beliefs, jobs, or educational backgrounds. Mobilization of an interest group on a particular issue requires the identifi-

cation of a problem common to a number of individuals and agreement among them on the need for collective action. Leaders must secure control over the resources necessary for collective action, develop strategies for accomplishing collective goals, and move the rank-and-file members toward achieving group goals. After a group has become established, it must maintain its organization, recruit and retain capable leaders, develop reliable membership and resource bases, and continue to influence policies of concern to the group (Cigler 1986).

An incentive model can be used to explain the development of interest groups and the exchange of benefits among groups and members. This model assumes that individuals participate in groups for specific benefits (Clark and Wilson 1961, Moe 1980, Olson 1971, and Salisbury 1961). Groups may offer three principal types of benefits (Cigler 1986, p. 47).

(1) [M]aterial benefits, the tangible rewards of participation such as income or services that usually have monetary value; (2) solidary benefits, the socially derived, intangible rewards created by the act of association, such as fun, camaraderie, status, or prestige; and (3) purposive or expressive rewards, those derived from advocating a particular cause or ideological orientation.

The incentive model of group development suggests that group leaders develop incentives to perpetuate their organizations and satisfy members. These incentives must change as groups evolve from new single-issue coalitions to enduring, broader groups. At the initial stages of development, groups tend to focus on government benefits that all individuals receive, whether they are group members or not (e.g., price supports for row crops). Seeking these collective benefits may be the initial issue causing groups to form, but nongroup members also may benefit. Thus, as groups mature, they must provide more selective benefits to group members, such as life insurance benefits, reduced publication prices, or special trips or camps available only to members. Otherwise, a "free rider" problem will develop—the few group members will obtain and pay for benefits enjoyed by many who are not group members.

STRUCTURE

Interest groups of all kinds generally are governed by elected officers who serve as volunteers in addition to their regular employment. Most interest groups also hire full-time, professional staff who carry out the daily business affairs of the organization.

The Society of American Foresters (1983) is one example of the organization of interest groups. The SAF is governed by an elected council that has 11 regional representatives and 3 national officers. The SAF full-time staff includes the executive vice-president; directors for resource policy, science and educa-

tion, member services, and publications; and other business and clerical staff. Members are divided into local chapters and state or multistate societies, each of which assesses its own dues in addition to national dues. State or multistate societies or divisions form a general governing body that reports to the council. As a professional society, SAF also has a Forest Science Board, which represents various areas of technical expertise in the society. It also has a Committee on Forest Policy that considers and adopts official position statements for the society or approves those formulated by states or local chapters (Society of American Foresters 1990).

Many interest groups have a structure similar to that of the SAF. The full-time staff is supervised by the organization's executive director or executive vice-president. The staff reports to the executive director, who is then responsible to the elected officers or governing board. Input from members at the local level theoretically is conveyed to the officers and staff of the organization, but in practice, rank-and-file members often have little to say about the operations of the national office. Member satisfaction (or dissatisfaction) is best expressed by the payment (or nonpayment) of annual dues.

PROCESS

Various factors influence the involvement of an interest group on a particular issue. Members or staff must identify issues germane to the group's interests. Some groups do this in a very rational, deliberate manner; others proceed more haphazardly. Members, officers, or policy committee members may identify issues. Groups must assess their ability to act on an issue. To affect policy outcomes, the groups must have adequate time, financial, and political resources. They must have staff or members who are knowledgeable about the issue. They also must consider the opportunity costs of acting on one issue versus another. Groups are apt to tackle an issue only if they have at least a moderate chance for success, and only if the issue will not be divisive among the membership.

Once issues are identified for action, an interest group must select the strategies and tactics it believes will be most effective. Some groups specialize in particular strategies or tactics. Strategies imply long-range approaches to issue advocacy, such as lobbying, litigation, publicity, or grass-roots support. Tactics imply the specific actions required to implement the strategy, such as organizing a letter-writing campaign or suing an agency for inadequate implementation of a federal law.

Most interest groups rely on their staff for issue selection and action. Many interest groups have little formal structure for gathering input from the membership at-large. One exception is Common Cause, which polls its members to select the issues in which it will become involved. In addition, many issues arise swiftly and require an immediate response from the organization. In these cases there may not be time for detailed membership input, even for well-organized groups.

STRATEGIES

Interest groups may adopt a number of strategies for influencing forest resource policies, including forming coalitions, initiating lawsuits, and providing information.

Coalitions involve a number of interest groups working together to achieve common goals. Coalitions are popular because they help increase the number of people who can contact policymakers, thus sharing costs as well as information. Also, different coalition partners may have unique advantages in dealing with certain policymakers. Coalitions provide an effective means of lobbying within the issue network process and help to involve more groups to push an issue toward agenda status. The Environmental Leadership Conference, Global Tomorrow Coalition, and American Forest Resource Alliance are examples of coalitions of groups with similar interests. Coalitions may be limited somewhat by staff who would rather

claim personal than joint credit for a successful effort. Also each group must maintain its ideological and functional niche in order to attract contributions and retain its members.

Some conservation groups often choose to litigate, such as the Environmental Defense Fund, the Natural Resources Defense Council, and the Sierra Club Legal Defense Fund. Other groups use court challenges as a backup strategy if other means fail, including the National Wildlife Federation, Sierra Club, and National Forest Products Association. Groups with few members may use litigation more than groups having a mass membership; large groups can use grass-roots lobbying more effectively.

Some groups try to use embarrassment and confrontation as a strategy, relying on the media to publicize the failure of government agencies or private corporations. Publicity about the Exxon Valdez oil spill in 1989 helped stop reauthorization of expanded drilling in the Alaska National Wildlife Refuge. During the 1970s Environmental Action received widespread publicity with the biennial publication of its "Dirty Dozen" list. These were 12 members of Congress who Environmental Action hoped would be defeated because of their poor records on environmental protection.

Environmental activists who release balloons near nuclear plants, drive spikes into trees or lie down in front of bulldozers epitomize the confrontational approach. Greenpeace members often use confrontation to stop unwanted actions. They pester large whaling ships by zooming about in rubber rafts and placing themselves between the harpoon cannon and a whale, or by trying to snarl harpoon lines that have missed their mark. Such actions are not without personal and legal hazards, however. A Greenpeace ship was blown up by French government agents, killing one activist. Earth First! members have been taken to court and forced to pay compensatory and punitive damages.

Many interest groups believe that providing reliable information on issues is their best long-term strategy. As the muddling-through model suggests, policymakers operate in an environment of imperfect knowledge. They rely heavily on interest groups to provide information on the subjects relevant to their interests because they do not have the time or resources to gather data themselves. Such information includes technical research data, political feedback on the effects on interest group members of proposed laws, speech material, or even drafts of proposed laws. Some groups, such as the Conservation Foundation, have enjoyed a reputation for providing unbiased nonpartisan information; others are unabashed advocates of certain positions. At the state level, registered lobbyists are relied on frequently by legislators to provide information about issues (Forest Farmer 1984).

Another strategy is to encourage group members to contact decision makers. Interest groups may try to activate rank-and-file members or key influential members of an organization, depending on the particular issue. Legislators are likely to respond more favorably to constituents' requests than to lobbyists'; therefore, group members' contacting their own legislators often is more effective than direct lobbying. The National Rifle Association is famous for its ability to flood Washington, DC legislators with calls and letters from "back home." The National Wildlife Federation has a network of members who receive periodic notices about crucial legislation and urges members to write their elected officials when appropriate. Successful grass-roots efforts require a large membership distributed across the districts of many legislators and, therefore, are less available to small trade associations. This strategy also requires sophisticated, expensive information networks to keep members informed.

Tactics

Tactics are the specific actions undertaken by interest groups to promote their policy preferences. Tactics include personal communication, influential member lobbying, and various other means.

Direct Communication

One principal tactic used by interest groups is direct communication between the group's staff and policymakers. Staff members may meet with agency heads, legislators, legislative staff, or state agency personnel. Lobbyists tend to meet more often with those who are friendly toward the group and to ignore enemies. It is easier to keep friends than convert enemies. Lobbyists have been criticized for ignoring swing or undecided voters in the legislature (Bauer, de Sola Pool, and Dexter 1968).

Most interest groups view personal presentations as an effective tactic. The famous three-martini lunch is one form of this approach. At the state level, personal discussions with state legislators often are the most effective way to affect lawmaking. Telephone calls are next best, and letter writing is least effective (Forest Farmer 1984).

However, letter-writing campaigns can catch the attention of Congress members and may influence their policy decisions. Some groups try to encourage personal mail because it is considered more effective than form letters, although many successful campaigns have used form postcards or letters. Groups may encourage letter writing by appeals to members and nonmembers published in newspapers and magazine articles. They also may appeal directly to members, either through the group magazine or newsletter or by a special mailing to members who have indicated an interest in a particular issue. They may use a telephone chain to urge members in a particular region to write to their legislator or to members of key committees.

A second broad communications tactic involves grass-roots contacts by interest group members or other interested people. Because of their constituency and reelection concerns, legislators usually monitor their mail and home-town opinions closely. Environmental groups, in particular, have been very effective at grass-roots lobbying, helping offset the often larger campaign contributions of business groups. Businesses now are trying to take greater advantage of grass-roots lobbying.

Appearances at legislative hearings may be considered a form of direct communication. However, most interest groups consider such appearances to be ineffective as a single tactic. One-on-one presentations are thought to be better methods of providing legislators and staffs with information. However, testifying at a hearing is considered important for its symbolic value, if not for its content. These appearances show policymakers and group members that the group is a key player in decisions. Most groups testify when possible so they can enter their views in the record. This may not be all that important in determining the content of legislation, but it may be useful if subsequent judicial or administrative proceedings seek to determine legislative intent. Also, a failure to appear at a legislative hearing might be construed as lack of interest in the outcome. Ellefson (1985) analyzed the congressional testimony of wood-based companies and found that wilderness allocation hearings drew the most participation—indicating that despite their opposition to wilderness, they did feel attending the hearings was important.

Legal action is a form of direct communication by interest groups. Some groups specialize in bringing court challenges, as noted before. The expense of lawsuits prohibits many groups from pursuing this tactic unless it is absolutely necessary. However, some of the larger conservation groups employ their own legal staff, which makes the expenses more reasonable, but only if spread over a number of legal actions. Groups also may become involved in lawsuits to which they are not parties through friend-of-the-court (amicus curiae) briefs.

Group Member Influence

Interest groups may try to influence policymakers through acquaintances or friends. The primary purpose of this tactic is to gain access; the group members need not necessarily have any expertise in the subject area.

Conservation groups and trade associations use this tactic particularly well at the state and local level. In fact, many companies encourage members to be active on local boards and commissions so that they are represented when issues arise. In states with large forest products industries, many company officials are social friends of local or national legislators. These contacts are used by interest groups whenever possible.

Campaign Contributions and PACs

One often hears that campaign contributions influence legislators. Political campaigns are costly, so contributions certainly are helpful. Forest products firms contributed nearly $5 million to presidential and congressional candidates from 1983 to 1990, according to records at the Federal Election Commission. Environmental groups contributed just over $2 million (Associated Press 1990). Both sides make direct contributions in order to further their causes as Congress struggles to decide the best use for the nation's forests. Forest products firms contributed 73 percent of their funds to Republicans; 93 percent of environmental group contributions went to Democrats. (Note that political parties certainly do seem to matter in forest resource issues!) More than $775,000 of the industry contributions went to members of the House and Senate from five northwestern states, presumably to influence decisions about public lands policies.

More than 40 forest products companies filed contribution records between 1983 and 1990. Westvaco led the industry with $716,700 in political action committee (PAC) contributions. Other large industry PAC contributions were made by International Paper, Union Camp, Weyerhaeuser, Georgia-Pacific, and the National Forest Products Association. The Sierra Club was the largest contributor of the environmental groups, spending $1.2 million from 1983 to 1990. The League of Conservation Voters was next, at $700,000. Eight other environmental groups that registered with the Federal Elections Commission each spent less than $300,000 (Associated Press 1990).

What do campaign contributions do? First, they may help keep "friendly" people in office. Alternatively, interest group contributions may help defeat legislators who are clearly opposed to an interest group's programs. More important, campaign contributions also help ensure access to legislators. At least the groups or individuals will be known when they express views on pertinent legislation. Being able to meet with and be recognized by a senator or representative can be valuable.

Political action committees are the newest major player in the realm of campaign financing. Since the 1970s, thousands of PACs have been organized to collect contributions that are then distributed to candidates whose policy views agree with those of the PAC. Labor unions, trade associations, individual corporations, citizen interest groups, and some politicians have PACs. In 1974 PACs raised $8.5 million; by 1986 this figure increased to $132.2 million (Smith 1988). By 1990, 40 forest products and paper industry PACs were registered with the Federal Elections Commission (Associated Press 1990).

The American Pulpwood Association (1981) clearly defines the now-prevalent political action committees.

"A Political Action Committee (PAC) is a voluntary group organized to support political candidates or issues of interest to a particular constituency." They are authorized by federal law and can be formed by corporations, labor organizations, nonconnected organizations, trade and business organizations, cooperatives, and "corporations without stock."

PACs operate under the jurisdiction of the Federal Election Committee (FEC) and must file detailed reports of their receipts, expenditures, and contributions with the FEC. All data reported to FEC are available to the public, and FEC also publishes periodic news reports and summaries.

Political action committees provide a means for any group of individuals to have a greater impact on the political process through a united effort than any one of them can have individually (p. 42).

PACs often have been criticized because of the vast sums of money they contribute to politicians and their purported influence. PACs have proliferated partially because election campaign reforms were designed to limit excessive individual or corporate campaign contributions and their political influence. As of 1989 the Federal Election Campaign Act of 1971, as amended in 1974, 1976, and 1979, limited an individual's or organization's contributions to a candidate for federal office to $1000 and to a political party to $20,000. A multicandidate PAC may give no more than $5000 directly to each candidate in each election. However, there is no limit on the total amount a PAC may spend on behalf of a candidate as long as the PAC does not coordinate its activities in any way with the candidate, the candidate's representatives, or the campaign committee (Conway 1986).

Business, labor, and conservation groups all have influential PACs. PACs help maintain friendly relations with Congress members, but PAC contributions do promote iron triangles. Despite criticisms of their role and influence, Conway (1986) and Green and Guth (1986) conclude that PACs probably are an improvement over large corporate, labor, or individual sponsorship of political campaigns and are an appropriate means for interest group involvement; furthermore, proposed reforms to the PAC system are likely to be worse than the problems.

Giving patterns of PACs are a source of frustration for challengers to incumbent members of Congress. Because the primary concern of PACs is having access to decision makers, there is little incentive to help challengers, who seldom beat incumbents anyway. Therefore both corporate and labor PACs give a disproportionate share of their funding to existing legislators.

Bribes are an often cited, but seldom proved, aspect of politics. Although the FBI was successful in stinging a few Congress members with operation ABSCAM in the late 1970s, bribes are probably rare. Less odious and perfectly legal rewards such as paid junkets, speech honoraria, and book deals can channel funds to supportive legislators. Perceived abuses of these rewards in the late 1980s led to calls for reform, and passage of legislation that eliminated honoraria for members of the House of Representatives, and gave them a large pay increase instead.

Endorsements and Voting Records

A few interest groups have publicly endorsed political candidates, but this has not been a particularly effective tactic. Labor unions endorsed Mondale in 1984 and Carter in 1980 for president, yet they barely delivered a majority of the labor votes. In 1984, for the first time in its history, the National Education Association endorsed a presidential candidate—Walter Mondale. Perhaps it helped him win in his home state of Minnesota, but he lost the other 49 states. Many environmental groups actively endorsed Democratic candidates Carter in 1980, Mondale in 1984, and Dukakis in 1988, to little avail. Endorsement by interest groups may carry more weight in state or local elections.

Some groups publicize part or all of a legislator's voting record as a means of generating support or opposition. Liberal groups that publish such records include the Americans for Democratic Action, American Civil Liberties Union, and Council on Political Education. Conservative groups include the National Taxpayers Union, Americans for Constitutional Action, the Committee for Survival of a Free Congress, and the Chamber of Commerce of the United States (Barone and Ujifusa 1986). Other groups also rank Congress members according to key votes that affect their interest groups. These ratings are intended to publicize the records of legislators' support for individual issues. The League of Conservation Voters rates Congress members' votes on environmental issues. Most states have coalitions of environmental groups that rate state legislators and encourage group members to vote for legislators supportive of interest group objectives.

Public Relations

Interest groups often use public relations to promote their causes. They may conduct advertising campaigns, issue research results, or promote causes through the media. Reports of protestors who only demonstrate while TV cameras are filming are common. Groups also send press releases to the radio and print media outlets in hopes that they will be used. If issues are extremely important, press conferences may be held, although this is uncommon in forestry. Groups also may conduct individual meetings with reporters. Forestry groups occasionally take reporters on woods or mill tours. Some forestry associations hold annual golf tournaments or other events with members of the media to promote good relations for forestry. Public organizations also recognize the value of such goodwill, as demonstrated by their hiring of information officers and similar public relations specialists. Further discussion of the importance of public relations is provided in Chapter 11.

PROBLEMS OF INTEREST GROUPS

Interest groups are obviously important in shaping public policy. However, like other organizations, interest groups face problems. First, they must establish priorities for acting on the many issues that may be relevant to their interests. They must have special knowledge and skills of the issue at hand. They also must have sufficient time and resources to attack the issue.

Poor selection of issues may foster ill-conceived group actions. Interest groups may become involved in too many issues. They may act on issues of little importance to group members, so politicians may ignore them without fear of electoral retribution. A related problem is that with heterogeneous interest groups, particularly professional societies, it is difficult to establish criteria for action that are acceptable to all members. In fact, many issues may prove so divisive that no official position can be adopted that is acceptable to the entire membership.

Controlling interest group representatives presents another problem. Difficulties may arise when individual members or staff speak on behalf of the group without official approval. Regional or local chapters sometimes wish to adopt positions contrary to those supported by the national society.

Responding adequately to policy issues is another concern. Like Congress, interest groups monitor thousands of issues each year, although only a few will be of great import to a particular group. Groups must choose their responses carefully to maximize their effectiveness and not spread their resources too thinly. Increasing staff size is tempting, but costly. Coercing talented members to work for the group is a cheaper but more difficult approach. Attracting and retaining members is another ongoing problem. As mentioned in the section on group development, leaders must convince members that membership provides unique benefits, be they tangible or ideological.

Maintaining adequate operating budgets poses a perpetual problem for most interest groups. Revenues may come from membership dues, contributions, publications and conferences, federal grants, professional services, or other sources. In 1985 trade associations relied mostly on dues, publications, and conferences—81 percent of their revenue sources. Nonprofit associations (including professional societies) garnered 70 percent of their income from these sources, citizen groups only 43 percent. Contributions, gifts, grants from government and foundations, and other nonrecurring, nonmember sources also provide funds for interest groups. In 1985 trade associations received about 8 percent of their income from these sources, nonprofit associations 18 percent, and citizen groups 41 percent. Investments, loans, rents, merchandise sales, and so forth comprise the remainder of the income sources for these groups (Peterson and Walker 1986).

Expenses for groups include publications, staff salaries, travel expenses, mailing costs, public relations, lobbying, clerical support, and legal fees. Expenditures increase with the rise in inflation, but membership dues seldom are raised comparably due to the fear of losing members, so other means of increasing funding are constantly sought. In periods of economic recession, membership in trade associations and professional societies often declines significantly. These losses must be accompanied by painful budget and staff cuts. This is particularly true in the cyclical forest products business. The National Forest Products Association, American Forest Institute, and Forest Products Research Society, to name a few, all had significant membership declines and budget crises during the early 1980s. In 1991 the National Wildlife Federation had a substantial staff reduction due to budget problems.

Most interest groups strive to maintain their IRS section 501(c)(3) tax-exempt status as a charitable, scientific, or educational organization. As such, they are classed as nonprofit organizations that need not pay taxes on revenues. Maintaining their tax-free status requires that they spend no more than a portion (roughly 5 percent) of their funds on lobbying, so some organizations have set up separate political action arms to do their lobbying. A nonprofit organization also qualifies for favorable postage rates. In 1991 regular bulk mail was 29 cents per piece; nonprofit organizations paid only 11.1 cents per piece. For large organizations, the difference of 18 cents could amount to a postage savings alone of millions of dollars per year.

Perhaps the most fundamental dilemma faced by interest group leaders is the collective action or free-rider problem. Often individuals will not contribute money and time to a group unless they can gain some benefit from their contribution. Thus interest group leaders must attempt to convince members that their contributions are necessary and effective. Some groups do this by offering their members selective incentives—material benefits available only to members. Trade associations offer members market information and technical assistance in addition to lobbying. Professional societies may sponsor certification programs leading to credentials and may offer reduced group rates on insurance. Environmental groups print high-quality magazines and offer member-only tours. All of these methods are used to attract and maintain members.

When selective incentives are unavailable or insufficient, members can be attracted by emphasizing the political purposes of the organization and the members' duty to contribute. Thus resource managers help to fulfill their professional obligations to society by being active members of professional associations; conservationists help preserve wildlife and habitat by sending annual dues and contributions to the National Audubon Society or the Nature Conservancy; and business employees help preserve competitive markets for their products by joining trade associations. Interest groups devote considerable resources to attracting and keeping members, sometimes at the expense of the declared purposes of the organization.

SUMMARY

Interest groups are the principal means available for individuals to influence public policies. The iron triangle political model suggests that groups work in narrow, specialized policy areas to seek specialized government favors, often at the expense of the larger public. These narrow subsystems—involving an interest group, a congressional subcommittee and its staff, and a government agency—have become more diffuse and less influential as group interests have proliferated and government budgets have tightened, forming a broader issue network.

Groups may be comprised of individual citizens (citizen interest groups), business interests (trade associations), nonprofit professional associations (professional societies), or researchers (informational organizations or "think tanks"). Most groups develop in response to a particular problem or common area of interest. They must maintain membership by successfully influencing government agencies, Congress, and state legislatures to enact favorable policies and by providing incentives for individual membership. Daily operations of interest groups are usually performed by paid, full-time staff; general policy directions may be determined by the grassroots membership or their elected officers in consent with staff members.

Interest groups use a variety of strategies and tactics to influence policy. Direct communication with policymakers is considered to be the most important. Campaign contributions, especially through political action committees, provide interest groups with access to elected officials and perhaps provide some influence in policy deliberations. Broad public relations efforts also help create a climate favorable for desired policy outcomes.

LITERATURE CITED

AFA. 1987. L-P offers $20,000 reward [for information on tree spiking that severely injured a sawmill worker]. *American Forests* 93(7, 8):10–11.

AFRA. 1989. Prospectus–Executive Summary. American Forest Resource Alliance. Washington, DC. 3 pp.

American Pulpwood Association. 1981. APA Legislative Handbook. Paper 81-A-2. Washington, DC. 46 pp.

Arnold, Ron. 1982. As the Eye of the Storm: James Watt and the Environmentalists. Regnery Gateway. Chicago. 282 pp.

Associated Press. 1990. Loggers, environmentalists square off at ballot box. *Atlanta Journal*, December 31, p. A3.

Barone, Michael, and Grant Ujifusa. 1986. The Almanac of American Politics 1986. National Journal. Washington, DC. 1593 pp.

Bauer, Raymond A., Ithiel de Sola Pool, and Lewis A. Dexter. 1963. American Business and Public Policy. Atherton. New York. 499 pp.

Black, Hugo L. 1935. The Lobby. P. 35 in L. Harmon Ziegler and Wayne Peak. 1972. Interest Groups in American Society, 2nd ed. Prentice Hall. Englewood Cliffs, NJ.

Boernor, Deborah A. 1987. Texas First! [Earth First! stalls silvicultural efforts in Sam Houston National Forest]. *American Forests* 93 (3, 4):29.

Borelli, Peter. 1987. Environmentalism at a crossroads: Reflections on the old old, new old, old new, and new new movements. *Amicus Journal* 9(3):24–37.

Browne, William P. 1986. Policy and interests: Instability and change in a classic issue subsystem. Pp. 183–201 in Allan J. Cigler and Burdett A. Loomis (eds.), Interest Group Politics, 2nd ed. Congressional Quarterly. Washington, DC.

Cahn, Robert (ed.). 1985. An Environmental Agenda for the Future. Island Press. Covelo, CA. 155 pp.

Cigler, Allan J. 1986. From protest group to interest group: The making of the American Agriculture Movement, Inc. Pp. 46–69 in Allan J. Cigler and Burdett A. Loomis (eds.), Interest Group Politics, 2nd ed. Congressional Quarterly. Washington, DC.

Clark, Peter, and James Q. Wilson. 1961. Incentive systems: A theory of organizations. *Administrative Science Quarterly* 6(September):126–166.

Conway, M. Margaret. 1986. PACs and congressional elections in the 1980s. Pp. 70–90 in Allan J. Cigler and Burdett A. Loomis (eds.), Interest Group Politics, 2nd ed. Congressional Quarterly. Washington, DC.

Devall, Bill. 1980. The deep ecology movement. *Natural Resources Journal* 20(April):299–322.

Dye, Thomas R., Lee S. Greene, and George S. Parthemos. 1980. Governing the American Democracy. St. Martin's Press. New York. 624 pp.

Ellefson, Paul V. 1985. Congressional testimony: Who presents wood-based industrial interests? *Journal of Forestry* 83(5):300–301.

Foreman, Dave, and Bill Haywood, (eds.). 1987. Ecodefense: A Field Guide to Monkeywrenching, 2nd ed. Ned Ludd Books. Tucson, AZ. 311 pp.

Forest Farmer. 1984. Forestry lobbying at the state level. 43(4):10–11.

Franklin, Karen E., and J. Sowell. 1987. The timber terrorists. *American Forests* 93(3, 4):41–42.

Green, John C., and James L. Guth. 1986. Big bucks and petty cash: Party and interest group activists in American politics.

Pp. 91–131 in Allan J. Cigler and Burdett A. Loomis (eds.), Interest Group Politics, 2nd ed. Congressional Quarterly. Washington, DC.

Grosvenor, Gilbert M. 1988. Will we mend our Earth? *National Geographic* 174(6):766–771.

Hayes, Michael T. 1986. The new group universe. Pp. 133–145 in Allan J. Cigler and Burdett A. Loomis (eds.), Interest Group Politics, 2nd ed. Congressional Quarterly. Washington, DC.

Heclo, Hugh. 1978. Issue networks and the executive establishment. Pp. 87–124 in Anthony King (ed.), The New Political System, American Enterprise Institute for Public Policy Research. Washington, DC.

Jordan, A. Grant. 1981. Iron triangles, wooly corporatism, and elastic nets: Images of the policy process. *Journal of Public Policy* 1(February):95–123.

Lancaster, John. 1991. The environmentalist as insider. *Washington Post Magazine*, August 4, pp. 17–20, 28–29.

Latham, Earl. 1952. The group basis of politics: Notes for a theory. *American Political Science Review* 46(June): 376–397.

Loomis, Burdett A., and Allan J. Cigler. 1986. Introduction: The changing nature of interest group politics. Pp. 1–26 in Allan J. Cigler and Burdett A. Loomis, (eds.), Interest Group Politics, 2nd ed. Congressional Quarterly. Washington, DC.

Milbrath, Lester W. 1984. Environmentalists: A Vanguard for a New Society. State University of New York Press. Albany. 180 pp.

Miller, Robert L. 1989. Planet of the year: Endangered Earth. *Time*, January 2, pp. 3, 24–73.

Moe, Terry. 1980. A calculus of group membership. *American Journal of Political Science* 24(November):593–623.

Montsma, Stephen V. 1969. American Politics: A Systems Approach. Holt, Rinehart & Winston. New York. 399 pp.

National Wildlife Federation. 1992. Conservation Directory, 37th ed. Washington, DC. 398 pp.

NFPA. 1982. Special [Congressional] report lashes environmental extremists. *Forest Industries Newsletter* 70-11-15(April 16). National Forest Products Association. Washington, DC.

Olson, Mancur. 1971. The Logic of Collective Action. Harvard University Press. Cambridge, MA. 186 pp.

Petersen, Philip V. 1982. An interview with Sierra Club executive director J. Michael McCloskey. *Journal of Forestry* 80(5): 276–279.

Peterson, Mark A., and Jack L. Walker. 1986. Interest group responses to partisan change: The impact of the Reagan administration upon the national interest group system. Pp. 162–182 in Allan J. Cigler and Burdett A. Loomis (eds.), Interest Group Politics, 2nd ed. Congressional Quarterly. Washington, DC.

Rose, Robert L. 1988. The urban conscience turns to the environment. *American Forests* 94(7, 8):17–20.

Russell, Dick. 1987. The monkeywrenchers: Whatever happened to the nice little old ladies in tennis shoes? *Amicus Journal* 9(4):28–42.

Salisbury, Robert H. 1969. An exchange theory of interest groups. *Midwest Journal of Political Science* 13(February):1–32.

Schattschneider, Elmer E. 1960. The Semisovereign People. Holt, Rinehart & Winston. New York. 147 pp.

Smith, Hedrick. 1988. The Power Game: How Washington Works. Random House. New York. 793 pp.

Smith, James A. 1991. The Idea Brokers: Think Tanks and the Rise of the New Policy Elite. Free Press, Macmillan. New York. 313 pp.

Society of American Foresters. 1983. SAF Manual. Bethesda, MD. 105 pp.

Society of American Foresters. 1990. SAF forest policies and positions. Society of American Foresters, SAF 90-01. Bethesda, MD. 63 pp.

TFA. 1988. Congress makes [tree] spiking a federal crime. *Texas Forestry* 29(12):3. Texas Forestry Association. Lufkin.

Tucker, William. 1982. Progress and Privileges: America in the Age of Environmentalism. Anchor Press/Doubleday. Garden City, NY. 314 pp.

Walsh, Barry W. 1985. After Watt: The environmentalists. *Journal of Forestry* 83(4): 212–217.

Walt, Harold R. 1986. Of forestry, tree spikers, and the dinosaur. S. J. Hall Lectureship in Industrial Forestry. University of California, Department of Forestry and Resource Management. Berkeley. 8 pp.

Chapter 10

Environmentalism, Conservation, Ethics, and Professionalism

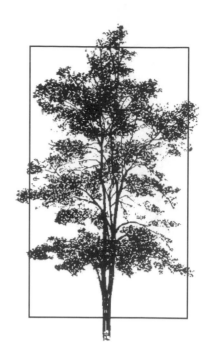

True conservation means not only protecting nature against human behavior but also developing human activities which favor a creative harmonious relationship between humans and nature.

—*Rene Dubos 1980*

It is a social goal, this land ethic of Aldo Leopold, and it must be expressed in "policy." And not only the abstract big-P Policy of Principle, but the workaday little-p policy of legislation, of statute, of government regulation and management practice.

—*Charles E. Little 1985*

INTRODUCTION

Forest policy processes and the participants in them have been described in the preceding chapters. This chapter focuses on *conservation*, a concept that has set the public agenda for natural resource management for well over a century. *Environmentalism*, a later term that expands the original idea of conservation, has been especially important since the 1960s and will continue to dominate natural resource policy discussions in the future. The role of natural resource managers in environmental issues is important for both the future of the profession and the forests that cover one-third of the nation's land.

This chapter also examines environmentalism and professionalism, thus leaving the domain of scientific fact and technical so-

lutions and entering the nebulous realm of values and beliefs. Participants in the policy process hold diverse personal philosophies concerning natural resources. These values and beliefs are perhaps the most important of all considerations when it comes to making forest resource policy.

ENVIRONMENTALISM AND CONSERVATION

Environmentalism has been defined as a set of ideas that emphasizes the interrelationship between humans and the ecosystem and the threats human activity poses to the continued viability of ecosystems (Mitchell 1980a). Environmentalism refers to the ideas and activities of those concerned with the protection or proper use of the natural environment or natural resources (Petulla 1980). Beauty, health, and permanence—the ideology of environmentalism is captured in these three words that are the title of Hays's (1987) historical treatise on the politics of the modern environmental movement. Environmentalism is a political and social movement concerned with the preservation of the environment (Pepper 1984). Environmentalists represent the entire spectrum of opinions on both the environment and natural resources (Mitchell 1980b).

Sometimes modern-day environmentalists favor managed forests; more often, they do not. Chapter 9 identified many of the interest groups that environmentalists join. This chapter is concerned with what environmentalists are about, and why the forestry, range, recreation, and wildlife professions must come to grips with environmentalism. Timber, grazing, and game management often are at odds with environmentalism over resource management issues, as are developed and dispersed recreation uses. Thus resource managers and environmentalists square off on many policy disputes. However, there is much in common between the two, and much to be gained by searching for areas of agreement.

Many segments of society that advocate changes in our relationship with natural surroundings use environmentalism as a rallying cry. The environmental movement is a force that is local, regional, national, and now global in its scope. It is important to realize that all sides in an environmental dispute desire a cleaner, healthier environment and a better life for the planet's inhabitants. It is their objectives, means, and underlying values that differ (Petulla 1980).

Environmentalism is not a single ideology or philosophy, but a manifestation of several. Buttel and Larson (1980) described the three-part character of environmentalism. First is public environmentalism: the preferences of the general public for healthier, aesthetically pleasing, and ecologically harmonious residential, work, and recreation surroundings. Second is bureaucratic environmentalism: the public institutions and agencies with ju-

risdiction over certain portions of the environment and related public policies. These include the EPA, National Park Service, Forest Service, Department of Energy, state agencies, and others—bureaucracies whose advocacy of environmental protection is tempered by philosophical and fiscal constraints on governmental action. The third aspect is voluntary environmentalism: the structure, ideology, and tactics of citizen interest groups, such as the Sierra Club, National Audubon Society, and a host of others. Milbrath (1984) claimed that more than 12,000 environmental and conservation groups exist in the United States, with 250 new groups being added each year.

Citizens are more concerned about the environment now than they were a decade ago. For example, Figure 10-1 illustrates the rise of interest in environmental affairs during the 1980s. By 1989, 80 percent of 1500 people polled in a *New York Times* survey agreed with the statement "Protecting the environment is so important that requirements and standards cannot be too high and continuing environmental improvements must be made regardless of cost" (Suro, p.18). In fact, environmental (and forest) protection has be-

Do you agree or disagree with the following statement: *Protecting the environment is so important that requirements and standards cannot be too high and continuing environmental improvements must be made regardless of cost.*

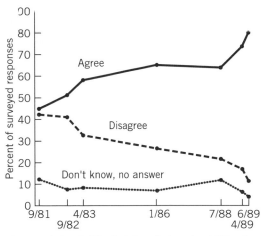

Figure 10-1. Public Opinion during the 1980s about the Importance of Protecting the Environment
Source: New York Times, July 2, 1989.

come one of the most important national issues and public agenda items in the late 1980s and early 1990s. Such public concern compels resource managers to come to grips with environmental issues.

In environmental debates concerning forestry and natural resource management, both disputants may claim to be conservationists. Yet their interpretations of natural resource conservation are in conflict. To understand the branches of the modern environmental movement, it is important to first examine its roots.

THE CONSERVATION MOVEMENT

Theodore Roosevelt can justifiably be called "the conservation president" (see Chapter 7). His attitude toward natural resources is one reason why his visage appears with those of Presidents Washington, Jefferson, and Lincoln on the Mt. Rushmore National Monument in the Black Hills of South Dakota (Eliot 1982). TR's colleague, Gifford Pinchot, was a leader in founding American forestry. He was the first American to be educated in forestry and the first American to practice forestry. He helped found the Society of American Foresters in 1900. He was the first chief of the USDA Forest Service. He was responsible for defining the national forest land management mission as providing the greatest good of the greatest number for the long run. He popularized the use of the term *conservation* to mean the "wise use" of natural resources (Hays 1959).

As the twentieth century began, conservation was a rallying cry for the progressive conservation movement. Forest policies spawned during this period were based on fears of a timber famine (Gray 1983). Until 1891 federal land policy largely had been one of divesting the public domain into private hands. At one time or another, the federal government had owned 80 percent of all the land in the United States; today, it owns almost 30 percent. During the nineteenth century, "cut out and get out" timber removal, sometimes accompanied by forest fires, had stripped the

only valuable natural resource from several regions, notably the Great Lakes and southern pine regions. The cry to stem the tide of forest devastation culminated in 1891 after a 15-year struggle in the U.S. Congress to get the remaining public forests of the West placed under federal protection. The American Forestry Association, the first of America's citizen conservation groups, played an instrumental role in the push for the creation of federal forest reserves.

ILLUSTRATION: THE AMERICAN FORESTRY ASSOCIATION AND THE CREATION OF THE NATIONAL FORESTS

The organizational meeting of the American Forestry Association (AFA) was held in 1875 in Chicago (Sparhawk 1949). One objective of the association was "the fostering of all interests of forest planting and conservation on this continent" (Clepper 1971, p. 20). At the same time, hunters and anglers interested in the future of fish and game populations also were quite active in promoting their ideas of conservation (Reiger 1975). These conservation efforts were triggered by George Marsh's (1864) *Man and Nature*, a work that pointed out that the decline of empires was in part traceable to the decline of their forests.

The AFA worked closely with the American Association for the Advancement of Science (AAAS), a group that represented the interests of the scientific community. The AAAS led the drive to establish a forestry agency in the U.S. Department of Agriculture in the 1870s. In the 1880s the AFA and AAAS also worked together to obtain congressional authority to reserve the remaining government-owned timberlands in the West as public forests. The first federal forest policy action was taken in 1876, when the USDA hired a special agent, Franklin B. Hough, to investigate forestry issues. The first forest reservation bill was proposed in 1878. Many others followed. These bills served to attract the attention of the public and of members of Congress and to demonstrate that a new federal policy for public lands was needed (Clepper 1971, 1975b).

The AFA was not very active until 1882, when Bernhard E. Fernow drafted a new constitution for the merger of the AFA with the American Forest Congress. Fernow, a trained Prussian forester who had emigrated to the United States in 1876, became a leader in the AFA. In 1886 he was appointed to Hough's former position as chief of the Division of Forestry in the USDA, where he remained through 1898. Under his leadership, the AFA was effective in urging the enactment of state and federal forest policies (Harmon 1983, Sparhawk 1949). As a leader of both the foremost citizen interest group and the government agency charged with assessing—but not, at that time, managing—the nation's forests, Fernow was in a strategic position to greatly influence the development of forest policy during these formative years (Dana and Fairfax 1980).

In 1889 Fernow addressed a meeting of the AAAS on the need for forest administration. The AAAS petitioned President Harrison to reserve some forest land in the public domain; the president conveyed that message to Congress in 1890. The American Economic Association added its support for forest conservation. Problems with timber trespass on western federal lands also were publicized. In 1891 Congress passed a revision of the general land laws. In the conference committee, a brief clause was inserted to authorize the president to create forest reserves by setting the land aside. The actual responsibility for the timber reservation clause is unclear, but many credit Fernow and his associates in the American Forestry Association (Clepper 1971).

Later, the AFA set the creation of national forests in the northeastern United States as a major goal. To this end, the AFA coordinated efforts that led to the passage of the Weeks Act in 1911, thereby authorizing federal purchases of forest land. In the 1920s the AFA sponsored and supported other federal forest policies, such as cooperative federal and state fire protection efforts. More recently, the AFA has occupied the middle ground in resource policy debates, advocating a reasoned balance between preservation and wise use

(Dana and Fairfax 1980). Today, the AFA provides leadership in urban forestry, forest policy, and global reforestation efforts.

UTILITARIANISM VERSUS PRESERVATION

Pinchot made it clear when he followed Fernow as chief of the Division of Forestry in 1898 that the purpose of forestry was service to people, not to trees (Zivnuska 1971). This utilitarian view of natural resources—that forests were to be used to benefit human economic welfare—drove a wedge into the conservation movement, causing a split that persists today.

John Muir, who is idolized by many modern environmentalists, worked side by side with Pinchot in the conservation movement to promote and establish federal forest reserves. Muir helped found the Sierra Club in 1892 to promote recreation in a primeval setting of scenic beauty, with objectives stressing aesthetics and nonuse. Pinchot, however, failed to recognize the importance of these objectives. Muir fought against Pinchot's desire to control and "properly utilize" the resources of national parks.

The conflict over preservation versus use erupted in 1913 after a 12-year struggle, when Congress permitted the city of San Francisco to construct a water supply reservoir in the Hetch Hetchy Valley in Yosemite National Park. The Hetch Hetchy reservoir issue split the conservation movement even further. Pinchot supported building the dam; Muir opposed it. (See Chapter 12 for more details.) An interesting postscript occurred in 1988 when the feasibility of draining the reservoir in order to reclaim the lost valley was studied. Even more interesting is that both President Reagan's secretary of the interior, Donald Hodel, and the Earth First! group supported undoing Hetch Hetchy. Although the project was technologically feasible, no alternative water supply source could be found.

Preservation of natural resources is recognized by some as desirable and by others as a waste of valuable resources. As Spurr (1982) explains, Muir and his present-day followers basically oppose the cutting of trees. Pinchot and his later disciples favor the growing of trees as renewable crops. The crux of the issue is whether federal (and private) forest lands should be actively managed for commodities, or whether they should be left as wilderness areas. A secondary issue is if these forests are managed, should it be for one use or multiple uses? The choice is an emotional one, and the case is strong for both sides. Certainly we need to preserve examples of our natural and cultural heritage, to set aside areas for scientific study, and to protect diverse genetic pools and the diversity of species. Certainly we need wood, a versatile and recyclable industrial material with useful structural properties, and paper for a host of purposes. The choice between the two cannot be solved by economic analysis alone, because many forest values consist of nonmarket goods that are difficult to quantify. This issue can be resolved only on a subjective basis (Spurr 1982) and through the public policy process.

Many battles for wilderness designation have been fought and won. Like any other organization, groups espousing wilderness preservation point to past successes and look toward further success in the future. Therefore, it is pointless to expect them to say when an adequate amount of wilderness has been preserved.

Preservationists have enjoyed success that has exceeded even their own expectations. Doug Scott, the Sierra Club's conservation director, said that

Our ambitions, plans, and visions about what was the art of the possible for preserving wilderness were feeble compared to today's reality. Eighty million of the 91 million acres in the wilderness system have been added since the Wilderness Act was passed [1964]. This is an enormous achievement, and most of the land was never on anybody's agenda. (Borelli 1988, p. 27)

In the late 1960s when Michael McCloskey (appointed chair of the Sierra Club follow-

ing his 1969–1985 reign as its executive director) held Scott's position, he wrote a letter to the Forest Service and enclosed a map of the club's ultimate plan for the Siskiyou wilderness area in northern California. Later Scott said that "Now it's three times as large and the Forest Service keeps hauling out this yellowed letter and saying, 'but you guys said.' Our fondest ambitions have underestimated the growth of our political clout" (Borelli 1988, p.27).

ENVIRONMENTALISTS AND CONSERVATION

Using the antagonism between John Muir and Gifford Pinchot as their model, historians have tended to categorize every environmentalist as either a preservationist or a conservationist (Reiger 1975). Although these labels are meaningful, they leave the distinctions among environmentalists, preservationists, or conservationists ill defined. In a review of the field of wildlife management, Peek (1986) stated that virtually everyone interested in wildlife can be considered a conservationist. Harry, Galer, and Hendee (1969) split conservationists into two groups: those with a conservation-utilization emphasis, and those with a conservation-preservation emphasis. The former group was identified as followers of Pinchot and the latter as followers of Muir. Peek (1986) further explained that environmentalism not only includes preservation, but also the movement to eliminate pollution and other human abuses of the planet.

Who Is an Environmentalist?

Were Pinchot and Muir environmentalists? To the extent that they cared deeply about the future of natural resources and their role in American life, yes, they were. But today, the term *environmentalist* has narrowed in meaning and generally describes the preservationist followers of Muir, but not necessarily Pinchot's utilitarian conservationists. It is confusing, but both preservationists and utilitarians refer to themselves as conservationists. Preservationists generally are comfortable with the environmentalist label; utilitarians generally are not. Utilitarians do not like the utilitarian label; they prefer to be called conservationists.

In another much broader sense, environmentalism is more than the preservation and permanence of natural beauty. A fundamental concern of environmentalism is the wise use of all earth's resources that is essential for human survival. The problem is that not everyone agrees on what constitutes wise use. Jackson (1983) describes the problem well: A farmer or industrial forester may be heard to claim that she or he is a good conservationist, and in the next breath confide that most environmentalists are radicals. This prejudice is common but is neither fair nor helpful in resolving the complex resource management problems facing our society. Placing conservationists and environmentalists in separate, antagonistic camps polarizes issues.

Who is an environmentalist? Many definitions have been offered. We will consider an environmentalist as a person who wants to protect the earth from harmful human actions. One recent public opinion poll found that 76 percent of all Americans considered themselves environmentalists (*Harper's* 1989). Those who consider themselves environmentalists generally favor preservation over development, and aesthetic considerations over economic ones, at least as long as they are not inconvenienced. Furthermore, environmentalists usually prefer nonconsumptive uses, such as wilderness, recreation, or aesthetics, to extractive uses, such as timber, grazing, or minerals.

The Environmental Movement

Environmentalism gathered new momentum during the 1960s. Nash (1968) said that protection of the environment for its nonmaterial values began to challenge utilitarianism as the central theme of conservation. People began to demand that land do more than just keep people alive. President Johnson in 1965 called this the "new conservation." Increased leisure time and mobility created an "outdoor recreation crisis" and a new awareness of federal lands in the West.

As mentioned before, the catalyst for environmental activism was Rachel Carson's (1962) *Silent Spring*, which documented the adverse effects of pesticides. People became uncomfortable with the air and water pollution resulting from the economic growth and industrial expansion following World War II. Young Americans felt disenfranchised during the bitter social struggle over the Vietnam War. Part of their reaction was to take up the cause of environmentalism. But the movement involved more than young radicals. A wide spectrum of groups was pulled into the environmental movement in the 1970s, including hunters and anglers with little or no political agenda, pragmatic reformers cast in the mold of Teddy Roosevelt and Gifford Pinchot, middle-class moderates newly awakened to the dangers of pesticides and industrial pollution, hard-line preservationists carrying on the anti-industrial tradition of John Muir, and elements of new and old leftist politics who viewed environmental problems as proof positive of the need for a new social order (Borelli 1988).

The benchmark of the new environmental era was the enactment of the National Environmental Policy Act (NEPA) in late 1969 that took effect on New Year's Day 1970. America marked the new decade of environmentalism on April 22, 1970, with Earth Day. NEPA has been identified by leading conservationists as the most "constructively influential" piece of conservation legislation in the twentieth century (Clepper 1975a). NEPA has been hailed as the keystone in the bridge between conservation and environmentalism (Kury 1985).

Environmental organizations increased in number and size throughout the 1970s. When President Carter was defeated in 1980, many groups feared that President Reagan's prodevelopment slant would halt environmental protection and group expansion. However, Reagan's zeal prompted the opposite reaction. James Watt, secretary of the interior from 1981 to 1984, became a lightning rod for renewed fervor regarding federal natural resource management. Membership in environmental organizations began to rise dramatically. For example, the Wilderness Society increased in size from 40,000 members when President Reagan took office in 1981 to more than 300,000 members when President Bush took office in 1989.

The Reagan administration and its supporters began to use pejorative adjectives to flavor the term *environmentalist*, conducting a war of words in an attempt to negate the influence of environmental groups. James Watt characterized environmentalist goals as "extremist" and announced the Reagan administration's intentions to "reverse twenty-five years of bad resource management" (Udall 1988).

Critics have been quick to indict the Reagan administration for its lack of vision concerning natural resources (Hays 1987) and lack of leadership in global environmental matters (Udall 1988). The Reagan scorecard reveals that he did sign many environmental bills into law, although often reluctantly, and had his veto overridden a few times. The Watt years—there were only three of them—spawned controversy but were followed by a spate of wilderness designations in 1984. President Reagan presided over the greatest expansion of the wilderness preservation system in the contiguous 48 states of any president (Hays 1987). The major environmental legacies of the Reagan era, though, were checks on the increases in staff and budget for natural resource and environmental agencies (Rose 1988) and a gargantuan debt that restricts his successors' options as well as those of the American people (Udall 1988). Congress, however, shares the blame or credit for these program decisions; it allocates funds among agencies and was responsible for developing and approving the unbalanced budgets of the 1980s and 1990s.

Critics of Environmentalism

Despite pervasive public support for environmental protection, many people have criticized environmentalism by stating that environmentalists seek to prevent additional economic growth, thus protecting their comfortable quality of life and their aesthetic sensibilities at the expense of those who are poorer (Arnold 1982, Popovich 1983, Tucker 1982). In Colorado, the saying goes that an environmentalist is someone who built a mountain cabin last year.

Opposition to the environmental movement came from people in both public and private life who were committed to material development and unregulated market allocation of resources. To them, environmental objectives were either secondary or unnecessary. Gains made by environmentalists were considered extreme by developers. Stunned in the 1960s and early 1970s, commodity and development groups, including private businesspersons, became hostile and developed strategies to thwart environmentalists, including attempts to influence administrative decisions and the use of lawsuits and courts to press their case (Hays 1983).

Developers have become particularly hostile about opposition from environmental or neighborhood groups. Developers have recently begun to employ a tactic called SLAPP (Strategic Lawsuit Against Public Participation), suing individuals or groups opposing development for monetary damages that run to millions of dollars. These SLAPPs have had chilling effects on groups opposing private development, but they have not helped public relations efforts of developers.

Challenges to the merits of environmentalism resurfaced in the 1990s. For example, political columnist George Will (1990, p. A-23) refuted the extreme environmental tenet of faith that human health and longevity are so valuable that they are superior to all other goods. He criticized this premise as crude biological materialism, writing that "Economic vitality produces jobs, wealth, and other satisfactions; economic vitality underwrites government, the arts, and the sciences, including sciences pertaining to health." In regard to the national debate approving new amendments to the Clean Air Act, congressional sponsors said that the cost to industry—estimated at $21 billion per year—would pay for itself, based on the prevention of lost productivity and of premature death. Will observed that almost all federal programs are sold as ones that will pay for themselves, but that consumers or the government usually spend the cash. Furthermore, to spend $21 billion on clean air means we probably cannot spend $21 billion on other health needs, such as immunization, infant mortality, or care for poor pregnant women. In the end, Will concluded that all aspects of life have some degree of cost and benefit, including environmental protection. He wrote, "The idea that 'life is priceless' comes under the category of useful nonsense."(p. A-23)

In opposition to the environmental movement, a burgeoning "wise use" movement expanded in the 1990s. This movement was started by Ron Arnold and others in the late 1980s and has become a profession for them, just as it has for the leaders of environmental groups. The wise use agenda includes 25 specific goals, including allowing mining and oil exploration in national parks and refuges, weakening the Endangered Species Act, protecting private property rights, protecting cattle ranching, and developing off-road trails (Krakauer 1991). (The wise use movement has been dubbed the "brown movement" by environmentalists, who are the "greens.")

The wise use movement encompasses a number of ideologically linked interest groups, including Arnold's Center for Defense of Free Enterprise in Bellevue, Washington, the Wilderness Impact Research Foundation, the Mountain States Legal Foundation, and the Multiple Use Land Alliance. These groups provide information, publish newsletters and magazines, campaign for laws that prohibit interference with business relationships, and litigate against perceived invalid regulation. Arnold stumps the country, advocating a fight for survival over commodity production or environmental strangulation (Krakauer 1991). The successes of the environmental movement have led to backlashes and helped create the wise use movement. This policy debate promises to become more acrimonious in the 1990s.

In essence, this ongoing debate about environmental protection versus private property rights is a variation of the community and government versus individualism and markets dichotomy discussed in Chapter 3. Some analysts have suggested that America swings between these points on a spectrum. De-

spite the successes of environmentalism in the early 1970s and its resurgence in the late 1980s, strong individual rights/free market groups are forming to push back the gains achieved by environmentalists. These groups may be aided by the many conservative federal judges appointed during the Reagan and Bush administrations, and perhaps by more conservative state and federal legislators.

Polls indicate that most people in the United States support environmental protection, even at a significant cost, and most people consider themselves environmentalists. In fact, the combination of nuclear mishaps, oil tanker spills, droughts, floods, pollution, and other natural and human disasters has created a pervasive feeling that we are fouling our own nest and should strive to clean it up. Coupled with media saturation and political support, the environment has leapfrogged into the spotlight as one of the premier national, state, and local agenda items of the 1990s.

However, the wise users, including a large complement of forestry interest groups, are taking a hard line in opposing further environmental protection inroads. In fact, many are attempting to turn back the environmental protection laws. Whether this strategy will serve commercial interests well, or further narrow their base of support, remains to be seen.

ENVIRONMENTAL VALUES AND THE NEEDS HIERARCHY

Environmentalism encompasses a nebulous set of ideas and diverse groups. One can analyze environmentalists by examining the values underlying the environmental movement. Values are learned early in life and strengthened, lost, or renounced as individuals are nurtured by social, economic, and political institutions. Values can be derived from class position, but also from political or social ideals as well as from a religious heritage. All of these will influence how individuals will view and act toward nature (Petulla 1980).

Issues of any type are characterized by two conflicting viewpoints and, thus, conflicting values. A *value*, as defined by Barbour (1980), is a general characteristic of a thing or a circumstance that a person views with favor, believes is beneficial, and is disposed to act to promote. Values are not held in isolation, but as components of a value system, or ordered set of values.

One of the most widely used and easily understood value systems was developed by psychologist Abraham Maslow and is called a hierarchy of human needs. There are five levels of needs ranging from the most basic to the most personally satisfying (Barbour 1980, Maslow 1943, 1954).

1. Survival (physiological needs): food, shelter, clothing, health.

2. Security (safety needs): protection from danger and threat.

3. Social (belonging needs): friendship, acceptance, love.

4. Self-esteem (ego needs): self-respect, recognition, status.

5. Self-actualization (fulfillment needs): creativity, realization of individual potential.

According to Maslow, lower level needs, such as survival and security, must be satisfied before people can give attention to the higher levels. Starving individuals have little interest in either artistic creativity or political liberty. Furthermore, they do not care about global climate change and external costs of tropical deforestation. They would much rather find food and the fuelwood to cook it than worry about self-fulfillment.

Once a need is satisfied, its motivating role diminishes; the next lowest level of ungratified need becomes the primary influence on a person's behavior. But some higher level needs always are present, if not always primary or achievable. Hungry people would miss their loved ones as much as the well-fed would. Many artists are able to create despite being very poor or living in impoverished societies. Enlightened policy should strive to meet basic human needs in ways that simultaneously promote community life and fulfillment of the human potential (Barbour 1980).

Once lower level safety and security needs have been fulfilled, there is a tendency to take them for granted and no longer consider them to be goal objects. Material possessions are no longer motivators and can even become repulsive once a person has met those needs. The higher up the hierarchy one moves, the more one tends to reconstruct his or her world view, and the more one tends to underestimate the value of lower level satisfied needs. People tend to take for granted what they have, once they no longer have to struggle for it (Arnold 1982, Inglehart 1977).

Duerr (1982) uses the needs hierarchy as a device to help explain how Americans found value in forest resources as our country developed. Timber (lumber) provided shelter. Forests harbored valuable game for food, and less desirable Indians. Taming the wilderness provided self-esteem. In modern times, forests have provided people with wood for shelter and, increasingly, habitat for self-actualization. Duerr then asks: Which forest resource is at the top of the hierarchy? Or, what can forests provide to fulfill self-actualization needs? (This concept also can be related to the stages of the development of forestry policy that evolved from exploitation to protection [see Chapter 2].)

However, the needs hierarchy alone cannot explain environmentalism. But the values and needs people have help explain the services and goods they want from forest lands. These values help drive forest, range, and wildlife policy deliberations and decisions. As Americans fulfill more of their basic personal needs, they seem to become more concerned about social needs, including environmental protection. As most Americans become older, more of their basic needs will have been fulfilled. Thus they will desire fewer market goods and want more nonmarket goods such as recreation, scenery, or ecological values.

ILLUSTRATION: ENVIRONMENTALISM— BUSINESS BECOMES A BELIEVER

The environmental movement has had tremendous impacts on business and may be the most important business issue of the 1990s. As this decade dawned, environmentalism had become a watchword for industry and was supported in about equal proportions by liberals and conservatives and by Democrats and Republicans (Kirkpatrick 1990). Demographic factors favor continuation of environmental concerns. Activists of the 1960s had become more establishment-oriented, but they still favored environmental causes. The prevalent Earth Day events each April and pervasive media coverage of environmental issues focused public attention on the environment and business practices. Environmental education became one of the de facto core requirements for students in primary and secondary schools and is required in many college and university curricula.

In response to increased calls for environmental protection and more environmental regulation, many industries are voluntarily working to act responsibly (and improve their image). McDonalds has become a crusading proponent of recycling, plans to be a leading environmental educator, has reduced its waste generation substantially, and is a major contributor to the American Forestry Association's Global ReLeaf tree planting program. In 1988 DuPont, a chemical manufacturing company, announced that it would voluntarily suspend all production of CFCs by 2000, or sooner if possible. That is a $750-million-a-year business for DuPont, the industry leader. Another large manufacturing company, 3M, is installing pollution controls beyond what the law requires. Procter and Gamble and many other astute marketers of consumer products are moving to produce, package, and promote their products in ways that are environmentally safe. Other businesses are enhancing their environmental divisions, putting representatives of environmental groups on their boards of directors, and contributing to or performing joint projects with environmental groups (Kirkpatrick 1990, Schwartz, Springen, and Hager 1990).

Many traditional environmental groups are eager to work with business, rather than rely only on confrontation tactics. In September 1989 a coalition of large institutional investors and environmental groups promulgated the Valdez Principles, named for the massive Alaskan oil spill that occurred that year. The 10 Valdez principles ask businesses to minimize environmental pollutants; make sustainable use of natural resources; reduce waste and dispose of it properly; use energy wisely; and reduce environmental, health, and safety risks to employees and communities. The Valdez Principles stipulate that businesses should market safe products and services, repair damage to the environment and compensate injured people, and disclose environmental problems or accidents. Businesses are to assess their compliance with the principles yearly. The principles state that at least one member of the board of directors is to represent environmental interests, and that a position of vice-president for environmental affairs (or its equivalent) be created and report directly to the chief executive officer (CEO) of the firm (Bavaria 1989).

Although environmentalism has moved up on the list of corporate issues of the 1990s, there are limits to the support business is willing to provide for environmental protection. As might be expected, not all businesses cheerfully comply with (or even pay any attention to) maxims such as the Valdez Principles. Citizen support also varies. In the November 1990 elections, voters in some states soundly defeated referendums that would increase taxes in order to provide greater environmental protection measures, including a complex set of proposals termed "Big Green" in California. Consumers are suspicious of dubious environmental claims made by businesses in their advertisements (e.g., "biodegradable"), or about the sincerity of their pollution cleanup efforts. Cooperative environmental groups such as the National Wildlife Federation and the Environmental Defense Fund have been criticized by more radical groups as collaborating with polluters. To the radicals who do not believe in most existing government and business practices, cooperation is an anathema.

Even "environmentally correct" choices are not always apparent. The choice of which grocery bag to use—paper or plastic—is confusing; the environmentally correct choice is a reusable canvas tote or a string bag, but both are less convenient than grocery bags. Recycling may reduce solid waste but costs more in terms of energy use. A detailed study found that foam cups may use less energy and take less landfill space than paper (Hocking 1991). Even benefits claimed by manufacturers are sometimes elusive. "Degradable" products should break down, but a well-maintained landfill does not let in the sun and air necessary to break down a paper bag. "Recycled" paper products may be called that if they include wood chips from a sawmill or edge trimmings from the paper line—but this "recycled" raw material has not previously been used by consumers.

As environmentalism matures it will be good business for firms to protect the environment and make the public aware of those efforts. Many consumers consciously try to purchase environmentally safe products. Recycling is becoming more widespread. Environmental seals of approval for safe products and packages are being developed, but they are competing for recognition in the United States. (Germany already has the accepted Blue Angel label denoting environmentally correct products.) Despite the recent clamor raised by the wise use movement, businesses and mainstream environmental groups are beginning to work together to ensure good products and environmental protection. State and federal laws will encourage environmentalism, tempered by the government's ability to tax citizens or impose unreasonable costs on individual business owners or large business firms (through the political process). Some resource commodity production groups—including forestry, ranching, and mining—are fighting environmental regulation, but more people in these businesses are opting to cooperate.

CONSERVATION ETHICS

Environmentalism is often linked to ethical behavior regarding natural resources and the planet earth. An *ethic* is a statement of a prin-

ciple of conduct. It is a systematic attempt to answer the question of what is right and what is wrong (Scherer and Attig 1983). The subject of ethics deals with those weighty matters of right and wrong, good and evil, duty and obligation. It tends to be a nebulous, abstract subject (Kaufman 1981). A conversation about ethics can turn into a sermon rather than a practical discussion. Ethics, though, do reflect the accumulated wisdom of experience. Sound ethical principles are those that promote long-term concerns, such as surviving on this planet, providing for succeeding generations, and maintaining the productive capacity of natural resources (Bruce 1981). In spite of the difficulties in putting ethical principles to work, they are too important for natural resource managers to ignore.

Interest in applied ethics has burgeoned during the environmental movement, arising out of the perception of a moral vacuum in our society. A greater sense of moral obligation and personal responsibility regarding the use of land resources is a good starting point for understanding ethics. If land custodians pay only lip service to ethical principles, then little progress will be made toward educating the general public (Kaufman 1981).

The pertinent questions that can be addressed with environmental or conservation ethics are: How should we think? and What values and attitudes should shape the concepts through which we define ourselves and the world in which we live? The premise is that some ways are better than others (Scherer and Attig 1983). Ethical forest resource management practices conform to social, moral, and religious norms and contribute to achieving society's goals. Unethical practices are those that may breach accepted norms and hinder the achievement of those goals (Lammi 1968).

Natural resource conservation is torn between the conflicting values of wise use utilitarian conservation and strict preservation. It is important that citizen conservationists and resource management professionals understand how the beliefs underlying these two different concepts of conservation arise, as well as their ethical implications. The perceived difference between them lies partly in differing views of the relationship of society and nature (Schwartz 1982).

ATTITUDES TOWARD NATURE

An *attitude* is a set of beliefs and values organized around a specific thing or situation. Attitudes toward nature are correlated with beliefs about resources, technology, and growth. Cultural attitudes are expressed in social institutions and in the structures of economic and political power. Broad cultural assumptions about nature have influenced the way we treat the environment (Barbour 1980).

Both now and in the past, attitudes toward nature have been quite diverse. Perhaps it is an oversimplification, but these attitudes may be arrayed along a continuum. At one end is domination over nature (anthropocentrism). At the other is unity with nature (biocentrism). An intermediate attitude is stewardship of nature. There are many variations within each of these positions, but they help in understanding environmental behavior (Barbour 1980).

Anthropocentrism focuses on nature and the environment in human terms. An extreme form of anthropocentrism might be human domination of nature, or humans first and nature second. A more moderate view is simply that only humans have senses and are capable of thought, so everything must be judged in human terms. *Biocentrism*, on the other hand, implies an attitude of caring for nature, but it also can mean a refusal to accept the argument that humans are part of nature. At the extreme, biocentrism may mean that *any* influence of humans on nature is "unnatural"—the action of an outside force.

Ecology describes these interrelationships within the natural world. The strict application of ecological principles underlies an environmentalist attitude that ecology is the appropriate worldview (ecocentrism). An even more restrictive facet of this viewpoint is that all biological entities have equal importance (biocentrism). Even further, all entities have equal rights.

A *Time* magazine feature article on the endangered earth captured and promoted the biocentric philosophy: "Man must abandon the belief that the natural order is mere stuff to be managed and domesticated, and accept that humans, like other creatures, depend on a web of life that must be disturbed as little as possible" (Linder 1989, p. 35).

Deep Ecology

Deep ecology is another way of thinking about resources. It is difficult to define deep ecology completely; its proponents resist attempts to fit them into a clear philosophy. Deep ecologists argue that a deep commitment to nature and to activism distinguish them from mainstream (shallow) ecologists.

Deep ecologists, including monkeywrenchers, regard the large national environmental organizations as being "too establishment"—too human-centered and utilitarian (Devall 1980). By working within the system, they have been co-opted by the system. John Muir is revered by deep ecologists who subscribe to a biocentric philosophy. One of their goals, attributed to Norwegian philosopher Arne Naess, is to reduce the population of Spaceship Earth (now at 5 billion plus) to 1 billion people, roughly the world's population in 1800.

Rain forest activist Pete Seed has said, "The basic idea of deep ecology is that humanity is only another member of the biotic community.... Other species have just as much importance and right to exist as we do." Seed envisions "working toward a situation where 99 percent of the land would be turned back into wilderness. The whole world would be a national park spinning through space, and there'd be small enclaves of human beings whose satisfactions come not from materialism but from the love of nature and spirit" (Stone 1989, p. 60).

The concept of *Gaia*, the Greek Goddess "Mother Earth," is one aspect of deep ecology. According to James Lovelock, an early Gaia proponent, the Gaia hypothesis is that "the biosphere is a self-regulating entity with the capacity to keep our planet healthy by controlling the chemical and physical environment" (Odum 1989). To the deep ecologist, the human species has no right to exert a disproportionate impact on Mother Earth. Even the notion of benevolent stewardship is distasteful, in that it implies human dominance over species and systems.

Another encapsulation of the deep ecology philosophy is that it is

a way of thinking about environmental problems that attacks them from the roots, i.e., the way they can be seen as symptoms of the deepest ills of our present society. This is to be contrasted with "shallow ecology"—treating merely the symptoms themselves, not the causes, through technological fixes such as pollution-control devices, regulations upon industry, etc. (Rothenberg 1987, p. 186).

It is easier to see how deep ecology adherents stand on different philosophical ground than the groups on the traditional preservation–conservation spectrum. Not yet imbued with enough impetus to be a movement, though, deep ecology is now a bundle of ideas (Russell 1987).

Resource Managers

Professional resource management interest groups, such as the Society of American Foresters, are out of the "vanguard of environmentalism." That is not to say, however, that resource managers, as environmental managers or *technocentrists*, are not influenced by many of the same quality of life concerns that motivate environmental activists, or *ecocentrists*. Professionals—either as citizens who care about natural resources or as actors dealing with citizens who care about natural resources—need to be aware not only that there are a variety of citizen interest groups, but also that the objectives and purposes of these groups are rooted in their attitudes toward the environment.

The attitudes of the two major factions of environmentalism represented as ecocentrism and technocentrism are organized and displayed in Figure 10-2. The place of natural resource managers—who are stewards of nature or the environment—in this scheme is clearly that of the technocentrist, under the

major subheading of environmental manager. Nonetheless, the natural resource manager needs a workable understanding of the range of environmental attitudes if conflict between two factions is to be resolved. Anyone who intends to *manage* natural resources will be damned by the deep ecology followers, but merely criticized by ecocentrics.

ENVIRONMENTAL ETHICS

The environmental movement does not have a carefully wrought creed. Those active in the movement do share some attitudes in spite of the great diversity of groups with different philosophies of political action and ecological priorities. These shared attitudes might be called the *ethos* of the movement.

Barbour (1973) listed five themes that characterized the environmental ethic, gleaned from a variety of ideas and writings at the beginning of the environmental era.

1. Interdependence of society and the environment.

2. Unity with nature—people are inseparable from it.

3. Finite resources, with limits that can be exceeded by exponential growth to the detriment of people and nature.

4. Control of technology to reduce effluents, recycle materials, and develop new and more appropriate technologies.

5. Social justice, which can be achieved with changes in political power structures and economic institutions such as private property rights.

The wilderness preservation ethic, as should be evident from this short list, is but one facet of the environmental movement. It has legitimate goals, but it is not the solution for all of our modern natural resource management problems, nor will it solve the unforeseeable problems of future generations.

In the past, some foresters have challenged the early ethos of preservation. Zivnuska

Figure 10-2. Environmentalism: Ecocentrism/Technocentrism
Source: O'Riordan 1981b.

Environmentalism

Ecocentrism		Technocentrism	
Deep ecologists	Self-reliance Soft technologists	Environmental managers	Cornucopians
Intrinsic importance of nature for the humanity of individuals	1. Emphasis on smallness of scale and hence community identity in settlement, work, and leisure	1. Belief that economic growth and resource exploitation can continue assuming:	1. Belief that humans can always find a way out of any difficulties either political or technological
Ecological (and other natural) laws dictate human morality	2. Integration of concepts of work and leisure through a process of personal and communal improvement	a. suitable economic adjustments to taxes, fees, and so on	2. Acceptance that progrowth goals define the rationality of project appraisal and policy formulation
Biorights – the right of endangered species or unique landscapes to remain unmolested	3. Importance of participation in community affairs and of guarantees of the rights of minority interests. Participation seen both as a continuing education and political function	b. improvements in the legal rights to a minimum level of environmental quality	3. Optimism about the ability of humans to improve the lot of the world's people
	4. Lack of faith in modern large-scale technology and its associated demands on elitist expertise, central state authority and inherently antidemocratic institutions	c. compensation arrangement satisfactory to those who experience adverse environmental and/or social effects	4. Faith that scientific and technological expertise provides the basic foundation for advice on matters pertaining to economic growth, public health, and safety
	5. Implication that materialism for its own sake is wrong and that economic growth can be geared to providing for the basic needs of those below subsistence levels	2. Acceptance of new project appraisal techniques and decision review arrangements to allow for wider discussion or genuine search for consensus among representative groups of interested parties	5. Suspicion of attempts to widen basis for participation and lengthy discussion in project appraisal and policy review
			6. Belief that all impediments can be overcome given a will, ingenuity, and sufficient resources arising out of growth

239

(1971) questioned the social justice and economic equity aspects of preservation. Boster (1971) challenged some of the tenets of environmentalism, including the usual assumptions of limits to growth and finite resources.

The goals of the earlier conservation crusade have been absorbed and expanded. The new concerns in the environmental ethic are (1) a concern for life's quality, (2) a sense of urgency, and (3) social reconstruction, based on a deep disillusionment with existing American values and institutions. It is more than a crusade to change public policy; it is meant to change the institutional structure underlying public policy (Rosenbaum 1977). Milbrath (1984) calls environmentalism the vanguard for a new society.

However, the preservation ethic of wilderness advocacy groups is appropriate for limited circumstances. One problem or paradox is that wilderness advocates more often than not are anthropocentric, promoting what Rodman (1983) calls religio-esthetic goals. They advocate wise use of wilderness areas, but that use is essentially for only one form of recreation, and its value diminishes if too many people use a particular wilderness area for spiritual renewal. Another paradox is the very notion of attempting to preserve natural ecological systems that are dynamic. Given time, even mountains erode.

Norton (1987) suggested that the anthropocentrism/nonanthropocentrism debate should be put aside, and that people interested in conservation and preservation issues should focus on more tractable value questions that relate to concrete policy issues and specific land use proposals.

LEOPOLD'S LAND ETHIC

The cornerstone of environmental ethics is most often attributed to Aldo Leopold's (1949) land ethic. Many historians and philosophers—but not all of them, as we shall see—maintain that the land ethic prescribes the biocentric view that nature should be granted rights equal to those of humans. Many professional foresters have identified Leopold's *A Sand County Almanac*, which

described the land ethic, as the most memorable and influential literature they have read (SAF 1988b). Leopold was trained as a forester and was a United States Forest Service officer. In 1924 he recommended that the first federal wilderness area be established in New Mexico's Gila National Forest. Leopold was one of the founders of the Wilderness Society in 1935. He was a widely respected professor of wildlife management (Walsh 1987) and literally founded the profession of wildlife management with his ecologically-steeped ideas.

What, exactly, is the message of Leopold's land ethic? It is profound, and it should be read in its entirety—from its discussion of repairing damage to the natural world of a cutover woodlot in central Wisconsin that Leopold so eloquently described to one of its concluding statements that an ethic is a product of social evolution rather than a written credo. But in short, the land ethic is essentially this, in Leopold's (1949) words:

An ethic, ecologically, is a limitation on freedom of action in the struggle for existence. An ethic, philosophically, is a differentiation of social from anti-social conduct. These are two definitions of one thing (p. 238).

All ethics so far evolved rest upon a single premise: that the individual is a member of a community of interdependent parts.... The land ethic simply enlarges the boundaries of the community to include soils, water, plants, and animals, or collectively: the land (p. 239).

Conservation is a state of harmony between men and the land. Despite nearly a century of propaganda, conservation still proceeds at a snail's pace; progress still consists largely of letterhead pieties and convention oratory (p. 243).

The "key-log" which must be moved to release the evolutionary process for an ethic is simply this: quit thinking about decent land-use as solely an economic problem. Examine each question in terms of what is ethically and aesthetically right, as well as what is economically expedient. A thing is right when it tends to preserve the integrity, stability, and beauty of the biotic community. It is wrong when it tends otherwise (p. 262).

The last two sentences are those most widely excerpted to represent the land ethic. It is strongly biocentric and has all the attendant problems of measuring natural systems when one tries to put the concept into operation.

Leopold has been characterized by many environmental ethicists as an "uncompromising preservationist," which the previous excerpt from *A Sand County Almanac* might well indicate. But if environmentalists were to delve into Leopold's life and the development of his ideas (see Flader 1974, Walsh 1987), they would see that he was more than a proponent of preservationist viewpoints (Clement 1987). Leopold's scientific training as a forester with its traditional utilitarian conservation viewpoint did indeed shift. Leopold did not reject the anthropocentric view of the world, but instead he lost faith in human management (Norton 1987).

Leopold was as suspicious of recreation as he was of logging and agriculture. But he had no romantic revulsion against plowing, or cutting trees, or hunting game, or any of the things that people do to make a living from the land. He was only against the excesses of exploitation, the willingness of people to live not on just land's interest, but the principal itself. Leopold's ideas were viewed as heresy in 1949 and still are by many today. They are viewed in some circles as antiprogress. They are said to dampen initiative and impose limits and restraints. They also are said to smack of socialism and the public good (Stegner 1985).

Economic and ecological perspectives on land ethics often conflict because of differing value bases (Burk 1980, Henderson 1973, Kaufman 1981). Some of these real-world environmental conflicts include (Kaufman 1981)

- The psychological and economic need to grow (e.g., need for jobs and material products) versus the need to conserve resources.

- Passive acceptance of nature versus preserving and improving nature.

- The philosophy of individual freedom versus collective restraint and decision making.

- Faith in human abilities and technology versus caution regarding human error (e.g., nuclear, oil drilling, and shipping accidents).

- Environmental protection versus equity and social justice for the have-nots.

- The growth ethic (more jobs, more goods, a better life) versus the ecological ethic (steady state economy, appropriate-sized technology).

Natural resource managers and planners must operate in this complex ethical milieu. These numerous ethical imperatives make it difficult to sort out right from wrong in any practical way (Kaufman 1981). Perhaps Leopold's concept of a land ethic can sort out these crosscurrents and achieve a stable footing in these turbulent waters. Many conservationists from both camps feel that it helps. The wise use camp of foresters is represented by Tombaugh (1985), Arnold (1982), and many others (SAF 1988b). The preservationist camp also is well represented (Little 1985, Stegner 1985). Leopold himself had a foot in both camps. Perhaps the recognition and application of the land ethic can help reconcile preservation and utilitarian views.

Today, the land ethic is something of an intellectual growth industry. Discussions of land stewardship range from those of prominent conservationists to a controversial pastoral letter issued by U.S. Catholic bishops in 1984. Stewardship underlies the beliefs of most professional resource organizations and environmental groups. Even forest products companies promote their stewardship efforts in their annual reports.

But there are other social goals that complicate efforts to create an American land policy. Many of these goals are viewed as being in conflict with the land ethic and include individual liberty, private property rights, social justice, and scientific progress (Little 1985).

A NEW ETHIC

Conservation of natural resources in the United States is one of our more consistent and long-standing national policies. Today's arguments are on how conservation will be practiced, not if it will be practiced (Reid 1983). Will conservation be practiced as scientific wise use management of resources or preservation in perpetuity? Or will the nations of the world scramble to outproduce and out-consume each other, with little thought for the future?

Reidel (1987a) urged foresters to consider what lessons can be learned not only from history, but also from the philosophies that underlie today's existing policies. The roots of these policies were value-laden debates with political, social, and ideological bases that were seldom scientific or factual in nature. Was there really a timber famine facing the United States at the end of the nineteenth century when it was decided that a federal forest reserve system was desirable? Professional foresters have sought to avoid continuing these debates about values by designing and seeking out technical, scientific, or planning strategies to "compute" forest management decisions. Perhaps it is time to grapple with basic values and to be willing to make some value judgments that do not necessarily compute, such as the biases of the past few decades against timber production and clearcutting.

Old Biases

Wondollcck (1988) identified the professional ethics of forestry as one of the factors contributing to the USDA Forest Service's persistent problem of "caring for the land and serving the needs of the American people." This traditional ethic stems from what Behan (1975) called the myth of the omnipotent forester, who by virtue of special technical training should be trusted with resource management decisions. Professionals can overcome this problem by focusing on ways to achieve clearly stated objectives, instead of determining what these objectives ought to be. The insistence on "multiple use" as a forestry objective is closer to sloganeering than it is to ethical management. "Sustained yield" is yet another such tenet of faith that needs to adapt to modern times and modern problems that cannot be so simply described by a catch phrase (Behan 1975, Duerr 1982).

Duerr (1982) described a consumer-oriented ethic for natural resource professionals to replace the traditional tenets of

forestry faith Americans inherited from sixteenth century Teutonic forestry and maintained through most of the twentieth century. By continuing to follow these traditional rules, foresters lost a measure of society's approval of their actions (Duerr 1986). Times have changed, but according to Duerr, foresters have not. Forest management decisions should be based on a new ethic that responds to the desires of people. This is an anthropocentric, utilitarian concept, but one that is flexible enough to accommodate the desires of recreationists as well as wildlife and wilderness enthusiasts—all those who want to enjoy a product of the forest.

Cooperation and Leadership

According to Tombaugh (1985), a land ethic is a prerequisite for conservation. As a nation, we have tended to emphasize the role of government in conservation and have not set out systematically to develop a land ethic within individual citizens that would complement public programs. This weakens attempts to motivate private landowners toward conservation of forest resources. Without a feeling for the land, citizens cannot intelligently involve themselves in the process that now, by law, guides public land management planning.

If forest resource managers are to succeed in changing the way that individuals think about and treat land and forests, there will have to be a high level of cooperation among members of the forestry community. We need to come to an agreement on goals and the means to reach them. The "sue them" mentality of the environmental decade of the 1970s is not appropriate for developing the land ethic in the individuals who will become leaders in the policy process. It is not likely that we will be able to meet the full potential of our forest resources without a new focus not only on ethics, but also on leadership, which is the scarcest resource of all (Tombaugh 1985). Reidel (1987a,b) reinforces the need for a stronger focus on leadership and less emphasis on managerial skills.

A new ethic, if there is to be one, will find useful building blocks from concepts of utilitarianism, preservationism, Leopold's land ethic, and the environmental ethic of the early 1970s. The challenge of a new ethic is to build upon Leopold's ideas to develop a workable concept of land stewardship. To some, a forest is a forest is a forest. To others, a forest is a collection of things that are useful to people. To still others, a forest is an ecosystem with a right to exist unmolested. Forest resource managers, trained to manage the forest to accommodate these conflicting desires, will therefore never be able to please everyone. But if resource managers can see the merit of Leopold's holistic view, they will not oppose all preservationist proposals because the value of species diversity for protecting genetic resources will be recognized. A compromise between utilitarian conservation and preservation has to be made in the minds of natural resource managers and users before it can be made on the land.

To paraphrase Dana (1974), forestry, by its very nature, is both environmental and ecological and cannot be practiced in a vacuum. However, as Hays (1987) pointed out, conflict arises from the views of environmentalists who emphasize "natural" forest management that promotes biological diversity and those who favor "scientific" forest management that emphasizes a monoculture of trees. This issue will refuse to die as long as timber resource managers select clear-cutting as a forest management technique, wildlife managers favor game over nongame species, and range managers fail to recognize resource carrying capacity.

PROFESSIONALISM AND ETHICS

Natural resource managers are professionals. But in the sense of some traditional professions—law, medicine, and the ministry—forestry, wildlife, fisheries, range, and recreation may seem "less" professional. There often is no specific skill that separates the professional from the technician or even the amateur in forestry, range, recreation, wildlife, and fisheries management. Techni-

cians or knowledgeable individuals may perform many of the jobs required in these fields without formal education. Pulpwood buyers can purchase timber, game managers can run hunting plantations, and local people can run parks without certification or licensing. Members of the natural resource professions usually do not have to pass an examination or acquire a credential in order to practice their profession. While strict standards are lacking, many specific types of knowledge, skills, and experience are needed by natural resource professionals.

DEFINITION OF A PROFESSION

One aspect of a profession is that its members are devoted to public service for altruistic as well as materialistic reasons. Furthermore, professionals have some competence in a special body of knowledge that is linked to fundamental needs and values of society (Steinbeck 1988). Of the many criteria that could be selected to identify a profession, the following six are common, and forestry meets all six to some degree (Barrett 1972, Steinbeck 1988).

1. Skill based on a unique body of theoretical knowledge.
2. Education and training in accredited schools.
3. Organization of members in a formal association.
4. Testing of the competence of individual members.
5. Adherence to a code of conduct that expresses ethical guidelines.
6. Service to a public need involving more than earning a livelihood.

By most standards, forestry, range, fisheries, wildlife, and recreation management are professions. In most southern and some western states, as well as in Maine and New Hampshire, foresters are required to obtain credentials such as a license, certification, or registration. California requires that a licensed, registered forester prepare a timber harvesting plan before harvests can be approved under its state forest practice act. However, even in states where registration exists, foresters do not have specific legal rights. And few, if any, other practitioners have been prosecuted for performing forestry work.

Other resource professions are generally less exclusive. Park managers do not have specific registration requirements. Wildlife and fisheries biologists, however, may become certified by their professional societies. The Wildlife Society certifies individuals as professional wildlife biologists if they have taken adequate college coursework in six programmatic areas—biological sciences, physical sciences, quantitative sciences, communications, humanities and social sciences, and policy, administration, and law. A certified wildlife biologist must meet the education requirements, have five years of experience, and uphold The Wildlife Society Code of Ethics. An associate wildlife biologist has met the educational requirements but not the experience requirement. The American Fisheries Society has similar requirements for a certified fisheries biologist.

Note how the wildlife and fisheries certifications differ from the Society of American Foresters' approach. The SAF accredits individual schools, departments, or forestry programs—and assumes that graduates of these programs are foresters. The Wildlife Society and American Fisheries Society certify individuals, based on their college coursework and experience. In accrediting programs, the SAF has become more lenient about the type of coursework that is necessary to constitute a forestry program. The fisheries and wildlife professional societies, however, define their expertise much more strictly. SAF has instituted a voluntary program in Continuing Forestry Education to help ensure that foresters update their skills. A minimum number of CFE credits are required in some states in order to remain a licensed, registered forester.

CODE OF ETHICS

Both the Society of American Foresters and The Wildlife Society (TWS) have adopted codes of ethics. The code for the SAF is older than that of TWS, and more detailed. Both are intended to ensure that professionals conform to high standards of integrity and conduct.

The Society of American Foresters

When the SAF was founded in 1900, its professional ethic—"the public good comes first"—was Theodore Roosevelt's motto, often cited by Gifford Pinchot (Argow 1975). Since then, the profession of forestry, its followers, and its critics have been trying to determine just what the "public good" is, and how "the greatest good of the greatest number" can be fulfilled. Statements such as these may be effective slogans for attracting the attention of the public or explaining, in broad general terms, what the purpose of forestry is. But they do not offer a sense of direction for professional foresters.

Clarifying the public good for foresters became easier after 1948, when the SAF enacted a code of professional ethics. The 15 canons in the code provide guidelines for forester–forester, forester–employee, forester–client, and forester–forest user relationships (Figure 10-3). The SAF Code of Ethics also offers guidance for maintaining the delicate relationship between the profession and those segments of the public that influence forest policy through their contact with policymakers yet have little knowledge or appreciation of forest resource management (Lammi 1968). Flanagan (1981) provided three reasons for a code of professional behavior: (1) promoting the pride of practitioners in their occupation, (2) protecting the consuming public, and (3) helping to guide the professional's personal decision-making process in difficult issues of professional conduct.

It is not enough just to have a code of ethics. A profession has an obligation to ensure that its members follow those ethics. Enforcement of the SAF Code of Ethics is a weak

Adopted by the Society of American Foresters by Member Referendum, June 23, 1976, replacing the code adopted November 12, 1948, as amended December 4, 1971, and November 4, 1986.

Preamble

The purpose of these canons is to govern the professional conduct of members of the Society of American Foresters in their relations with the public, their employers, including clients, and each other as provided in Article VIII of the Society's Constitution. Compliance with these canons help to assure just and honorable professional human relationships, mutual confidence and respect, and competent service to society.

These cannons have been adopted by the membership of the Society and can only be amended by the membership. Procedures for processing charges of violation of the canons are contained in Bylaws established by the Council. The cannons and procedures apply to all membership categories in all forestry-related disciplines, except Honorary Members.

All members upon joining the Society agree to abide by this Code as a condition of membership.

Canons

1. A member's knowledge and skills will be utilized for the benefit of society. A member will strive for accurate, current and increasing knowledge of forestry, will communicate such knowledge when not confidential, and will challenge and correct untrue statements about forestry.

2. A member will advertise only in a dignified and truthful manner, stating the services the member is qualified and prepared to perform. Such advertisements may include references to fees charged.

3. A member will base public comment on forestry matters on accurate knowledge and will not distort or withhold pertinent information to substantiate a point of view. Prior to making public statements on forest policies and practices, a member will indicate on whose behalf the statements are made.

4. A member will perform services consistent with the highest standards of quality and with loyalty to the employer.

5. A member will perform only those services for which the member is qualified by education or experience.

6. A member who is asked to participate in forestry operations which deviate from accepted professional standards must advise the employer in advance of the consequences of such deviation.

7. A member will not voluntarily disclose information concerning the affairs of the member's employer without the employer's express permission.

8. A member must avoid conflicts of interest or even the appearance of such conflicts. If, despite such precaution, a conflict of interest is discovered, it must be promptly and fully disclosed to the member's employer and the member must be prepared to act immediately to resolve the conflict.

9. A member will not accept compensation or expenses from more than one employer for the same service, unless the parties involved are informed and consent.

10. A member will engage, or advise the member's employer to engage, other experts and specialists in forestry or related fields whenever the employer's interest would be best served by such actions, and members will work cooperatively with other professionals.

11. A member will not by false statement or dishonest action injure the reputation or professional associations of another member.

12. A member will give credit for the methods, ideas, or assistance obtained from others.

13. A member in competition for supplying forestry services will encourage the prospective employer to base selection on comparison of qualifications and negotiation of fee or salary.

14. Information submitted by a member about a candidate for a prospective position, award, or elected office will be accurate, factual, and objective.

15. A member having evidence of violation of these canons by another member will present the information and charges to the Council in accordance with the Bylaws.

Figure 10-3. Code of Ethics for Members of the Society of American Foresters
Source: SAF 1988a

point. The need to convince the public that foresters are competent and desire to serve society's needs has been and still is a matter of urgency (Barrett 1972). Banzhaf (1981), after serving four years on the SAF Ethics Committee, noted that very few formal charges were brought for review. His hope was that this reflected high standards of ethical practice; more realistically, he stated that it probably reflected a lack of the members' understanding coupled with some disinterest.

Many forestry decisions are gray-area judgment calls, not obvious yes-or-no decisions. In recognition of this problem, the SAF published an Ethics Guide for professional foresters that contained interpretations and brief elaborations on the 15 canons as well as hypothetical case examples (SAF 1985). Discussions of ethical problems for foresters have appeared in the literature, including whistle-blowing by public agency foresters (Banzhaf, Burns and Vance. 1985), conflict of interest (Stuart 1981), and pesticide use—a case that Irland (1983) related to Leopold's land ethic. Stuart (1975) cited six actual cases of ethical breaches that were brought to the attention of the Association of Consulting Foresters, which adopted a code of ethics in 1952 that is stronger than that of the SAF.

The Wildlife Society

The Code of Ethics for The Wildlife Society is much briefer than that of the SAF. The code first states the objectives of TWS and then briefly states its seven points.

Objectives

The principal objectives of The Society are

1. To develop and promote sound stewardship of wildlife resources and of the environments upon which wildlife and humans depend.

2. To undertake an active role in preventing human- induced environmental degradation.

3. To increase awareness and appreciation of wildlife values.

4. To seek the highest standards in all activities of the wildlife profession.

Code of Ethics

Each member, in striving to meet the objectives of The Society, pledges to

1. Subscribe to the highest standards of integrity and conduct.

2. Recognize research and scientific management of wildlife and their environments are primary goals.

3. Disseminate information to promote understanding of, and appreciation for, values of wildlife and their habitats.

4. Strive to increase knowledge and skills to advance the practice of wildlife management.

5. Promote competence in the field of wildlife management by supporting high standards of education, employment, and performance.

6. Encourage the use of sound biological information in management decisions.

7. Support fair and uniform standards of employment and treatment of those professionally engaged in the practice of wildlife management.

In addition to a code of ethics, TWS adopted Standards for Professional Conduct (Figure 10-4), which are similar to the more detailed SAF code. Again, these standards attempt to ensure that wildlife professionals act professionally. TWS, like the SAF, has prosecuted few, if any, violations of its code of ethics and Standards for Professional Conduct.

ILLUSTRATION: APPLICATIONS OF PROFESSIONAL ETHICS

It is not easy to define ethics; applying ethical standards is even more difficult. A few examples of situations posing ethical questions that professionals may experience illustrate the importance and the complexity of the subject. Consider the foresters on the Bit-

The following tenets express the intent of the Code of Ethics as prescribed by The Wildlife Society and traditional norms for professional service.

Wildlife biologists shall at all times:

1. Recognize and inform prospective clients or employers of their *prime* responsibility to the public interest, conservation of the wildlife resource, and the environment. They shall act with the authority of professional judgment, and avoid actions or omissions that may compromise these broad responsibilities. They shall respect the competence, judgment, and authority of the professional community.

2. Avoid performing professional services for any client or employer when such service is judged to be contrary to the Code of Ethics or Standards for Professional Conduct or detrimental to the well-being of the wildlife resource and its environment.

3. Provide maximum possible effort in the best interest of each client/employer accepted, regardless of the degree of renumeration. They shall be mindful of their responsibility to society, and seek to meet the needs of the disadvantaged for advice in wildlife-related matters. They should studiously avoid discrimination in any form, or the abuse of professional authority for personal satisfaction.

4. Accept employment to perform professional services only in areas of their own competence, and consistent with the Code of Ethics and Standards for Professional Conduct described herein. They shall seek to refer clients or employers to other natural resource professionals when the expertise of such professionals shall best serve the interest of the public, wildlife, and the client/employer. They shall cooperate fully with other professionals in the best interest of the wildlife resource.

5. Maintain a confidential professional client/employer relationship except when specifically authorized by the client/employer or required by due process of law or this Code of Ethics and Standards to disclose pertinent information. They shall not use such confidence to their personal advantage or to the advantage of other parties, nor shall they permit personal interests of other client/employer relationships to interfere with their professional judgment.

6. Refrain from advertising in a self-laudatory manner, beyond statements intended to inform prospective clients/employers of qualifications, or in a manner detrimental to fellow professionals and the wildlife resource.

7. Refuse compensation or rewards of any kind intended to influence their professional judgment or advice. They shall not permit a person who recommends or employs them, directly or indirectly, to regulate their professional judgment. They shall not accept compensation for the same professional services from any source other than the client/employer without the prior consent of all the clients or employers involved. Similarly, they shall not offer a reward of any kind or promise of service in order to secure a recommendation, a client, or preferential treatment from public officials.

8. Uphold the dignity and integrity of the wildlife profession. They shall endeavor to avoid even the suspicion of dishonesty, fraud, deceit, misrepresentation, or unprofessional demeanor.

Figure 10-4 The Wildlife Society Standards for Professional Conduct
Source: The Wildlife Society, personal com., 1991.

terroot National Forest in Montana during the 1960s. If they felt the Forest Service was damaging the health of mountain ecosystems and wasting taxpayer's money, should they have blown the whistle on the agency to citizens or Congress members, at the risk of losing their jobs?

During the 1980s and early 1990s, biologists in the United States Fish and Wildlife Service often have faced similar questions regarding listing plant and animal species un- der the Endangered Species Act. Ecologists in the Army Corps of Engineers face similar pressures in granting or refusing permits to fill wetlands for development. Should the agency biologists/ecologists declare species endangered, or wetlands inviolate, as perhaps their scientific training leads them to conclude? Or should they acknowledge the economic potential for development, loss of local jobs, or pressure from their administrators and local Congress members (or state representatives)—and allow development, harvest, and so on? These are not easy questions. Unbending adherence to purely scientific knowledge, with no recognition of human trade-offs and politics, will ultimately lead one to be fired or transferred to a dark hole. But one must at times stand up for truth, beauty, flora, or fauna. Choosing between unbending principles and wishy-washy politics is an ongoing ethical dilemma. No one can be effective if all of his or her time is spent arguing points of principle. But one cannot be professional without principles.

Private wildlife biologists and foresters often face ethical questions. Is it ethical to manage a hunting preserve stocked with pen-raised quail, domesticated deer, and no cover? Is it ethical for a consulting forester to advise private landowners, buy their wood, and operate a pulpwood dealership at the same time? If these actions seem unethical, consider the family that depends on these jobs.

Even university forestry and wildlife programs are faced with ethical questions. In the continuing debate concerning plant and animal preservation versus timber and game production, where should teachers and researchers stand? Many forestry schools owe their legislative financial support to lobbying by strong timber industry interest groups. University range resources programs in the West sometimes have a similar commodity orientation and clientele. And even wildlife departments often have focused on game species and been supported by hunting and fishing groups, including state fish and game agencies. Should department heads, deans, and academic faculty risk alienating their traditional commodity group supporters in order to broaden their natural resource programs, or even reorient their programs to focus on teaching environmental values and performing environmental research? Academic administrators and faculty are no better equipped to resolve such difficult ethical issues than are other public or private resource professionals.

In short, the application of ethics is fundamental to the practice of all natural resource professions. One should do what is right. But there are many shades of gray between right and wrong. The hope is that by practicing one's profession ethically, clearly wrong actions will be prevented, and possibly wrong actions will be minimized. Discerning right from wrong and acting correctly are the challenges of any professional career.

SUMMARY

The environmental movement began more than a century ago in the United States as a means of protecting natural resources from overexploitation. One group of conservationists at that time sought to protect lands for wise use (the utilitarians); another group sought to preserve lands in their natural state (the preservationists). Conflicts between use and preservation continue today. Protection of the environment from degradation has become a local, national, and global policy objective.

Environmentalists seek to protect nature from adverse effects of resource exploitation. Some prefer to work through existing institutions; radicals advocate overthrow of the current institutions. Leopold's call for a land ethic—taking responsibility for good stewardship by all landowners—has been advocated by many as one means to solve environmental problems. Professionals have an ethical responsibility to manage and protect natural resources, as well as to conduct their business activities with high moral standards.

LITERATURE CITED

Argow, Keith A. 1975. Professionalism and ethics: A history within SAF. *Journal of Forestry* 73(8):460–463.

Arnold, Ron. 1982. At the Eye of the Storm: James Watt and the Environmentalists. Regnery Gateway. Chicago. 282 pp.

Banzhaf, William H. 1981. Professional ethics. *Consultant* 26(3):65–68.

Banzhaf, William H., A. F. Burns, and J. Vance. 1985. Ethics and forestry: Can a forester facing a moral dilemma get help from a piece of paper called a code of ethics? *Journal of Forestry* 83(4):219–223.

Barbour, Ian G. 1973. Western Man and Environmental Ethics: Attitudes toward Nature and Technology. Addison-Wesley Publishing Co. Reading, Mass. 276 pp.

Barbour, Ian G. 1980. Technology, Environment, and Human Values. Praeger. New York. 331 pp.

Barrett, J. W. 1972. Forestry—A profession. *Journal of Forestry* 70(12):752–753.

Bavaria, John. 1989. An environmental code for corporations. *Issues in Science and Technology* (Winter 1989–1990), pp. 28–31.

Behan, Richard W. 1975. Forestry and the end of innocence. *American Forests* 81(5): 16–19, 38–49.

Borelli, Peter. 1987. Environmentalism at a crossroads: Reflections on the old old, new old, old new, and new new movements. *Amicus Journal* 9(3):24–37.

Borelli, Peter. 1988. The ecophilosophers: A guide to deep ecologists, bioregionalists, Greens, and others in pursuit of radical change. *Amicus Journal* 10(2):30–39.

Boster, Ron S. 1971. A critical appraisal of the environmental movement. *Journal of Forestry* 69(1):12–16.

Bruce, J. P. 1981. Choices in resource use: ethical perspectives. Pp. 12–19 in Walter Jeske, ed. Economies, Ethics, Ecology: Roots of Productive Conservation. Soil Conservation Society of America. Ankeny, Iowa.

Burk, Monroe. 1980. Economists and ecologists: Dialogue of the deaf. *Business* 30(1):47–52.

Buttel, Frederick H., and Oscar W. Larson III. 1980. Whither environmentalism? The future political path of the environmental movement. *Natural Resources Journal* 20(2):323–344.

Carson, Rachel. 1962. Silent Spring. Houghton Mifflin. Boston. 368 pp.

Clement, Roland C. 1987. Comment: The relationship of conservation and preservation. *Environmental Ethics* 9(3):285–286.

Clepper, Henry. 1971. Professional Forestry in the United States. Resources for the Future. Johns Hopkins Press. Baltimore, MD. 337 pp.

Clepper, Henry. 1975a. What conservationists think about conservation. *American Forests* 81(8):28–29, 46–47.

Clepper, Henry. 1975b. Crusade for conservation: The centennial history of the American Forestry Association. *American Forests* 81(10):entire issue.

Clepper, Henry. 1983. American Forestry Association. Pp. 16–18 in Richard C. Davis (ed.), Encyclopedia of American Forest and Conservation History, Vol. I. Macmillan. New York.

Dana, Samuel T. 1974. On environmental redundancy. *Journal of Forestry* 72(4): 200–201.

Dana, Samuel T., and Sally K. Fairfax. 1980. Forest and Range Policy: Its Development in the United States, 2nd ed. McGraw-Hill. New York. 458 pp.

Devall, Bill. 1980. The deep ecology movement. *Natural Resources Journal* 20(2):299–322.

Dubos, Reneé. 1980. The Wooing of Earth. Charles Scribner's Sons. New York. 183 pp.

Duerr, William A. 1982. Criteria for forest management. Pp. 57–66 in William A. Duerr, Dennis E. Teeguarden, Neils B. Christiansen, and Sam Guttenberg (eds.), Forest Resource Management: Decision-Making Principles and Cases. O.S.U. Bookstores. Corvallis, OR.

Duerr, William A. 1986. Forestry's upheaval: Are advances in Western civilization redefining the profession? *Journal of Forestry* 84(1):20–26.

Eliot, John L. 1982. T.R.'s wilderness legacy. *National Geographic* 162(3):340–363.

Flader, Susan L. 1974. Thinking like a Mountain: Aldo Leopold and the Evolution of an Ecological Attitude toward Deer, Wolves and Forests. University of Nebraska Press. Lincoln. 284 pp.

Flanagan, David T. 1981. Legal considerations of professional ethics. *Consultant* 26(3):59–64.

Gray, Gary C. 1983. Conservation movement. Pp. 105–113 in Richard C. Davis (ed.), Encyclopedia of American Forest and Conservation History, Vol. I. Macmillan. New York.

Harmon, Frank J. 1983. Fernow, Bernard Edward (1851–1923). Pp.168 in Richard C. Davis (ed.), Encyclopedia of American Forest and Conservation History. Vol I. Macmillan. New York.

Harper's. 1989. Harper's Index (Percentage of Americans who consider themselves environmentalists). Volume 279, Number 279(1675):11.

Harry, Joseph, Richard Gale, and John Hendee. 1969. Conservation: An upper-middle class social movement. *Journal of Leisure Research* 1:246–254.

Hays, Samuel P. 1959. Conservation and the Gospel of Efficiency: The Progressive Conservation Movement, 1890–1920. Harvard University Press. Cambridge, MA. 297 pp.

Hays, Samuel P. 1983. Environmental movement. Pp. 144–148 in Richard C. Davis (ed.), Encyclopedia of American Forest and Conservation History, Vol. I. Macmillan. New York.

Hays, Samuel P. 1987. Beauty, Health and Permanence: Environmental Politics in the United States, 1955–1985. Cambridge University Press. New York. 630 pp.

Henderson, Hazel. 1973. Ecologists vs. economists: A heated debate ranges from environmental issues to the legitimacy of the United States economic system. *Harvard Business Review* 51(4):28–30, 32ff.

Hocking, Martin B. 1991. Paper versus polystyrene: A complex choice. *Science* 251(4993):504–505.

Inglehart, Ronald. 1977. The Silent Revolution: Changing Values and Political Styles among Western Publics. Princeton University Press. Princeton, NJ. 482 pp.

Irland, Lloyd C. 1983. Pesticides: Ethical problems for foresters. *Consultant* 28(1):17–20.

Jackson, James P. 1983. What's happening to the conservation ethic? *American Forests* 89(11):49–51.

Kaufman, Jerome L. 1981. The land planning urgency: An ethical perspective. Pp. 51–57 in: Walter E. Jeske (ed.), Economics, Ethics, Ecology: Roots of Productive Conservation. Soil Conservation Society of America. Ankeny, IA.

Kirkpatrick, David. 1990. Environmentalism: The new crusade. *Fortune* 121(4):44–52.

Krakauer, Jon. 1991. Brown fellas. *Outside* 16(12):68–72, 114–116.

Kury, Channing (ed.), 1985. Enclosing the environment: NEPA's transformation of conservation into environmentalism. *Natural Resources Journal* 25th anniv. anthology. Univ. of New Mexico School of Law. Albuquerque. 180 pp.

Lammi, J. O. 1968. Professional ethics in forestry. *Journal of Forestry* 66(2):111–114.

Leopold, Aldo. 1949. A Sand County Almanac, and Sketches Here and There. Oxford University Press. New York. 226 pp.

Linder, Eugene. 1989. Biodiversity—The Death of Birth. The problem: Man is recklessly wiping out life on Earth. *Time*, January 2, pp. 32–35.

Little, Charles E. 1985. The once and future land ethic: In a landscape of hope. *Wilderness* 48(168):21–30.

Marsh, George Perkins. 1864. Man and Nature; or, Physical Geography as Modified by Human Action. Scribner. New York. (republished 1965, Harvard University Press. Cambridge, MA.) 472 pp.

Maslow, Abraham H. 1943. A theory of human motivation. *Psychological Review* (July) pp. 370–396.

Maslow, Abraham H. 1954. Motivation and Personality. Harper & Row. New York. 411 pp.

Milbrath, Lester W. 1984. Environmentalists: Vanguard for a New Society. State University of New York Press. Albany. 180 pp.

Mitchell, Robert C. 1980a. Introduction to symposium on "Whither Environmentalism?" *Natural Resources Journal* 20(2): 345–358.

Mitchell, Robert C. 1980b. How "soft," "deep," or "left?" Present constituencies in the environmental movement for certain world views. *Natural Resources Journal* 20(2):345–358.

Nash, Roderick. 1968. Conservation as quality of the environment. Pp. 155–156 in R. Nash (ed.). The American Environment: Readings in the History of Conservation. Addison-Wesley. Reading, MA.

Norton, Bryan G. 1987. Conservation and preservation: A conceptual rehabilitation. *Environmental Ethics* 8(3):195–220.

Odum, Eugene P. 1989. Ecology and Our Endangered Life-Support Systems. Sinauer Associates, Inc. Sunderland, MA. 283 pp.

O'Riordan, Timothy. 1981a. Environmentalism. Pion. London. 409 pp.

O'Riordan, Timothy. 1981b. Environmentalism and education. *Journal of Geography in Higher Education* 5(1):3–18.

Peek, James M. 1986. A Review of Wildlife Management. Prentice Hall. Englewood Cliffs, NJ. 486 pp.

Pepper, David. 1984. The Roots of Modern Environmentalism. Croom Helm. London. 246 pp.

Petulla, Joseph M. 1980. American Environmentalism: Values, Tactics, Priorities. Texas A&M University Press. College Station. 239 pp.

Popovich, Luke. 1979. Letters: "Environmentalist" vs. "Conservationist." *Journal of Forestry* 77(8):467.

Popovich, Luke. 1983. Environmentalism and the new conservatives. *American Forests* 89(3):18–20, 50–51.

Reid, Richard G. 1983. What's happening with the conservation ethic? *American Forests* 89(11):10, 60–61.

Reidel, Carl H. 1987a. Roots, ruts, revolution. *American Forests* 93(5, 6):14–16, 73–74.

Reidel, Carl H. 1987b. Leadership land. *Journal of Forestry* 85(8):17–21.

Reiger, John F. 1975. American Sportsmen and the Origins of Conservation. Winchester. New York. 316 pp.

Rodman, John. 1983. Four forms of ecological consciousness reconsidered. Pp. 82–92 in Donald Scherer and Thomas Attig (eds.), Ethics and the Environment. Prentice Hall. Englewood Cliffs, NJ.

Rose, Robert L. 1988. Reagan vs. the environment. *American Forests* 94(3,4):17–20.

Rosenbaum, Walter A. 1977. The Politics of Environmental Concern, 2nd ed. Praeger. New York. 311 pp.

Rothenberg, David. 1987. A platform of deep ecology. *The Environmentalist* 7 (3): 185–190.

Russell, Dick. 1987. The monkeywrenchers: Whatever happened to the nice little old ladies in tennis shoes? *Amicus Journal* 9(4):28–42.

SAF. 1985. Ethics guide. Society of American Foresters, SAF 85-07, Bethesda, MD. 35 pp.

SAF. 1988a. Code of ethics for members of the Society of American Foresters. *Journal of Forestry* 86(2):58.

SAF. 1988b. Who's reading what: Results of a quick survey. *Journal of Forestry* 86(9): 46–49.

Scherer, Donald, and Thomas Attig (eds.). 1983. Ethics and the Environment. Prentice Hall. Englewood Cliffs, NJ. 236 pp.

Schwartz, John, Karen Springen, and Mary Hager. 1990. It's not easy being green. *Newsweek*, November 19, pp. 51–52.

Schwartz, Peter. 1982. Changing values and the environment. Pp. 27–41 in Dennis L. Little, Robert E. Dils, and J. Gray (eds.), Renewable Natural Resources: A Management Handbook for the 1980s. Westview, Boulder, CO.

Sparhawk, W. N. 1949. The history of forestry in America. Pp. 702–714 in Trees—The Yearbook of Agriculture. U.S. Department of Agriculture. Washington, DC.

Spurr, Stephen H. 1982. North American forests: Converging forces and emerging trends. Pp. 29–34 in Charles E. Hewett and Thomas E. Hamilton (eds.), Forests in Demand: Conflicts and Solutions. Auburn House. Boston.

Spurr, Stephen H., and R. Keith Arnold. 1971. The forester's role in today's social and economic changes. *Journal of Forestry* 69(11):795–799.

Stegner, Wallace. 1985. The once and future land ethic: Living on our principal. *Wilderness* 48(168):15–21.

Steinbeck, Klaus. 1988. My chance: Reflections on forestry as a profession. *Journal of Forestry* 86(3):65.

Stone, Pat. 1989. John Seed and the Council of All Beings. *Mother Earth News* (117):58–63.

Stuart, Edward, Jr. 1975. Professional ethics and the Association of Consulting Foresters. *Consultant* 20(2):32–35.

Stuart, Edward, Jr. 1981. Conflict of interest: A question of ethics. *Consultant* 26(4):85–87.

Suro, Roberto. 1989. Grass-roots groups show power battling pollution close to home.

The New York Times 138(47,19):A1,A18. July 2.

Tombaugh, Larry W. 1985. Is conservation outmoded? *American Forests* 92(4):58, 66–71.

Tucker, William. 1982. Progress and Privilege: America in the Age of Environmentalism. Anchor Press/Doubleday. Garden City, NY. 314 pp.

Udall, Stewart L. 1988. Encounter with the Reagan revolution. *Amicus Journal* 10(3):5–7.

Walsh, Barry W. 1987. Aldo Leopold: SAF Fellow, councilman, editor, author, and activist. *Journal of Forestry* 85(1):5–7.

Will, George. 1990. Environmentalism is only one concern among many. *Atlanta Journal/Atlanta Constitution*, March 8, pp. A-23.

Wondolleck, Julia M. 1988. Public Lands Conflict and Resolution: Managing National Forest Disputes. Plenum Press. New York. 263 pp.

Zivnuska, John A. 1971. Conservation—For whom? *American Forests* 77(7): 8–9, 37–42.

Chapter 11

Mass Media and the Forestry Message

One who molds opinion is greater than one who enacts laws.

—Abraham Lincoln

The hand that rules the press, the radio, the screen, and the far-spread magazine rules the country.

—Supreme Court Judge Learned Hand

MASS COMMUNICATION

We are often said to be living in the age of communication. Whether it be through television, radio, newspapers, magazines, movies, or junk mail, mass communication activities dominate our lives, along with sleep, work, and school. On average, media-related activities consume about one-third of a typical day (Hiebert, Ungurait, and Bohn 1988).

Communication through the mass media is a central part of political life as well. Earth Day, the modern environmental movement, and most environmental and land management laws of the 1970s were spawned by a series of issues that were amplified and expanded through the media. Use of the mass media is important for gaining or retaining policy leadership in natural resources. Public and mass media involvement in resource issues will undoubtedly increase in the future.

Communication of facts, ideas, beliefs, and values is the essential purpose of the mass media. *Communication* is a broad term that has many meanings, so perhaps it is better viewed as a process rather than a single event. In thinking about things, we practice self-communication. A few individuals talking (or writing) with (or to) each other are practicing interpersonal communication. Group communication occurs as the number of participants increases and the level of involvement changes. Some participants in group communication are more active than others; listeners may drift in or out; and the total group experience often is less intense and immediate than with interpersonal communication. Mass communication occurs when a mass medium such as a newspaper or a radio or television station is used to convey messages to a very large audience (Hiebert, Ungurait, and Bohn 1988).

American mass media have pervasive impacts on societies around the world. In Africa and Europe, one is more likely to hear American music or see American television shows than native fare. In fact, European countries have tried to legally limit broadcasts of American television and radio shows, in order to preserve their own cultures (Hiebert, Ungurait, and Bohn 1988).

ILLUSTRATION: HERBICIDE PROTESTS AND THE MEDIA

The issue of herbicide use in forest management illustrates the media's role in making public policy. The herbicide 2,4,5-T was disallowed for forestry use by the Environmental Protection Agency (EPA) in 1979 and then revoked for all uses in 1985. For two decades before this, 2,4,5-T had been the forester's most cost-effective tool for controlling hardwood trees and brush that compete with softwoods. The scientific evidence regarding the hazards of 2,4,5-T and other herbicides had been debated for decades. Media publicity played an important role in the issue expansion process leading to the 1979 ban of 2,4,5-T. The issue included social and biological factors interacting to affect policy (Weesner 1983). The pros and cons of chemicals as a forestry tool are described by Grier (1985), who represented a citizens' group that was instrumental in the 2,4,5-T case, and Witt (1985), who represented a chemical manufacturing company.

HERBICIDE HAZARDS

In the 1970s citizens in Alsea, Oregon, claimed that miscarriages had resulted from aerial spraying, and national media attention became focused on this issue. The use of phenoxy herbicides also has been criticized in other areas, including Arizona, Virginia, Idaho, and Vietnam (Agent Orange) (Hayes 1987, Weesner 1983). The same concerns about herbicides have been expressed in Maine, Minnesota, and Canada (Dunster 1987, Irland 1983, Marcouiller and Ellefson 1987).

The scientific evidence supporting the banning of 2,4,5-T was adequate enough for the EPA in 1979, but it was less convincing to timber management groups.

Later studies have confirmed a linkage between herbicide use and cancer. For example, Stokes and Brace (1988) looked at data from 1497 rural counties in the United States. Their statistical analysis indicated that herbicide use was the strongest predicting variable for incidences of genital and lymphatic cancer, and the second best predictor of digestive cancer. The *New York Times* (June 20, 1990) reported results of a research project linking testicular cancer in military dogs to their exposure to Agent Orange in Vietnam. It also stated that human cancers of non-Hodgkins lymphoma and soft-tissue sarcoma were associated with chemicals in Agent Orange, and that the U.S. Veterans Administration would begin to compensate Vietnam veterans with those diseases (Associated Press 1990). But these findings were made relatively recently.

MEDIA INVOLVEMENT

Many actions helped attract media attention and expand the issue. In 1977 a company employee sprayed a group of protestors near Rose Lodge, Oregon, which was observed by a journalist. Perhaps the company was responding to protestors' camping out on company lands and inhibiting the company's site preparation work; perhaps the action was a response to vandalism done to barrels of herbicide and shots fired at helicopters (Stiak 1988). Whatever the rationale, publicly dousing the protestors was a poor public relations tactic. Protestors responded by vandalizing a company helicopter to publicize their grievances.

A company helicopter pilot said during an interview that reporters seek sensationalism. His firm often contacted news agencies before aerial herbicide applications to invite them to observe their operations. The invitations always were refused. But if someone were to claim that a water supply or a person had been sprayed, the story, regardless of its validity, would be covered immediately, leading to further problems for herbicide applicators and timberland owners (Lautenschlager 1985).

PUBLIC RELATIONS

Weesner (1983) suggests the following ways to avoid protests: Identify segments of the public, and analyze how they will be affected by the use of a tool such as herbicides. In the Oregon herbicide protests, 10 segments of the public were identified; 4 would be likely to protest—rural residents, forest workers, environmentalists, and marijuana growers and dealers. The other 6 "publics" were either neutral or in favor of aerial spraying of herbicides.

The responses of the different groups to this issue depended on their personal opinions and economic stake in herbicide use. Because phenoxy herbicides may pose health risks, some rural residents may protest. Those who use pesticides on their farms may not perceive herbicides as harmful. Tree planting companies could oppose aerial spraying of herbicides because of perceived health threats in areas where they would plant trees and because aerial spraying is a competitive threat to their own labor-intensive hand-planting business. Environmentalists and deep ecologists certainly oppose herbicide spraying because they are concerned with the preservation of natural environments; any intensive forestry method will therefore be opposed. Others may see the need for intensive silviculture on some land areas in order to preserve other areas and might be neutral on the herbicide issue. Marijuana growers will adamantly oppose herbicide spraying of forested areas. However, they will not likely admit their reason for protest, using health threats or some other reason to cover their actual concern.

Walstad and Dost (1986) list six steps for responding to public concerns. These tactics could be applied in any sensitive forest management program.

1. Establish communication networks with the community in advance. Questions dealing with sensitive areas then can be dealt with and resolved. Guided tours and door-to-door visits with neighboring landowners are very effective.

2. Identify sources of reliable information and expertise to answer questions raised during interaction with the community.

3. Establish news media contacts. This is essential for success, regardless of inconvenience or aggravation.

4. Encourage prompt, thorough, and impartial investigation of alleged pesticide exposure incidents.

5. Ensure consistent and firm enforcement by regulatory agencies concerning pesticide use infractions.

6. Execute pesticide applications with extreme care and proficiency, from planning, training, and supervision through implementation, using appropriate security and safety precautions.

The scientific issues regarding the relative safety of 2,4,5-T are moot now. However, public opinion regarding natural resources management will continue to play an important role in forest policy. Public perceptions of adverse environmental consequences can result in policies that eliminate almost any management technique. Professional credibility suffers when neighbors believe that improper management methods have been used. That goes not only for chemicals use, but also for prescribed burning, which adversely affects air quality. The ongoing environmentalists' attacks on clear-cutting, and professionals' advocacy of the method, are more likely to have a negative impact on foresters than their own critics. Perhaps foresters should use selective cutting methods whenever possible, even if they are not biologically or economically optimal. The only way for resource managers to retain an array of land management options, and to project an image of credibility and responsible resource stewardship, is to deal effectively with the concerns and perceptions of the public.

MEDIA ROLES

The various mass communications media are unofficial participants in the policy-making process. They have had some influence and have been criticized for their role in shaping public policy. The media interact with interest groups and elected officials to publicize and expand issues beyond the narrow confines of interest group meetings and legislatures. Mass media always have been important in American politics. They helped inflame the passions of our revolutionary forebears against the British. The Federalist papers were instrumental in the debate over adopting the U.S. Constitution. Mass media also played a key role in the progressive conservation movement in the late nineteenth and early twentieth centuries, as well as the environmental movement that began in the 1960s.

The media have had a strong impact on forest policies. Without the media, issues could not get widespread public attention. Most public and private natural resource organizations seek good public relations and a favorable public image, so they employ full-time information specialists. The Society of American Foresters ran an extensive public relations campaign about the benefits of forests in 1983 and 1984. Public service announcements about forestry were produced for television, radio, and print media. They featured Ralph Waite, the patriarch of the "Waltons" television family. The Sierra Club carries on an extensive advertising program and has bought time on MTV (a cable music station) and space in newspapers and magazines to deliver its message (Figure 11-1). Forest products firms, acting both individually and collectively through trade associations, use public relations efforts. Many state forestry organizations and wildlife agencies have mass media production facilities in addition to the traditional state agency information and education programs.

Mass media serve many roles. They may increase people's knowledge, influence their opinions, or shape their actions. Media influence most aspects of life, including consumer behavior, political or voting behavior, and natural resource management on public and private lands.

What do mass media communicate? Hiebert et al. (1988) classify media roles into several components. Media convey news and information and provide analysis and interpretation. They also attempt to persuade and to promote good public relations, as well as advertise specific goods and services. Media are involved in education, entertainment, and art. They help form social norms and establish public policy agendas.

NEWS REPORTING AND INTERPRETATION

The media report news and information to the interested public. The economic, political, and cultural relationships among individuals, groups, and countries depend on the communication of factual information. As suggested in Chapter 9, many interest groups "lobby" by providing information. Policymakers need information to make decisions. Similarly, individuals need information to form opinions and act in their own political or economic self-interest. The mass media provide this information, either in exchange for money from consumers of information (e.g., newspaper readers), or from advertisers (e.g., on radio or television) who hope to influence consumer behavior.

For information to become news, it must meet various criteria. To be reportable, information should be objective, accurate, balanced, and fair. These standards help to separate news from analysis, advocacy, or public relations. To become news, information must be of interest to news consumers. Journalists use many criteria to determine the suitability of information to be news. It must be timely; old news is dull. The events also must be of interest to the media outlet's audience—local or national consumers, specialized groups, or the general public. News also must have eco-

Figure 11-1. Sierra Club Public Relations Advertisement
Source: Sierra Club, personal com., 1992

nomic, political, or human interest and have some consequence for the audience (Hiebert et al. 1988).

Most people are more interested in news that gives them immediate satisfaction or affects their basic livelihood or safety. As a result, sensational news, crime, and other "bad" news tends to be reported most often, which distorts the reality of everyday life. Longer-term issues, such as environmental protec-

tion and natural resource management, also are reported as news. These issues affect our quality of life and are of immediate concern to many interest groups and individuals in the attentive segment of the public.

The news media also analyze and interpret facts and information. Facts can be manipulated and news distorted, intentionally or inadvertently. American newspapers have traditionally separated facts appearing in news sections from opinions on the editorial pages and provide separate sections for business, sports, life-style, and the arts where opinions are clearly identifiable in separate authored columns. News, business, trade, and personal interest magazines provide facts, interpretations, and opinions in their articles. Radio tends to present more facts; television presents a mix of facts, reporters' opinions, and attention-getting images.

The media often have been accused of bias and sensationalism in their coverage. To the extent that opinions are explicitly stated as analysis or interpretation, such charges are unfair. In America the subtle slant achieved by the mixture of facts and values is deemed inappropriate, unlike its accepted use in many European countries (Hiebert et al. 1988). Sensationalism, too, is not new. William Randolph Hearst, a newspaper titan at the turn of the twentieth century, became rich and famous by publishing sensationalist, muckraking, "yellow journalism" articles. Ironically, progeny Patty Hearst was exploited by members of the Symbionese Liberation Army in the 1970s. They kidnapped and brainwashed her, using the media to promote their cause. The growing importance of television coverage and reduced censorship in the late 1980s and early 1990s have exacerbated tendencies toward sensationalism.

ADVERTISEMENTS AND PUBLIC RELATIONS

The media can help to promote good public relations for politicians, firms, or interest groups; to persuade people to act favorably or purchase certain goods and services; or to mold personal opinions and set societal agendas. In a democratic society, all individuals have a right to persuade others to follow their points of view. In early American politics, lobbyists were said to use "bribes, booze, and women" to peddle influence. As politics and society have become more complex, more sophisticated means of persuading politicians and constituents are required. Most interest groups and office seekers now employ public relations professionals and firms to under-

stand and influence public opinion and develop favorable policies.

Interest groups use the mass media to shape opinion. In addition to the traditional print and electronic media (see the next section), they also use direct mail, pamphlets, brochures, graphic materials, audiovisual materials, and mixed-media presentations. Advertising is perhaps the best known technique to influence public opinion. Advertising pays the bills for commercial network television, and much of the cost of newspapers and magazine production as well. Political campaigns rely on advertising to help elect candidates, often at great expense. Corporations advertise to sell products and services. Some corporations advertise to shape public policy.

Public relations is a systematic process of communication that involves the identification of discrete publics and the tailoring of specific messages to them (DeFleur and Dennis 1988). Public relations, like advertising, is a communications process and depends in part on mass media to carry its messages. Public relations consists of more than just buying media space or time. Sometimes other, more indirect, means are used to build a favorable climate of opinion. Public relations efforts often cannot be identified, as such, in the way that a magazine advertisement is easily recognized as promoting a product. The source for a news article or a demonstration by protestors might have been part of a public relations campaign. Press releases from interest groups are often printed as news; "spontaneous" protests are often carefully staged to enlarge issues (see Chapter 4). Public relations involves the manipulation of meanings; however, that manipulation is not necessarily deceptive.

Public relations efforts use advertising, publicity, and promotion to persuade the public. They are crucial in politics, government, business, education, religion, entertainment, and all other forms of public life (Hiebert et al. 1988). Massive public relations campaigns are not unique to democratic countries, nor are they confined to our modern era. Countries without freedom of expression use public relations—referred to as propaganda. One definition of propaganda is the attempt by the government to control opinion through the use of significant symbols in stories, rumors, reports, music, pictures, threats, or other forms of social communication (Lasswell 1927). To some extent, this definition of propaganda and the techniques used apply to forms of persuasion common in democratic societies as well. However, in free societies, access to the media is not restricted to the government alone, but rather by the ability to pay, and the messages conveyed may be more disparate in nature (Severin and Tankard 1988).

It is interesting to note that not even sustained propaganda, such as that common in the former Soviet Union and Eastern Europe before the downfall of communism, is ultimately successful in convincing oppressed or deprived people that they are well off or politically free. Politicians, public policies, and products must have some intrinsic merits for public relations efforts to be successful.

What are the "discrete publics" referred to in the preceding definition of public relations? The recognition of segments of the general public is a way of targeting where the message will be delivered. Publics should be identified in relation to a resource manager's situation and to a specific issue (Fazio and Gilbert 1981). For example, Force and Williams (1989) have identified different groups of people who participate in national forest planning activities. These publics can be identified by forest planners, and specific planning activities can be designed to ensure their active participation.

For example, in Texas, the Lone Star Trail for hikers winds through portions of the Sam Houston National Forest, including a wilderness area. Adjacent motorcycle trails (outside the wilderness, of course) support as many as a thousand vehicles per weekend. A district forester would view the recreation maintenance crew members, the district ranger, staff forestry specialists, and forest supervisor as internal publics, in the jargon of public relations. The Lone Star Chapter of the Sierra Club and the Trail Riders Association of Houston would be external publics, as would various news media representatives such as newspaper and television reporters. All these publics would have some interest in a change in recreation plans on a particular ranger district. Some segments of the external public might favor the change; others might not. These segments need to be identified because they can help or hinder resource management efforts. Dealing effectively with these publics is important because much of the trail maintenance work on the hiking and motorcycle trails is accomplished by volunteers from external public groups.

EDUCATION AND ENTERTAINMENT

With the single exception of books, the use of mass media for formal education has had a checkered history. American education relies mostly on textbooks, with some sporadic use of public television programs, films and videos, and filmstrips. Informal education, however, uses the mass media extensively and very successfully. Motion pictures help convey ideas, reflect public opinion, and even set the public agenda. Dramatized television series may do the same. Nature shows, such as "Wild Kingdom," "The Undersea World of Jacques Cousteau," many "Nova" specials, and National Geographic Society documentaries have sensitized people to fish, wildlife, and environmental issues.

The general press and specialized magazines have played an important educational role in natural resource issues and policies. Magazines such as *National Geographic*, *National Wildlife*, *Audubon*, and *American Forests* feature articles on wildlife and plant biology, sometimes advocating species and habitat protection or preservation. These popular outlets summarize factual knowledge and public issues in terms understandable by nonprofessionals, furthering informed policymaking.

Art and entertainment are conveyed through mass media. Americans use entertainment media for recreation, escape, and stimulation. All media have an entertainment focus, in order to keep their audience.

But entertainment is often intertwined with concepts and ideology designed to provoke thought, discussion, and action. Poetry and prose, both classical and contemporary, remain influential for entertainment value and for content. The plays of Shakespeare and Ibsen have endured for their timeless insights about people and social values, not only for their entertainment value. Classical literature remains instructive today and continues to be adapted to other media. Current and historic events are presented in the media in ways that promote public discussion and action.

MEDIA TYPES

Print and electronic broadcasting are the two basic types of mass media. Both have some effect on forest resource policies. A third major media type is film, or motion pictures. Films usually are thought of as an entertainment medium. However, educational films can affect public attitudes about forestry and forest policies.

Mass media such as newspapers, magazines, television, and radio are instrumental in helping natural resource agencies communicate with their various publics. Fazio and Gilbert (1981) reported on a survey of natural resources agencies in which 308 information and education executives ranked the relative importance of various communication methods in helping them achieve their agency goals. In order of importance (1 – most important to 6 – least important), they were

	Score
1. Newspaper articles	2.6
2. Field contacts	2.8
3. Publications (magazines and brochures)	3.6
4. Television programs	3.7
5. Scheduled personal appearance programs	3.8
6. Radio	4.1

PRINT MEDIA

The print media—newspapers, magazines, and books—are channels of mass communication. As profit-making businesses, they also play an important economic role. All three, especially newspapers, were very profitable in the 1980s. They competed well with electronic media for advertising revenue dollars and are likely to continue to do so (DeFleur and Dennis 1988).

Newspapers

Newspapers generally deliver detailed current information to citizens, which facilitates the discussion of public affairs necessary in a democracy. They also depend on advertising revenue and direct sales to people who will read the ads. Newspapers have a special responsibility to inform the public, and freedom of the press is specifically granted in the U.S. Constitution. In serving the public interest, newspapers are important social watchdogs, commenting on abuses of power by government, businesses, and other institutions that may be violating laws or perceived public values (DeFleur and Dennis 1988).

Newspapers also deliver telling messages through cartoons. Political cartoons are standard fare on most editorial pages and are effective at lampooning politicians, business executives, and bureaucrats alike. Many cartoons have dealt with forestry issues, including dozens about the spotted owl issue in the 1990s and clear-cuts for many years. Cartoonist Ding Darling, of the *Des Moines Register,* campaigned endlessly and effectively through his front-page cartoons for conservation causes (see Figure 4-2). Cartoons help create an image or impression that will provoke a response. Posters and pictures of beautiful scenery, cuddly animals, ugly clear-cuts, poisoned waters, and trash in the streets may do the same.

Natural resource issues are not always as exciting and newsworthy as other basic social issues or tragedies, but they are covered often. The *New York Times,* whose motto is "All the news that's fit to print," often runs natural resource articles of global, national, and local significance. During the fall of 1988, the *Times* ran stories on the effects of deforestation in the Amazon rain forest of Brazil, the efforts of a Kansas man to plant trees in India, the Indian government's attempts to "save dwindling forests" in its fuel-starved regions, the "poor shape" of the National Wildlife Refuge System, the Christmas tree industry and biotechnology, the effects of a protracted paper mill strike in Maine, workers buying a plywood mill in Washington state, and President Reagan's veto of a 1.4 million acre wilderness bill for Montana. It also reported the proposed listing of the spotted owl as an endangered species as an attempt by environmentalists to prevent logging of old-growth timber in the Pacific Northwest; the extensive forest fires in Yellowstone National Park; and private property regulation in New York's 6 million acre Adirondack Park, which is three times the size of Yellowstone. On one single weekday (Friday, November 18, 1988), the *New York Times* had a front page story on a federal judge's ruling that the northern spotted owl should be listed as an endangered species, which would reduce logging of old-growth forests in the Pacific Northwest; on page 7, an article on a fence in Wyoming that killed 700 pronghorn antelope in one winter, illustrated with a gruesome picture; and on page 10, an article on proposals that would more than double the size of the nation's Wild and Scenic Rivers System by 1993.

Local newspapers may cover natural resources issues frequently or infrequently, depending on their location and general reader interest in that subject. The *Portland Oregonian* ran many detailed articles on the spotted owl/old-growth/logging issues in the early 1990s.

Magazines

Published less often than newspapers, magazines can look into issues more extensively. There is less need to focus on the events of the day, and more room for interpretation and analysis in a broader context. Specialization is the specialty of the magazine industry. Some widely read general interest magazines occasionally may cover forestry and wildlife issues.

In the 1980s *National Geographic*, with a paid circulation exceeding 10 million, featured national forest management problems and Theodore Roosevelt's wilderness legacy in separate articles in the same issue (Eliot 1982, Findley 1982). *Newsweek* magazine, with a paid circulation of 3 million, had a cover story on the "Battle over the wilderness," which included an interview with James Watt, President Reagan's controversial interior secretary (Beck et al. 1983). The cover of the magazine carried that title over a picture of Secretary Watt in a pristine setting in Glacier National Park, accompanied by a telling subtitle: "Uncle Sam owns one-third of the country, and Americans are fighting over every acre." *Newsweek* revisited the problems in the West in a 1991 cover article on "The War for the West," exploring the clashes between recreational and amenity users and mineral, timber, and livestock interests (Turque 1991). Both *Time* and *Newsweek* ran feature stories on global climate change in 1988. The U.N. Conference on Environment and Development dominated magazine coverage in May and June of 1992, with cover features in *Newsweek*, *Time*, and *Business Week*. Politics, of course, is a perpetual topic in general interest magazines.

General news magazines, specifically *Time* and *Newsweek*, occasionally contain paid advertisements from conservation groups and forest industry firms. One effort was a series of corporate image advertisements by Boise Cascade, one of which portrayed timber harvesting as a magical event, and invited the public to come see company harvests (Figure 11-2). The American Forest Resource Alliance, in cooperation with the American Forest Council, began a nationwide publicity campaign to promote wise forest use and the industry's image, via full-page advertisements in major newspapers and *National Geographic*. One ad (Figure 11-3) notes that threats of running out of trees have occurred

Figure 11-2. Boise Cascade Advertisement
Source: Boise Cascade, personal com., 1992

for decades, but have been false, inferring that similar claims made today are untrue.

One of the more memorable image advertisements was International Paper's campaign to help Americans become better communicators. Throughout the 1980s the company published a series of two-page magazine ads featuring celebrities and noted literati giving some how-to lessons. These included Bill Cosby on "How to read faster," Steve Allen on "How to enjoy the classics," George Plimpton on "How to give a speech," Malcolm Forbes on "How to write a business letter," Kurt Vonnegut on "How to write with

Figure 11-3. American Forest Council Advertisement
Source: National Geographic 1989.

style," John Irving on "How to spell," and James Michener on "How to use a library." Remarkably, the name of the company appears only in the lower right-hand corner of the piece, in almost a parenthetical manner (similar to the famous Nike ads in 1990 through 1992), carrying the message "We believe in the power of the printed word."

Scientific magazines also play an important part in public policy formation and evaluation. Research helps establish new knowledge, which is conveyed through peer-reviewed journal articles, professional speeches and proceedings, and many other outlets. Scientists testify at national and local legislative hearings and provide information used by professionals, interest groups, and all three branches of government. Published research results help convey the effects of public policies. Government, private, and academic research publications have been crucial in resource policy-making, as well as in social policy-making. Many groups concentrate heavily on producing and providing research information favorable to their policy goals.

Books

Like newspapers and magazines, books inform, persuade, and entertain. Unlike the other print media, they seldom contain advertising. Books often persuade influential people and therefore have impacts beyond the mere number of copies sold. Books can promote powerful ideas and inspire changes, even revolutions, in people and institutions. They transmit a culture's heritage. Books are seen as delightful, and also as dangerous; they have been banned by libraries and burned by foreign dictators and American parents (DeFleur and Dennis 1988).

One such "dangerous" book with a forestry message caused a small furor in 1989. Parents of schoolchildren in a timber-dependent community in Montana were upset when their progeny were asked to read and report on *The Lorax*, one of the many children's stories by Dr. Suess (Suess and Geisel 1971). When asked what his purpose was, the Lorax replied, "I speak for the trees." When the Once-ler, a prototypical entrepreneur, discovered that people would buy Sneeds manufactured from Truffula trees, the Lorax cautioned against overcutting the trees. But alas, the trees disappeared and so, too, did the Lorax. The forest was replaced by fouled air and abandoned factories.

General interest books, called "trade" books in the industry, have had huge impacts on environmental and resource management issues. As discussed before, Leopold's *A Sand County Almanac*, published posthumously in 1949, articulated the land ethic; Rachel Carson's (1962) *Silent Spring* exposed the dangers of chemical pesticides accumulating in the food chain and poisoning many animals and people and triggered the modern environmental movement. Stewart Udall's (1963) widely read *The Quiet Crisis* focused attention on federal land management, general land use, and environmental problems. The messages of environmentalism were carried to millions of people by Paul Ehrlich's (1968) *The Population Bomb*; Barry Com-

moner's (1971) *The Closing Circle* helped to make ecology a household word; *The Limits to Growth* by Meadows et al. (1972) dramatized the potential for shortages of natural resources as population exploded. Bill McKibben's (1989) *The End of Nature* predicted that pollution and environmental destruction soon would lead to an apocalypse.

Other general interest books have examined environmental attitudes and values. John McPhee's (1971) *Encounters with the Archdruid* is a literate and revealing portrait of modern environmentalism, featuring a series of interviews with David Brower. The charismatic leader of the Sierra Club in the 1950s and 1960s, Brower was forced out and started Friends of the Earth and then in the late 1980s, Earth Island Institute. Edward Abbey achieved literary fame with *Desert Solitaire* (1968), a paean to the wilderness qualities of the American Southwest. Later, Abbey achieved infamy due to the ecotage (ecological sabotage) tactics described in *The Monkey Wrench Gang* (1975).

Poets and writers have been awed and inspired by the beauty and vitality of trees and nature. Early pagan religions revered trees and sacrificed wildlife to appease their gods. In medieval England, the Druids worshiped trees and the spirits within them. The Bible contains many references to different trees with distinctly reverent connotations of their importance to life. In each quarterly issue of the *Amicus Journal*, the Natural Resources Defense Council publishes a poetry section.

References to trees and forests in general literature have some influence on public attitudes toward them. Many people have a strong emotional attachment to trees and forests. The idea of managing a tract of forest land as a farmer manages a field of corn stirs these emotions and presents foresters with a deep-seated public relations problem. As Spurr (1977, p. 72) put it, "In Tolkien's *The Lord of the Rings* fantasy, it was Treebeard and his fellow human trees of Fanghorn Forest who, when finally aroused, tipped the scales of battle against the forces of evil. What have we [foresters], who mark trees to be cut down, to look forward to ... ?"

Special interest books and reports carrying natural resource management messages have been used with success. The Sierra Club has furthered its cause by producing high-quality books featuring beautiful photographs of wild places accompanied by evocative prose descriptions or poetry. Hays (1987) concludes that the images portrayed in these large format books have helped shape the environmental perception of the landscape for millions of Americans. In 1988 and 1989 the Wilderness Society published a series of six resource reports that were very successful at setting the public agenda for discussions on national forest management and biological diversity. These reports have been used in congressional hearings and in writing bills proposed in Congress.

Each of the three largest citizen conservation interest groups publishes books to help Americans discover and become more knowledgeable about their natural heritage. The Sierra Club publishes a series of regional guides designed to help visitors interpret natural resources. The National Audubon Society publishes a popular series of field guides to American wildlife. The National Wildlife Federation also publishes a series of guidebooks for plants and wildlife.

ELECTRONIC BROADCASTING MEDIA

Broadcast media are a constant presence in the lives of Americans. Broadcasting has a vast potential to bring beautiful sounds and images and a wealth of information to us. Yet the content of broadcasting, especially on television, has drawn many criticisms, ranging from poor quality, to negative effects on children, to tasteless commercials, to biased or poor news coverage. Some of the criticism reflects a belief in the power of broadcasting, and some a legacy of fear (DeFleur and Dennis 1988). For example, 1988 marked the fiftieth anniversary of Orson Welles's radio broadcast of the landing of aliens from Mars and the beginning of a war of the worlds. The broadcast was fiction, but this was not initially revealed to the listeners. The public was outraged by this abuse of broadcasting power.

Broadcast news media are the self-appointed defenders of the public faith, and society seems to have accepted this role for them. Their role is limited by the short time demands of radio and TV. In the electronic media, news reports tend to be 60 seconds in length, regardless of the subject's complexity, and this pressure for compactness means that issues must be kept simple. Reporters try to summarize in one minute what may take volumes of print. Politicians respond by packaging policy statements in short "news/sound bites" that stations can clip and run on broadcasts. This does not, however, help lead to informed public discourse on and policymaking for complex issues.

Radio

Radio has the largest composite audience of any communication medium; there are almost 489 million radio sets in the country. Radio experienced a rebirth in the 1980s that surprised many media specialists. The continuing appeal of radio involves many economic, cultural, and psychological factors. Radio is a more cost-effective advertising medium than television—costing less per audience member reached. Radio takes in more revenue than do magazines, but only one-third as much as television, and one-fourth as much as newspapers. Dull television programs and endless reruns turn many viewers to their radios. Many listeners enjoy using their imagination, which radio requires and television often stifles (DeFleur and Dennis 1988). Radios are inexpensive and easy to listen to in a vehicle or almost anywhere else.

Radio news coverage of forestry and environmental issues often occurs at the local level. Many talk shows; public service announcements; or discussions of forestry, hunting, fishing, or their impact on the local economy are broadcast on the radio.

National radio coverage for resource issues is of two types. Commercial radio networks seldom carry forest resources news. When they do, the coverage will not be detailed because of time limitations. The National Public Radio (NPR) network does cover forest resource issues and news in detail. On one day (November 4, 1989), two in-depth stories were reported. One featured a U.S. Forest Service archaeologist who had discovered remnants of the most extensive Chinese terraced gardens outside of China in a remote section of Idaho's Payette National Forest. The other story discussed clear-cuts, biological diversity, jobs, and forest policies in Southeast Alaska's Tongass National Forest. This occurred at a time when the U.S. House of Representatives had passed a bill to revise the 1980 Alaska National Interest Land Conservation Act provisions for the Tongass, and the Senate version of the bill had not yet been deliberated.

Although official radio coverage for forestry and wildlife issues is limited, media broadcasting of music and songs are important in molding public opinion. The protest against the war in Vietnam, the expansion of the environmental movement, and the revolt against the establishment in the 1960s were fostered and enhanced by folk songs and rock music. The music, the rock groups, the concerts, and the protests of the Woodstock generation all helped trigger protests of the war and demands for environmental protection. "Make love, not war!" and "Goin' Up the Country" became the ideals of a generation that were expressed in music and helped set the American policy agenda in the late 1960s and early 1970s.

Music continues to help define public perceptions and expand social issues. In the late 1980s, the popular Irish rock band U2 sang about peace in Northern Ireland; Paul Simon and native artists sang against apartheid in South Africa on a Grammy award–winning album; Midnight Oil promoted Aboriginal rights and environmental protection in Australia; Indiana native John Cougar Mellencamp's rock songs helped dramatize farm problems; and the Indigo Girls' album covers asked buyers to support Greenpeace, one of their favorite causes. The advent of music video and the MTV and VH1 cable channels has broadened the appeal of and audience for such messages. Concerts have been targeted at particular social issues, such as farm aid, AIDS, apartheid, and "Our Common Future— The Global Environment."

Television

Television has become an intimate part of American life. Almost 98 percent of all American households have at least one television set; 57 percent have more than one. On the average, a household TV set is on for a staggering seven hours a day (DeFleur and Dennis 1988). The sheer size of the viewing audience makes television a scapegoat for many societal ills, as well as a vehicle for paid commercial advertisements. Some critics call television a "vast wasteland." There are high-quality programs, but far too many unimaginative spin-offs, knock-offs, and copies of popular programs. News programs also are the subject of criticism, often for their "happy talk" formats—serious attention to important issues is displaced by the search for entertaining stories. News and entertainment content is greatly influenced by visual appeal, spectacle, and entertainment, say critics. Defenders say television does not create American values, but mirrors them (DeFleur and Dennis 1988).

Television broadcasting delivers forestry messages via newscasts and specials, although public service announcements (PSAs) and advertisements can have some influence on public opinion. Television news coverage and issue expansion of national forest policy issues is uncommon, with a few notable exceptions. TV news covered high-profile problems such as the clear-cutting issues in West Virginia and Montana during the 1970s, Yellowstone National Park fires in 1988, acid rain, and global environmental problems. Local television coverage may be slightly more extensive, particularly in areas with forest-based economies.

In the 1990s television networks expanded environmental coverage. Many shows began focusing on environmental problems, especially during Earth Day each April. In short, the environment has reached status as a national agenda item, worthy of even extensive television coverage.

Television broadcasting stations devote a small percentage of their commercial messages to public service announcements. These time slots are free opportunities to deliver promotional or public relations messages. The USDA Forest Service's Smokey the Bear anti–forest fire and Woodsy the Owl clean environment campaigns have been PSA staples for many years. Woodsy the Owl has been shelved since the northern spotted owl became an official endangered species and symbol for forest preservation. In 1991 and 1992 MTV and VH1 ran PSAs or short specials on how to save the environment via activism, including recommendations to join groups such as Greenpeace.

In 1989 Turner Broadcasting System (TBS) carried an hour-long National Geographic Society special on clear-cutting and spotted owls in national forests in the West. The program was initially to be sponsored by Stroh's beer. However, when loggers and others in the Pacific Northwest threatened to boycott the beer, the firm withdrew its support. In fact TBS ran the entire special without any paid advertisements. Forest industry groups claimed the special was biased; environmentalists approved of the selection of material. A similar event occurred in 1991 with an Audubon special on public rangeland management in the West.

Over the past 30 years thousand of wildlife TV films and documentaries have educated American children and parents to appreciate wildlife. By making a niche for itself in television programming, wildlife programming may have done more to save wildlife itself than the work of all the organizations devoted to its cause (Stegner 1985). The popularity of sport fishing programs also has reinforced public desires for fisheries management and recreation.

MOTION PICTURES

The film or motion picture industry usually is thought to reside in Hollywood, California, and to produce lavishly expensive forms of entertainment. But many other movies are made for educational or other purposes, including public relations. Movies air not only in movie theaters, but also on broadcast television or videocassettes that can be purchased or rented. Forestry issues usually are portrayed in educational films or videotapes that can be broadcast on television or housed in the film libraries that virtually every natural resource agency maintains. According to Fazio and Gilbert (1981), the average fish and game agency had 42 different film titles in 1981. USDA Forest Service regional offices averaged 206 available titles at that time.

Forestry and Hollywood

Only a few recent movies have featured forestry themes, which usually have been tangential to the main plot. Nonetheless, some messages regarding forestry are brought to the attention of millions of moviegoers and viewers of late-night television.

Movie star Kirk Douglas played a lumber baron intent on cutting a stand of old-growth redwoods in a 1952 movie called *The Big Trees*. The tract was purchased from a family that had nurtured its forest resource and family income with infrequent and carefully selected timber harvests. Before the big trees were felled, the protagonist was shown the error of his ways by the daughter of the family, who became the love interest in the movie.

In the 1980s *The Big Trees* story jumped off the screen and become a reality. The Pacific Lumber Company, analogous to the family that practiced careful resource stewardship, was acquired by the Maxxam Group, Inc., a financial conglomerate that saw dollar signs in the redwood groves. Maxxam stepped up the timber harvest, apparently intent on liquidating the trees in order to pay off some portion of the corporation's heavily leveraged debt (Ahlfeld 1987, Anderberg 1988a, Garlington 1988). This story did not have the happy ending that the movie did, unless you are a Maxxam shareholder. But protestors, including local citizens, the California Department of Forestry, Earth First! and other activists, as well as the media helped force some concessions from the corporation (Mitchell 1988), and the planned clear-cutting of old-growth timber has been restricted to selective cutting (Anderberg 1988b).

The classic Disney feature-length animated film *Bambi* has influenced American attitudes toward wildlife for many years. Wildlife managers speak of the "Bambi syndrome" that has closed the minds of many to wildlife population management through controlled harvest by hunters (Schectman 1978).

The Emerald Forest enjoyed a modest commercial success in 1985. This film had no major stars other than the magnificent tropical rain forest setting. The story involved an American engineer working on a hydropower development project in a tropical forest jungle. His young son was kidnapped and raised to adolescence by rain forest natives and was eventually found by the father. The film documents the ecological, anthropological, and sociological problems in cultivating the less developed regions of the world and perhaps has had some subtle influence in popularizing the plight of tropical forests. But all things considered, movies have given us a view of tropical forests that is more romantic than realistic. As Boerner (1988, p. 15) has said, "We can't even begin to take wise action until we shed our movie-image views of the far-off forests."

Educational Films and Videotapes

Hollywood movies may enlighten as well as entertain, but their primary purpose is to enthrall mass audiences and make money for the production company. Educational films are produced by a variety of organizations that are not as concerned with commercial success as are Hollywood's movie moguls. Resource-related messages have been the substance of a number of educational films. For example, the biological diversity of the Costa Rican rain forest was featured in a 1983 National Geographic Society special. Many educational films are broadcast thanks to the voracious appetites of television stations for something to send out over the airwaves.

Interest groups sometimes use motion pictures to convey messages. The Conservation Foundation, an organization that engages in special studies and disseminates the results,

produced *Common Ground: Changing Values and the National Forests*. The title of this 28-minute film is self-explanatory; its timeless message, delivered by Dr. Carl Reidel of the University of Vermont, offers insight into forest policy deliberations: "What you want from a forest tends to influence how you see it." The Society of American Foresters produced *To Work with the Forest* in 1981. The film depicted the complexity and challenges of modern forestry and was of the right length (18 minutes) and scope to present to general or specialized audiences. The Sierra Club has produced several films highlighting the beauty and values of the American wilderness. The National Wildlife Federation produced a 19-minute videotape in 1988 featuring tropical rain forest problems called *Our Threatened Heritage*. The National Audubon Society produced a 23-minute videotape in 1987 called *What Is the Limit?* It dealt with the disturbing questions of global population issues as they relate to natural resources and was accompanied by written materials designed to be used in discussion groups.

THE MEDIA AND FOREST RESOURCES

Advertising and public relations all depend on mass media to deliver their messages. In and of themselves, they are not media but roles that media perform. This section explores in more detail those roles and their important relationship with forest resource management.

ADVERTISING

Advertising is a means of presenting and promoting ideas, goods, and services that is paid for by an identified sponsor. The objective of advertising is to inform consumers and persuade them to take some action, usually to purchase a particular product (DeFleur and Dennis 1988). Advertising also is used to create favorable attitudes toward a firm, organization, or individual. Politicians spend vast sums on advertising in order to get elected, so they may pursue policy choices that they or their constituents find desirable. Firms use advertising to sell products as well as their image; environmental groups use it to seek funds and protect plants, animals, and ecosystems.

ILLUSTRATION: THE RIO EARTH SUMMIT

An innovative use of advertising related to environmental issues occurred before the June 1992 Earth Summit in Rio de Janiero sponsored by the United Nations. The Rio summit was the largest environmental conference ever held, and had official representation from leaders from over 150 countries. The leaders were supposed to confer and sign treaties regarding the future of the global environment—covering subjects such as carbon dioxide emissions, global warming, and protection of plant and animal species. As of April 20, 1992, however, the Bush administration had steadfastly refused to send an official U.S. delegation to the global conference. Critics of the administration said that the U.S. negotiators who were helping set the agenda before the conference were remarkably uncooperative and inflexible. Administration officials contended that more scientific information was needed before taking actions that might hurt economic growth (Bronstein 1992).

In response to this inaction on the part of the president who campaigned as an environmentalist, a national citizens ad campaign was developed to try to persuade President Bush to attend the UN Earth Summit. Film clips that pictured tropical forest destruction were shown and citizens were asked to call an "action" line (1-800-LEAD-RIO) that would send a telegram for $6.95 urging Bush to attend the conference. The clips were shown as a trailer before popular films in many theaters nationwide, as well as on Fox television, VH1, and several other cable networks. Public service announcements were made on many radio stations, and ads were placed on about 300 billboards in 10 cities (Bronstein 1992).

As of Earth Day, April 22, 1992, more than 10,000 citizens heeded the message and called the action line number to send their telegram to President Bush. This ad campaign apparently helped prompt official U.S. participation at the summit; in May Bush agreed to attend. The campaign certainly illustrates an innovative application of environmental activism/advertising. It also is indicative of the fairly broad-based support for worldwide environmental protection and cleanup efforts.

The political aspects of U.S. participation in the Earth Summit are worth noting. Many developed countries, who were participating, hoped that George Bush would continue to refuse to sign a tough treaty on global warming. Despite their public statements, many European countries and Japan were not enthused about binding reductions in carbon-dioxide emissions, which could seriously disturb their economies. Bush was thus taking the heat, and they could make greener-than-thou speeches blasting the United States ("Passing the Buck" 1992). In the end, all other major countries did support stronger emission controls, but U.S. opposition did lead to a weak agreement (see Chapter 18). This issue illustrates how complex the choices about environmental protection and economic development are, and how politics and public relations are integrally involved.

PUBLIC RELATIONS

Public relations are complex and important, as discussed earlier in the chapter. We seldom observe public relations efforts directly, except in political campaigns. Few public relations leaders are known to the general populace. Public relations specialists try to overcome the barriers between the mass media and an individual or group desiring to deliver a message and try to foster favorable impressions in people's minds about a person, product, or service.

Probably more land managers have failed due to public relations problems than have ever failed because of technical limitations. The purpose of a public relations program is not only to understand public attitudes and promote public understanding of a land management program, but also to maintain an atmosphere in which issues can be resolved. Public relations represent, in many ways, a systematic approach toward being a good neighbor (Connaughton 1982). If neighbors dislike land management activities, they will protest them. Public relations can help reduce the incidence and severity of the protest.

Being a good neighbor means knowing what your neighbors like and dislike. Fortmann (1987) conducted several studies of protests of timber harvests from private lands in Northern California, which debunked the negative stereotypes of environmental protestors and their motivations. For example, Fortmann found that:

1. Not everything that the timber industry does gets protested.

2. Most protestors are neighbors, not die-hard environmentalists.

3. Protestors include long-term area residents as well as newcomers.

4. Land use issues such as erosion, water quality, and roads are more important to neighbors than are their scenic views.

5. People can tell the difference between good and bad logging jobs.

6. Protestors are willing to use legitimate channels of protest.

The implications of these finding are especially important in forests near urban areas. Timber harvesting probably will be protested on private lands (at least in California), and more so on public lands. Challenges and protests will be made through government channels where and when they are available. Protests are not a form of recreation but represent real concerns of the public. If they are not heard, people are likely to gather up some spikes and matches and head for the woods (Fortmann 1987).

Public relations efforts may be divided into two major approaches: the mass approach and the key approach. The mass approach used by natural resource managers targets people in an immediate locality and the public at large, using the media to sustain the flow of information. Resource managers must remember to direct special attention to urban and suburban areas. The key approach is directed to opinion makers or opinion leaders—key individuals who need to be consulted and kept informed so they can interject their influential judgments. These leaders understand and guide public opinion and can serve as effective bridges between natural resource managers and either the general public or policymakers (Connaughton 1982).

Fazio and Gilbert (1981) outline seven principles to be used in planning public relations efforts.

1. Every action makes an impression.

2. Good public relations is a prerequisite of success.

3. The public is actually many publics.

4. Truth and honesty are essential.

5. Offense is more effective than defense.

6. Communication is the key to good public relations.

7. Planning is essential.

ILLUSTRATION: FERNOW AND PINCHOT—EARLY FORESTRY PROMOTERS

The use of public relations and the media is an integral part of American forestry. Bernhard Fernow, chief of the Department of Agriculture's Division of Forestry from 1886 to 1898, and Gifford Pinchot, who followed Fernow in that position and then became the first chief of the Forest Service, respectively illustrate ineffective and effective use of public relations.

First, let's consider the case of Fernow's public relations failure. Fernow knew how to use print media effectively, but he used them primarily to create and disseminate information on trees and their use. In total, some 6000 pages of government publications, including 40 bulletins, 20 circulars, and annual reports, produced an embryonic national awareness of forestry by 1898 under Fernow's leadership (Ponder 1987). The number of reports was a trifle compared to the deluge that would follow during the Pinchot years.

When Fernow left the reins of the Division of Forestry to Pinchot in 1898, he became dean of the first forestry college in the United States at Cornell University in upstate New York. Enrollment grew quickly, exceeding the largest forestry schools of France—where Pinchot, an American educated at Yale, received his abbreviated forestry training in 1889–1890; and Germany, where Fernow, a Prussian, received his training before his love for a Philadelphian woman brought him to America in 1876 (Behan 1975, Fazio and Gilbert 1981, Pinchot 1947).

Fernow acquired for Cornell a 30,000-acre tract of land in the Adirondack Mountains to be used for demonstration purposes, much like the school forests administered by many universities today. The forest was dominated by low-grade hardwoods with a mixture of spruce. Fernow designed a series of 30 different cutting systems to demonstrate scientific forestry, obtain new knowledge, and achieve his goal of reconstructing the forest to produce the largest amount of the most useful wood. Fernow acknowledged aesthetic and recreation values of the forest, but he regarded them as secondary to wood production. His plan, begun in 1899, would require 15 to 30 years to implement, at which time the forest would become financially self-supporting (Fazio and Gilbert 1981).

Although the Cornell forest was isolated, it did have neighbors, some of whom were wealthy and influential. They were displeased with the noise, smoke, and fire danger brought to the woods (their favorite hunting ground) by Cornell's forestry expert. Their outcry found its way into the newspapers and reached the governor. The concern focused on the intentional "denuding" of the land. Cornell's president supported Fernow's actions. But when the appropriation bill for Cornell reached the governor's desk the next year, he vetoed funds for the school. With the stroke of a pen, the New York State College of Forestry at Cornell ceased to exist,

and Fernow was out of a job. Years later, a forestry school was reinstituted in New York, but at Syracuse, not Cornell (Fazio and Gilbert 1981).

The public relations lesson here is that the media did not report the scientific merits of Fernow's efforts, but the outcry of the Cornell forest's neighbors. To both Behan (1975) and Duerr (1986), this classic example illustrates the danger of relying too heavily on technical resource management. Fernow went wrong by applying traditional European rules to an American situation. He wrote to one of his former professors in Germany, asking his opinion. The reply was, "Your management plan was obviously sound. Laymen ignorant of forestry shouldn't interfere. The episode exposes the shady side of the much-praised democratic system" (Duerr 1986, p. 21).

Two bits of wisdom may be gleaned from this example. First, per philosopher George Santayana's sage advice: Those who ignore the failures of the past are doomed to repeat them. Second, an adaptation of Santayana: Those who try to emulate the successes of the past should be mindful that the programs and policies of the past will be evaluated with the criteria of the present.

Now let's turn to Pinchot's success story in public relations and effective use of the media. When he took over Fernow's position as chief of the Division of Forestry in 1898, Pinchot sought to transfer the nation's forest reserves from the Department of the Interior to his own Department of Agriculture. He succeeded in 1905, but not by any accident or fortuitous circumstance. He campaigned for his goal and understood the need for a constant flow of publicity. Pinchot repeatedly overcame opposition by using personal letters, leaflets, circulars, and a constant stream of news releases. Each month, an estimated 30 to 50 million newspaper copies carried forestry items (Fazio and Gilbert 1981).

Pinchot's skillful publicity campaign for government forestry promoted his doctrine of utilitarian conservation at the expense of the preservationists, led by John Muir. Pinchot's efforts also provide a benchmark in the important historical development of the role of the executive branch in leading public opinion. Pres. Theodore Roosevelt and Pinchot not only promoted utilitarian conservation, but also turned it into a crusade. Pinchot's aggressive use of government resources to present his conservation policy to newspapers and magazines in a form acceptable as news allowed Pinchot to dominate natural resources management discussions at the beginning of the twentieth century and to remain an influence in those discussions today. But alas, Pinchot's use of the media may have been his undoing as well. His later attacks against Secretary of the Interior Ballinger, carried on in the media, are cited as one reason why he was fired by President Taft in 1910 from his position as the first chief of the USDA Forest Service (Ponder 1987).

RESOURCE MANAGERS' PUBLIC IMAGE

Many if not most forestry and wildlife professionals feel that they have a negative public image. Innumerable cartoons about clearcuts, dead owls, frightened animals and the like are rampant on the comics and editorial pages of newspapers. The animal rights movement has besmirched the reputation of wildlife managers and fur growers, casting them in as dark a light as loggers and foresters who practice clear-cutting.

The forestry profession has tried to enhance its image through many public relations campaigns. The Forest Service initiated a "Forests for US" campaign in the 1980s, and the American Forestry Association started a "Friends of the National Forest" campaign to improve public understanding at the local level (Sampson 1988). As mentioned, the Society of American Foresters' public relations campaigns also are designed to promote professional management. So are the efforts of forest industry and many local professional groups.

If foresters often are equated with loggers in the public's mind, the fate of wildlife managers may be even worse. The evolution of wildlife policy, described in Chapter 15, has

been paralleled by the evolution of animal rights and antihunting groups. Constant criticism has put the ethics of hunting into the national spotlight.

The attacks of animal rights advocates on hunting and scientific research using animals is intense and is accompanied by graphic language, photos, and images of the plight of helpless dead animals. For example, an *Esquire* article on "The Killing Game" (Williams 1990) excoriated hunters. The polemic exposed "why the American hunter is bloodthirsty, piggish, and grossly incompetent." Two captions in the article stated that "The chief attraction of hunting is the pursuit and murder of animals" and "Sport hunting is immoral. Hunters are persecutors to be prosecuted." Not only did Williams oppose hunting, she also criticized wildlife management, wildlife refuges and restoration, and hunting season mismanagement, damning the profession as well as the hunters. A 1990 cover story in *U.S. News and World Report* discussed the "American Hunter Under Fire," and "Uncle Sam's War on Wildlife" (Satchell 1990).

Many different animal rights groups oppose hunting, research, or fur-growing. People for Ethical Treatment of Animals (PETA) has a membership of more than 200,000 and a budget of several million dollars. Friends of Animals organized active opposition to hunting and the fur trade in the 1980s. Many groups oppose hunting in other areas, including Europe, Africa, Asia, and South America. Tactics of antihunting groups have included harassment of hunters and scaring game in the field. Those opposing animal research have broken into research labs, freed animals, and destroyed equipment. Fur-free Friday has been sponsored yearly since 1986 by animal rights activists, on the Friday after Thanksgiving. Radicals have begun throwing red paint on furs (to symbolize blood) and carrying leghold traps to protest at wildlife meetings.

Hunters, fish and game managers, fur growers, and scientists all receive adverse publicity from these groups. Certainly the groups have valid points—crippling game by accident is unfortunate, using leghold traps is inhumane, and giving cancer to monkeys seems cruel as does confining minks in pens. The challenge for resource managers and scientists is to develop successful publicity campaigns illustrating that the benefits of controlling game populations, avoiding synthetic (oil-based) fabrics, and curing illness and avoiding death of people outweigh the discomfort or death of animals.

PROFESSIONALS AND THE MEDIA

Part of the public image problem of foresters and wildlifers is the way the media depict resource management. Part of the solution therefore rests in changing how the media portray resource issues. Professional managers and societies must learn to anticipate controversy and seek out the news media instead of waiting to react to emotional charges with facts and figures. They must take the offensive rather than defend themselves.

News gathering is not the same as truth seeking. Journalists have many limitations, so what we get as news consumers are selected facts. News is not just a reflection of what is happening around us, but a manufactured report of selected events. News is tailored to the medium that will deliver it, the audience that will hear it, and the news organization that will produce it (DeFleur and Dennis 1988).

Natural resource managers often are frustrated with the mass media, especially with news reporters. "I didn't say that!" or "I was misquoted!" are common statements, which may result from adversarial contacts or too few contacts *before* crises erupt. Resource agencies need publicity to convey their message to the public. The media need news, and resource agencies are engaged in interesting and sometimes exciting stories, which are the raw material of the media. There is an opportunity for a mutually beneficial relationship (Fazio and Gilbert 1981).

But as information moves from a scientific environment into the media environment, it inevitably suffers alteration and filtration that will affect public perceptions. Three major problems result from the media's filtration process: (1) The public's level of anxiety is raised through the media's attempt to create suspense; (2) false or inaccurate information may be conveyed and may persist; and (3) scientific knowledge may be misinterpreted or misrepresented. These problems can occur innocently, accidently, or purposely. Scientists or technical specialists and media representatives must learn to work together. The technocrat has to try to simplify without overgeneralizing. The reporter has to learn to differentiate between fact and fantasy without missing a deadline. The public has to use its intelligence (Baskerville and Brown 1985).

In regard to some environmental issues, Singer (1987) says that scientists are perhaps as guilty as the media of distorting issues and have frightened the public with prophecies of impending doom. There are many examples of such issues: timber famine, nuclear winter, depletion of the ozone layer, the "ozone hole" over the Antarctic, the supersonic transport (SST) debate of the 1970s, and now, global warming. Scientists have a responsibility to be voices of reason, not of alarm (Singer 1987). The same is true of natural resource managers.

Since the 1960s the public no longer is reluctant to speak out on complex resource management issues. Foresters and wildlifers have been reluctant to express their views and have not always made the effort to understand public needs. They must be willing to do this if the public is to be convinced that they have the ability to get the job done. Many people view natural resource management as "evil" manipulation. Only effective communication can change these opinions.

Use of Symbols

When our natural resources face an apparent crisis—forest fire, flood, the logger's saw, pollution—the media pay attention. Symbols are very effective in attracting the media to an issue. Few people can think far enough ahead to see how a forest will change over decades and centuries; everyone can imagine the walls of flame and clouds of thick smoke generated by forest fires. Few can appreciate the complexity of air pollution's effect on forests; everyone can understand the image of "acid rain" pouring from the sky on immobile trees.

Many interest groups use symbols to attract the media. The militant Earth First! group uses large banners at their demonstrations: "Save this Forest," "Save Our Old Growth," "Ax Maxxam," "Save the Redwoods," "Pacific Lumber Stop the Plunder," "Stop the Tree Crusher," "Stop the Tree Nazis" (Klimko 1986, Miles 1987, Mitchell 1988, Russell 1988). The Rainforest Action Network affixed a huge 20 by 30-foot banner to the side of the World Bank building in 1986, proclaiming that the "World Bank Destroys Tropical Rainforests" (Russell 1988). The World Bank now at least seems to be more sensitive to the environmental impacts of economic development projects and has hired more ecologists for project reviews. Loggers have effectively used banners and large posters when they assemble their rolling stock in protest of environmental activism. Signs such as "Timber, our life blood" and "Wilderness—Land of No Uses" help attract media attention (Gale 1987, Simons 1988).

Foresters have effectively used symbols, most notably Smokey the Bear, to deliver messages to the public. Other positive symbols of forestry—Spunky Squirrel, Lassie, Mark Trail, and actor Ralph Waite—have helped sell forestry and wildlife conservation (Hendee 1984). More recently, Andy Griffith and Jimmy and Rosalyn Carter have touted the benefits of tree farming. Former President Carter has had his tree farm certified in the American Forest Council's Tree Farm system.

But these efforts may be too staid to attract the mass media and the general public. According to Michael McCloskey, the Sierra Club tries to sensationalize issues so that constituencies interested in environmental protection can be mobilized to persuade their governmental representatives to get Congress to "vote right" on issues—to pursue what the Sierra Club thinks are the best policies. To move people to that point, they must be motivated by appeals to their convictions and to their commitments (Petersen 1982).

Meet the Press

To avoid frustration when dealing with media representatives, natural resource managers need to meet the press with confidence. Remember that the function of the press is to inform the public. Reporters are most sympathetic to people who bring them the story first. Natural resource managers would do well to follow these preparatory tips in dealing with the media (Anonymous 1980, Barber 1982):

- Check your attitude
    —recognize the public's need to know
    —understand reporters' problems
- Get ready
    —get the facts straight
    —brace for controversy
    —prepare to do some teaching
- What to do at an interview
    —get important points across first
    —do not put on airs
    —do not be on the defensive
- Relax and be yourself
    —speak for yourself
    —make your points
    —make yourself clear
    —do not fake it
    —do not say anything "off the record"
    —tell the truth, always
    —do not rise to the bait
    —offer to check the transcript for technical accuracy
    —maintain a professional attitude
    —do not lobby for your employer

These tips for dealing with the media in an interview also will help the natural resource manager prepare for any public contact. Foresters may directly influence policy as expert witnesses in a courtroom setting or a legislative hearing. In these situations, Appler (1982) offers some advice: Be qualified, prepared, and careful. Managers need to listen carefully, respond only to the question that is asked, and be sure the question is understood before an answer is given. Above all else, they need to be themselves. Their greatest assets are their ability, experience, and judgment.

MEDIA EFFECTIVENESS

How influential are the media? They are omnipresent in our life. Are they omnipotent as well? Do they not only sell goods, but also mold opinions and shape action? Or do they merely report and sensationalize contemporary trends that would occur with or without their participation?

MEDIA POWER RESEARCH

Many studies have examined the effectiveness of the media in influencing opinions during three time periods. The first extended from the turn of the century until the late 1930s (McQuail 1983). Theories and research during this time credited the media with considerable power to shape opinion and belief, change habits of life, and actively mold behavior more or less according to the will of those who controlled the media and their content. These views were not based on scientific research, but on observation of the enormous popularity of the press, the news media, radio, and film as well as their intrusion on daily life. These beliefs were shared and reinforced by advertisers and by government propagandists during World War I (Bauer and Bauer 1960).

The possibilities of using film and other media for active persuasion or information were studied in the 1930s, 1940s, and 1950s. Klapper (1960) summarized this second research phase and concluded that the use of mass media alone was not enough to cause people to change opinions or to induce action. Instead, media acted in concert with other influential social and cultural factors. Media research during the 1930s to 1950s could find no specific short-term cause-and-effect relationship between media presentations and public responses.

The third and current phase of media research, begun in 1960, has suggested that the power of the media to influence people has become more significant. Indeed, the effect of the media in arousing opposition to the Vietnam War and in publicizing environmental concerns suggests that this is the case. Studies in the 1940s and 1950s measured immediate effects of the media in changing personal beliefs or actions. Modern research has suggested that media effects are more subtle and long term in nature (McQuail 1983).

Media may have several long-term effects on people. Media advertising is intended to change some people's opinions and actions. Media may create effects that are external to its message or even negative backlashes against perceived distortions or bias. For example, charges of liberal bias in reporting may have weakened the media's credibility in attacking President Reagan's conservative agenda and his prodevelopment policies. Media may enhance feelings, make changes occur faster, or confirm existing beliefs and policies. Media may be used to block or prevent change as well (McQuail 1983).

AGENDA SETTING

In fostering long-term change, the media serve an agenda-setting role (McCombs and Shaw 1972). Agenda setting suggests that the power of the media lies not in telling people what to think, but rather selectively reporting facts and issues about which to think. By so doing, media set the general agenda of items considered worthy of public debate, action, and policy-making. Empirical studies have shown that media have the ability to direct attention and to affect cognition—the selective awareness of public issues—but proving direct cause and effect remains difficult (Lowery and DeFleur 1988).

The agenda-setting theories of media effectiveness conform well with the issue expansion process discussed earlier in Chapter 4. To change policies, an awareness of the problem is developed first as a systemic or general agenda issue, and then efforts are made to get that issue placed on a specific agenda for action. Intuitively, the media have an important role in this process. For example, based on his experiences in promoting forestry in the United States, Gifford Pinchot said that one should "Use the press first, last, and all the time if you want to reach the public." Public awareness is the first step toward public policy.

A prominent theory about how the media influence public opinion is termed the *spiral of silence* (Noelle-Neumann 1974). Most people have a natural fear of being isolated in their opinions and actions and will try to identify and then follow the majority opinion or consensus. The main source of information about such a consensus will be media journalists, who have considerable power to define and promulgate the "majority climate of opinion." The more dominant the version of the consensus opinion disseminated, the more individual voices of dissent will remain silent— hence a "spiraling" process.

The media help define and structure reality by their bias, be it unwitting or purposeful. The presence of television cameras always sparks exaggerated actions on the part of protestors, political aspirants, and issue creators. Many "pseudo-events" are created to manufacture impressions for the public. Just as the media may manipulate the public, the public may manipulate the media. For example, both Presidents Reagan and Bush choreographed their public images, taking advantage of the media as well as being subjects of media attention.

FORESTRY AND WILDLIFE INFLUENCES

How influential are the media in forestry and wildlife? In reply to that question, Burch (1977) suggested avoiding two conceptual errors regarding news media and the press.

One erroneous school of thought holds that the press is relatively unimportant and that newspapers are merely ordered gossip generating handsome financial returns (Burch 1977). This jaundiced view is extreme and can be refuted with some classic forestry examples. Through the clever use of the popular and scientific press, Gifford Pinchot and Theodore Roosevelt fostered the conservation movement in the first decade of the twentieth century. Later in his career, Pinchot

made astute use of the media. He campaigned for and was elected governor of Pennsylvania in 1924 on the theme "Get the farmer out of the mud." During his term of office, he proceeded to pave every pigpath in the state. For decades afterwards, blacktop roads still were called "Pinchot roads" in rural Pennsylvania.

A second error regarding the press is to assume that it has enormous power to influence public opinion (Burch 1977). Presidential elections refute this thesis. In 1948 only 15 percent of the newspapers in the United States endorsed Harry Truman; 65 percent endorsed Dewey; Truman was elected president. In the 1960s and 1970s most newspapers favored Republican platforms and candidates. However, the majority of voters were Democrats. One poll in 1980 found that 87 percent of the newspaper reporters favored President Carter, the incumbent; Ronald Reagan was elected president. A more graphic illustration of the failure of the media occurred in Eastern Europe in 1989 and Russia in 1991. Even after four decades of media saturation and propaganda, young and old people alike rejected the tenets of communism as a political or economic system and sought free elections, free expression, and freer markets. As another example, the *Atlanta Journal/Atlanta Constitution* ran a series of front-page articles in 1990 blasting a proposed tax change, calling it a "Tax Break for the Timber Barons." Despite the adverse publicity, a constitutional amendment authorizing such a change was approved in a statewide referendum by 60 percent of the votes cast.

Arnold (1982) claims that many news media have a liberal bias. Research results cited by Arnold reveal that 80 percent of the 240 journalists and broadcasters surveyed in a 1981 had voted "liberal" in the last four presidential elections. More than half of those surveyed agreed with the statement that "The United States exploits the Third World and causes poverty"; more than half agreed that the use of natural resources by the United States is "immoral" (Lichter and Rothmann 1981). These biases suggest that the media will tend to favor resource preservation, not use or management, in their news coverage.

Even so, Behan (1977) believes that the press affects the power system somewhat, but is apt to be largely ignored by the mass public. Forestry news is often rather dull compared with other stories and usually affects fewer people than problems in large urban areas. Thus, news coverage of forestry issues will be more limited and probably not have much effect on forestry policy (Behan 1977, Burch 1977). Environmental issues with a forestry component, such as acid rain, tropical deforestation, and global climate change, are becoming much more newsworthy now.

Overall, the media, particularly newspapers and magazines, will have some effect on forest resource issues, but they probably will not govern the outcome. The media will continue to make celebrities of creative persons who articulate emerging concerns in society—such as Gifford Pinchot, Rachel Carson, Ralph Nader, or Chico Mendes, who was assassinated for opposing tropical deforestation in Brazil (Brooke 1989). The media can serve as a conduit for increasing the controversy that polarizes issues. It also will continue to validate and enhance social movements related to forestry. It will tend to be more influential with politicians, bureaucrats, and academics than with the masses. Like all modern institutions, it will not be completely trusted, but it will still have some effect on policy outcomes (Burch 1977).

SUMMARY

The mass media are pervasive and influential participants in our lives and in the political process. Media report and interpret news; advertise goods, services, and politicians; promote good public relations; educate people; and provide entertainment. Media include print media (newspapers, magazines, and books), broadcast media (radio and television), and entertainment or recording media (movies, videotapes, and music).

The mass media are involved in forest resource management concerns in varying degrees. Environmental and natural resource issues often are covered in news and inter-

pretative media. Broadcast news media probably cover resource issues to a lesser extent because they are often less eye-appealing. Wildlife, hunting, and fishing programs, however, are common on network and public TV. Broadcast media and music recordings also have been influential in setting the agenda for much of contemporary American politics, including the environmental movement. Popular movies deal with forestry and wildlife topics only infrequently, seldom attaining a great mass appeal.

Forestry and wildlife interests rely on the mass media to convey their messages about resource management. Forest products companies advertise their products and promote their image in the media. Wildlife conservation groups rely on prevailing favorable opinions and public relations to promote their goals. In general, the media are effective in enhancing existing predilections about resource policy and helping to set the public agenda. Media are relied on extensively by interest groups trying to protect trees and animals, and with some success. Media seem to favor environmental protection and thus will help foster favorable public opinion of programs to promote and enhance environmental quality.

LITERATURE CITED

Abbey, Edward. 1968. Desert Solitaire: A Season in the Wilderness. McGraw-Hill. New York. 269 pp.

Abbey, Edward. 1975. The Monkey Wrench Gang. Lippincott. Philadelphia. 352 pp.

Ahlfeld, Bill. 1987. Ancient redwoods and a modern merger—A story that pits facts versus emotion. *Forestry Industry Affairs Newsletter* 20(15):1–4.

American Forest Council. 1989. By 1945, America's forests will be history. *National Geographic* 176(4): facing back cover.

Anderberg, Robert K. 1988a. Wall Street sleaze: How the hostile takeover of Pacific Lumber led to the clear-cutting of coastal redwoods. *Amicus Journal* 10(2):8–10.

Anderberg, Robert K. 1988b. Pacific Lumber's liquidation plans delayed. *Amicus Journal* 10(4):7.

Anonymous. 1980. Foresters, meet the press. *Forestry Chronicle* 56(6):287–288.

Appler, Charles I. 1982. The forester as an expert witness: Some tips on litigation. *Southern Journal of Applied Forestry* 7(3): 170–173.

Arnold, Ron. 1982. At the Eye of the Storm: James Watt and the Environmentalists. Regnery Gateway. Chicago. 282 pp.

Associated Press. 1990. Herbicides linked to cancer in military dogs. *New York Times* 39(48, 272): A18, June 20.

Barber, John C. 1982. How we can control a media burn. *Journal of Forestry* 80(11):700.

Baskerville, G. I. and K. L. Brown. 1985. The different worlds of scientists and reporters. *Journal of Forestry* 83(8):490–493.

Bauer, R. A. and A. Bauer. 1960. America, mass society, and mass media. *Journal of Social Issues* 10(3):3–66.

Beck, Melinda, Mary Hager, Jeff B. Copeland, Darby Junkin, Shawn Doherty, and Peter McAlevey. 1983. Battle over the wilderness. *Newsweek* 102(4):22–30, July 25.

Behan, Richard W. 1975. Forestry and the end of innocence. *American Forests* 81(5):16–19, 38–49.

Behan, Richard W. 1977. A political, historical, and irresponsible view of the forest policymaking process. Pp. 125–132 in Frank J. Convery and Jean E. Davis (eds.), Centers of Influence and U.S. Forest Policy. Duke University, School of Forestry and Environmental Studies. Durham, NC.

Boerner, Deborah A. 1988. Tarzan's jungle and other misconceptions. *American Forests* 94(11,12):15, 76–77.

Bronstein, Scott. 1992. Ads attempt to pressure Bush to attend Earth Summit. *The Atlanta Journal/The Atlanta Constitution*, April 21, p. A9.

Brooke, James. 1989. In death, Brazilian [leader of rubber tappers] inspires a script. *New York Times*, April 12, p. 5.

Burch, William R., Jr. 1977. The influence of the press on U.S. forest policy. Pp. 133–136 in Frank J. Convery and Jean E. Davis (eds.), Centers of Influence and U.S. Forest Policy. Duke University, School of Forestry and Environmental Studies. Durham, NC.

Carson, Rachel. 1962. Silent Spring. Houghton Mifflin. Boston. 368 pp.

Commoner, Barry. 1971. The Closing Circle: Nature, Man, and Technology. Knopf. New York. 326 pp.

Connaughton, Charles A. 1982. Planning a public-relations program. Pp. 391–402 in Frank J. Convery and Jean E. Davis (eds.), Centers of Influence and U.S. Forest Policy. Duke University School of Forestry and Environmental Studies. Durham, NC.

DeFleur, Melvin L., and Everette E. Dennis. 1988. Understanding Mass Communication, 3rd ed. Houghton Mifflin. Boston. 565 pp.

Deurr, William A. 1986. Forestry's upheaval: Are advances in Western civilization redefining the profession? *Journal of Forestry* 84(1):20–26.

Dunster, Julian A. 1987. Forestry conflicts in Canada. *Ambio, A Journal of the Human Environment* 16(1):59–63.

Ehrlich, Paul R. 1968. The Population Bomb. Ballantine. New York. 223 pp. (Also published in 1969 as a Sierra Club book.)

Eliot, John L. 1982. T.R.'s wilderness legacy. *National Geographic* 162(3):340–363.

Fazio, James R., and Douglas L. Gilbert. 1981. Public Relations and Communications for Natural Resource Managers. Kendall/Hunt. Dubuque, IA. 375 pp.

Findley, Rowe 1982. Our national forests: Problems in paradise. *National Geographic* 162(3):307–339.

Force, Jo Ellen, and Kevin L. Williams. 1989. A profile of national forest planning participants. *Journal of Forestry* 87(1):33–38.

Fortmann, Louise. 1987. At issue: People and processes in forest protest. *American Forests* 93(3,4):12–13, 56–57.

Gale, Richard P. 1987. The U.S. Forest Service and the evolution of the environmental movement. *Western Wildlands* 11(4):22–26.

Garlington, Phil. 1988. The predator's maul: California's last giant redwoods can stand up to anything except a Wall Street raid. *Outside* 13(12):38–42ff.

Grier, Norma. 1985. At issue: Herbicides in forestry—Risks, benefits, perspectives. *American Forests* 91(11):10, 58.

Hays, Samuel P. 1987. Beauty, Health, and Permanence: Environmental Politics in the United States, 1955–1985. Cambridge University Press. New York. 630 pp.

Hendee, John C. 1984. Public opinion, and what foresters should do about it. *Journal of Forestry* 82(6):340–344.

Hiebert, Ray Eldon, Donald F. Ungurait, and Thomas W. Bohn. 1988. Mass Media, 5th ed. Longman. New York. 721 pp.

Irland, Lloyd C. 1983. Pesticides: Ethical problems for foresters. *Consultant* 28(1): 17–20.

Klapper, Joseph T. 1960. The Effects of Mass Communication. Free Press. New York. 302 pp.

Klimko, Frank. 1986. Six arrested in protest against tree burning. *Houston Chronicle,* October 22, pp. 1, 10.

Lasswell, Harold D. 1927. Propaganda Technique in the World War. Peter Smith. New York. 233 pp.

Lautenschlager, R. A. 1985. Herbicides and the media. *American Forests* 91(11):47.

Leopold, Aldo. 1949. A Sand County Almanac, and Sketches Here and There. Oxford University Press. New York. 226 pp. (Also published in 1970 as a Sierra Club book by Ballantine, New York.)

Lichter, S. Robert, and Stanley Rothmann. 1981. Media and business elites. *Public Opinion* 4(5):42–46, 59–60.

Lowery, Shearon A., and Melvin L. DeFleur. 1988. Milestones in Mass Communication Research, 2nd ed. Longman. New York. 472 pp.

Marcouiller, David W., and Paul V. Ellefson. 1987. Forest land use and management conflicts: A review and evaluation of approaches for management. University of Minnesota, Dept. of Forest Resources Staff Paper No. 65 College of Forestry. St. Paul. 70 pp.

McCombs, Maxwell E., and Donald L. Shaw. 1972. The agenda-setting function of the mass media. *Public Opinion Quarterly* 36(2):176–187.

McKibben, Bill. 1989. The End of Nature. Random House. New York. 226 pp.

McPhee, John. 1971. Encounters with the Archdruid. Farrar, Strauss, and Giroux. New York. 245 pp.

McQuail, Dennis. 1983. Mass Communication Theory: An Introduction. Sage. Beverly Hills, CA. 245 pp.

Meadows, Donnella H., Dennis L. Meadows, Jorgen Randers, and William W. Behrens III. 1972. The Limits to Growth. Signet Publishing/New American Library. New York. 207 pp.

Miles, Bruce R. 1987. Environmental issues and the press. *Forest Farmer* (Manual Edition) 46(5):48–49.

Mitchell, John G. 1988. Tree-sitters protest as old redwoods fall to corporate raider. *Audubon* 90(5):78–79.

Noelle-Neumann, Elisabeth. 1974. The spiral of silence: A theory of public opinion. *Journal of Communication* 24(2):43–51.

Passing the buck. Periscope. 1992. *Newsweek,* April 27, p. 3.

Petersen, Philip V. 1982. An interview with Sierra Club Executive Director J. Michael McCloskey. *Journal of Forestry* 80(5): 276–279.

Pinchot, Gifford. 1947. Breaking New Ground. Harcourt, Brace, and Company. New York. 522 pp.

Ponder, Stephen. 1987. Gifford Pinchot: Press agent for forestry. *Journal of Forest History* 31(1):26–35.

Russell, Dick. 1988. The monkeywrenchers. *Amicus Journal* 9(4):28–42.

SAF. 1983. "Trees don't just drink water, they clean it." [Advertisement] *Journal of Forestry* 81(6):391.

Sampson, Neil. 1988. A new charter for the National Forests? *American Forests* 94(5,6):17–20.

Satchell, Michael. 1990. The American hunter under fire. *U.S. News and World Report*, February 5, pp. 31–36.

Schectman, Susan M. 1978. The "Bambi syndrome": How NEPA's public participation in wildlife management is hurting the environment. *Environmental Law* 8(2): 611–643.

Severin, Werner J., with James W. Tankard, Jr. 1988. Communication Theories: Origins, Methods, Uses, 2nd ed. Longman. New York. 351 pp.

Simons, Jay. 1988. The great Northwest log haul. *American Forests* 94(9,10):17–20.

Singer, S. Fred. 1987. My turn: Lowering the gloom—too many scientists have learned the political lesson that frightening the public gets results. *Newsweek,* September 14, p. 12.

Spurr, Stephen H. 1977. Use of professional forestry competence by the judiciary. Pp. 72–75 in Dennis C. Le Master and Luke Popovich (eds.), Crisis in Federal Forest Land Management. Society of American Foresters. Bethesda, MD.

Stegner, Wallace. 1985. Living on our principal. *Wilderness* 48(168):15–21.

Stiak, Jim. 1988. The pesticide wars: A grassroots coalition takes on the industry. *Amicus Journal* 10(3):8–9.

Stokes, C. Shannon, and Kathy Brace. 1988. Agricultural chemical use and cancer mortality in selected rural counties in the U.S.A. *Journal of Rural Studies* 4(3):239–247.

Suess, Dr., and A. S. Geisel. 1971. The Lorax. Random House. New York. 61 pp.

Turque, Bill. 1991. The war for the West. *Newsweek* 118(14):18–32.

Udall, Stewart L. 1963. The Quiet Crisis. Holt, Rinehart & Winston. New York. 209 pp.

USDA Forest Service. 1988. Let us tell you about America's "Forever Forests." [Advertisements] *American Forests* 94(1,2):16; 94(5,6):11.

Walstad, John D., and Frank N. Dost. 1986. All the king's horses and all the king's men: The lessons of 2,4,5-T. *Journal of Forestry* 84(9):28–32.

Weesner, Margaret. 1983. Land managers and the public: The herbicide protests. *Western Wildlands* 9(1):30–33.

Williams, Joy. 1990. The killing game. *Esquire*, October, pp. 113–128.

Witt, Terry. 1985. At issue: Herbicides in forestry—Risks, benefits, perspectives. *American Forests* 91(11):11, 50–51.

PART III

PROGRAMS

Chapter 12

Public Ownership and Management of Land

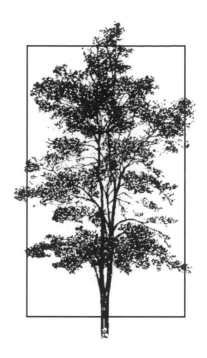

The scenic splendors of Yellowstone, the arid lands of the Desert Game Range in Nevada, sand dunes on the Pea Island National Wildlife Refuge in North Carolina, a mountain meadow in the Deschutes National Forest in the Pacific Northwest—these are typical of the contrasting nature of land types held by the federal government. Some lands were reserved from general disposal; others were purchased for particular purposes; and still others remained in public ownership when otherwise available to private owners, because of their low apparent value.

—Marion Clawson and Burnell Held 1957

INTRODUCTION

Ownership and management of public land via governmental agencies is one broad means of implementing resource policy. Public ownership implies that the resources associated with the public lands will be allocated largely by political processes, not private markets. Some government agency is responsible for the management and use of all public lands in the United States.

Public lands provide a wealth of both market and nonmarket goods. One can use the types of goods classification scheme discussed in Chapter 3 (Savas 1982) to note the diversity of goods produced on public lands. First, they produce private goods, such as timber or minerals, that can be and are distributed through the market system. Second, they produce toll goods, such as wildlife man-

agement areas or national parks, that individual hunters or recreationists may use jointly, and where exclusion is possible. They also produce common-pool goods such as open range, salmon, or elk that are hard to exclude from individual use. Public lands also contribute to collective goods, such as picturesque scenery and air and water pollution control.

The public owns roughly 36 percent of the nation's land. The federal government holds 29 percent, and state and local governments 7 percent. Native Americans hold 2 percent of the nation's land area, but this is not considered public lands. Private landowners hold the remaining 62 percent of the U.S. forest land (Statistical Abstract of the United States 1989, U.S. General Services Administration 1989). As Clawson and Held (1957) suggested in the opening quote for this chapter, the reasons for public ownership vary widely. So do the diverse goods and services provided by these public lands. Furthermore, so do the laws and policies that govern the use and management of public lands.

These laws and policies are an expression of and are guided by the public interest (Coggins and Wilkinson 1987). However, the public interest cannot always be definitely determined (Worrell 1970). Nonetheless, policymakers try to balance the many products and values associated with public lands with what they perceive the public interest to be. The task is daunting and among the most difficult public policy problems because public lands are vast and provide a wide variety of resources, each with its own subset of issues and policies. For example, Coggins and Wilkinson (1987) structured two-thirds of their text on public land and resources law into chapters on individual resources: water, minerals, timber, range, wildlife, recreation, and preservation. Resolution of public land issues requires finding an acceptable balance of resource outputs. Each and every American has a stake in the outcome. These lands belong to all of us, and our tax dollars are used to manage them not only for our benefit, but also for our heirs as well. Thus federal public land issues produce intense conflicts and require resolution through the public policy process.

Much of the federal land holdings are reserved for natural resource purposes. The majority (56.7 percent) of the 662.2 million acres of federal land are used for forests and wildlife. A large portion is used for grazing (22.8 percent) and for parks and historic sites (14.7 percent). Military reservations and airfields make up 3 percent, and flood control, navigation, reclamation, and irrigation projects 1.7 percent. Other uses account for the remaining 1.1 percent of the federal acres (U.S. General Services Administration 1989).

This chapter reviews the development of public land ownership and management in the United States. Innumerable books and articles have been written about U.S. public lands. We provide an overview of the public lands, the agencies and laws governing their use, and a few brief summaries of current issues.

EARLY AMERICAN LAND POLICY

Early American land policy had its roots in European cultures, but developed some distinctly different branches. Native Americans generally used lands in the Americas as a commons, revering them as part of their spiritual beliefs. Native Americans practiced a nomadic type of sustained yield, often based on hunting, not farming. However, their sustainable practices probably were linked more to their small populations than to a particular conservation philosophy. The white colonial settlers brought with them a much different concept of land tenure and management.

The European countries fought for dominion over the New World based on the claims of their early explorers and their established settlements in the Americas. The British crown established 13 Atlantic Seaboard colonies, in part by setting up plantations for settlers. The lure of land was powerful to the colonists, who were usually fleeing from the English feudal tradition where a limited number of aristocratic families had controlled land resources for centuries. Land ownership became an important right in the colonies and drove the colonists to subdue the wilderness and defy British attempts to control colonial resource development. Contrary to the British traditions of careful husbandry, the colonists exploited natural resources wantonly, clearing land for farms and for producing wood, furs, fish, and tobacco for trade with England. The resources seemed limitless, and a colonist could always move to a new farm if the land gave out or game became scarce.

Land ownership and control were two of the reasons the colonists went to war with Britain, and they were explicitly protected in the U.S. Bill of Rights. Land ownership also was crucial in uniting the original 13 colonies. Six of the smaller colonies refused to ratify the original Articles of Confederation until Virginia, Massachusetts, and five other colonies yielded their extensive and overlapping western land claims to the Confederation Congress. To form a union, New York and Virginia gave in by 1781, and the Articles were then quickly ratified. Georgia finally complied in 1802, bringing the total amount of land ceded to the national government to 236 million acres between the Appalachians and the Mississippi River. This public domain formed a bond among the confederated states, provided the basis for settlement of many new states, and brought some sales revenue to the newly formed U.S. federal government (Arrandale 1983).

EXPANDING THE PUBLIC DOMAIN

The public domain expanded rapidly after the cessions of the original states (Table 12-1, Figure 12-1). With some initial reluctance, in 1803 President Jefferson negotiated the Louisiana Purchase with France and acquired the area extending from present-day Louisiana northwest to Montana. Florida and the western portion of the state of Louisiana were obtained in a treaty with Spain in 1819. The United States annexed Texas in 1845 and purchased a portion of Texas for the public domain in 1850. The Oregon Compromise of 1846 brought the present-day areas of Washington, Oregon, and Idaho under federal control as territories. After the Mexican war, most of present-day California, Nevada, Utah, Arizona, and New Mexico were ceded to the United States. Alaska was purchased from Russia in 1867, and Hawaii was annexed in 1898.

In total, public land acquisitions accounted for 1463 million acres, or 75.5 percent of the territory of the continental United States. The original 13 states totaled over 305 million acres, or an additional 15.7 percent of

TABLE 12-1.   Origin of Original Public Domain Lands

Land	Date of Acquisition	Total Area (land and water)	
		Million Acres	% of U.S. Continent
Original Public Domain			
Cessions by original states	1781–1802	237	12.2
Louisiana Purchase, Red River Basin	1803	560	28.9
Florida Purchase	1819	46	2.4
Oregon Compromise	1846	183	9.4
Mexican Treaty	1848	339	17.5
Purchase from Texas	1850	79	4.1
Gadsden Purchase	1853	19	1.0
Subtotal		1463	75.5
Never Public Domain:			
Original states		305	15.7
Texas		170	8.8
Subtotal		475	24.5
Total area of Continental United States		1937	100.0
Alaska	1867	375	—
Hawaii	1898	4	—
Total Area of United States (land and water)		2316	—

Source: Adapted from Table 1, Clawson and Held 1957, Statistical Abstract of the United States 1989. Totals may not equal column sums due to rounding.

Figure 12-1. Territorial Expansion of the United States
Source: Statistical Abstract of the United States 1989.

the land area. Finally, Texas added another 170 million acres (8.8 percent) to the territory (Waggener 1984).

The expansion of the public domain often resulted from wars (with the Native Americans, British, Spanish, Mexicans), and displacement of the Native American tribes through dubious treaties. For nearly a century after the adoption of the Constitution, the Native American tribes were legally regarded as sovereign nations residing within the limits of the United States, whose right of occupancy of their tribal lands could be legally adjusted only by treaty. However, continual pressure from settlers, harassment by and battles with the army, and violations of treaties eventually forced them from their na-

tive lands onto reservations (U.S. Department of the Interior 1976).

Tecumseh, Native American leader of the early 1800s, helped lead many nations to successfully oppose American expansion into Wisconsin in the decade before the War of 1812, but he was killed in battle by the forces of William Henry Harrison, later a U.S. president. The Seminole Indians in Florida also proved difficult to remove, even after a removal treaty of 1823. It was not until 1841, following the death of the resistance leader, Osceola, that most of the Seminoles were successfully removed from Florida. From 1825 to 1840 many other tribes were forced to move west by the signing of new treaties. The Creeks and the Cherokees were also removed from the Southeast by force, including the infamous forced march to Oklahoma in the winter of 1827 to 1828, called the Trail of Tears (U.S. Department of the Interior 1976). The continual breaking of treaties, forced displacement, and ongoing mismanagement of Native American lands continue to provide bases for animosity, public policy debates, and lawsuits over land tenure and resource management today.

DISPOSING OF THE PUBLIC LANDS

Although the U.S. government was eager to acquire all lands within its present borders, it was just as eager to sell or give those lands to private landowners or firms in order to spur development and generate revenues for the fledgling government (Table 12-2). At one time or another the federal government has held title to 82.5 percent of the land in the United States. Today 29 percent of the nation's land still remains in federal control; title to the remaining 53.5 percent of the land once held by the federal government has been transferred to private entities and state institutions for a variety of specific purposes based on encouraging or supporting the settlement of the American frontier.

The Land Ordinance of 1785 helped disposition efforts by establishing a means of selling national lands and of gaining clear land title. This included clearance of the Native American title, survey of the land, then public sale. The Public Land Survey that began in 1785 established the well-known method of dividing property into square sections (1 mile

TABLE 12-2. Public Land Disposals, 1781–1981

	Acres
Homesteaders	287,500,000
Railroads	94,400,000
Military veterans	61,000,000
Land grants to individuals by foreign governments before U.S. acquisition of territories	34,000,000
Sold or granted under 1873 Timber Culture Act	10,900,000
Sold under 1877 Desert Land Sales Act	10,700,000
Sold under 1878 Timber and Stone Act	13,900,000
State land grants	
to support common schools	77,600,000
to reclaim swamplands	64,900,000
to build railroads	37,100,000
to support universities, hospitals, asylums, and so on	21,700,000
for public improvements, reservoirs, irrigation	117,600,000
for canals and rivers	6,100,000
for wagon road construction	3,400,000
Total granted to states	328,400,000
Land sales, mineral claims and entries, other methods	303,500,000
Total land disposals	1,144,300,240

Source: Arrandale 1983.

square, 640 acres) and townships (6 miles square, 36 sections), departing from the traditional metes and bounds division that relied on physical landmarks and resulted in odd-shaped parcels. Quarter-sections or eighth-sections were common units for land sale.

The General Land Office was created as a branch of the Treasury Department in 1812 to help sell the public lands. Public land sales began to boom after 1820, when the price was set at $1.25 per acre and tracts as small as 80 acres (an eighth-section) could be purchased. The selling of land proved to be a fairly efficient, swift, and lucrative undertaking— immortalized by the idiom "doing a Land Office business" (U.S. Department of the Interior 1976). The sale of quarter-sections worked well in the East and the Midwest, where 160 acres could easily support a farm family. However, squatters and speculators still obtained a large portion of the land. In the Great Plains and the mountainous West, however, land sale procedures were much less successful because the land was too arid or rugged for farming, and other land disposal programs were initiated, as described below.

In 1862 Congress passed the Homestead Act, which granted free title of 160 acres to any citizen willing to settle the land and cultivate it for five years. Some 287 million acres were claimed by homesteaders. Congress also granted alternate sections of land adjoining the railroads to various companies, especially the Union Pacific and Central Pacific railroads. The railroad grants totaled more than 94 million acres when the last grant was made in 1871 (Arrandale 1983).

In total, the largest divestiture of federal land was made when states were admitted to the Union. The grants to the states were part of a political compromise under which newly admitted states agreed not to contest or tax the federal land holdings within their borders in exchange for school and other grant lands (Fairfax and Yale 1987, Gates 1968). Grants to the states totaled over 328 million acres (see Table 12-2), almost 15 percent of America's land. Grants to the states also were made to reclaim swamplands, to support universi-

ties and hospitals, to build reservoirs, and for other reasons. One type of grant to the states was for the specific purpose of supporting public education in the "common schools." Such grants totaled 77.6 million acres, almost 3.5 percent of America's land.

In an attempt to promote equity and harmony among the new states and the old, each state was given one-thirty-sixth of the land in the territory as school lands—specifically section 16 in each 36-square-mile township. With the admission of California in 1850, grants of one-eighteenth of the land (sections 16 and 36) were made to the new western states in appreciation of their vastness. Utah (1896) and New Mexico and Arizona (1912) received four sections per township (Fairfax and Yale 1987) because of the arid, and presumably less valuable, land in those territories (Bassett 1989).

Other programs listed in Table 12-2 also attempted to encourage public land development. The 1873 Timber Culture Act offered 160 acres to any person who would plant 40 acres with trees. The 1877 Desert Land Sales Act authorized sale of 640 acres to a settler who would irrigate it within three years. The 1872 Mining Law, still in effect in 1992, granted title to valuable minerals on public lands to any prospector who discovered a deposit and staked a claim. The law also offered full title to surrounding lands at $5.00 per acre. However, the 1872 law imposes no requirement that mineral production be proved within a stipulated time period following the staking of a claim. Consequently, thousands of acres of public land have become tied up in long-term nonproducing claims (U.S. Department of the Interior 1976).

ILLUSTRATION: LOOTING THE PUBLIC DOMAIN

Lawlessness prevailed as the public domain was transferred to private hands. As chronicled by Puter (1908/1972) in his classic *Looters of the Public Domain*, land frauds were common and widely known. The Timber and Stone Act of 1878, designed to transfer lands to individual farmers, resulted in a massive transfer of prime timberland to sawmillers and loggers at a fraction of its potential value (Alston 1983). Bernard Devoto (1953), an ardent conservationist with *Harper's* magazine in the 1950s, documented some of the frauds prevalent in the late 1800s. Such deceptions as placing a 12 by 14 *inch* cabin on forest land in order to acquire title were common under the act. Sometimes a more scrupulous corporation would build a genuine log cabin 12 by 14 feet and drive it from claim to claim or place it on the corner of four sections. Another swindle involved "bringing water to a tract" (by throwing cupfuls on it)—which was an improvement required of homesteaders—. "Shingled residences" were established on the land by fastening a shingle to a tent below the ridgepole. Often, "homesteaders" used aliases to obtain dozens of quarter-sections at $1.25 per acre by fraudulent means, waited the obligatory six months, and transferred the land to a corporation. Lumber companies could operate even more cheaply. Their employees could pay a claim location fee, perhaps about $16 per half-section, and the company could forthwith cut all the timber. Then they would let the claims lapse (Devoto 1953).

These deceptions were only a small part of the fraud that occurred. Devoto (1953, p. 58) writes that

These are typical, routine, second-magnitude land frauds in the history of the public domain out West—to describe the bigger ones would require too much space. Enough that in the golden age of landgrabs, the total area of the public domain proved up and lived on by actual homesteaders amounted to only a trivial fraction of the area fraudulently acquired by land companies, cattle companies, and lumber companies. Among the compelling reasons why the present public-land reserves had to be set aside was the headlong monopolization of the public domain that was threatening the West with peonage. Those reserves were also made to halt the waste of natural resources which the United States had dissipated more prodigally than any other nation. They had to be made so that a useful part of our national wealth could be preserved, developed, wisely managed, and intelligently used in future times. They had to be made so that the watersheds which control the destiny of the West could be safeguarded. But no one should forget for a moment that they were, besides, necessary to prevent Eastern and foreign corporations from taking over the whole West by fraud, bribery, and engineered bankruptcy.

Widespread problems such as these in the West led everyone but the beneficiaries to doubt the merits of laissez faire. As the United States became an industrial nation in the second half of the nineteenth century, large corporations began to dominate the economic and political scene throughout the country. Many people feared that too much economic power was becoming concentrated in the hands of the "robber barons." In particular, people feared that large corporations would take over public forest resources and destroy them for profit. By 1890 much of the public believed that large corporations should not be allowed to abridge the freedom of individuals. Followers of the progressive movement initiated and achieved laws (such as the Sherman Antitrust Act) designed to guarantee economic freedom in the marketplace by controlling power in big business and supporting small business (Alston 1983). At the same time as the calls for control of monopoly power, the growing conservation movement called for reservation of some public forest lands.

RETAINING PUBLIC LANDS

George Perkins Marsh, a scholar, diplomat, and Congress member who operated a sawmill in the Green Mountains of Vermont, triggered the first conservation movement with the publication of *Man and Nature* (Marsh 1864). The book examined history, geography, and ecology from the perspective of people's use and abuse of land and advocated land planning. Marsh attributed the fall of great ancient empires to human abuse of the land, and promoted preservation. He summed up his own thesis in words that could well relate to beliefs common today: "...we are never justified in assuming a force to be insignificant because its measure is unknown, or even because no physical effect can now be traced to it (p. 465)." He applied this rule to the destruction already visible in America's forest lands in the nineteenth century.

After a century of land sales and giveaways, dubious success of the existing programs in the West, and substantial demands for change in and out of government, Congress began to act to reverse federal land policies. In the 1870s a small movement started to protect some forested lands in the West from land sales. Carl Schurz, secretary of the Department of the Interior from 1877 to 1881, became a leading proponent of protection of forest lands via government control.

In 1877 Schurz stated in his annual report that "[The government] can preserve the forests still in its possession by keeping them under its control…all the timberlands still belonging to the United States should be withdrawn from the operation of the preemption and homestead laws" (Waggener 1984, p. 6).

The statement by Schurz reflected serious concerns with the federal disposition policies of the time. Free market advocates have criticized Schurz, calling him a German-influenced socialist (Dowdle 1984, Hanke 1984). Leman (1984) debunks such a caricature, noting that Schurz was a founder of the Republican party, a monetarist, a Civil War general, and a Missouri senator before arriving at Interior. Leman (1984, p. 99) continues, "His first statement as secretary was a promise to 'conduct this department upon business principles, and one of his first reforms was to institute a system of competitive bidding for government contracts.'"

Federal Forest Reserves

After considerable public debate regarding forest practices, Congress enacted the General Revision Act of 1891 in order to reverse the massive land disposal programs. Section 24 of the act was slipped into the bill in conference committee without being in either the House or Senate legislation of that year (Dana and Fairfax 1980). It authorized the president to "set apart and reserve, in any State or Territory having public lands wholly or in part covered with timber or undergrowth, [such lands] as forest reserves."

Despite the unusual insertion in conference committee, Section 24 was not a new concept. Dating back to 1871, there had been over 50 bills introduced into Congress to reserve timber or forests on the public domain, and three such versions of the law had passed the Senate, and one the House, in prior years. By the end of 1893, Presidents Harrison and Cleveland had set aside about 17.5 million acres. Most reservations established between 1891 and 1897 were created after petitions were submitted by local citizens. Thereafter Cleveland took no action because of the lack of provision for the protection or administration of the reserves.

In 1897, just before leaving office, President Cleveland issued a hastily developed proclamation creating 13 new reserves with a gross area of 21.3 million acres. He did not consult with representatives from many of the affected areas, so his proposal was received with an immediate, virtually unanimous burst of anger in Congress. Congress members debated revoking presidential authority to set aside reserves. But instead, they passed an amendment of the appropriations bill giving the president authority to modify the reserve boundaries to exclude towns, cities, or important developments—such as those Cleveland had included. However, Cleveland used a pocket veto on the entire appropriations bill, so the amendment did not pass (Dana and Fairfax 1980).

President McKinley placed a moratorium on creating new forest reserves immediately after taking office in 1897. Subsequent congressional appropriations legislation in the summer of 1897 finally provided authority for managing the forest reserves. The law, commonly referred to as the [Forest Service] Organic Act of 1897, defined the purpose of the forest reserves and authorized the secretary of the interior to establish rules for their utilization. The lands were to (1) be preserved and protected, (2) secure favorable conditions of water flows, and (3) furnish a continuous supply of timber for the use and necessities of the people of the United States. After the Organic Act, more reserves were established.

Roosevelt Expands the Reserves

Theodore Roosevelt (TR) became president when McKinley was assassinated in 1901, and the conservation movement remained on the national agenda for the duration of his presidency. Gifford Pinchot became a friend and confidante of Roosevelt's, and a leading force of the progressive conservation movement. Pinchot and TR collaborated to establish many more forest reserves in the West. Despite vocal opposition to his actions, Roosevelt set aside 95 million acres of reserves from 1901 to early 1907. As mentioned in Chapter 7, Congress enacted legislation in 1907 rescinding presidential authority to set aside national forests in the West. However, in the 10 days before signing the bill, TR, in collaboration with Pinchot, added another 16 million acres (McGeary 1960). Congress disputed his authority to do so. Pinchot (1947, p. 300) wrote that TR replied, "The opponents of the Forest Service turned handsprings in their wrath, and dire were their threats against the Executive; but the threats could not be carried out, and were really only a tribute to the efficiency of our action."

By 1907 President Roosevelt had increased the area in national forests from 38.8 to 140 million acres. He also worked with Pinchot to gain congressional passage of the Transfer Act of 1905, which authorized transfer of the forest reserves from the Department of the Interior to the Department of Agriculture. The reserves were renamed national forests in 1907, and the policy regarding their management shifted more toward one of "wise, scientific use" than one of preservation. The move to Agriculture was prompted by desires that forest reserves be less politicized, as was common in Interior, and more professionally managed. Friction between the agencies has continued since that time.

EASTERN NATIONAL FOREST PURCHASES

Large areas of the West were placed into forest reserves, but conservationists felt that the East was neglected. Most of the lands in the East were privately owned and had been cut over and left barren. Devastating forest fires were common. Millions of acres were burned and hundreds of people were killed by wildfires in the late 1800s, especially in Wisconsin and Minnesota. Massive and fatal floods occurred from the 1880s to 1910, such as the 1889 Johnstown flood in Pennsylvania, which killed 2200 people. Many people believed that denuded forest lands contributed to floods, and some (but not all) scientific evidence supported the notion.

Based on beliefs that improved forest management and fire protection would be forthcoming, preservationists proposed acquiring national parks in the East. Eventually these proposals evolved into an eastern national forest purchase bill. These efforts proved successful in 1911, when the Weeks Law authorized the federal *purchase* of private forest lands in the East along the headwaters of navigable streams, for watershed protection purposes. In the 1924 Clarke-McNary Act, the purchase authority was extended to practically all lands in the East and purchases for timber production purposes also were authorized. Amendments in the 1928 McNary-Woodruff Act limited the purchases to less than 1 million acres per state but authorized increased funding for acquisitions. However, purchases did not increase significantly until the depression of the 1930s. This purchase of formerly private land by the federal government began a new public policy approach, which continues today.

The new national forest land was widely considered to be useless at the time, and average per acre purchase costs remained less than $5.00 until after World War II. Shands (1977) called the purchases the "Lands Nobody Wanted." The Monongahela National Forest was called the great cut and burn patch. Today, these lands are valuable for timber, recreation, and wildlife production and are the center of important forest management and preservation debates.

FEDERAL LAND MANAGEMENT AGENCIES

As the review of U.S. land policy and the discussions in prior chapters suggest, many federal agencies manage public lands and represent the public as "owners" of the land. Table 12-3 summarizes the current land ownership for the principal federal agencies. The Forest Service owned 184 million acres in 1983 and now controls almost 191 million acres. In 1989 the Department of the Interior owned about 430 million acres, including 266 million acres owned by the Bureau of Land Management, 81 million acres by the Fish and Wildlife Service, and 68 million acres by the National Park Service. The holdings in Alaska boosted these totals con-

TABLE 12-3. Public Land Areas by Agency Ownership

Agency	Total Area (million acres)
Federal	
Department of Agriculture	201.9
Forest Service	190.8
Department of the Interior	432.4
Bureau of Indian Affairs	2.7
Bureau of Land Management	266.3
Bureau of Reclamation	5.7
Fish and Wildlife Service	83.4
National Park Service	74.2
Department of Defense	26.0
Army Corps of Engineers	5.5
Other	1.9
Total federal	662.2
State and local	155.0
Total government	817.2
Total area of United States	2316.0

Note: Department total area includes the areas reported for subsidiary agencies.

Source: Bureau of Land Management 1983, Statistical Abstract of the United States 1989, U.S. General Services Administration 1989.

siderably, because much of the state's 375 million acres are in federal or state ownership. Note that state and local governments also own 155 million acres.

The history, policies, and current issues involving these public land agencies are fascinating. They cannot be covered in detail in one chapter, but an overview is helpful.

THE DEPARTMENT OF THE INTERIOR

HISTORY

Despite the vast acquisitions and disposals of public lands in the first half of the nineteenth century, the federal government had no specific agency to manage these lands. The General Land Office in the Department of Treasury dealt with disposal of public lands. War pension land activities and Native American affairs were managed by the War Department. After efforts of many groups to build support for a separate federal department, the Department of the Interior was authorized in 1849.

Agency Evolution
The new Department of the Interior combined several disparate activities. It administered the General Land Office (from Treasury), the Bureau of Indian Affairs (from the War Department), the Pension Office (from the War and Navy departments), and the Patent Office (from the Department of State). Agriculture received its first federal recognition, albeit only as a division in the Patent Office. Several other departments that came into being later, such as Education and Labor, resided in Interior at one time. Many other important bureaus and divisions also became part of Interior.

New agencies often were withdrawn from or added to the original Department of the Interior. The Department of Agriculture was created by Congress in 1862 and raised to cabinet level in 1889. In 1879 the Geological Survey was created as a bureau in the Interior Department. John Wesley Powell, a strong advocate of settlement and development of the arid West, became director of the Geological Survey in 1881. He said that farming could occur successfully only with irrigation and that land grants should be four sections large in the West, not a quarter-section as in the Midwest. He advocated major dams and storage reservoirs, with the government advancing the money and supervising the work. Powell proposed that local communities should pay for the irrigation because they would stand to benefit from the public works. Powell was assisted in his reservoir and dam work by W. T. McGee and Frederick Newell.

The 1900s

Powell was unsuccessful at gaining funding for his plans, but his thesis lived on. In 1902 Congress established a Reclamation Service within the Geological Survey. Newell became Reclamation Service chief under TR, and McGee became Pinchot's and TR's "scientific brains of the Conservation movement" (Pinchot 1947, p. 359). The Reclamation Service became the Bureau of Reclamation in 1906 and developed both irrigation and hydropower water management systems in 17 western states over the next several decades (U.S. Department of the Interior 1976).

As mentioned before, the first forest reserves were created from Interior lands. Pinchot sought and eventually achieved transfer of these lands from Interior into the Department of Agriculture. Pinchot advocated wise use of the national forests, which meant production of useful products. But he also favored regulation of resource use, including range. He successfully imposed regulation of livestock grazing on the forests. Two 1911 Supreme Court decisions, *Grimaud* v. *United States* and *United States* v. *Light*, upheld the grazing regulations and confirmed congressional authority to establish the forests and assign the Forest Service to manage them (Arrandale 1983).

Yellowstone National Park was created by Congress in 1872, and 13 more national parks were reserved by 1912. Roosevelt also had proclaimed 18 national monuments under authority of the Antiquities Act of 1906, including the Grand Canyon and three other areas

that became national parks. The national park superintendents reported to the secretary of the interior. The Forest Service attempted to gain administrative authority for the national parks in the early 1900s. But at the urging of preservationists, who detested the utilitarian orientation of the Forest Service, Congress established a National Park Service within the Department of the Interior in 1916 and directed the Park Service "to conserve the scenery and the natural and historic objects and the wildlife therein and to provide for the enjoyment of the same in such manner and by such means as will leave them unimpaired for the enjoyment of future generations" (Arrandale 1983, p. 31).

The Department of the Interior continued to be involved in public land management issues for the next three decades as well, but no new major issues were spawned. As the white settlers spread throughout the West, the Native Americans were disenfranchised from their lands in Oklahoma, a wealth of wildlife species became extinct or threatened, mineral and oil exploitation boomed, and the western range deteriorated rapidly. Many steps were taken in the 1930s in an attempt to remedy some public land problems.

In the 1930s the Great Depression caused almost one-quarter of the eligible work force to become unemployed. The economic collapse was initiated by the stock market crash of 1929 and endured throughout the 1930s. In addition, the driest, hottest decade on record to date caused crops to wither and wind and rainstorms to cause massive erosion. Pres. Franklin Delano Roosevelt proposed a host of social and natural resource programs to revive the economy, care for people, and protect the land.

One of these new programs was the Civilian Conservation Corps (CCC), which was established by federal legislation in March 1933 in order to provide jobs for unemployed young men, World War I veterans, Native Americans, and local experienced laborers. The corps was an interdepartmental cooperative effort and an example of effective federal–state relationships. The U.S. Department of Labor, functioning through state selection organizations, had jurisdiction over the enrollment of workers, while the Department of the Interior, the Department of Agriculture, and the Army Corps of Engineers had final authority over the work done, depending upon whether it was fire fighting, reforestation, timberstand improvement, soil conservation, wildlife restoration, land reclamation, park development, or flood control. In most areas, state forestry or parks agencies had immediate charge over these projects. The army commanded and supplied the CCC camps and supervised their recreational activities. The U.S. Office of Education helped with educational programs, while religious programs found support from local sources.

In 1935 Roosevelt raised the enrollment goal from 250,000 to 600,000 people. The corps reached a total of slightly under 560,000 in October and thereafter declined to a level of about 300,000, which it held until 1941. The CCC's strength gradually waned and Congress ended it in June 1942 as part of the general cutback of New Deal relief agencies (Potter 1983).

In 1934 the Taylor Grazing Act reversed almost three centuries of unfettered settlement of the American public domain. The act curtailed homesteading by stating that the Homestead Act and public land sales acts would be subject to the judgment of the secretary of the interior of whether the lands were suitable for the purpose stated in the patent application. Furthermore, the act authorized the secretary to organize grazing districts—to be managed by a newly formed Grazing Service—to preserve the land from destruction or unnecessary injury, to provide for its orderly use, and to perform the work necessary to protect and rehabilitate the public grazing lands.

The events of the 1930s and 1940s also led in the 1950s to the development of many of the massive western dams, creation of the Tennessee Valley Authority (TVA), and establishment of the Bureau of Land Management and Fish and Wildlife Service, thus creating most of the federal agencies that still exist in the Department of the Interior, and in the De-

partment of Agriculture as well. The most important Interior agencies, laws, and issues regarding public lands are discussed next.

NATIONAL PARK SERVICE

The National Park System had its origins with the reservation of the 2.25-million-acre Yellowstone National Park in the territories of Montana and Wyoming in 1872. It was established as a public park or pleasuring ground for the benefit and enjoyment of the people and was placed under exclusive control of the Secretary of the Interior. Reserving Yellowstone did not guarantee protection, however. Concessionaires operated the park ineffectually, and in 1886 the secretary of the interior was forced to ask the army to take over the park's protection and supervision. The army's generally successful job satisfied the public, paved the way for more national parks, and created the model for future park rangers. Yosemite National Park was created in 1890, as were Sequoia and General Grant, all in California's High Sierra. Mount Rainier became a National Park in 1899, Crater Lake in 1902, Wind Cave in 1903, Mesa Verde in 1906, and Glacier in 1910 (Wirth 1966).

The National Park System

At the same time that these parks were established, a national controversy arose over the building of a water power and electric generating dam in the Hetch Hetchy Valley. The beautiful valley was proposed as the best site for water supplies for San Francisco and created a major split between utilitarians and preservationists. Building of the dam was approved reluctantly in 1908 by Theodore Roosevelt, but John Muir and other preservationists launched a national campaign to prevent its construction. After a long and bitter public debate, Congress finally approved building of the dam, and President Wilson signed the bill authorizing the reservoir in 1913. A year later, broken by the struggle, John Muir died. The preservationists lost the battle, but their movement was inspired by the fight, making them much more prepared for the next battle. Furthermore, the controversy changed public opinion from generally favoring conquering and developing the wilderness to opposing such actions (Wellman 1987).

After Hetch Hetchy, a movement began to develop a system for the national parks, similar to that for national forests. Stephen T. Mather, a self-made Chicago millionaire, became the Department of the Interior director for all the separate national parks in 1915. He and his new assistant, Horace M. Albright, drafted legislation that established the National Park System in 1916. The initial system included 11 national parks, 18 national monuments, and 2 other reservations. Mather promptly began the work of staffing and securing Civil Service protection for the parks' landscape architects, building architects, foresters, naturalists, historians, and engineers (Wirth 1966). Mather and Albright, who succeeded him, sought to build an extensive constituency base and to develop the parks. A large expansion occurred in 1933, when a presidential order transferred 63 national monuments and military sites from the Forest Service and War Department to the Park Service. By 1964 there were 32 national parks, 77 national monuments, and 93 other areas administered by the Park Service, totaling 26 million acres.

The National Park system has gradually expanded since then and now contains about 75 million acres. Gradual additions to the system have occurred, and it expanded greatly with the addition of land in Alaska, which now comprises more than half of the total National Park System land area.

Park Land Types

In addition to national parks, the park system includes national monuments, national memorials, national historic sites, national seashores, national battlefield parks, and national trails. In 1964 the areas of the park system were classified into natural, historical, and recreational areas. Table 12-4 summarizes the National Park System areas as of 1987. Well over half the land area is in Alaska,

however, so the totals are somewhat deceptive.

Natural areas are unspoiled examples of the primeval heritage of the nation. Natural areas must be an expanse or feature of land or water of substantial scenic or scientific value and quality. National park natural areas may consist of forests, tundra, grasslands, deserts, estuaries, or river systems. National parks are established by congressional action alone, as noted in Chapter 6. A national monument— such as Mount Saint Helens National Volcanic Monument—is generally smaller than a national park and is established by presidential proclamation. It is designed to preserve at least one nationally significant resource and generally lacks the diversity of attractions found in a national park. National preserves are authorized to protect resources, but hunting or extraction of minerals or oil may occur when they do not conflict with a preserve's purpose (Jensen 1977).

Historical areas in the National Park System preserve places and commemorate persons, events, and activities important in the nation's past. They range from Native American archaeological sites to modern American historical buildings. National historical parks, such as old battlefields, are generally much larger than national historic sites. National memorials, such as the Lincoln Memorial, are unique places which are commemorative in nature (Jensen 1977).

Many other types of park areas exist. Recreation areas are set aside primarily for intensive outdoor recreation use. National Recreation Areas were originally Park System units surrounding dams built by other federal agencies. The Forest Service and Park Service also manage some National Recreation Areas. Wild and Scenic Rivers preserve ribbons of land bordering on free-flowing streams that have not been dammed, channelized, or otherwise altered by humans. National Lakeshores and Seashores are established to preserve natural values and provide water-oriented recreation. National trails protect hiking routes through scenic areas (Jensen 1977).

TABLE 12-4. The National Park System by Type of Area, 1987

Type of Area	Number of Units	Federal Acreage	Recreational Visits (in millions)
National Park System	343	76,055,373	287.2
National parks	49	45,875,126	56.6
National historical parks	26	94,815	29.5
National monuments	78	4,626,647	23.5
National military parks	9	33,099	4.5
National battlefields	11	9,358	2.1
National battlefield parks	3	7,449	1.7
National battlefield site	1	1	(NA)
National historic sites	64	16,454	10.6
National memorials	25	7,865	20.1
National seashores	10	476,215	18.5
Parkways	4	159,648	39.3
National lakeshores	4	143,282	3.4
National rivers	12	237,137	3.6
National capital parks	1	6,469	8.1
Parks, other	10	31,953	8.0
National recreation areas	17	3,338,848	56.5
National trails	3	91,103	(NA)
National preserves	12	20,899,872	0.1
National Mall	1	14	(NA)
White House	1	18	1.1
Other	2	(NA)	(NA)

NA = not available.

Source: Statistical Abstract of the United States 1989.

Current Outdoor Recreation Programs

The National Park Service is the best known agency that provides public recreation. But several other federal agencies also provide recreational opportunities. In fact, the Forest Service is the largest provider of recreation on a total visitor basis, with about 40 percent of the total number of visitor hours on federal lands. The Army Corps of Engineers provides about 25 percent of the visitor hours, and the Park Service 20 percent. The Bureau of Land Management provides about 7 percent, the Bureau of Reclamation 5 percent, and the Tennessee Valley Authority and the Fish and Wildlife Service about 1 percent each of the federal total (Statistical Abstract of the United States 1989).

National Park Service policies in the 1960s began to shift away from the development and elite-oriented focus initiated by Mather and Albright in the early years. Environ- mentalists grew to oppose the materialistic orientation of the service, and this trend be- came magnified by the appointment of Stew- art Udall as secretary of the interior in the Kennedy and Johnson administrations. In *The Quiet Crisis*, Udall (1962) decried America's misuse of its natural resources and suggested that the National Park Service should manage the parks by adopting a land ethic.

An Outdoor Recreation Resources Review Commission (ORRRC) had been chartered in 1958 to study the problems resulting from greatly increased recreation visitation on fed- eral lands. The ORRRC report, 27 volumes in all, was published in 1962. It identified the lack of a coherent federal policy as the princi- pal cause of the outdoor recreation crisis. The report concluded that the National Park Ser- vice administered mostly natural areas, which were not the focus of the crisis. ORRRC stated that more emphasis was needed on urban-oriented recreation, thus helping draw the Park Service into the confusing new domain of the urban national parks and recreation areas (Wellman 1987).

The ORRRC report, coupled with Udall's influence, prompted many new federal actions. The 1965 Land and Water Conservation Fund Act (LWCF) helped obtain funds for state and federal recreation land acquisition, development, and planning (LWCF is discussed in detail in an illustration at the end of this chapter). ORRRC also recommended creation of a new federal outdoor recreation agency to coordinate federal programs and to provide technical and financial assistance to states and localities. A Bureau of Outdoor Recreation was established due to Udall's influence, but it did not remain important for long. President Carter changed its name to the Heritage Conservation and Recreation Service, and President Reagan dismantled it in the early days of his administration. ORRRC also endorsed wilderness, which was being considered as a federal land management concept in the early 1960s and has since flourished (Wellman 1987).

As ORRRC redirected national recreation efforts away from development, the Park Service found itself out of step. Udall forced Conrad Wirth, director of the Park Service, out of the job and replaced him with George Hartzog. Udall also appointed many new members of the Park Service advisory board, rather than relying on Park Service recommendations. Congressional control of parks also increased. The president's Bureau of the Budget (now the Office of Management and Budget) controlled Park Service budgets more tightly.

Many of the same issues regarding outdoor recreation remain as concerns today. Wellman (1987) summarizes many of them. They include external threats to the federal parks and recreation, such as air pollution; energy needs; water development; wildlife protection and hunting; private land inholdings; and new laws. Internal policies may include political appointments taking precedence over professionalism, park responses to use pressures, recreation's effect on wildlife, recreational damage to vegetation and soils, vandalism and crime in the parks, recreational carrying capacity, and user fees. These issues will be crucial to development of federal outdoor recreation in the future.

One attempt to address these problems was made by another national review of recreation in America—the 1985 President's Commission on Americans Outdoors (PCAO). It included virtually no representation from any of the major environmental groups. It took several efforts before the final report was issued in 1987, however, because the committee still came out with draft recommendations too strong for the Reagan administration. These included greater land use regulation and a national recreation policy, as well as proposals for over $1 billion in additional funding. Even the final report was suppressed by the Reagan administration for many months. In the end, the administration issued a response (Task Force on Outdoor Recreation Resources and Opportunities 1988) that indicated the administration would focus on more community effort and less regulation, without an increased federal role. As of 1991 the eventual impact of the PCAO report is still moot. It called for more federal action, but whether the president and Congress will want to or be able to afford to respond remains to be seen.

BUREAU OF RECLAMATION

John Wesley Powell pioneered the development of the arid West. His report on the *Lands of the Arid Regions of the United States* (1879) stated that the region had potential for limited development and cultivation if the federal government supported extensive irrigation projects. In 1902, the year that Powell died, Congress passed the Reclamation Act, which led to the extensive system of dams in the West and the establishment of the Reclamation Service in the Geological Survey in 1907. The Bureau of Reclamation was established in 1906; the 1930s and 1940s may be called the Reclamation Era because of the huge size and number of multipurpose water projects that were begun. The water projects served two fundamental purposes: (1) They reclaimed and brought water to millions of acres of land, as well as opening millions of acres to agriculture, and (2) they provided employment to millions of workers during the depression.

The first major project began during Hoover's administration as the Boulder project on the Colorado River on the Nevada–Arizona border. The dam provided irrigation, flood control, and electric power generation, as well as irrigation to the Imperial Valley in California. Boulder was later renamed the Hoover Dam in honor of the president who helped initiate the project. Lake Mead (behind Hoover Dam) became a magnet for recreation in the area and was designated a National Recreational Area, as were other large western reservoirs.

Other dam projects include the massive Central Valley Project in California, started in the 1930s, and Grand Coulee and Bonneville dams on the Columbia River in Washington, which were authorized in 1935 and 1937. The Corps of Engineers also built dams in the Bonneville system. Extensive flood control and power generation dams in the central United States and Southeast were developed in this time period. The bureau owned 6 million acres of land and water in 1987 and provided electricity in all 17 western states, as well as substantial amounts of water-based recreation on its 355 recreation areas.

BUREAU OF LAND MANAGEMENT

The modern Bureau of Land Management was created in 1946 by combining the General Land Office (GLO) and the Grazing Service, which had been created by the Taylor Grazing Act of 1934. The history of the General Land Office was mentioned earlier in this chapter. The controversies surrounding the grazing service bear further examination.

The Grazing Service
Management of the Department of the Interior lands had no legislative authority until passage of the Taylor Grazing Act of 1934. Throughout the 1910s and 1920s, the Forest Service successfully implemented programs to control and charge for grazing use on national forest lands, and beginning in 1916, it gradually increased grazing fees. Congressional committees forced the Forest Service to rapidly bring its fees up to fair market value in 1924, which created a storm of protest from livestock owners, who had supported the agency until that time. This controversy permanently alienated most livestock owners from the Forest Service, and from any federal range regulation at all. This rift effectively prohibited transfer of any more Interior rangelands to the Forest Service (Culhane 1981).

Sen. Edward Taylor of Colorado introduced a grazing district bill in 1933, which was opposed by some livestock owners and the Forest Service but favored by others. Secretary of the Interior Harold Ickes campaigned aggressively for the bill, threatening to withhold federal funding for CCC camps, and even threatening to withhold grazing access to the public domain. However, to help procure passage for the bill, Ickes promised the livestock industry that grazing fees would be kept low and grazing would be administered without an extensive bureaucracy such as the Forest Service. The act was passed in 1934 and authorized the Grazing Service in the Department of the Interior, as well as refining Forest Service policy (Arrandale 1983, Culhane 1981).

The Taylor Grazing Act's major provision established the grazing districts and the leasing of forage in the districts to local stock owners who had a prior use of the range. The basic administrative policies were similar to those of the Forest Service: confinement of each livestock operator's grazing operations to a specified area; prohibition of use by ranchers without permits; and payment of fees for use of a specified number of animal unit months (AUMs) of grazing (Section 3). Section 15 of the act provided for leasing of small scattered tracts not included in the grazing districts to local adjacent ranchers. Section 9 was subsequently interpreted to allow formation of stock owners' advisory boards, which eventually set leasing policies in local districts with considerable discretion. The act also gave the secretary of the interior considerable discretion to classify lands according to their best use or to sell them (Culhane 1981).

The Taylor Act ended the era of disposal of federal public domain lands. Homesteading was withdrawn for all western lands except in Washington and Alaska. The act also established within the Department of the Interior the Division of Grazing—renamed the Grazing Service in 1939—to administer the act's provisions.

The first director of Division of the Grazing Service, Farrington Carpenter, administered grazing regulations via the district advisory boards. He relied on the boards because they were familiar with the local conditions and because he wanted to avoid the bureaucratic approach of the Forest Service that was disliked by so many ranchers.

A former Forest Service grazing specialist, Richard Rutledge, became head of the Grazing Service in 1939. This helped blunt Forest Service drives to gain control of Interior grazing lands and brought professional management to Interior. It also helped Harold Ickes in a campaign he started to create a Department of Conservation, which would include Interior and the national forests. In the end, Ickes and the Forest Service were stalemated, and the two natural resource agencies have remained separate, despite further attempts (the latest in the waning years of the Carter administration) to consolidate federal natural resource agencies.

Rutledge tried to increase grazing fees and reduce the number of livestock on overgrazed and deteriorated ranges. These efforts met with strident opposition from cattle ranchers and led to congressional hearings and criticism of the grazing service, led by Sen. Pat McCarran of Nevada. McCarran carried on a successful congressional fight to drastically cut Grazing Service appropriations so that the agency would be unable to administer the Taylor Grazing Act. Grazing Service employees were forced to depend on the grazing advisory boards for funds for their salaries and therefore were literally paid by the very users they were supposed to regulate. In 1946 President Truman put the Grazing Service out of its misery by signing a reorganization plan that consolidated the Grazing Service and the General Land Office into a new Bureau of Land Management (Culhane 1981).

The New BLM
The Bureau of Land Management was first directed by Marion Clawson, an agricultural economist, insightful analyst, and prolific author on a wide variety of natural resource subjects, including his 1975 classic *Forests for Whom and for What?* Clawson had to try to merge the weak, decentralized Grazing Service and the rigid, centralized GLO into one agency. He continued the struggle to reduce overgrazing on the Interior range and to increase grazing fees to reasonable levels. However, the BLM and its district managers still were hobbled by interest groups and Congress members who cooperated to prevent any agency control to improve conservation. As an economist, Clawson continued to try to raise grazing fees, as well as reduce range use, improve conservation, and enhance the BLM administration (Clawson 1971), albeit without much success.

The BLM continued to seek control of the range through Clawson's departure in 1952 and throughout the 1950s. A Public Land Law Review Commission (PLLRC) was created in 1964 to review public lands, especially those administered by Interior. The Classification and Multiple-Use Act of 1964 gave the secretary of the interior and the BLM authority to inventory the public domain lands and classify them for either disposal or retention in federal ownership. In 1970 the PLLRC issued its final report, which firmly asserted that the public lands should, with minor exceptions, be retained and managed by the federal government. Given the significant pro-industry tenor of the rest of the report, this helped solidify these lands as western *public* lands.

The Federal Land Policy and Management Act of 1976

Although the BLM had received an imprimatur to retain its lands from the PLLRC, it still lacked official authority to manage them; that is, the agency did not have an organic act. This deficiency was rectified with the 1976 Federal Land Policy and Management Act (FLPMA), which gave the BLM statutory status as a permanent federal agency and made its director a presidential appointee subject to Senate confirmation. FLPMA also gave the BLM a multiple-use mandate similar to what the Forest Service has under the Multiple-Use Sustained-Yield Act of 1960. FLPMA authorized multiple-use advisory councils in the hope of counterbalancing the stock owners' advisory boards. FLPMA, similar to the National Forest Management Act, required comprehensive long-range planning. Under FLPMA, grazing fees are subject to review and increase, but they have remained an enduring source of controversy between ranchers, agency personnel, and conservation groups.

FLPMA also authorized a wilderness review of BLM lands, as had occurred earlier on Forest Service lands. Last, it recodified many of BLM's responsibilities for land withdrawal, classification, and disposal. FLPMA marked the final closing of disposal of the public domain (Culhane 1981).

Current BLM Programs

The use of BLM lands varies more than in other agencies. As of 1989 the agency managed about 266 million acres in the United States, with about half in the western states and half in Alaska (Task Force on Outdoor Recreation Resources and Opportunities 1988). Grazing remains the predominant use of BLM lands, and ranching is a major economic contributor in almost all the western states. But BLM lands, which comprised about 7 percent of the federal recreation visitor days in 1985, are increasingly used for hunting, fishing, camping, hiking, off-road vehicles, and other recreation activities (USDA Forest Service 1987).

BLM management occurs at three levels of intensity. The huge block of Alaska land receives only custodial management and remains essentially wilderness. Second, the BLM owns 2.6 million acres of prime Douglas-fir timberland, spread in a checkerboard pattern throughout the Coastal Range and Cascade Range of western Oregon. In 1913–1916 these timberlands reverted to the federal government when several railroad companies violated the terms of their land grants. These "O & C lands" are now managed primarily for timber production. Third, most of the rest of the land in the lower 48 states is managed within grazing districts established under the Taylor Grazing Act. The BLM proportion of land within these grazing districts ranges from up to 90 percent in parts of Utah and Nevada to 25 percent in areas such as eastern Montana (Figure 12-2).

BLM remains in charge of leasing the mineral and oil rights on most federal lands, the outer continental shelf, and grazing. In 1977 the BLM took in receipts of $2.4 billion from the outer continental shelf leases, $344 million from other mineral leases, $212 million from timber sales on the O & C lands, and $17.6 million from grazing leases. The agency remains widely decentralized and is generally oriented toward development, as evidenced by its leasing revenues (Culhane 1981). The BLM began to respond to pressure from environmental groups in the 1980s and sought to expand its recreation and other multiple-use programs.

Rangeland Issues

Issues involving public rangelands in the United States, particularly in the West, focus largely but not exclusively on BLM management. U.S. forests and rangelands provide forage and browse for more than 70 million cattle, 8 million sheep, 55,000 wild horses and burros, 20 million deer, 400,000 elk, and 600,000 antelope (Gardner 1991). Private rangelands provide nearly 86 percent of the total forage consumed by domestic livestock nationwide, as measured by the animal unit month (AUM). Public rangelands managed by state and federal governments provide about 7 percent of the total AUMs. Many private ranchers depend on nearby public lands as

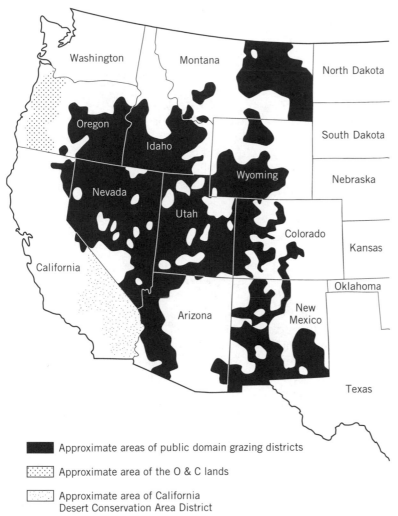

Figure 12-2. Public Domain Administration Districts of the Bureau of Land Management, 1981
Source: Culhane 1981, p. 99.

part of their total livestock management enterprises. Most of the rangeland is concentrated in the 17 western states. More than 40 percent of the rangeland is owned by the federal government, mostly in the West (Joyce 1989).

One of the basic issues in range management is whether the land is in good or poor condition. But even this involves a value judgment regarding the use of rangelands. Early surveys of range conditions merely measured how good the rangelands were at producing forage for domestic livestock and classed

them as excellent, good, fair, or poor. However, this criterion did not account for the quality of rangelands for other purposes, including wildlife. Thus in 1978 the Society for Range Management established a Range Inventory Standardization Committee (RISC) to reclassify range conditions. The 1983 RISC report recommended classifying rangelands on the basis of their ecological status, rather than their ability to produce livestock forage. The committee recommended that the old Soil Conservation Service criterion be replaced with four new ecological indicators: potential natural community or climax, late seral, mid seral, or early seral. These are measures of the composition of the forage toward its highest or climax value (Gardner 1991).

In 1988 the Forest Service and the Bureau of Land Management decided to adopt the seral stages approach to range evaluation. The BLM described range condition on its land as a comparison with a potential natural community: excellent, 75–100 percent similarity with the potential natural community; good, 50–75 percent; fair, 25–50 percent; and poor, 0–25 percent. The Soil Conservation Service, however, elected to retain its use of the old excellent to poor classes based on livestock use criteria (Gardner 1991, Joyce 1989).

Differing definitions of rangelands among agencies imply that even assessments and discussions of range quality remain complex. Furthermore, trying to state what is the "optimal" range condition depends on one's criteria and the purpose for which that range is used. Most range scientists, environmental groups, and even western ranchers do agree, however, that public *and* private rangelands in the West are overgrazed—which one could class as "suboptimal." Gardner (1991) chronicles the problems with rangelands throughout the nation's history, including the many attempts to measure quality and to improve range conditions by controlling overgrazing. Furthermore, he notes that competition between domestic livestock and wildlife on western range lands has increased significantly in recent decades.

FISH AND WILDLIFE SERVICE

The Fish and Wildlife Service is charged with the protection and restoration of migratory and endangered species of wildlife. Fish and wildlife management also has its origins in the early conservation movement of the late nineteenth century. The slaughter of game and nongame animals alike threatened many species with extinction. Ducks, geese, cranes, plovers, and snipes were killed and sold for food. Egrets, herons, ibises, and other wading birds were killed for millinery plumage. Any bird with colorful feathers was at risk, including orioles, warblers, and swallows. The vast western herds of American bison were almost eliminated, and deer and other big game were almost extirpated from many states in the East.

Early Legislation

The Fish and Wildlife Service traces its origins to the earlier (1886) USDA Bureau of Economic Entomology and Mammology and the USDA Biological Survey. Congress members tried at one time to include wildlife protection as part of the mission of the national parks. But despite other successes, the U.S. Army had failed to prevent the killing of wildlife in Yellowstone. Rep. John Lacey of Iowa sponsored the Yellowstone Park Protective Bill, which provided jail sentences of up to two years for anyone convicted of killing wildlife in Yellowstone Park. This prompted Pres. Theodore Roosevelt (an avid hunter himself) to consider making the forest reserves inviolate wildlife refuges. Pinchot convinced TR that this would be impractical, but that parts of the federal domain should be designated as such refuges. Roosevelt thus established many wildlife refuges when he was president and created many national forests as much for their wildlife value as for their timber value (Trefethen 1966).

The decline of wildlife in the nineteenth century also prompted Congress to enact the first federal wildlife law in 1900. The Lacey Act of 1900 made the interstate shipment of game killed in violation of state law a federal offense, thus curtailing much of the traffic in wild meat and plumage that the market gunners had conducted in defiance of state law.

The 1900s saw an increase in state wildlife protection as well. In fact, excessive protection occurred in some places. Unchecked wildlife populations endangered natural food supplies because most large predators had been exterminated. Elk threatened habitat in Yellowstone, and the mule deer in Arizona's Kaibab Plateau almost destroyed the habitat. These events led to the birth of game management, pioneered by the publication of Aldo Leopold's (1933) *Game Management*.

Leopold became the first professor of game management (at the University of Wisconsin) in America (Trefethen 1966).

A New Agency

In the 1930s wildlife conservationists focused on waterfowl protection and habitat. FDR's first appointee to head the Bureau of Biological Survey was Jay N. "Ding" Darling of Iowa. Darling fought enthusiastically for wildlife program funding. He launched the Cooperative Wildlife Research Unit Program in 1935—a system of training and research stations for advanced students in wildlife management at various land-grant colleges across the nation. Darling also helped establish the National Wildlife Federation to unify and coordinate the activities of state and local conservation groups, hunters, and anglers. Additionally, he helped promote enactment of the Pittman-Robertson Federal Aid in Wildlife Restoration Act of 1937. Pittman-Robertson authorizes an 11 percent excise tax on sporting arms and ammunition and allocates funds back to the states based on the number of licensed hunters and the area of the state (Trefethen 1966).

In 1940 the U.S. Fish and Wildlife Service was established in the Department of the Interior by consolidating the former Bureau of Biological Survey from the Department of Agriculture and the Bureau of Fisheries from the Department of Commerce. The role of the agency expanded to include many conservation, propagation, and regulatory activities. Ira Gabrielson, who succeeded Darling as chief of the Biological Survey, became its first director.

Current Programs

These basic developments led to modern federal and state wildlife policies. Most states have strong wildlife agencies as well, staffed by specialists in research, management, law, and administration. Hunting seasons are based on sustainable wildlife population levels. Nearly all states maintain wildlife refuges and extensive habitat restoration programs on public and private lands. The Fish and Wildlife Service is responsible for protecting migratory birds that cross state or national borders, as well as threatened and endangered species.

The Fish and Wildlife Service now oversees 443 national wildlife refuges, totaling more than 90 million acres. About 77 million acres are in Alaska, the rest are in the continental United States (Task Force on Outdoor Recreation Resources and Opportunities 1988). It also operates about 75 fish hatcheries, 50 cooperative research units at state universities, and several research laboratories. It monitors U.S. wildlife populations, sets migratory bird hunting seasons and limits, and distributes excise tax funds. The Pittman-Robertson program also has been expanded to include a wider range of items. A similar bill (Dingle-Johnson) provided a tax on fishing equipment in 1950 and was expanded to include boats and boating fuel in 1985 by the Wallop-Breaux amendments. The Fish and Wildlife Service also plays a crucial role in reviewing federal Environmental Impact Statements and in enforcing the Endangered Species Act. These roles are discussed in more detail in Chapter 15.

BUREAU OF INDIAN AFFAIRS

The Bureau of Indian Affairs (BIA) manages more than 3 million acres of federal land on behalf of Native Americans, including the Inuits (Eskimos). The BIA was created in 1824 by the War Department and was added to the new U.S. Department of the Interior in 1849. Its early mission was to assimilate Native Americans into white American culture, but by the 1930s it had succeeded only in drastically disrupting Native Americans' lives. It now is charged with providing technical assistance to tribal governments, as well as helping to obtain maximum benefits from Native American resources.

Most of the BIA's employees and resources are scattered among its 83 agency offices on Native American reservations. The BIA employs about 10,000 people, most of whom are Native Americans. Because the Native Americans own considerable mineral, forest, and fishery resources, they employ many resource managers. Indeed, the Native Americans often have some reserved rights to hunt, fish, and gather wood on other public lands. These rights range from unlimited hunting and fishing in many western states to logging timber ("gathering wood") on some public lands in the Lake States and have caused interesting policy issues in many states. The broken treaties of the past also have recently led to lawsuits by some Native American tribes against the government and individual landowners, which in some cases have resulted in large settlements in favor of the Native Americans.

THE USDA FOREST SERVICE

The management of the national forests has served throughout this book as an example of the development and implementation of forest resource policy. The early history of the national forests and the agency that manages them has been cited in several illustrations. Today, the National Forest System encompasses an area as large as California and Montana combined, and it is troubled by many management issues and public policy questions. Because we have used the agency for many illustrations and its planning methods are discussed in Chapter 13, our review here will be brief.

LAND AREAS

The Forest Service, which is a part of the U.S. Department of Agriculture, owned 190.8 million acres of land in 1987 (Table 12-5). The National Forest System boundaries encompassed about 230 million acres. The remaining lands within the boundaries were owned by other private or public entities.

The National Forest System is spread among 44 states and Puerto Rico, and among all regions of the country. Most area is in the West (Figure 12-3). Alaska, with 22.7 million acres, has the largest amount of land in National Forest System, followed by California (20.5 million acres), Idaho (20.4 million), Montana (16.8 million), Oregon (15.6 million), and Colorado (14.4 million). Several other states, including Arizona, New Mexico, Utah, Washington, and Wyoming have close to 10 million acres of national forest land. Some states in the Midwest have no national forest land. Most states in the East and the South have less than 1 million acres of national forest land.

Not all of the National Forest System is forest land. Some of the national forest area is reserved for wilderness or other purposes, and some is rangeland. Approximately 4 million acres of the National Forest System are formally designated as National Grasslands, not National Forests.

Not all the forest land is classed as capable of growing commercial timber crops (defined as the potential growth rate of at least 20 cubic feet per acre per year of wood). In 1987 only 85 million acres of the National Forest System were classed as timberland (Waddell, Oswald, and Powell 1989). Thus the actual timber-growing base of the National Forest System is smaller than one might presume from the aggregate agency acreage figure of 191 million acres. In fact, the Pacific Coast (Alaska, Oregon, Washington, and California) had only 28 million acres of timberland, despite having 68 million acres of national forest land. The South had a much higher proportion of timberland, at 11.7 million acres out of a national forest base of 12.6 million acres.

POLICIES AND ISSUES

A brief summary of some of the Forest Service policy issues is appropriate. As our prior illustrations indicate, the Forest Service must contend with a bewildering variety of resource management issues.

Perhaps the preeminent issue today in Forest Service policy is—as it has been for several decades—the use of clear-cutting as a silvicultural tool. The issue also includes questions of timber harvesting, regardless of cutting method. National debates about harvesting of the old-growth timber or ancient forests

TABLE 12-5. Areas of National Forest System Lands by State, 1987

State	Gross Area Within Unit Boundaries (thousand acres)	National Forest System Lands (thousand acres)	Other Lands Within Unit Boundaries (thousand acres)
Total	230,220	190,830	39,390
AL	1,274	649	625
AK	24,228	22,750	1,477
AZ	11,933	11,276	657
AR	3,502	2,484	1,019
CA	24,384	20,524	3,860
CO	16,030	14,458	1,572
CT	0	0	—
FL	1,224	1,100	125
GA	1,855	867	988
HI	0	0	—
ID	21,705	20,455	1,250
IL	840	263	576
IN	644	188	456
KS	117	108	9
KY	2,102	665	1,436
LA	1,023	600	422
ME	94	53	40
MI	4,872	2,802	2,070
MN	5,467	2,806	2,661
MS	2,310	1,148	1,162
MO	3,082	1,473	1,609
MT	19,097	16,796	2,301
NE	442	352	90
NV	5,364	5,103	261
NH	823	715	109
NM	10,384	9,326	1,058
NY	13	13	—
NC	3,165	1,220	1,946
ND	1,106	1,106	0
OH	833	179	654
OK	461	296	166
OR	17,488	15,621	1,867
PA	743	511	232
SC	1,376	606	769
SD	2,348	1,997	351
TN	1,212	626	586
TX	1,994	753	1,242
UT	9,128	8,040	1,087
VT	630	326	304
VA	3,226	1,638	1,588
WA	10,044	9,144	900
WV	1,861	1,003	858
WI	2,023	1,507	516
WY	9,717	9,255	463
PR	56	28	28

Source: Statistical Abstract of the United States 1989.

NATIONAL FOREST SYSTEM LANDS
(191 million acres)

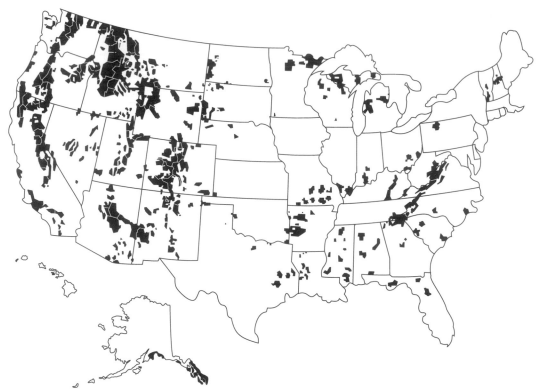

Figure 12-3. National Forest System Lands
Source: USDA Forest Service, 1992

in the West have been the center of attention for the past decade and will continue to be so until the last ancient tree is either cut or placed in a preserve. An illustration of this issue appears later in this chapter. The Forest Service still relies predominantly on clear-cutting in the East as well as in the West and continues to be roundly criticized for its seemingly single-minded pursuit of this widely disliked silvicultural method.

This debate over clear-cutting has actually crystallized somewhat in recent years. Critics challenge timber harvesting on national forests and even question the agency's responsibility to maintain a productive timberland base. A limited amount of old-growth trees are left in the West, and citizen conservaton groups question whether old-growth forests should all be harvested just to keep local mills in operation for a few extra years.

Instead, these groups propose that the remaining old-growth forests be preserved and that more timber be produced on private lands, with government assistance to help retrain displaced forest industry workers. In the South, national forests comprise less than 10 percent of the timberland area and timber harvest. Conservation groups in the South, as in the West, argue for management aimed at producing biological diversity and habitat through natural stand management, which cannot be expected for private landowners. These arguments are countered by the forest products industry, whose representatives and supporters maintain that the timber, jobs, and income from national forests are crucial to local communitites and to the nation.

Other controversies on national forest lands abound. Some are related to timber management practices; others are not. Road building on national forests, below-cost timber sales, herbicide and pesticide use, allowable sale quantities of timber, site conversions, and silvicultural systems all have many critics. Withdrawals of multiple-use lands for wilderness are debated continually, as is the use of timber sale revenues to fund wildlife and recreation management under the Knutson-Vandenburg Act. The same issues discussed by Wellman (1987) for national parks also are relevant in national forests— inholdings, recreation pressure, visitor safety, wildlife management—as well as problems with off-road vehicles, marijuana growing, timber trespass, and other issues. Financing the individual forests with federal appropriations or Knutson-Vandenberg funds and giving local counties payments-in-lieu-of property taxes remain matters of ongoing debate. The national forest planning process is at the center of many policy debates. These issues ensure that discussions of policy for and management of the national forests will continue to be interesting in the future.

OTHER PUBLIC LANDS

Various other federal, state, and local government agencies are responsible for significant amounts of land and manage them for various resources. The U.S. Department of Defense owns land principally for military purposes. The Army Corps of Engineers has built dams for flood control and energy generation, which currently provide many outdoor recreation opportunities. State and local governments also own and manage lands for many purposes.

THE DEPARTMENT OF DEFENSE

The military was the first protector of the major national parks. The Department of Defense manages 26 million acres of land in the United States; 5.5 million acres of this land and inland waters are owned and managed by the U.S. Army Corps of Engineers. Most of the other 20.5 million acres

are in military bases spread throughout the country. Although the lands are not open for public use, each base is managed for timber and wildlife habitat to the extent possible by a staff of civilian resource managers. Because maneuvers generally are held on these bases, resource management takes special talents. Timber buyers must be aware that there may be bullets and shrapnel in their logs; forest regeneration must take place around mock battlefields and tank routes; and wildlife must adapt to loud noises. Nevertheless, these lands provide valuable forest and wildlife resources in many parts of the country, including a significant amount of forests for threatened and endangered species.

Military needs have had great historical significance in affecting U.S. forest resource policy. In colonial days the English crown reserved white pine trees in New England with the broad-arrow policy, which marked the tallest and straightest trees for use as masts for the Royal Navy's ships. In the nineteenth century the extremely tough live oak trees in the South provided excellent material for war ships and led the United States to withdraw the first lands ever from the public domain in 1817—a live oak preserve in Florida. These precedents helped establish the right to regulate private landowners and to retain public domain lands for public purposes.

THE CORPS OF ENGINEERS

The U.S. Army Corps of Engineers (COE or the corps) was established by Congress in 1802. Creation of the corps coincided with and complemented the nation's expansion. From its beginning, the corps assumed a major role in the protection and use of the U.S. waterways. It helped in exploring the United States and locating viable wagon and railroad routes to aid settlement of the West.

The duties of the corps expanded significantly in 1824 when Congress passed the first rivers-and-harbors bills, mandating that the corps improve navigation on the Mississippi and Ohio rivers. This led to channelization projects and dredge-and-fill activities to maintain water-based transportation. In 1850 Congress made the corps responsible for determining the most practical plan for flood prevention in the Mississippi River Basin, leading to its present role in river basin planning. In 1909 Congress gave the corps authority to develop hydroelectric power projects.

By 1917 the concept of comprehensive water resources projects had become firmly established and was expanded over time to include navigation improvement, flood control, and hydroelectric power generation—wherever appropriate (Clarke and McCool 1985).

The COE has gleaned huge amounts of public funding to build a variety of water-related structures and projects. In the 1970s the corps greatly expanded its previously limited involvement in water pollution control by authority granted in the 1972 amendments to the Federal Water Pollution Control Act. President Carter tried to reduce agency budgets and new water projects throughout his term in office, but he was not particularly successful. He criticized project waste and was concerned that the beneficiaries of the corps' projects, unlike those for Bureau of Reclamation dams, did not share in their cost. The iron triangle relationships among the corps, members of Congress, and water-using constituents proved extremely difficult to break (Clarke and McCool 1985).

The Reagan administration tried to reduce the budget and power of the Corps of Engineers, but Congress usually restored much of these cuts in the early 1980s. President Reagan also unsuccessfully proposed that states share part of the cost. In the 1980s the corps expanded its wetlands protection program, mostly because of court decisions that found the Clean Water Act was not being implemented as required by federal law.

Currently, the Army Corps of Engineers manages its 5.5 million acres of land and water for flood control, water basin planning, hydroelectric power, recreational, and other uses. These projects include more than 4000 recreation sites that supply more recreational visits than do the national parks (Task Force

on Outdoor Recreation Resources and Opportunities 1988, U.S. General Services Administration 1989).

STATE AND LOCAL

State and local governments owned about 155 million acres of land in the United States in 1982, or 6.8 percent of the total land area (Statistical Abstract of the United States 1989). Much of this land is in parks, wildlife refuges, highways, and urban property. Much of it also is in forest and timberland. In 1987 the states owned 26.7 million acres of timberland, and county and municipal governments owned 7 million acres of timberland (Waddell et al. 1989).

The geographical distribution of timberland in state and local ownership varies widely. In the Northeast, Pennsylvania has almost 3 million acres of timberland in state and local ownership, and New York has more than 1 million acres. All the other northeastern states have less than 500,000 acres. The Great Lake States of Michigan, Wisconsin, and Minnesota all have large timberland areas in state, county, or local government ownership. Michigan has 3.7 million acres, Wisconsin 2.7 million, and Minnesota 3.1 million. Florida has the largest state and local timberland ownership in the South, at 583,000 acres in 1987. In the West, Alaska has 4.6 million acres of state and local-owned timberland, Oregon 929,000 acres, Washington 2.25 million, Idaho 1.09 million, and Montana 640,000 (Waddell et al. 1989).

The origins of these public timberlands and other public lands have varied by region of the country. Public lands in the East are comprised of some lands that were held by states or communities, and some lands that have been repurchased by governments. The Adirondack Preserve in New York, for example, was initiated in 1885 when the state legislature set aside 750,000 acres of wild forest land; purchases since then have brought its area to more than 2.6 million acres. Many wildlife refuge areas also have been purchased in the 1900s. Several states maintain active programs of buying land for wildlife protection and habitat. Each of the states in the Pacific Northwest has several hundred thousand acres of state-owned land expressly for wildlife purposes (Table 12-6). Florida has been exceptionally active recently, buying wetlands and land along stream corridors in order to protect water quality.

Most of the state and local land in the Lake States was initially given to private landowners but then reverted to the state or local governments. Some of the forest land was deeded to the state after the timber had been cut. Other land was forfeited to county governments when the owners were unable to pay the property tax burdens. Much of the state lands in the Midwest and West were deeded to the states by the federal government as land grants at statehood. Recall that one section in each township was given to the territory for public education funding in the Midwest, and two or four sections in the western states. Midwestern states generally sold this land for revenue, but some western states retained these lands and continued to manage them to provide benefits for the exclusive use of public schools or other public institutions to which the land was granted (O'Laughlin 1990).

State public land issues are similar to federal public land issues, but the politics are obviously more local. Issues include the intensity of management, managing for multiple benefits, the use of public lands for economic development versus resource protection, appropriate methods for game and nongame management, and conflicts between developed and extensive outdoor recreation.

State lands, in particular, provide great amounts of recreation use and fish and wildlife habitat. Clawson and Harrington (1991) write that from 1920 to 1987 state parks provided as many visits to outdoor recreation areas as did the national parks and national forests combined. In 1981 state parks included an area of 1,097 million acres and had an attendance of 618 million persons. State and county lands provide extensive areas for fishing, hunting, and amenity uses.

MODERN PUBLIC LAND RESERVATIONS

One issue regarding public land management is the modern tendency to reserve forest or other public land for a primary use. The initial forest reserves, national wildlife refuges, and national parks were given multiple-use management missions that were reinforced and broadened over time. Three federal acts in the 1960s—The Wilderness Act (1964), the National Wild and Scenic Rivers Act (1968), and the National Trails System Act (1968)—initiated the modern federal policy of creating dominant use reserves for protecting unique areas or special uses.

WILDERNESS

The concept of preserving wilderness predates the Civil War, but a specific wilderness policy did not come about until much later. In 1832 George Catlin proposed that the government preserve lands in their pristine beauty and wilderness. Henry David Thoreau wrote in 1855: "Why should not we...have our national preserves...not for idle sport or food, but for inspiration and our own true recreation?" Various actions to reserve city and state parks began in the 1800s (Wirth 1966).

The two premier national parks—Yosemite and Yellowstone—were originally established to preserve their unique natural beauty and wildness. After the first white explorers entered Yosemite Valley in California in the 1840s, the area became famous for its beauty and splendor. Many people, especially the influential park planner Frederick Law Olmsted, proposed to preserve the valley. Through the efforts of Olmsted and others, Congress in 1864 gave California roughly 40 square miles in the Yosemite Valley and the Grove of Sequoias as a public park to be administered by the state. The park was not yet "national" but would become so in 1890 due to the efforts of John Muir and others. The little known area of Yellowstone was explored by a party of private citizens in 1870. The expedition leaders began a movement to preserve the area for the benefit of all the people, culminat-

TABLE 12-6.   Lands Owned and Controlled by State Wildlife Agencies in Selected Western States

State Wildlife Agency	Acres Owned	Percent of Land in State Owned by Agency	Acres Controlled (by lease, easement, or other agreement)	Percent of Land in State Owned and Controlled by Agency
Idaho Department of Fish and Game	116,101	0.22	91,113	0.39
Montana Department of Fish, Wildlife, and Parks	207,743[a]	0.22	124,102[a]	0.36
Oregon Department of Fish and Wildlife	131,525	0.21	210,660	0.56
Utah Division of Wildlife Resources	361,204	0.69	data unavailable	> 0.69
Washington Department of Wildlife	395,229	0.93	411,254	1.89
Wyoming Department of Game and Fish	119,132	0.19	165,980	0.46

[a]Includes only lands managed for fish and wildlife purposes.
Source: Wise and O'Laughlin 1990.

ing in the designation of Yellowstone National Park by President Grant in 1872 (Bartlett 1983, Clements 1983, Wirth 1966).

The initial forest reserves and the national parks were supported and set aside largely due to the efforts of naturalists. However, management of the forest reserves became infused with the wise use conservation philosophies of Pinchot and Roosevelt, to the chagrin of those who would prefer these areas be preserved in a natural state. The battle for Hetch Hetchy in California further embittered the naturalists and probably led to the death of John Muir. One of Muir's legacies is the Sierra Club, which still is a leading factor in the cause for wilderness preservation. Fuel was added to the fire as Stephen Mather charted an ambitious program to develop the national parks for outdoor recreation, not preserve their naturalness. These disappointments prompted efforts to seek setasides of specific public lands to preserve their wilderness character by forbidding any development.

Early Efforts

Protection of "wilderness" in the national forests began to crystallize when the writings and actions of forester Aldo Leopold (1921) led to the establishment of a 574,000-acre wilderness recreation area in the Gila National Forest in New Mexico in 1924 (Nash 1967). This first wilderness area was to be protected in its natural state and kept roadless. In 1926 the secretary of agriculture decreed that not less than 1000 square miles of the best lakes and waterways in the Superior National Forest of Minnesota would be kept as wilderness recreation areas—the region now called the Boundary Waters Canoe Area Wilderness.

In 1930 Robert Marshall joined the crusade for wilderness. Marshall was an innovative thinker and writer who obtained a master's degree from Harvard, specializing in forestry. In 1933 he wrote a treatise on the need to expand public ownership of forests, and he wrote part of a comprehensive survey of the forestry situation in the

United States, called the Copeland Report after its Senate sponsor. Marshall felt that 45 million acres of forest land in the United States could be chiefly valuable for recreation, 22.5 million acres of which might be considered primeval or wilderness. In 1935 Marshall and other wilderness preservation advocates formed the Wilderness Society. In 1937 Marshall became head of the Forest Service Recreation and Lands Division—one of the very few cases of an entry into the Service at a high-level position. He campaigned for additional wilderness areas in the national forests and helped initiate a classification scheme to identify and protect national forest wilderness areas (Davis 1983a, Wellman 1987).

Marshall died of a heart attack in 1939, at the age of 38, but the new Forest Service "U-Regulations" he instigated two months before his death were designed to protect more wilderness areas. Lands designated U-1 were "wilderness" areas of more than 100,000 acres and timber harvesting and most developed uses were to be prohibited on them. U-2 lands were "wild" lands so designated by the chief that were from 5000 to 100,000 acres in size and were to be managed as wilderness. U-3 "recreation" lands were roadless areas where timber cutting could occur away from scenic routes and recreation zones. The U-regulations, however, were not well implemented, to the disappointment of preservation groups such as the Wilderness Society and the Sierra Club (Wellman 1987). In 1940 the U.S. Forest Service created a memorial to Marshall by reclassifying three primitive areas in Montana as the Bob Marshall Wilderness Area (Davis 1983a).

Continuing controversies over development of potential wilderness areas prompted wilderness groups to seek specific federal legislation. The proposed Echo Park Dam led to a famous dispute. It involved a 1949 plan by the Bureau of Reclamation to build a reservoir on Utah's Green River that would have submerged what today is Dinosaur National Monument. Howard Zahniser of the Wilderness Society and David Brower of the Sierra Club led an extended congressional fight against the dam, including a media blitz, letter-writing campaigns, and pictures of Hetch Hetchy before and after the dam (with the reservoir at low levels, and the shore awash in mud). The Bureau of Reclamation's massive Colorado River Storage Project was eventually implemented, but without the Echo Park Dam.

Wellman (1987) notes that the coalition of interests that defeated the Echo Park Dam illustrates the old saying that "politics makes strange bedfellows." The wilderness interests were joined by the National Park Service, the Army Corps of Engineers (possibly to frustrate the Bureau of Reclamation), southern California water interests, and budget-balancing conservatives. Wellman also notes that although Echo Park was saved, Arizona's Glen Canyon was later lost to a water project.

The Wilderness Act of 1964

Echo Park galvanized the preservationist groups seeking federal protection for wilderness lands. They did not trust Forest Service motivations, which were manifested by increases in road building and timber harvests. Nor were they enthusiastic about Park Service recreational development policies. In 1956 Hubert Humphrey of Minnesota introduced what would be the first of many wilderness bills. Reserving areas for exclusive noneconomic use proved to be a difficult precedent to set. Mining, lumber, and livestock industries strongly opposed a revised 1957 Humphrey bill. Howard Zahniser of the Wilderness Society led preservationists in the legislative struggle.

After 66 modifications and resubmissions of the wilderness bill (Nash 1967), and many compromises regarding permitted uses and areas to be included, the Wilderness Act of 1964 was signed into law four months after Zahniser's death. The act designated 54 areas totaling 9.1 million acres as immediate wilderness, all on Forest Service land. The Forest Service was directed by Congress to review all unroaded or primitive areas within 10 years. All the Forest Service lands that had been administratively classed under Marshall's U-regulations as wilderness, wild, and recreational were included. This Roadless Area Review Evaluation became known as RARE I. The secretary of the interior was directed to review all Park Service and Fish and Wildlife Service roadless areas larger than 5000 acres and all islands within 10 years (Wellman 1987).

Wilderness designation continues to be controversial. The degree of wildness was relaxed after considerable debate in 1975 to allow the creation of eastern wilderness areas. President Carter and his Department of Agriculture Assistant Secretary for Natural Resources Rupert Cutler initiated a second major Roadless Area Review Study (RARE II) in 1977. The plans for using RARE II to make wilderness allocation decisions were crushed, however, by a federal court in California when it was found that the RARE II Final Environmental Impact Statement violated the National Environmental Policy Act (Mohai and Verbyla 1987). The failure of RARE II eventually led to state-by-state bills to complete the wilderness review and allocation process, such as the Washington State law illustrated in Chapter 6. Between 1968 and 1987, 102 additional state-by-state laws were passed, until the National Wilderness Preservation System had grown to 467 areas in 44 states and totaled 89 million acres (Browning, Hendee, and Roggenbuck 1988). Another 3 million acres were added by 1990.

The state-by-state allocation process worked well in most, but not all, states. This process broke down for some states where conservative Congress members submitted proposals that were actively opposed by national environmental organizations. Environmentalists argued for large designations and for further study and restricted use of many nondesignated areas. Commodity interests proposed small designations and "release" of undesignated areas for resource extraction and development. The state-by-state negotiation process left the Forest Service with a small role in wilderness *allocation* on the national forests.

Nevertheless, the Forest Service is responsible for *managing* 80 percent of the lands in the National Wilderness Preservation System in the 48 contiguous states. But as Table 12-7 indicates, there is much more wilderness in Alaska than in the "lower 48." The Forest Service manages a small portion of it, but it is a highly significant portion. In Alaska, the 5.5 million acres of wilderness in the 16.7 million acre Tongass National Forest (the nation's largest) are the responsibility of the Forest Service. The Fish and Wildlife Service controls a large share in Alaska.

WILD AND SCENIC RIVERS

The efforts leading to enactment of the Wilderness Act in 1964 also led to calls for separate legislation to protect wild and scenic rivers and to establish a national trail system. The Wild and Scenic Rivers Act of 1968 established a U.S. policy that certain rivers of national significance should be preserved in their free-flowing condition for the benefit and enjoyment of present and future generations because they possess outstanding and remarkable scenic, recreational, geographic, fish and wildlife, historic, cultural, or other values. The act clearly states that there are intrinsic values in the protection of rivers against dams and other human structures, the lifeblood of the Bureau of Reclamation and Army COE.

Like the Wilderness Act, the Wild and Scenic Rivers Act designated a small number of rivers initially and prescribed methods by which additional components could be added to the system in the future. Ten rivers or sections of rivers were set aside first, and many more have been added to the National Wild and Scenic Rivers System since. As of 1987 the federal government had designated 75 river segments, totaling 7709 miles, for protection under the act. Federal agencies administer the rivers that run through their lands. States administer 753 miles of the system. States also report that they have provided some protection to an additional 6000 miles of rivers (Task Force on Outdoor Recreation Resources and Opportunities 1988).

Additions to the National Wild and Scenic Rivers system are made either directly by Congress or by designation by state legislatures and acceptance by the secretary of the

TABLE 12-7. National Wilderness Preservation System by Federal Land Management Agency, 1989 (in millions of acres)

	"Lower 48"	Alaska	Total
U.S. Department of the Interior			
National Park Service	6.1	33.0	39.1
Bureau of Land Management	0.5	0.0	0.5
Fish and Wildlife Service	0.7	18.7	19.3
U.S. Department of Agriculture			
Forest Service	27.8	5.5	33.3
Total	35.1	57.1	92.2

Source: Hendee et al. 1990.

interior (Davis 1983b). *Wild* rivers are free of impoundments and are generally inaccessible except by trail, and their watersheds or shorelines are essentially primitive with unpolluted waters. *Scenic* rivers are primitive, free of impoundments, and largely undeveloped but accessible in places by roads. *Recreational* rivers are accessible by road or railroad, may have some development along their shorelines, and may have undergone some impoundment or diversion in the past (Jensen 1977).

NATIONAL TRAILS

The National Trails System Act of 1968 recognized the need for a system of national trails to accommodate outdoor recreation needs. The act is designed to preserve scenic and otherwise interesting trail routes throughout the United States for present and future use.

The trail system has three classes of trails: (1) national recreation trails, (2) national scenic trails, and (3) connecting or side trails. The authorizing law initially established two trails—the 2100-mile Appalachian Trail, extending from Maine to Georgia; and the 2300-mile Pacific Crest Trail, extending from the Mexican to the Canadian borders. As of 1987 there were 14 designated federal trails, stretching more than 23,500 miles. Local and state agencies officially operated an additional

35,000 miles of trail (Task Force on Outdoor Recreation Resources and Opportunities 1988).

National trails may be designated only by an act of Congress. They may be administered by the secretary of the interior or the secretary of agriculture. Except for the Appalachian Trail, which is administered by the Department of the Interior despite extensive mileage on national forest lands, administration usually depends on land ownership.

ALASKA NATIONAL LANDS

The largest modern public lands reservation occurred in 1980 when Congress enacted the Alaska National Interest Lands Conservation Act, or ANILCA. The title of the act itself is a clue to the controversy and purposes surrounding the legislation.

Alaska became the forty-ninth state on January 3, 1959. Alaska's economy developed slowly until the 1960s, despite the Klondike and Nome gold rushes of 1896 and 1898, which brought thousands of people eager for a quick fortune. Oil deposits were found on the Alaska North Slope in 1968. In the 1970s exploration and extraction of oil began along the Arctic shore, including construction of the 800-mile Trans-Alaska Pipeline from Prudhoe Bay to the ice-free port of Valdez, where the first oil arrived in July 1977. By 1989 oil from

Prudhoe Bay provided about 25 percent of the nation's domestic production. These rapid developments in the exploitation of natural resources in Alaska prompted opposition to more development by environmental groups.

Statehood and Native Claims

Prior to becoming a state in 1959, 99 percent of Alaska was federally owned. The new state received 103 million acres as a grant, to be selected over a period of 25 years (Rakestraw 1983). Because most of Alaska was still in the public domain, the public debate and conflicts over land designation, management, and preservation were placed on Congress's agenda to be resolved. A large variety of interest groups were involved in the struggle. Alaskan natives wanted guarantees of land, upon which their culture and life-style were based. Pioneers in the "last frontier" wanted unlimited settlement and exploitation rights. Commercial fishing industries wanted unlimited fishing; forest products firms wanted to harvest timber; and oil companies wanted to explore and drill for oil. On the other hand, conservationists—some in Alaska and many in the lower 48 states—wanted to preserve as much of Alaska in as natural a state as possible.

By 1968, 26 million acres had been transferred to the state. Conflicts and pressure from Alaskan natives resulted in the Alaska Native Claims Settlement Act (ANCSA) of 1971. Congress provided native groups with a $1 billion cash settlement and the right to select 44 million acres of federal land from a pool of mostly national forest lands. Alaskan natives wanted lands with highly valued resources. But a section of ANCSA authorized the secretary of the interior to withdraw up to 80 million acres of federal land for study as possible national parks, wildlife refuges, and wild and scenic rivers.

Recommendations for disposal of these "d-2" lands were to occur by 1978. Congress failed to meet the deadline, and by executive decree President Carter set aside 107 million acres from selection, pending legislation. He created 56 million acres of new national monuments from d-2 lands under the authority of the 1906 Antiquities Act. Further, the secretary of the interior was instructed to withdraw 40 million acres from selection under emergency authority in the 1976 Federal Land Policy and Management Act and place them in 12 national wildlife refuges. President Carter also instructed the secretary of agriculture to withdraw 11 million acres in the Tongass and Chugach National Forests (Rakestraw 1983). Citizens and officials in Alaska and Alaskan natives were less than happy about Carter's actions. But Congress basically concurred and settled the controversy by passing ANILCA.

The diversity of the groups and the significance of the Alaskan lands issue made expansion and congressional deliberations unavoidable. These characteristics did not, however, lead to an easy solution. ANILCA took years to formulate and contained many compromises between local, state, and national interests in Alaska, as well as between development and preservationist sentiments. In the end, the act reserved some lands for use by Alaskan natives, some for state agencies, and some for federal resource agencies. The act provided for the establishment of 10 new national parks, 9 new wildlife refuges, and 35 new wilderness areas. Over 56 million acres, larger than the total area of Ohio and New York, were reserved as wilderness.

Many of the residents of Alaska felt ANILCA served the national interests excessively—note "National Interest" and "Lands Conservation" in the title. Environmental groups thought that the act did not accomplish enough. Much land was still outside of wilderness and therefore unprotected. The act also validated many ongoing mining rights and logging interests, which environmental groups opposed greatly. In the end, the act has a number of the traits of political decision making: consensus without substantive conviction and no group totally pleased or totally dissatisfied. Management of the national forests and wildlife refuges remains a crucial issue in Alaska.

The Tongass National Forest

National forests are managed for multiple uses, but ANILCA aimed to reach a compromise that could provide both wilderness and jobs from timber harvesting on the Tongass National Forest in Southeast Alaska. Specifically, section 705(a) of ANILCA sets harvest levels by providing

the sum of at least $40,000,000 annually or as much as the Secretary of Agriculture finds is necessary to maintain the timber supply from the Tongass National Forest to dependent industry at a rate of four billion five hundred million board foot measure per decade.

Timber harvests on the Tongass have spurred massive protests by environmental groups, who have lobbied to have section 705(a) repealed. Environmentalists claim that the section was hastily inserted at the behest of industry groups without any formal review. Environmental groups make strong arguments against timber harvesting on the Tongass. They claim that the "taxpayer-subsidized destruction of Alaska's rainforest defies belief" (Laycock 1987, p. 111). They oppose clear-cutting on the Tongass, pointing out that revenues from harvests are far below cost and that the value of the fisheries destroyed by silt far exceeds the timber value. The deal to provide the Forest Service with $40 million to help sell 450 million board feet per year—much of it used to construct roads—was made when timber prices were at an all-time high and principally benefits the two pulp mills in Southeast Alaska. However, in 1983, for every dollar spent to sell Tongass timber, only nine cents were returned to the U.S. Treasury. For the five years beginning in 1982, the Timber Supply Fund pumped $234 million into Alaska, and timber sales returned a total income of $31 million, for a net loss of $203 million (Laycock 1987).

On the other side, the Forest Service supports the Tongass sales, saying that it is merely carrying out congressional intent in the ANILCA compromises. The two pulp mills were lured to Alaska in the 1950s with 50-year timber contracts, and the service points out that failure to supply them with logs would be breach of contract. Conservation groups will continue to struggle to repeal section 705(a), to preserve the ancient forests in the Tongass, and to protect the wildlife they feel is threatened by roads and clear-cutting.

Between 1980 and 1988 native corporations provided roughly 40 percent of all the timber harvested in southeast Alaska. This proportion is expected to decline in the future as native timber supplies dwindle (O'Laughlin and Rule 1990).

The Arctic National Wildlife Refuge

The second major national controversy regarding ANILCA is oil drilling in the Arctic National Wildlife Refuge (ANWR), in the northeast corner of Alaska on the Arctic Ocean, next to Canada. The ANWR is close to Prudhoe Bay on the North Slope, promises to be rich in oil, and could easily hook into the Trans-Alaska Pipeline. Alaska depends on oil more than any other state, deriving about 85 percent of its state income from oil taxes and revenues. Additionally, the nation's need for oil and the pressure from oil companies had nearly prodded Congress into allowing more exploration in the late 1980s. Environmental groups vehemently opposed drilling in a wildlife refuge, arguing that the ecosystems were so fragile that more drilling would harm them irreparably and stressing the adverse impact on fauna ranging from tiny aquatic animals to caribou calves.

Congress was close to reporting legislation out of the Senate Energy and Natural Resources Committee in 1989 that would allow drilling. But on March 24, 1989, an Exxon oil tanker ran aground leaving the Port of Valdez, spilling crude oil over much of Prince William Sound. Innumerable pictures of oil-soaked beaches, dead birds, blackened seals, and so on were used by environmental groups to publicize the problems with oil exploration and galvanize opposition to drilling in the ANWR. The oil spill prompted consideration and passage of several bills in the Alaska state legislature that raised oil industry taxes and spill fines and strengthened spill prevention and cleanup.

The Exxon Valdez spill delayed congressional approval of drilling in the ANWR. Support for opening the refuge to exploration remained strong in Alaska, despite the Valdez incident. Congress has cooled to the idea, especially after several more oil tanker spills occurred throughout the world in 1989 and 1990. The environmental groups now can more credibly ask if the possible increase in domestic oil production is worth the risk. They also have made more points in questioning the safety and cleanup assurances based on the fiasco at Valdez. This debate will continue to pit preservationists against development interests in Alaska and, to some extent, continental U.S. interests against local Alaskan interests.

ILLUSTRATION: OLD GROWTH, WILDLIFE, AND VALUES

The management and protection of old-growth or ancient forests is one of the most compelling forest resource issues that will face the public and professionals in the 1990s. The fate of these forests has tremendous environmental, economic, and political ramifications for the nation and for public and private forest land management. The issue is not confined to the West—members of Congress from Indiana, Minnesota, New York, and other states have sponsored bills to resolve preservation of the ancient western forests. This illustration helps provide information on this current policy debate and indicates how many of the political principles discussed in the first 11 chapters of this book are being used in setting old-growth policy.

FACTS AND VALUES

The old-growth controversy involves different definitions of ancient forests and the lack of agreement on how many remain. These technical issues can be resolved because they are matters of definition and measurable fact. But it will be difficult to decide how much ancient forest should be preserved because that involves the conflicting and deeply held values of many people. Some ancient forests already are in the National Wilderness Preservation System, and some people feel that they

are more than adequate to preserve our heritage. Other people feel that an inadequate amount of ancient forests is under protection. Preservationists feel that ancient forests have more spiritual, environmental, and perhaps even commercial (except for timber) value when left uncut. Loggers and mill owners believe trees have more value when used for lumber and indeed cringe at the thought of just watching trees grow old and die.

The need to protect habitat for the threatened northern spotted owl, which depends on a forest structure similar to that of old-growth forests, led to mandated preservation of more ancient forests. Other species that may be listed as threatened or endangered, such as the marbled murrelet, also may lead to additional preserves. The trade-off for preserving the vestiges of our ancient forest heritage and its denizens is a reduction in the amount of public timber available for commercial harvest. Some observers translate that into the loss of jobs. At the same time, logs harvested from private lands in the Pacific Northwest attract premium prices from overseas buyers and continue to be exported to Japan and other Pacific Rim countries. Public policy prohibits the export of logs harvested from public lands.

Estimates of job losses in the region due to preserving spotted owl habitat conservation areas vary widely. The industry interest group, the American Forest Resource Alliance, estimated that 147,000 jobs would be lost. The Forest Service and the Wilderness Society, on the other hand, estimated that 30,000 and 37,000 jobs, respectively, could be lost due to reduced old-growth harvests. These job losses in either case would be significant but must be viewed in the context of a long-term downward trend in the regions' timber-related employment (Sample and Le Master 1992).

Some observers say the protection of spotted owl habitat is a "surrogate" issue and that preservationists are using the Endangered Species Act to help achieve their objective of "locking up" ancient forests. This is undeniably true. How much is a pair of threatened owls worth in terms of timber harvests and woods and sawmill jobs foregone? The same "surrogate" label also can be applied to arguments that saving owls will result in the loss of jobs and social hardships in timber-dependent communities. Mill operators want cheap public timber. Mills operating near the margin of success will likely close anyway, as they always have. Jobs are being lost for reasons other than increased forest preserves, such as log exports and improvements in technology that displace human capital with machinery. How far should society go to preserve particular jobs in distressed industries? These questions defy value-free analysis and require resolution in the public policy process.

PARTICIPANTS

The players and the issues in the old-growth harvest debate have crystallized over time. The tactics and strategies also have been honed from past confrontations. Virtually all environmental groups positioned to the left of the American Forestry Association on the political spectrum oppose cutting the ancient forests in the West. Preservationists believe that the ancient forests are significant ecosystems harboring considerable biological diversity, including rare and endangered species such as spotted owls; help ameliorate global warming; and possess intrinsic spiritual values. Furthermore, the groups have lobbied hard, noting that only a fraction of the original U.S. old-growth timber remains and that we should not sacrifice it to keep the industry afloat for a few more years before the mills will close anyway. The groups have used means such as research and information releases, media campaigns, challenges to national forest management plans, appeals of the timber sales, and the Endangered Species Act to try to stop the clear-cutting of national forests.

The forest industry and the Forest Service were unprepared for these challenges to their customary timber sales practices in the early 1980s. Most of the Forest Service plans became tied up in appeals, and the industry was unable to frame cohesive responses to

these challenges. However, by the late 1980s the industry formed an umbrella lobbying organization to oppose the loss of public timber and the spillover effects on private industry. This group, the American Forest Resource Alliance (AFRA), quickly gained the support of forest products firms. AFRA used national publicity campaigns, member influence, and issue expansion to further its utilitarian goals. In 1992 it was folded back into its parent organization, the National Forest Products Association.

By 1989 the old-growth issue had expanded throughout the nation, and national forest management was on the congressional agenda and hearings were held in several places. Conservation groups, with dynamic leaders such as Jay Hair of the National Wildlife Federation, George Frampton of the Wilderness Society, and even David Brower (formerly of Sierra Club and Friends of the Earth), extolled the virtues of ancient forests and the evils of clear-cutting. And they backed their claims with well-prepared and well-publicized analyses of wildlife *and* economic issues that favored their views and values.

The AFRA/industry coalitions, led by a host of new technical specialists, lobbied in favor of continuing harvests of old-growth forests in the West and newer growth in the East. They stated that the environmental protection standards on national forests were the strictest in the world and that curtailed timber harvests would in effect export jobs and lead to more environmental destruction abroad. AFRA also sought to build coalitions with allied commercial interest groups, such as railroad, trucking, or home-building associations.

CONTINUING ISSUES

The spotted owl was listed as a threatened species by the Fish and Wildlife Service in 1990. A series of Forest Service reserves, national forest plan appeals, court cases, and congressional actions attempted to resolve the owl protection–timber harvest conundrum in the late 1980s. The issue had expanded throughout the nation by then and into the early 1990s as well. Listing the owl as a threatened species, however, changed the nature of these debates. After that action, the relevant question became how much old-growth habitat would need to be reserved from timber harvests to protect the owl? Millions of acres would be involved—perhaps up to 12 million or more.

The debate in 1990 shifted away from the traditional lumber groups–Congress member–Forest Service iron triangle relationships. Many Congress members, such as Senator Leahy of New Hampshire (chair of Agriculture, Nutrition, and Forestry) and Senator Fowler of Georgia (chair of the Subcommittee on Conservation and Forestry) clearly began to support environmental groups. But they also supported private forestry funding, in order to retain support from the private forest production sector and weaken forestry support for national forest timber sales. Additionally, many Forest Service employees formed an informal network in 1989 called the Association of Forest Service Employees for Environmental Ethics (AFSEEE). This reform group within the service, comprised of more than 2000 members by 1991, publicly opposed harvest of much old-growth timber, at the risk of their jobs (McLean 1990). Ned Fritz's Forestry Reform network also began campaigning influentially for changes in national forest management, especially an end to clear-cutting.

Part of a solution to the forest harvesting/preservation debates may come by striking a balance between harvesting either all or none of the old trees in a given stand. That will require a different professional attitude toward forest practices. Many foresters have been taught that the most rational way to manage Douglas-fir—the major Pacific Coast timber species, with trees reaching astonishing sizes and astounding volumes of timber per acre—is to clear-cut it. That conventional wisdom is no longer so widely accepted. Jerry Franklin, a Forest Service research ecologist, has shown that these forests may be managed using something other than even-aged methods. He termed these methods *new forestry*.

New forestry methods offer the promise of cutting some timber and creating desirable wildlife habitat characteristics after a partial timber harvest.

In response to public displeasure with timber-oriented individual national forest plans produced in the 1980s, and the criticism of some of its own employees, the U.S. Forest Service began developing a *new perspectives* program for land and resource management, based on the new forestry paradigm. The agency, its critics, and its supporters hope that its managers can change along with the changing needs and interests of society. Most people want more than just economic products from their public forests; they want ecological integrity within them. In fact, they probably want ecological protection primarily, and timber harvests only if they do not harm that integrity.

The new forestry or new perspectives programs attempt to develop ecological forest management regimes in the West that would allow some periodic timber harvests. This approach involves modifying traditional management so as to allow practices that more nearly mimic natural conditions and forest disturbances. Such an approach would allow for the retention at harvest of standing live trees, both in riparian zones and elsewhere; increase reliance on natural regeneration; and provide for the management of dead wood. This approach would promote a forest structure on managed forests that has characteristics similar to those found in the old-growth forests of the region. These would include, for example, a multilayered canopy; a range of tree sizes, ages, and species; and the occurrence of dead wood in the form of both snags and downed wood. New forestry also looks at the unit of management analysis as the landscape, as opposed to the usual timber stand. This allows for the introduction of harvest-free set-asides, which, for example, may by in the form of expanded riparian zones or other strategic locations.

These public debates and silvicultural/wildlife developments are likely to lead to several outcomes. Timber harvests of old growth will decline and more old-growth timber will be preserved. Various proposals will attract more support for protection, as will the revolt in the Forest Service against timber dominance. AFRA and the industry groups will oppose public timber reservations, but they seem to have a dwindling congressional support base and poor success in court challenges to protect timber harvest levels. Just how large a share of the ancient forests will be protected will depend on the strength of these groups. But because endangered species listings, court decisions, and pervasive public sentiments favor preservation of the ancient forests, harvest levels will be reduced and more stands will be retained in their present condition.

LAND ACQUISITIONS

Ongoing Purchases

It also is worth noting that increased land acquisition by government agencies has been and continues to be a viable public policy for forest resources. The Weeks Act purchases, which were authorized in 1911 and continued actively through the depression in the 1930s, resulted in the purchase of millions of acres of national forest land in the East.

The Land and Water Conservation Fund Act (LWCF) of 1965 also authorized funding for purchases of land in order to develop outdoor recreational facilities and has continued to provide significant funding since its enactment. The funds under LWCF may be used to assist states in developing recreational facilities and in acquiring and developing federal land. For example, millions of dollars of LWCF funds were used to acquire private lands around Lake Tahoe, especially on the Nevada side, and also at Sylvania in Michigan.

Federal, state, and local land acquisition efforts have continued in the 1980s and 1990s. Several states have proposed increased purchase of forest lands for parks, water quality, and wildlife protection purposes. These purchases have been constrained by tight budgets, but the area of state-owned forest land has increased substantially. For example, state-owned timberland in the United States increased from 19.2 million acres in 1952 to 26.7 million in 1987 (Waddell et al. 1989). Furthermore, many state and local purchases involved forest, range, and wetland reservations, which are not included in the timberland totals.

The public sector also has gained much more control of many forest uses via the purchase and transfer of development rights from private owners to government agencies. These transfers limit the rights of landowners to develop lands. The federal Food Security Act of 1985 (the farm bill) allowed forgiveness of some farm debts in exchange for transfer of all development rights on wetlands to the government—a means of protecting wetlands. Some local land use planning agencies have purchased development rights in order to protect (preserve) scenic vistas or rural characteristics. The transfer of development rights will continue to be one means of extending public control over land use, without outright purchase of all rights (e.g., the land itself).

The continuing purchase of lands for public ownership has been challenged recently by new private property rights groups. In 1992, 12 senators introduced legislation to prevent some federal agencies from increasing public land holdings in the 12 western states having more than 25 percent of their area in federal ownership. The senators contended that the western United States was too much like Russia and that state and local governments need private land for taxing. The proposal was titled "No Net Loss of Private Lands," reflecting the national counterattack against natural resource laws that restrict land development. The bill, however, had no Democratic cosponsors and was not considered likely to go far in Congress (Williamson 1992). The proposal does indicate that property rights groups are having some success at placing their issues on the national legislative agenda, as well as the courts' agenda. Whether they will be successful at obtaining new policies remains to be determined.

ILLUSTRATION: THE LAND AND WATER CONSERVATION FUND

During the Great Depression of the 1930s, the federal government purchased millions of acres of forest land under authority of the 1924 Clarke-McNary Act, bought abandoned farm land under the 1933 Bankhead-Jones Act and purchased and comdemned farm and forest land in the Tennessee Valley Authority rural development program. Massive reversion of private lands to the states and counties for failure to pay taxes also was common in the Lake States and, to a lesser degree, on the West Coast.

Large-scale federal and state acquisitions of forest, farm, and range land were halted shortly after World War II began. However, the federal and state governments continued to acquire lands for special purposes. Building the interstate highway system required substantial land condemnation and acquisition. Military bases and weapon testing sites required special use reservation of existing public lands. State land acquisitions for parks and other purposes continued.

The largest continuing government land acquisition program—The Land and Water Conservation Fund—was enacted in 1964. This fund has provided several billion dollars for the acquisition and management of public lands for recreation and wildlife purposes. Its history and status provide a good illustration of how the public policy of land acquisition for recreation and wildlife has developed. An article by Mantell, Myers, and Reed (1988) reviews the history and issue of the LWCF and is paraphrased in this illustration.

Establishment and Structure

Creation of a federal grants program for recreation planning and land acquisition was one of the principal recommendations of the Outdoor Recreation Resources Review Commission (ORRRC) report of 1962. Unlike those from many blue-ribbon commissions, the reports from ORRRC met with approval from Congress and the president, and the Land and Water Conservation Fund Act was passed in 1964, as one of several ORRRC recommendations that formed the basis for public policies. The LWCF was intended to provide a predictable, stable flow of earmarked funds for recreation purposes that would be insulated from the year-to-year competition for congressional appropriations. Advocates for establishing the LWCF believed that it would operate like a true trust fund (such as the Highway Trust Fund) where its revenues would be earmarked by Congress and not used for other purposes; Congress would merely appropriate money from the fund as it was needed. In theory, this would remove the flow of revenues into the LWCF from the political appropriation process, although political factors would still influence the LWCF spending.

In practice, the LWCF is not an independent trust fund. Revenue in the LWCF can and has been used for other purposes, and funds cannot be spent without the advance approval of the relevant appropriations committees in Congress. However, the LWCF has been funded by a specially designated source, different from the general appropriations process followed for most federal programs. Additionally, the fund's existence has apparently made it easier for Congress to appropriate money for federal land acquisition.

Funding of the LWCF is unique for natural resource programs. LWCF has two accounts—a receipts account and an appropriations account for distributing state grants and acquiring federal lands. The receipts account grows by $400 million each year, less whatever is transferred to the appropriations account. The receipts account, however, is only a bookkeeping account. For example the account had $1.8 billion in 1982, but only on paper. The LWCF receipts fund was actually held as part of the general treasury fund and included in the budget as an "offsetting receipt." However, the LWCF "paper account" does allow the money to be carried over from year to year, unlike most federal appropriations.

The LWCF carryover feature may cause variations in LWCF appropriations. If an agency accumulates unspent funds, Congress may withhold or reduce appropriations and direct the agency to spend the funds. On the other hand, the carryover feature can be used by agencies to blunt the destabilizing effect of large shifts in appropriations.

Revenue Sources and Disbursements

The LWCF originally received revenues from the sale of surplus property, the motorboat fuel tax, and user fees from recreation activities on federal lands. These funds amounted to about $100 million in 1967 and 1968, which the supporting interest groups deemed to be inadequate. They sought additional funding, which was granted by Congress in 1968. The 1968 amendments provided that the LWCF would receive at least $200 million per year. The difference between the original funding sources and $200 million would be gleaned from oil and gas lease revenues on the Outer Continental Shelf. Congress raised the floor to $300 million annually in 1970 and $900 million in 1977. Approximately 90 percent of the LWCF receipts now come from the oil and gas lease revenues.

A share of the LWCF goes to the federal government and a share goes to the states. The state share provides matching grants to state governments for acquisition and development of recreational facilities. States may use the funds themselves or pass them on to local governments. The federal share is used mostly for acquisition by the NPS, BLM, FS, and FWS.

States must prepare a State Comprehensive Outdoor Recreation Plan (SCORP) to receive a share of the LWCF pool. These plans are updated periodically. The SCORP documents must inventory all federal, state, county, and local recreational lands and facilities; analyze present and projected recreation demands; and lay out a program for implementing the plan. The LWCF was amended in 1986 by the Emergency Wetlands Resources Act (Public Law 99-645) to allow wetland acquisition, which was formerly allowed only under the Migratory Bird Conservation Act (Duck Stamp Act).

Accomplishments

The LWCF has been a key federal law and funding source for acquiring, managing, and protecting outdoor recreation lands, wildlife habitat, and scenic and historic resources. The blend of federal, state, and local assistance in the LWCF resembles other federal–state forest resources programs and even extends the model to local governments, which provided a powerful political appeal to many interest groups and government agencies. In the late 1970s and early 1980s, states provided less cost-sharing funds in general and shifted more toward facility development than land acquisition. On average, state projects received about one-third of the LWCF funds received by each state, and localities received about two-thirds.

Since it was initiated in 1964, the Land and Water Conservation Fund has spent $3.2 billion of federal funds, which have been matched in various proportions by state and local governments, to help these levels of government plan, acquire, and develop more than 32,000 projects providing parks and outdoor recreation facilities in some 14,000 communities. By 1986 the National Park Service had spent $2.1 billion in LWCF money to acquire 1.6 million acres of land for national parks. The Fish and Wildlife Service spent $350 million by 1986 to acquire 390,000 acres of land, and $3.6 billion of LWCF funds were spent to purchase 3.2 million acres of other land for the Departments of the Interior and Agriculture (Mantell et al. 1988).

Despite its success, the LWCF has been criticized. The state SCORP documents have been fairly general and have not been all that useful for community planning and priority setting. Some lands purchased by the states have proven to be inaccessible without easements from private landowners, which could not be purchased with LWCF money. And despite a reasonable funding basis, the interest groups support for LWCF has been fairly modest.

Ongoing Issues

In 1987 the LWCF was reauthorized without change for 25 years more. But ongoing debate about the program began in the same year after release of the recommendations from the President's Commission on Americans Outdoor (1987) report. The PCAO commission recommended the establishment of a true trust fund.

Administration of the LWCF also has been contentious. Following a recommendation of the ORRRC groups, a federal Bureau of Outdoor Recreation was created within the Interior Department to help administer the LWCF, provide technical assistance to state and local governments with LWCF grants, and prepare a National Outdoor Recreation Plan. During the Carter administration, the bureau was converted into the Heritage Conservation and Recreation Service, which assumed LWCF administration. During the first year of the Reagan administration, Secretary of the Interior James Watt abolished Carter's agency and transferred its LWCF responsibilities to the National Park Service. Critics of Reagan, Watt, and eventually President Bush felt that the Park Service direct administration was unwise. They felt that the agency was too politicized, ignored historic preservation, provided little help to the states, and had too large an interest in keeping funds for National Park System use. These complaints and others have provided ongoing issues about revision of the LWCF fund.

The PCAO report recommended some reorganization of the granting methods, including more cooperation with the private nonprofit groups that have developed since 1962. Most major national conservation groups, led by the National Parks and Conservation Association and the Wilderness Society, adopted 13 recommendations as the basis for congressional action. These efforts to revise the LWCF, however, did not meet with success. Their implementation depended on budget increases to a large degree, which proved difficult to obtain when deficits of $200 billion occurred every year in the 1980s, despite the Gramm-Rudman-Hollings deficit reduction legislation. The blue-ribbon PCAO recommendations also were opposed by the Reagan and Bush administrations, both for their adverse budget implications and because they further impinged on the privatization movement promoted by the Reagan executive officials and the private property rights move-

ment supported by Bush and Dan Quayle. The early 1990s saw continued debate about revising the LWCF structure and revenues, as well as the spending of the growing surplus of carryover funds, but no major action was taken.

SUMMARY

The federal government owns and manages about 28.6 percent of the land and water area in the United States, and state and local governments own an additional 6.7 percent. Thus only 64.7 percent of the land in the United States is held by private owners. The U. S. Department of the Interior (USDI) Bureau of Land Management is the largest federal landowner, with almost 266 million acres, mostly in the West and in Alaska. The USDA Forest Service owns about 190 million acres of forest and range land. Two other agencies with large land holdings include the USDI Fish and Wildlife Service (83 million acres) and the National Park Service (74 million acres), although much of this land is in Alaska. The Department of Defense, including the Army Corps of Engineers, owns almost 26 million acres of land. State and local governments also own more than 150 million acres of land.

The early colonists in the United States revered land ownership as one of the crucial rights in America. Many colonists and new settlers moved west in America in order to find better lands to farm and exploit for their natural resources. The new United States of America gained control of the lands from the Atlantic Coast to the Pacific Coast by revolution, war, intimidation, and purchase from European countries and Native Americans. For its first century as a nation, the U.S. government tried to dispose of these public domain lands as expeditiously as possible, via land sales; gifts to railroads; establishment of territories; grants for veterans, homesteading, and mining; or other means. The diminishing quality of public domain in the West along with the wanton destruction of timber and wildlife in the 1800s prompted the first American conservation movement and the reservation of national parks, forest reserves, and wildlife refuges in the late 1800s and early 1900s.

Our modern federal natural resource agencies evolved over the last century. The U.S. Department of the Interior housed many agencies that have since become separate departments but still contains several important public lands agencies. The Bureau of Land Management controls much of the western rangelands, which are important for grazing and mining. The Bureau of Reclamation builds and maintains dams for irrigation, flood control, hydropower generation, and outdoor recreation in the western states. The National Park Service manages many natural, historic, and scenic areas for public recreational use and protection of natural ecosystems. The Fish and Wildlife Service regulates the taking of migratory birds, helps protect threatened and endangered species, performs research, and manages the extensive National Wildlife Refuge System. Last, the Bureau of Indian Affairs helps Native American tribes manage the lands they own.

The U.S. Department of Agriculture contains the Forest Service, which manages the 190-million-acre National Forest System. The Department of Defense holds millions of acres in military reservations, which provide wildlife protection and timber supplies in local areas. The U.S. Army Corps of Engineers also owns and manages millions of acres of land and water, due to its involvement in massive water projects and dam building throughout the nation. State and local governments own land for public buildings, parks, wildlife preserves, forest reserves, and many other purposes.

Many federal lands have been reserved by congressional action for dominant use mandates. Separate wilderness lands were proposed for almost 50 years before their eventual authorization in the Wilderness Act of 1964. Many wild and scenic rivers have been protected by federal law under legislation passed in 1968, and a national trail system was set up then and has expanded greatly since. The lands in Alaska were most recently legislatively allocated to different public and private owners based on 1980 congressional action.

LITERATURE CITED

Alston, Richard M. 1983. The Individual vs. the Public Interest: Political Ideology and National Forest Policy. Westview Press. Boulder, CO. 250 pp.

Arrandale, Tom. 1983. The Battle for Natural Resources. Congressional Quarterly, Inc. Washington, DC. 230 pp.

Bartlett, Richard A. 1983. Yellowstone National Park. Pp. 735–737 in Richard C. Davis (ed.), Encyclopedia of American Forest and Conservation History, Vol. 2. Macmillan. New York.

Bassett, Kedric A. 1989. Utah's School Trust Lands. *Journal of Energy Law and Policy* 9(2):195–212.

Beuter, John H. 1990. Social and economic impacts of spotted owl conservation strategy. American Forest Resource Alliance Technical Bulletin No. 9003, Washington, DC. 37 pp.

Browning, James A., John C. Hendee, and Joe W. Roggenbuck. 1988. 103 Wilderness Laws: Milestones and Management Direction in Wilderness Legislation, 1964–1987. Bulletin No. 51, University of Idaho, College of Forestry, Wildlife and Range Sciences. Moscow. 73 pp.

Bureau of Land Management. 1983. Public Land Statistics 1982. U.S. Department of the Interior, Bureau of Land Management. U.S. Government Printing Office. Washington, DC. 216 pp.

Clarke, Jeanne Nienabar, and Daniel McCool. 1985. Staking Out the Terrain: Power Differentials among Natural Resource Agencies. State University of New York Press. Albany. 198 pp.

Clawson, Marion. 1971. The Bureau of Land Management. Praeger Publishers. New York. 209 pp.

Clawson, Marion. 1975. Forests for Whom and for What? Resources for the Future/John Hopkins University Press. Baltimore, MD. 175 pp.

Clawson, Marion. 1976. The Economics of National Forest Management. RFF Working Paper EN-6. Resources for the Future/Johns Hopkins Press. Baltimore, MD. 117 pp.

Clawson, Marion, and Winston Harrington. 1991. The growing role of outdoor recreation. Pp. 249–282 in Kenneth D. Frederick and Roger A. Sedjo (eds.), America's Renewable Resources—Historical Trends and Current Challenges. Resources for the Future/Johns Hopkins Press. Baltimore, MD.

Clawson, Marion, and Burnell Held. 1957. The Federal Lands: Their Use and Management. Resources for the Future/Johns Hopkins Press. Baltimore, MD. 501 pp.

Clements, Kendrick A. 1983. Robert Marshall (1901–1939). Pp. 406–408 in Richard C. Davis (ed.), Encyclopedia of American Forest and Conservation History, Vol. 2. Macmillan. New York.

Coggins, George C., and Charles F. Wilkinson. 1987. Federal Public Land and Resources Law, 2nd ed. Foundation Press. Mineola, NY. 1066 pp.

Culhane, Paul J. 1981. Public Land Politics: Interest Group Influence in the Forest Service and Bureau of Land Management. Johns Hopkins Press. Baltimore, MD. 398 pp.

Dana, Samuel T., and Sally K. Fairfax. 1980. Forest and Range Policy, 2nd ed. McGraw-Hill. New York. 458 pp.

Davis, Richard C. 1983a. Robert Marshall (1901–1939). Pp. 406–408 in Richard C. Davis (ed.), Encyclopedia of American Forest and Conservation History, Vol. 2. Macmillan. New York.

Davis, Richard C. 1983b. Wild and scenic rivers. Pp. 690–691 in Richard C. Davis (ed.), Encyclopedia of American Forest and Conservation History, Vol. 2. Macmillan. New York.

Devens, Carol. 1983. Indian forest use. Pp. 308–311 in Richard C. Davis (ed.), Encyclopedia of American Forest and Conservation History, Vol. 1. Macmillan. New York.

Devoto, Bernard. 1953. The easy chair—the sturdy corporate homesteader, western land grabs. *Harper's* 206(1236):57–60, May.

Dowdle, Barney. 1984. The case for selling federal timberlands. Pp. 21–46 in Selling the Federal Forests. Contribution No. 50. University of Washington, College of Forest Resources. Seattle.

Fairfax, Sally K., and Carolyn E. Yale. 1987. Federal Lands. Island Press. Washington, DC. 252 pp.

Gardner, B. Delworth. 1991. Rangeland resources: Changing uses and productivity. Pp. 123–166 in Kenneth D. Frederick and Roger A. Sedjo (eds.), America's Renewable Resources—Historical Trends and Current Challenges. Resources for the Future/Johns Hopkins Press. Baltimore, MD.

Gates, Paul. 1968. History of Public Land Law Development. Public Land Law Review Commission. Washington, DC. 828 pp.

Hanke, Steve H. 1984. On privatization. Pp. 84–92 in Proceedings, Symposium on Selling the Federal Forests. Institute of Forest Resources Contribution No. 50. University of Washington, College of Forest Resources. Seattle.

Hendee, John C., George H. Stankey, and Robert C. Lucas. 1990. Wilderness Management, 2nd ed. Fulcrum. Golden, CO. 546 pp.

Jensen, Clayne R. 1977. Outdoor Recreation in America: Trends, Problems, and Opportunities, 3rd ed. Burgess Publishing Company. Minneapolis. 269 pp.

Joyce, Linda A. 1989. An analysis of the range forage situation in the United States: 1989–2040. A Technical Document Supporting the 1989 USDA Forest Service RPA Assessment. USDA Forest Service, Rocky Mountain Forest and Range Experiment Station. Fort Collins, CO. 130pp.

Laycock, George. 1987. Trashing the Tongass. *Audubon*. November, pp. 110–127.

Leman, Christopher K. 1984. The revolution of the saints: The ideology of privatization and its consequences for the public lands. Pp. 93–162 in Selling the Federal Forests. Contribution No. 50. University of Washington, College of Forest Resources. Seattle.

Leopold, Aldo. 1921. The wilderness and its place in forest recreational policy. *Journal of Forestry* 19:718–721.

Leopold, Aldo. 1933. Game Management. Scribner. New York. 481 pp.

Lippke, Bruce R., J. Keith Gilles, Robert G. Lee, and Paul E. Sommers. 1990. Three-state impact of spotted owl conservation and other timber harvest reductions: A cooperative evaluation of the economic and social impacts. Based on independent studies at the University of Washington, University of California, and Oregon State University Institute of Forest Resources. Contribution No. 69. University of Washington, Seattle. 43 pp.

Mantell, Michael, Phyllis Myers, and Robert B. Reed. 1988. The Land and Water Conservation Fund: Past experience, future directions. Pp. 257–281 in William J. Chandler, (ed.), Audubon Wildlife Report 1988/1989. The National Audubon Society. New York.

Marsh, George Perkins. 1864. Man and Nature. Belknap Press/Harvard University Press. (1965 Reprinted Version). Cambridge, MA. 472 pp.

Marshall, Robert. 1933. The People's Forests. Harrison Smith and Robert Haas. New York. 224 pp.

McClean, Herbert E. 1990. A very hot potato. *American Forests* 96(3,4):30–31, 65–67.

McGeary, Nelson M. 1960. Gifford Pinchot. Princeton University Press. Princeton, NJ. 481 pp.

Mohai, Paul, and David L. Verbyla. 1987. The RARE II Wilderness Decisions. *Journal of Forestry* 85(1):17–24.

Nash, Roderick. 1967. Wilderness and the American Mind. Yale University Press. New Haven, CT. 256 pp.

O'Laughlin, Jay. 1990. Idaho's Endowment Lands: A Matter of Sacred Trust. Idaho Forest, Wildlife and Range Policy Analysis Group Report No. 1. University of Idaho. Moscow, 18 pp.

O'Laughlin, Jay, and Lita C. Rule. 1990. The future of Alaska's forest products industry. *Journal of Forestry* 88(12):16–22.

Outdoor Recreation Resources Review Commission. 1961. Final Report of the Outdoor Recreation Resources Review Commission to Congress. 27 volumes. U.S. Government Printing Office. Washington, DC.

Pinchot, Gifford. 1947. Breaking New Ground. Harcourt, Brace. New York. 522 pp.

Potter, Barrett G. 1983. Civilian Conservation Corps. Pp. 82–83 in Richard C. Davis (ed.), Encyclopedia of American Forest and Conservation History, Vol 1. Macmillan. New York.

Powell, John Wesley. 1879. Lands of the Arid Regions of the United States, 2nd Ed. Document No. 73, 45th Congress, 2nd session. 208 pp. U.S. Government Printing Office. Washington, DC.

President's Commission on Americans Outdoors. 1987. Report and Recommendations to the United States. 4 vols. U.S. Government Printing Office. Washington, DC.

President's Commission on Americans Outdoors. 1987. The Report of the President's Commission—Americans Outdoors: The Legacy, the Challenge. Island Press. Washington, DC. 426 pp.

Public Land Law Review Commission. 1970. One Third the Nation's Land. Report to President and to Congress of the Public Land Law Review Commission. U.S. Government Printing Office. Washington, DC. 342 pp.

Puter, Stephen A. Douglas. 1908. Looters of the Public Domain, Embracing a Complete Exposure of the Fraudulent Systems of Acquiring Title to Public Lands of the United States. Da Capo Press. New York. (reprinted 1972).

Rakestraw, Lawrence W. 1983. Alaska forests. Pp. 9–13 in Richard C. Davis (ed.), Encyclopedia of American Forest and Conservation History, Vol. 1. Macmillan. New York.

Sample, V. Alaric, and Dennis C. Le Master. 1992. Assessing the Employment Impacts of

Proposed Measures to Protect the Northern Spotted Owl. Forest Policy Center, American Forestry Association. Washington, DC. 65 pp.

Savas, E. S. 1982. Privatizing the Public Sector. Chatham House. Chatham, NJ. 164 pp.

Shands, William E. 1977. The Lands Nobody Wanted: Policy for National Forests in the Eastern United States. The Conservation Foundation. Washington, DC. 282 pp.

Statistical Abstract of the United States. 1989. U.S. Department of Commerce. U.S. Government Printing Office. Washington, DC.

Task Force on Outdoor Recreation Resources and Opportunities. 1988. Outdoor Recreation in a Nation of Communities. U.S. Government Printing Office. Washington, DC. 169 pp.

Trefethen, James B. 1966. Wildlife regulation and restoration. Pp. 16–37 in Henry Clepper (ed.), Origins of American Conservation. Ronald Press. New York.

Udall, Stewart. 1962. The Quiet Crisis. Holt, Rinehart & Winston. New York. 209 pp.

USDA Forest Service. 1987. Report of the Forest Service, Fiscal Year 1986. U.S. Government Printing Office. Washington, DC. 172 pp.

U.S. Department of the Interior. 1976. America 200: The Legacy of Our Lands. Conservation Yearbook II, Special Bicentennial Edition 1975–1976. U.S. Government Printing Office. Washington, DC. 160 pp.

U.S. General Services Administration. 1989. Summary Report of Real Property Owned by the United States throughout the World as of September 30, 1989. Unnumbered report of the Office of Governmentwide Real Property Relations, Public Buildings Service, GSA. Washington, DC. 68 pp.

Waddell, Karen L., Daniel D. Oswald, and Douglas S. Powell. 1989. Forest Statistics of the United States, 1987. Resource Bulletin PNW-RB-168. USDA Forest Service, Pacific Northwest Research Station. Portland, OR. 106 pp.

Waggener, Thomas R. 1984. Federal commercial forest lands: Origins, status and issues. Pp. 1–20 in Selling the Federal Forests. Contribution No. 50. University of Washington, College of Forest Resources. Seattle.

Wellman, J. Douglas. 1987. Wildland Recreation Policy. Wiley. New York. 284 pp.

Williamson, Lonnie. 1992. Senators would limit federal estate. *Outdoor News Bulletin.* 46(3):1–2.

Wirth, Conrad L. 1966. Parks and wilderness. Pp. 146–159 in Henry Clepper, (ed.), Origins of American Conservation. Ronald Press. New York.

Wise, Carla, and Jay O'Laughlin. 1990. Idaho Department of Fish and Game's Land Acquisition and Land Management Program. Idaho Forest, Wildlife and Range Policy Analysis Group Report No. 3. University of Idaho. Moscow. 26 pp.

Worrell, Albert C. 1970. Principles of Forest Policy. McGraw-Hill. New York. 243 pp.

Chapter 13

Federal Forest Policy: Multiple-Use Forestry and Forest Planning

1. The management of the Nation's renewable resources is highly complex and the uses, demand for, and supply of the various resources are subject to change over time.

6. The Forest Service…has both a responsibility and an opportunity to be a leader in assuring that the Nation maintains a natural resource conservation posture that will meet the requirements of our people in perpetuity.

—National Forest Management Act of 1976, Section 2

Chapter 12 discussed public land management agencies and issues. This chapter traces the development of modern federal forest policy in the United States as enacted in the Multiple-Use Sustained-Yield Act (MUSYA) of 1960, the Forest and Rangeland Renewable Resources Planning Act (RPA) of 1974, and the National Forest Management Act (NFMA) of 1976. RPA and NFMA are the principal methods for U.S. forest planning, and they merit separate examination here. Additionally, the chapter illustrates the interaction of the American people and government institutions as participants in the policy process.

FOREST MANAGEMENT PLANNING POLICY

MUSYA and RPA/NFMA were designed principally to govern the management of our na-

tional forests. But the laws are important for private forestry as well. The public's desire for forest resources that cannot be satisfied from public lands will need to be fulfilled on private lands, and vice versa. The public's image of the forestry profession is partly a function of how federal forestry is conducted. Bolle (1982 p. 339) addressed the importance of forest planning by saying, "The planning must include all woodlands, public and private, and for leadership we look to the government, the only body stable enough to plan for decades and centuries." The USDA Forest Service is the government's lead agency for forest planning.

The Forest Service always considered planning necessary for good management, from the time of Gifford Pinchot, the first chief of the Forest Service, to the current NFMA planning regulations. The main difference is that until NFMA was enacted in the mid-1970s, there was virtually no congressional direction other than broad mandates (Wilkinson and Anderson 1987).

Pinchot believed that wise use and preservation of forest resources were compatible. To implement Pinchot's philosophy of conservation, two traditions of planning—utilitarian and protective—developed for timber, range, and watershed areas. Under Pinchot's leadership, four features of planning became fundamental parts of Forest Service policy. All four components are still followed today in NFMA: (1) prepare detailed inventories, (2) monitor the condition of the reserves, (3) determine sustainable use levels, and (4) exclude use from specific areas where necessary to protect watershed and other resources (Wilkinson and Anderson 1987).

Despite the Forest Service's planning history, its efforts did not lead to public acceptance of the results. RPA/NFMA is the legislative reply of Congress to public protests of the 1960s and 1970s regarding federal forest management. NFMA gives the Forest Service fairly specific planning instructions. Sen. Hubert H. Humphrey, one of the two principal sponsors of NFMA, identified the central problem as a predominance of timber production activities over protection of other resources. He wanted to prevent the Forest Service from "turning the national forests into tree production programs which override other values" (Wilkinson and Anderson 1987, p. 70).

RPA/NFMA also represents a statement of American forest policy that many forestry professionals of that time advocated (Clawson 1975, Connaughton 1975, Craig 1975, Glascock 1977a, Spurr 1976). Glascock (1977b p. 306) said that "this planning and goal-setting law may well be, in disguise, the American forest policy so avidly sought by a number of forestry spokesmen." Sen. Patrick J. Leahy, in his keynote address to the 1979 Society of American Foresters' national convention, said that "America needs a federal forest policy to give direction, guidance and consistency to all federal programs that affect the woodlands" (Leahy 1980, p. 2). RPA/NFMA fulfills part of that need. During the Reagan presidency, the forestry community was relatively

silent on the need for an American forest policy, perhaps because of the daunting challenges that have developed in implementing RPA/NFMA.

RPA/NFMA is concerned primarily with planning, but that is only one part of policy. Perhaps the realization will come someday, as Behan (1981a, 1981b, 1988) says it should, that planning is only a precursor to management, and that better forest planning does not necessarily mean better forest management. Put simply, RPA/NFMA was designed by Congress to provide the framework and method for allocating forest resources to their various uses in the face of competing demands (Krutilla and Haigh 1978). RPA/NFMA provides an assessment of U.S. forest resources and an analysis of federal forest policy alternatives; programmatic decisions among alternatives remain a congressional responsibility.

RPA and NFMA are attempts at rational-comprehensive planning. But in practice, these policy tools are inherently political. RPA contains many detailed analyses in each of its assessments and program recommendations. However, the RPA recommendations are shaped by interest group input, by the current presidential administration, and by Forest Service objectives and culture. The individual forest plans, despite the use of the sophisticated FORPLAN computer program, public comments, and planning sessions, are even more likely than national RPA plans to result from the efforts of competing interests to shape their directions. Local commodity, recreation, and amenity groups seek their own goals, and the national forest groups promotes theirs. Overall national interests may complement or conflict with local interests.

MULTIPLE-USE PLANNING

The beginnings of our current national forest planning stemmed from the concept of *multiple use*. Multiple use is a difficult notion to define, let alone administer. Federal land management agencies have always had the multiple responsibilities of developing policies for timber sales, watershed protection, and grazing permits. Multiple use in the Forest Service evolved from both legislative intent and a need to broaden support for forestry. In 1905 Gifford Pinchot declared that the agency would strive to achieve "the greatest good of the greatest number in the long run." This philosophy continues to shape the agency's policies today (Clary 1986).

Pinchot's statement is unequalled in describing the need for and wisdom of sustained yield. But as a formulation of multiple use, it was ill defined and biased. Of primary importance to Pinchot were the needs of the home builder and the timber industry; he did not speak to recreation, wildlife, and aesthetic needs. Modern multiple-use conceptions are as ill defined as Pinchot's nebulous principle (Huffman 1978).

Foresters understand multiple use as a concept, but they have been perplexed when it comes to implementing it in a management scheme. Forestry professionals who have tried to define, clarify, or apply the concept of multiple use run the gamut, literally, from A to Z: Altson (1983), Alward (1986), Barber (1984), Behan (1981b), Coggins (1982), Connaughton (1962), Convery (1980), Crafts (1970), Davis (1969), Fight (1980), Glascock (1968, 1970, 1972), Gregory (1955, 1987), Hall (1963), McArdle (1970), Popovich (1979), Ridd (1965), Risbrudt (1986), Robinson (1975), Teeguarden (1982), Whaley (1970), Worrell (1970) and Zivnuska (1961, 1980). This alphabetic sequence could be readily completed using the quarterly *Social Sciences in Forestry* bibliography section on multiple use that averages 11 citations per quarter (Albrecht et al.).

Even the media recognize that multiple use is little more than what Clawson (1975) calls a slogan. A *Newsweek* cover story on federal lands had this to say: "Much of the remaining [federal] land is held by law for 'multiple use'—a somewhat implausible doctrine that requires federal land managers to juggle hunting, fishing, timbering, grazing, oil, gas and mineral development, watershed protection, wildlife preservation and recreation on the same lands" (Beck et al. 1983, p. 23).

PUBLIC DEMANDS ON NATIONAL FORESTS

A century ago, the American public expressed more concern for fish and game management than it did for forest, watershed, and land management. The focus of the first conservation efforts by the public was on wild animals (Reiger 1975). It was not until the 1930s that advocates for wild animals began to consider forests, waters, and land as habitats for wildlife rather than as commodities. This view is compatible with modern environmental interests but conflicts with earlier utilitarian conservation ideas, described by Hays (1959, 1987) as efficient commodity production. Concern for the habitat of wild animals became an important feature of multiple use and made the job of forest resource managers more difficult.

But it was not until after World War II that the concept of multiple use received much attention outside the Forest Service (Clary 1986). Prior to the 1950s Forest Service planning was relatively uncomplicated because the management of range, timber, and noncommodity resources seldom interfered or conflicted with each other, so there was little need to accommodate one use to the needs of another. Recreation and wilderness uses were not yet controversial because there was little pressure to reconcile them with other national forest uses (Wilkinson and Anderson 1987).

Until the post–World War II period, Americans were confident that their national forests were being protected from fire, insects, disease, and rapacious developers. In the first half of the nineteenth century, the nation's timber needs were met from private lands—holdings of both large industrial firms and smaller independent forest landowners. The national forests became an important supplier of timber during the postwar housing boom. For the first time, timber harvesting became a major activity of the Forest Service. The "greatest good" policy was interpreted to mean maximizing timber production. Congress began to view the Forest Service primarily as a commodity-producing as well as an income-producing agency for the national treasury (Bolle 1987). Between 1950 and 1959 annual timber harvests from national forests increased from 3.5 to 8.3 billion board feet (Wilkinson and Anderson 1987).

With the development of the interstate highway system during President Eisenhower's administration in the 1950s and the increasing amounts of affluence and leisure time, more people were able to use America's once-remote natural resources. More use of public forests led to more conflicts regarding resource allocation. An increasing sense of dissatisfaction with the war in Vietnam led many to question virtually every other area of governmental involvement in their lives.

The previously harmonious, administrative national forest planning framework began to crumble because of the increased demand not only for timber but also for all other resources. Annual recreational visitor days increased from 26 to 81.5 million between 1950 and 1959. Forest Service planners responded to increasing demands by attempting to coordinate resource planning, based on the intuitive judgments of forest supervisors and district rangers concerning the best use for each part of the forest (Wilkinson and Anderson 1987).

MULTIPLE-USE SUSTAINED-YIELD ACT (MUSYA) OF 1960

When the American people began to demand resources other than timber from the national forests, the Forest Service answered by preaching about "multiple use," but practices changed little (Clary 1986). Multiple use had been around for a long time. The Organic Act of 1897 acknowledged timber and water control as purposes of the forest reserves. The national forests served other interests as well. Grazing was the most important of the uses until the 1940s. Mining and various forms of recreation had required some attention since the inception of the reserves. From the 1920s on the Forest Service managed wildlife and water resources. A formal, but unsystematic, program of designated wildernesses and primitive areas had been developed. Dur-

ing World War II, the Society of American Foresters produced a formal policy document calling for multiple use to ensure "adequate recognition of all resources and benefits," including recreation. But a decade later in the 1950s, the Forest Service had no systematic approach to accommodate conflicting interests (Clary 1986).

During the late 1950s the Forest Service faced increasing pressure to change its management policies. Forest products manufacturing interests wanted to cut more timber; preservation interests wanted to prohibit timber harvests. The agency responded to these pressures by proposing legislation mandating multiple use (Wilkinson and Anderson 1987). During the 1950s Congress considered a multiple-use proposal for management of the national forests during each of its sessions. By 1960, 53 bills proposing multiple-use and sustained-yield management of national forest lands had been introduced in the House of Representatives (Huffman 1978). The Forest Service itself had written virtually all of the legislation dealing with forestry and the administration of the agency, up to and including the Multiple-Use Sustained-Yield Act of 1960.

Confronted by conflicting pressures from timber, grazing, recreation, and wilderness interest groups, the Forest Service requested clarification of its mission from Congress in the hope of strengthening the agency's hand in balancing competing pressures from different interest groups. The Forest Service was wary of losing land to the National Park Service, so it also sought affirmation from Congress of its legitimacy as a provider of recreation facilities on the national forests. The Forest Service wrote and lobbied for MUSYA. This was an awkward position for it to be in, because Congress had to be convinced on the one hand that the legislation was needed, and on the other that the authority to practice multiple use already existed. After considerable discussion, Congress passed MUSYA nearly unanimously (Dana and Fairfax 1980).

MUSYA was a legislative milepost in a period of gradual change. It recognized new uses and new pressures, but it did so in a traditional way. MUSYA reserved discretionary authority in the hands of Forest Service technical experts who were imbued with a concept of conservation defined in the earlier, simpler era of Gifford Pinchot. MUSYA failed to recognize the challenges of the strongly dissenting faction of lovers of forest aesthetics who had earlier risen up behind John Muir to challenge Pinchot. It failed to realize that there is more to conservation of natural resources than technically defined wise use (Dana and Fairfax 1980).

The passage of MUSYA in 1960 marked the beginning of a new and unsettled era of Forest Service planning. Outdoor recreation, range, wildlife, and fish were given equal statutory footing with timber and watershed uses. However, MUSYA only required equal "consideration" to all resources, begging the question of how to administer such resources equally (Wilkinson and Anderson 1987). The Multiple-Use Sustained-Yield Act of 1960, in the end, was not a seminal piece of legislation, but rather a codification of the Forest Service management policies that had evolved to that point in time. Rather than a benchmark, it proved to be a milepost as agency policy evolved. As a guide for decision making or as a standard for evaluating the performance of programs, MUSYA is not very helpful. Little guidance for setting priorities is given in the law.

MULTIPLE CRITICISMS

Bolle (1987) wrote that the concept of multiple use tilted so that timber harvesting was pronounced beneficial to wildlife, water production, and other forest uses. But nontimber uses were neglected in the budget and in the field. The structure of the Forest Service and its reward system were wedded to timber because only timber meant money, growth, and power for the agency. Iron triangle relationships among Congress members who appropriated harvest and road budgets; the forest industry, which supported them; and the For-

est Service, which sought more growth, led to timber primacy. Multiple use ran afoul of multiple demands. Multiple use seemed to delude the Forest Service into believing that all interests were being accommodated, but dividing the forest into five categories—outdoor recreation, range, timber, water, and wildlife and fish—is simplistic. Increasing demands made on federal land managers could not be easily pigeonholed into a few uses. The grip that timber production held on the Forest Service was not loosened by MUSYA (Clary 1986).

The environmental movement of the 1960s and 1970s brought a new ethic and a new set of laws into natural resource management. Bolle (1987) wrote that the Forest Service was out of step with these changes and suddenly found itself perceived as an enemy of the environment and the people. Logging methods, timber supply, and recreation represent the value conflicts that the Forest Service had to deal with in the MUSYA era and today. Barely was the presidential ink on MUSYA dry when the environmental storm broke across the nation. The Forest Service not only had a whole new set of policies to contend with, but also a bevy of watchdogs following at its heels. It is ironic that the Forest Service would become unnerved by such close scrutiny. Foresters had long lamented the lack of public interest in their work; now that the public was interested, foresters were dodging brickbats instead of catching long-awaited bouquets (Steen 1976).

The Sierra Club objected to the lack of specific management standards in MUSYA and was the only major interest group that did not support its passage. The Sierra Club argued that foresters, with their predisposition to timber production, were unqualified to make value decisions regarding which and how many acres should be set aside and left unmanaged (Dana and Fairfax 1980, McCloskey 1961). The Sierra Club withheld active opposition to MUSYA in return for a statement in the act that wilderness was consistent with the purposes and provisions of MUSYA

(Le Master 1984). The Wilderness Society and other groups also had sought federal wilderness authorizations, based on a bill first introduced by Senator Humphrey in 1956. These efforts eventually led to the Wilderness Act of 1964, which reflected an absence of faith in multiple use in the Forest Service (Clary 1986).

MUSYA is primarily important for the precedent it set. In the 1950s the timber industry began claiming that the multiple use policy of the Forest Service was in error, that under the Organic Act the national forests were set up only for timber, water, and forage. The Forest Service requested and got from Congress authorization for equal consideration for recreation, range, timber, watershed, and wildlife and fish.

In this bill, wilderness as a resource was defeated, but the Wilderness Society and Sierra Club managed to obtain insertion of a final sentence in Section 2: "The establishment and maintenance of areas of wilderness are consistent with the purposes and provisions of the act." This is the first mention of wilderness in a federal statute (Le Master 1984).

In implementing MUSYA, the courts and the Forest Service agree that MUSYA "breathes discretion." The statute now says that "In the administration of the national forests, due consideration shall be given to the relative values of the various resources in particular areas" (16 U.S.C. 529 [1985]).

This language is a license to compromise, and most organizations accept it. There have been few lawsuits involving MUSYA. Today the act serves mostly to mark the formal, albeit indirect, acceptance of the value that public forests are for the public.

COMPREHENSIVE PLANNING

New environmental laws passed in the 1970s threatened to reduce not only timber harvests but also the Forest Service's decision-making authority. These laws were written by others but affected the Forest Service, putting the agency in a new and uncomfortable relationship with the public and Congress. Members of many interest groups and many forestry analysts argued that we needed to deal with public forest land management problems in a rational-comprehensive planning process—in other words, we needed an American forest policy.

Legislation enacted after MUSYA had major impacts on forest planning, chiefly the National Environmental Policy Act (NEPA) of 1969 (42 U.S.C. 4321) and the Endangered Species Act (ESA) of 1973 (16 U.S.C. 1531).

If MUSYA has important but somewhat indirect effects on forest planning under the NFMA, the scope of NEPA's application to the Forest Service cannot be overestimated. The Council on Environmental Quality, established as the rule-making body for NEPA, requires that all federal agencies integrate NEPA compliance with their decision-making processes. Thus all forest plans must be accompanied by Environmental Impact Statements that "shall be prepared using an inter-disciplinary approach which will insure the integrated use of the natural and social sciences and the environmental design arts" (1502.6). NEPA also provides that the agency "affirmatively [solicit] comments from those persons or organizations who may be interested or affected" (1503.1.a.4).

The Endangered Species Act provides a program for the conservation of endangered and threatened species and for the ecosystems upon which they depend for survival. This act had major effects on many forest plans in the first round of planning and promises to have an even greater effect in the next round.

FOREST AND RANGELAND RENEWABLE RESOURCES PLANNING ACT (RPA) OF 1974

Influential legislators also were concerned about conflicts affecting the National Forest System. In the winter of 1972, Sen. Hubert H. Humphrey introduced a legislative amendment that dealt with three particular concerns: (1) the lack of long-term planning in the federal government, (2) polarization of forestry issues—the timber industry and conservation groups were at odds with each other, and both distrusted the U.S. Forest Service, and (3) the threat to natural resource conservation by the president's Office of Management and Budget, stemming from its impoundment of funds that had been appropriated by Congress (Le Master 1984). The desire on the part of Humphrey and other members of Congress to increase congressional control over national forest management and budgetary decisions was, according to Le Master (1984), the most important driving force that ultimately led to the passage of the RPA.

During Senate agricultural and forestry subcommittee hearings in late 1973, Senator Humphrey's introductory remarks captured the essence of this legislation:

Now, as far as this bill is concerned, if you are looking at the language in this bill expecting to find quotas for wildlife, timber or recreational areas, or wilderness, you will not find it.

If you are looking for a condemnation of some particular method of timber management, or the endorsement of another, you will not find it.

If you are looking for a magic formula that resolves land use conflicts, you will not find it here either. If you are looking for a statement on what the condition of our renewable resources will be in the year 2000, you will not find it in S. 2296.

However, if you are looking for a means or a vehicle that will get the facts needed to make wise decisions, this is your bill. If you are looking for a way to set national goals, to get public input into policy-making, and if you believe that setting policy is the function of the Congress, and implementing policy is the function of the Executive, then this bill should have some appeal to you.

On August 2, 1974, the House and Senate agreed to a conference committee version of the bill and it was sent to President Nixon. He resigned from office on August 9, 1974, and Gerald R. Ford succeeded to the presidency. Ford signed RPA into law without ceremony on August 17, 1974, lauding its objectives but citing some objections expressed by the Office of Management and Budget.

Since its enactment, RPA and the National Forest Management Act of 1976, which amended RPA, have become the principal laws governing American forest policy. Although these laws have not been implemented without problems, they nevertheless provide the principal legislative direction for how the national forests—and to a much lesser extent, private forest lands—will be managed.

RPA has three major procedural requirements, the first two are the responsibility of the Forest Service as the lead agency: (1) an assessment, which includes an inventory of all resources, every 10 years, (2) a program, proposing resource goals, every five years, and (3) a presidential statement of policy, to be used in framing budget requests, also every five years.

RPA requires an assessment of all the forest and range resources in the United States, public and private. Current data on resource supplies and demands for the next 50 years are to be collected and summarized. Furthermore, the assessment must describe the institutions and laws involved in forest resources. Based on the decennial assessment, the Forest Service is required to develop and examine alternative means to meet the nation's forest resource needs and to estimate the costs and benefits of these alternatives. The agency must then present its suggested program to the president, who will consider it and send it to the Congress with budget recommendations (Shands 1981). The presidential statement of policy is, essentially, a cover letter for the budget recommendations.

Clary (1986) believed that RPA was an answer to a bureaucrat's prayer. The Forest Service had long dreamed of a comprehensive national plan for forestry based on a comprehensive inventory, and RPA was that, but only superficially. The RPA assessment and program provisions authorized the generation of tons of paperwork. The program documents effectively defused arguments that the agency concentrated too much on timber and not enough on other things. In the name of multiple use, the Forest Service assembled "impossibly expensive" plans to manage everything at a high level. When Congress failed to fund the entire proposed program and instead chose to keep the Forest Service budget at a level "within reason," it was not the Forest Service's fault. Now any failure to realize multiple use, any emphasis on timber at the expense of other programs, could be attributed to congressional reluctance to fund the proposed program (Clary 1986).

However, RPA could not help the Forest Service deflect all criticism. Wilderness enthusiasts demonstrated the futility of an administered planning approach to wilderness use by scuttling the Roadless Area Review and Evaluation (RARE) processes. And the clear-cutting controversies refused to die: During the Monongahela crisis, clear-cutting was stopped by a federal judge, who suggested that new national forest management legislation would be required (Clary 1986).

National Forest Management Act (NFMA) of 1976

The National Forest Management Act (P.L. 94-588; 16 U.S.C. 1600) was passed in 1976 as a five-page amendment to the 1974 RPA (P.L. 93-378). On one level the NMFA was classic iron triangle legislation hammered out among the Forest Service; the House Committee on Agriculture, Nutrition, and Forestry; the Senate Committee on Energy and Natural Resources; and the various national conservation groups and trade associations of the timber industry (Le Master 1984).

The Forest Service wanted legislative sanction for its planning efforts and for retention of professional management discretion; the House and Senate Committees sought to wrest control over national forest planning and budgetary decisions from the Nixon White House; conservation groups were pushing for planning and management that would consider not just timber but all renewable resources on the basis of sustained yield and that would be done with a guarantee of public input; and the timber industry

wanted a resumption of clear-cut harvesting on the national forests (Le Master 1984).

As with most or all compromise legislation, the NFMA was an incremental, negotiated law, with little pretense of resolving more than an immediate congressional and judicial logjam. As a timber industry spokesperson pointed out shortly after its passage:

> ...several people have commented that the [NFMA] sets the stage for forest management for the next 75 years. I must add that it also sets the stage for litigation and judicial involvement in forest management decisions for the next 10 years at least. I caution you when the Chief of the Forest Service, the Sierra Club's Washington D.C. representative, and I say that the 1976 Act is generally a reasonable and workable statute—each of us may be reading a different act. (Hall 1977, p. 17)

The resulting National Forest Management Act provided some general principles under which national forests were to be managed, but it avoided specific prescriptive language regarding silvicultural methods. The bill did, however, mandate that clear-cuts be minimized in size. Further, it stated that timber rotations should be based on the criterion of maximum mean annual increment—a biological measurement that would usually lead to longer rotations than economic criteria. More important, NFMA mandated that national forest plans that integrated all multiple uses be developed for each forest. The plans were to be prepared by interdisciplinary teams of specialists in forestry, wildlife, recreation, social sciences, and other relevant disciplines. NFMA also initiated procedures and rules for widespread public input, public review, and appeal of the plan.

Contents

The most significant provisions of the 1976 NFMA are its fundamentally new amendments to the 1974 RPA. The RPA directed the secretary of agriculture to develop land and resource management plans for units of the National Forest System, using a "systematic interdisciplinary approach to achieve integrated consideration of physical, biological, economic, and other sciences." The 1974 act, however, failed to specify how such individual land management plans were to be prepared, and what they were to contain. The 1976 NFMA fills those gaps in copious detail (Bean 1983).

Section 6 of the NFMA specifically sets new standards for national forest system resource planning (USDA Forest Service 1983). It requires the secretary of agriculture to provide for public participation in the development, review, and revision of land management plans and to promulgate regulations describing the process of development and revisions of land management plans, pursuant to the informal rule-making procedures of the Administrative Procedures Act. NFMA also requires that the regulations specify procedures that ensure compliance with NEPA in the preparation of land management plans. And the secretary of agriculture was to identify land unsuitable for timber production.

Section 6 also requires specific guidelines for land management plans. The guidelines must "provide for diversity of plant and animal communities based on suitability and capability of specific land area in order to meet overall multiple-use objectives" [Section 6(g)(B)] and ensure consideration of economic and environmental aspects of various systems of renewable resource management [Section 6(g)(A)]. The guidelines [Section 6(g)(E)] were to "insure that timber will be harvested from National Forest System lands only where—"

Soil, slope, or other watershed conditions will not be irreversibly damaged.

There is assurance that the lands can be adequately restocked within five years after harvest.

Stream protection is provided.

The harvesting system to be used is not selected primarily because it will give the greatest dollar return or the greatest unit output of timber.

The guidelines also specified [Section 6(g)(F)] that clearcutting, seed tree cutting, and shelterwood cutting be used only where–

For clearcutting, it is determined to be the optimum method to meet the land management plan objectives.

The potential environmental, biological, aesthetic, engineering, and economic impacts on each advertised sale area have been assessed.

Cut block, patches, or strips are shaped and blended to the extent practicable with the natural terrain.

Maximum clearcut size limits are established.

Cuts are made in a manner that protects soil, watershed, fish, wildlife, recreation, and esthetic resources, and timber regeneration.

Section 11 of NFMA amends the 1974 RPA with regard to limits on timber removals—referred to as the allowable cut or the allowable sale quantity (ASQ). The law states that the sale of timber from each forest shall be limited "to a quantity equal to or less than a quantity which can be removed from such forest annually in perpetuity on a sustained-yield basis." Two provisos further qualify this ASQ. First, in order to meet overall multiple-use objectives, the ASQ may depart from the projected long-term average quantity allowed. Second, any such planned departure must be consistent with multiple-use management objectives of the land management plan. An earlier proviso in Section 6 of NFMA does allow increase in harvest levels (the ASQ) based on intensified management practices, such as reforestation, thinning, and tree improvement, if they are consistent with MUSYA and can be sustained.

Section 14 of NFMA further elucidates the requirements for public participation in planning for and management of the National Forest System. The secretary of agriculture, by regulation, was to develop procedures to allow all levels of government and the public adequate notice and opportunity to comment on the formulation of standards, criteria, and guidelines applicable to Forest Service programs. The secretary was authorized to prescribe such regulations as determined necessary to carry out the provisions of the act.

Implications

As the preceding paraphrasing of part of NFMA indicates, the act wrought major changes in the way the Forest Service planned and managed its lands. As the illustration on clear-cutting in Chapter 2 indicated, NFMA was a response to the Monongahela court decision that stopped clear-cutting in West Virginia. NFMA was then shaped at the peak of the environmental movement in the 1970s, following NEPA in 1969, the Federal Water Pollution Control Act Amendments in 1972, and the Endangered Species Act in 1973.

In NFMA debates, environmentalists fought for bans on clear-cutting, detailed restrictions on forest management, more wildlife protection, and greater opportunities for public participation. Many of these goals were related to the three preceding federal laws and were included as part of the NFMA. Clear-cutting, even-aged management, and forest management discretion remained as professional options, but they were more narrowly circumscribed than before NFMA. Optimal rotation ages were defined in biological (culmination of mean annual increment) rather than economic terms. The timber allowable sale quantity (ASQ) for each forest was not to exceed the sustainable harvest in perpetuity; however, determining these ASQs has proved a continuing point of contention. The requirements for planning guidelines to protect the diversity of plant and animal communities and for detailed public participation were strict and have proved crucial since in the implementation of the law.

NFMA combines the statutory authority of the Forest Service that dates from the beginning of the twentieth century with modern environmental laws, specifically the National Environmental Protection Act of 1969. Each multiple use is treated separately and collec-

tively. In effect, Congress said to the Forest Service:

> Give us a different concept of good forestry, one that gives full respect to recreation, wildlife, and watershed values. You decide what good forestry ought to be within that framework, but state it publicly and get public acceptance, and it will then become the yardstick by which you will be measured. (Bolle 1987, p. 4)

The changes included many specifics, but more important, NFMA required a change in the way the Forest Service viewed its responsibilities.

NFMA greatly reduced the Forest Service's established autonomy and tampered with agency discretion in ways that MUSYA and RPA did not. There are various restrictions, almost all revolving around timber harvesting. But NFMA goes even deeper by requiring Forest Service planners to do two other things: (1) bring in the public as participants in the planning process and (2) reach out to disciplines other than forestry and road engineering, which always had dominated the roster of professional employees within the agency (Wilkinson and Anderson 1987).

NFMA required an uneasy marriage of science, economics, history, public administration, abstract values, and the rule of law. By modifying traditional Forest Service policies, NFMA will play a large role in determining whether the national forests will make substantial contributions to the quality of life in the United States. In so determining the role of the Forest Service to meet the nation's need for all forest resources, RPA/NFMA also will have substantial impacts on the private forestry sector. Ellis and Force (1987) provide a guide to the sizable body of literature that NFMA has generated.

In summary, NFMA and RPA impose legal requirements on the Forest Service that are the mold for policy. NFMA, NEPA, MUSYA, the Endangered Species Act, the Clean Water Act, and other environmental laws establish the arena in which policy is made and set the limits of discretion for the Forest Service. NFMA

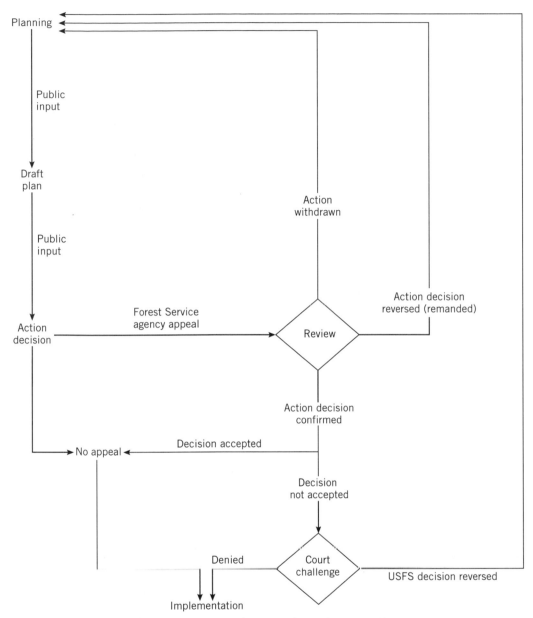

Figure 13-1. The National Forest Management Planning and Appeal Process, 1991

forest plans are the vehicle for compliance with federal environmental law. That is why the plans are so complex and often the basis for administrative appeals or legal challenges.

THE PLANNING AND APPEAL PROCESS

The national forest management process that has evolved since 1976 is very complex and involves many levels of planning, required planning considerations, and agency actions. A simplified version of the planning and appeals process (as of 1991) for a national forest plan is shown in Figure 13-1.

In addition to the individual forest plans, the NFMA regulations also required two other levels of plans—the national and regional. The national RPA assessment provided information and management objectives for regional guides, which did the same for individual national forest plans. The Forest Service regulations provide detailed and complex regulations for developing, amending, and revising forest plans. Plans must be revised at least every 15 years. The planning and administrative appeal process was developed by the Forest Service and the U.S. Department of Agriculture, as required by NFMA. The process is maintained at the discretion of the agency and may be changed as long as any revision does not violate the intent of the enabling legislation.

The crux of the planning process to date lies in the development of the individual national forest plans, perhaps with modest guidance from the regional guides and related Environmental Impact Statements. The forest planners have begun with various amounts of public input and used data from the forest, FORPLAN linear programming computer runs, agency analyses, and a slew of other inputs to produce a draft forest plan. Each draft forest plan also must have an associated draft forest Environmental Impact Statement (EIS). After the draft plan and EIS are released, more public comment is allowed. Based on the review comments, a final forest plan can be written. (A similar process is followed at the regional level.) The individual forest supervisor is responsible for preparing the forest plan and the EIS; the regional forester is responsible for approving them. District rangers actually are responsible for performing actions, preparing timber sales, and writing the briefer Environmental Assessments.

Groups that oppose forest plans may appeal to the regional forester to disapprove the plan unless specific plan components are changed. In examining the appeals, the regional foresters, Forest Service Land Management Planning staff, and the chief are advised by lawyers—most of whom also have forestry degrees—employed by the U.S. Department of Agriculture. If the regional forester denies the appeal, the groups may then appeal to the chief of the Forest Service. The chief may reverse the objectionable components of the forest plan and remand it back to the for-

est for correction. The supervisors, regional foresters, and chief are advised by their land management planning staff and U.S. Department of Agriculture lawyers in responding to appeals. At any one time, various portions of a plan may be under appeal or revision at different levels of the administrative appeals chain of command. If a plan is approved by the forest supervisor, and confirmed by the regional forester and the chief, then groups that still oppose it must seek judicial action. The Environmental Impact Statement process is similar to that for the plans.

At the individual forest level, each timber sale or other specific action must be prepared by the district forester and his or her employees. An Environmental Assessment (small EIS) also must be prepared for each timber sale. In the 1980s individual timber sale Environmental Assessments were "tiered" to the forest-level or regional-level plans and Environmental Empact Statements. This means that the environmental impacts for land management were thoroughly described in the forest plan and then cited as the basis for individual actions (e.g., timber sales). This general approach does, however, present some problems, considering that many of the plans have been declared deficient by the agency, are still under appeal, or are subject to court challenge. Tiering to a deficient plan places individual forest management actions on shaky ground.

ILLUSTRATION: THE ADMINISTRATIVE APPEAL OF THE HARPER CLIFFS TIMBER SALE

The preceding discussion of NFMA, the forest planning process, and the NFMA regulations is somewhat complex, as is the law. An illustration of an administrative appeal of the NFMA may help illustrate how the process works and is presented in the following summary of one significant case concerning the use of clear-cutting for an individual timber sale. This case consisted of an administrative appeal of a proposed timber sale on the Warm Springs Ranger District in the George Washington National Forest in Virginia.

The Process

On February 20, 1990, the forest supervisor of the George Washington signed a Decision Notice, which contained a Finding of No Significant Impact (FONSI), to proceed with a planned timber harvest and its associated management practices on the Harpers Cliffs area (Kelley 1990). The FONSI was based on the Environmental Assessment of the effects of the proposed timber sale. Part of the harvest included clear-cutting 77 acres in four cutting units. Per the administrative regulations that had been issued for appeals, the Decision Notice could be appealed to the regional forester in Atlanta within 45 days of the date of the decision.

On March 22, 1990, the Natural Resources Defense Council, Virginia Wilderness Committee, and the Wilderness Society did file an administrative appeal of the timber sale decision (NRDC et al. 1990). The brief 14-page appeal stated that the Environmental Assessment failed to meet the legal requirement to justify the use of clear-cutting and requested that the timber sale be withdrawn and the EA rewritten with improved analysis to comply with legal requirements. The appellants brought the case because they believed that the George Washington staff prescribed the use of clear- cutting in nearly all situations and without adequate justification, and they asked the regional forester to redress this problem.

The Issues

According to Harper Cliffs EA, the forest supervisor found that clear-cutting was the optimum method for the following reasons:

1. Clear-cutting provides early successional stages of deer habitat.
2. Other harvest methods would not ensure regeneration of the described oak types.
3. Clear-cutting is the least expensive method to use and still accomplish plan direction.
4. The Forest Final Environmental Impact Statement led to the conclusion that clear-cutting was needed to regenerate the stands.

The appellants rebutted each of these contentions. First, in response to number 4, they pointed out that in an earlier appeal of the George Washington National Forest Plan, the chief of the Forest Service found that the clear-cutting was not justified in the forest plan and EIS programmatic documents. Thus the contention that an individual sale EA could rely on ("tier to") the analysis in the deficient Forest Final EIS was discredited. Instead, if the EIS fails to meet the legal or regulatory requirements, the individual project analysis must contain the complete environmental analysis.

Second, the appellants refuted that clear-cutting is optimum for deer habitat because such a contention was not supported by the analysis in the EA. The EA indicated that shelterwood would result in exactly the same number of deer as clear-cutting and that group selection would decrease the number of deer compared with the preharvest conditions. These inconsistencies were stated to render the supposed deer habitat benefits of clear-cutting moot.

Third, the appeal refuted that oak regeneration would not occur without clear-cutting. The stands already had advanced regeneration of oak species, and Forest Service research had shown that clear-cutting is less desirable than shelterwood or group selection in maintaining oak regeneration under these circumstances. Thus clear-cutting not only was not optimum, it was even inferior.

Last, the appeal refuted the rationale that clear-cutting should be used because it was the least expensive harvesting method and would help prevent the timber sale from being a below-cost sale. The appellants wrote that this type of reasoning was exactly what NFMA's limits on clear-cutting prohibited. In fact, as noted before, NFMA states that timber will be harvested only where "the harvesting system to be used is not selected primarily because it will give the greatest dollar return" (16 U.S.C. 1604 [g][3][E]).

The Outcome

The NRDC et al. (1990) appeal was reviewed by the regional forester, with assistance from the timber management staff, the planning staff, and then the USDA legal staff. On June 29, 1990, the regional forester and his staff responded to the appeal (Alcock 1990). The letter to NRDC et al. conceded that the Harper Cliffs EA failed to adequately tier to the environmental effects disclosed in the EIS relevant to the proposed clear-cutting and also failed to disclose the anticipated site-specific impacts. The regional forester's response concurred that the EA and Decision Notice failed to support the decision that clear-cutting was best for deer habitat, or that it would be best for oak regeneration where advance reproduction already was adequate. Furthermore, the response agreed that basing the harvest method choice strictly on economic grounds could not serve as the sole reason for clear-cutting.

In the end, the regional forester and timber staff reversed the forest supervisor's decision, with regret. The sale would have to be reanalyzed and new NEPA documents (a new EA) would have to be prepared to explain why clear-cutting is the optimum harvest method.

The broader implications of this appeal are significant. This was one of the first successful direct challenges to clear-cutting and could serve as a model for others in the East or West. It does indicate how the specific language of NFMA, the administrative appeals process, the NEPA requirements, and current scientific knowledge were used to change policy at the forest level. Note also that 14 years after the passage of NFMA, debates over clear-cutting persist, as they do today. The Forest Service still preferred its use, and opponents used the regulatory tools available—with great skill and cogency—to attempt to change this policy. Although not totally enamored with the process, environmental groups still support the administrative appeal process and agency review as a less expensive and less adversarial way than lawsuits to resolve differences and change Forest Service policy. Whether or not the Forest Service will retain this process remains to be determined, as discussed in the following section on national forest planning today.

RPA/NFMA Debates

Criticisms of RPA/NFMA have been prevalent since their enactment. The laws represent a massive experiment in rational-comprehensive planning and have met with as much approbation as acclamation. Criticisms have focused on both the size and lack of utility of the RPA documents; the extreme difficulties in getting forest plans implemented; and the lack of coordination between RPA assessments, RPA programs, and national forest plans. RPA/NFMA has its defenders as well, though.

Critics

Although few critics say so directly, it is clear that RPA and NFMA were the result of a political process. Compromises among groups in enacting the laws and conflicting values about the national forests prevent any rational-comprehensive approach from resolving all differences on the use of public lands. Thus critics often will focus on the problems of the laws, not on the political conflicts that are unavoidable, and perhaps unresolvable.

Criticisms of RPA/NFMA began soon after implementation. Fairfax (1981) questioned the benefits of the RPA/NFMA rational decision-making process. She argued that the immense amounts of data collected would outstrip the utility or inherent good sense to use them. The massive computer programming requirements would increase centralization, thwart citizen involvement, and let major decision-making authority within the agency slip to computer technicians. Convery (1983) expressed similar concerns that management authority had been usurped from ground managers, whose idealism had been supplanted by rigid management guidelines.

Fairfax (1981) also was less than sanguine about the benefits of multidisciplinary planning and believed that the process had become more important than the decisions, and that the net effect was actually the reverse of rational decision making. She did suggest a few silver linings—the process may improve over time, the computer technology may actually work, and multidisciplinary planning may help the Forest Service—but overall she remained unconvinced. The forest industry expressed dissatisfaction with national forest planning because of the approach, costs of planning, deficient economic analyses, and overemphasis on wildlife, not to mention the fact that it often led to the "wrong" results—lower timber removal allowable sale quantities (ASQs). The RPA plans also presented a series of alternative output levels, but they made no specific recommendations, thus placing the failure to fully fund programs on Congress.

Behan (1981a, 1985) examined the RPA/NFMA process and criticized the extraordinary amounts of time, effort, and money required to implement the law. Additionally, he believed that the detailed procedural requirements and public input process provided easy bases for litigation. Indeed, most forest plans released in the 1980s were appealed by environmental or forest industry groups to the chief of the Forest Service, and litigation on many others seems likely. By 1985 the Forest Service had spent $2 billion for the national forest plans, yet most were being challenged. This represents a hefty cost for planning, especially in a time of budget austerity. Behan concluded that we need better administration, not comprehensive planning, and we should repeal the laws.

Advocates

In a rebuttal to Behan, James Giltmier (1981), legislative assistant on the Senate Committee on Agriculture, Nutrition, and Forestry, defended the merits of RPA. He argued that litigation would occur with or without RPA/NFMA and that planning and decision making strictly by local Forest Service officials would not be successful. In fact, NFMA was enacted in response to the Monongahela National Forest lawsuit in which the district and appellate courts ruled that the Forest Service's timber-cutting practices violated the authorizing statute. He contended that (1981, p. 806) "The planning it [RPA] mandates, though costly, is helping national forest personnel to improve their management, and the data generated will increasingly provide a rational basis for deciding issues."

John R. McGuire (1985), former chief of the U.S. Forest Service, also rebutted the criticisms made by Behan. He pointed out that the plans in the future would cost less than 50 cents per acre per year, which was well justified, considering the public interest in the natural resource decisions that have to be made. (Actually, the plans now probably cost at least $1.00 per acre, and perhaps $3.00 to $5.00 per acre per year.) McGuire also believed that repeal of NFMA would not reduce lawsuits, as suggested by Behan, but only lead to more confusion. Although conceding that the process has been costly and ponderous, McGuire argued that only a Pollyanna would have expected otherwise, considering the many activities and competing interests involved. To him, the forest planning process was clearly worth the expense.

Le Master (1982) reminded critics that budgeting purposes had prompted RPA. According to Senator Hubert Humphrey, RPA would (Le Master 1982):

[R]equire Congress and the Executive Branch to set long- and short-term goals for national forest use and jointly to translate these goals each year into action programs through the annual budgeting process.

This approach is designed to open up the long-range national planning on our forests to greater public participation by using the law and the forum of Congress to set our nation's goals.

Le Master said RPA was designed to protect the Forest Service from budget cuts from the Office of Management and Budget. The Forest Service budget is particularly vulnerable to cuts because 71 percent of its budget is discretionary—within the immediate control of the president and Congress. After examining the Forest Service and Bureau of Land Management appropriations, Le Master concluded that RPA had been successful at increasing forest land management appropriations, but not agency appropriations as a whole.

However, the use of RPA to coerce the Office of Management and Budget and Congress into approving greater budgets probably backfired in the long run. The 1975, 1980, and 1985 RPA recommended high levels of management (and funding), which then cast lawmakers, OMB, and the president in a negative light for underfunding Forest Service programs. They responded by criticizing RPA and ignoring its funding level requests. The ill will generated also contributed to poor executive and congressional relationships with the Forest Service.

The 1990 RPA program, however, proved to be dramatically different in purpose and scope from its predecessors. The 1990 program placed less emphasis on making specific budget amounts and program alternative mixes and more on serving as a strategic planning document. The 1990 program discussed basic directions of the agency and responses and policies regarding issues such as below-cost timber sales and ceded to Congress and the executive branch the specific implementation of these directions. The broad Regional Forest guides, which had been mandatory, became optional. In short, with the same statutory mandate, the Forest Service developed a new policy-making process.

NATIONAL FOREST PLANNING TODAY

NFMA and NEPA contained many substantive requirements and a complex web of procedural requirements. By 1986, 10 years after NFMA was signed into law, the Forest Service had produced the required 123 plans for the 155 national forests (some plans cover more than one forest). In 1986 only 50 of these plans were in final form; the remainder were drafts (Hunt 1986).

The NFMA requirements led to a host of national forest plan appeals. By 1990 the Forest Service had received over 1200 plan appeals and 1800 lawsuits (Robertson 1990). In fiscal year 1991 there were 1249 administrative appeals pending at the beginning of the year and an additional 1386 were made during the year. Of the 1182 appeals decided that year, 57 percent were affirmed in the agency's favor, 18 percent were dismissed for various procedural reasons, 19 percent were withdrawn or resolved through negotiations, and 6 percent were remanded to the deciding

Forest Service official for reconsideration. Almost half of the appeals (46 percent) involved timber sales (Gray 1991). These problems led Forest Service Chief Dale Robertson to seek to change the appeals process, and the agency officially proposed dropping the administrative appeals entirely in 1992.

In general, most environmental groups would rather use administrative appeals, and not have to resort to lawsuits. Agency discretion still makes it difficult to win lawsuits regarding forest management practices. Generally, national environmental groups have focused more on administrative appeals of individual national forest plans. Local groups have tended to focus on making individual timber sale appeals. By early 1991, 114 of the 123 plans were finalized and in the process of being implemented. Of these 65 had been cleared of all administrative appeals (Federal Register 1991).

The Forest Service is not the only federal agency that has been subjected to mandated planning requirements. All of the major land management agencies are involved in land and resource planning. The other multiple-use agency, the Bureau of Land Management, follows explicit guidelines in the Federal Land Planning and Management Act (FLPMA) of 1976 that parallel NFMA planning requirements. The National Park Service and the U.S. Fish and Wildlife Service face somewhat less difficult planning problems because of their dominant-use orientation. Neither agency needs to consider the full range of commercial development that the Forest Service and BLM must review. But both still do have conflicts between preservation (of ecosystems or wildlife) and developed uses (such as parks or hunting).

The Forest Service sponsored a comprehensive evaluation of its planning process in 1989, which was performed by the Conservation Foundation and the Purdue University Department of Forestry. The results were published in an 11-volume report in 1990. Major findings include adjustments that are needed in the following areas (Federal Register 1991, p. 6511):

- Citizens', lawmakers', and the agency's expectations of planning.
- The agency's attitude toward and conduct of public involvement.
- How the agency conducts planning.
- Simplification and clarification of planning procedures.
- Implementation of plans, particularly to ensure that they are followed and used.
- Connections between appropriations and forest plans.

The report was, however, generally positive in its assessment of the National Forest Management Act planning process. For example, it states that

Planning is the gateway to meeting both the spirit and intent of the many laws governing natural resources, particularly the National Forest Management Act and the National Environmental Policy Act. *The real challenge has been that each law changes the way the agency does business, and change is not easy.* That the struggle in forest planning was difficult attests not to flaws in the basic legislation, but instead to the high-reaching goals expressed in various laws... (p. vii–viii).

Great strides have been made in Forest Service planning. Citizens were involved to an unprecedented extent. Interdisciplinary teams became a standard way of doing business. A broader range of resources was considered than ever before. Many issues were resolved, and unresolved issues have become more sharply focused. *Citizens' awareness of national forests is higher than ever before.* Analytical tools and procedures have been improved. Many important relationships, with citizens, local officials, other agencies, and Indian tribes, have been formed. And finally, our Forest plans are the best we have ever developed. (USDA Forest Service 1990; emphasis in original) (p. viii).

In many ways the ultimate effect of the NFMA, an effect totally unsought and unanticipated, is a transformation in the personnel, orientation, and mission of the Forest Service. Foresters and "timber beasts" of old are now becoming less dominant in the organization as new emphasis and new hiring have focused on wildlife biologists, landscape architects, hydrologists, engineers, and, lately,

even botanists and professional planners. A major push toward work force diversity has added a number of women and minorities to Forest Service ranks (Tipple and Wellman 1991).

The orientation of the agency also has transformed—or, more accurately, is in the process of transformation—from that of technical expert in sustained timber production to that of environmental planner. Concomitantly its mission has become much more broadly defined and increasingly ecosystem-based, replacing the narrow primary focus on timber as the main resource. This shift has not come without considerable opposition and morale problems in the agency, especially in the West where many jobs are slated to be lost if timber harvests decline. Forest industry user groups also continue to oppose this change and are supported by many western Congress members.

In the 1990 RPA assessment, some of the earlier criticisms of RPA also were addressed. The Forest Service largely conceded that there could not be specific linkages between RPA national program goals and output levels and individual forest plans. They also used the RPA more as a strategic plan and omitted any budget data or requests until after 1995, thus avoiding congressional and executive ire. Furthermore, they proposed five alternative program mixes in the draft but eventually adopted only one recommended program in the final document. These changes led to a much better reception of RPA by Congress and the president and facilitated discussions of national directions for the agency. The president (and OMB) clearly supported the document in the 1990 letter of transmittal to Congress.

By 1991 and 1992 changes also were being considered for the NFMA forest planning process. The administrative appeal process for individual timber sales or other forest practices was proposed for elimination by the secretary of the Department of Agriculture on March 19, 1992. (The administrative appeals process would be retained for forest plans.) The secretary and the Forest Service believed that dropping the lower-level administrative appeals would reduce frivolous appeals. Environmental groups opposed the loss of this opportunity for public involvement, and claimed that it would lead to many more lawsuits. Furthermore, they felt that modifying the appeals system to reduce access or expedite process would further polarize national forest management. This appeals process issue is critical and difficult. The challenge is to find a way to maintain citizens' rights to appeal agency decisions but also allow agencies to implement decisions in a responsible manner (Gray 1991).

Proposals to drop the required use of the FORPLAN computer program in planning also were made in the draft revised guidelines. Greater limits on clear-cutting were being proposed. The outcome of the March 1992 proposed changes had not been decided by mid-1992. In fact, Senator Fowler of Georgia even introduced a bill in July to prevent the Forest Service from dropping the appeal process. Other changes in NFMA will continue and will cause controversy in future years as well. Even proposals to repeal or to amend NFMA were common by 1991.

FOREST PLANNING AND CONFLICT RESOLUTION

One might hope that national forest planning ultimately will resolve conflicts that occur among various user groups. Clawson (1987) listed three avenues for resolving natural resource user conflicts: (1) reliance on markets, (2) appeals to the legislature/judiciary, and (3) negotiation between the disputing parties. Each method has its strengths and limitations. In practice, conflict resolution likely will combine all of these approaches in varying proportions, depending on individual circumstances. The forest planning process mandated by NFMA is essentially a legislative solution that has elements of both the market and negotiation approaches in it. The relatively new NFMA process may eventually result in management of the national forests that is in keeping with modern times and needs. Or perhaps the planning process will continue indefinitely to focus attention on process and documents rather than resource outputs and the expressed needs of many different people. Whichever the case may be, many suggestions for improving the process have been offered.

Market Approach

O'Toole (1988) advocates radical market-based reforms to solve national forest problems. He proposes the repeal of RPA/NFMA. To solve perennial budget problems, he proposes that each national forest be restructured into an independent quasi-public corporation responsible for generating its own revenues and profits from a full range of multiple forest uses.

O'Toole (1988) maintains that much of the charged mismanagement of national forests can be attributed to perverse "market" signals. He particularly faults the Knutson-Vandenburg Act of 1936 for these problems. The act required the deposit of a portion of the total timber sale price in a fund for reforestation, which could be controlled directly by local Forest Service administrators. Allowable expenses for K-V funds have since been expanded to include wildlife habitat management, recreation, and even general office administration. Thus all Forest Service employees have incentives to cut timber, which yields money without the need for congressional appropriations.

O'Toole suggests that the Forest Service sought and obtained this expanded use of K-V funds to promote its own ends—consistent with the public choice theory that views bureaucrats as utility-maximizers. Sample (1988), however, believes that K-V funds and other incentives that lead to wasteful national forest management are due to congressional, not agency, intent. Although the agency may not be a neutral player in making policy, he believes that interest groups and Congress members should receive much more credit (or blame) for current policies.

Nevertheless, the market approach could help move the national forests toward more accepted public policies. Reduction of below-cost timber sales would be approved of by most interest groups, although defining below-cost is a very technical issue. Privatization, as discussed in Chapter 3, seems unlikely to occur soon, if ever. But perhaps management leases, concessions, or other market-based approaches may see greater use in national forest planning in the future.

Legislative-Judicial Approach
NFMA is a legislative approach that tries to resolve the many conflicts facing the Forest Service as it attempts to administer multiple-use forest management in the national forests. The law leaves many opportunities for challenge through the administrative and judicial appeal systems. Until the late 1980s judges tended to allow the Forest Service much administrative discretion as long as the plans required by NFMA were produced by following the mandated procedures. This conforms to general principles favoring judicial restraint unless agencies have been arbitrary and capricious. However, the late 1980s and 1990s have seen significant legal challenges to forest plans in many parts of the country.

Negotiated Approach
The NFMA forest planning process, with its requirement for public participation, may be viewed as an opportunity to resolve national forest management conflicts through negotiation by disputants. Methods of negotiation were described in Chapter 4. Negotiation is likely to happen only if the Forest Service begins to focus on the planning process itself rather than the document that is the output of the process. If disputes over national forest use are to be resolved, Wondolleck (1988) recommends five objectives to guide the process.

- Building trust.
- Building understanding.
- Incorporating conflicting values.
- Providing opportunities for joint fact-finding.
- Encouraging cooperation and collaboration.

Wondolleck (1988) describes three examples of negotiated approaches that have proven successful in resolving land use conflicts in national forests. First, mediation was used to resolve a conflict on the San Juan National Forest in Colorado. Local citizens voiced concerns about scenic beauty and tourism in response to Forest Service plans to build 50 miles of roads to support timber harvests. Professional mediators were able to find areas of agreement that led to a compromise solution in only two days, after public hearings had produced nothing but shouting matches.

Second, a consensus-building process was used to resolve a conflict on the Willamette National Forest in Oregon. Citizen concerns regarding recreation trails, scenic beauty, and access to a nearby wilderness area were pitted against planned timber sales. A public hearing followed by a field trip to proposed harvest sites did nothing to alleviate these concerns. Adjustments to harvest plans, followed by more meetings and site visits, did not satisfy hikers and environmentalists. Following a Forest Service suggestion, a citizens' task force was formed. Six months later, a series of proposals and counterproposals finally led to a compromise solution. The key to success was allowing citizens to actually develop the plan, rather than respond with "input" to Forest Service alternatives.

Third, an ad hoc negotiation process was used on the Bridger-Teton National Forest in Wyoming to resolve a conflict involving an application for an oil-drilling permit on a lease in a roadless area. The company's lease predated the RARE II (Roadless Area Review and Evaluation) process for identifying potential additions to the National Wilderness Preservation System. The Sierra Club filed an appeal, reasoning that a decision on the permit should be delayed until a final wilderness decision was made. The company, anticipating a long delay while the RARE II process unfolded, established a dialogue with the Sierra Club and the Forest Service. A mutually acceptable drilling plan resulted from upfront, good faith negotiations and accommodation by the company regarding specific concerns that the Sierra Club had.

A public participation technique that will not work is the "jack-in-the-box" approach described by Behan (1981a): Produce a draft plan, pop out of the box and call for public comment, gather the public comment, go back in the box, and pop out some time later with a final plan. As Wondolleck (1988) puts it, interest "airing" is not the same thing as interest "accommodation." The jack-in-the-box approach to forest planning is characteristic of foresters' traditional reliance on technically trained experts who determine how the forests should be managed, out of sight and earshot of the public.

A Retrospective View

The National Forest System has produced timber with great success. The national forests survived national crises—the Great Depression of the 1930s and two world wars. When the nation needed timber, it was available. Today the national forests provide about one-fourth of the nation's need for raw forest products. Most of the rest of the nation's timber supply comes from private lands, which is a credit to the influence and example of the Forest Service. The feared timber famine never developed (Clary 1986).

With less than 20 percent of the nation's productive timberlands, the national forests contain almost half of the nation's inventory of softwood timber. Although far from self-supporting, the Forest Service goes further toward paying its own way than any major federal agency except the Internal Revenue Service. As Popovich (1988) points out, the timber program is responsible for this, returning a net profit to the U.S. Treasury of $229 million in 1987, not counting the additional $254 million received by local counties for schools and roads in lieu of property tax payments. But critics of the Forest Service timber program continue to argue about below-cost sales on many forests. The Forest Service still does not produce more revenue than it expends, failing to meet Gifford Pinchot's promise that the national forests would pay their own way.

Senator Humphrey's goal, and the idea behind NFMA, was to get forest management out of the courts and back into the woods (Hall and Wasserstrom 1978, Humphrey 1976). This goal likely will not be achieved until the forest planning process evolves, if ever. Criticism of NFMA has been intense and voluminous. Foresters, the Forest Service, and the forest industry almost universally dislike the expense and legal/judicial interference in agency discretion, and the planning outcomes that may not favor their interests.

On the other hand, by legislating a forest planning process, Congress gave citizens many statutory bases to challenge plans for managing federal forests. RPA/NFMA has addressed many forestry issues, especially clear-cutting, but it has not resolved many. Those who abhor clear-cutting or any cutting have found many bases on which to challenge forest managers. In fact, despite the morass of appeals, most environmental groups view NFMA as a success. It has allowed them to stop timber sales, change agency priorities, and by the 1990s, perhaps even change agency direction and philosophy. To them, this is just what NFMA was intended to accomplish.

Forest policy is now being decided by the legislature, implemented by executive agencies (or bureaucracies), and interpreted by courts. Groups of citizens alert the government to perceived abuses. This is how RPA/NFMA is working, and it seems consistent with American democratic ideals. However, it does not make the job of resource stewardship any easier. Complex problems have resulted in complex laws with complex interpretations, making for complex management. Will RPA/NFMA result in better resource stewardship? The answer is being debated now.

The American Forestry Association (AFA), a citizens' interest group that has championed the cause of American forestry since 1875, has called for decentralized planning and management as a solution to planning problems. AFA has proposed a citizens' program called "Friends of the National Forests" to focus on the needs of localized interests who know and care about each national forest (Sampson 1988). Shands (1988) has a related suggestion: Replace the broad concept of multiple use with management for the unique values of each national forest. Locally developed plans would thus provide a range of values and uses. National forests should not compete with other public and private forests in the same locality. Surely there are unique elements that each national forest provides and for which they should be managed. The Wilderness Society goes even further, suggesting that whole regions of national forests should be managed for unique natural values that markets will not produce.

How will forest planning evolve? What will it become? That is a matter of policy, and a matter of lively discussion both within and outside the forestry community. Many people and institutions have a stake in the outcome.

SUMMARY

Multiple use has been one of the principal concepts underlying American forestry and national forest management for more than three decades. Passage of the Multiple Use Sustained Yield Act (MUSYA) of 1960 served to affirm evolving multiple use Forest Service policies, recognizing the importance of a broad range of forest resources—outdoor recreation, range, timber, water, and wildlife and fish. While MUSYA codified the importance of multiple use management, it did not provide an adequate basis for resolving complex management debates that occurred in the 1960s and 1970s.

Demands for improved national forest management and better balance among multiple resources—not just timber dominance—and for increased public input prompted enactment of the Renewable Resources Planning Act (RPA) of 1974. RPA mandated improved planning for national forests, including periodic assessments of the nations' public and private forests and rangelands, and submissions of the Forest Service recommended forest and rangeland programs to Congress. RPA was soon amended by the National Forest Management Act (NFMA) of 1976, which was passed in response to the Monongahela court decision that banned clear-cutting. NFMA mandated new rules and regulations for preparation of individual national

forest management plans, including guidelines for required use of interdisciplinary planning teams; restrictions on clear-cutting; mandates for biologically-based rotation ages and protection of biodiversity; and enhanced public input.

The RPA/NFMA laws have led to greatly increased national- and forest-level planning efforts and public involvement, perhaps to a fault. Critics have questioned the effectiveness of the national RPA process and programs, as well as the merits of detailed forest planning. Developing national forest plans has been time-consuming and expensive and the massive public input efforts have not prevented numerous administrative appeals to most plans. Traditional timber interest groups have been dismayed that the planning results have gradually reduced allowable sale quantities on national forests. Proponents of RPA/NFMA suggest that it would be naive to expect RPA/NFMA to solve intractable public debates. Environmental groups support the laws, the public input, and the administrative appeals process because they have allowed the public to gradually shift Forest Service management to a more ecologically-oriented philosophy. Controversy about RPA/NFMA—including its rules, regulations and appeals processes—and about national forest management itself will surely endure and evolve in the 1990s.

LITERATURE CITED

Albrecht, Jean, et al. (eds.). Various dates. Social Sciences in Forestry: A Current Selected Bibliography and Index. University of Minnesota, College of Forestry. (quarterly) St. Paul.

Alcock, Jack. 1990. Letter RE Appeal #90-08-01-0028, 2/20/90 Decision Notice for Harper Cliffs Timber Forest, Warm Springs Ranger District, George Washington National Forest. USDA Forest Service, Region 8. Atlanta. June 29. 4 pp.

Alston, Richard M. 1983. The Individual vs. the Public Interest: Political Ideology and

National Forest Policy. Westview. Boulder, CO. 250 pp.

Alward, Gregory S. 1986. Assessing the socioeconomic implications of multiple use forestry. Pp. 192–201 in Proceedings, IUFRO 18th World Forestry Congress, Division 4.

Barber, John C. 1981. A national policy on forestry: Can we write one? *Journal of Forestry* 79(2):68, 116.

Barber, John C. 1984. Who invented multiple use? *Journal of Forestry* 82(7):387.

Bean, Michael J. 1983. The Evolution of National Wildlife Law. Praeger. New York. 449 pp.

Beck, Melinda, Mary Hager, Jeff B. Copeland, Darby Junkin, Shawn Doherty, and Peter McAlevey. 1983. Battle over the wilderness. *Newsweek*, July 25, pp. 22–30.

Behan, Richard W. 1981a. Forest planning viewed askance: A plea for better management. *Western Wildlands* 7(1):9–12.

Behan, Richard W. 1981b. RPA/NFMA—Time to punt. *Journal of Forestry* 79(12):802–805.

Behan, Richard W. 1985. National forest planning: Will it ever end? *American Forests* 91(3):11, 50–53.

Behan, Richard W. 1988. A plea for constituency-based management. *American Forests* 94(7,8):46–48.

Bolle, Arnold W. 1982. Quoted in Findley, Rowe. 1982. Our national forests: Problems in paradise. *National Geographic* 162(3):307–339.

Bolle, Arnold W. 1987. Foreword. Pp. 1–6 in C. F. Wilkinson, and H. M. Anderson (eds.), Land and Resource Planning in the National Forests. Island Press. Covelo, CA.

Clary, David A. 1986. Timber and the Forest Service. University Press of Kansas. Lawrence. 252 pp.

Clawson, Marion. 1975. Forests for Whom and for What? Resources for the Future/Johns Hopkins University Press. Baltimore, MD. 175 pp.

Clawson, Marion. 1987. Achieving agreement on natural resource use. H. M. Albright Lectureship in Conservation. University of California, Department of Forestry and Resource Management. Berkeley. 22 pp.

Coggins, George C. 1982. Of succotash syndromes and vacuous platitudes: The meaning of "multiple use, sustained yield" for public land management (Part I). *University of Colorado Law Review* 53:229–280.

Connaughton, Charles A. 1962. Multiple use as a concept of land management. *Forest Farmer* 21(12):18–19, 21–22.

Connaughton, Charles A. 1975. Where do we go from here? First step—A national forest policy. *American Forests* 81(4):7.

Convery, Frank J. 1980. The case for multiple use. Pp. 44–48 in Proceedings, Society of American Foresters 1979 Annual Convention. Bethesda, MD.

Convery, Frank J. 1983. Determinants in futures planning. Pp. 91–95 in Gerald R. Stairs and Thomas E. Hamilton (eds.), The RPA Process: Moving along the Learning Curve. Duke University, School of Forestry and Environmental Studies. Durham, NC.

Crafts, Edward C. 1970. Saga of a law; "behind-the-scenes story of the Forest Service" and MUSY. *American Forests* 76(6):13–19, 52, 54; 76(7):29–32, 34–35.

Craig, James B. 1975. The need for an American forest policy. *American Forests* 81(12):8.

Dana, Samuel T., and Sally K. Fairfax. 1980. Forest and Range Policy: Its Development in the United States, 2nd ed. McGraw-Hill. New York. 458 pp.

Davis, Kenneth P. 1969. What multiple forest land use and for whom? *Journal of Forestry* 67(10):718–721.

Ellis, Donald J., and Jo Ellen Force. 1987. National forest planning and the National Forest Management Act of 1976—An annotated bibliography, 1976–1986. SAF Publ. 87.11, Society of American Foresters. Bethesda, MD. 125 pp.

Fairfax, Sally K. 1981. RPA and the Forest Service. Pp. 181–200 in A Citizen's Guide to the

Forest and Rangeland Renewable Resource Planning Act. Publication FS-365. USDA Forest Service. Washington, DC.

Federal Register. 1991. Part III, Department of Agriculture, Forest Service, 36 CFR Part 219. National Forest System Land and Resource Management Planning; Advance Notice of Proposed Rulemaking. February 15.

Fight, Roger. 1980. Multiple use reexamined. Pp. 42–43 in Proceedings, 1979 Society of American Foresters Annual Convention. Bethesda, MD.

Giltmeier, James W. 1981. In response to "RPA/NFMA–Time to Punt." *Journal of Forestry* 79(12):806, 810.

Glascock, Hardin R., Jr. 1968. What multiple use really means. *Forest Farmer* 28(2): 34, 36.

Glascock, Hardin R., Jr. 1970. Multiple use at the crossroads. *Journal of Forestry* 68(3):132.

Glascock, Hardin R., Jr. 1972. A concept [multiple use] in search of a method. *Journal of Forestry* 70(4):194.

Glascock, Hardin R., Jr. 1977a. "Why not an American forest policy—Now?": A dialogue. *American Forests* 83(4):22–25.

Glascock, Hardin R., Jr. 1977b. Policy, profession, and leadership. *Journal of Forestry* 75(6):306, 347.

Gray, Gerald J. 1991. Senate panel examines Forest Service appeals. Resource Hotline. *American Forestry Association* 7(18):1–4.

Gregory, G. Robinson 1955. An economic approach to multiple use. *Forest Science* 1(1):6–13.

Gregory, G. Robinson 1987. Multiple use: Theory and application. Pp. 357–404 in Resource Economics for Foresters. Wiley. New York.

Hall, George R. 1963. The myth and reality of multiple use forestry. *Natural Resources Journal* 3: 276–290.

Hall, John F. 1977. National forest timber obligation. Pp. 15–18 in D. C. Le Master and L. Popovich (eds.), Crisis in Federal Forest Land Management: Proceedings of a

Symposium. Society of American Foresters. Washington, DC.

Hall, John F., and Richard S. Wasserstrom. 1978. The National Forest Management Act of 1976: Out of the courts and back to the forests. *Environmental Law* 8: 523–538.

Hays, Samuel P. 1959. Conservation and the gospel of efficiency: The progressive conservation movement, 1890–1920. Harvard University Press. Cambridge, MA. 297 pp.

Hays, Samuel P. 1987. Beauty, health, and permanence: Environmental politics in the United States, 1955–1985. Cambridge University Press. New York. 630 pp.

Huffman, James L. 1978. A history of forest policy in the United States. *Environmental Law* 8(2):239–280.

Humphrey, Hubert H. 1976. "...in the courts, or in the woods?" *American Forests* 82(1):14–15, 62.

Hunt, Frances A. 1986. We asked for it [RPA/NFMA], or did we? *American Forest* 92(10):60–63.

Kelley, George W. 1990. Decision Notice and Finding of No Significant Impact, Harpers Cliff Timber Sale. USDA Forest Service, Region 8, George Washington National Forest, Warm Spring Ranger District. February 20. 5 pp. Mimeo.

Krutilla, John V., and John A. Haigh. 1978. An integrated approach to national forest management. *Environmental Law* 8(2): 373–416.

Leahy, Patrick J. 1980. Keynote address ["The prosperity and greatness of America is founded in our forests"]. Pp. 2–5 in Proceedings, 1979 Annual Convention, Society of American Foresters. Bethesda, MD.

Le Master, Dennis C. 1982. Forest funding under RPA. *Journal of Forestry* 80(3): 161–163.

Le Master, Dennis C. 1984. Decade of change: The remaking of Forest Service statutory authority during the 1970s. Greenwood Press. Westport, CT. 290 pp.

McArdle, Richard E. 1970. Why we needed the multiple use bill. *American Forests* 76(6):10, 59.

McCloskey, J. Michael. 1961. Natural resources—national forests—the Multiple Use–Sustained Yield Act of 1960. *Oregon Law Review* 41(1):49–78.

McGuire, John R. 1985. National forest planning: Will it ever end? *American Forests* 91(3):10, 44–45.

NRDC et al. 1990. Notice of Appeal, Re Administrative Appeal of Forest Supervisor's Decision to Approve the Harper Cliffs Timber Sale, George Washington National Forest. March 22, 1990. 14 pp. Mimeo.

O'Toole, Randal. 1988. Reforming the Forest Service. Island Press. Covelo, CA. 247 pp.

Popovich, Luke. 1979. RAT in the woodpile— A study of dashed [multiple use] expectations. *Journal of Forestry* 77(1):33–38.

Popovich, Luke. 1988. Roads redux. *American Tree Farmer* 7(2):6.

Reiger, John F. 1975. American Sportsmen and the Origins of Conservation. Winchester. New York. 316 pp.

Ridd, Merrill K. 1965. Multiple use. Pp. 178–183 in R. Nash (ed.), The American Environment: Readings in the History of Conservation. Addison-Wesley. Reading, MA.

Risbrudt, Christopher. 1986. The real issue in below-cost sales: Multiple-use management of public lands. *Western Wildlands* 12(1):2–5.

Robertson, F. Dale. 1990. Demands on public lands may affect private forestry practices. *Forest Farmer* 49(9):18.

Robinson, Glen O. 1975. The Forest Service: A study in public land management. Resources for the Future/Johns Hopkins Press. Baltimore, MD. 337 pp.

Sample, V. Alaric. 1988. Not for the faint-hearted [a review of O'Toole (1988)]. *Journal of Forestry* 86(12):41.

Sampson, Neil. 1988. A new charter for the national forests? *American Forests* 95(5,6):17–20.

Shands, William E. (ed.). 1981. A Citizen's Guide to the Forest and Rangeland Renewable Resources Planning Act. USDA Forest Service Publication FS-365. Washington, DC. 200 pp. + append.

Shands, William E. 1988. At issue—Beyond multiple use: Managing national forests for distinctive values. *American Forests* 94(3,4):14–15, 56–57.

Spurr, Stephen H. 1976. The need for an American forest policy. *American Forests* 82(3):8–9, 55–58.

Steen, Harold K. 1976. The U.S. Forest Service: A history. University of Washington Press. Seattle. 356 pp.

Teeguarden, Dennis E. 1982. Multiple services. Pp. 276–290 in William A. Duerr et al. (eds.), Forest Resource Management: Decision-Making Principles and Cases. O.S.U. Bookstores. Corvallis, OR.

Tipple, Terence J., and Douglas J. Wellman. 1991. Herbert Kaufman's Forest Ranger thirty years later: From simplicity and homogeneity to complexity and diversity. *Public Administration Review* 51(5):421–428.

USDA Forest Service. 1983. The Principal Laws Relating to Forest Service Activities. Agricultural Handbook No. 453, Revised September 1983. U.S. Government Printing Office. Washington, DC. 591 pp.

USDA Forest Service. 1987. Report of the Forest Service, Fiscal Year 1986. Washington, DC. 172 pp.

USDA Forest Service. 1990. Synthesis of the critique of Land Management Planning, Vol. 1. Document FS-42. U.S. Government Printing Office. Washington, DC. 24 pp.

Whaley, Ross S. 1970. Multiple-use decision making—Where do we go from here? *Natural Resources Journal* 10(3):557–565.

Wilkinson, Charles F., and H. Michael Anderson. 1987. Land and Resource Planning in the National Forests. Island Press. Covelo, CA. 389 pp. (Originally in 1985 *Oregon Law Review* 64(1,2):1–373)

Wondolleck, Julia M. 1988. Public Lands Conflict and Resolution: Managing National Forest Disputes. Plenum. New York. 263 pp.

Worrell, Albert C. 1970. Principles of Forest Policy. McGraw-Hill. New York. 243 pp.

Zivnuska, John A. 1961. The Multiple Problems of Multiple Use. *Journal of Forestry* 59(8):555–560.

Zivnuska, John A. 1980. The case for dominant use. Pp. 49–53 in Proceedings, 1979 Annual Convention, Society of American Foresters. Bethesda, MD.

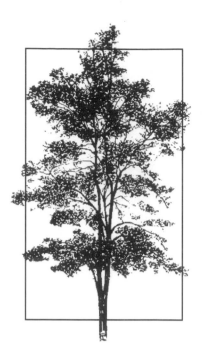

Chapter 14

Federal Environmental Protection and Regulation

The issue is real and immediate because forest devastation increases with appalling rapidity; because the need for governmental control on private timberlands is now self-evident; because without such control the general practice of forestry in this country will never become a reality; and because unless enough forestry is practiced to prevent forest devastation the danger to our prosperity in peace and safety in war will grow steadily worse. The field is cleared for action and the lines are plainly drawn. He who is not for forestry is against it. The choice lies between the convenience of the lumbermen and the public good.

—Gifford Pinchot 1919

The progressive conservation movement in the 1800's led to congressional authorization for establishing the national forest lands in the West in 1891 and purchasing those in the East in 1911. In addition, the nation's first wildlife protection laws were enacted— The Lacey Act of 1900 and the Migratory Bird Treaty Act of 1918. In 1919 the first concerted efforts for federal regulation of private forestry began, spearheaded by Gifford Pinchot. These efforts were initially unsuccessful but became the forerunners of much of the present-day forestry and environmental laws that regulate private forest landowners. This chapter reviews the development and extent of these federal natural resource laws.

EARLY FOREST AND ENVIRONMENTAL POLICY

Current environmental law and policy have their roots in statutes enacted by the first settlers of the United States. Regulation of forest practices was not new, even in 1600. Measures designed to protect forests were decreed in Germany as early as the 1400s. England has protected forest lands from unrestricted use for centuries, including the crown lands. Other European and Scandinavian countries also began to develop their now extensive system of laws that regulate public and private forestry. In colonial America, the English heritage was reflected in British common law that was designed to protect forests and game but was tempered by the abundance of natural resources found in America (Siegel and Cubbage 1984).

COLONIAL AMERICA

Since the beginning of the colonization of North America, statutes regarding forests and the environment were enacted by both the English crown and the settlers themselves. Early colonists generally regarded forests as a liability and cleared them for the more highly valued farms and towns. Many colonial laws actually promoted clearing land, draining swamps, or otherwise "improving" land in its natural state.

However, overexploitation of easily accessible timber, game, and agricultural resources prompted some protective and regulatory statutes by the early seventeenth century. Public regulation of private forest lands was initiated in North America in 1626 in the Plymouth Colony, which prohibited selling or transportation of timber out of the colony without the approval of the governor and the council (Huffman 1978). Various other conservation laws were passed by the mid-1600s (Kawashima and Tone 1983). In 1668 the Massachusetts Bay Colony reserved for the governor all white pine trees in parts of the town of Exeter that were fit for ship masts. In 1681 Gov. William Penn proclaimed that for every five acres of forest land cleared, one acre should be kept—which is the basis for the name Pennsylvania (literally, Penn's forest). In 1739 Massachusetts attempted to halt the encroachment of sand dunes on parts of Cape Cod by regulating timber cutting, burning, and grazing.

In addition to the general forest conservation efforts made by the early colonists, the English crown made specific efforts to reserve white pine trees in the colonies for use as masts for naval ships. In 1691 the English rulers, William and Mary, issued a new charter for the Massachusetts Bay Colony. Among other things, it codified the earlier prohibition of cutting white pine trees—including all trees 24 inches or more in diameter growing on land not granted to a private person, unless permission had been obtained from the British government. This became known as the Broad Arrow policy because the white pine trees reserved under it were marked with a broad arrow that was the symbol of sovereignty. The Broad Arrow policy was extended to all public lands in the colonies north of New Jersey in 1721, and the rest of America in 1729. In 1783, after the United States won independence, Massachusetts passed an act substantially equivalent to the Broad Arrow policy of the British (Dana 1956).

Some officials in the South also felt the need to preserve some of the vast stands of timber in order to prevent scarcity. A proclamation issued by a government official serving in 1735, during the tenure of Colonial Gov. William Oglethorpe of Georgia, illustrates this need (Lane 1975, p. 210):

> Whereas divers timber trees have been cut down without just cause, by which great waste hath been made, and if not prevented would in a short time disappoint everyone of the great advantages they would otherways enjoy in having timber so near the town for finishing and improving their respective building and whereas a great nuisance also arises from the falling such trees by the stopping up the passages to the plantations of the several respective freeholders, and the branches thereof covering the pastures which would otherways be useful for the feed of cattle and in a great measure prevent their rambling,
>
> This is therefore to give notice that if any person after the publication hereof shall at any time cut down any timber trees without my license or do not immediately after such cutting down such trees remove, burn or destroy all laps, tops, chips and brush occasioned by the falling, hewing or using such timber or trees will be prosecuted for the same with utmost severity,
>
> Or if any person shall presume on any pretense to cut down, deface or destroy any tree or shrub anywhere about the spring or make any fires there or make it a place to wash clothes they will have their tubs, pots & c. broke and be also prosecuted for the same.
>
> N. Jones, Ranger and Surveyor.

The early colonial and state acts set the precedent that government had the power to regulate tree cutting, forest burning, and hunting practices on public and private land. In addition, the English common law concept of *nuisance*—an unreasonable interference in the use and enjoyment of an interest in land—was applied in the colonies. Courts often heard nuisance cases, such as those concerned with placing a gate across a rural road, damming a stream, or operating foul-smelling businesses near residences. The courts usually required a remedy wth the best technique available to correct a nuisance—a precursor of modern environmental approaches.

THE UNITED STATES

Despite the colonial conservation statutes and the English heritage of conservation of natural resources, early policies of the independent United States reverted almost exclusively to exploitation of most forest and game resources. Little effort was expended to prevent or even fight fires, let alone regulate hunting or timber cutting. Disposition, development, and private use were the official policies; conservation was ignored (Schieber 1983).

As the nation expanded westward, the perception of unlimited forests and game fostered little concern for protection or regulation. A few forest protection laws existed in the 1800s, but none was enforced. However, some live oak forest reserves in the South were set aside to ensure an adequate supply for the U.S. Navy. The vast timbering operations of the Nineteenth century, combined with many massive and destructive forest fires, eventually led to the nation's first conservation movement and creation of forest reserves in 1891.

Proposed Federal Forestry Regulation
National debate over public regulation of private forestry began in the early 1900s, shortly after the national forests were established. Separate but similar drives to bring about public regulation of cutting on privately owned lands were started by the U.S. Forest Service and the Society of American Foresters. Forest Service Chief Henry S. Graves called for regulation by the states in 1919. At the same time the Society of American Foresters appointed a Committee for the Application of Forestry, chaired by Gifford Pinchot. The committee was charged with recommending action for prevention of forest devastation on privately owned timberland in the United States (Dana 1956).

Among other things, Pinchot's committee recommended national legislation to prevent such devastation. This effort spawned the national debate presented as an illustration in Chapter 3—the debate between Pinchot and Wilson Compton of the Lumber Manufacturers' Association. A bill was introduced into Congress to regulate private forestry according to the committee's recommendations. Opponents of federal regulation introduced a bill emphasizing fire control and state regulation of forestry activities. Opposing arguments and lack of leadership eventually brought congressional action on both bills to a halt (Greeley 1951). However, the impetus generated by the debates eventually led to further study, compromise, and passage of the Clarke-McNary Act in 1924. Clarke-McNary fostered federal–state cooperation in fire protection, forestry extension, and tree planting, but it avoided regulation. The act was essentially implemented by individual states enacting their own forest fire control laws. Similar federal and state administrative arrangements exist in current federal environmental legislation, such as water and air quality laws.

Federal Wildlife Law
At the same time that state and federal legislation governing private forest landowners began to be debated, several efforts were initiated to introduce national legislation to protect wildlife and game resources. The extinction of the carrier pigeon, devastation of the buffalo, and threatened status of a variety of other species led to federal efforts to regulate wildlife resources. Traditionally, ownership of wildlife and regulation of its taking were rights reserved to the states (Bean 1978). More recently, these rights have be-

come subordinate to federal law. States still control wildlife within their borders, but the exportation of game subordinates most state game laws to federal jurisdiction (Schoenbaum 1982).

Initial justification of federal involvement proved difficult, but that intervention was necessary because state laws were ineffective in protecting species. Like most other laws regulating individuals or states, legislation first was enacted under the federal authority to regulate interstate commerce. The Lacey Act of 1900 made it a federal offense to transport wild animals or birds that were killed in violation of state laws across state lines. This helped halt the illegal sales of pelts, plumes, feathers, and quills. The act also prohibited the importation of foreign species without a permit from the secretary of agriculture.

In 1913 the Weeks-McClean Act (Migratory Bird Law) placed migratory birds under federal protection. It was enacted as a rider on the general agricultural appropriations bill, and its constitutionality was challenged in the courts. President Taft later said he would have vetoed the entire bill had he been aware of the Weeks-McClean provision. Two federal district courts considered the constitutionality of the act and found it wanting, despite the government's claim of constitutionality under the interstate commerce clause. Fearful of an adverse Supreme Court ruling on the Weeks-McClean Act, proponents of the act initiated a treaty with Great Britain, on behalf of Canada for the joint protection of migratory birds, that would be constitutional under the treaty-making powers of Congress. This was signed in 1916 and enacted in 1918 as the Migratory Bird Treaty Act. It superseded the Weeks-McClean Act. Mexico finally signed the treaty in 1937 (Bean 1978).

Beginning Forest Practice Law
After enactment of the Clarke-McNary Act in 1924, the forest practices regulation debate temporarily abated. However, in a 1931 referendum, the membership of the Society of American Foresters reaffirmed that public control of private forestry was necessary to protect community interests (Hamilton 1965).

The issue persisted throughout the New Deal. A succession of U.S. Forest Service chiefs who followed William Greeley supported federal regulation of private forestry, at least in principle. At the time, even the forest industry supported self-regulation.

The federal attempts at forest regulation were actually enacted as Title 10 (the Lumber Code) of the National Recovery Administration (NRA) Codes, promulgated under the National Industrial Recovery Act (NIRA) of 1933. Title 10 was promoted by some forestry trade associations. It included provisions for the conservation of forests and prevention of destructive cutting practices. Administration of the law was delegated to a board composed primarily of forest industry representatives (Vaux 1985). However, the NRA codes were declared unconstitutional by the Supreme Court in 1935, as an unlawful delegation of legislative power to the executive. This eliminated overt federal regulation of forestry, as well as about 500 other industries.

In 1939 Earle H. Clapp became acting chief of the Forest Service. Greeley (1951, p. 212) wrote that Clapp was "wholly sincere and forthright in wanting forest regulation and single-minded in his pursuit of it." The Bankhead report issued by the U.S. Congress in 1941, following an extensive study concerning regulation of private forestry practices, noted widespread damage to forest resources caused by private timber harvests. The report recommended a combined federal–state regulatory system. Federal legislation was introduced on several occasions but never seriously considered. The latest federal effort was the proposed Forest Lands Restoration and Protection Act of 1971 that covered a wide range of regulatory practices, including mandatory harvesting plans for private owners.

The clamor for regulatory action in the 1930s and 1940s prompted 13 states to pass seed tree laws or state forest practice laws in order to ensure productivity of private forest lands. The seed tree laws requiring that trees be left standing after a harvest were passed mostly in the East. Many of these, however, were either voluntary or not enforced. More comprehensive seed tree laws—the precursors of modern state forest practice acts—were passed in California, Oregon, and Washington.

By 1950 interest in the movement toward federal regulation had come to a complete standstill (Society of American Foresters 1956). A 1945 forest inventory indicated that forest lands owned by private forest industry were better managed than Forest Service lands. Suddenly the spotlight of regulation, long aimed at the forest industry, shifted to private owners of small woodlots —who were still deemed to be poor stewards. (Greeley 1951). In addition, a 1950 Society of American Forester's referendum strongly opposed regulation. The referendum, coupled with the rising strength of industrial forestry, halted serious consideration of federal regulation of private forest lands (Society of American Foresters 1956).

Mid-Century Conservation

Despite the depression in the 1930s and world war in the 1940s, public interest in conservation in the United States continued to increase. The Civilian Conservation Corps put millions of young people to work building and protecting the facilities in America's parks and forests. Many of these facilities still exist today. Widespread wind and water erosion during the dust bowl years spurred the establishment of the federal Soil Erosion Service, now the Soil Conservation Service. New groups, led by people such as wilderness advocate Robert Marshall (1933) and naturalist Aldo Leopold, began to split away from the utilitarians who had earlier dominated national forest policy. They supported land preservation and stewardship and dismissed strictly economic criteria for land use decisions as being rapacious and shortsighted (Leopold 1949). Two influential citizen interest groups formed in the 1930s—the Wilderness Society (1935) and the National Wildlife Federation (1936). Other private conservation organizations broadened their focus and geographical base during 1940s and 1950s, including the Sierra Club and the Na-

tional Audubon Society. All of these groups provided grass-roots support for wildlife and land conservation laws at the time, and they increased in size and influence during the 1950s and 1960s.

With increasing affluence and leisure time, Americans began to spend more time in outdoor recreation activities during the 1960s. Membership in conservation organizations increased, and environmental protection became more important. The publication of *Silent Spring* in 1962 triggered environmental protection as a national issue and focused legislative attention on laws to protect the environment. Increasing industrial production and pervasive water and air pollution contributed to the demand for environmental protection laws.

The Taking Issue

Many current policy debates center on how far we can go in regulating private persons in order to to protect the environment. This question—called the *taking issue*—is not new. Early colonial and U.S. policy established that public regulation of private landowners was legitimate. The early laws were based on the premise that in order to protect and promote the public health, safety, morals, and general welfare, society can—through its police power—restrict the freedom with which owners may use their land (Bosselman, Callies, and Banta 1973, Roberts 1974). Use of police power to restrict landowners' actions stems from the common law of private nuisance or, less frequently, from the doctrine of waste (Carmichael 1975).

Common law and legal doctrine have established that individuals may not use their property in a manner that will injure the real property rights of others. The statutory and judicial law covering such injuries is classified under the concept of private nuisance (Freeman 1975). For example, nuisance laws prevented foul-smelling businesses from locating near residences or firms from dumping wastes in waters used by downstream owners. The nuisance principle applies not only to private property owners, but also may be expanded to protect the public (Troup 1938). Forest practice laws fall within this expanded version of private nuisance, as do most land use statutes, zoning regulations, and environmental protection legislation enacted in recent years.

The courts fashioned the doctrine of waste in an attempt to balance the desire of a current owner to make productive use of his or her property against future owners' desires to receive the property essentially unimpaired. The doctrine has been applied beyond the context of present and future or public and private owners to ensure that natural resources are not improvidently depleted or destroyed. The doctrine of waste implies that owners only have *usufructuary* rights: They may use their land as they will as long as they do not damage or destroy it (Spurr 1976). In the United States, as a general rule, the doctrine requires that existing owners not materially decrease the value of their property and that they use good husbandry in managing it (Carmichael 1975). Most early forest practice laws were based largely on this doctrine of waste.

The police power exercised by the states to protect the public health, safety, morality, and general welfare should not be confused with eminent domain. Under eminent domain, property is taken for a public purpose and just compensation—often determined by a jury—is paid. Regulation by police power—such as zoning areas for only residential developement, or to restrict development on coastal areas—may decrease a property's value or earning potential, but land is not physically taken nor is compensation paid. Such police action is clearly legitimate. However, excessive regulation that would take all the value of a piece of property without just compensation is proscribed by the Fifth Amendment of the U.S. Constitution and its state counterparts (Roberts 1974).

Despite thousands of judicial decisions, the line between compensable and noncompensable taking remains uncertain. The question is

critical in land use control and environmental quality regulation. The Fifth Amendment is generally applied to the states through the due process and equal protection clause of the Fourteenth Amendment (Paster 1983), which specifies that no state shall "deprive any person of life, liberty, or property without due process of law." The courts have held this to mean that regulation is an appropriate exercise of police power if it does not discriminate among owners and is applicable to all persons in a like manner. Most successful constitutional challenges to zoning and forest practice laws have been based on violations of the Fourteenth Amendment (Paster 1983, Siegel 1974).

Early Decisions

In the late 1800s and early 1900s the courts broadly endorsed the use of state police power to regulate private forestry and land use actions in the public interest. Judicial interpretation of the federal Constitution placed few, if any, limits on exercising police power for the general public welfare, even if it meant regulating actions of private owners on their own land. The courts during these years widely upheld the power of the "state" (the government) to regulate private landowners to protect the health, safety, morals, and general welfare of society.

The courts generally ruled that laws encouraging timber production could be enacted for the public welfare, but not for private benefit (*Deal* v. *Mississippi County*, 107 Mo. 464, 18 S.W. 24 [1891]). Later, the Supreme Court ruled that the state could use its police powers to guard the public welfare and interest to "protect the atmosphere, the water, and the forests within its territory, irrespective of the assent or dissent of the private owners of the land most immediately concerned" (*State of Georgia* v. *Tennessee Copper Co.*, 27 S.Ct. 618, 206 U.S. 230 [1907]).

In 1908 (*Opinion of Justices*, 103 Me. 506, 69 A. 627 [1908]), the Maine Supreme Court responded to a legislative query to determine if a law regulating actions on private forests would be constitutional.

[W]e do not think the proposed legislation would operate to "take" private property within the prohibition of the constitution. While it might restrict the owner of wild and uncultivated lands in his use of them, might delay his taking some of the product, might defer his anticipated profits, and even thereby might cause him some loss of profit, it would nonetheless leave him his lands, their product, and increase untouched, and without diminution of title, estate, or quantity. He would still have large measure of control and large opportunity to realize values. He might suffer delay, but not deprivation. While the use might be restricted, it would not be appropriated or "taken."

The justices further concurred that the proposed forest regulation would not violate the due process and equal protection provisions of the Fourteenth Amendment.

In 1919 a landowner challenged a North Carolina law that required people who cut timber near streams that supplied water to cities and towns to remove or burn all treetops within 400 feet of the stream (*Perley* v. *North Carolina*, 173 N.C. 783, 39 S.Ct. 357, 249 U.S. 510 [1919]). He claimed that tops were harmless and not a nuisance, that the required cleanup of his land deprived him of property without due process of law or just compensation, and that the law did not bear equally on everyone because it did not apply to local governments. The North Carolina Supreme Court affirmed that the statute was a constitutional exercise of the police power, violating neither the Fifth nor Fourteenth Amendments. The U.S. Supreme Court upheld the state court.

These early decisions established that state and local governments could exercise police power to achieve a natural resource objective in the general public interest. Several decisions also stressed that no matter how inconvenienced, restricted, or even damaged a particular landowner may be, general laws and regulations should be held valid unless specifically prohibited by the federal or a state constitution.

Diminution of Value and Public Interest

Although many court decisions involved the use of state police power, the degree of per-

missible regulation was not clearly defined by the U.S. Supreme Court until the 1920s. A test of a state's power to regulate a private coal company led to the benchmark Supreme Court definition of taking by Justice Oliver Wendell Holmes in 1922 (*Pennsylvania Coal* v. *Mahon*, 274 Pa. 489, 118 A. 491, 43 S.Ct. 158, 200 U.S. 393 [1922]). Holmes concurred that the state may use its police powers to regulate private property owners, but he placed stricter limits on those powers than did earlier court decisions: "While property may be regulated to a certain extent, if the regulation goes too far it will be considered as a taking."

Holmes established a two-part test (Paster 1983). Taking without just compensation occurs when (1) diminution in property value is great enough, and (2) the public interest disclosed in a statute is not sufficient to extensively impair the constitutionally protected property rights.

Individual courts have since had to determine subjectively whether value losses are great enough and if there is sufficient public interest. If a statute met these requirements, the regulation would be considered a taking and the law unconstitutional. The Holmes opinion has led to a balancing test—a weighing of the public benefits of regulation against the extent of loss of property values. This test reduced the taking question to a matter of degree and to a mixture of fact and law (Stoebuck 1982).

A number of judicial opinions during the four decades following the *Mahon* decision clarified state legislative authority to regulate private forests. In 1928 the Idaho Supreme Court vigorously affirmed the validity of fire protection provisions (*Chambers* v. *McCollum*, 47 Idaho 74, 272 P. 707 [1928]). The court held that state law prohibiting the setting of fires, allowing the state forester to determine the adequacy of fire protection, charging landowners for fire protection, and holding administrative appeals instead of court hearings did not take property without compensation or due process. *Conway* v. *New Hampshire Water Resources Board* (89 N.H. 346, 199 A. 83 [1938]) justified the use of police power to regulate private forest owners to protect other natural resources.

State v. *Dexter* (32 Wash.2d 551, 202 P.2d 906, 70 S.Ct. 147 [1947]), the only litigation involving a state forest practice act to reach the U.S. Supreme Court, addressed taking from the standpoint of conservation of resources over time. In 1945 Washington enacted a forest practice act regulating timber harvesting on private land. In 1947 the state shut down Avery Dexter's logging operation for failure to comply with the act. Dexter had refused to leave uncut all ponderosa pine less than 16 inches in diameter and to apply for a cutting permit. He maintained that the law permitted the equivalent of taking without compensation, thus destroying private property rights (Siegel 1974). The trial court ruled for Dexter, but the Washington Supreme Court reversed the decision and held the law to be constitutional. The judges broadly defined police power, writing:

Edmund Burke once said that a great unwritten compact exists between the dead, the living, and the unborn. We leave to the unborn a colossal financial debt, perhaps inescapable, but incurred, nonetheless, in our time and for our immediate benefit. Such an unwritten compact requires that we leave the unborn something more than debts and depleted natural resources. Surely where natural resources can be utilized and at the same time perpetuated for future generations, what has been called "constitutional morality" requires that we do so.

The majority held that the law violated neither the Fifth Amendment taking strictures nor the Fourteenth Amendment due process clause. The court refuted Dexter's claim of financial loss as grounds for a constitutional challenge, stating: "It frequently happens that regulatory laws, enacted under the police power in furtherance of some appropriate purpose, impose hardships in individual cases, due to special and peculiar circumstances; but this fact will not subject the law to constitutional objection."

The state supreme court opinion was upheld by the U.S. Supreme Court without comment. *Dexter* has been used frequently to support laws for regulation, preservation, promotion, and development of natural resources. The Washington Act also was held to apply to state as well as private land (*West Norman Timber* v. *State*, 37 Wash.2d 467, 224 P.2d 635 [1950]). The legislature could enact laws to prevent indiscriminate damage to, or destruction of, forest and water resources of the state, even though they might involve some regulation and control over private ownership of property.

Most of these court decisions indicate that laws regulating forest practices in the public interest were likely to be held constitutional, even if a landowner lost some value of her or his property. Forest and land use cases decided from the 1960s to the 1980s affirmed, and even extended the limits of, allowable regulation (Cubbage and Siegel 1985).

Modern Regulatory Powers

In the 1970s and 1980s, the number of federal and state environmental laws increased greatly, and the number of administrative rules and regulations increased by the thousands. Many of these laws and regulations have been challenged in court, in order to invalidate them, reduce their extent, clarify unclear legislative intent, or increase their authority. The body of common law that has stemmed from these court decisions has generally found regulation to protect the environment to be a valid exercise of the state's police power and often supported expansion of administrative legal authority based on unclear statutory wording (i.e. Malone 1991, Novick, Stever, and Mellon 1988).

Each presidential administration has also affected modern regulatory powers. Nixon created the Environmental Protection Agency in 1970 and presided over the largest expansion of federal environmental laws in our history in the early 1970s. Carter's Executive Order 11990 in 1980 directed all government agencies to work for environmental protection. Executive Order No. 12630, signed by Reagan on March 15, 1988 [53 Federal Register 8859] instructed federal agencies to examine the taking implications of their actions in relation to the Fifth Amendment of the Constitution. Federal agencies must file a "Taking Impact Assessment" with the Office of Management and Budget prior to introducing legislation into Congress. This gives landowners a mechanism to raise questions, but the agency still makes the decisions on taking implications.

President Bush and Vice-President Dan Quayle have also been very active in the regulatory arena, largely through attempts to turn back the tide of new regulations. Bush created a Council on Competitiveness, which Quayle chaired. The probusiness council focused largely on reducing or weakening regulations that adversely affect business, including wetlands and private property regulations. The council and Quayle's ongoing role became a significant issue in the 1992 presidential campaign.

With the economy lagging and the business community protesting regulation in 1991, Bush responded in his State of the Union address on January 28, 1992, by declaring a 90-day freeze on all new regulations. On April 29 Bush extended the moratorium for several more months. The president promised a top-to-bottom review of all regulations to eliminate those that will hurt growth and speed up those that will help growth. Much of the effect of the Bush freeze was felt on environmental rules. For example, the administration halted identifying rare plants and animals under the Endangered Species Act, delayed rules to carry out the Clean Air Act, floated proposals to reduce appeals under NFMA, and limited the liability of banks and other lenders for cleaning up toxic wastes generated by firms to which they had loaned money (Rosenbaum and Schneider 1992).

Although the number of environmental laws and regulations expanded greatly during the 1970s and 1980s, public sentiment and presidential discretion have placed limits on their power and extent. Furthermore, the growing wise use/private property rights movement has begun a concerted campaign to curtail environmental regulations. These efforts have been abetted by the conservative judiciary appointed during the Reagan and Bush presidencies.

Recent Court Decisions

A number of decided or pending court decisions in the late 1980s and early 1990s indicated that some limits would be placed on the extent of public regulation of private landowners, or indeed that the balancing test might swing further back toward private property rights and less toward public welfare rights. Several federal court decisions found that public regulations could go so far as to constitute an impermissible taking of private land.

In one case, *First Evangelical Lutheran Church of Glendale* v. *County of Los Angeles* (482 U.S. 304 [1987]), the Supreme Court ruled that an ordinance prohibiting construction of any buildings in a flood plain was confiscatory. The Supreme Court did not decide that a taking had in fact occurred. Instead, the Court remanded the case to the lower court for that determination. The Court, likewise, did not change the criterion that is used in deciding takings cases—that all use of property has to be denied.

In *Nollan* v. *California Coastal Commission* (483 U.S. 825 [1987]), the California Coastal Commission granted a permit to appellants to replace a small bungalow on their beach front lot with a larger house upon the condition that they allow the public an easement to pass across their beach. This was an attempt by the commission to address public concerns over visual access to the shoreline. Upon appeal, the U.S. Supreme Court held that the commission's imposition of the access–easement condition cannot be treated as an exercise of land-use regulation power because the condition does not serve public purposes related to the permit requirement.

In *Tull* v. *United States* (481 U.S. 412 [1987]), the U.S. Supreme Court ruled that jury trials were required to assess civil penalties *when* monetary damages are sought under common law. Edward Lunn Tull, a real estate developer, was enjoined and assessed a civil penalty for illegally dredging and filling a wetland area on Chincoteague Island, Virginia. Tull appealed to the Supreme Court, arguing that the lower court failed to separate the civil penalty issue from the request for an injunction and that he should be afforded a jury trial. Civil penalties under the Clean Water Act closely resemble the remedy in actions to recover a debt and thus require a jury trial. The Supreme Court concurred but ruled that judges retain power to determine the amount of penalty to be imposed. This ruling could substantially complicate future enforcement actions under the Section 404 wetlands permit program (see the *Water Pollution Control Act* section).

The number of cases challenging that regulations constitute a taking has mushroomed in the last few years. In addition, many cases have been filed in the U.S. Claims Court by owners seeking to receive payment for the loss of use of their land due to regulations. Under this approach, which is termed *inverse condemnation*, instead of trying to prove that an unconstitutional taking occurred, landowners just try to receive payment for their financial loss. The court had 52 cases filed involving allegations of the taking of property in 1991, the most in at least a decade. About 200 property-taking cases were pending in 1992. These included cases challenging the government's authority to clean up toxic wastes, regulate fishing and water rights, buy land for national parks, restrict mining in wilderness areas, and prevent development on private land to protect wetlands. In 1991 the U.S. Claims Court did rule that landowners affected by environmental regulations are entitled to compensation (Schneider 1992).

These efforts in the courts will surely affect the rate at which environmental regulation proceeds. They will at least make regulators wary. Environmental group leaders go further and say that the lawsuits could cripple the government's ability to enforce its basic environmental laws by making such enforcement too expensive. They contend that the real intention of the movement is to eliminate three decades of environmental protections that are broadly supported by the American public (Schneider 1992).

In addition to pursuing a judicial and executive branch strategy, landowners and businesses have sought legislative relief from environmental regulations. Bills have been enacted in Congress to limit wetlands regula-

tion and to provide compensation for owners whose land values are decreased by regulation. These bills have had wide sponsorship in Congress but to date have been successfully opposed by environmental groups, and even the National Governor's Association. Environmental groups strongly support use of the state's police power to prevent harm to the environment or to other individuals. Similar legislation limiting regulation in order to protect private property rights has been introduced in many state legislatures as well. In 1992, 27 property rights protection laws were introduced in state legislatures, and passed by two. Under the new Delaware law, for instance, no rule or regulation will become effective until the state attorney general reviews its potential for taking private property (Wildlife Digest 1992).

NATIONAL ENVIRONMENTAL POLICY

The current debates about regulatory limits reflect the rapid growth of environmental laws in the last three decades. The environmental interest groups of the 1930s and 1940s grew rapidly in the 1960s, and many new groups were formed. By the 1970s environmentalists and preservationists had become more influential in setting the public policy agenda for conservation than were utilitarians and foresters. These interest groups had greater numbers, good organizations, successful public relations efforts, and effective grass-roots and national lobbying. Widespread popular support for the environmental movement and the groups' effective lobbying efforts led to enactment of strong federal environmental laws in the 1970s. An overview of these policies follows.

NATIONAL ENVIRONMENTAL POLICY ACT

The turning point for modern environmental law was the passage of the National Environmental Policy Act (NEPA) of 1969. As discussed in earlier chapters, the act's purposes were to (1) encourage harmony between people and the environment, (2) promote efforts that prevent or eliminate damage to the environment and biosphere and stimulate the health and welfare of humanity, and (3) enrich the understanding of the ecological systems and natural resources so important to the nation. NEPA requires the preparation of an Environmental Impact Statement for all federal actions significantly affecting the environment. Therefore, such actions as national forest planning, wilderness designations, or dam construction require comprehensive impact statements. Failure to meet NEPA strictures has been the basis for many lawsuits.

Details on NEPA were discussed in the illustration in Chapter 8 and in Chapter 13 (national forest planning). NEPA follows earlier federal–state cooperative patterns by recommending guidelines that each state could use in enacting its own environmental legislation. Several states have now passed environmental protection statutes that regulate forest and other natural resources to some extent. NEPA prompted some states to go further and require environmental impact reports for activities on private lands as well as for state actions. California, Oregon, Washington, and several states in the northern and eastern United States have enacted rigorous state environmental acts. The California act in particular has created controversy regarding forest management practices.

As discussed before, NEPA can stall projects until adequate environmental impact studies are done, but once an EIS is satisfactorily completed, courts cannot force an agency to choose one alternative over another, even if one is clearly superior environmentally. Agencies still may choose environmentally poor projects even after a NEPA analysis. Nonetheless, NEPA has spared a considerable amount of wild land from oil and gas drilling, from road construction and logging, and from strip mining and flooding. NEPA lawsuits bought enough time for legislative action that eventually kept the land from being developed. NEPA also added so much delay and litigation cost that it helped kill many already marginal

projects. Examples of such projects include (Turner 1988)

- Mineral King Valley, California—leased for a ski development, now in Sequoia National Park.

- Admiralty Island, Alaska—timber harvest contracts signed by the USDA Forest Service, now mostly protected as a national monument.

- Redwood National Park, California—upslope logging delayed until area could be added to park.

- Blue Creek, California—proposed national forest road and timber sale in remote area sacred to Native Americans; lawsuit stopped road on environmental grounds, Supreme Court will consider religious freedom arguments.

- Gore Range Eagles Nest Primitive Area, Colorado—proposed national forest timber sale area, now in National Wilderness Preservation System.

- Canaan Valley, West Virginia—proposed for reservoir flooding; Supreme Court declined to review decision that halted development, may become a national wildlife refuge.

- Misty Fjords National Monument, Alaska—plan for world's largest open pit mine (for molybdenum), eventual fate still unresolved.

The indirect expansion of the NEPA process to private lands was proposed by the Tennessee Valley Authority (TVA) in 1991. TVA decided to perform an EIS on three proposed hardwood chip-barge mills on the Tennessee River, which would obtain wood from adjacent private lands. The mill owners, who would chip the wood and barge it down river, need a permit from TVA to transport their logs across TVA domain at the river's edge. One of the proposals for the EIS was that private landowners who cut timber to supply the mills would need approved forest management plans. This EIS could set a precedent—if the six acres of public land could lead to regulation of timberland owners in the surrounding 7 million acres.

Apparently, environmental groups convinced TVA that the EIS on mill location must contain a mitigation plan requiring mill owners to prepare preharvest management plans for landowners from whom they buy logs. The management plans would need to reflect BMPs and be reviewed by state agencies and the Fish and Wildlife Service. A new landowner and industry interest group committee was formed to oppose this administrative application of the EIS. The final TVA actions were still pending in 1992.

THE ENVIRONMENTAL PROTECTION AGENCY

Prior to 1969 federal environmental protection efforts were spread among many agencies. Federal reorganization of environmental agencies was initially proposed by the 1969 President's Advisory Council on Executive Reorganization. Two proposals for departments of the environment and natural resources suggested consolidating parts of the Departments of Interior and Agriculture. But the secretaries of agriculture and interior and their supporting interest groups opposed consolidation.

A third alternative also was proposed— an independent Environmental Protection Agency (EPA) to oversee pollution monitoring, research, standard setting, and enforcement activities. Specifically, EPA would consolidate water quality administration from Interior, air pollution control and the environmental control administration from Health, Education and Welfare, pesticide registration from Agriculture, and some radiation protection from the Atomic Energy Commission. The proposal for a Department of Environment and Natural Resources was eventually rejected, and the EPA proposal became more appealing. President Nixon submitted the EPA reorganization plan to Congress in July 1970; Congress raised no objections, so the agency was formally established in December 1970 (Dana and Fairfax 1980).

Since then, EPA has become the lead agency for federal regulation of public and private landowners in order to prevent environmental damage. EPA administers the legislative programs for water, air, radiation, and pesticide protection. EPA was assigned several important roles, including (35 Federal Register 15623, 84 Stat. 2086)

The establishment and enforcement of environmental protection standards consistent with national environmental goals.

The conduct of research on the adverse effects of pollution and on methods and equipment for controlling it, the gathering of information on pollution, and the use of this information in strengthening environmental protection programs and recommending policy changes.

Assisting others, through grants, technical assistance, and other means, in arresting pollution of the environment.

Assisting the Council on Environmental Quality in developing and recommending to the President new policies for the protection of the environment.

The Council on Environmental Quality (CEQ), which was created by NEPA, was to work with EPA. CEQ serves to advise the president and is concerned with all aspects of environmental quality—wildlife preservation, parklands, land use, population growth, and pollution. EPA became an operating "line" organization (rather than a merely advisory agency) charged with protecting the environment by abating pollution.

FEDERAL WATER POLLUTION CONTROL ACT

A flood of federal environmental laws followed NEPA. Many of the rivers and lakes in the nation were little more than open sewers, full of industrial and municipal waste. Several even caught fire and burned, and many were devoid of life. To help correct these severe water quality problems, Congress abandoned the laissez-faire approach to water quality protection. It enacted the Federal Water Pollution Control Act (FWPCA) Amendments of 1972, overriding President Nixon's veto. This act and its amendments in 1977 and 1987 remain among the most comprehensive and expensive pieces of legislation ever enacted by Congress. The basic water quality objective expressed in FWPCA is to restore and maintain the chemical, physical, and biological integrity of the nation's waters. The law was intended to accomplish this broad goal by eliminating the discharge of point sources of pollutants into navigable waters by 1985 and by developing an interim level of water quality for 1983, for both point and nonpoint sources, that permitted swimming and fish propagation—often referred to as the *fishable/swimmable* goal. The law also prohibits degradation of existing water quality levels (termed *nondegradation*). These federal laws and amendments are generally referred to as the Clean Water Act.

Section 402 of the 1972 law clearly defined point source pollution as any discrete conveyance such as a pipe, ditch, or other identifiable source with a distinct origin. Nonpoint source pollution was not clearly defined, leaving much to administrative interpretation. Over time, definitions of both have evolved. Point pollutants have discrete, identifiable sources, and nonpoint sources originate from a widespread land area, such as silvicultural, agricultural, mining, or construction activities. Section 208 of the 1972 amendments deals with nonpoint source pollution, including forest land management activities; a new Section 319 promulgated in the 1987 amendments also is relevant. Section 404 of the 1972 Clean Water Act governs operations in wetlands.

SECTION 402–INDUSTRIAL POINT SOURCE POLLUTION

Section 402 of the 1972 FWPCA established the National Pollutant Discharge Elimination System (NPDES), administered by the EPA, to control industrial point source discharges. In 1972 EPA proposed to use Section 402 permits to control almost all sources of pollution, including agriculture and forestry. The prospect of permits for all forestry and farm-

ing activities led to immediate, adverse reactions, causing EPA to withdraw the proposal. In 1973 EPA published regulations excluding small animal feedlot operations and small agricultural, and silvicultural activities from requiring a Section 402 discharge permit. Mostly due to concern over animal feedlot pollution, the Natural Resources Defense Council (NRDC) contested EPA's authority to exempt classes of activities from 402 permit requirements. The federal court for the District of Columbia ruled in favor of NRDC, requiring EPA to promulgate regulations extending the NPDES permit system to include all point sources in the concentrated animal feeding operation, separate storm sewer, agriculture, and silviculture categories (*Natural Resource Defense Council* v. *Train*, No. 1629-73, D.D.C. 1975). The court decision forced EPA to make a distinction between point and nonpoint sources that would be regulated under Section 402 (Rey 1980).

EPA subsequently published final regulations in 1976 identifying those silvicultural activities that constitute Section 402 point sources of pollution. Most forestry pollution activities were considered nonpoint in nature, but four activities were considered point sources and subject to permits: (1) rock crushing, (2) gravel washing, (3) log sorting, and (4) log storage facilities (all are activities occuring mostly in the western United States). The regulations also provided criteria for determining nonpoint sources: (1) pollution induced by natural processes such as precipitation, seepage, percolation, and runoff; (2) pollution not traceable to any discreet or identifiable facility, and (3) discharged pollutants that are better controlled through the use of management practices (Rey 1980).

SECTIONS 208 AND 319–NONPOINT SOURCE POLLUTION

Section 208 of the 1972 amendments mandated state planning in order to control nonpoint source pollution from mining, agricultural, development, and silvicultural activities. EPA originally interpreted Section

208's state planning requirement as applying only to problem areas designated by the governor. However, litigation initiated by the Environmental Defense Fund and the Natural Resources Defense Council led to a court decision that Section 208 planning should apply to all rreas of the state, including non-designated forest and agricultural lands (*Natural Resources Defense Council v. Train*, 396 F. Supp. 1386 [1975]). Although this ruling was affirmed upon appeal, the appeals court held that the intensity of planning for non-designated areas need not be as great as for designated areas (*Natural Resources Defense Council v. Costle*, 564 F.2d 753 [1977]).

EPA pursued Section 208 implementation aggressively, particularly during the 1970s. These efforts included recommendations for formal regulation of private forest practices via state forest practices legislation (Agee 1975). EPA drafted a model law in 1974 that contained strict regeneration standards, water quality protection measures, and even amenity protection guidelines. Vocal criticism from the forestry community caused EPA to withdraw the model act in favor of less overt implementing mechanisms, particularly in the eastern United States, where forestry–related water quality problems were perceived as being less severe than in the West. Nevertheless, a number of eastern states, such as Maine, Massachusetts, and Florida, have some regulatory legislation that includes measures to control silvicultural nonpoint source pollution. These statutes, however, are not comprehensive forest practice laws (Cubbage, Siegel, and Lickwar 1989; Haines, Cubbage, and Siegel 1988).

Despite the efforts in the 1980s that have stemmed from Section 208, many interest groups and members of Congress continued to believe that nonpoint source pollution was still an impediment to achieving the nation's water quality goals. In addition, many other aspects of the federal water quality laws were being considered for revision in 1985 and 1986. Congressional deliberations in 1986 eventually led to a major revision of the 1972 and 1977 amendments. The new statute was passed unanimously by both houses of Congress in 1986. However, President Reagan pocket-vetoed the legislation after Congress adjourned. As an indication of their resolve to revise the federal water quality protection law, many Congress members reintroduced the legislation as the first bill of 1987. It was swiftly enacted in February by overriding President Reagan's veto.

Section 319 of the 1987 Water Quality Act required each state to prepare by August 1988 detailed water quality management plans that identify bodies of water not in compliance with water quality standards because of nonpoint source pollution. States were required to identify categories and individual nonpoint sources that violate water quality and to describe control mechanisms. States could devise either regulatory or voluntary programs to control nonpoint source pollution. State control plans had to target resources on the most heavily impacted waters, develop management programs on a watershed-by-watershed basis, and identify best management practices (BMPs) to be applied to mitigate impacts (U.S. Environmental Protection Agency 1987).

In implementing their nonpoint source control mechanisms—whether voluntary or regulatory—states may base compliance on use of BMPs or on state water quality standards. BMPs are the optimal methods, measures, or practices for preventing or reducing water pollution, including, but not limited to, structural controls, operation and maintenance procedures, and scheduling and distribution of activities. Water quality standards (WQS) are specific water quality criteria, both narrative and numeric, for the water bodies of a state. There has been considerable debate regarding which of these approaches will be used in the case of forestry, and indeed some question of whether WQS can be used without completely halting some forestry operations. In 1987 EPA released a memorandum stating that BMPs generally should serve as adequate implementing mechanisms to meet water quality goals, which somewhat ameliorated forestry fears of excessive regulation.

Most states have submitted their Section 319 plans to EPA. In the South, all states except Florida and North Carolina elected to use nonregulatory mechanisms, such as voluntary BMPs, education, and monitoring of forest practices to control water pollution. Florida and North Carolina used a mix of regulatory and educational programs. Most of the western states already have incorporated water quality protection measures in their existing state forest practice acts. Northeastern and midwestern states relied mostly on BMPs and educational programs, but some were considering regulations (Haines et al. 1988). By 1992 many states were making substantial efforts to reduce forestry nonpoint source pollution. This included extensive educational programs, responding to citizens' complaints about water quality violations, and fining individuals who violated water quality standards. Use of BMPs approached required status in several eastern states, in addition to their explicit inclusion in western forest practice laws.

A recent enforcement action in Florida illustrates the application of the nonpoint source pollution provisions of the FWPCA to forestry operations. A major forest products firm was harvesting a large bottomland hardwood stand during the wet winter months in 1990. The loggers were using the state BMPs as prescribed in Section 404, but the water quality and flow were nevertheless considerably impaired. The state water quality agency initiated a nonpoint source pollution enforcement action against the firm, stating it had violated the FWPCA Section 208/319 nonpoint pollution requirements. The firm initially fought this interpretation but eventually conceded that the water quality protection measures did apply, and it has been negotiating an agreeement to cease harvesting operations during excessively wet weather and to protect water quality.

SECTION 404 – WETLAND POINT SOURCE POLLUTION

Wetlands protection became an important issue in the 1980s. Section 404 of the 1972

FWPCA mandated that the U.S. Army Corps of Engineers develop regulations governing permits and their jurisdiction in wetlands areas and allowed a broad definition of wetlands. The corps, however, was somewhat ambivalent about the possibility of expanding its regulatory role and opted instead for a narrow jurisdictional definition of traditional navigable waters in its subsequent 1974 regulations. It chose to limit its coastal jurisdiction to wetlands below the mean high-water mark, leaving much of the coastal wetlands unregulated. Most freshwater wetlands and tributary streams also remained outside the corps' jurisdiction, as did many lakes and prairie potholes (Stine 1983).

The corps' narrow definition of the applicable water areas was promptly challenged by the NRDC, which argued that Congress intended to control pollution at its source, and that the whole aquatic ecosystem must be protected and could not be arbitrarily divided if the statute was to work. The NRDC further argued that the preservation and protection of wetlands are essential to help restore and maintain the chemical, physical, and biological integrity of the nation's waters, as required by FWPCA (*Natural Resources Defense Council* v. *Callaway*, 392 F. Supp. 685 [1975]).

The court ruled in favor of NRDC, stating that Section 502(7) of the FWPCA intended that federal jurisdiction over the nation's waters be exercised to the maximum extent permissible under the Commerce Clause of the U.S. Constitution and not restricted to traditional definitions of navigability. The court instructed the corps to revise and expand its regulations to protect wetlands, including ephemeral streams. However, the specifics of a broadened wetlands definition has remained an unresolved political and scientific issue through 1992.

The corps promptly complied, and broadened its wetlands jurisdiction, but not all personnel agreed with the decision. On May 6, 1975, four alternative wetland regulations were released by the corps. Simultaneously, many dissenting people in the corps launched a negative publicity campaign to expand the issue and get the regulatory scope reduced to traditional navigable waters. The campaign was triggered by a corps public affairs office press release stating that federal permits could be required for stock ponds, stream erosion protection, or even plowing fields. The press release further warned that millions of people might be violating the law and be subject to fines and imprisonment (Stine 1983).

The furor created by the corps' 1975 press release led to predictable adverse reactions from farm, forestry, development, and other interests and intense criticism of the corps' tactics by conservation groups and Congress. Nevertheless, the corps finally adopted the expanded Section 404 wetlands definitions in 1977 and tried to ensure that recalcitrant field offices implemented them sincerely (Stine 1983).

A broad interpretation of navigable waters and wetlands as proposed in 1977 could have led to permits being required for forestry activities such as logging and road building, even near an intermittent stream. The 1977 Clean Water Act Amendments to the FWPCA, however, specifically exempted normal silvicultural activities from the permitting requirement. Also, construction and maintenance of forest roads was exempted when done in accordance with approved BMPs. Section 404 is still relevant, however, because controversy remains as to what constitutes a "normal" silvicultural practice.

Permit Authority *(coE)*

The basic authority of the corps to issue 404 permits is summarized in Section 320.2(f) of the 1986 Federal Register. Permits may be issued, after notice and opportunity for public hearing, for the discharge of dredged or fill material into the waters of the United States at specified disposal sites. Section 320.4 of the final regulations lists an extensive number of general policies for evaluating permit applications. These include numerous factors that should be considered under the public interest review, such as conservation, aesthetics, economics, general environmental concerns, fish and wildlife values, water quality, energy needs, property rights, and the needs and welfare of the people. Other broad classes of criteria to be considered in granting or denying a permit include minimizing unnecessary alteration or destruction of wetlands; consulting with regional U.S. Fish and Wildlife personnel and similar state agencies; evaluating the impact on water quality; considering historical, regional, scenic, and recreational values; considering property ownership; and evaluating other factors (51 Federal Register 219 [Nov. 13, 1986]: 41206-260).

There are three types of Section 404 permits: nationwide, regional, and individual. Nationwide and regional permits are sometimes referred to as general permits, whereas individual permits are sometimes called standard permits.

A nationwide permit may authorize certain activities throughout the country. These wide-ranging permits help simplify the permitting process by allowing certain activities, such as discharge of material for utility lines, to occur in wetlands. These permits help reduce the tremendous amount of paperwork involved in the permit process and allow more time to be spent on individual permits. A complete list of activities authorized under the nationwide permits has been compiled in the Federal Register (33 CFR Part 330.5), and includes the controversial *Nationwide Permit 26* which allows for no individual review by the corps of isolated wetlands or wetlands above the headwaters of rivers or streams.

Regional permits are similar to nationwide permits except that they are issued by COE district engineers on a regional basis. Regional conditions can vary and copies of these modifications can be acquired from the district engineers (33 CFR Part 330.1).

Individual permits are authorized on a case-by-case basis. These kinds of permits take up the most time for the COE permitting staff. According to the Federal Register, Part 325.5, individual or standard permits are ones that have been processed through the public interest review procedures.

Silvicultural Exemptions

Except for several explicitly enumerated exceptions, Department of Army (corps) permits are required for deposit of dredged or fill material in the nation's waters. Section 323.4 of the final Section 404 regulations continues to exempt normal silviculture activities from permit requirements. However, activities which bring an area into farming, silviculture, or ranching use are not exempt from permit requirements. These limitations were determined based on the court decision of *Avoyelles Sportsmen's League* v. *Alexander* (473 F. Supp. 525 [1979], 511 F. Supp. 278 [1981]), which was discussed as the "Wetlands Clearing in Louisiana" illustration in Chapter 8.

Section 404 is still relevant, however, because some controversy remains as to what constitutes "normal" silvicultural practice. In brief, the implementation of the mandate requiring permits for designated forestry operations has been slow and difficult. The regulations dictating when permits would be required were not released until 1986 and considerable debate remains about when permits are required. Additionally, many states have not yet developed forestry BMPs.

An additional ongoing debate centers on the "recapture" provision of Section 404(f)(2). This section states that notwithstanding the 404(f)(1) exemption, if an operation does noticeably alter the flow, circulation, and hydrology of a site, the silvicultural exemption from the permit requirement is voided, or recaptured. Thus, the silvicultural exemption is conditioned on the premise that the wetlands will not be altered. The recapture clause specifically states that the exempt activities would still require a permit if their purpose were "to convert an area of the waters of the United States into a use to which it was not previously subject, where the flow or circulation of waters of the United States may be impaired or the reach of such water reduced." Discernible alteration to flow or circulation are presumed to be impairments. The regulations continue: "For example, a permit will be required for the conversion of a wetland from silvicultural or agricultural use when there is a discharge of dredged or fill materials into waters of the United States in conjunction with construction of dikes, drainage ditches, or other works or structures used to effect such conversion."

1986 Regulations

Fourteen years after passage of the 1972 FW-PCA, the Corps of Engineers issued its final rules on Section 404 dredge and fill permits and related regulatory programs (51 Federal Register 219 [13 November 1986]: 41206-260). The rules continued to exempt normal silvicultural activities from permit requirements but stated that "Activities which bring an area into farming, silviculture, or ranching use are not part of an established operation." Thus these activities are not exempt from permit requirements. Additionally, while normal harvesting is exempt, this "does not include the construction of farm, forest or ranch roads."

Wetlands that are managed for timber production must follow state approved BMPs in order to be exempt from federal and/or state permit requirements. Roads and skid trails that meet the state BMP guidelines established under Section 208 of the FWPCA and also meet 15 additional Section 404 criteria are exempt from permits. To qualify for an exemption, they must be (1) minimized in number, width, and length; (2) located sufficiently far from streams or other water bodies; (3) bridged or culverted so as to not impede expected flood flows; and (4) properly maintained and stabilized to prevent erosion. In addition, (5) use of equipment in U.S. waters must be minimized; (6) vegetation disturbance in waters should be minimized during road construction; (7) road construction and maintenance should not disrupt movement of aquatic life; (8) borrow material should be taken from upland sources; (9) fill discharges cannot jeopardize endangered species; (10) discharges should avoid wildlife nesting, breeding, and spawning areas; and (11) they should not be located near a public water supply intake. Furthermore, discharge should not (12) occur in areas of concentrated shellfish production; (13) occur in scenic or wild rivers; and (14) contain toxic pollutants in toxic amounts. Last, (15) all temporary fills should be removed in their entirety, and the area restored to its original elevation.

The final 404 regulations also reiterate that the Clean Water Act allows the administrator of the EPA to transfer administration of the 404 permit program for discharge into certain waters of the United States to qualified states. Once a state's 404 program is approved and in effect, the corps will suspend its application processing and turn it over to the responsible state agency. But as of 1991, only Michigan had assumed this responsibility.

Court Cases

Several significant court cases have been decided or are pending regarding the forestry implementation of Section 404 (f)(1)—the silvicultural exemption—and Section 404 (f)(2)—the recapture provision. These decisions will be crucial in helping to define what is or is not exempt from the permit requirements, and indeed what management actions may or may not be allowed. The definition of wetlands also remains unclear and relevant (Cubbage, Siegler, and Flather 1992).

A 1989 decision in Florida addressed the extent of the silvicultural exemption (*Bayou Marcus Livestock and Agricultural Company* vs. *U.S. Environmental Protection Agency and U.S. Army Corps of Engineers*, Civil Action No. 88-30275 [N.D. Fla. 1989]). In this case, a land developer attempted to use the silvicultural exemption in order to avoid obtaining a permit for what was clearly a development activity. He performed extensive draining and ditching activities to build roads into a pine plantation and harvested trees as part of the operation. The plantation had been previously used for a naval stores operation, and the last harvesting had occurred in 1974. The developer contended that these activities demonstrated that the site was an ongoing silvicultural operation and that his harvest and road building operations should be exempt. The Florida District Court, however, ruled that the activities did not constitute an ongoing silvicultural operation and that they also were subject to the recapture provisions of Section 404(f)(2) because the activities on the site constituted a new use. The court ordered the developer to fill in the ditches on the site and revegetate and return it to its initial condition to the extent possible.

Part of the court's opinion in *Bayou Marcus* might suggest a definitional narrowing of "normal silviculture." The plaintiff had argued that the management gap between 1974 and 1985 was not unusual because slash pines had a 12-to-15–year growing cycle; therefore, letting the trees grow was part of an ongoing operation. The court, however, characterized this attempt to bridge the gap where no management occurred as a "novel contention having no merit."

Both the forest industry and environmental organizations recognize the problems with this precedent because the developer was clearly trying to circumvent the Section 404 permit requirements. However, the points of law still stand. The period of time between the entries into the stand was relatively short for forestry; but based on the particulars of the case, the court ruled that the harvest was not an ongoing forestry operation. Furthermore, it ruled that the extensive ditching and drainage of the site made it subject to the Section 404 recapture provisions, so a permit was required. Despite its concern with this decision, the forest industry did not seek further involvement or an appeal, perhaps fearing a concurrence at the appeals court level, which would set a firmer precedent.

A more recent case filed in North Carolina may have even more substantial implications for forestry operations in wetlands. Although the *Avoyelles* decision made it clear that conversion from bottomland hardwoods to croplands was not exempt from the 404 permit requirements, changes in forest types remain a point of contention among forest industry, environmental groups, and the administering agencies. In this litigation, several environmental organizations have brought suit against Weyerhaeuser Company—stating that the company's conversion of natural pine stands in the East Dismal Swamp of North Carolina into loblolly pine plantations is not exempt from the permit requirements (*Environmental Defense Fund et al. v. Tidwell*, Civil Action No. 91-467-CIV-5-D). The case for the plaintiffs is being handled by the Southern Environmental Law Center. Other plaintiffs include the National Audubon Society, the

Sierra Club, the North Carolina Wildlife Federation, and the North Carolina Coastal Association.

Several key points are under consideration in the North Carolina case. The first question is whether the area in question is indeed a wetland. In this instance, all parties agree that the dismal swamp area is a wetland, under any reasonable definition. The second issue is whether Weyerhaeuser's operations are an ongoing silvicultural operation, implying that owners must maintain a management plan and produce timber on a regular basis. All parties concerned agree that this is occurring. In the third issue, however, the plaintiffs contend that changing the land use from natural pine to planted pine impairs the functions and reduces the values of a wetland and impedes or alters water flow. They thus claim that a tree farm is not an ongoing silvicultural operation on this particular site, but rather a special, "permittable" (one that requires a permit) operation, subject to the recapture provisions. The environmental groups agree that a pine plantation still may be a wetland, but they contend that in this situation the land is impaired and its functions have changed from its natural state, so that establishing a plantation should require a permit before it can occur. Weyerhaeuser and the industry groups in North Carolina disagree strongly with this interpretation.

This distinction regarding conversion or type change becomes crucial in applying Section 404. In earlier years, and occasionally now, forestry groups have contended that pine plantations were not wetlands and thus would be exempt from the 404 regulations. However, in recent years this stance has been reversed because it would imply that many sites have been converted from natural pine wetlands to planted pine uplands. Thus the North Carolina suit seeks to clarify whether change of forest types in a wetland—which usually only occurs with intensive site preparation, bulldozing, soil movement, and disturbance—should trigger the recapture clause and thus require a permit.

Wetlands Definition

The scientific and legal definition of wetlands has been the subject of an ongoing debate since the late 1980s. Because wetlands are areas that are periodically or continuously inundated by water, they fall along a transitional zone between permanently wet aquatic ecosystems and dry terrestrial ecosystems. From one end to the other, this zone varies considerably in the associated hydrologic conditions, vegetation, and soil characteristics. Consequently, wetland boundaries are not easily identified. A definition that is both practical and legally precise and accurately reflects ecological reality is problematic.

The legal definition of wetlands, as enacted by Section 404 of the Clean Water Act is stated as

[T]hose areas that are inundated or saturated by surface or groundwater at a frequency and duration sufficient to support, and that under normal circumstances do support, a prevalence of vegetation typically adapted for life in saturated soil conditions. Wetlands generally include swamps, marshes, bogs, and similar areas.

After considerable scientific and public debate about wetlands, three distinguishing features were settled on as defining their extent: (1) the presence of water (2) unique soils and (3) vegetation adapted to wet conditions (based on Cowardin et al. 1979). In 1989, the four federal agencies with wetlands protection and permitting responsibilities—the Environmental Protection Agency, Fish and Wildlife Service, Corps of Engineers, and the Soil Conservation Service— released the official *Federal Manual for Identifying and Delineating Jurisdictional Wetlands* (Interagency Cooperative Publication 1989). The manual stated that all three of these criteria: (1) wetland hydrology (water at or near the surface for some part of the growing season), (2) hydric soils (seasonally wet or saturated), and (3) hydrophylic vegetation (plants adapted for life in saturated soil) were required for an area to be classed as a wetland.

Implementation of the 1989 manual still led to a broad definition of wetlands, so that much of the coastal plain in the South and flatwoods pine resource and wet areas in the North Central region were included. The 1989 definition created potentials for considerably increased regulatory impacts and permit requirements/wetland reservations.

In 1991 the protests over the broad definition of wetlands prompted strong reactions, embodied in many proposed bills from southern Congress members and from federal agencies. Several bills sought to limit wetlands definition to very wet sites and some sought to eliminate EPA authority and involvement in the process. The 1989 *Federal Manual for Wetlands Delineation* was withdrawn in 1991, after criticism from President Bush's staff and from some members of Congress that it was too far-reaching. This criticism resulted in passage of an amendment to the Energy and Water Development Appropriations Act of 1991. The amendment prohibits the Corps of Engineers from delineating wetlands using the 1989 manual because that report did not first undergo Administrative Procedures Act (APA) rule making. The corps is required to use its 1987 manual until adoption of a new manual that complies with APA rule-making procedures. The 1987 regulations generally require consideration of the same three factors for wetlands classification, but they rely more on hydrology than did the 1989 manual.

In 1991 EPA released proposed revisions to the 1989 manual. The 1991 proposals, which were closed for public comment on October 15, 1991, contained more stringent requirements for wetlands. In particular, the proposed revisions included changing the time frame of the growing season to consider the dates of first and last killing frosts; requiring saturation to the surface; changing the hydrology criteria from 7 to 21 days of coverage by water during the growing season; and limiting the use of facultative-dominated plant communities as indications of hydrology.

The release of the changed wetlands definition proposals created more national controversy. Protests over the 1989 manual were lodged by the forest industry and by developers. Protests over the 1991 proposals were made with equal vehemence by environmental groups. These groups were particularly upset because they said that the Bush administration reneged on the president's stated policy of "no-net-loss" of wetlands, and that the new definitions would significantly reduce the areas classed as wetlands, perhaps causing up to one-half the jurisdictional area to be lost (EDF and WWF 1992).

The largest impetus for withdrawal of the 1989 manual was provided by the Council on Competitiveness, a probusiness advisory group led by Vice-President Dan Quayle. As part of the Bush administration efforts to reduce regulations, the council reviewed the wetlands issue and wrote specific proposed recommendations regarding criteria used for delineating wetlands. The administration proposals were examined by government scientists, who estimated that the stricter regulations would cause up to one- half the area currently classed as wetlands to become dryland. The adverse reaction from environmental groups and the public caused the administration to revise the proposed regulations. In the end, the three criteria of hydrology, soil, and vegetation will continue to be used, but the total of about 100 million acres of wetlands in the United States may be altered. The specifics of wetland delineation, however, had not yet been decided as of 1992. The Clean Water Act will be considered for reauthorization in 1993, and wetlands protection will be one of the principal issues.

Wetlands Area

The total area of wetlands, given various criteria, has been estimated by various agencies and organizations. Cubbage et al. (1992) review the various data sources and summarize forested wetland areas by region of the country (Figure 14-1, Table 14-1).

Dahl (1990) estimated the wetland losses that have occurred over the last 200 years, based on the wetlands definitions from Cowardin et al. (1979). The United States had about 104 million acres of wetlands in 1980,

Figure 14-1. Wetland Analysis Regions

only about one-half the estimated wetland area in the 1780s. The South had over one-half of this area (57 million acres), followed by the Lake States (19.6 million acres).

The Soil Conservation Service conducts a Natural Resource Inventory (NRI), which Cubbage et al. (1992) used to estimate forested wetland areas. According to the NRI survey (USDA Soil Conservation Service 1987, 1992), there were about 81.9 million acres of non-federal wetlands in the contiguous United States in 1987, down from 83.1 million in 1982. Approximately 300,000 acres were lost from the statistics because their title transferred to the federal government—these areas probably remained wetlands. The 1987

TABLE 14-1.   Wetland Areas in the Contiguous United States, According to Selected Data Sources (in acres)

			Source, Types, and Date		
	USFWS[a]	**SCS Natural Resource Inventory**[b]			
	1980s	*1987*		*1982*	
Region	*All Wetlands*	*All*	*Forests*	*All*	*Forests*
South	56,909,325	42,426,100	29,348,700	43,118,200	29,770,700
Northeast	9,548,314	7,834,500	5,179,300	7,891,100	5,206,900
Lake States	19,614,792	17,148,800	8,750,300	17,212,300	8,733,000
Midwest	3,552,833	2,828,800	1,146,500	2,851,600	1,169,900
Great Plains	6,610,900	5,509,300	24,800	5,521,300	28,00
Mountain	5,352,250	3,583,800	198,000	3,877,200	197,200
Pacific Coast	2,785,900	2,584,400	354,100	2,638,400	353,800
Total	104,374,314	81,915,700	45,001,700	83,110,100	45,459,500

Source: Adapted from Cubbage et al. 1992

[a]Dahl 1990

[b]USDA Soil Conservation Service 1987, 1992

NRI survey classed 45.0 million acres of the nation's nonfederal wetlands as forested wetlands, a drop of nearly 458,000 acres from 1982. In 1987, 29.3 million acres of the forested acres were in the South, about 65 percent of the total. The Lake States had 8.7 million acres of forested wetlands, and the Northeast 5.2 million acres. The Great Plains had only about 25,000 acres of forested wetlands, the Mountains 198,000 acres, the Pacific Coast 351,000 acres, and the Midwest about 1.1 million acres. Obviously, the East contains most of the forested wetlands in the United States—over 95 percent.

Wetlands Mitigation

With today's emphasis on no-net-loss of wetlands, the concept of *mitigation* has become important. Wetlands mitigation is the creation, enhancement, or restoration of a wetlands area. It also can refer to preserving wetlands or leaving them alone.

The U.S. Council on Environmental Quality (40 CFR Part 1508.20a-e) has listed five types of mitigation:

1. Avoiding the impact altogether by not taking a certain action or parts of an action.

2. Minimizing impacts by limiting the degree of magnitude of an action and its implementation.

3. Rectifying the impact by repairing, rehabilitating, or restoring the affected environment.

4. Reducing or eliminating the impact over time by preservation and maintenance operations during the life of the action.

5. Compensating for the impact by replacing or providing substitute resources or environments.

Of all these types of mitigation, the most controversial is the creation of wetlands, or the replacement of natural wetlands with artificial wetlands. The concept of wetlands mitigation, of any type, seems to have originated as a means to allow development in wetlands to occur without a net loss of wetland acreage.

The EPA and the corps signed a Memorandum of Agreement (MOA) on November 15, 1989, which provides guidance on the type and level of mitigation required to determine compliance with the Federal Water Pollution Control Act 404(b)(1) guidelines. This agreement introduces a concept called *sequencing*—a three-step process used by the EPA and the corps to evaluate Section 404 permit applications concerning mitigation. The steps are (1) to avoid impacts by exploring alternatives, (2) to minimize potential impacts through project modifications, and (3) to compensate for any unavoidable impacts that remain.

Two mitigation techniques that bear explanation are a wetlands value system and mitigation banking. A *wetlands value system* would consist of identifying wetlands in a particular area (i.e., topographic quadrangle, county) through mapping and then placing the wetlands on a numerical value system. This would demarcate wetlands where no development could occur and allow development on the lower valued wetlands with mitigation and enhancement. However, this system has been criticized for two reasons: (1) it could result in loss of diversity of wetlands by allowing use of the lower valued wetlands, and (2) human value judgments of which value is more important than another are difficult to contest—they depend on who is performing the valuation. Some proposed legislation—for example, the Comprehensive Wetlands Conservation and Management Act of 1991—sought to amend Section 404 of the FWPCA by requiring the classification of wetlands into three tiers according to their functions and values.

Mitigation banking involves compensating for wetland alterations by acquiring or improving "off-site" land. banking can take many forms: (1) acquiring, protecting, and managing large areas of wetlands as a "bank" against which credits can be withdrawn in exchange for altering wetlands elsewhere; (2) enhancing and restoring degraded or former wetlands in exchange for credits to alter other wetlands; and (3) establishing a bank account into which cash is contributed for wetland acquisitions in exchange for permits to alter wetlands.

Criticisms of mitigation banking include that (1) bank lands may not be managed carefully and may not provide the wetland functions they are intended to replace; (2) scientific methodologies for quantifying wetland functions are presently crude and imprecise; (3) long-term ownership of bank lands may not be possible, leading to destruction of the lands by subsequent landowners; (4) it may not be ecologically sensible to replace wetlands lost in one geographic zone with wetlands in another (i.e. different states or physiogeographical regions); and (5) mitigated bank lands could be expensive to manage and monitor.

Mitigation banking also has advantages: (1) Large wetland areas (the banks) will benefit from protection; (2) banking encourages upfront mitigation (i.e., mitigation before development); and (3) it increases ease of monitoring by decreasing the number of sites to monitor.

Both of these mitigation techniques, a value system and banking, have been addressed by federal agencies working with Section 404. Both will probably become viable wetland policies.

RELATED WETLANDS LEGISLATION

Other federal laws also may affect wetlands protection as part of their other purposes. These include the Coastal Zone Management Act as amended in 1990 and the 1985 and 1990 farm bills (Cubbage et al. 1992).

Coastal Zone Management

A related issue that could affect even more area than wetlands alone is the promulgation of new forestry rules and regulations under the 1990 federal amendments to the Coastal Zone Management Act. The 1990 amendments require enhanced measures to control nonpoint source pollution from forest operations in coastal counties—defined as areas where 15 percent or more of the precipitation in an area would reach the ocean or Great Lakes. This definition of a coastal county implies that the regulations could apply two to

four counties deep in many of the approximately 38 states affected by the act.

The states were to develop regulations to implement the Coastal Zone Act pollution prevention measures by 1992. The EPA was required to identify forest practices likely to contribute to pollution, identify BMPs that could be used to control it, and evaluate the costs of their implementation. This effort was due in the summer of 1992. If such BMPs are adopted by the states, they could greatly affect wetlands (and drylands) forest management.

Farm Bill

The 1985 and 1990 amendments to the federal farm bill also can affect forestry operations in wetlands areas. The farm bill contains provisions that prohibit landowners from converting wetlands to nonwetland uses without losing cost-share or subsidy payments from other federal farm programs (termed *cross-compliance*). The farm bill also requires that by 1995 all farmers have farm management plans in place in order to continue to receive federal subsidies and cost-share payments authorized by the farm bill. These sets of requirements can be used to prevent wetland (swampbuster) loss or loss of untilled dry prairie lands as well (sodbuster).

The swampbuster provisions were applied in early 1992 to a timber harvest on a wetlands site in Georgia. In this situation, a large forest landowner was harvesting timber on a forested wetland site on a tract separated from his principal farm. The Soil Conservation Service (SCS) found out about the harvest and informed the landowner that he would need a specific SCS wetlands timber harvesting permit. Furthermore, it informed him that he would need an approved SCS farm plan before harvests could occur in the wetlands, or else he would face loss of his other farm bill–related government payments on his other farm lands. The Soil Conservation Service also has compounded the confusion by advising tree farmers that they could not use Forestry Incentives Program (FIP) or Agricultural Conservation Program (ACP) funds to cost-share reforestation when it involves mechanical site preparation in wetlands, if tree stumps are removed and soil is disturbed.

This application of the farm bill cross-compliance strictures to timber harvesting in forested wetlands is new, but it certainly promises to generate more regulatory control of private forestry operations and more controversy. To date, the cross-compliance provisions have been interpreted to imply that landowners could lose payments from other federal programs contained in the farm bill, such as those for crop subsidies, planting trees or grass cover on erodible soils, and agricultural conservation practices. The Forestry Incentives Program was a separate forestry cost-share program from 1974 to 1990. But the 1990 farm bill authorized a new program—the Stewardship Incentives Program—to be phased in to replace FIP by 1995. Thus all forestry cost-share payments could eventually be subject to cross-compliance measures as well.

CLEAN AIR ACT

After studying the steadily worsening problem of air pollution for 15 years, in 1970 Congress passed a comprehensive Clean Air Act (42 U.S.C. 7401-7642) to regulate pollution. The 1970 law amended earlier weak laws enacted in 1955 and 1967, which delegated all authority to the states to meet suggested federal guidelines. The 1970 act authorized the federal government to impose controls if the states did not satisfy national standards. As a result of the sweeping reforms of the 1970 Clean Air Act, from 1979 to 1988 approximately $300 billion was spent on air pollution (Malone 1991).

AIR POLLUTANTS

Air pollutants may be described as substances or particles that may be harmful to human, animal, or plant health by causing growth problems, mortality, or economic losses. As with water pollution, some pollutants occur naturally, such as hydrocarbons or hydrogen sulfide. Even trees emit hydrocarbons that may contribute to pollution, and burning of wood for residential or commercial purposes causes air pollution.

A host of health or environmental problems may be caused by air pollution, and the Clean Air Act attempts to conrol many of them. Suspended particulates (TSPs) are solid or liquid particles that remain suspended in the air. They come mostly from large industrial sources (about 67 percent), motor vehicles (18 percent), or solid waste disposal (5 percent). Smaller particles present more of a health risk than larger particles (Malone 1991).

Sulfur dioxide increases death rates and heart and lung disease and adversely affects plant growth. In the 1980s it was linked to acid precipitation and alleged to cause agricultural problems, forest growth reductions, and acidified soils and lakes in the eastern United States and Canada. Sulfur dioxide can be reduced by the use of low-sulfur fuels, scrubbing emissions before release, or catalytic conversion to sulfuric acid. Nitrogen dioxide, which comes mostly from automobile and power plant emissions, causes respiratory problems and other diseases and contributes to acid precipitation. Carbon monoxide and hydrocarbons form from the incomplete combustion of fossil fuels or from forest fires. Ozone is the principal component of smog and is formed by a photochemical reaction between nitrogen dioxide and volatile organic compounds. Lead also is a pollutant (Malone 1991). Methane, caused by burning fossil fuels or by natural biodegradation, has been linked with global warming, as has excessive release of carbon dioxide and other trace gases. Particulate matter emitted from prescribed fires or wild fires may harm human health as well.

CONTROL METHODS

The 1970 Clean Air Act instituted a series of environmental standards and controls to reduce air pollutants. Section 108 of the 1970 Clean Air Act (CAA) required the administrator of the EPA to publish a list of pollutants that had an adverse effect on public health or welfare. This step initiates the process for EPA to establish standards to control a pollutant, including documenting the adverse effects of the pollutant, control techniques, and control costs.

Officially listing a new pollutant takes substantial effort on the part of EPA and usually is met with substantial opposition by interest groups who stand to face more regulations. As of 1982 the listed pollutants were sulfur oxides, particulate matter, carbon monoxide, ozone, hydrocarbons, nitrogen dioxide, and lead. Other chemicals have been listed or considered since then, including calcium, arsenic, polycyclic organic matter, and formaldehyde (which is used in plywood and other structural board products).

Section 109 of the CAA requires EPA to establish national ambient air quality standards (NAAQS) for each pollutant officially listed with a safety criteria document under Section 108. Two sets of NAAQS exist. Primary NAAQS are the levels of air quality, based on the Section 108 criteria and allowing an adequate margin of safety, that will protect the public health. Secondary NAAQS consist of the level of air quality sufficient to protect the public welfare from any known or anticipated adverse effects. Public welfare includes anything other than human health, such as soils, crops, vegetation, animals, buildings, and so forth (Holmes 1982).

Section 107 of the Clean Air Act requires that the country be divided into air quality control regions (AQCRs), and 247 AQCRs were designated. Air pollution control plans were developed to meet NAAQS within each region. The 1977 amendments to the CAA required the states and EPA to designate which AQCRs meet NAAQS, which do not, and for those which there are insufficient data. Some of the areas designated were counties or areas that do not correspond to the AQCR boundaries (Holmes 1982).

The CAA required EPA to promulgate ambient air quality standards. The states were required to develop specific state implementation plans (SIPs) to achieve the national ambient air quality standards by a series of emission limitations for existing sources and other control strategies. A series of legal controls was used to ensure that the states met federal requirements. The CAA, Section 111, authorizes EPA to identify sources that contribute to air pollution and develop new source performance standards (NSPS), based on the best available technology to reduce pollution. This approach was designed to set uniform performance standards for all industries, rather than a particular pollutant. This approach helps prevent states from using "easy" air pollution regulations to attract new industry. However, there were less restrictive controls on existing sources compared to "new" sources. These rules tended to favor or protect plants in the more polluted Northeast from the environmental advantages of locating new plants in the cleaner Sun Belt (Holmes 1982).

LAND USE CONTROLS

The Clean Air Act has had obvious direct and indirect impacts on the manufacturing sector in forestry. Lumber mills stopped burning waste wood in tipis; plywood and particle board manufacturers have reduced formaldehyde emissions in plants and from structural lumber in houses; and pulp and paper mills have reduced chemical emissions into the air. The CAA also has affected land use and management. Of course, it is hoped that it also has positive effects on human health and plant and animal vigor as well.

The Clean Air Act gives states a choice between banning major new sources in nonattainment areas (areas where NAAQS are not met) or preparing a state implementation plan more stringent than statutory requirements for the area. There are 11 statutory requirements for SIPs in nonattainment areas. One is a preconstruction review for any new project in an area. New projects must (1) achieve the lowest achievable emission rate, (2) have their emissions offset by another pollutant source in the area, (3) have other company-owned sources meeting the SIP, and (4) have the SIP for the nonattainment area being carried out by the state.

The 1977 amendments to the 1970 Clean Air Act require prevention of air quality loss in areas where the ambient air quality standards were already better than the NAAQs. These areas are called prevention of significant deterioration areas (PSDs), and as the name implies, they cannot suffer a decline in air quality. The superior air quality in PSD areas is primarily maintained through preconstruction review of proposed land uses. To receive construction permits, proposed facilities (1) must utilize the best available pollution contol technology (BACT), (2) cannot cause air quality to exceed the NAAQS, and (3) cannot violate any other applicable emission limit (Novick et al. 1988).

To meet criteria (2) above, each PSD is placed within one of three baseline air quality classes. Class I areas, which include national parks and wilderness areas, have the strictest limits—ambient air cannot exceed a narrow allowable increment in pollution above the baseline. Class II areas are allowed a moderate increment above the baseline, and Class III areas are given an allowable increment almost to the level of the NAAQS for the PSD pollutant (Visibility also is protected under the CAA, which is relevant for natural areas). The state implementation plans are supposed to include long-term plans to prevent impairment in Class I areas, but EPA protection efforts to date have been feeble (Malone 1991).

The NAAQS that affect forestry operations most directly are for particulate matter. The particulate standard has changed from measuring total suspended particulates (TSP) to measuring particulates 10 microns in size or smaller (PM10). The PM10 standard was adopted in 1987 after almost a decade of debate, even though there was widespread agreement that fine particles posed the greastest hazard by penetrating deep into the lungs. This standard will be used to develop rules governing prescribed burning and residential wood combustion (Randle and Bosco 1991).

THE 1990 AMENDMENTS

Despite its complexity, the 1970 Clean Air Act was only partially successful. Under the act, states in one area remained unable to stop air pollution emanating from other states. Many areas failed to meet the NAAQS, despite a series of statutory extensions. Congress clearly intended that land use controls would be a significant implementing mechanism in the SIPs in 1970, but the reference to land use controls was deleted in the 1977 amendments (Malone 1991).

In response to these shortcomings, the 1990 CAA Amendments reformulated the nonattainment program and made significant changes in the regulation of toxic air pollutants, acid rain, and ozone depletion. Title I of the 1990 amendments sets requirements for nonattainment areas to meet the NAAQS, for various pollutants and levels of noncompliance. Title III of the bill lists 189 chemicals for which EPA must set standards requiring the maximum achievable control technology (MACT) within 10 years of enactment.

The acid rain controls of Title IV were controversial. The provisions essentially set a cap on allowable emissions of sulfur dioxide and established a system by which EPA distributes allowances (equivalent to one ton of sulfur dioxide emissions) to existing sources, thus creating a market for the right to emit sulfur dioxide (Malone 1991). This market approach to pollution control has been advocated by economists for decades. They contend that it is an efficient means of obtaining a desired level of pollution control for the least cost. Title IV also mandated that EPA formulate emission controls for nitrogen oxides for utilities subject to sulfur-dioxide controls. An assistance program for workers displaced due to these provisions also was included in the act.

Title VI of the 1990 amendments responds to concerns with ozone depletion and climate changes. It requires the phaseout of five ozone-depleting chemicals, three halons, and carbon tetrachloride by the year 2000. Methyl chloroform production is to be prohibited by

2002. For other regulated hydrochlorofluo-rocarbons, production is frozen in 2015 and prohibited entirely by 2030 (Malone 1991).

EPA's adoption of the PM10 standard in 1987, and its delayed implementation, led Congress to adopt separate PM10 nonat-tainment area requirements. All areas were classed as moderate in the 1990 CAA amend-ments and need to comply with the PM10 standards by December 1994. Reasonably available control measures (RACM) must be adopted by December 1993 for moderate nonattainment areas; serious nonattainment areas must use the best available control measures (BACM) instead of RACM. EPA was to issue guidlines for the RACM and BACM practices by April 1992, including those for residential wood combustion, agricultural and forestry burning practices, and other sources of particulates (Randleman and Bosco 1991). These were deferred until at least late 1992 by the Bush administration regulation freeze, however.

OTHER FEDERAL LAWS

Many other federal laws regulate forest re-sources in some fashion, but not to as great an extent as those discussed so far. NEPA, the Clean Water Act, and RPA/NFMA have been discussed in this or earlier chapters. Federal wildlife laws will be discussed in Chapter 15. Occupational health and safety laws also in-clude environmental protection components, although they are not discussed in this text. Other federal laws are enumerated in Ap-pendix A. Brief discussions of coastal zone protection and pesticide and herbicide con-trol follow in this section.

COASTAL ZONE MANAGEMENT ACT

States and local governments have tradition-ally had control over land use regulation. However, the Coastal Zone Management Act of 1972, as amended in 1990, provides a means for federal involvement to help states plan for coastal zone protection. The act pro-vides funds to participating states (a few states

have declined to enroll in the program). The general purpose of the Coastal Zone Manage-ment Act is to encourage states to devise land and water use plans for coastal protection. It is designed to preserve, protect, develop, and restore or enhance coastal resources. Pro-tection of natural resources; access to coasts for recreation; protection of historic, cultural, and aesthetic features; and assistance for plan-ning and conservation were among the rele-vant resource objectives of the act.

The 1990 amendments to the Coastal Zone Management Act require every state with a federally approved program to develop a plan to control coastal nonpoint source pollution. EPA must publish national guidelines on man-agement measures—economically achievable measures to control nonpoint pollution us-ing the best available control practices. States must submit their plan to EPAs within 30 months of publication of the national guide-lines. State failure to develop plans may result in EPA's withholding portions of the Coastal Zone and FWPCA Section 319 planning grant funds (Malone 1991).

The 1990 amendments to the Coastal Zone Act extended the requirements for protec-tion to silvicultural, agricultural, develop-ment, and septic systems, which had previ-ously been exempt under the act. For forestry, the EPA proposed a number of best man-agement practices that should be consid-ered in controlling forest nonpoint source or point source pollution in the Coastal Zone. These included protection of streamside man-agement zones (SMZs), road construction and maintenance measures (i.e., bridges, cul-verts, water bars), timber harvesting practices (landings and their revegetation), site prepa-ration, reforestation methods; prescribed fire; and pesticide and fertilizer applications. The EPA list and evaluations of these BMPs could provide the basis for pollution control mea-sures to be adopted by individual states.

FEDERAL ENVIRONMENTAL PESTICIDE CONTROL ACT

The first major U.S. pesticide control act was the Federal Insecticide, Fungicide, and Rodenticide Act (FIFRA) of 1947. FIFRA required that pesticides used in the United States be registered with the U.S. Department of Agriculture. However, the act gave the secretary of agriculture no power to refuse registrations, nor power to prevent misuse. With the growth of the environmental movement in the 1960s, environmental groups filed a host of lawsuits relating to major pesticides such as DDT and aldrin and the herbicide 2,4,5-T. The rapid development of toxic pesticides, without meaningful regulation, prompted the need for better control.

On December 2, 1970, President Nixon signed Reorganization Order No. 3, which created EPA and transferred the USDA pesticides division (and other agencies' divisions) to EPA. EPA inherited the many lawsuits seeking better regulation as well. The judges in these suits concurred that the federal agencies had not adequately examined health and environmental problems associated with pesticides. These numerous criticisms helped mold the new EPA's resolve to be more aggressive (Miller 1991).

FIFRA was amended by the Federal Environmental Pesticide Control Act (FEPCA) of 1972, amended again in 1975, 1978, 1980, and 1988. FEPCA was virtually a new law. The 1972 amendments instituted strong federal control over the application of pesticides and placed EPA in charge of pesticide regulation.

FIFRA/FEPCA authorized EPA to classify and register the uses of most herbicides, pesticides, fungicides, and rodenticides. EPA had to rule on the safety of each existing chemical, based on the available scientific evidence, and list the specific allowable applications for which the chemicals could be used. Chemical formulations deemed to be environmentally hazardous could be banned completely, and chemicals could only be used legally for their EPA-approved applications. The acts convert the product label of a pesticide from a guide to its use into a binding legal document. No one can use a registered chemical in a manner inconsistent with its label. Any damage caused while a pesticide is used in accordance with label instructions is attributable to the manufacturer, who is held liable (Dana and Fairfax 1980). Additionally, the acts set up

a procedure for testing and licensing the people who apply chemicals, in order to ensure that the chemicals are used safely.

EPA had no constituency relationship with chemical and pesticide users, and its aggressive implementation of the act led to displeased chemical users. Based on lobbying by these interest groups, the act was amended in 1975 to (1) require EPA to advise the secretary of agriculture before taking action with respect to a pesticide, (2) provide the Department of Agriculture with specific authority to comment on pesticide regulations, and (3) require EPA to assess the economic impact of any action proposed or taken against a pesticide. The 1975 amendments thus ensured some coordination among EPA, the Department of Agriculture, and the relevant user groups (Dana and Fairfax 1980).

Various amendments to FIFRA and administrative interpretations continue to be important. A 1978 amendment to the law influenced the availability of minor uses such as for forest tree nurseries, seed orchards, and greenhouses. The act required EPA to issue simplified regulations for registration of all chemicals and to define minor uses (such as forestry uses of agriculture chemicals) in a flexible manner. The 1980s also have seen EPA place more focus on protecting employees from chemicals in the workplace, such as the use of lindane as a pesticide for lumber preservation.

The Federal Insecticide, Fungicide, and Rodenticide Act now includes the following major provisions:

1. Registration of all pesticides with the Environmental Protection Agency (EPA).

2. Classification of pesticides into two categories
   a. General use—available to the general public
   b. Restricted use—available only to certified individuals

3. Requires certification of applicators by two groups
   a. Private—apply pesticides on own or leased property

    b. Commercial—apply restricted-use pesticides for hire (10 different categories)

4. Minimum standards of competency for both private and commercial applicators

5. Misuse of pesticides made unlawful with provision for enforcement and penalties when appropriate

6. Enforcement of regulations delegated to the designated state agencies

FIFRA also authorizes the responsible state enforcement agencies to impose greater regulations on the sale or use of any pesticide that has been registered with the EPA. For this reason, the requirements for certification vary to some degree among the states.

In addition to the requirements for commercial forestry herbicide applications (i.e., where payment for application is involved), some states also require a business license for the company that performs the applications. Also, several states require special licenses for public or government agency work.

SUMMARY

Public regulation of forestry and wildlife has evolved continually in the United States. Some rudimentary statutes in colonial America protected game from exploitation and timber from wanton destruction. The British crown also reserved some pine trees for ship masts and naval stores. However, once America became a nation, few efforts were made to protect forests or game for almost a century—not until the late 1800s. But the next three decades saw a substantial expansion of purposeful federal retention of forest lands and enactment of wildlife protection laws. Efforts also were begun in the early 1900s to regulate timber cutting practices of private landowners. Although not successful, they did lead to a number of state forest practice acts or seed tree laws that were enacted in the 1930s and 1940s.

In the 1970s many federal regulatory laws were enacted or amended to provide environmental protection. The National Environmental Policy Act, implemented in 1970, required federal agencies to prepare Environmental Impact Statements justifying the effect of their actions. The Federal Water Pollution Control Act Amendments (FWPCA) of 1972 mandated control of point and nonpoint sources of pollution. FWPCA Section 208, and Section 319 of its 1987 amendments mandated and enhanced control of pollution from silvicultural activities, leading to the development and implementation of best management practices (BMPs). Section 404 of FWPCA was designed to protect wetlands and required that persons depositing dredged or filled material obtain a permit from the U.S. Army Corps of Engineers. The Air Pollution Control Act of 1970 established federal regulations to protect air quality and was reauthorized in 1990. The Federal Environmental Pesticide Control Act of 1972 established federal control over the registration and use of chemical herbicides and pesticides, and the Coastal Zone Management Act provided federal assistance to states to protect coastal resources on the oceans and Great Lakes.

LITERATURE CITED

Agee, James L. 1975. A suggested State Forest Practices Act: One implementing mechanism for improving water quality on forest lands. *Journal of Forestry* 73(1):40–41.

Bean, Michael J. 1978. Federal wildlife law in: Howard P. Brokaw, (ed.), Wildlife and America. Council on Environmental Quality. Washington, DC.

Bosselman, Fred P., David Callies, and John Banta. 1973. The Taking Issue. U.S. Government Printing Office. Washington, DC. 329 pp.

Carmichael, Donald M. 1975. Fee simple absolute as a variable research concept. *Natural Resources Journal* 15(4):749–764.

Cowardin, Lewis M., Virginia Carter, Francis C. Golet, and Edward T. Laroe. 1979. Classification of Wetlands and Deepwater Habitats of the United States. Publication No. FWS/OBS-79/31. USDI Fish and Wildlife Service. Washington, DC. 103 pp.

Cubbage, Frederick W., and William C. Siegel. 1985. The law regulating private forestry. *Journal of Forestry* 83(9):538–545.

Cubbage, Frederick W., William C. Siegel, and Peter M. Lickwar. 1989. State water quality laws and programs to control nonpoint source pollution from forest lands in the South. Pp. 8A-29–8A-37 in: Proceedings, AWRA 1989 Conference on Water: Laws and Management. Technical Publication 89-4. American Water Resources Association. Bethesda, MD.

Cubbage, Frederick W., William C. Siegel, and Curtis H. Flather. 1992. Forested wetlands in the United States: Geographic distribution, federal regulations, and management implications. In Proceedings, Conference on Forestry and the Environment, an Economics Perspective. Forestry Canada, and Department of Rural Economy, Faculty of Agriculture and Forestry, University of Alberta. Edmonton, Canada. Unnumbered.

Dahl, Thomas E. 1990. Wetland losses in the United States 1780's to 1980's. U.S. Department of the Interior, Fish and Wildlife Service. Washington, DC. 21 pp.

Dana, Samuel T. 1956. Forest and Range Policy. McGraw-Hill. New York. 455 pp.

Dana, Samuel T., and Sally K. Fairfax. 1980. Forest and Range Policy, 2nd ed. McGraw-Hill. New York. 458 pp.

EDF and WWF. 1992. How wet is a wetland?—The impacts of the proposed revisions to the Federal Wetlands Delineation Manual. Environmental Defense Fund and World Wildlife Fund. New York and Washington. 175 pp.

Freeman, Alan D. 1975. Historical development of public restrictions on the use of private land. Pp. 5–17 in Public Control of Privately Owned Land. University of Minnesota, Center for Urban and Regional Affairs. Minneapolis.

Gates, Paul W. 1968. History of Public Land Law Development. Written for Public Land Law Review Commission. U.S. Government Printing Office. Washington, D.C. 828 pp.

Greeley, William B. 1951. Forests and Men. Doubleday. Garden City, NY. 255 pp.

Haines, Terry K., Frederick W. Cubbage, and William C. Siegel. 1988. Recent developments in state water quality laws affecting forestry in the East. Pp. 457–467 in Proceedings, 1988 Environmental Conference. TAPPI. Atlanta.

Hamilton, Lawrence S. 1965. The federal forest regulation issue. *Forest History* 9(1):2–11.

Holmes, Eugene T. 1982. Introduction to Environmental Law for Pulp and Paper Managers. Technical Association of the Pulp and Paper Industry. Atlanta, GA. 74 pp.

Huffman, James L. 1978. A history of forest policy in the U.S. *Environmental Law* 8(2):239–280.

Interagency Cooperative Publication. 1989. Federal Manual for Identifying and Delineating Jurisdictional Wetlands, an Interagency Cooperative Publication. Fish and Wildlife Service, Environment Protection Agency, Department of the Army, Soil Conservation Service. Washington, D.C. 76 pp. + appen.

Kawashima, Yasuhide, and Ruth Tone. 1983. Environmental policy in early America, a survey of colonial statutes. *Journal of Forest History* 27(4):168–179.

Lane, M. (ed.) 1975. Pp. 208–211 in General Oglethorpe's Georgia: Colonial Letters 1733–1743, Vol. I. Beehive Press. Savannah, GA.

Leopold, Aldo. 1949. A Sand County Almanac, and Sketches Here and There. Oxford University Press. New York. 226 pp. (reprinted 1968)

Malone, Linda A. 1991. Environmental Regulation of Land Use. Clark Boardman Company. New York. 14 chaps. + appen.

Marshall, Robert. 1933. The People's Forests. Harrison Smith and Robert Hags. New York. 233 pp.

Miller, Marshall Lee. 1991. Toxic substance control act. Pp. 280–327 in Environmental Law Handbook, 11th ed. Government Institutes, Inc. Rockville, MD.

National Wildlife Federation. 1988. *Conservation 88 Newsletter* 6(13):13–15.

Novick, Sheldon M., Donald W. Stever, and Margaret G. Mellon (eds.). 1988. Law of Environmental Protection, Vol. II. Environmental Law Institute/Clark Boardman Company. New York. 18 chaps. + appen.

Paster, Janice D. 1983. Money damages for regulatory "takings." *Natural Resources Journal* 23(3):711–724.

Pinchot, Gifford. 1991. The lines are drawn. *Journal of Forestry* 17(8):899–900.

Randle, Russell V., and Mary Elizabeth Bosco. 1991. Air pollution control. Pp. 524–628 in Environmental Law Handbook, 11th ed. Government Institute, Inc. Rockville, MD.

Regens, James L., and Robert W. Rycroft. 1988. The Acid Rain Controversy. University of Pittsburgh Press. Pittsburgh. 228 pp.

Rey, Mark. 1980. The effect of the Clean Water Act on forestry practices. Presented at Symposium on U.S. Forestry and Water Quality: What Course in the 80's? Sponsored by the Water Pollution Control Federation, June 19–29, 1980. Richmond, VA. 20 pp. Mimeo.

Roberts, E. F. 1974. A basic introduction to land use control and doctrine. Pp. 13–53 in Proceedings, Conference on Rural Land-Use Policy in the Northeast, Northeast Regional Center for Rural Development. Cornell University. Ithaca, NY.

Rosenbaum, David E., and Keith Schneider. 1992. Bush is extending regulation freeze with a fanfare. *New York Times*, April 29, pp. A1, A12.

Schieber, Harry N. 1983. Law and the forest. Pp. 336–343 in Encyclopedia of American Forest and Conservation History. Macmillan. New York. Richard C. Davis, ed.

Schneider, Keith. 1992. Environmental laws face a stiff test from landowners. *New York Times*, January 20, pp. A1, A8.

Schoenbaum, Thomas J. 1982. Environmental Policy Law. The Foundation Press. Mineola, NY. 1065 pp.

Siegel, William C. 1974. State forest practice laws today. *Journal of Forestry* 72(4): 208-211.

Siegel, William C., and Frederick W. Cubbage. 1984. Environmental protection law and forest management regulation on private lands in the United States. Pp. 140–156 in Forestry Legislation—Report No. 2 of the IUFRO Working Party S4.06-04. Zurich. 176 pp.

Society of American Foresters. 1956. Forest Practice Developments in the United States, 1940 to 1955. Washington, D.C. 39 pp.

Spurr, Stephen H. 1976. American Forest Policy in Development. University of Washington Press. Seattle. 86 pp.

Stine, J. K. 1983. Regulating wetlands in the 1970s: U.S. Army Corps of Engineers and the environmental organizations. *Journal of Forest History* 27(2):60–75.

Stoebuck, William B. 1982. Police power, taking and due process. *Land Use and Environmental Law Review* 13:349–392.

Troup, Robert S. 1938. Forestry and State Control. Clarendon Press. Oxford, England. 87 pp.

Turner, Tom. 1988. The legal eagles. *Amicus Journal* 10(1): 25–37.

USDA Soil Conservation Service and Iowa State University Statistical Laboratory. 1987. Basic Statistics 1982 Natural Resource Inventory. Statistical Bulletin Number 756. Washington, DC. 153 pp.

USDA Soil Conservation Service and Iowa State Unversity Statistical Laboratory. 1992. The 1987 Natural Resource Inventory. Computer database. Washington, DC.

U.S. Environmental Protection Agency. 1987. Nonpoint source guidance and clean lakes guidance, memorandum. Office of Water. 28 pp. + appen. Mimeo. Washington, DC.

Vaux, Henry J. 1985. Private forestland regulation—current issues and future trends. Speech presented at Western Forest Economists Meeting, Rippling River Resort. Wemme, OR. May 8.

Wildlife Digest. 1992. "Property-rights" laws threaten environment. *National Wildlife* 30(5):26.

Chapter 15

Wildlife Management and Protection Policy

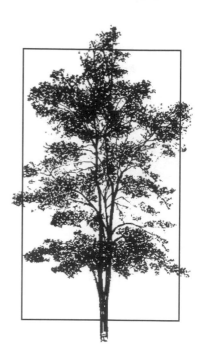

Throughout most of human history, animals (like trees) were thought to exist only to support human life in ways that humans determined. In Genesis, God commanded Man to assert dominion "over every thing that moves." This injunction has been observed much more closely than other biblical lessons.

—George Cameron Coggins 1991a

The intricate problems and issues that now surround wildlife are not solved by clamor. They lend themselves more and more to reasoned compromise, where inescapable relationships between the needs of humans and wild creatures are aired, and decisions are made with deep understanding that all living things have similar ecological requirements.

—Lonnie Williamson 1988a

INTRODUCTION

Wildlife includes not just game animals, but the entire range of vertebrate and invertebrate species (Peek 1986). Species ranging from minute insects to blue whales, and from ugly toads to majestic bald eagles are included. Some species have tremendous commercial value, some are valued primarily for aesthetic reasons, and some merely contribute to ecological stability (Coggins 1991b).

The history of fish and wildlife conservation in America includes a chronicle of laws passed to protect wildlife from the greed and

carelessness of humans (Reed and Drabelle 1984). Wildlife policy in America has evolved from a laissez-faire philosophy, to recognition of dwindling resources, to management of individual species and populations. It is now moving in the direction of ecosystem management. Until fairly recently, wildlife policy was aimed almost exclusively at the conservation of game and fish that could be taken in sporting activities. Now other aspects of wildlife—ecology, aesthetics, and ethics—are becoming more important in American society. Wildlife protection policy for ecological purposes as embodied in the Endangered Species Act of 1973 has become one of the most controversial resource management policies in the 1990s.

Throughout history, we humans as an individual species have been uncertain about our relationship with the rest of the natural world and the many other species with which we share the planet. Whereas our ancestors spoke of animating spirits or God's personal intervention, today we speak in scientific terms and invoke such concepts as ecosystems and predator–prey interactions. For centuries the ruling idea was that humans must dominate nature, but there have always been those who have disagreed. Science has made such dissent more popular. Today we are much less fearful of nature and not as subject to its harsher realities, which were pervasive even a century ago (Dunlap 1988).

Science is supposed to guide wildlife policy, but the reality is that policy-making involves choices and values more than decisions of fact. Scientific findings can, after all, be interpreted in different ways. Nonetheless, scientific knowledge has played an important role in policy shifts affecting wildlife in the past 100 years, beginning with Darwin's theory of evolution. Scientists have played important roles in the public debate concerning humans and nature and have fostered an appreciation of wilderness and wildlife (Dunlap 1988).

OWNERSHIP OF WILDLIFE

Determining the ownership of wildlife, or more properly wildlife property rights, provides insights into policy-making. Among other things it reveals the complexity of the process. Institutional and cultural constraints modify the outcomes that natural resource managers and planners desire. Wildlife may be publicy or privately owned. Property rights can be assigned to individual private decision makers who would, in theory, manage the resources in society's best interests as they simultaneously promoted their own best interests. This approach would mean limiting the customary freedom of hunters that always has been recognized as an im-

portant American right. So the second general approach is to assign property rights to an agency of the government. In theory, an administrator could determine an optimal level of harvest for each species and devise means to regulate the harvest while providing equality of access not always possible under the private rights alternative. This governmental approach is the essence of the American system of property rights in wildlife, an explicit rejection of the traditional private rights in English game law (Tober 1981). Thus wildlife and its management involve political issues that center on the rights of the individual versus the general social welfare (Peek 1986). Complicating the picture is the *wild* nature of wildlife.

In reality, wildlife cannot be truly owned by any person, private or governmental, a conclusion only recently arrived at by the Supreme Court in Hughes v. Oklahoma [441 U.S. 322 (1979)]. In this case, the Supreme Court overruled an Oklahoma law that prohibited the export of "natural" minnows, which was presumably done for the purposes of conservation. The Court held that wildlife in commerce was to be treated the same as any other article of commerce and that states could not claim actual ownership of creatures not actually possessed or controlled. Consequently, no private, corporate, or governmental entity has true property interests in wildlife before legal capture. The federal government might be able to assert an ownership claim, but it has not chosen to do so. This ruling by the Court represents the demise of the long-accepted traditional state ownership doctrine. The Court, however, was careful to point out that states remain free to legislate fully for wildlife conservation, subject only to federal law and the U.S. Constitution (Coggins 1991b).

Wildlife regulation has a long and bitter history of state and federal conflicts over wildlife jurisdiction. A 1976 Supreme Court opinion in Kleppe v. New Mexico 426 U.S. 529 established that Congress can legislate however it wishes for wildlife on federal lands and can override contrary state law. But because federal wildlife legislation falls far short of being comprehensive, wildlife regulation is primarily a state prerogative (Coggins 1991b), except that the federal government, in cooperation with the states, controls the hunting of migratory birds and waterfowl (Siegel 1982). A number of federal laws do protect wildlife and promote wildlife conservation, but wildlife hunting remains primarily a state function even on federal lands. States set hunting seasons and conditions and issue licenses for taking most game species. The National Park Service can, and usually does, choose to ignore state hunting and fishing regulations. The U.S. Fish and Wildlife Service can choose to manage wildlife refuges in ways inconsistent with state wildlife law. On national forests and lands under the BLM's management, state wildlife law dominates. The wildlife responsibilities of the Forest Service and the BLM are directed more toward habitat protection and enhancement, with wildlife and fish as one of several coequal resources under multiple-use mandates that receive a portion of resource management funds (Coggins 1991b).

Regardless of who owns wildlife, the ultimate control over wildlife rests with the landowner who manages habitat (Leopold 1930). Landowners may do a number of things to influence wildlife populations and to provide opportunities for the public to access wildlife resources. Landowners can encourage hunting and fishing access and perhaps even charge for the privilege. In states with little public land, such as Texas, markets for hunting opportunities are strong, and landowners may obtain substantial revenue from hunting leases. This encourages wildlife habitat management to enhance game populations. Landowners may purchase fish and game for stocking on their land, and most states tightly regulate such private stocking and the operation of private hunting and fishing preserves. Because responsibility for wildlife is split between the stewards of the resident wildlife populations (the state) and their habitat (the landowners), a number of wildlife policy problems arise concerning harvest regulation and habitat management (Davis and Wagner 1982).

WILDLIFE MANAGEMENT OBJECTIVES

Wildlife management consists of the science, art, and practice of making the land produce wildlife. The overriding reason for managing wildlife is the obligation to do so. That obligation stems from the combination of human exploitation of wildlife populations and land use practices that alter wildlife habitat (Peek 1986).

Wildlife management policy has four major goals that are derived from English law. The first is to provide for the sustained periodic harvest of wildlife. The second is to regulate human behavior, including the use of weapons and methods of taking wildlife that challenge primitive skills. Third, policy favors particular groups of individuals. Wildlife is not ordinarily subject to human control, the basis for most views of ownership, so privileges to hunt or fish may be granted without provoking issues of fairness among different classes of people. While special hunting privileges are granted in England, they are the antithesis of American democratic values. Fourth, wildlife regulations can try to promote what may be perceived as the rights of animals (Lund 1980). An illustration on the antihunting or humane movement later in this chapter explores this last goal.

Among the states, the following six wildlife management goals are common: (1) preserve all species and ecosystems, (2) provide nongame wildlife enjoyment opportunities, (3) provide hunting opportunities for state residents, (4) promote economic development by attracting out-of-state hunters, (5) make wildlife management self-supporting through user fees, and (6) look to appropriated funds and other sources besides license fees to support wildlife management activities. These goals often conflict. For example, the historical emphasis in wildlife management has been to provide hunting opportunities for state residents. Limited wildlife resources put this goal in conflict with attracting out-of-state visitors for economic development (Davis and Wagner 1982).

Four categories of activities constitute wildlife management: (1) habitat management, (2) predator control, (3) species introduction, and (4) regulation of wildlife consumers. All involve policy issues, especially the last category that includes regulating the take of wildlife, acquiring and developing land, concentrating animals for hunting or viewing, and providing information (Davis and Wagner 1982).

Wildlife agencies at both the state and federal levels have broadened their management horizons. Most wildlife experts now have discarded the idea that by eradicating predatory species such as wolves, harvests of game species such as deer can be enhanced. New legislation protecting endangered species and recognizing the importance of "nongame" species, coupled with public scrutiny and opinion, have downplayed the creation of game surpluses and emphasized the importance of more balanced ecosystem approaches to management (Coggins 1991b).

ILLUSTRATION: ALDO LEOPOLD, PROFESSOR OF GAME MANAGEMENT AND CONSERVATIONIST

The life of Aldo Leopold provides an interesting illustration of how wildlife management and protection evolved in America. Leopold was born in Iowa on the banks of the Mississippi River in 1887. He began his distinguished conservation career as a forester with the U.S. Forest Service. His field observations led him to develop a comprehensive way of thinking about the relationship between the natural world and human activity. He wrote the first book on game management and helped launch that new profession, which he taught at the University of Wisconsin. He helped establish the first administratively protected wilderness area in America and helped establish the Wilderness Society. A year after he died in 1948, "A Sand County Almanac" was published. This collection of essays eloquently describes the intricate interrelationships of all things and leads the reader to contemplate the effects of his or her actions on the land that ultimately supports all living creatures.

The lives of individuals who have made a difference serve as an inspiration to the rest of us. Aldo Leopold made a difference and has inspired professional resource managers and citizens alike. His life story illustrates the close relationship among all natural resource professions. This illustration traces his accomplishments and is a synopsis of the first chapter of historian Susan Flader's (1974) book, "Thinking Like a Mountain," which describes the evolution of Leopold's thinking about deer, predators, and the forest.

A YOUNG FORESTER

By the late nineteenth century many species were in danger of extinction and the future of sport hunting appeared bleak. In 1900 the Yale Forest School was established with an endowment from Gifford Pinchot's family to provide graduate education for American foresters for work in American forests. Aldo Leopold enrolled at Yale University in 1906 to begin studies for a forestry career, the newest and most appealing of the outdoor professions because of the recent transfer of the national forests to Gifford Pinchot's newly designated U.S. Forest Service in the Department of Agriculture. Leopold received his master's degree in 1909, joined the Forest Service, and went off to work in the Arizona and New Mexico territories. The scarcity of wildlife was just beginning to be noticed there. The stock of native wildlife had been depleted—as it had been throughout America—by indiscriminate hunting, whether for market or sport, and in some instances by wholesale destruction of habitat. In the Southwest most of the remaining game animals, especially deer and turkeys, were on national forest lands. But the Forest Service lacked a legislative mandate to administer its lands for either wildlife or recreation, or indeed for anything but timber production and watershed values, as provided in the Organic Act of 1897.

Leopold became interested in wildlife conservation work when after four years on his job in the Carson National Forest in northern New Mexico he fell ill with acute nephritis. The recuperation period provided time to think about his future. The illness made extended fieldwork a life-threatening endeavor. But the forced respite and introspection forced him to commit to wildlife conservation and his zealous efforts in the unconventional field attracted public attention. The Forest Service, however, remained reluctant to commit people and money to the game restoration program Leopold envisioned.

Nonetheless, Forest Service officials took notice of Leopold's work, perhaps because they believed it would strengthen the position of Forest Service in its struggle with the new National Park Service, established in 1916. Anything the Forest Service could do to demonstrate the potential for forms of recreation—including hunting and fishing—that were compatible with other uses of the forest might help the agency keep the national forest lands coveted by Department of the Interior for new national parks. Hunting was not allowed in the national parks, nor was the leasing of sites for summer homes and commercial recreation as authorized by the Agricultural Appropriations Act of 1915. (Incidentally, that was the first significant congressional recognition of recreation as a legitimate use of forests.)

Leopold also was in charge of planning recreation on the southwestern national forests. His reluctance to see certain areas subdivided for recreation would lead him in a few years to promote the establishment of a system of roadless wilderness areas. Although he took his recreation responsibilities seriously, the conservation of game remained a goal that Leopold continued to promote within the Forest Service. It also was an all-absorbing hobby in his spare time.

A GAME MANAGER

In 1924 Leopold accepted a transfer to the U.S. Forest Products Laboratory in Madison, Wisconsin, the principal research institution of the Forest Service at the time. By 1928 he was determined to leave that post for a position more in line with his consuming interest in wildlife and conservation. He declined other opportunities with the Forest Service and some with various universities, choosing instead to launch into a new profession, game management. With funding from the sporting Arms and Ammunitions Manufacturers' Institute, a trade association, he conducted game surveys in the Lake States. He saw this work as the first step in game management; it involved appraising the environmental factors affecting the productivity of game in a particular region and recommending policy measures necessary to restore game. The work illustrated the difference between the old idea of restricting the kill and the new idea of building up a supply of game through the management of habitat. Leopold became established as one of the country's foremost authorities on native game.

In 1929 and 1930, Leopold chaired a committee of the American Game Conference, which considered formulating a new policy concerning game in America. The policy sought to wrest control over game away from hunters in favor of the public, and met with great debate. Like his game survey, the new policy stressed the idea of production in the wild, encouraging game protection and management of habitat by the landowner, and cooperation with the conservation movement. Leopold promoted the need for solid scientific foundations in training individuals for administration, management, and research (Leopold 1930). In short, he made the management of game a profession, and today Aldo Leopold is widely acknowledged as the "father" of the profession of wildlife management in America (Meine 1988).

The depression years, a time when many Americans were bewildered and without hope, found Leopold unemployed. He applied his optimism and discipline to write a textbook for the new field, published in 1933 under the title *Game Management*. It is a basic statement of the science, art, and profession of wildlife management and has been in print continuously since then. The compelling idea for Leopold (1933, vii) at that time was resource management. Producing sustained yields of wild game had always been the thrust of his efforts: "The central thesis of game management is this: game can be restored by the creative use of the same tools which have heretofore destroyed it— axe, plow, cow, fire, and gun." Leopold applied to wildlife a faith in the possibility of wise resource management akin to that of Gifford Pinchot and the progressive conservation movement.

In 1933 the University of Wisconsin created a chair of game management for Leopold in the Department of Agricultural Economics. In 1934 he served on the President's Committee on Wildlife Restoration, charged with developing a proposal for restoring wildlife habitat on submarginal farmland, which was abundant and abandoned during the depression. Leopold thought the states would be in a better position than the federal government to encourage the practice of game management by private landowners, and he promoted the idea of research and program administration at the state level. His efforts were rewarded in 1935 with the creation of the Cooperative Wildlife Research Unit Program that established research units in nine of the nation's land-grant colleges. He was disappointed when Wisconsin failed to get one of the federally funded wildlife research units because the Wisconsin Conservation Commission did not support his program. His political efforts proved more successful at the federal than state level in this case.

A WILDLIFE ECOLOGIST

Three events in 1935 set the tone for the remaining 13 years of Aldo Leopold's life. In January he joined with Robert Marshall and others to found the Wilderness Society to protect and extend the fledgling system of wilderness areas that they had helped to create. Leopold was attracted to the Wilderness Society's philosophy of fostering a new attitude in the relationship between humans and nature. This reoriented his thinking from historical

and recreational ideas about wild areas to a predominantly ecological and ethical justification for wilderness. In April Leopold acquired an abandoned farm that became his weekend and vacation retreat and was to provide the setting for most of the nature sketches in "A Sand County Almanac." He invested his energy to restore ecological integrity to the land and learned many lessons while doing it. The third event was a fellowship that took Leopold abroad to study German methods of forestry and wildlife management. The highly artificial German system—which included even-aged forest monocultures and supplemental deer feedings—challenged some of his most basic assumptions and showed him the ecological and aesthetic costs of controlling environmental factors. That led him to reevaluate the objectives of wildlife management.

As his philosophy evolved, Leopold began to think in terms of systems. The key idea became the relationship between the complex structure and the smooth functioning of the whole system, between the evolution of ecological diversity and the capacity of the land as a self-renewing organism. Rather than protecting individual animals or producing a shootable surplus of them as had been done in early game management programs, the objective of conservation became preserving the capacity for healthy functioning of the land system. After three decades of trying to "control" wildlife populations by manipulating selected environmental factors, Leopold realized the importance of ecological diversity as the proper function of management. Added to this was a belief in the responsibility of the individual for the health of the land. In perhaps his most widely quoted essay, "The Land Ethic," he said, (1949 p. 224–225) "A thing is right when it tends to preserve the integrity, stability and beauty of the biotic community. It is wrong when it tends otherwise."

"A Sand County Almanac" is Aldo Leopold's greatest legacy. It represents the essence of a lifetime of observation and reflection on the interrelations of ecology, aesthetics, and ethics. Ecological perception, he believed, was a matter of careful observation and critical thinking, wherein complexity reveals a sense of relatedness. Aldo Leopold was deeply concerned with causes and consequences. He was not afraid to ask Why? but he did not formulate a reply while seated at his desk.

STATE WILDLIFE POLICY

From the colonial period through the late nineteenth century, the principal goal of American wildlife policy was unrestricted taking. Animals were slaughtered at incredible rates throughout the nineteenth century—for fashion, for fun, and occasionally for food. Programs were designed to hunt and poison all major predators in the United States. Deer almost were eliminated on the East Coast. Railroad travelers across the Great Plains were reported to never be out of sight of a dead buffalo, and never in sight of a live one. Beaver hats for men nearly caused the extinction of that animal. Feathered hats did nearly the same for many species of plume birds. Cannons were used to slaughter sleeping ducks, and commercial netters could capture 3000 birds in a single effort. Competitions were held to who could kill the most ducks with one shot; one claim boasted 81 ducks killed, and 46 crippled by a single blast (Lund 1980).

These depredations against wildlife, which often occurred despite legislation mandating protection, prompted calls throughout the nation for real protection and for enforcement. Sports hunters helped to change the unrestricted taking policy by promoting the sporting values of wildlife and saying that hunting and killing wildlife should be regulated. (Lund 1980). Nature lovers also helped develop different attitudes about wildlife (Dunlap 1988), but it took a transition from economic to sport values to institute a policy of wildlife conservation. Once the view that wildlife would be hunted for personal game use rather than slaughtered for market meat or fun was accepted, the alarming trend of wildlife depletion could be altered (Lund 1980). The policy turnabout was initiated in the states. By 1880 all the states had enacted laws protecting fish and game, and most had

hired game protectors (Leopold 1933, cited by Gottschalk 1978). By 1912 salaried game wardens were employed in 41 states (Bavin 1978).

Hunters were concerned primarily with game animals, but they helped protect nongame species, too. They joined with nature lovers and ladies' clubs in the 1890s to campaign against the slaughter of plume birds and played a role in the movement that resulted in the Lacey Act, the first general federal wildlife statute. Sports hunters helped nature lover organize the Audubon Society in 1886 for those interested in protecting and enjoying birds (Dunlap 1988).

CONTROLLING THE TAKE

Wildlife was more or less a free good before 1850. There were a few state laws that protected some species by closing the hunt during breeding season, but the laws were seldom, if ever, enforced. Without widespread support or enforcement, the wisest of laws will fail. Enforcement was the weak link in the early development of protective legislation for wildlife, in part because it was costly, and in part because conviction often required a guilty verdict from peers who also may not have respected the law. States began to initiate concerted efforts to enforce game laws in 1885. Until then, hunting clubs often were effective at bringing game law violators to the attention of prosecuting officals (Tober 1981).

A key consideration that was necessary in the early days of wildlife conservation in America was the need to diminish the pressure to take wildlife populations. This was first accomplished at the end of the nineteenth century through a policy that eliminated hunters killing for mass markets. The lobbying efforts of sports hunting organizations were instrumental. Forceful arguments were made that market hunting was less efficient as a food source than animal agriculture and that civilized people no longer needed to depend on the methods of primitive people for sustenance. Forest and Stream, a hunters' publication proposed in 1894 that "The sale of game should be forbidden at all seasons." Commerce in game had been regulated to some degree prior to that time. The first major victory came with New York's 1911 Bayne Law which prohibited the sale of game mammals and birds. Other states soon followed this precedent, leading to the demise of market hunting. Since then, the states have characteristically prohibited commerce in game animals except for those raised in captivity (Lund 1980). Today, Native Americans can still sell fish taken from the wild, which has caused walleye wars in the Lake States and salmon skirmishes in the Pacific Northwest.

The next step in the development of state wildlife law was controlling the number of sport takers. License requirements were initiated for this purpose, but they are more important for revenue generation. Licenses do provide states with estimates of the numbers of hunters and anglers. Some states restrict the number of licenses to protect scarcer species. The restriction of methods of taking—via traps, rifles, shotguns, bows, or other approved means—also is important (Lund 1980).

Two essential items were required to make wildlife laws more than meaningless gestures on the statute books: funding and then enforcement personnel. Funds were generated by the sale of hunting and fishing licenses. Initially considered an unwanted tax, the fees were levied at first only on nonresidents, but they quickly were extended to residents. Licenses have proved to be an effective technique for funding state agencies because revenue for programs increases proportionally with consumers' desires for fish and game. State license fees were supplemented by federal excise taxes beginning in the 1930s. The adequate funding base allowed the employment of enforcement specialists or game wardens. They were paid with a percentage of the fines extracted from wildlife law offenders, a policy that spread to other states and persisted until the 1930s when salaries were drawn from license sales revenues (Lund 1980). Lawren (1989) estimated that at least 70 percent of the $1 billion plus per year allocated to management of game species comes

from license fees and from excise taxes and guns, ammunition, and fishing equipment.

State and federal laws continue to protect game and nongame species from being killed or captured illegally. Although such actions pose less of a threat of extinction now than in the past, they are still a problem. State fish and game departments have large enforcement staffs who try to prevent illegal hunting and fishing. Programs such as Turn in a Poacher (TIP) are used to get public involvement and support for game law enforcement. Game wardens still face threats, injury, and death when they try to control those armed hunters who do not believe their rights should be limited.

The continuing problems of protection could be illustrated by many enforcement actions. For example, in the late 1980s, dwindling continental duck populations prompted the Fish and Wildlife Service to increase its poaching enforcement efforts, with spectacular results. In December 1988, after three years of investigations, federal wildlife law enforcement officers arrested 23 people and returned felony indictments against 50 others in Texas. Additionally, more than 130 law violators in six other states were charged with misdemeanor violations of hunting regulations. Undercover agents documented over 1300 violations of wildlife laws at 41 Texas hunt clubs. Violations included taking waterfowl illegally, as well as killing ibises, herons, hawks, and other nongame birds. This massive federal sting operation was instituted because of pervasive law breaking, as well as population declines caused by the drought in the late 1980s (Williamson 1988b).

Wildlife law enforcement comprises a significant portion of state wildlife agency personnel and budgets. In 1984 conservation officers (game wardens) constituted 33% of all state fish and wildlife employees, and law enforcement operating budgets averaged 30% of all agency expenditures (Chandler 1986, Morse 1984). Enforcement programs rely heavily on patrol by foot, automobile, boat, or airplane by uniformed field officers. Patrols help protect wildlife by catching violators and by creating the belief that officers may be anywhere at any time and that violators are likely to be apprehended (Bavin 1978).

The deterrence of illegal acts and apprehension of violators are immense tasks. Conservation officers must cover vast areas; there are many hunters and anglers; and crimes against wildlife usually have no human victims. In 1984, 40 states reported 381,496 arrests by their wildlife agencies; about 70% were violations of fish and game laws. Only 1.9% were for violations of laws pertaining to nongame or endangered species (Morse 1984).

INCREASING POPULATIONS AND MANAGING HABITAT

The principal goal of wildlife management is to maintain populations at levels that are best for the animals themselves and consistent with the social, economic, and cultural needs of people. This is not easy. What may be acceptable populations of deer for hunters may be excessive for farmers and horticulturists harassed by deer depredations or for motorists who run into deer. Dense flocks of birds may gratify the birdwatcher but alarm farmers. The distant sight of a grizzly bear may thrill the backpacker, but too many of these unpredictable animals raise threats to human property and life. The best the wildlife manager can do is strive to balance conflicting interests and maintain populations at viable levels without excessive economic damages, thus satisfying the desire of the public for a diversity and relative abundance of species (Poole and Trefethen 1978).

Along with programs to reduce hunter takes, there have been programs to increase game stocks by transplanting wildlife from areas with adequate populations and by rearing captive wildlife for subsequent liberation. The introduction of exotic species dates to efforts by a New York colonial governor to import the English pheasant. The first successful transplant, however, was the Chinese ring-necked pheasant in 1881 (Lund 1980).

The brown trout was transplanted successfully from Europe in the same year.

State programs to augment natural game populations by releasing animals raised in captivity into the wild achieved little success, although they were vigorously pursued between 1930 and 1950. Statistics on cost and capture rates revealed inefficiency. Programs for stocking cold-water fish have a better economic profile (Lund 1980).

In contrast, programs to reintroduce native animals have been very successful. Local habitats where species were devastated by hunters have been replenished. Success stories include the small band of elk in Yellowstone National Park at the turn of the century that have provided stock for large herds throughout the West. Beaver, nearly extinct in 1900, now are abundant. Wild turkey, nearly extinct in 1930, now are hunted in many areas. Antelope and bison have been brought back from the edge of extinction (Lund 1980).

Animals receive protection from wanton killing by a myriad of laws, both state and federal. Habitat destruction, however, remains mostly unregulated. State wildlife management programs began to focus efforts on habitat, once taking was under control and wildlife populations had been augmented. Habitat management efforts include policies aimed at improving habitat productivity and access to land. Both of these goals can be accomplished by the acquisition of land for wildlife purposes, and such lands have been so earmarked since the eighteenth century. Land acquisition programs have been greatly enhanced by federal revenue sharing funds that come from federal taxes on hunting gear and fishing tackle (Lund 1980).

NONGAME CONCERNS

Historically wildlife programs have been driven by hunting and fishing interests. But state wildlife law also has sought to achieve and regulate commercial exploitation, predator control, aesthetics, and ethical goals. State law regulating the commercial exploitation of nongame wildlife is concerned primarily with the trapping of wild fur bearers. In concert with international and federal laws, states also may regulate the harvest of food fishes (Lund 1980).

Predator control has been a state goal since colonial days. Aimed primarily at protecting agricultural interests, predator control has been enthusiastically endorsed by sports interests to reduce wild competitors for game species (Lund 1980). Both agricultural and sports interests benefit from programs that diminish species such as coyotes that prey upon livestock and game species. Both interests benefit from programs such as Idaho's controlled depredation hunts for elk that raid farmers' field crops.

Policies to protect wildlife, rather than consume it, respond to aesthetic, ethical, and ecological interests. State law has historically not made these interests a major focus. However, songbirds have been protected for more than a century, in part due to aesthetics, and in part for the practical reasons that they control insect pests. Unnecessarily cruel treatment of animals—especially the domesticated varieties—is dealt with in state laws and reflects ethical concerns. Regulations on trapping also have some ethical dimensions. Some states such as New York and California have followed the recent federal lead by enacting legislation to protect endangered species. Other states have not, especially those states where the influence of ecological interests is weak compared to that of sport and agricultural interests (Lund 1980).

Nongame wildlife programs have not been funded well compared to the more traditional game programs. In 1986 state agencies spent 20 times as much money (about $1.1 billion) to manage game species as they did on nongame species ($43 million), despite the fact that nongame animals comprise more than 90 percent of the more than 2000 vertebrates found in the United States. By 1989 all states in the United States had nongame management programs, but their funding levels were still poorly funded and staffed compared to traditional game pro-

grams. The nongame income tax checkoff programs in many states, however, were starting to provide improved funding, but the total amount remained small compared to game program funding.

FEDERAL WILDLIFE POLICY

Beginning in 1900 Congress put together a plethora of wildlife protection statutes. Some apply everywhere; others are limited to federal lands. All have withstood challenges to their constitutionality. Taken together, federal statutes are an impressive but fragmented and incomplete body of law. All of the laws preserve important roles for states, but most also set limits on state management discretion (Coggins 1991b). The U.S. Supreme Court has validated federal authority in wildlife management. In Kleppe v. New Mexico (426 U.S. 529 [1976]), the Supreme Court ruled that Congress can legislate however it wishes for wildlife on federal lands, and congressional actions override contrary state law. States retain control over wildlife within there borders but may exercise power only within the framework of federal constitutional and statutory law. State wildlife law has been supplemented by federal legislation (Schoenbaum 1982); however, Congress seldom attempts to preempt the traditional state wildlife management prerogative (Coggins 1991b).

A principal thrust of federal wildlife policy has been cooperation with the states to facilitate sport goals. Assistance has provided lands for hunting and fishing, money for state fish and game programs, and law enforcement. Increasing federal sensitivity to aesthetic, ethical, and ecological considerations regarding wildlife has resulted in conflicts with agricultural and sport interests (Lund 1980).

Federal wildlife policies including those for predators, nongame animals, and species preservation, which have long been implemented in national parks, now are being extended to other areas. These new policies reflecting ecological concerns for species preservation are some of the most controversial natural resource issues of the 1990s. Other issues reflecting ethical and aesthetic concerns also require the attention of wildlife resource managers.

U.S. FISH AND WILDLIFE SERVICE

Many of the federal laws protecting wildlife are administered by the U.S. Department of the Interior, Fish and Wildlife Service (FWS). An overview of the agency was presented in Chapter 12 and is reviewed here.

The federal interest in protecting wildlife surfaced at approximately the same time as the states' interests. An independent Bureau of Fisheries was established in 1871 and later became part of the Department of Commerce. In 1886 the Division of the Biological Survey was established under another name in the Department of Agriculture. These two agencies were transferred to the Department of the Interior in 1939 and renamed the Fish and Wildlife Service. In 1956 Congress renamed the agency the U.S. Fish and Wildlife Service and divided it into two bureaus—the Bureau of Sport Fisheries and Wildlife and the Bureau of Commercial Fisheries. In 1970 yet another reorganization transferred the Bureau of Commercial Fisheries to the Department of Commerce; ocean fisheries now are governed by the National Marine Fisheries Service. In 1974 Congress redesignated the Department of the Interior's Bureau of Sport Fisheries and Wildlife as the U.S. Fish and Wildlife Service (Reed and Drabelle 1984).

The mission of the FWS is "to conserve, protect, and enhance fish and wildlife and their habitats for the continuing benefit of the American people." The agency has seven principal functions: (1) managing the national wildlife refuge system of 400 refuges covering almost 89 million acres, (2) protecting endangered species, (3) protecting habitat, (4) conducting research, (5) enforcing fish and wildlife laws, (6) providing recreational fishing, and (7) advising other agencies. Sporting hunting is permitted on many refuges, an anomaly that some people consider inappropriate even though it generates revenue for future acquisitions and can be an effective technique for reducing excess populations (Reed and Drabelle 1984).

PRINCIPAL LAWS

Brief descriptions of the principal federal wildlife laws follow. These statutes are designed to protect wildlife and fish and regulate landowners, hunters, business, federal agencies, and resource managers to various extents. We generally discuss these federal laws in the order in which they were initially enacted. Bean (1977, 1983) thoroughly summarizes the federal wildlife laws and the court decisions involving them. He classes the federal laws into several major themes and discusses each in a chapter.

Federal laws regulate the taking of wildlife, regulate commerce in wildlife, allow the government to acquire and manage wildlife habitat, and encourage wildlife conservation through mandating consideration of wildlife impacts. Federal laws also provide means of funding wildlife programs, controlling damage from predators and pesticides, and requiring international cooperation in wildlife conservation. Federal laws require protection of marine mammals and the conservation of endangered species. In addition to laws that are directly enacted to conserve wildlife, many others include wildlife protection purposes, including the Federal Water Pollution Control Act Amendments, the National Forest Management Act, the Wilderness Act, National Park Service regulations, and a host of other laws and rules (Bean 1983).

Lacey Act

The Lacey Act of 1900 was America's first nationwide wildlife statute (Cart 1973). Part of the wildlife crisis at the turn of the century reflected the inability of the states to enforce laws against wildlife taking. State marketing restrictions were seen as a remedy for inadequate field enforcement. Poachers effectively sidestepped market restrictions by shipping their quarry to states that had not restricted the sale of game. There was some doubt that a state could constitutionally prohibit the sale of game taken outside the state. Federal legislative action intervened and addressed this problem with the Lacey Act, making interstate shipment of wildlife taken in violation of state law a federal crime (Lund 1980).

The Lacey Act as originally passed had two purposes. The first was to strengthen and supplement state wildlife conservation laws. The second was to promote agricultural and horticultural interests by prohibiting the import of injurious wildlife. Both of these purposes have been expanded considerably in the 90 plus years since the act's passage. The Lacey Act was an indirect expedient and a bit clumsy, but it worked. Within a decade of its passage, traffic in bird plumes was choked off, and herons and egrets in their breeding plumage were no longer attractive prey as they reared their young in the rookeries, because there was no longer a market (Dunlap 1988). The constitutionality of the Lacey Act was upheld in several federal court cases, although none reached the supreme court (Bean 1983).

The act currently prohibits import, export, transport, or sale of any fish, wildlife, or plant species taken in violation of any law, treaty, or regulation of the United States. In 1960 Congress amended the act, extending the ban on animal importation beyond those deemed injurious to agriculture or horticulture to those injurious to native wildlife, thus recognizing the protection of native wildlife as a worthy goal (Bean 1978). In 1981 Congress again amended the act, consolidating it with the Black Bass Act of 1926—a parallel statute for fish. The amendments strengthened criminal penalties for violators to up to five years imprisonment and a $420,000 fine, plus civil penalties of up to $410,000 in fines. The consolidated law is triggered only when there is interstate or foreign traffic in fish and wildlife items taken, bought, or sold in violation of some other law, usually a state fish and game law (Reed and Drabelle 1984).

Migratory Bird Treaty Act

The Migratory Bird Treaty Act of 1918 prohibits the taking of any species of migratory bird unless it is done under federal permit or regulation. The U.S. Fish and Wildlife Service in close cooperation with states annually designs hunting limits and regulations on migratory game bird species. Regulations are enforced jointly by federal and state officials (Schoenbaum 1982).

The 1918 Act established a treaty with Great Britain, Mexico, and Japan for the protection of migratory birds. The act authorized the secretary of the interior to determine when such birds may be taken, killed, or possessed. It also outlaws transportation of migratory birds, nests, or eggs possessed in violation of the statute. Numerous court decisions have held that restrictions authorized by the act are constitutional and are not a taking of private property rights, nor unreasonable in regulating methods of hunting or in even denying (or *allowing*) hunting to occur (Bean 1983). The law has remained a partial basis for continued protection of migratory birds and regulation of their hunting (Bean 1978). One example is the ban on lead shot for hunting waterfowl, which was begun in 1981, in order to stop lead poisoning of birds who ate the spent shot from marsh bottoms. Replacing lead with steel shot was implemented nationwide after considerable controversy and a court decision upholding the ban in the 1980s.

Migratory Bird Conservation Act and Duck Stamp Act

The Migratory Bird Conservation Act of 1929 authorizes the secretary of the interior to acquire land for bird sanctuaries, conditioned on the approval of the state in which the land is located. Funds for such acquisitions were hard to come by in the depression era, so Congress passed the Migratory Bird Hunting and Conservation Act of 1934. This "Duck Stamp Act," which was promoted by political cartoonist and conservationist Ding Darling, provides that anyone hunting migratory birds must purchase a hunting stamp. Revenues from these sales are placed into a special fund used to acquire refuge areas and waterfowl production areas. This law was the first major federal statute to establish a special fund to be used exclusively for wildlife purposes.

The federal duck stamp program has been very successful at both raising funds for conservation purposes and promoting conservation awareness. As of 1989 the federal duck stamp program had collected $326 million, which has been used to preserve 4 million acres of habitat for ducks and geese (Turbak 1989). The Wetlands Loan Act of 1961, as amended in 1976, authorized loans to the Duck Stamp Fund of up to $200 million, which could be used immediately for land purchase and repaid in the future (Bean 1983).

The artists who draw the winning duck stamp each year also are guaranteed fame and sales of art prints worth up to a $1 million art prints based on the stamp competition. The federal program also has spawned similar state art competitions, stamp sale requirements, and art reproductions, which also generate millions of dollars in fees and art sales each year. The stamp programs also have expanded beyond waterfowl to help fund nongame management programs as well (Turbak 1989). In fact, the wildlife competitions have become an industry themselves and help promote interest in wildlife throughout the country.

Animal Damage Control Act

The Animal Damage Control Act of 1931 authorizes the U.S. Department of Agriculture to eradicate or suppress animals injurious to agriculture, horticulture, forestry, animal husbandry, game, furbearers, or birds. It was passed by Congress as a confirmation of federal predator-killing authority. Attempts to control predators with bounty systems were plagued with fraud and ineffectiveness, and poisons long ago replaced bounties as the preferred lethal agent. By the turn of the nineteenth century, most large carnivores had been eliminated in the East, and the focus shifted to the West. Ranchers demanded protection from wolves, bears, mountain lions, eagles, and coyotes. The federal government responded to the ranchers' desires, departing from the notion that wildlife man-

agement was a state prerogative. Congress appropriated money for predator control beginning in 1909 and began massive strychnine poisoning campaigns in 1915 (Coggins 1991b). The Animal Control Act was passed to formally recognize the federal programs started years before.

Aldo Leopold recognized that the eradication of predators can permanently disrupt the stability of ecosystems, as it had on Arizona's Kaibab Plateau. A 1964 study by A. Starker Leopold (Aldo's son) for the National Park Service heavily criticized federal predator control programs. The 1972 Cain Report helped President Nixon decide to issue an executive order barring the use of predator poisons on public lands. President Reagan revoked the order in 1982 (Coggins 1991b).

Although the 1931 act is still on the books, it has lost much of its force, and federal predator control is only a shadow of its former self. Most of the assumptions underlying the policy of predator control have been discredited by various studies, and the Endangered Species Act of 1973 now prevents the killing of wolves, grizzly bears, and bald eagles. The primary focus of current efforts is the coyote, but some observers say that the program is ineffective and is more a subsidy for ranchers than a realistic attempt to solve a problem (Cogging 1991b). Of course, ranchers disagree. Reintroduction of wolves in some states and bobcats in others has made predator control a reemerging issue in the 1990s.

Fish and Wildlife Coordination Act

The Fish and Wildlife Coordination Act of 1934 as amended in 1946 and 1958 requires federal water resources development agencies to consider the impact of their actions on wildlife. Before the act little consideration had been given to the effects of such projects on fish and wildlife (Gottschalk 1978). The act as originally written called for an investigation of the effects of pollution on wildlife, encouraged wildlife programs federal lands, and promised a national program of wildlife conservation and rehabilitation. The promise was little more than rhetoric, because the law only required consultation upon dam construction authorization and "if economically practicable" fish passage was to be provided (Bean 1978).

The 1946 amendments to the act require consultation with the U.S. Fish and Wildlife Service for all government or private water resources projects. The 1958 amendments put wildlife values on "equal consideration" with other water resources development project purposes. Consultation by federal construction agencies was mandated not only to prevent loss or damage to wildlife, but also to develop and encourage wildlife resources. Agencies were directed to give "full consideration" to the recommendations of wildlife agencies. In practice, however, the policies of the act have not been effectively carried out, from its initiation throughout the Reagan administration (Bean 1978, 1983, Reed and Drabelle 1984).

Taylor Grazing Act and Forest Wildlife Refuge Act

Federal lands—especially those under the management authority of the BLM, as well as Forest Service lands—produce vegetation that provides forage for ungulates (hooved animals). Either wild ungulates (sheep, deer, elk, etc.) or domesticated ungulates (sheep, goats, and cattle) may use this forage. The Taylor Grazing Act of 1934 established policies for managing public range lands and thus affects wildlife. The act also mandates state regulation of all hunting and fishing on grazing districts. The background of the 1934 act was discussed in Chapter 12; details are contained in Dana and Fairfax (1980). The Forest Wildlife Refuge Act of 1934 gave the U.S. Forest Service statutory authority and a mission to protect game on its lands (Dunlap 1988).

Federal Aid in Wildlife Restoration Act

During the depression, wildlife interest groups sought to improve federal and state wildlife programs. In addition to the Duck Stamp Act, they also proposed that hunters be taxed to support game management programs. Eventually, the efforts led to passage of the Federal Aid in Wildlife Restoration Act of 1937 (more commonly known as the Pittman-Robertson Act), which places a federal excise tax on hunting gear and remits the proceeds to the states according to a formula reflecting the state's geographic size and the extent of its sales of hunting licenses. These funds must provide "benefits to hunters and fishermen." A state's eligibility for funding is conditioned on the requirement that proceeds from game licenses be appropriated by state law in their entirety to wildlife agencies. This federal intrusion into state policy was designed as a carrot-and-stick approach to avoid the diversion of license revenues into school budgets and highway funding (Lund 1980).

Pittman-Robertson authorized the U.S. Department of the Interior to cooperate with states in wildlife restoration projects in two rather narrow areas: (1) selection and restoration of areas adaptable as feeding, nesting, or breeding places including construction of works thereon; and (2) research into wildlife management problems, including hunter education. These restricted choices for using the funds were gradually expanded by state political pressure for greater latitude. Amendments in 1946 allowed states to include maintenance of completed projects to fall within the definition of a "wildlife restoration project." A 1955 amendment allowed the expenditure of funds for the management of wildlife areas and resources, exclusive of law enforcement and public relations activities. A 1970 amendment allowed states to spend their funds based on an official "comprehensive fish and wildlife resource management plan" in lieu of the traditional individual restoration projects (Bean 1983). State wildlife agencies still may not use the funds for law enforcement, public relations activities, or game farms and stocking programs (Peek 1986).

Pittman-Robertson funds are generated from an 11 percent federal excise tax on sporting arms and ammunition and archery gear and a 10 percent tax on handguns (Reed and Drabelle 1984). The act generated about $120 million per year on the 1980s and financed large amounts of habitat acquisition and extensive management programs.

According to Coggins (1991b), a side effect of this program and the similar Dingell-Johnson program on fishing tackle begun in 1950 is that state game and fish agencies are highly sympathetic and responsive to the desires of hunters and anglers.

Bald Eagle Act

In spite of Benjamin Franklin's condemnation of the bald eagle as a "rank coward," it is a majestic symbol of America. At one time, eagles were destroyed as alleged enemies of agriculture. Because some states left eagles unprotected and considered them as predators. The Bald Eagle Act of 1940 was passed to protect this national symbol (Schoenbaum 1982). The act made it a criminal offense for any person to take or possess a bald eagle or any part, egg, or nest thereof.

The act was revised as the Bald Eagle Protection Act of 1972, extending protection to golden eagles. The revised act prohibits the killing, molesting, or poisoning of bald and golden eagles except with federal permission. Such permits are available for the religious practices of Native Americans and the protection of domestic livestock against depredations of golden eagles (Coggins and Wilkinson 1987). A rancher who kills eagles can lose his or her federal grazing permit and be fined $5000 (Peek 1986).

Fish Restoration and Management Act

The Fish Restoration and Management Act of 1950 (better known as the Dingell-Johnson Act) places a 10 percent federal excise tax on sport fishing tackle and remits the proceeds to the states. It was enacted after general satisfaction with the Pittman-Robertson Act and because a special wartime tax on certain fishing equipment was likely to be terminated unless it could be earmarked for fish restoration purposes (Bean 1983).

The act was designed to be administered similar to the Pittman-Robertson program and has the same requirement that proceeds from fishing licenses be appropriated by state law to the state fish and game agency. Funds are distributed to the states, with 40 percent of the allocation based on geographical area and 60 percent on the basis of the licenses issued, after deducting 8 percent for federal administration.

The funds may be used to purchase land and water for fisheries development or rehabilitation, to develop access sites and facilities for fishing, and for fisheries management research (Peek 1986, Reed and Drabelle 1984). The act generated about $35 million per year in the early 1980s. It was amended by the Wallop-Breaux Trust Fund import duties in 1984, which added a tax on pleasure boats and yachts and boating fuel and supplies as well and significantly increased revenues and spawned a substantial expansion of state fishery programs. The new revenue sources increased revenue generation to about $100 million per year.

Sikes Act

The Sikes Act of 1960 authorizes the Department of Defense to expend money for wildlife on lands under its jurisdiction. Amendments in 1974, 1978, and 1982 mandated cooperation between federal agencies, especially the Departments of the Interior and Agriculture, in the conservation and rehabilitation of public lands, including the development of comprehensive plans for the protection of wildlife and fisheries resources in consultation with state wildlife agencies (Gottschalk 1978). The act has not been well funded, but it does serve as one mechanism for wildlife management on federal lands.

Land and Water Conservation Fund Act

The Land and Water Conservation Fund (LWCF) Act of 1965 provides funds to plan, acquire, and develop land and water areas, including facilities for recreation purposes and the preservation of native wildlife. Revenues come from the sale of surplus federal property, motorboat fuel taxes, certain national parks and national recreation area fees earmarked to "enhance and administer," receipts from offshore oil leases, and general treasury funds. Each state must develop a comprehensive outdoor recreation plan to be eligible for these 50-50 matching funds (Douglas 1982, Peek 1986, Dunlap 1988). An illustration in Chapter 12 provides much more detail on the LWCF.

The LWCF provides substantial funds for the purchase and management of public lands for recreation, wildlife, and other purposes. Between 1967 and 1986 the Fish and Wildlife Service alone spent more than $350 million of LWCF monies for land acquisition and habitat management programs. It also provided funds for all federal agencies to purchase about 3.2 million acres of recreational lands, which also preserve considerable wildlife habitat values (Mantell, Myers, and Reed 1988).

Anadromous Fish Conservation Act

The Anadromous Fish Conservation Act of 1965 directs the secretary of the interior to make studies and recommendations for the conservation and enhancement of anadromous fisheries resources (Schoenbaum 1982). It did not seem to afford migrating salmon any real protection (Coggins and Wilkinson 1987). The Pacific Northwest Power Planning and Conservation Act of 1980 attempts to meet this shortcoming, but it, too, has failed to adequately protect fish from hydroelectric dams.

National Wildlife Refuge System Administration Act

The National Wildlife Refuge System Administration Act of 1966 is the "organic" law under which national wildlife refuges are managed, and it allows use of these areas for any purpose, including but not limited to hunting, fishing, public recreation (Coggins 1991b). The first such refuge, Pelican Island, Florida, was designated by Pres. Theodore Roosevelt's proclamation in 1903 (Coggins and Wilkinson 1987). The refuge system was described in Chapter 12. Many issues about its management persist, including, the amount of hunting allowed; management for game versus nongame species; use for recreation; mining, or grazing; and even the amount of management control allowed to the FWS.

Wild Free-Roaming Horses and Burros Protection Act

The Wild Free-Roaming Horses and Burros Protection Act of 1971 declares that these feral ungulates are an integral part of western natural systems and symbols of western history. Like the Bald Eagle Protection Act, its objective was to protect the symbolic value of a vanishing type of wildlife, and humanitarian concerns also figured prominently in its passage. The act's focus on the animals as an important part of the natural system also afforded them more protection than would just a prohibition on their taking (Bean 1983).

To most ranchers and federal land managers, these animals are "a royal pain in the backside." They have no natural predators; they compete with livestock for forage and make general nuisances of themselves (Coggins 1991b). The act abolishes private killing and commerce in wild horses and burros. Federal agencies are allowed to remove the minimum feasible number of these animals from BLM and Forest Service lands (Schoenbaum 1982).

The act was among the first federal wildlife laws to establish a specific mandate for federal land managers to practice wildlife management, and it affects the BLM the most. The act also contains numerous management requirements designed to protect the animals but which actually make management very difficult. Wild horses and burro populations burgeoned rapidly after the act, causing considerable damage to the western range. Subsequent amendments in 1978 allow the BLM to use motorized equipment to control population levels, which has helped range improvement (Dana and Fairfax 1980). The BLM adopt-a-horse program has been the focus of adverse publicity because critics feel capturing and shipping horses was inhumane (Coggins 1991b). In a challenge to the act, the Supreme Court affirmed the power of the federal government to control all wildlife species on its lands (Kleppe v. New Mexico, 426 U.S. 529 [1976]). This ruling is significant because prior to the 1970s, the federal government relied almost exclusively on state game laws and enforcement officers to govern operations on federal lands.

Federal Water Pollution Control Laws

One important indirect law affecting fish and wildlife is the Clean Water Act. Although the Clean Air Act makes almost no mention of wildlife protection, the Clean Water Act focused much more on wildlife. In fact, one of the two initial goals of the 1972 amendments was to obtain by 1983 a level of water quality "which provides for the protection and propagation of fish, shellfish, and wildlife and provides for recreation in and on the water."

As discussed in Chapter 14, the Clean Water Act prescribes a series of policies designed to improve the quality of the nation's water. Sections 208 and 319 mandate control on nonpoint source pollution; the National Pollutant Discharge Elimination System (NPDES) helps control industrial point sources of pollution; and Section 404 permits are intended to control pollution of or loss of wetlands. Permits may be denied for point source emission or for wetland fill actions if they will result in unacceptably adverse impacts on municipal water supplies, shellfish beds, wildlife, fisheries (including spawning and breeding areas), or recreational areas. The determination of the impacts of proposed actions on fish and wildlife has been an integral component of federal water quality laws and implementation. furthermore, this focus has carried over to the language and implementation of state laws. The protection of water quality for fish, wildlife, and humans is the primary purpose of all the state laws. In fact, it was problems with dead, deformed, or toxic fish that prompted many of the early calls for water pollution control, and the health of fish remains a crucial indicator of our success at eliminating water pollution.

Marine Mammal Protection Act

The Marine Mammal Protection Act (MMPA) of 1972 declares a total moratorium on the taking of certain marine mammals—whales, porpoises, seals, and polar bears (taking is defined in the same way as in the Endangered Species Act). The act prohibits the possession, sale, or transportation of such animals in interstate or international commerce unless permits have been granted by the secretaries of the interior or commerce, which can only be done after detailed scientific studies of the impact of the proposed action. The key management concept under the act is the requirement to maintain an "optimum sustainable population," meaning "the number of animals that will result in the maximum productivity of the population or species, keeping in mind the carrying capacity of the habitat and the health of the ecosystem of which they form a constitutional element." The act extends protection 200 miles into territorial seas. It preempts state law, except within state boundaries if the secretary of commerce certifies compliance with major provisions of federal law (Schoenbaum 1982). The MMPA is the first major conservation act to be based on ecosystem principles (Norris 1978).

The Marine Mammal Protection Act was reauthorized in 1988. The 1988 revision allowed commercial fishing operations to take a small number of depleted marine mammals in their catches. In exchange, there would be greater monitoring on incidental take, development of management plans for species most affected by commercial fishing, and an industrywide education program focusing on the mammals' importance to the marine ecosystem.

Endangered Species Act

The Endangered Species Act (ESA) of 1973 is intended to protect species from becoming extinct (Tobin 1990). In a nutshell, the ESA creates two main processes: (1) the designation of species and their critical habitat through *listing*, and (2) protection (Coggins 1991b). Listing is important because it triggers the four major provisions of the ESA, which are to *conserve* listed species, avoid *jeopardization*, avoid destruction of *critical habitat*, and avoid *taking* (Coggins 1991a). Definitions of these key terms are at the heart of understanding the ESA and are provided in the last major section of this chapter, which is devoted to the ESA as a policy for protecting biological diversity.

Fishery Conservation and Management Act

The Fishery Conservation and Management Act (FCMA) of 1976 extends federal management to marine fisheries by declaring federal jurisdiction over all fish within 200 miles, anadromous species throughout their migratory range, and all fishery resources of the continental shelf. Marine mammals and "highly migratory" species (e.g., tuna) are specifically excluded. Unlike the MMPA, state jurisdiction over marine fisheries is preserved. The principal management concept under the act is the requirement that regulations should achieve the "optimum yield" from each fishery, defined to mean "the amount of fish (A) which will provide the greatest overall benefit to the nation, with particular reference to food production and recreational opportunities; and (B) which is prescribed as such on the basis of maximum sustainable yield from each fishery, as modified by any relevant economic, social, or ecological factor." At issue is the relationship of the FCMA with the MMPA, because marine mammals compete with humans for certain stocks of fish (Schoenbaum 1982).

Fish and Wildlife Conservation Act

The Fish and Wildlife Conservation Act of 1980 may properly be called the Nongame Act. It sets in motion a process whereby states are encouraged with federal financial assistance to develop plans for the conservation of species formerly neglected by state fish and game agencies (Coggins and Wilkinson 1987). Also known as the Forsythe-Chaffee Act, the law calls for each state desiring federal assistance to develop a conservation plan identifying species, ranges, problems, and a plan of action for nongame species, which are defined as those species not ordinarily taken for food, fur, or sport. The plan does not need to consider threatened or endangered species or marine mammals, which are protected under other laws (Peek 1986).

The act provided for the federal government to reimburse states at up to 90 percent of the costs of developing a nongame conservation plan and up to 75 percent of the conservation measures specified in the plan that pertain to nongame fish and wildlife. Unlike Pittman-Robertson and Dingell-Johnson, however, the act relies on direct congressional appropriations, not excise taxes. Given the budget balancing problems of the 1980s and the opposition of OMB, the act received no funding for many years and only token amounts later. These difficulties do illustrate that appropriations are just as important as authorizations.

Pacific Northwest Planning Act

The Pacific Northwest Power Planning and Conservation Act of 1980 established a regional council. One of its tasks was to develop plans to ensure that fish and wildlife receive "equitable treatment" with the other objectives of hydroelectric projects. But since stocks of salmon in about 200 areas are on the decline, groups have petitioned to protect some of them under the Endangered Species Act. The winter run of Chinook salmon on the Sacramento River was the first salmon species to be so protected when it was listed as threatened in 1989 by the National Marine Fisheries Service. The Snake River Sockeye Salmon was listed as endangered in 1991. More imperiled Salmon stocks will undoubtedly be listed in the future.

Federal Land Management

A large number of federal laws also cover wildlife conservation and management on federal lands, as discussed in Chapter 12. The National Wildlife Refuge System Administration Act of 1966 consolidated many different federal wildlife refuges into the National Wildlife Refuge System. NWRS lands incorporated areas formerly administered as part of the Fish and Wildlife Service and the Bureau of Land Management. These areas included game ranges, wildlife ranges, wildlife management areas, waterfowl production areas, and wildlife refuges. The 1966 act did not provide much management direction, but it did authorize the secretary of the interior to "permit the use of any area within the system for any purpose, including but not limited to hunting, fishing, public recreation and accommodations, and access wherever he determines that such uses are compatible with the major purposes for which such areas were established." The authorization of "compatible" uses made it clear that the national wildlife refuges were not to be managed as single-use lands, but more properly as "dominant-use" lands (Bean 1983).

Debates do occur over what uses are appropriate on National Wildlife Refuge lands. Some refuge lands allow grazing by domestic livestock, some allow motor boating and water skiing, and of course, most allow hunting. Wildlife conservation groups often have opposed an expansive definition of compatible uses, in hope of providing greater wildlife protection by restricted use. Animal rights groups often have opposed hunting, albeit without much success.

The National Forest System and the Bureau of Land Management holdings are managed under the doctrine of multiple use, which requires that fish and wildlife are indeed among the management objectives. As discussed in Chapter 13, the Multiple-Use Sustained-Yield Act required that the Forest Service give due consideration to the various uses of the national forests, although the decision as to the proper mix of uses within a particular area is left to the discretion and expertise of the agency.

The National Forest Management Act of 1976 contains much more specific guidelines about national forest management plans and the interactions among multiple resources. NFMA requires compliance with NEPA and states that the NFMA regulations must include guidelines that

Provide for diversity of plant and animal communities based on the suitability and capability of the specific land area.

Insure consideration of the economic and environmental aspects of various systems of renewable resource management, including the related systems of silviculture and protection of forest resources, to provide for outdoor recreation (including wilderness), range, timber, watershed, wildlife and fish.

Insure that timber will be harvested... only where... protection is provided for streams, streambanks, shorelines, lakes, wetlands, and other bodies of water from detrimental changes... where harvests are likely to seriously and adversely affect water conditions or fish habitat.

Finally, clearcutting or other even-aged management is to be permitted only if

The potential environmental, biological, esthetic, engineering, and economic impacts on each advertised sale area have been assessed and such cuts are carried out in a manner consistent with the protection of soil, watershed, fish, wildlife, recreation and esthetic resources.

The preceding NFMA diversity requirements alone have substantially affected how national forests can be managed. A large amount of attention has focused on the Endangered Species Act in preserving species and restricting national forest management options. But in practice, managers on the forest believe that the NFMA diversity regulations alone are sufficient to protect most flora and fauna and are the greatest constraints on their management.

The Federal Land Policy Management Act (FLPMA) of 1976 requires that the Bureau of Land Management perform multiple-use planning. FLPMA requires the secretary of the interior to "use a systematic interdisciplinary approach to achieve integrated consideration of physical, biological, economic, and other sciences" in developing land use plans. FLPMA directs that half the monies received by the United States as fees for grazing livestock be put in a special fund to be spent solely for "range betterment," including "fish and wildlife habitat enhancement." FLPMA also authorizes exchanges of public for private lands, which must include a consideration of the fish and wildlife aspect of the proposed exchange (Bean 1983). These provisions ensure that fish and wildlife management are incorporated in BLM plans and actions.

TRENDS

Two trends in federal wildlife law are worth noting. One is the requirement that agencies consult with the U.S. Fish and Wildlife Service in planning the development of land and water resources in order to consider wildlife needs. Two laws mandate this consultation: the Fish and Wildlife Coordination Act of 1934, as amended in 1946 and 1958, and the Endangered Species Act of 1973. The second trend is the combination of public participation and ecosystem management on the planning process. This trend is consistent with the concept of wildlife as a "public trust" resource, and the belief that the use of such resources is to be accomplished with the broadest possible public participation. Both the Marine Mammal Protection Act of 1972 and the Endangered Species Act of 1973 open up the body of wildlife law to the interested citizenry, and both assume that a well-balanced ecosystem offers the greatest potential for good to the greatest variety of wildlife (Bean 1978).

MANAGING HABITAT AND ECOSYSTEMS

Congress allows some hunting and fishing on most federal land systems, including wilderness areas. Federal law primarily leaves the regulation of taking to the discretion of the states. The National Park System places the most restrictions on hunting and fishing. National parks are closed to hunting, but it is allowed in other units of the park system such as national monuments and national reserves, preserves, or recreational areas (Coggins 1991b).

On the multiple-use lands managed by the U.S. Forest Service and the BLM, a fraction of the agencies' budgets is specifically earmarked for wildlife programs (see Swanson 1978). The agencies generally abide by long-standing informal agreements with state hunting and fishing laws and devote their efforts to wildlife habitat enhancement (see Gottschalk 1978). Habitat management by federal agencies has been criticized on the grounds that such practices were narrowly aimed at game species for human harvest to the detriment of other species. Although wildlife management is less than an exact science, many wildlife managers have broadened their focus in recent decades in response to intense public scrutiny, nongame legislation, and advances in science (Coggins 1991b).

Today, public land management is undergoing a challenging transformation to ecosystem-based management. Although the concept is in its formative stages and not yet well defined, four important characteristics are evident. First, interagency cooperation is the cornerstone of ecosystem management. Natural phenomena such as watersheds, airsheds, and wildlife habitats are the appropriate management focus; and because they do not respect jurisdictional boundaries, consultation and coordination among agencies is required. Second, managers must identify and analyze the full geographic and cumulative impacts of management proposals to minimize the disruption of fragmentation of ecosystem processes. Third, ecosystem management is closely linked to modern theories of conservation biology; therefore, it encompasses a commitment to the protection of biological diversity. Fourth, in national parks and wilderness areas the natural integrity and appearance of the areas are to be retained and preserved (Keiter 1990).

This management transformation is occurring, but it is by no means doing so without opposition or pain. The Forest Service's New Perspectives Program, which promote ecological management, has created considerable confusion within the agency, virulent opposition from timber industry groups, and prevalent suspicion from wary environmental groups. The shifts to new paradigms for public land management will be a crucial policy issue in the 1990s.

ILLUSTRATION: THE ANTIHUNTING ISSUE

A HISTORY OF CONFLICT

In the 1850s Americans had different ideas about nature and wild animals than we have today. It was widely accepted then that animals were put on the face of the earth in a flurry of activity that lasted six days. People thought of animals as "dumb brutes" without thoughts, emotions, or the capacity to feel pain. Wildlife was judged to be good or bad, useful or worthless, only as it suited human needs. Wildlife existed to be fully exploited. Those attitudes have changed. Today a more scientific view of creation is widely accepted. Many people believe that animals have feelings and can in some way think. A significant minority is willing to grant rights to animals and seeks to have society do the same. Most of us shun cruelty and pain inflicted on animals. The popularization of ecological thinking means that many see species as interdependent parts of the ecosystem, with each part playing some role in sustaining the whole (Dunlap 1988).

The hunting controversy characterized by Reiger (1975) is a manifestation of the change in the way we view the role of wildlife. The controversy, said Peek (1986), is ages old and defies resolution because it stems from two fundamentally different philosophies. One is rooted in religion, morals, and ethics, the other, in the biological sciences. The former view is that it is wrong to kill individual animals because they have a right to live. The latter view is that a biological surplus of animals is produced, and the welfare of the population takes precedence over the welfare of the individual animal (Peek 1986).

Reiger (1975) described the issue as a bitter struggle between two groups: (1) a large group of "animal lovers" who claim that killing is wrong and must be stopped, and (2) "sportsmen and sportswomen"—the 20 million or so hunters. Reiger, a historian, claimed

that sports hunters are the victims of fashion, and he wrote a book in their defense. In it he attacked some colleagues for succumbing to "the wishful thinking of the tenderhearted (p. 14)." He reminded them that the "awful truth is that in order to live, all of us kill continually, directly or indirectly (p. 15)." Reiger pointed out that Aldo Leopold was an avid hunter. Reiger recognized that the hunting controversy is a moral issue, meaning that some will find it impossible even to consider that hunters played an important role in wildlife conservation. Dunlap (1988), also a historian, felt that Reiger overstated his claim that hunters originated the progressive conservation movement. The men in the movement were hunters, but so were most (but not all) adult men in the late nineteenth century.

The activities of the American Society for the Prevention of Cruelty to Animals (ASPCA) typify the interests of the humane movement. Dating back to 1872, the ASPCA intervened in pigeon shoots, a popular pastime of gunners. The sporting press labelled such efforts as eccentric but recognized the potential for such eccentricity to generate political support. Continued pressure brought concessions from New York hunters and outright prohibition of pigeon shoots in at least three other states (Tober 1981).

As Peek (1986) indicated, progress in North American wildlife management can be determined to some extent by comparing the American Game Policy of 1930 (Leopold 1930) with the North American Wildlife Policy of 1973 (Allen 1973). One of the basic actions recommended in 1930 was the recognition that the nonshooting protectionist and the scientist shared with hunters and landowners the responsibility for wildlife as a whole. This action has not been well implemented. Not until 1980 was federal legislation enacted that recognized the importance of nongame wildlife. The formation of antihunting groups attests to the continued polarization between hunters and protectionists. The 1973 policy recognized antihunting as a by-product of increasing urbanization and called for continuing public relations programs for fish and wildlife agencies. By ignoring the antihunting faction, agencies risk constraining legislation (Peek 1986).

PUBLIC SENTIMENT

Attitudes of the general public toward hunting are important in wildlife management. Public opinion survey research conducted in 1980 indicated that hunting for meat, subsistence, or the combination of recreation and meat is generally approved. Hunting for recreation alone, especially trophy hunting, receives much less approval. It appears that people approve of utilitarian uses of wildlife more than purely sporting goals. As might be expected, survey research showed that rural residents are more likely to approve of hunting than are urban residents (Peek 1986).

The traditional arguments for hunting include the following points (Klein 1973): (1) It is generally more humane to kill outright than to allow death by starvation or by predators; (2) humans have evolved as hunters and modern sport hunting reenacts the traditional drama; (3) hunting keeps wildlife populations healthy and generally replaces other types of mortality; (4) hunting does not endanger populations; (5) hunted species are among the most abundant; and (6) hunters tend to be in close touch with the environment and environmental realities. Some of these arguments are human-centered and subject to immediate challenge and rapid dismissal by those who reject imposing human values on the natural world (Peek 1986).

Some humane groups are antihunting and antifishing, and they reject the common goals of wildlife management. The formation of two new humane organizations in 1954 set the stage for the modern debate over hunting. The Society of Animal Protective Legislation gave the movement a continued presence in Washington, lobbying at the federal level. The Humane Society of the United States (HSUS) split off from the American Humane Association (founded in 1877) because the parent organization was not sufficiently "radical." The Humane Society was against hunting and was willing to say so, believing that the public was

ready for a radical argument. Shortly thereafter, the Anti-Steel Trap League was revived by some old adherents under the name Defenders of Wildlife. It quickly grew into a national organization with national goals, a journal ("Defenders"), a Washington office, a permanent staff, and the backing of a number of scientists (Dunlap 1988).

The humane movement has developed a philosophical and ideological base centered on the concept of *pain*. By the 1970s humane advocates concluded that all animals are able to suffer pain. By the 1980s some went even further and attempted to construct ethical systems that took into account all forms of life and even landscapes. Humane advocates drew parallels between opposition to their cause and other forms of prejudice and discrimination such as those based on race or sex. They saw specieism as analogous to racism or sexism. Animal rights arguments are used to justify actions such as freeing experimental animals and destroying laboratories (Dunlap 1988).

As in earlier days, the modern humane movement depended on women for the majority of membership and for leadership as well. The movement also reflected demographic and social changes that have occurred since World War II. The young, city dwellers and the college-educated were disproportionately likely to agree with humane goals and join humane societies. A generation raised in the city and educated in urban culture was breaking its ties with a rural society that still accepted and even celebrated hunting, fishing, trapping, and the conquest of the wilderness (Dunlap 1988).

In the 1960s the wildlife wing of the humane movement developed its own action agenda. One of its first causes was the protection of the West's wild horses, some of which were being turned into dog food. A dedicated few set out to oppose such activity and make it a national cause. In addition, wildlife managers wanted to remove introduced species, including burros in the Grand Canyon. The Wild Free-Roaming Horses and Burros Protection Act of 1971 is a testament to the successful challenge of these practices. The poisoning and trapping of predators was another enemy of the cause. Since 1968 almost 350 antitrap bills have been introduced at various levels of government. Thirty-three states have taken action to ban leg-hold and other "inhumane" traps. Predator control remains a platform plank of the humane cause. Efforts to ban hunting, once the dream of a few radicals in the humane movement, are extensive and respectable, and sporting organizations and hunting magazines take them seriously (Dunlap 1988).

The new humane groups put pressure on the U.S. Fish and Wildlife Service and they served as a foil for more traditional conservation organizations. With groups such as the Defenders of Wildlife speaking out to abolish predator control programs and advocating the cessation of the killing of any wildlife, the National Wildlife Federation and National Audubon Society seemed by comparison to be the voices of moderation, whatever their demands were (Dunlap 1988).

LEGAL AND INSTITUTIONAL ISSUES

Coggins (1991b) discusses several legal issues relating to hunting rights, which are paraphrased in this section. Federal constitutional law holds that the hunter's interest in pursuing game as a sport is at best minor. Sport hunting is not a constitutionally protected endeavor, but commercial harvesting of wildlife is. In 1948 the Supreme Court struck down a state statute charging nonresident commercial shrimpers 100 times the license fee of residents. However, in 1978 the Court allowed a Montana law that heavily discriminated against out-of-state elk hunters with high license fees on the ground that sport hunting unrelated to livelihood is not a fundamental interest protected by the Constitution, even though the ruling did affect the plaintiffs, who were hunting guides trying to protect their livelihoods.

Other cases make more or less the same point on the ground of the Endangered Species Act of 1973. Courts have required agencies to take actions that have impinged

upon hunting time and restricted hunting means, without any deference to the affected sports interests. The steel-shot issue is one such case. Courts have affirmed that the Congress can forbid the shooting of grizzly bears even when private property has been harmed. On the one hand, courts have implicitly assumed that the interests of hunters were not worthy of much consideration; on the other hand, a court has indicated that recreational hunting is an important and valuable use that should not be impaired without strong evidence of the need to do so.

Most organizations that support hunting promote conservation as a guiding principle, so overt conflicts with organizations not devoted to wildlife harvesting have been rare. Some organizations, such as humane societies or the Fund for Animals, have antihunting orientations, and several mainline conservation organizations are less than enthusiastic about viewing wildlife as a crop to be harvested. These philosophical differences could erupt into several types of legal problems.

Congress, and to a lesser degree, state legislatures can enhance of limit the right to hunt wildlife. Congress has done so in Alaska, where subsistence hunting is considered more important than in the lower 48 states. Generally, though, Congress leaves the regulation of hunting, fishing, and trapping to federal land management agencies and the states. The states have mostly divorced hunting privileges from land ownership, and landowners cannot harvest wildlife on their own property when it is not consistent with general state hunting regulations.

The U.S. Fish and Wildlife Service has long acted on the belief that hunting is a valuable management tool and an appropriate use of wildlife refuges under the National Wildlife Refuge Administration Act of 1966. In 1978 the secretary of the interior rejected a recommendation from an advisory committee that the propriety of all refuge hunting be judged on a beneficial-to-wildlife standard and, therefore, has not had to establish scientifically the proposition that killing animals is good for them. In 1990 Congress considered, and hunting groups opposed, legislation that would ban "harmful" uses of national wildlife refuges.

Following FWS decisions to open more refuge land to hunting, the Humane Society filed a lawsuit challenging FWS hunting policies. On remand, a federal district court is faced with the question of conflicting values akin to the compatibility of mining and wilderness. Congress certainly contemplated some limited refuge hunting, but it also specified that species' welfare takes precedence. If the plaintiffs are successful, FWS wildlife management refuges will be forced into new and more preservationist directions, even without new legislation (Coggins 1991b).

THE PROFESSIONAL VIEW

Wildlife management agencies have a large constituency that includes people motivated by aesthetic and nonconsumptive aspects of wildlife as well as the traditional hunters and anglers. Wildlife professionals must recognize that they answer to a much larger group of interests than do hunters and trappers. Their constituency is a large proportion of the public at large. Wildlife management that demonstrates responsible stewardship while providing benefits for people will more and more be the standards by which the profession is judged (Peek 1986).

The question remains. How can wildlife resource managers reconcile the polarization between hunters and antihunters—between those who view wildlife as populations and those who see individual animals? Perhaps it is best to start by recognizing that both viewpoints are ingrained in personal value systems and will be stoutly defended by personal commitments and actions. Therefore, criticism or defense of either point of view is unprofessional. We should realize that there is a common ground in the conservation of wildlife resources even if we cannot agree about their uses (Peek 1986). Hunters and nonhunters have a common enemy—the economic forces that alter the habitats necessary to sustain diverse and abundant populations of wildlife (Lund 1980).

PROTECTING BIOLOGICAL DIVERSITY

Darwin's theory of evolution implies that species adapt to the environment. Changes in the environment change the distribution of species and may endanger their very existence. Recent actions by humans seem to have drastically increased the rate at which species become extinct. Since 1600 at least 700 animal species have become extinct—290 mammals, 200 birds, and 210 reptiles and amphibians. By one estimate, only 1 percent of all the species that have ever existed is alive at present—99 percent have become extinct, mostly through natural processes. This is not a valid argument for allowing species to become extinct; rather, it indicates the importance of preserving the species that remain (Hoban and Brooks 1987).

People have led species to the point of extinction by two principal methods. The most obvious method is unrestrained killing, which exterminated the great auk and the dodo, whose lack of fear made them easy prey for sailors. Habitat deprivation has now become the more prevalent means of eliminating species. Loss of cover, habitat, forage, or prey will destroy viable breeding populations of animals, as will overhunting. Run-ins with vehicles also have caused the loss of many animals in developed countries. Loss of plant species may be caused by harvesting, clearing, or converting forest lands.

Efforts were made at the end of the nineteenth century to save some of the nation's most beautiful, useful, or historic animals. The public paid little attention to species other than egrets, herons, bison, or antelope, even though the extinction of the passenger pigeon saddened many. Extinction became an important issue after World War II when economic development flourished, accompanied by habitat destruction. The public's new appreciation of ecosystems made people want to save all species as parts of a whole, arguing that they all have a place and purpose on earth. These ideals were enthusiastically written into law as Congress passed endangered species acts in 1966, 1969, and 1973 (Dunlap 1988).

Much has changed since the initial policy efforts to prevent premature extinction in 1966, when a small protection program was envisioned at a time when extinction was neither a pressing scientific problem nor a hot political issue as it was at the beginning of the 1990s. Now the pace of extinction throughout the world has led some scientists to fear the onset of an irreversible environmental catastrophe. Several agencies share the responsibility for implementing the U.S. policy, and they must cope with inadequate financial support, poor organizational resources, uncertain public support, and, frequently, political antagonism and interference. The protection of biological diversity—the actual purpose of the Endangered Species Act—raises fascinating economic, political, and institutional problems that will not soon fade (Tobin 1990).

ENDANGERED SPECIES ACT

The Endangered Species Act (ESA) of 1973 is at the cutting edge of not only wildlife law, but also public natural resources law in general. The presence of a threatened or endangered species on federal lands drastically affects management. Protection provisions in the ESA have provided courts with grounds to enjoin proposed dams, roads, hunting regulations, and timber harvesting plans (Coggins 1991a,b). The spotted owl controversy in the Pacific Northwest and the litigation involving the protection of the red-cockaded woodpecker in the South challenge traditional timber management practices and timber sales in the national forests.

The purpose of the ESA is a compelling statement of national policy:

The Congress finds and declares that the United States has pledged itself as a sovereign state in the international community to conserve to the extent practicable the various species of fish or wildlife or plants facing extinction [ESA section 2(a)(4)].

The purposes…are to provide a means whereby the ecosystems upon which endangered species…depend may be conserved, to provide a program for the conservation of such endangered species [ESA section 2(b)].

For some, perhaps these statements of policy and purpose are adequate to understand what the ESA is all about. As a nation we are committed to protecting from extinction what remains of our plant and animal heritage. But in practice, we seem to be trying to do more than protect species from extinction. Biologists have effectively argued that to protect a species, we must conserve its genetic diversity by protecting subspecies or even distinct individual populations of species and their ecosystems. And the ESA language says that is the way it shall be. In effect, we have made an ethical commitment to protecting aspects of the natural environment that could be eradicated, and doing so everywhere that a federal agency says we should. Why? Because the law says so? Just exactly what does the law say?

Look first at the objective or purpose of the ESA. Tobin (1990, p. 228) described it unambiguously: "All of the effort associated with the implementation of the Endangered Species Act is ultimately directed at a single goal—the recovery of endangered species to the point where their continued existence is no longer in doubt." Tobin's (1990, p. 235) interpretation of the FWS's stated ESA objective seemed quite clear: "The Service's goal is to improve the status of endangered or threatened species so that they can be delisted."

These simply stated objectives depend entirely upon how an endangered species is identified and designated for listing. The listing decision is therefore very important because it sets the protection mandates of the ESA in motion. Yet the listing process and the discretion it allows agencies seem to be taken for granted, perhaps because the listing process defies simple explanation.

The ESA creates two main processes: (1) the designation of species and their critical habitat through "listing" and (2) protection. These processes are fundamental to understanding the ESA.

Listing

The ESA begins with listing—selecting species to be put on the endangered species list. As of March 1991, 360 U.S. animal species, 246 U.S. plant species, and 522 foreign species were on the list. Coggins (1991a) considers listing to be important because it triggers the four major provisions of the ESA, which are to conserve listed species, avoid jeopardization, avoid destruction of critical habitat, and avoid taking.

The first of the four provisions—conservation of listed species—requires action by federal agencies. Conservation is defined as "the use of all methods and procedures which are necessary to bring any endangered species or threatened species to the point at which the measures–are no longer necessary" [ESA section 3(3)].

Two federal agencies and their cabinet officers have the authority to list species: the U.S. Fish and Wildlife Service (FWS) under the secretary of the interior, and in the case of salmon, other anadromous fish, and most marine species, the National Marine Fisheries Service (NMFS, or "Nimfs") under the secretary of commerce. The secretaries are to make listing determinations "...solely on the basis of the best scientific and commercial data available after conducting a review of the status of the species and after taking into account those efforts, if any, being made by any state or foreign nation.... to protect such species" [ESA section 4(b)(1)(A)].

The definition of species is broad and ambiguous (Rohlf 1989): "The term 'species' includes any subspecies of fish or wildlife or plants, and any distinct population segment of any species of vertebrate fish or wildlife which interbreeds when mature" [ESA section 3(16)]. Species may be listed as endangered or threatened or both. The distinction between listing a species as endangered or threatened is subtle [ESA section 3]: An endangered species is "any species which is in danger of extinction throughout all or any significant portion of its range." A threatened species is "likely to become an endangered species within the foreseeable future." As a practical matter, the difference is that a threat-

ened species may be taken under certain circumstances that would promote conservation; an endangered species may not be taken except under very limited and explicit circumstances.

Listing involves 16 steps to be followed over a period that can take up to two years (Tobin 1990). The law defines five criteria for listing [ESA section 4(a)(1)]:

The Secretary shall...determine whether any species is an endangered species or a threatened species because of any of the following factors:

A. The present or threatened destruction, modification, or curtailment of its habitat of range.

B. Overutilization for commercial, recreational, scientific, or educational purposes.

C. Disease or predation.

D. The inadequacy of existing regulatory mechanisms.

E. Other natural or manmade factors affecting its continued existence.

There have been criticisms of the FWS implementation of the listing process in three key areas: (1) biological and nonbiological variables included in listing decisions, (2) the handling of petitions, and (3) priorities to determine which species to list first and protect with scarce resources (Tobin 1990). Actions have been taken in the past decade to remedy the situation, but listing still has its problems, as the species backlog indicates. With only 606 North American species on the list, not all those in danger of extinction are protected. The inspector general of the U.S. Department of the Interior (1991) concluded that about 600 domestic species that probably merit listing have not been listed. According to Kohm (1991a,b) the FWS has a list of roughly 3900 candidate species that possibly could be listed.

Critical Habitat

Critical habitat is to be designated when a species is listed. It is an important sounding but ambiguous concept. Yaffee (1991) identified the endangered species problem as principally a land-use one. The habitat needs of endangered species are therefore the paramount concern and source of conflict. By definition, critical habitat should play a vital role. Coggins (1991b, p. 15-25) cut through the legalese of the ESA and defined critical habitat as "the area occupied by the species at the time of listing and essential to its conservation." Only about 20 percent of the species now listed have had critical habitat designated.

The designation of critical habitat is among the most controversial aspects of FWS activities (Tobin 1990). Although Congress made critical habitat an important feature of species protection, agency regulations have reduced its significance. As Rohlf (1989, p. 152) put it, "Since a jeopardy finding alone is sufficient to constitute a section 7 violation, the ESA's critical habitat mandate, as interpreted by the regulations, adds nothing to Section 7's substantiative protection and is therefore simply redundant."

Nevertheless, critical habitat designation is called for by the ESA, and nonbiological factors, including economics, are to be used in determining critical habitat. From 1978 to 1982 the listing decision included the designation of critical habitat, which effectively forced economic considerations into the listing decision. Critical habitat is to be designated "after taking into consideration the economic impact, and any other relevant impact, of specifying any particular area as critical habitat" [ESA section 4(b)(2)]. Only 65 new species were listed during that four-year period. Amendments were made to the ESA in 1982 to delink listing and critical habitat designation. The amendments stated that listing decisions will be based "solely on the basis of the best scientific and commercial data available" [ESA section 4(b)(1)(A)]. The Senate and House conference report clarified that to mean that economic considerations would have no relevance in determining the status of species and that economic analysis would not be applied to any phase of the listing process (Tobin 1990).

Since 1982 the designation of critical habitat has been treated as optional at the time of listing (Coggins 1991b, Rohlf 1991). A recent ruling makes the optimal feature questionable. On a motion filed by the Sierra Club Legal Defense Fund, Federal District Judge Thomas Zilly ruled on February 26, 1991, that the FWS should have designated critical habitat when it listed the northern spotted owl as threatened in June 1990 (Gray 1991).

Because the social and economic impacts of species protection are for the most part predictable, social uncertainty could be reduced by including at the time of listing, an analysis of economic and social impacts along with the biological decree for species protection, the way things were done between 1978 and 1982. This seems to be more consistent with the National Environmental Policy Act (NEPA) of 1969—the cornerstone of all environmental laws—than the way things are done now. According to Reed and Drabelle (1984), the Department of the Interior has never found that listing a species is a major federal action, and the endangered species program as a whole is considered to comply with NEPA because it "almost by definition improves the status of listed species and thus enhances the natural environment" (Reed and Drabelle 1984, p. 99). Almost forgotten, it seems, is that NEPA also requires economic and social impact analysis.

Because of the ambiguous way critical habitat is used in ESA protection processes, the designation of critical habitat is a shaky foundation upon which to build an argument for better protection of species. That is unfortunate, because all species depend on their habitat.

Protection

Once a species has been listed, agencies must do whatever they can to see that the species will be delisted sometime in the future. Part of that mandate is to protect listed species and their habitat, critical or otherwise. Protection involves several things, all intended to promote the conservation of listed species. Coggins (1991b) describes the ESA as having three main prohibitions and requiring consultation among agencies. The prohibitions and consultations are briefly covered in this section. In addition, the ESA requires agencies to draft regulations for implementing the ESA and to develop recovery plans for listed species.

Two of the three prohibitions apply to individuals. First, trade in endangered species is prohibited without a permit, grantable only in a few narrow situations. Second, no person may take an endangered species. *Taking* can be defined very broadly—far beyond merely killing an animal or plant, (Coggins 1991b), and it has a double meaning in the ESA context (see Rolston 1991). The ESA definition does not refer to the broader issue of taking private property rights but instead, "The term 'take' means to harass, harm, pursue, hunt, shoot, wound, kill, trap, capture, or collect, or to attempt to engage in any such conduct" [ESA section 3(19)]. Furthermore, the FWS defined *harm* to include "an act which actually kills or injures wildlife [including] significant habitat modification or degradation where it actually kills or injures wildlife by significantly impairing essential behavior patterns, including breeding, feeding, or sheltering" [50 C.F.R. section 17.3 (1986)]. A forest products industry trade association is challenging the definition of harm as it pertains to habitat modification, asserting that the FWS acted arbitrarily (Murray 1991).

The third key prohibition is that a federal agency may not act unless it ensures that its action will neither jeopardize a species nor adversely affect the designated critical habitat of the species (Coggins 1991b, ESA section 7[a][2]). Definitions of these terms and court interpretations are the teeth of the ESA (see Coggins 1991b, Rohlf 1989). *Jeopardize* has been defined by the FWS to mean "to engage in an action that reasonably may be expected, directly or indirectly, to reduce the reproduction, numbers, or distribution of the species" [50 C.F.R. section 402.02 (1986)].

The failure to designate critical habitat does not in any way diminish the protection available to listed species. A jeopardy opinion that a proposed activity might destroy or adversely modify habitat may be issued regardless of whether or not the activity is to take place within designated critical habitat (Tobin

1990). For example, consider a case involving a possible conflict between the gray wolf and a proposed road in Idaho's Nez Perce National Forest. No critical habitat has been designated for the gray wolf. An appellate court ruled that the U.S. Forest Service failed to perform the required consultation procedure with the FWS (*Thomas* v. *Peterson* 753 F.2d 754 [1985]), even though no proof was offered that wolves actually inhabited the area (Coggins and Wilkinson 1987). Protection is extended to endangered species where they roam, and wherever a federal agency thinks they might roam.

Interagency consultation is the mechanism for implementing the prohibition in ESA section 7 against jeopardizing a species or its habitat (Yaffee 1991). The teeth of the ESA are used to chew on agency actions in the required consultation process. Agencies planning actions in an area used by an endangered species must consult with either the FWS or NMFS (Coggins 1991b, Kohm 1991b). Coggins (1991b, p. 15-33, 15-34) described the process concisely:

If a proposed activity will take place in an area harboring, or possibly harboring, a listed species, the responsible agency must provide the Interior [or Commerce] Secretary with the best available data in a "biological assessment." The FWS [or NMFS] then consults with the agency in forming biological opinions about the extent of probable harm to the species. New information at subsequent stages of the proceedings may trigger a requirement to reinitiate consultation within a reasonable time. The action agency cannot make "irreversible or irretrievable commitments or resources" during the consultation process. If the FWS [or NMFS] concludes that the project will jeopardize a species or harm its habitat, the project must be modified to avoid such harm. If modification is infeasible or futile, the project cannot proceed unless the "God Committee" decides that the national interest in project completion outweighs the species' welfare.

Violation of the Endangered Species Act may be prosecuted as a criminal activity. Individulas may be prosecuted for trading in endangered species without a permit or for taking an endangered species or its habitat on public or private land. A precedent-setting enforcement action occurred in 1992. Three civilian employees of the army, who were responsible for forestry and environmental protection, were indicted in January 1992 by a federal grand jury. They were charged with conspiracy to violate the ESA by allegedly allowing timber harvests that harmed the red-cockaded woodpecker (RCW) population on the military reservation. The indictment alleges that the defendants concealed the known presence of RCW cavity trees and colonies and submitted false documents and maps, therby permitting cavity trees to be destroyed and RCW colonies to be left without sufficient habitat. This resulted in a take of the RCW by disturbing natural behavior patterns, including breeding, feeding, and sheltering, such that RCWs were injured and died (Rolston 1992).

The charges in the RCW case against the three defendants—who are required to bear their own defense costs—were brought by the U.S. Fish and Wildlife Service. It is believed they were prompted by the threat of a lawsuit by Sierra/Audubon/Wilderness groups over RCW mismanagement at Fort Benning. The case has potential for similar enforcement of takings cases on private land, and for future criminal prosecution of professional foresters and wildlife management prescriptions, investigation about damage to RCW populations, and application of the ESA. The trial was scheduled for the fall of 1992; whatever the results the case will be watched closely by resource professionals and environmentalists.

ILLUSTRATION: THE SNAIL DARTER AND THE DAM

The ESA is a policy for protecting biological diversity that conflicts with economic reality and has produced social uncertainty. Looking back to the 1970s, Greenwalt (1991, p. 32) said:

During rounds of congressional hearings, many legislators came forward to say that they did not know this new act would protect everything; they thought they were voting for legislation to protect eagles, bears, and whooping cranes. They professed not to understand at the time of passage that this law might raise questions about irrigation projects, timber harvests, the dredging of ports, or the generation of electricity.

The ESA has not combined the disciplines of biology and law very well (Rohlf 1991). Nor has it smoothly blended biology with economics. As written in 1973, the ESA focused only on biological concerns, expressly and purposely ignoring economics. Things have changed since then.

In 1978 the strictly biological focus of the ESA changed because of the snail darter, the first species to confront economic development in a big way. The 1975 listing of the snail darter as an endangered species threatened to call a halt to the Tellico Dam, a Tennessee Valley Authority hydroelectric project that was nearing completion when this previously unknown three-inch fish was discovered in the Little Tennessee River. The case was heard by the Supreme Court, which said:

It may seem curious to some that the survival of a relatively small number of three-inch fish among the countless millions of species extant would require the permanent halting of a virtually completed dam for which Congress has expended more than $100 million...We conclude, however, that the explicit provision of the Endangered Species Act requires precisely that result.

Congress intended endangered species to be afforded the highest of priorities...The plain intent of Congress in enacting this statute was to halt and reverse the trend toward species extinction, *whatever the cost.* (*Tennessee Valley Authority* v. *Hill*, 437 U.S. 153, 174, 184, [1978]; emphasis added)

The Court's opinion is cited today to mean that endangered species conservation excludes economics (see Rolston 1991). Such an argument, however, ignores subsequent amendments that Congress made to incorporate economics in the ESA. Because of the

Court's ruling on the snail darter, the ESA was amended in 1978, 1979, and 1982.

Another three-inch fish has been proposed for listing and could take a place next to the snail darter and spotted owl high up on the list of species that conflict with development activities. On September 27, 1991, the FWS proposed listing the delta smelt. This fish inhabits brackish water in the Sacramento River estuary in San Francisco Bay. Actions to protect the delta smelt may change the irrigation regime in one of the nation's most productive agricultural areas. In 1992 several species of salmon were listed, affecting more areas in the Pacific Northwest.

Economics and the ESA

As a direct result of the snail darter case, the ESA now includes economic concerns, but until the spotted owl listing those provisions had not been tested. Amendments to the ESA in 1978 guaranteed that economic issues are considered in the designation of critical habitat after a species has been listed. But as mentioned earlier, critical habitat is not always designated. Even so, economics are to be considered in the development and implementation of recovery plans: "The Secretary, in developing and implementing recovery plans, shall to the maximum extent practicable incorporate in each plan estimates of the time required and the cost to carry out those measures needed to achieve the plan's goal" [ESA section 4(f)(1)(B)]. Furthermore, as the ESA was amended in 1988, the FWS is to report annually on a species-by-species basis all federal expenditures and grants to states for the conservation of species under the act (ESA section 18).

The FWS had a total budget of $905 million in fiscal year 1990, of which it spent $35 million (3.9 percent) on endangered species programs. Twelve other federal agencies spent $61 million, and states were allocated $6 million in federal grant funds, for a total of $102.3 million reported spent for the conservation of 477 listed species. At $9.7 million, the northern spotted owl accounted for more expenditures than any other species. These

cost figures do not include law enforcement, consultation, or recovery coordination (U.S. FWS 1991).

The God Committee

Economics may be considered because the 1978 amendments created a high-level committee with the authority to decide if a particular species could be exempted from the ESA. Officially called the Endangered Species Committee, it is more widely known as the God Committee or God Squad: "The Committee shall review any application submitted to it pursuant to this section and determine...whether or not to grant an exemption from the requirements [of the Act]" [ESA section 7(e)]. The God Committee may be convened when there is an irreconcilable conflict between a development project and species conservation needs. The committee includes the chairperson of the Council of Economic Advisors and at least six others: the secretaries of agriculture, the army, and the interior (who chairs the committee); and the administrators of the Environmental Protection Agency and the National Oceanic and Atmospheric Administration; also, the president appoints one individual from each affected state.

The God Committee might have been feared by environmentalists when first authorized in 1978, but it has proved to be an essential political pressure valve (Yaffee 1991). Until now the committee has been convened only twice, both times in response to the 1978 ESA amendment creating the committee. Those two cases were the snail darter/Tellico Dam conflict in Tennessee and the less well known whooping crane/Grayrock Dam conflict in Wyoming. In the snail darter case, the committee unanimously concluded that reasonable alternatives to the Tellico Dam existed and did not exempt the project from the ESA. Sen. Howard Baker (R-TN) pushed legislation through Congress to build the dam anyway; President Carter disregarded the advice of Secretary of the Interior Cecil Andrus and signed the bill. Fish were transplanted above the dam before it was completed and established themselves successfully there. Later, biological surveys discovered additional snail darter populations in other streams and the species was downlisted from endangered to threatened status in 1984. In the whooping crane case, the committee voted to exempt the project from the ESA, but only because the applicants had agreed to alter the project to mitigate its harmful effects and to establish a $7.5 million trust fund to maintain and enhance whooping crane habitat (Ono, Williams, and Wagner 1983, Reed and Drabelle 1984, Tobin 1990, Yaffee 1991).

With the support of the Bush administration, Republican Sen. Bob Packwood of Oregon tried unsuccessfully to amend the ESA in 1990 to make it easier to convene the God Committee so it could address the spotted owl case. It is not clear whether the committee could deal effectively with the entire spotted owl problem because of the large geographic scope of spotted owl habitat and the remedy of modified timber harvest levels that are involved, rather than a specific development project such as a dam. Nevertheless, in September 1991, the director of the Bureau of Land Management requested that the committee be convened because of the postponement and likely cancellation of 44 planned timber sales on 4570 acres of BLM lands in Oregon. In October 1991 the Secretary of the Interior Manuel Lujan, Jr., said he reluctantly would convene the God Squad. Critics stated that the move by Lujan was merely an effort by the Bush administration to undermine federal environmental laws.

Lujan, who was responsible for serving as the chair of the Cabinet-level committee, had 140 days to hold a hearing and examine evidence. He then had 30 days to report to the committee and 30 days to deny or approve the BLM request for an exemption to the ESA. However, the waiver would apply only to the 4570 acres requested by the BLM director, not to the millions of acres Northwest forests inhabited by the spotted owl. The God squad decision, released in May 1992, was voted to exempt 13 of 44 sales, but the BLM was not to offer any new sales until it developed a credible recovery strategy for the owl.

In 1992, however, a federal district court judge enjoined all of the BLM's timber sales on the O & C lands in Orgeon, until such time as BLM could complete an acceptable Environmental Impact Statement for the sales. This decision shut down the BLM timber sale for the region, including 44 sales that the God Squad was reviewing, until at least the spring of 1993. Thus the "God Squad" decision regarding permissible sales was largely symbolic, regardless of its outcome.

SOCIAL AND POLITICAL REALITIES

Regarding the ESA, Tobin (1990, p. ix) observed that "most social scientists are consistent in their total neglect of this topic." Why is this so? That is a good question, given that a conservation biologist (Soule 1985, p. 727) recognized "the dependence of the biological sciences on social science disciplines."

There are two obvious reasons why up until now the protection of biological diversity has been left to biologists. First, except for localized cases of conflict with economic development—including the snail darter, orange-footed pearly mussel, Hawaiian palila, and many others–the concept of species protection met with either general acceptance or indifference. Recently, interest groups and judges have forced the issue of listing and protecting species, raising substantial economic and social issues that go far beyond local impacts and affect multistate regions and major industries. Only now are we beginning to see what the costs of protecting biological diversity entail, and policymakers face two questions: Is it worth it? and Where do we draw the line? The ESA can severely limit economic development. It allows citizens to file petitions to protect species—and the ecosystems upon which they depend—for any conceivable reason. It allows biologists a great deal of latitude in determining what population segments of what species need to be protected. It produces years of uncertainty while the policy process tries to summon a response.

Second, no one knows what *biodiversity* means. Although the definition in the previous section is understandable, it is difficult for many to comprehend the importance of conservation biology. Recent developments with spotted owls and other species proposed for listing have many people wondering about the purposes and costs of species protection. As the ESA is about to enter the political arena once again, Tobin's (1990) basic observations about political reality are worth remembering.

Political systems place the burden of proof on those who want to change the status quo. Those favoring change must produce persuasive... evidence that a problem exists,... especially when change threatens the well-being of those who profit from the status quo (p. 19).

A sense of urgency about extinction... is not yet widely shared in the political community or among the general public... [S]cientists have not communicated successfully the adverse effects of past extinctions,... and they are woefully uncertain of the likely consequences of projected extinctions... [I]t is difficult to communicate whatever information is available... [because] the issues are as complex and little understood as any modern society has ever faced (p. 19).

[S]cientists and conservationists have been warning of an impending crisis of biological diversity for at least twenty years... [W]hen nothing seems to happen, scientists lose their credibility and are labeled as eccentric, publicity-seeking doomsayers (p. 20).

[T]he conclusion [is] that endangered species do not now possess the attractive features to make them prime candidates for sustained political attention,... [and] needs for resources, authority, and political capital may quickly exceed the political system's desire, capacity, and willingness to provide them (p. 25–26).

The social perspective has the last word here, as it should in public policy matters. Lee's (1991) comments summarized the importance of the social perspective.

Concerned citizens, especially in a democracy, will not accept resource management decisions that disrupt their way of life, including their livelihood, recreation pursuits, and sense of commu-

nity. This social scientific fact is often overlooked by proponents for preserving biological legacies, just as it was overlooked by proponents for maximizing the economic value of forests. Biological legacies cannot be maintained unless social and cultural legacies are also maintained (p. 14).

ESA REAUTHORIZATION

The Endangered Species Act was due for reauthorization in 1992, although passage of a bill seemed unlikely. Various bills were introduced to reauthorize the law, and the legislative debates promised to be acrimonious. Environmentalists rallied behind bills that would strengthen various components of the law, including:

- Giving federal officials a deadline to develop and implement recovery plans for ecosystems containing threatened, endangered, or candidate species.

- Encouraging officials to develop conservation plans for whole ecosystems instead of single species.

- Expanding citizens' rights to file lawsuits against violators of the ESA in emergency situations.

- Increasing funding levels for chronically underfunded federal endangered species programs.

- Initiating a revolving fund to help communities create plans to balance local development needs with habitat protection for endangered species.

Opponents of the ESA oppose its costs, infringements on private property rights, and extension of protection to a rapidly expanding list of species and habitats. They observe that not all species can be protected, or no lands will be left for development and production. Furthermore, they contend that threats of more protection or listing are counterproductive because they prompt private landowners to hastily and needlessly destroy habitat, cut trees, or develop sites to avoid regulatory takings. The opponents of strengthening ESA include developers, farmers, the forest products industry, western water districts, public utilities, and even Native Americans. They want the ESA reauthorization to have greater recognition of economic costs and private property rights—a platform of the wise use movement.

The debates over the ESA have revealed interesting information. As mentioned, Section 7 of the ESA requires federal development agencies to consult with the FWS or National Marine Fisheries Service (NMFS) before proceeding with projects that may affect threatened or endangered species or their habitats. The provision has been accused of derailing hundreds of needed federal projects in the United States. A study by the World Wildlife Fund found that from 1979 through 1986, the FWS conducted 71,650 informal and 2000 formal Section 7 consultations. Of those, only 18 resulted in projects being terminated. NMFS conducted 788 informal and 248 formal consultations during the period; only one project was blocked. The WWF study concluded that irreconcilable conflicts occurred rarely under Section 7 consultation. The vast majority of federal consultataions led to successful complction of projects while accommodating the needs of endangered and threatened species (Williamson 1992).

On the other hand, there are individuals who, due to ESA habitat protection, have lost part or most of the income they anticipated. Much of this evidence is anecdotal rather than thoroughly compiled, but it is still compelling. Landowners in Florida have reportedly razed oak habitat to avoid requirements to protect the blue and bray scrub jay; California residents have been forced to leave trees to protect endangered animals; and Maryland landowners have been prohibited from harvesting timber to protect endangered plants. The potential for large or total timber losses on private lands, perhaps to poor or elderly individuals, or perhaps loss of multimillion dollar development projects is used as evidence that the ESA needs a better methods of dealing with economic considerations short of convening the God Squad. The ESA reauthorization debates will be lively in 1992 and probably beyond.

SUMMARY

Throughout most of colonial times and the first century of U. S. history, wildlife was exploited by killing it for food, furs, and fun. The conservtion movement at the end of the nineteenth century began efforts to protect wildlife from humans by enacting and enforcing state and federal laws. In general, wildlife in the United States has belonged to the government—usually to the states for game animals or to the federal government for migratory species. The principal objectives of wildlife management include preservation of species and ecosystems, nongame protection, and hunting, which can be funded in various ways. Government control of hunted populations was the first wildlife policy. Increasing populations and managing habitat became the objectives of wildlife management in the mid-1900s, after the profession of wildlife management was fostered by Aldo Leopold. Nongame concerns have become more important during the 1980s, but they still comprise a modest share of state and federal wildlife program budgets.

A host of federal laws have been enacted to protect wildlife and their habitat. Waterfowl-related laws regulate hunting and garner revenues for habitat acquistion. Federal lands management laws and federal agencey mandates help protect wildlife species and habitat on federal lands. State laws regulate hunting and help manage public and private lands. Perhaps most important, the Endangered Species Act makes it illegal to kill threatened or endangered species or destroy their habitat on public or private land. The complex web of federal and state laws helps protect wildlife from ever-increasing population and commercial pressures. But they often are the center of debates about the values of wildlife versus the values of developed human uses, providing the basis for evolving public policy.

LITERATURE CITED

Allen, Durward L. 1973. Report of the Committee on North American Wildlife Policy.

Transactions of the North American Wildlife and Natural Resources Conference 38: 152–181.

Bavin, Clark R. 1978. Wildlife law enforcement. Pp. 350–364 in Howard P. Brokaw, (ed.), Wildlife and America. Council on Environmental Quality. Washington, DC.

Bean, Michael J. 1977. The Evolution of National Wildlife Law. Prepared for the Council on Environmental Quality. U.S. Government Printing Office. Washington, DC. 485 pp.

Bean, Michael J. 1978. Federal wildlife law. Pp. 279–289 in Howard P. Brokaw (ed.), Wildlife and America. Council on Environmental Quality, Washington, DC.

Bean, Michael J. 1983. The Evolution of National Wildlife Law. Praeger. New York. 449 pp.

Cart, Theodore Whaley. 1973. The Lacey Act: America's first nationwide wildlife statute. *Forest History* 17 (October): 4–13.

Chandler, William H. 1986. State wildlife enforcement. Pp. 593–628 in Audubon Wildlife Report, 1986. The National Aubudon Society. New York.

Coggins, George Cameron. 1991a. Snail darters and pork barrels revisited: Reflections on endangered species and land use in America. Pp. 62–74 in Kathryn A. Kohm, (ed.), Balancing on the Brink of Extinction: The Endangered Species Act and Lessons for the Future. Island Press. Washington, DC.

Coggins, George Cameron. 1991b. Public natural resources law. (Release #2, 6/91) Clark Boardman. New York. Looseleaf

Coggins, George Cameron, and Charles F. Wilkinson. 1987. Federal Public Land and Resources Law, 2nd ed. Foundation Press. Mineola, NY. 1066 pp.

Dana, Samuel T., and Sally K. Fairfax. 1980. Forest and Range Policy, 2nd ed. McGraw-Hill. New York. 458 pp.

Davis, Larry S., and Frederic H. Wagner. 1982. Forest wildlife. Chapter 20 in William A. Duerr et al., (eds.), Forest Resource Management: Decision-making Principles and Cases. Oregon State University Bookstores. Corvallis, OR. 612 pp.

Dunlap, Thomas R. 1988. Saving America's Wildlife. Princeton University Press. Princeton, NJ. 222 pp.

Ernst, John P. 1991. Federalism and the act. Pp. 98–113 in Kathryn A. Kohm (ed.), Balancing on the Brink of Extinction: The Endangered Species Act and Lessons for the Future. Island Press. Washington, DC.

Flader, Susan. 1974. Thinking like a Mountain: Aldo Leopold and the evolution of an Ecological Attitude Toward Deer, Wolves and Forests. University of Nebraska Press. Lincoln. 284 pp.

Gottschalk, John S. 1978. The state–federal partnership in wildlife conservation. Pp. 290–301 in Howard P. Brokaw, (ed.), Wildlife and America. Council on Environmental Quality. Washington, DC.

Gray, Gerald J., (ed.). 1991, May 23. F&WS proposes critical habitat for the spotted owl. American Forestry Association, Resource Hotline. Washington, DC.

Greenwalt, Lynn A. 1991. The power and potential of the act. Pp. 31–36 in Kathryn A. Kohm, (ed.), Balancing on the Brink of Extinction: The Endangered Species Act and Lessons for the Future. Island Press. Washington, DC.

Hoban, Thomas M., and Richard O. Brooks. 1987. Green Justice: The Environment and the Courts. Westview Press. Boulder, CO. 250 pp.

Keiter, Robert B. 1990. NEPA and the emerging concept of ecosystem management on the public lands. *Land and Water Law Review* 25(1):43–60.

Klein, David. 1973. The ethics of hunting and the anti-hunting movement. *Transactions of the North American Wildlife and Natural Resources Conference* 38:256–266.

Kohm, Kathryn A. 1991a. Introduction. Pp. 1–9 in Kathryn A. Kohm, (ed.), Balancing on the Brink of Extinction: The Endangered Species Act and Lessons for the Future. Island Press. Washington, DC.

Kohm, Kathryn A. 1991b. The act's history and framework. Pp. 10–22 in Kathryn A. Kohm (ed.), Balancing on the Brink of Extinction: The Endangered Species Act and Lessons for the Future. Island Press. Washington, DC.

Lawren, Bill. 1989. The high cost of neglecting wildlife. *National Wildlife* 27(3):4-8.

Lee, Robert G. 1991. Biological legacies are only part of the answer. *Forest Perspectives* 1(3):13–14.

Leopold, Aldo. 1930. Report to the American game conference on an American game policy. Pp. 284–309 in 17th American Game Conference Transactions.

Leopold, Aldo. 1933. Game management. Scribners, New York, NY. 482 pp.

Leopold, Aldo. 1949. A Sand County Almanac, and sketches Here and There. Oxford University Press. New York, NY. 226 pp.

Leopold, A. Starker. 1978. Wildlife and forest practice. Pp. 108–120 in Howard P. Brokaw, (ed.), Wildlife and America. Council on Environmental Quality. Washington, DC. 532 pp.

Lund, Thomas A. 1980. American Wildlife Law. University of California Press. Berkeley. 179 pp.

Mantell, Michael, Phyllis Myers, and Robert B. Reed. 1988. The Land and Water Conservation Fund: Past experience, future directions. Pp. 257–281 in William J. Chandler. (ed.) Audubon Wildlife Report 1988/1989. The National Audubon Society. New York.

Meine, Curt. 1988. Aldo Leopold. University of Wisconsin Press. Madison, 638 pp.

Morse, W. B. 1984. Wildlife law enforcement, 1984. Wildlife Management Institute. Washington, DC. Unpublished manuscript.

Murray, William R. 1991. Industry's full court press. National Forest Products Association in *Focus* (September), 6 pp.

Norris, Kenneth S. 1978. Marine mammals and man. Pp. 320-338 in Howard P. Brokaw, (ed.), Wildlife and America. Council on Environmental Quality, Washington, DC.

Ono, R. Dana, James D. Williams, and Anne Wagner. 1983. Vanishing Fishes of North America. Stone Wall Press. Washington, DC. 257 pp.

Peek, James M. 1986. A Review of Wildlife Management. Prentice Hall, Englewood Cliffs, NJ. 486 pp.

Poole, Daniel A., and James B. Trefethen. 1978. Maintenance of wildlife populations. Pp. 339–349 in Howard P. Brokaw, (ed.), Wildlife and America. Council on Environmental Quality. Washington, DC.

Reed, Nathaniel P., and Dennis Drabelle. 1984. The United States Fish and Wildlife Service. Westview Press. Boulder, CO. 163 pp.

Reiger, John F. 1975. American Sportsmen and the Origins of Conservation. Winchester Press. New York. 316 pp.

Rohlf, Daniel J. 1989. The Endangered Species Act: A Guide to Its Protections and Implementation. Stanford Environmental Law Society. Stanford, CA. 207 pp.

Rohlf, Daniel J. 1991. Essay: Six biological reasons why the Endangered Species Act doesn't work—and what to do about it. *Conservation Biology* 5(3):273–282.

Rolston, Holmes, III. 1991. Life in jeopardy on private property. Pp. 43-61 in Kathryn A. Kohm, (ed.), Balancing on the brink of extinction: The Endangered Species Act and Lessons for the Future. Island Press, Washington, DC.

Rolston, Ken. 1992. A report on the federal criminal conspiracy prosecution of three civilian employees of the U.S. Army over alleged mismanagement of red-cockaded woodpecker habitat on Fort Benning. Technical Paper 92-A-7. American Pulpwood Association. Washington, DC. 18 pp. + appen.

Scheonbaum, Thomas J. 1982. Environmental Policy Law: Cases, Readings, Text. Foundation Press. Mineola, NY. 1065 pp.

Siegel, William C. 1982. Forest management and the law. Chapter 25 in William A. Duerr et al., (eds.), Forest Resource Management: Decision-making Principles and Cases. Oregon State University. Bookstores, Corvallis, OR.

Soule, Michael E. 1985. What is conservation biology? *BioScience* 35:727–734.

Swanson, Gustav A. 1978. Wildlife on the public lands. Pp. 428–441 in Howard P. Brokaw, (ed.), Wildlife and America. Council on Environmental Quality. Washington, DC.

Tober, James A. 1981. Who Owns the Wildlife? The Political Economy of Conservation in Nineteenth Century America. Greenwood Press. Westport, CT. 330 pp.

Tobin, Richard J. 1990. The Expendable Future: U.S. Politics and the Protection of Biological Diversity. Duke University Press. Durham, NC. 325 pp.

Turbak, Gary. 1989. Licking the costs of conservation. *National Wildlife* 27(1:)34–41.

U.S. Department of the Interior. 1991. Federal and state endangered species expenditures in 1990. Fish and Wildlife Service. *Endangered Species Technical Bulletin* 16(5):3.

U.S. Fish and Wildlife Service. 1991. Federal and state endangered species expenditures in fiscal year 1990. *Endangered Species Technical Bulletin* 16(5):3.

Williamson, Lonnie. 1988a. Foreword. In William J. Chandler (ed.), Audubon Wildlife Report 1988/1989. The National Audubon Society. New York.

Williamson, Lonnie. 1988b. *Outdoor News Bulletin* 42(5):1–2.

Williamson, Lonnie. 1992. *Outdoor News Bulletin* 46(3):2–3.

Yaffee, Steven L. 1991. Avoiding endangered species/development conflicts through interagency consultation. Pp. 86–97 in Kathryn A. Kohm, (ed.), Balancing on the Brink of Extinction: The Endangered Species Act and Lessons for the Future. Island Press. Washington, DC.

Chapter 16

Regulation of Forest Practices

[I]t is doubtful that federal [forest practice] regulation will ever become an issue again. State regulation will be the central theme of any future public controversy.

— Lawrence Hamilton 1965

A recent survey identified 359 local ordinances that regulate forestry activities in the eastern United States.... The statutes vary greatly in terms of their regulatory requirements, but many are highly restrictive and prescribe significant penalties.

— Clifford Hickman et al. 1991

As these quotes suggest, state and local regulation of forest practices is prevalent throughout the United States. State forest practice acts predominate in the West; local laws are more common in the East. Chapters 14 and 15 discussed the bases for public regulation of private landowners and wildlife protection programs, respectively. This chapter discusses state and local regulation of forest practices in the United States and briefly outlines the regulations that affect forest business practices. State and local regulation of private forestry, in concert with federal environmental laws, is at the center of many current public policy debates.

STATE FOREST PRACTICE LAWS

In addition to federal and state environmental laws enacted during the 1970s, several states either passed new state forest practice laws or strongly revised old ones, in order to strengthen environmental protection (Cubbage and Ellefson 1980). Comprehensive forest practice statutes passed by the western states were designed to achieve broad purposes. One purpose of an Oregon law is to assure "the continuous growing and harvesting of forest tree species to protect the soil, air, and water resources, including but not limited to streams, lakes, and estuaries." California's Z'berg-Nejedly Forest Practice Act contains similar provisions. The Washington Forest Practice Act of 1974 authorized a statewide system of regulations to achieve many objectives, including encouraging timber growth, protecting forest soils, avoiding duplication of forest practice regulations, complying with all federal and state laws regarding nonpoint source water pollution, and considering reasonable land use planning goals contained in local comprehensive plans and zoning regulations.

Some forest practice laws have attempted to consolidate all environmental regulation of forest management into one statute administered by one agency, but such laws have not been completely successful. The California requirement for Environmental Impact Statements was applied to timber harvesting operations by a 1975 court ruling (*Natural Resources Defense Council* v. *Arcata National Corporation*, 131 Cal. Rptr. 172, 59 Cal. App. 3rd 959 [1975]). After considerable debate, approval was given for the timber harvesting plans required under the forest practice law to serve as the functional equivalent of the state Environmental Impact Statements. Thus, the plans now must have considerably more detail than before.

The new laws contain detailed requirements for forest practices and also extensive administrative requirements. Depending on the state and the type of forest practice, forest landowners may (1) not be regulated at all, (2) have to comply with standards set out in the law, (3) have to notify the state forestry agency and comply with applicable standards, (4) be required to receive a permit from the forestry agency before beginning operations, or (5) have to prepare a timber harvesting plan or an Environmental Impact Statement and receive a permit. Forestry agencies may inspect a portion of any activities, or even all activities, before, during, and after the forestry operation. For example, in the state of Washington, the Department of Ecology may inspect operations to ensure that water quality is maintained.

Few comprehensive state forest practice laws have been enacted in the eastern United States. Most eastern statutes are for fire control; some include seed tree laws. However, almost all forested states have developed and promoted voluntary best management practices in an attempt to meet the area-wide planning requirements of Section 208 of FWPCA. The BMP guidelines often contain provisions regarding stream protection, logging practices near waterways, and herbicide applications that are similar to those found in the western statutes. In addition, some eastern states have passed specific laws governing certain of these practices. In the early 1990s at least 10 additional states had at least considered state forest practice acts in some fashion.

Table 16-1 summarizes the chronology for states' enactment of some type of forest practices legislation from 1903 to 1992. Much of the early legislation was either voluntary or required that a minimum number of seed trees be left on a site, but it was poorly enforced. Most of the modern laws enacted or revised since 1970 include stricter environmental protection measures and have been reasonably well implemented. Not all of these laws are comprehensive state forest practice laws per se, but each regulates forest pratices such as timber harvesting, regeneration, or use of Best Management Practices (BMPs) in some manner.

Older Laws

Most pre-1969 forest practice laws approached regulation in a narrow sense, addressing only timber harvesting practices. Their stated purpose was primarily to ensure future productivity of forest lands and to prevent forest devastation. Usually the laws mandated that a specific number of desirable trees be left for regeneration purposes— consequently, they were labeled "seed tree laws" (Society of American Foresters 1956). Some of the older forest practice laws are still in effect: Some have been slightly modified; seven have been strongly revised or superseded; and one has been repealed.

The Louisiana Turpentine Seed Tree Law, enacted in 1922, was the first legislation in the East that regulated forest cutting practices. The law was very limited in scope, aimed primarily at preserving a minimum number of pine trees as a seed source for regeneration of stands used for turpentine manufacture. The still-existing law has never been widely used or enforced, but it was the precursor of legislation enacted in the South and East in the 1940s.

TABLE 16-1. Chronology of State Forest Practices Legislation

State	Initial Enactment	New Laws or Major Revisions
Nevada	1903	1955, 1971
Louisiana	1922	
Idaho	1937	1974, 1986
New Mexico	1939	
Oregon	1941	1971, 1987, 1991
Florida	1943	
Massachusetts	1943	1982
Minnesota	1943	repealed 1967
Mississippi	1944	
California	1945	1973, 1991
Missouri	1945	
Vermont	1945	
Washington	1945	1974
New York	1946	
New Hampshire	1949	
Virginia	1950	
Maine (zoning)	1969	
Maryland	1977	
Alaska	1978	1990
Maine (forestry)	1989	
Connecticut	1991	
West Virginia	1992	

In response to widespread demand for federal regulation of private forestry in the 1930s and 1940s, ten states in the East and five in the West sought to preempt federal legislation by enacting forest practice laws of their own during the 1940s. These statutes were a response to the perceived threat of timber shortages, so most requirements pertained to ensuring adequate regeneration after harvest. Most eastern laws remain on the books; all the western laws have been superseded and/or strengthened.

The impact of these initial laws in the East was generally mild. Statutes ranged from mere exhortation to modest requirements for leaving seed trees, and—unlike in the three West Coast of California, Orgeon, and Washington—enforcement was minimal. Florida had a voluntary law, under which landowners could designate trees they desired to be saved, but there is no evidence

that it was used. Maryland established a statutory framework that allowed district forest practice boards to adopt mandatory forest practice guidelines for all landowners and operators. The boards, however, were strictly advisory. They suggested, but did not require, desirable forest practices. (Maryland now does require timber harvesting plans in every county, however, under a separate law.) New York and Vermont legislated some moderately detailed harvest and seed tree guidelines that still exist, but the statutes are voluntary and carry no penalties for noncompliance. New Hampshire regulates cutting practices and waste disposal near highways and waters and also requires timber operators to obtain a permit before altering the shape of the land, such as by building ski trails or log roads. Missouri's law, still on the books, uses tax incentives as an inducement for voluntary participation.

In each of these latter four states, technical forestry advice was or is available from the state in return for landowner participation.

The seed tree laws enacted in Massachusetts (1943), Minnesota (1943), Mississippi (1944), and Virginia (1950) included specific requirements for the size, species, and number of trees that were to be left per acre after a harvest cut. All carried nominal penalties for noncompliance, but none was enforced with vigor. Minnesota required leaving most trees less than 10 inches in diameter in order to provide seed, but the statute was ignored. A review of forestry legislation in Minnesota led to repeal of the law in 1967 because its management prescriptions were considered unrealistic given the prevalence of modern practices such as thinning and planting. Mississippi requires the leaving of pine seed trees after harvest, but enforcement was delegated to the county sheriffs and was nonexistent. In the 1990s some state environmental groups did seek enforcement of the act. Virginia's seed tree law, which requires leaving two 14-inch yellow poplar trees and eight 14-inch or greater pine trees per acre on harvest sites where these species predominate, has been the most consistently enforced. The law is still used and requires landowners to leave the seed trees or, alternately, to enter into a regeneration contract with the state in which they guarantee that the harvested land will be artificially regenerated. Maryland passed a well-enforced seed tree law in 1977 modeled after the Virginia law. The older laws, passed between 1943 and 1950, provided the basis for the more rigorous ones enacted in the 1970s.

MODERN LAWS

Since 1969 many states have substantially revised or replaced their old forest practice laws, or enacted new ones (see Table 16-1). Some states have revised their forest practices legislation more than once. A brief discussion of the general components of these major acts follows. More details can be obtained from Cubbage

and Ellefson (1980), Ellefson and Cubbage (1980), Henly and Ellefson (1986), Cubbage and Siegel (1988), and other references cited in this chapter.

The modern laws generally contain a statement of purpose, means of administration, specifications of owners and actions governed, authority to correct violations or impose penalties, and type of forest practices regulated. The degree of strictness in these regulations affects how well the environment is protected, how much government programs cost, and the expenses that private landowners must bear. The steadily increasing efforts to control nonpoint source water pollution under Section 208/319 of the Clean Water Act have prompted some states to enact or to consider forest practices legislation. States with forest practice laws often consider revisions; states considering new laws must decide what components to include. Debates over protection, strictness, and cost form the crux of forest practice regulatory policy. Thus a discussion of the possible components in these laws follows.

Purpose

Modern forest practice laws such as those enacted in California, Oregon, and Washington usually include a purpose or policy statement decreed by the state legislature. Most laws are aimed at protecting environmental quality and ensuring continuous productivity of forest lands. Most regulate forestry activities so as to protect water, wildlife, fisheries, soil productivity, recreation, and aesthetics. Some laws explicitly recognize the economic contribution of timber harvesting to the economy. Massachusetts, Nevada, and California laws primarily regulate timber harvesting and reforestation, whereas laws in Oregon, Idaho, and Washington regulate virtually all forest management activities. New Hampshire does not have a comprehensive state forest practice, but many forest practices are regulated.

Not all statements of policy or purpose actually can be fulfilled by regulations contained in the laws. The California law, for example, declares numerous broad environmental protection goals but emphasizes only timber harvesting activities. The Washington law lists several goals, not all of which are effected by the law. For example, one of its objectives is to eliminate unnecessary duplication of forest practices regulation, but the law fails to supersede most existing forestry regulations or eliminate the necessity of landowners' having to deal with up to eight different agencies when performing a forest practice. Ideally, a state forest practices law should state its purpose clearly and provide the means to fulfill it within the law itself.

Administration

Forest practices regulations can be established by one of two general methods. They can be specified in the law by the state legislature, or they can be promulgated by some other official body delegated the authority to do so by an enabling law. Regulations were written directly into the law in most of the older forest practices laws. All the modern laws, except in New Hampshire, provide for some form of subsequent agency rule making. Nevada combines the two methods by having most of the regulations written into the basic law and providing for a few to be promulgated at a later date by the State Board of Forestry and Fire Control. The California law combines the two methods by providing for subsequent rule making, while specifying minimum stocking standards that later rules must meet or exceed.

The modern western state forest practice laws, except Alaska's and Idaho's, delegate the rule-making authority to an existing or newly created forest practice board. Alaska's law and several of the old forest practice laws delegated the authority to existing state agencies such as a department of natural resources or a division of forestry. So did the 1989 Maine law and 1991 Connecticut law. Idaho has an advisory board but rules are made by the state forestry agency. Rule-making boards may receive technical advice from the state division of forestry, state or regional technical advisory boards, other state agencies, and public hearings and written testimony.

A forest practices law may require compliance with standards, notifications, or permits to control forestry activities. Modern forest practice laws encompass all three. The 1969 Maine land use law covers the "Unorganized Territory" in the state that has no local government, including forest land (Pidot 1982). Similar protection of forest resources and restriction on forest practices were extended to the state's organized municipalities as well. In Maine's regulated land use zones, some activities need only comply with standards, whereas other zones require a permit before operations may begin. In organized municipalities, the Department of Environmental Protection administers laws that regulate timber harvesting to protect water resources. The 1989 Maine state forest practice law governs forestry operations throughout the state, as does the 1991 Connecticut law. Alaska, Oregon, Idaho, Maine, Connecticut, and West Virginia all require only notification before forest practices (usually harvesting) may begin. If state agencies do not respond within a set time—say 3 to 10 days—operations may begin.

The New Hampshire forestry law relies on compliance with forest practice standards except for altering land along streams or other bodies of water, which requires a permit. Washington classes operations by their potential for environmental damage. It requires compliance with standards for Class I actions, notification for Class II actions, and permits for Class III and IV operations. Massachusetts requires submission of a detailed timber harvesting plan and logging permits. By requiring timber harvesting plans prepared by a registered forester and approved by the Department of Forestry, California employs a de facto permit scheme for timber harvesting. Nevada has the strictest administrative framework, requiring timber harvesting plans and performance bonds before a logging permit will be granted.

In administering their laws, states requiring notification usually inspect a percentage of the operations to ensure compliance with the practice regulation. They most often inspect operations with the greatest potential for environmental damage. Nevada foresters inspect operations before and after harvest. In Washington and California, the state forester must inspect operations before, during, and after they begin. The state forester also must inspect operations after regeneration has been completed and may inspect at any other time deemed necessary. West Virginia may inspect harvesting operations at any time, but plans to inspect all operations after harvest.

Different government agencies may administer the law. Usually the authority is delegated to the state natural resources department or forestry division. Washington's law is administered primarily by the Department of Natural Resources, but the Department of Ecology and the pertinent county also must be consulted before operations begin. The Department of Ecology also is authorized to make field inspections to ensure adequate water quality control. Maine's forest practice law is administered by the Maine Bureau of Forestry. Three different New Hampshire agencies administer the tax provisions, water control provisions, and slash and mill waste provisions in the state.

Applicability and Exemptions

Forest practice regulations usually apply to all private landowners and operators. The West Virginia laws apply only to loggers. In addition, laws also may apply to all public, nonfederal landowners, as do the laws in Alaska, Oregon, Idaho, Maine, Nevada, Washington, Massachusetts, and California. Massachusetts, Connecticut, and West Virginia require logger registration or certification. Connecticut requires foresters to be certified; California requires plans to be prepared by registered foresters.

The degree to which state laws take precedence over local laws also is important. California allows local laws that may be stricter than the state law; Oregon's and Washington's local zoning laws must conform to their forest practice acts. Connecticut's 1991 state act allows municipalities to regulate forest practices only if their ordinance or regulation conforms with the intent of the state law—in the opinion of the commissioner of the state's Department of Environmental Protection. In

Maine, which has a strong home rule tradition, towns must consult the Department of Conservation before enacting a law but need not follow its recommendation. The precedence of state laws was one of the key issues in the three Pacific Coast states and was generally resolved in favor of state supremacy (Salazar and Cubbage 1990). The plethora of county laws, which were all different and often contradictory, was one of the main factors prompting passage of the Connecticut, Maine, and Massachusetts laws. In 1990 the three West Coast states had only 18 county laws in total; the three northeastern states with state laws had at least that many each when they enacted their state forest practice acts.

Most of the laws exempt constructing rights-of-way, firewood cutting for personal use, and harvesting of minor forest products such as fruits, nuts, and berries. Christmas tree culture and salvage of insect- and disease-damaged trees also is usually exempt. Idaho exempts land use conversion and Oregon allows it for legitimate purposes. Washington, California, and Nevada severely restrict forest conversion. Massachusetts exempts small harvests of less than 25,000 board feet or 50 cords.

Violations and Penalties

In Oregon, Washington, California, and Idaho, enforcement authority ranges from personal conferences with violators to corrective action taken by the state agency that can include placing a lien on the landowner's or timber operator's property. Citations for violations and restraining or stop work orders are the intermediate enforcement tools in the four states. Violation of the law in the states usually is a misdemeanor punishable by fines of up to $1000 or jail sentences of up to one year, or both. In addition, Washington may ban loggers from operating for up to one year after violation, and California can deny, suspend, or revoke a logging operator's license until the violation is corrected. Some loggers and landowners have been jailed for violations of the state forest practice acts in Oregon and Washington.

Nevada, New Hampshire, and Maine use fines or imprisonment as their primary enforcement tools. Fines in Nevada range up to $500 and jail sentences up to six months. Operators also may forfeit their performance bond if they do not comply. The Maine Land Use Regulation Commission may levy fines up to $500 and also can issue stop work orders and take corrective action. New Hampshire fines may range up to $1000 for disposal of waste in waters or up to $25,000 for illegally altering land near bodies of water. Fines in Massachusetts are $100 per acre of violation. Loggers must be licensed or certified in Massachusetts, Connecticut, and West Virginia; violators of the law may be punished by suspension of their licenses.

Regulated Forest Practices

A complete listing of all forest practices regulated by law would be prohibitively long and subject to change, but a description of the general categories addressed is informative. New Hampshire regulates timber harvesting and forest road construction near waters and highways in piecemeal fashion through modern regulations. Maine's land use regulations generally regulate only timber harvesting and road construction in sensitive areas such as recreation sites, steep slopes, high elevation, or near streams and lakes. West Virginia requires loggers to use BMPs during timber harvests. State forest practice laws in Massachusetts, California, Nevada, and Maine address reforestation, timber harvesting, and the concomitant transportation networks required to guarantee restocking and to protect water quality.

Oregon, Idaho, and Washington address a broad array of forest management activities including timber harvest, road construction, chemical and fertilizer use, slash management site preparation, and precommercial thinning. Massachusetts' law also incorporates wetland protection regulations into its Cutting Practices Act. Oregon revised its act in 1987 and in 1991 to provide stricter regulation of practices near riparian zones. Oregon's and Maine's forest practice regulations also mandate maximum clear-cut sizes and buffer areas around clear-cuts. Clear-cuts larger than 250 acres are permitted only upon proof of "unusual hardship or extraordinary difficulties" due to physical facts of the site or forest condition. Proposed revisions to the western laws in the 1990s considered including requirements that no more than a small percentage of any watershed could be harvested in one year, in order to protect water quality.

ILLUSTRATION: THE OREGON FOREST PRACTICE ACT

In order to provide a better overview of how state forest practices develop and evolve, a brief discussion of the Oregon Forest Practice Act follows. The process described illustrates some of the politics and compromises that are involved in enacting forest practices legislation and provides more specific examples of the regulations contained in such laws.

The Oregon Conservation Act of 1941 required landowners in the state to leave seed trees to ensure regeneration. The act was reasonably well enforced throughout the 1950s and 1960s. However, public concerns about the environment and forestry led to the establishment of a special forest practices study committee, which proposed a new state forest practice law in 1970 (Anderson 1977). The committee proposed general legislation, which was given wide review by interest groups in the state and formed the basis for the legislation. The new legislation was enacted as the Oregon Forest Practice Act of 1971 and became effective on July 1, 1972.

The 1971 Law

The 1971 Oregon act was a general enabling law that required the State Board of Forestry to establish at least three forest regions and a nine-member forest practices committee for each region. The committees recommended appropriate regional forest practices to the State Board of Forestry, which was then responsible for promulgating the appropriate rules and regulations. The 16-member State Board of Forestry had 13 voting members, including the dean of the School of Forest

Resources at Oregon State University and 12 other members appointed by the governor with state Senate confirmation. Six members must work in the administration or production of forest products, one must be from the Association of Oregon Counties, one from a farm association, one from a range association, one from a conservation or labor group, and two from the public at large. The regional forester of the U.S. Forest Service, the state director of the Bureau of Land Management, and the president of the Oregon Forest Protection Association serve as advisory, nonvoting members.

The Oregon law is administered and enforced by the Oregon Department of Forestry. Any appeals to actions taken by the state forester in enforcing the law must be made to the State Board of Forestry. Operators, timber owners, or landowners must notify the state forester on forms provided by the department before commencing operations. Plans that deviate from the rules are acceptable if they propose equivalent or better forest practices and receive the written approval of the state forester.

The Oregon law applies to all nonfederal public lands and to all private lands. Notification is required for harvesting of forest crops, road construction or reconstruction, site preparation, application of chemicals, conversion of forest lands, treatment of slash, and precommercial thinning. Notification is not required for routine road maintenance, recreational uses, grazing, tree planting and direct seeding, Christmas tree culture, or harvesting of minor forest products. Waiver of notification does not relieve the owners or operators from the responsibility of complying with all applicable forest practice rules.

When violations are identified, the state forester may encourage compliance via informal conferences with the violators or may order the violator to cease the illegal activity. When practical and economically feasible, the state forester may direct the operator to cease all work in the area where the violation is occurring. If the operator refuses to repair the damage, the state may take corrective action and bill the operator accordingly. If not reimbursed, the state may attach a lien to the operator's, timber owner's, and landowner's property.

Failure to give notice or to follow the rules established by the board is a misdemeanor. Each day in violation after receiving a stop work order is considered a separate offense. Misdemeanor penalties consist of fines of not more than $1000 or imprisonment in the county jail for not more than one year, or both.

The law requires the State Board of Forestry to establish minimum practices for each region relating to reforestation, road construction and maintenance, timber harvesting, application of chemicals, and slash disposal. The subsequent regulations promulgated by the board require reforestation of at least 100 desirable seedlings per acre after harvest, or a basal area exceeding 80 square feet per acre of trees greater than 11 inches in diameter. The board also established regulations regarding road location, specification, construction, and maintenance. Harvesting rules cover the quality of the residual stand, soil protection, location of landings, skid trails, fire trails, drainage systems, treatment of waste materials, and stream protection. The regulations also control surface mining practices, protection of water quality during mixing and application of chemicals, and maintenance of productivity by proper disposal of slash.

Implementation and 1987 Revisions

Of the three West Coast states, most timber industry interest groups considered the Oregon regulatory law to be the most acceptable. The enabling legislation was the briefest of the three enacted during the 1970s; the administration of the law (notification, not permits or timber harvesting plans) was the least complicated; and interagency cooperation and problem prevention, not confrontation, were stressed. However, environmental groups criticized many perceived weaknesses of the law. Many viewed the Board of Forestry as being dominated by timber interests and having excessive discretion in writing forest practice standards. They also believed that enforcement of the law was inadequately funded and that there should be better cooperation and communication between the Oregon Department of Forestry and other state agencies. Furthermore, by the 1980s, environmental groups believed that the forest practices regulations themselves were too lenient. On the other hand, industry believed that new county land use laws were restricting forestry too much.

These perceived shortcomings in the 1971 Oregon law and regulations led to proposals for substantial revisions, which were effected by amendments in 1987. The interest groups involved in forest practice regulation went through a dispute resolution process to develop a new law, which contained some revisions favored by industry groups and some favored by environmental groups. The legislation imposed stricter requirements for riparian zone protection, including wider buffer strips and a greater percentage of trees being left in the zones. The law clarified that the Board of Forestry did have exclusive authority over forestry regulation (forestry would not fall under the county zoning laws and commissions), except in urban growth areas. Threatened and endangered species protection also was clarified under the 1987 revisions.

The 1991 Amendments

Despite the revisions in 1987, many groups, especially the forest industry, remained dissatisfied with the Oregon Forest Practices Act. The Oregon Forest Industries Council—a group representing private forest industry and private forest landowners—sought legislation to better control adverse impacts of forest regulation on private forest landowners. They wanted to clarify the Department of Forestry role and prevent the threat of increased regulation by the Department of Environmental Quality. They also wanted to update regulations and make them more rigorous, while preventing an excessive number of rules. They also wanted to prevent forestry regulation by public referendum—such as the "Big Green" ballot proposals in California that proposed detailed regulation of forest practices.

The Oregon Forest Industries Council helped introduce legislation without an elaborate public consensus or dispute resolution process. In fact, it did not believe that it could get environmental groups to agree with many of its proposals, so it opted instead to fight directly for the initiative in the state legislature. Note the difference between this approach and the environmental "mediation and negotiation" approach that was illustrated in Chapter 4. The Washington State consensus approach to changing its forest practice act dissolved in 1990, and no legislation could be passed in 1991. In Oregon, however, the industry-backed proposals eventually were enacted without prior consensus.

The 1991 Oregon Forest Practice Law amendments set new clear-cut limits of 120 acres, with the possibility of extension to 240 acres if no environmental harm were likely. They also tightened the requirements for reforestation and "green-up" after a clear-cut. The areas must be reforested within two years and have established seedlings at least four feet tall and free from overtopping competition after 4 years. The law also requires that on any clear-cut greater than 10 acres, at least two live trees and two downed trees per acre must be left for wildlife habitat. These requirements reflected the belief that more residual material should be left, as espoused by the advocates of "new forestry."

The 1991 law also required that stream classes/protection zones be reviewed, that forest corridor management zones be established along 29 state scenic highways, and that the exemption criteria for land use change be stricter. The 1991 law set interim standards that Class I streams be protected by buffer zones of up to three times the stream width, for a maximum of 100 feet, and that some merchantable conifers be left. The law also granted the Oregon Board of Forestry the authority to regulate to protect against cumulative adverse effects of harvesting, based on what is scientifically justifiable.

The 1991 forest practice revisions did make the law stricter, but the private landowners and industries felt that the increased costs were manageable and would help reduce risk from antiforest management initiatives such as those in California. The rules also centered water quality and all other forestry regulation in the Department of Forestry, rather than in an environmental agency. Furthermore, the industry groups and foresters were able to take the initiative away from environmental groups in the Oregon legislature. As a rule, industry's standing with legislators in the public policy arena increased substantially (Armstrong 1991).

LOCAL FORESTRY REGULATION

In addition to state forest practice laws, many localities have enacted their own environmental protection measures that affect forest management, especially in the East. Local zoning laws also are becoming more important in regulating some forestry activities (Cubbage and Siegel 1988). Some people believe that county governments are more prone to regulate private lands in the public's interest. In addition, more people living in rural areas no longer depend on production from the land for income, but rather "consume" it for amenity values. As such, they do not hesitate to regulate land use. As of 1991 there were about 400 local laws in the United States. More than 70 percent of these were passed in the last 10 years; 50 percent in the last five.

TYPES OF LAWS

Most local regulation of forest practices has occurred in the East. Western state laws often preclude local regulation. The mere hint of local regulation in Idaho led to such a state law in 1992. The types and amount of local regulation of forestry in the East were surveyed by Hickman and Martus (1991). They found that in 1990 there were about 360 local ordinances in the East that regulated forestry activities.

About three-quarters of the local ordinances found by Hickman and Martus (1991) occurred in the Northeast. Most of the other ordinances occurred in the South; only a few were found in the North Central states (Figure 16-1, Table 16-2). In the South, almost all the local ordinances reported occurred at the county or parish level of government. Georgia and Louisiana are the two southern states with the most county or parish ordinances (Cubbage 1989). A 1991 survey in Georgia found 47 out of the 169 counties in the state had some type of county logging ordinance (Greene, Jackson, and Baxter 1992).

In the Northeast, only about 13 percent of the local ordinances were enacted by counties. Forty-one percent of the ordinances were enacted by townships—a political subdivision of county governments that is common in the East. Local municipalities enacted 38 percent of the ordinances in the Northeast, boroughs 8 percent (Table 16-3). New Jersey alone has almost 100 local forestry ordinances, and New York, Connecticut, Maine, and Pennsylvania have dozens as well (Hogan 1984, Popovich 1984, Wolfgram 1984, Youell 1984).

Of the 18 local ordinances found in the West, municipalities accounted for about half and counties most of the remainder. Nearly 90 percent of the western ordinances were adopted in the last 10 years, and more than half in the last five years. General environmental protection and urban/suburban environmental protection were equally important as legislative goals, together accounting for 88 percent of the laws (Hickman, Siegel, and Martus. 1991).

Hickman and Martus (1991) divided local ordinances into five categories based on their primary reason for enactment (Table 16- 4): (1) public property/safety protection ordinances, (2) urban/suburban environmental protection ordinances, (3) general environmental protection ordinances, (4) special feature/habitat protection ordinances, and (5) forestland preservation ordinances.

Public Property/Safety Protection

Public property/safety protection ordinances are intended to (1) protect public investments in such things as roads, bridges, drainage ditches, and rights-of-way or (2) limit interference with normal traffic flows and protect local motorists from potentially hazardous driv-

Figure 16-1. Geographical Subregions Used in Review of Local Forestry Ordinances

ing conditions that might result from damaged road or bridge surfaces or the presence of mud or other logging debris on or in close proximity to public roadways and bridges. Ordinances typically regulate both the transport of roundwood products and logging-related equipment and also any harvesting activities (e.g., felling and skidding) that are conducted in the immediate vicinity of public roads, bridges, drainage ditches, and rights-of-way.

Public property ordinances may require operators to obtain a permit or license; post a surety or performance bond; remove debris, including mud, from roads, rights-of-way, and drainage ditches; and notify the administering agent or agency at the start and end of oper-

ations. Laws also may prohibit loading and unloading of logs and logging-related equipment along public roadways, require culverts or bridges at water crossings, restrict the use of unimproved roads during wet weather, require graveling of access points to prevent tracking mud onto roadways, prohibit skidding across public roadways, and prohibit use of tracked or lugged vehicles on roads.

Urban/Suburban Environmental Protection

Urban/suburban environmental protection ordinances attempt to protect the environmental values provided by trees and forests in urban and suburban settings. These benefits include improved aesthetics, reduced

TABLE 16-2. **Distribution of Local Forestry Ordinances in the East, by Time of Enactment and Subregion (January 1, 1991)**

Time Period	Northeast		North Central		Southeast		South Central	
	Number	Percent	Number	Percent	Number	Percent	Number	Percent
1970 or before	6	2	0	0	0	0	1	3
1971–1975	31	12	1	10	4	9	1	3
1976–1980	49	19	1	10	1	2	2	6
1981–1985	62	23	1	10	12	27	10	30
1986–1990	116	44	7	70	28	62	19	58
Total	264[a]	100	10	100	45	100	33	100

[a]Enactment dates were indeterminant for seven ordinances.

Source: Hickman and Martus 1991

erosion and sedimentation, improved water quality, improved air quality, amelioration of climate, reduced energy consumption, and reduced noise. Often, a secondary objective of such ordinances is the protection of urban and suburban property values. To achieve these goals, laws of this type generally regulate timber harvesting associated with land clearing and development. In many instances, the removal of individual trees is restricted.

The ordinances may require owners or operators to obtain a permit or license or post a surety or performance bond; require an erosion and sediment control plan prepared by a professional engineer; require a site plan prepared by a professional engineer or landscape architect; prohibit the removal of historical or large trees; or require replacement of trees removed or payments to a replanting fund.

General Environmental Protection

General environmental protection ordinances are intended to protect the environ-

mental values associated with well-managed commercial forestlands. These values include natural beauty, low erosion and sedimentation, water and air quality, diverse habitat for wildlife, and sustained soil productivity. To achieve their goals, most laws of this type regulate timber harvesting and harvest-related road construction practices. A smaller number of ordinances broaden the regulatory umbrella to include other forestry activities that cause soil disturbance—for example, site preparation and planting, dredging, and site drainage. Finally, a few laws go so far as to impose controls on all forest practices with the potential to harm the environment—such as prescribed burning and the use of fertilizers and pesticides.

The laws may require owners or operators to obtain a permit or license; leave buffers along property lines and roadways; post a surety or performance bond; remove slash and debris from drainages and culverts; or obtain a harvest plan prepared by a professional forester. Ordinances may require use

TABLE 16-3. **Distribution of Local Forestry Ordinances in the East, by Type of Local Government Enacting and Subregion (January 1, 1991)**

Type of Local Government	Northeast		North Central		Southeast		South Central	
	Number	Percent	Number	Percent	Number	Percent	Number	Percent
County or parish	36	13	5	50	43	96	33	100
Municipality	102	38	5	50	2	4	0	0
Township	111	41	0	0	0	0	0	0
Borough	22	8	0	0	0	0	0	0
Total	271	100	10	100	45	100	33	100

Source: Hickman and Martus 1991

TABLE 16-4. Distribution of Local Forestry Ordinances in the East, by Type of Ordinance and Subregion (January 1, 1991)

Type of Local Ordinance	Northeast Number	Northeast Percent	North Central Number	North Central Percent	Southeast Number	Southeast Percent	South Central Number	South Central Percent
Public property/safety protection	2	1	3	30	14	31	32	97
Urban/suburban environmental protection	91	33	2	20	20	45	1	3
General environmental protection	133	49	4	40	5	11	0	0
Special feature/habitat protection	38	14	1	10	6	13	0	0
Forestland preservation	7	3	0	0	0	0	0	0
Total	271	100	10	100	45	100	33	100

Source: Hickman and Martus 1991

of recognized BMPs; require buffers along streams and lakes; require culverts or bridges at water crossings; prohibit clear-cutting without a special variance from the administering agent or agency; or require that roads, skidtrails, and landings be properly retired when harvesting is completed.

Special Feature/Habitat Protection

Special feature/habitat protection ordinances are intended to protect features or habitats that are "special" because of their scenic value, their environmental sensitivity, or the natural functions that they perform. Examples of such special areas include scenic river corridors, shoreline and coastal zones, wetlands, and habitats occupied by threatened or endangered species. To achieve their intended purpose, most laws of this type—like the general environmental protection ordinances—regulate timber harvesting and harvest-related road construction activities. Once again, however, a number of laws broaden the regulatory umbrella to include all potentially harmful forest practices, or at least those than can cause soil disturbance.

These laws also may require permits or licenses; harvest plans prepared by a professional forester; or uncut buffers along streams and lakes or other zones. The laws also may limit the percent of timber volume that can be harvested in designated zones during some specified period of time or the size of openings that can be created, or harvesting may be prohibited altogether.

Forestland Preservation

Forestland preservation ordinances are intended to perpetuate forestlands in forest use and to maintain a relatively undisturbed forest condition. To achieve these goals, ordinances regulate land use, generally by zoning restrictions.

The laws may prohibit a change in land use without approval of the administering agent or agency; prohibit timber harvesting without approval of the administering agent or agency; require a permit or license; or require a public hearing.

Most forestland preservation statutes do include a mechanism by which landowners may be allowed to make a change in land use or to conduct a limited timber harvest with a permit or license. Typically, however, a very stringent process is required to obtain the necessary permit or license. Normally a public hearing must be held, and in some cases the landowner must show that the proposed change in land use or harvest would be in the public interest.

Penalties for Noncompliance

Penalties vary for violations of local forestry ordinances. About one-third of the laws do not explicitly set penalties; instead they state that violation of the ordinance constitutes a misdemeanor, the possible consequences of which are described elsewhere in the legal code of the local governmental entity. Where penalties are explicitly mentioned, they generally consist of a fine or a combination of fines and imprisonment; but other types of penalties are employed, such as requirements for corrective action.

Hickman and Martus (1991) state that

Fines are of varying types and amounts, and typically increase for repeated violations. Some fines are a specified amount, which may range from $250 to $5,000, per offense. Other fines are assessed on a daily basis, with the amounts ranging from $250 to $2,500 per day of violation. The fines associated with urban/suburban environmental protection ordinances are often levied on the basis of each tree illegally cut. In these cases, the amount of the fine may vary from $100 to $3,000 per tree. Imprisonment is usually for a period of 90 days or less, but in some cases violators can receive up to 1 year of jail time. The cost to restore adversely impacted property to its pre-existing condition is often mentioned as a penalty in public property/safety protection ordinances. The cost to install needed erosion and sedimentation controls is a common penalty in urban/suburban environmental protection ordinances. In these cases, some laws mandate that violators pay a multiple of the actual costs—e.g., 2 times or 4 times. Finally, some other penalties that are employed include forfeiture of the individual's or company's permit to operate, forfeiture of any posted bonds, and the cost to replant any illegally removed trees.

REASONS FOR LAWS

The Northeast

Private landowner regulation in the Northeast has been prompted primarily by concerns about logging and its effects on water quality, wildlife, and aesthetics. Water qual-

ity concerns include the nutrients in water, erosion from road building and log landings, streambed disruption by skidders, accidental fuel and lube spills, and removal of shade (Irland 1985). In addition, many citizens in the Northeast also are concerned about aesthetics, noise, increased truck traffic on town roads, and cutting practices. Frequently, local regulations are enacted in response to a clash between urban and rural values (Popovich 1984, Wolfgram 1984, Youell 1984).

The more comprehensive local ordinances require loggers to obtain a permit before harvesting a tract. They usually do not prohibit logging, but rather encourage desirable practices. The regulations are designed to protect border properties, streams, and soils; to protect county culverts, roads, and bridges; to ensure adequate maintenance of haul roads; and to control road slope. The permits allow municipalities to gather information on the type of cut (i.e., clear-cut, shelterwood, diameter limit), the location and the number of acres to be harvested, the dates of the operation, and the measures being used to ensure soil stability and stream protection. On the other hand, "informational" ordinances may require only notification coupled with adherence to a few minor regulations in order to let a township know when and where logging will occur (Provencher and Lassoie 1982).

Forestry may be regulated at the local level in a comprehensive and detailed manner by a separate distinct ordinance or by concealment in a related ordinance. For example, an ordinance regulating tree harvesting may be a small part of a larger ordinance, such as a soil excavation statute. In addition, the application of the ordinance to tree harvesting may not be apparent in its language. For instance, an existing or new ordinance that regulates the extraction of natural resources may be intended or construed to apply to timber cutting. The enforcement and interpretation of these laws often is left with a local building inspector or transportation official (Provencher and Lassoie 1982).

Local laws in the Northeast have been passed in response to aesthetic concerns and urban/rural conflicts. Viewsheds (the entire area one can see) are becoming important to urban planners, and local use of aesthetically based regulations is spreading. Noise, mud, and trucks also have been cited as reasons for local regulation (Goodfellow and Lea 1985, Wolfgram 1984). Pesticide use on forestlands has been a problem but has not been specifically regulated (Provencher and Lassoie 1982). Faced with these concerns, citizens and local government officials in some states have enacted various types of forest harvesting regulations.

The South

Despite the South's traditional conservatism, many southern states also have enacted logging regulations or regeneration standards. Broader state and national issues have led to regulations that may affect southern forestry and logging operations. Federal water pollution control laws instigated the development and promotion of voluntary best management practices in most southern states in the last decade. A few counties have required loggers to use BMPs in their operations; federal wetlands law requires road building in accordance with BMPs.

State highway departments and county governments are the principal proponents of logging regulation in the southern states. Highway departments primarily attempt to prevent damage to state roads and shoulders caused by logging trucks and harvesting equipment, in addition to their continual concern with truck weight limits and safety. Rural county governments usually are more concerned with preventing damage to roads, shoulders, culverts, and bridges than with timber cutting regulations. Urban counties are apt to have similar concerns. They also may regulate logging in order to preserve trees, control unbridled development, eliminate trash-covered logging sites, and protect aesthetic values. In addition, most southern states have specific legislation regarding slash disposal and stream blockage (Cubbage and Raney 1987, Cubbage and Siegel 1988, Haines, Cubbage, and Seigel 1988).

The West

Unlike the East, most forest practice acts in the West limit the role of local governments in the regulatory process. But local governments face pressure to expand regulatory controls on logging and other forest practices. Thus legislatures and courts in these states have been involved in the process of delineating state and local governments' responsibilities.

In Oregon the state/local regulation issue has been related to the state's comprehensive land use planning statute. In 1973 the Oregon legislature required local governments to develop comprehensive plans in order to protect natural resources. The Land Conservation and Development Commission and the Department of Land Conservation and Development were established to oversee and coordinate local planning. The planning law created a list of goals that local plans were required to achieve. The most pertinent of these deals with "Goal 5 resources," which include scenic areas, natural areas, open space, historic areas, fish and wildlife habitat, wetlands, watersheds, and cultural areas. Counties are required to inventory Goal 5 resources, to identify conflicting uses, and to develop a program to protect these resources.

Oregon counties began to construct their plans in the mid-1970s. There has been controversy since then about whether Goal 5 authorized or even required counties to regulate forest practices. The Oregon Department of Forestry and landowner representatives argued that the forest practices act preempted local government from regulating forestry. Some local citizen groups and a statewide group called 1000 Friends of Oregon argued that the forest practices program did not provide adequate protection for wildlife habitat, municipal watersheds, and scenic resources. The legislature amended the forest practice act in 1979 in order to resolve the controversy. However, the language of the amendment led to conflicting interpretations.

By the end of 1986, only Hood River county had actually implemented its own forest practice rules. Tourism is an important economic factor there, and the county forest practice ordinance regulated timber harvests to protect scenic qualities. Multnomah County, which includes Portland, also had adopted rules to protect scenery. Several other counties had considered regulating forest practices during their planning processes and the possibility of "39 different forest practice laws" roused Oregon's forestry community (Salazar 1989).

In a case pitting 1000 Friends of Oregon against Tillamook County, the Oregon Supreme court heard arguments regarding local regulation of forest practices. The court ruled that although counties had the authority to prohibit forest practices in particular zones, counties could not regulate forest practices in zones where forestry was a primary use; the forest practice act preempted county authority in this regard (737 P.2d 607 [Or. 1987]). In 1987 the Oregon legislature affirmed this interpretation by amending the forest practice law to clearly prohibit counties from using their land use planning authority to regulate forest practices. This interpretation was further strengthened in the 1991 Oregon State Forest Practice Act Amendments.

Perhaps nowhere has the issue of state versus local control of forest practice regulation been more contentious than in California. Counties have regulated harvesting in California since the 1930s (Arvola 1976). The California Board of Forestry dealt with proposals for county logging ordinances throughout the 1950s. In 1957 the board prevailed upon the legislature to amend the 1945 forest practice act so that it could preempt local governments.

There was no further local action until 1969 when Marin County and local governments in the Lake Tahoe Basin considered proposals to regulate logging (Arvola 1976). In the same year San Mateo County denied Bayside Timber company logging and road-building permits for a planned timber harvest. Bayside appealed the denial arguing that the California Forest Practice Act preempted county authority. The state courts sidestepped the preemption issue and ruled the state

law unconstitutional because it delegated rule making authority to individuals with a pecuniary interest in logging. The forest practice law in effect at the time allowed regional forest practice rules (Lundmark 1975). The turmoil surrounding forest practices set the stage for new state legislation in 1973.

The Z'berg-Nejedly Forest Practice Act of 1973 explicitly permitted counties to adopt rules "stricter than" those promulgated by the state. Six California counties exercised their authority to adopt separate rules (DeMaria 1983). Loggers and owners of forest lands perceived some of the county rules as unduly restrictive and costly. They proposed an amendment to the forest practice act that would eliminate county authority to adopt separate rules.

In 1982 the state legislature enacted this amendment, including a provision that allowed each county to petition the Board of Forestry to promulgate special rules. The board must adopt the proposed rules if they are consistent with the intent and purposes of the forest practice act and they are necessary to protect the "needs and conditions" of the county. The board has generally responded affirmatively to county requests for special rules. But the issue remains contentious as residents and officials of several suburban counties fight for greater local authority.

OTHER STATE REGULATIONS

Many other state laws regulate forestry and wildlife in some fashion but will not be discussed in detail here. The most significant of these are state environmental quality acts, fish and game regulations, and water and air quality laws. Prescribed burning, herbicide application, business practices, and highway transportation also are regulated by states. These laws interact with or supplement the existing federal laws and the state forest practice laws already discussed in this chapter. In some cases, they conflict with forest practice laws, and the courts must resolve the differences.

For example, the state environmental quality acts passed in the 1970s, and some provisions of state forest practice laws, often contain provisions that conflict with the timber production provision of the forest practice statutes—reflecting the tension between protecting aesthetic and recreational forest uses and preserving a viable forest products industry (Hansen 1978).

The courts have generally ruled that environmental protection for the public welfare takes precedence when conflicts occur. For example, both the California and Washington environmental protection acts were held to prevail when they conflicted with the state forest practice acts. In *Noel v. Cole* (No. 9806 Wash. Super. Ct. [1977]), the court ordered the defendant to prepare a detailed Environmental Impact Statement under the Washington Environmental Policy Act for a timber harvest, even though it was not required by the Forest Practice Act. In *Natural Resources Defense Council v. Arcata National Corporation* (131 Cal. Rptr. 172, 59 Cal. App. 3rd 959 [1975]), the court held that the principles and some of the procedures embodied in the California Environmental Quality Act apply to forest practice regulation. It ruled that when the two statutes overlap, the Forest Practice Act must be construed in ways consistent with the Environmental Quality Act and with other state and federal environmental legislation—such as that dealing with water quality, endangered species, coastal protection, and wild and scenic rivers. In *Arcata Redwood Co. v. State Board of Forestry* (No. 61910 Cal. Super. Ct., Humboldt City. [1977]), the court prohibited cutting on lands near the Redwood National Park. It held that harvesting would foreclose possible future federal action to expand the park and thus constitute a significant impact on the environment. The ruling was made even though the Forest Practice Act is intended to regulate only the manner of timber cutting, rather than whether or not it should be allowed. The fact that the plaintiffs would suffer serious monetary losses was not a consideration.

WATER QUALITY

State water pollution control laws also affect forest land management practices (Cubbage, Siegel, and Lickwar 1989, Guldin 1988, Haines et al. 1988). The laws are designed to control point and nonpoint source pollution and are the implementing mechanisms for the federal water pollution control laws discussed in Chapter 14. In the East, most states have relied on voluntary BMPs to achieve forestry nonpoint source pollution control objectives. Many also have laws prohibiting disposal of logging slash in streams or lakes. They also have broad water quality statutes that either apply directly to forestry operations or could be invoked to do so. State water quality laws have not been very restrictive to date, but they could be implemented more stringently without additional legislation. Based on their water quality laws, in the 1990s several states in the East began prosecuting operators who violated state water quality standards during timber harvesting operations, especially when there were complaints about the violations.

Water quality laws in the West usually have been invoked through direct regulation, often through incorporation in a state forest practices act. These laws are designed to protect streamside zones and fish habitat, often requiring operators to leave significant amounts of timber in the zones. At least 10 states in the United States have enacted their own wetlands laws, designed to protect crucial habitat and endangered species by restricting land management practices. Many other states are considering separate wetlands legislation.

BUSINESS PRACTICES

When discussing forestry regulation, it is appropriate to note that a host of business regulations affect private forestry firms. Federal laws for social security insurance (and taxes), unemployment insurance, and workers' compensation insurance affect private firms and public agencies. Private firms must withhold income and social security taxes from their employees and submit them to the state and federal treasuries. Firms also must pay taxes on their profits. Social insurance taxes such as unemployment insurance and workers' compensation represent large costs for all employers. Workers' compensation costs for loggers, in particular, are extremely expensive—averaging $41 for every $100 of payroll in 1991. In Colorado, Montana, and Rhode Island, logging workers' compensation rates were more than $70 per $100 of payroll (Culhane 1992).

Private firms and public agencies must comply with federal and state laws governing employment practices. These laws regulate hiring and firing, benefits, promotion, equal opportunity/affirmative action, minimum wage, child labor, overtime, and other concerns. They require that all firms and agencies comply with certain employment standards. Failure to comply with these laws can lead to lawsuits by dissatisfied employees. The Forest Service, in particular, has been beset by legal problems in failing to recruit and promote enough women and minority group members to upper level management positions. From the late 1980s, the agency operated under a consent decree, administered by a judge in Region 5 (California), that required the Forest Service to improve its desultory performance. The decree was conditionally lifted in 1992.

A host of other business regulations affect forestry firms in some fashion. Open burning laws require notification before prescribed fires can be made in some states. A number of states, including North Carolina and West Virginia, explicitly require that operators meet water quality standards by using BMPs or other satisfactory measures, or they face prosecution. Some states require permits for hauling wood products or minor forest products such as pine straw. All states have laws that allow prosecution of people who start forest fires or steal timber. Some states require foresters to be registered if they provide consulting advice or prepare official forest management plans. Landowner liability laws define conditions under which forest landowners may or may not be held responsible for actions or accidents on their land.

The state and federal laws that govern the business of forest resource management are extensive. Enumerating them all would be too time-consuming for this textbook. But one should be aware that they have a crucial effect on how markets operate and that these rules are determined by public debate and legislation, just as the more visible forest practice regulations are.

POLICY RESPONSES

A trend toward increasing regulation of public and private forest and resource management is readily apparent. Some view this trend with favor, others with dread. Those who place a high value on protecting many species of plants and animals are likely to favor greater regulation of forestry, especially in sensitive areas such as in wetlands, near streams, or in endangered species' habitat. Wildlife managers and interest groups usually agree that more farm land should be left for wildlife habitat, greater measures should be taken to protect the nation's waters from soil and chemical pollution, and most wetlands should be protected to the greatest extent practicable. People who earn a living from growing and harvesting food or timber, or from buying and selling land for residential or commercial development, are less apt to favor increased regulation. Such regulation is apt to either prohibit some commercial activities or at least increase their costs. Thus, trade associations representing farmers and forest products firms usually oppose increased regulation of land management practices. Other interests are not as well represented in regulation debates but do contribute to the discussion. The general public continues to favor strong laws to protect the environment, even at a substantial cost. However, critics contend that such expenses may be borne disproportionately by poor people who will sacrifice more of their meager standard of living than will middle- or upper-income people.

ALTERNATIVES

Given society's preferences and the potential conflict of these preferences with commercial forestry enterprises, what policies should forest and wildlife policymakers pursue to deal with regulation? First, forestry and wildlife interest groups can simply accept the status quo—a moderate tendency toward increased regulation—and continue to disagree often in legislative and administrative disputes. Wildlife groups are likely to continue to favor preservation; forestry groups timber production.

A second alternative in dealing with regulation might be further scientific research to determine the effects of forest management practices on wildlife and fish populations. With luck, these research efforts could better quantify the benefits of undisturbed wetlands, the impacts of timber harvesting on aquatic fauna, and the types of management practices needed to provide adequate protection for plants and animals. Research interest groups—academic and government alike—often attribute poor policies to inadequate knowledge and believe that more research funding would help.

Third, public education about the merits of forest management may help reduce some unnecessary conflicts based on misinformation. Educating foresters to avoid performing environmentally harmful practices also may be beneficial. Aggressively implementing voluntary BMP programs is one means of educating foresters and landowners. Virginia implemented an aggressive, statewide voluntary BMP program in 1989 that could serve as a model for conscientious voluntary programs (Hawks, Cubbage, and Newman 1991). Continuing forestry education is another approach.

Another means of dealing with increased regulation might well be to accept this inevitable trend and have forestry, wildlife, and environmental groups work together to develop reasonable laws (including regulation) that will meet the objectives of most landowners and conservationists. Such efforts could lead to model local ordinances designed to protect rural county roads and urban forest amenity values. Further, the forest industry and citizen conservation groups could strive to reach a consensus on individual state forest practice acts, which could serve to implement BMPs, require minimum regeneration requirements, or establish other environmental protection measures. The forest industry usually opposes such proposals, but it may be to its advantage to pursue favorable enabling legislation now, while the industry is still relatively powerful in the state legislatures. In another decade, environmental groups are more likely to successfully propose such state legislation and probably will have enough political clout to dictate terms of forest regulation that the industry and many forest landowners would like even less than those that could be determined now. However, industry groups fear that enactment of a law now will just lead to increasingly tougher laws once the framework is established, and such a position is supported by history.

In recent years, some state forest industry associations have become more aggressive and have enacted laws that either contain more tolerable regulations (such as in Oregon in 1991) or prevent outright regulations (such as a 1989 North Carolina forest water quality law). These efforts are a reversion to traditional legislative lawmaking, rather than a reliance on consensus and cooperation.

Two other, opposing alternatives for coping with regulatory demands remain—confrontation and mediation. Environmental groups will continue to pursue court challenges to ensure stricter enforcement of existing environmental protection laws. Forest industry associations and loggers may also challenge the legality of regulatory measures or try to block administrative regulation. One local logging ordinance was challenged successfully in Louisiana. However, legal challenges are expensive and risky. Legal costs are substantial and especially inhibiting for groups with modest funds, such as state forestry associations. Furthermore, loss of a legal challenge sets the precedent that regulation is a valid exercise of the state's police power, which may lead to further proliferation of such laws. Litigation and confrontation are reactive, create ill will, and undermine the industry's public relation efforts to appear to be good land stewards, not rapacious loggers.

As discussed in Chapter 4, another means of dealing with regulation might be to strive to achieve more cooperation and consensus rather than regulation. The Timber-Fish-Wildlife (TFW) agreement forged in Washington State in 1987 exemplified a consensus management approach to dealing with disagreements among the three principal interest groups. This agreement brought together forest industry (who wanted a stable regulatory environment), Native American tribes (who wanted to protect fish habitat), and state agencies (who wanted to reduce conflict and uncertainty associated with forest practice regulation). In a series of meetings, the groups agreed to a three-element strategy to help achieve all their goals. These included better riparian zone protection; more cooperative efforts to coordinate harvest and road planning and wildlife habitat protection; and implementation of a series of reforms designed to expedite the efficiency and effectiveness of the regulatory process. However, the subsequent Washington forest practices roundtable discussion in 1990 fell apart after the disparate interest groups had difficulty agreeing on desirable practices, and several environmental groups then failed to ratify the eventual agreements that were reached by their negotiators.

All these alternatives may be used to address regulatory issues in the future. In any case, the issues will not be resolved but will continue to involve differences in beliefs and values, desired policy outcomes, and impacts on forest management practices. Our skill in dealing with these issues will determine the success in protecting plant and wildlife species; providing safe water supplies; ensuring private property rights; maintaining professional credibility; and retaining a competitive, profitable forest products industry.

ILLUSTRATION: ENACTING THE MAINE FOREST PRACTICE LAW

Groups may either oppose or support forest practice regulation using the policy approaches discussed in the text. In 1989 Maine enacted a new forest practice law to deal with many forestry problems that were occurring in the state. A review of the politics, process, and outcome of the Maine deliberations illustrates the merits and hazards of taking a proactive approach to forestry regulation. In a meeting of the Michigan SAF, which also was considering forest practice regulation, Ludwig (1990) provided a thorough review of the process and players involved in enacting a new Maine state law. His discussion is paraphrased in this illustration.

Forestry Issues

Maine has about 17 million acres of forest land; 11 million acres (65 percent) of it is owned by 15 forest products firms (mostly paper manufacturers) or controlled by land management companies. Industry owns much of the forest land in the northern and eastern parts of the state. Roughly 80,000 landowners hold 10 to 1000 acres each, amounting to about 30 percent of the commercial forest land base. Public ownerships comprise less than 5 percent of Maine's forest land.

Demands on Maine's forests increased in the 1980s. More forest roads were built to remote places. Paper companies increased output via expanding paper mills and opening new sawmills. The spruce budworm arrived in the state in 1974 and reduced growth or killed spruce and fir. Projections of a timber shortfall based on increased timber harvest and mortality were widely publicized.

Prohibition of river driving of logs, increased paper mill demand, the salvage of insect-killed timber, and 10 new wood-fired boilers prompted a rapid expansion of Maine's logging road systems and increased clear-cutting. (So did change in ownership of some land, which was then harvested in order to support Canadian mills.) The industry also increased herbicide and pesticide use to ward off the projected timber shortage.

The new roads helped lead to dramatic increases in recreational use of once-remote forest lands. "People from away," all seemingly outfitted by L.L. Bean and having an excellent state atlas, migrated into Maine by the thousands, searching for permanent homes or vacation spots. Environmental awareness soared, as did media coverage of acid rain, ozone, wildlife crises, pesticide abuse, and the dangers of monoculture.

Public scrutiny led to sharp criticism of intensive forest practices. Maine's widely read environmental weekly publicized forestry issues; the Portland newspaper ran a four-part feature titled "Forest in Crises." Various towns began to develop their own timber harvesting ordinances—27 of them by 1990. The Maine Forest Service drafted an ill-fated model ordinance. Diamond International Corporation was bought out by corporate raider James Goldsmith in the early 1980s and dismantled, including the sale of much land for development. The Great Northern Nekoosa Paper Company, a stalwart employer, was acquired in 1990 by Georgia-Pacific Corporation in a hostile takeover. (This did not prompt passage of the 1989 Maine Act but probably did affect the rules that were eventually adopted.)

Issue Responses

The great number of issues created controversy among environmentalists, the forest industry, and small private forest landowners. In 1986 the Maine Audubon Society, which is affiliated with National Audubon but differs strongly with it on forest policy, invited participation in an industrial forest forum to address the projected spruce/fir shortfall. Forest industry joined in because the forum was not tied to a specific legislative initiative. Also, the Audubon Society had a track record of responsible positions on forestry matters, and some of the industry hardliners had given way to a new generation of managers more open to discussion.

Other interest groups were involved in the Maine issues and participated in the Audubon conference and subsequent events. Forest industry was represented by the Maine Forest Products Council, with more than 300 members. The Small Woodlot Owners Association of Maine (SWOAM) represented other private landowners. The Maine Audubon Society and the Natural Resources Council of Maine each had interests in forestry and Audubon employed a forester. The state agencies involved in the Maine Department of Conservation included the Land Use Regulation Commission (responsible for the state zoning laws in the state's Unorganized Territory) and the Bureau of Forestry. The Department of Environmental Protection controlled harvesting in conjunction with shoreland zoning in organized towns, and the state planning office administered a "Critical Areas" program of voluntary protection.

The 1986 Audubon forum was based on similar objectives among many groups: (1) a clearer definition of the public interest and the state's role in Maine's forest economy; (2) more public support for the small forest landowner; (3) extending the Land-Use Regulation Commission's water quality regulations statewide for consistency; (4) better reporting of forest activities; and (5) removing disincentives (taxes) or providing incentives for forestry investments. Environmental groups also felt that a viable forest industry would be a good defense against forest fragmentation and wanton development.

The 1989 Law

The 1986 forum discussions continued for more than a year and were broadened to include the sustainability and health of the entire forest resource. The Audubon discussions did not, however, lead to a consensus on how to proceed, so in 1988 Audubon unilaterally drafted and sponsored the introduction of a forest practices bill. That breach of faith created hard feelings. An opposing bill was drafted by the Maine Forest Products Council. Both bills were introduced in 1988, and interest groups heatedly discussed alternatives for agreement in a 1989 bill. These debates led to the Maine legislature's enacting "An Act to Implement Sound Forest Practices" in 1989.

The 1989 law called for the commissioner of the Department of Conservation to promulgate rules by January 15, 1991, to set mandatory standards for regeneration after timber harvests (which will pass with title to the land), determine performance standards for clear-cuts, and require management plans for certain clear-cuts. Municipalities may set standards that exceed those set by the state but must use the same definitions for forestry terms that are established in the act. The act also mandates preharvest notification of the Bureau of Forestry for all timber harvests (good for two years); detailed reporting of harvesting, silvicultural, and timber sale activities; and annual wood processing reports. The law also authorized an increase in the Bureau of Forestry field staff and made several changes in forestry taxation that benefited small and large forest owners.

Forest Practice Regulations

The law authorized the Department of Conservation to promulgate rules for forest practice regulation. The legislature provided only minimum standards for subsequent rule making. Regeneration must occur within five years and clear-cuts (less than 30 square feet of basal area remaining) of more than 50 acres required a management plan. Towns still could regulate harvesting. Violations of the law could draw fines of up to $1000 per day.

To come up with these rules in the short time allotted, the Bureau of Forestry first held 15 hearings to gather public input from around the state. Two groups advised the bureau as the draft rules were then developed: an ad hoc technical committee consisting of landowners, foresters, and wildlife professionals; and the Citizens Forestry Advisory Council, a panel appointed by the governor to direct the state's "Forests for the Future Program." Other state agency input was sought, especially that of the Department of Inland Fisheries and Wildlife. Rules were drafted and aired at three location hearings in August. Final rules became effective January 1, 1991, and govern the following tasks:

1. Minimum regeneration stocking standards.
2. Mitigation methods for inadequate regeneration.
3. Commercial tree species definitions.
4. Size limitations on clear-cuts and performance standards regulating clear-cuts.

As it turned out, regeneration became a consensus item, and the real controversy swirled around the size and distribution of clear-cuts. The performance standards key in on two issues: biological diversity for wildlife and timber yield sustainability.

The regeneration standards state that landowners must have a residual basal area of at least 30 square feet per acre or the area must be successfully regenerated within five years after harvest. Success is met when at least 60% of randomly distributed one-five-hundredth–acre plots contain at least one tree of acceptable growing stock. Exemptions from regeneration standards are allowed if failures occur due to natural disasters, or if land is being converted to some other use (Maine Forest Service 1990).

The final clear-cutting standards provided for three size categories: 5 to 35-acres, 36 to 125 acres, and 126 to 250 acres. A 35-acre or smaller clear-cut must be separated from other clear-cuts by 250 feet. Category 2 clear-cuts—from 36 to 125 acres—require the 250 feet of separation zone as part of a non–clear-cut area amounting to one-and-a-half times the clear-cut area. Clear-cuts greater than 125 acres must be surrounded by a separation zone totaling *twice* the clear-cut area, with a 500-foot minimum buffer. There also are some very restrictive regeneration standards.

Policy-Making Implications

Industry was displeased with the final clear-cutting rules, and that attitude tended to subsume its positive feelings about the effort. The clear-cutting reserves concept had already stretched some players to the limits and to have the automatically exempt clear-cut size drop from 50 to 35 acres, accompanied by substantial tightening of the rules—all since the final hearings—gave the process a surprise ending. What had allowed industry to compromise to get the act passed in the first place was a strong faith in the Department of Conservation's ability to understand its interests and make reasonable decisions. Industry was keenly disappointed with the fairly restrictive final rules.

The environmental and forest sustainability advocates were more pleased with the final results; however, they recognized industry's displeasure and did not want the fruits of their labor to be that burdensome. Small woodlot owners appear neutral or slightly positive in reaction. Most expect that the act will not affect them in a substantial way. There is some concern that field foresters' efforts could shift to an enforcement role because education was not clearly mandated in the act.

Ludwig (1990) summarized the benefits of the act as follows:

What's the feeling on the validity of a forest practice act from the Maine landowner's perspective? The big gain is in public and political credibility. The very existence of an act provides a sense of security to those who had worried that things were out of control. It would be naive to assume that additional control initiatives are dead in the water—Audubon is already planning further work on the sustainability issue—but hopefully there is a period of relative calm and stability in our near future. We expect the act will be given a chance to work and that tinkering will focus on improving workability.

An abuser is caught up in a frustrating exercise to meet the law, and gets no answer to his question, "Where is the societal benefit?" Adding to his frustration is the additional nagging question, "Will anybody be checking my actions?"

There is a brighter aspect to the opinion on the process (namely dialogue, consensus building and the proactive approach). Most feel we probably have a better product because all parties talked. Some with the extreme viewpoint disagree with the mainline environmental organizations, saying, "This is policy handed down from the top behind closed doors, and that an old-fashioned shoot-out would have stirred greater public emotional involvement." I view this as evidence we did the right thing.

There is a perceived carry-over advantage. The bridge building and mutual respect will aid in future efforts to resolve issues, such as the protectionism which looms around the corner.

A biting caution rides with these positive sentiments. Beware of getting stuck in a collaborative mode, and keep both eyes on the other players, especially as the effort comes down to the wire. Some feel that the rules of the game changed unannounced and that the opposition's reversion to an aggressive polarized position swayed the decision makers in the final hour. On the other hand, I think that familiarity and trust played a role in Audubon's decision not to use their potentially biggest emotional tool, the herbicide issue, at the time of crafting the law.

A final word of wisdom: It helps to draw a hard line on key reasonable demands, up front. Industry's position was not seriously challenged when they said:

- "We will accept controls only on clear-cutting and regeneration."
- "We will not accept a permit system."
- "We will accept performance standards, not mandated practices."

CURRENT PROSPECTS

By 1992 the debates over state forest practice acts were approaching status as a national issue. Approximately a dozen states had considered state forest practice acts, either via professional forestry meetings, environmental group proposals, or actual legislative bills. Consideration by some states was prompted by desires to consolidate environmental regulations (on the part of the forestry sector), to tighten environmental controls (by environmental groups), or to increase the role of foresters (by forestry professionals, especially hard-pressed state agencies and consulting foresters).

The forestry sector in most states in the South, however, remained steadfast in its opposition to state forest practice acts. In fact, several state forestry associations and industry groups became strong proponents for unregulated private property rights and began warning of excessive California-style applications, permits, and regulations (e.g., Shaffer 1991). The wise use movement was invoked as a model to oppose creeping regulatory socialism and leaders in most southern states and industry associations took a hard line on regulation. They feared that acceptance of any regulation would only lead to stricter rules in a short time.

In a move that helped corroborate the worst fears of southern industry groups, the Southern Environmental Law Center in Virginia prepared a strict draft state forest practice act, which leaked out in 1991. The discussion draft proposed minimum standards for harvesting timber, regeneration, species diversity, and clear-cuts. It also included controls on forest conversions, required management plans for tracts over 100 acres, specified penalties, and provided for citizen civil lawsuits to correct alleged violations. In addition to the Southern Environmental Law Center proposal, the possibility of the TVA's requiring forest management plans as part of its chip mill EIS further incited southern forest industries and landowner interest groups.

In short, regulation has again moved to the forefront of public debates. The state forestry regulations in the West have become stricter in order to provide greater amounts of environmental protection. State acts have been widely considered in the Northeast and Midwest for consolidating laws related to forestry—especially water quality rules and BMPs—and for curtailing the proliferation of local laws. Several states in the South and the national forest industry have mounted strident campaigns against regulation, linking the issue to the property rights/wise use movement. These groups feel that confrontation will protect their operating freedom better than cooperation. The environmental protection/landowner regulation issue and the appropriate policy responses will be crucial in determining how well the environment is protected, how much forest management will cost, the amount of public versus private rights in timber management and environmental law, and the stature of the forestry and wildlife professions in the future.

SUMMARY

Most of the existing state forest practice laws were first enacted in the 1940s. Those in the East were usually simple seed tree laws, with few penalties and little enforcement. Laws in the West were stricter and were strengthened considerably in the 1970s and 1980s. New acts also were passed in several western states; modern laws were intended to protect the environment and to ensure adequate regeneration. State forest practice acts require landowners or operators to obtain permits or notify state forestry agencies before timber harvests and other forest operations. They require regeneration, mandate strict water quality protection standards, and may require timber harvesting plans and performance bonds.

In the East, most states have relied on market forces, education, or technical assistance to protect the environment and to obtain adequate regeneration. However, local regulation of logging and urban tree protection ordinances have become prevalent in the Northeast and are beginning to appear in the South. Four new eastern state forest practice laws were enacted in the 1980s and 1990s.

Policy responses to regulation could range from outright opposition and legal challenges to active education programs to sponsorship of state forest practice acts. The response of forest and wildlife managers to these regulatory trends will determine the level of success at protecting the environment, encouraging wildlife protection and management, retaining profitable operating conditions for forest landowners and forest products firms, and maintaining professional credibility.

LITERATURE CITED

Anderson, Gordon B. 1977. Oregon's forest conservation laws—part I. *American Forests* 83(3):16-19, 52-56.

Armstrong, Ward S. 1991. Oregon forest practices regulation: Impacts on private landowners. Speech presented at the 1991

Society of American Foresters Convention, August 4–7. San Francisco.

Arvola, T. F. 1976. Regulation of Logging in California 1945–1975. State of California, Division of Forestry. Sacramento. 98 pp.

Cubbage, Frederick. 1989. Local regulation of forestry in the South. *Forest Farmer* 48(3):15–20. January.

Cubbage, Frederick W., and Paul V. Ellefson. 1980. State forest practice laws: A major policy force unique to the natural resources community. *Natural Resources Lawyer* 13(2):421–468.

Cubbage, Frederick W., and Kevin P. Raney. 1987. County logging and tree protection ordinances in Georgia. *Southern Journal of Applied Forestry* 11(1):76–82.

Cubbage, Frederick W., and William C. Siegel. 1985. The law regulating private forestry. *Journal of Forestry* 83(9):538–545.

Cubbage, Frederick W., and William C. Siegel. 1988. State and local regulation of private forestry in the East. *Northern Journal of Applied Forestry* 5(2):103–108.

Cubbage, Frederick W., William C. Siegel, and Peter M. Lickwar. 1989. State water quality laws and programs to control nonpoint source pollution from forest lands in the South. p. 8a-29–8A-37 in Proceedings, AWRA 1989 Conference on Water: Laws and Management. Technical Publication 89-4. American Water Resources Association. Bethesda, MD.

Culhane, John C. 1992. Workers' compensation insurance rates by state for logging. Technical Release 92-R-19. American Pulpwood Association. Washington, DC. 2 pp.

DeMaria, S. L. 1983. The legislative and regulatory environment for forestry enterprises in California. The S. J. Hall Memorial Lectureship in Industrial Forestry. University of California. Berkeley.

Ellefson, Paul V., and Frederick W. Cubbage. 1980. State forest practice laws and regulations: A review and case study for Minnesota. Station Bulletin 536-1980. Minnesota Agricultural Experiment Station, University of Minnesota. St. Paul. 42 pp.

Goodfellow, John W., and Richard V. Lea. 1985. A town and its harvesting ordinance. *Journal of Forestry* 83(3):159–161.

Greene, Dale, Ben Jackson, and Martha Baxter. 1992. County-level logging regulation in Georgia. Technical Release 92-R-20. American Pulpwood Association. Washington, DC. 2 pp.

Guldin, Richard W. 1988. An analysis of the water situation in the United States, A Technical Document Supporting the 1989 RPA Assessment. Draft. USDA Forest Service. Washington, DC. 5 sections + appen.

Haines, Terry K., Frederick W. Cubbage, and William C. Siegel. 1988. Recent developments in state water quality laws affecting forestry in the East. Pp. 457–467 in Proceedings, 1988 Environmental Conference. TAPPI. Atlanta.

Hamilton, Lawrence S. 1965. The federal forest regulation issues. *Forest History* 9(1): 2–11.

Hawks, Laurie J., Frederick W. Cubbage, and David H. Newman. 1991. Regulatory versus voluntary forest water quality programs in Maryland and Virginia. Pp. 333–338 in Proceedings, 1991 Society of American Foresters Convention. Bethesda, MD.

Hansen, Brian L. 1978. Protection of recreation and scenic beauty under the Washington Forest Practices Act. *Washington Law Review* 53:443–470.

Henly, Russell K., and Paul V. Ellefson. 1986. State forest practice regulation in the U.S.: Administration, cost, and accomplishment. Station Bulletin AP-5B-3011. University of Minnesota, Agricultural Experiment Station. St. Paul. 154 pp.

Hickman, Clifford A., and Christopher E. Martus. 1991. Local regulation of private forestry in the eastern United States. Pp. 73–90 in Proceedings, 1991 Southern Forest Economics Workers Meeting. Published by Louisiana State University, Department of

Forestry. Agricultural Experiment Station. Baton Rouge.

Hickman, Clifford A., William C. Siegel, and Christopher E. Martus. 1991. Forest practice regulatory developments in the East. Pp. 327–332 in Proceedings, 1991 Convention, Society of American Foresters. Bethesda, MD.

Hogan, Edward A. 1984. Catch-22 in New Jersey. *American Tree Farmer* 3(3):14–15.

Irland, Lloyd C. 1985. Logging and water quality: State regulation in New England. *Journal of Soil and Water Conservation* 40(1):98–102.

Ludwig, Peter. 1990. The Maine state forest practice law. Speech presented at the Michigan Society of American Foresters, Annual Meeting. October 17–18. Traverse City. Mimeo

Lundmark, T. 1975. Regulation of private logging in California. *Ecology Law Quarterly* 5(1):139–188.

Maine Forest Service. 1990. Forest regeneration and clear-cutting standards, MFS Rules Chapter 20. Department of Conservation. 15 Pp. Mimeo

Pidot, Jeffrey R. 1982. Maine's Land-Use Regulation Commission. *Journal of Forestry* 80(9):591–593, 602.

Popovich, Luke. 1984. Whither regulations? *American Tree Farmer* 3(3):9.

Provencher, R. W. and J. P. Lassoie. 1982. Pros and cons of local logging ordinances. *Conservation Circular* 20(3). Extension Publication. New York State College of Agricultural and Life Sciences at Cornell University. Department of Natural Resources. Ithaca, NY. 9 pp.

Salazar, Debra J. 1989. Counties, states, and regulation of forest practices on private lands. In R. G. Lee, W. R. Burch and D. R. Field, (eds.) Community and Forestry: Continuities in the Sociology of Natural Resources. Westview Press. Boulder CO. 301 pp.

Salazar, Debra J. and Frederick W. Cubbage. 1990. Regulating private forestry in the west and the South. *Journal of Forestry* 88(1): 14–19.

Shaffer, Robert M. 1991. Forestry by regulation. *The Consultant* 36(4):24–27.

Society of American Foresters. 1956. Forest Practice Developments in the United States, 1940 to 1955. Washington, DC. 39 pp.

Wolfgram, Steven. 1984. Regulations grow in New York. *American Tree Farmer* 3(3): 13–14.

Youell, Carol E. 1984. Connecticut forests are ready: The citizens aren't! *American Tree Farmer* 3(3):11.

Chapter 17

Public Assistance for Private Forest Owners

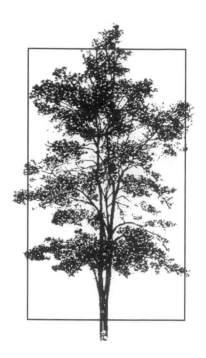

First, *how important is it that timber output from non-industrial private lands be increased?* Second, *if it is important, is public intervention, including subsidies, justified?* Third, *if public intervention is justified, are present programs relatively efficient and adequate?* Fourth, *if they are not adequate, how could we improve present programs or what new programs should we consider?*

—*Hans M. Gregersen 1977*

INTRODUCTION

Gregersen (1977) captured the essence of the issues regarding the provision of public assistance for nonindustrial private forest (NIPF) landowners. These owners hold about 60 percent of the timberland in the United States and are expected to contribute most of the increases in timber supplies in the future. The reasons for public intervention and consideration of the appropriate programs for increasing timber from NIPFs began in the early 1900s. Policies for production of nontimber outputs from NIPFs have become important recently, as evidenced by the forest stewardship program (a multiple-use program for private owners) that was enacted as part of the 1990 farm bill. As discussed in the previous chapter, regulation has been adopted to protect both timber and nontimber resources on public and private lands and is apt to increase. As an alternative to regulation, a wide variety of education and assistance programs have been developed to promote timber production, wildlife habitat creation, and soil conservation on NIPF lands. These educational approaches often are favored by forest landowners over regulation.

Straka and Bullard (1987) note that many studies have described the importance of nonindustrial private lands to U.S. forestry, and several have reviewed the success and potential of policies to stimulate nonindustrial private forestry investments. Prominent studies include Clawson (1974, 1979) and a seven-article series by Anderson (1975), Gould (1975), McComb (1975), McKillop (1975), Mills (1975), Skok and Gregersen (1975), and Worrell and Irland (1975), as well as reports by Sedjo and Ostermeier (1978), the Forest Industries Council (1980), and Meeks (1982).

Many federal and state programs have been developed to encourage NIPF management. The Clarke-McNary Act of 1924 was the forerunner of most cooperative state and federal programs designed to assist private forest landowners. It authorized federal–state cooperation to protect private forest lands from fire, to study the effects of taxes on conservation and timber production, to produce and distribute seeds and seedlings, and to educate farmers about the use and management of farm woodlots. Other federal legislation specifically provides forest management assistance to private forest landowners (Cooperative Farm Forestry Act of 1937, Cooperative Forest Management Act of 1950, Cooperative Forestry Assistance Act of 1978), assists in controlling forest pests (Forest Pest Control Act of 1947), and provides forestry extension advice (Smith-Lever Act of 1914, Renewable Resources Extension Act of 1978).

In addition to providing technical assistance in the form of advice to private forest landowners, the government also provides financial assistance to private landowners under a variety of laws. Both the Agricultural Conservation Program (ACP) and the Forestry Incentives Program (FIP) provide cost-share payments to nonindustrial private forest landowners who plant trees or perform timber stand improvement. Several states also offer cost-share programs. In 1943 Congress authorized long-term capital gains treatment of income from timber sales, which applied to industrial and nonindustrial timber owners alike. Reforestation tax benefits were enacted by Congress in 1980 but are limited to investments of $10,000 per year.

Most public assistance to private forest landowners is designed to promote increased production of timber outputs—production at levels that would be greater than those dictated by equilibrium market conditions. Generally, this has meant increasing the attractiveness of financial returns, often by reducing the cost of financial investments to the private forest landowner.

Skok and Gregersen (1975) divide public approaches to motivate U.S. nonindustrial timber production into two broad classes (Table 17-1). Direct incentive approaches, such as taxation or subsidies, provide identifiable monetary benefits to forest landowners who perform certain forest practices. Indirect approaches provide forest landowners with programs such as education, research, or fire protection that are subsidized with government funds. These same broad approaches of taxation, subsidies, education, research, and protection may be used to motivate landowners to adopt wildlife habitat management or environmental protection measures. These policy tools try to provide incentives ("carrots") to induce desirable private landowner behavior, as opposed to direct regulation (a "stick").

Skok and Gregersen also note that although most of these programs are based on the premise of divergent social and market values, efficiency is still important. At the very least, public programs should be socially desirable, with the social benefits exceeding the social costs. The following review examines the prevalent government programs other than regulation that affect privately owned forest resources.

TAXATION

State and federal tax benefits received by forest landowners include the exemption, remission, or deferred payment of taxes. Tax policy has been an important concern in forestry for over a century and was even identified as needing study as long ago as the 1924 Clarke-McNary Act. The timber tax sections of the U.S. Internal Revenue Service Code are important and complex, as is our federal tax system. Capital gains treatment of timber income, investment credits, yield taxes, and modified property tax laws are the principal tax treatments that affect timber production. Timber tax exemptions and rebate laws also have been tried by some states but have been of rather limited effectiveness (Skok and Gregersen 1975). Reduced property tax laws for forest lands are common in most states. Tax benefits are indirect financial approaches, in that forest landowners in most cases must apply and wait for tax relief. They still must

TABLE 17-1. Principal Public Incentive Programs for Private Forestry in the United States

Category	Comments
Taxation (exemption, remission, or deferred payment of taxes)	
1. Capital gains treatment for timber	1. Used the most by industrial ownerships—complex procedures reduced use by small private forest land owners; Tax rate advantage eliminated in 1986; slight advantage restored in 1990
2. Reforestation tax incentives	2. Amortize up to $10,000 investment per year over 8 years; receive 10% investment tax credit.
3. Yield taxes	3. Declining in use
4. Modified Property Tax Laws (current use valuation, modified assessment rate)	4. Now adopted by almost every state in nation
5. Tax exemptions and rebate laws	5. Limited effectiveness and applications
Financial Assistance (subsidization of production through cost-sharing, provision of material, etc.)	
1. Agricultural Conservation Program (ACP)	1. General agricultural conservation program that includes timber and wildlife components
2. Forestry Incentives Program (FIP)	2. Forest timber production program with cost-sharing for planting and management
3. Stewardship Incentive Program (SIP)	3. Multiple-use forest stewardship program designed to replace FIP by 1995
4. State incentives programs	4. Publicly and/or privately funded programs with cost-sharing for mostly timber and some wildlife production and management practices
5. Soil Bank and Conservation Reserve Programs	5. Conservation Reserve Program from 1956 to 1960 (Soil Bank) and from 1986 to 1995 (CRP) that converted erosive farm land to permanent grass or tree cover, with annual payments to participating owners

pay taxes, but not as much as without the benefits.

Although taxation and its subtleties are complex and technical, public debates over federal income taxes or state property taxes are among the hottest political issues. Millions of landowners are affected by federal income tax laws. Property taxes affect thousands of landowners in each state, and county tax revenues make forest tax receipts of great in-

terest to the other residents who want good schools, roads, and other public services. Small changes in tax levels can have large impacts on management costs and on federal or county revenues. Thus tax debates, such as the Georgia property tax issue illustrated in Chapter 8, can lead to strong emotions and acrimony. Many state and regional forestry associations monitor tax legislation continually and lobby to reduce taxes for

TABLE 17-1. Continued

Category	*Comments*
6. FHA loans	6. Low-interest, long-term loans, very limited availability for forestry
7. Low cost seedlings	7. Grown by state nurseries with some federal financial support
Technical Assistance (on-the-ground advice, extension programs)	
1. State technical assistance programs (and SCS soil conservationists)	1. Provide on-the-ground advice to forest landowners, with some federal funding and support from State and Private Forestry
2. State extension programs	2. Provide educational programs, and field demonstrations, and disseminate research results
3. State and Private Forestry, USDA Forest Service	3. Provide federal assistance to state forestry agencies, who advise landowners
Indirect (government research, training, marketing information, etc.)	
1. State Fish and Wildlife Agencies	1. Administer game management laws and nongame programs; provide wildlife habitat and management advice; receive support from U.S. Fish and Wildlife Service
2. USDA Forest Service, USDA Fish and Wildlife Service, state and university applied research programs	2. Research on basic and applied forestry and wildlife topics of value to private owners
3. Public cooperative forest protection programs such as Clarke-McNary Act, Forest Pest Control Act	3. Necessary because fire, insects, and disease spread across ownership boundaries and present large risks
4. Production and marketing cooperatives	4. Limited use and success to date
5. State income tax checkoff systems	5. Provide state taxpayers opportunity to designate portion of tax refund for nongame wildlife management

Source: Adapted from Skok and Gregersen (1975)

their members or fight tax increases. A number of forest economists have been involved in these debates—as analysts and advocates—and many have become pariahs in their states if their studies do not support the position of the forestry interest groups.

INCOME TAXES

Federal and state income taxes must be paid on receipts from timber income just like ordinary income from jobs or other investments.

These taxes usually must be paid at the person's or corporation's marginal tax rate based on the total timber income received, less any deductions that may be taken based on the costs of acquiring or planting and managing timber up to the time of harvest. The total tax due may occasionally be reduced by tax credits, which are direct subtractions from the tax bill.

Reducing income taxes by providing tax deductions or tax credits for timber growing is a way of favoring such investments. This section describes the federal income tax benefits related to timber, as of 1990. Many state income tax laws are based on federal law, but they vary so much that no generalizations will be made about them here.

Capital Gains

In 1943 Congress passed legislation, over President Roosevelt's veto, that allowed timber growing income to be treated as long-term capital gains for tax purposes. Prior to that time, only individuals who were not in the business of growing timber and who made infrequent sales could claim capital gains. The 1943 legislation, which went into effect in 1944, extended this treatment to individuals and corporations engaged in the business of growing timber. Based on the 1943 legislation, for both corporate and personal income taxes, revenue from timber sales could be taxed as capital gains under Section 631 of the Internal Revenue Service Code (Siegel 1978).

Before 1987 capital gains treatment allowed timber income to be taxed at more favorable rates than ordinary income, similar to the treatment for investments in the stock market. For individuals, capital gains income was subject to a 60 percent exclusion. Thus, only 40 percent of the gain was taxed. For example, individuals who were typically taxed at the 50 percent maximum marginal rate on ordinary income would pay only (40 percent) × (50 percent), or 20 percent, on timber sale income and other capital gains. (The marginal tax rate is the tax rate on the last amount of income earned—the highest tax rate an individual or firm pays.) There was no exclusion for corporations, but there was a tax rate differential between ordinary income (46 percent marginal tax rate) and capital gains (28 percent marginal tax rate); this tax treatment was intended to and did benefit investors in a long-term endeavor such as timber growing. Long-term is defined in the Internal Revenue Code as a six-month investment period; timber investments are obviously much longer.

In the Tax Reform Act of 1986, Congress eliminated the preferential taxation rate for capital gains income, including timber, by re-

ducing the amount of income excluded from taxation to zero. It also reduced the maximum marginal tax rate for individuals from 50 percent to 28 percent (there was a special bracket of 33 percent in some cases). The landmark 1986 act was intended to eliminate many tax breaks, such as capital gains, in order to reduce tax rates for most individuals (Siegel 1987). Timber income still may be treated as a capital gain if sold according to Section 631 of the Internal Revenue Code, but from 1986 to 1990, it was taxed at the same rate as ordinary income. However, the 1987 tax law did lower tax rates for all corporations and most individuals, so the loss of preferential treatment of capital gains did not represent an immense tax increase on timber income. Many organizations and legislators have proposed reinstating a preferential tax treatment of timber capital gains, but they remained unsuccessful as of 1992. Some of these proposals have linked capital gains treatment of timber income to wetlands protection or management plan requirements.

In 1990 Congress again revised the federal income tax laws, which did have implications for timber income. Most individuals would be taxed at their current marginal income rate for most income, including timber (Cubbage, Gunter, and Olsen 1991). This was either 15 or 28 percent of sale income less the cost basis of timber sold (capitalized expenses and a pro rata share of the original purchase cost of any standing timber) at the time of sale. Higher income taxpayers—those making approximately more than $100,000 per year—were taxed at a 31 percent marginal rate on most income. Timber income, however, still could be taxed at the 28 percent capital gains rate, providing a slight advantage. Corporations were still taxed at the new standard corporate rate of 34 percent.

Capital gains treatment of timber income is based on the idea that timber growing is a long-term investment. As such, it should receive the same tax benefits as other long-term capital investments, such as buying stock in corporations. Capital gains treatment is said to help private landowners produce more timber for the future, helping to overcome any long-term market inefficiencies. It also offsets nominal increases in value that are caused only by inflation of assets held for long time periods. The extension to corporate ownership, however, is unusual. No other industrial sectors received capital gains tax treatment of income from the sales of their product (nor does any other sector involve such a long-term production process).

Despite more than 40 years of capital gains use, very few empirical studies were performed to measure the actual effects of the policy in the forestry sector. Indeed, for nonindustrial private forest owners, it was difficult to even estimate the number of people using capital gains, let alone its effects on timber supplies. The capital gains provisions are complex, so forest industry probably took more advantage of the laws than did nonindustrial private owners (Skok and Gregersen 1975). In 1976 Sunley estimated that capital gains treatment of timber income amounted to a $215 million subsidy (loss of federal revenues)—$155 million from reduced corporate tax payments, the remainder from individuals. The forest products industry has been a vocal supporter of capital gains since its passage. In the 1980s the U.S. Treasury estimated that capital gains treatment costs about $500 million per year in forgone revenues, with most gains accruing to forest products companies. Capital gains provisions for timber were continually under threat of modification or elimination.

In one empirical study on the effects of corporate income taxation in the forest industry, Singleton (1983) found that the investment tax credit had the most significant stimulative impact on investment expenditures, tending to favor investments in short-lived assets. Capital gains income tax provisions also stimulated investments somewhat, favoring assets that appreciated in value. Singleton also found that the 1979 corporate tax rate decrease had little measurable effect in stimulating investment. Capital gains did reduce the effective tax rate of timber income.

In a stand-level analysis of the impacts of the 1986 elimination of capital gains treatment for timber, Guertin and Rideout (1987) found that the higher taxes did reduce investment returns on all sites, resulting in some low-site lands becoming economically unproductive. Boyd and Newman (1991) performed an econometric study to assess the economywide changes expected from the 1986 Tax Reform Act. Although they did find that forestry sector output was affected more than other industrial sectors by the act, the net change was only −1.4 percent, which was much less than that predicted by other studies. These more modest effects of the capital gains loss were caused by changes in demand for forest products and substitution of inputs, which were not considered in stand-level analyses alone.

Management Cost Deductions

In order to claim a tax deduction, individuals and corporations must "capitalize" their regeneration expenses—that is, record any site preparation, planting, and vegetation control costs and carry these costs on the books until harvest, when they are deducted from harvest income as a cost of timber sold. Alternatively, the first $10,000 of reforestation expenses may be amortized over an 84-month period (see next section on reforestation incentives). Any harvest sale costs, such as timber marking charges, advertising expenses, or consulting fees, also may be deducted from stumpage revenues. Income tax must then be paid on the net returns. This treatment of capitalizing regeneration costs was consistent with both the pre- and post-1986 tax revision.

Before the 1986 law, all corporate and individual forest landowners could "expense" management costs—that is, deduct the costs of management, such as property taxes, administration, and timber stand maintenance from their income taxes in that current year. When management costs cannot be expensed, they must be capitalized. If intermediate harvests are made, capitalized expenses can be deducted then as well. Regeneration costs must be capitalized, but management costs could be expensed before 1986.

Corporate owners may still expense management costs as of 1992, as well as any interest costs incurred. However, the new law, through the use of passive loss rules, also attempted to eliminate the practice of deducting expenses of one activity against income earned from other sources. The status of taxpayers may fall into at least three categories, depending on whether they are determined by the IRS to perform active versus passive activities, and whether they are making investments or are actually in the trade or business (Cubbage, Gunter, and Olsen 1991).

1. *Active trade or business*: All management costs, property taxes, and interest are fully deductible against income from any source if the owner "materially participates" in timber management activities.

2. *Investor*: Expenses can be recovered as miscellaneous itemized deductions to the extent they exceed 2 percent of adjusted gross income—similar to the floor for charitable contributions—or they can be capitalized as carrying charges. The latter avoids the permanent loss of the deductions that fall below the 2 percent floor. However, landowners cannot both expense and capitalize in the same year. Property taxes are deductible against income from any source. In addition, interest on debt incurred to buy or carry property held for investment is limited to net investment income for the year.

3. *Passive trade or business*: Expenses can be offset only against passive income. However, any net passive loss can be carried forward to be recovered against future passive income.

Determining passive and active status for NIPF landowners is a complex and still evolving process. Limited partnerships—in which landowners do not help manage the land—clearly are passive. Absentee owners who receive most of their income from other sources—such as doctors, lawyers, or airline pilots—would probably be considered investors, rather than in the trade or business. Farmers who manage and harvest their timber as part of a farming enterprise are likely to qualify as active in the trade or business. However, these generalizations may vary considerably from case to case. Even though capital gains income is usually taxed at the same rate as ordinary income, landowners may still want to claim their timber sales as capital gains to help demonstrate "active" management status.

Individuals or advisors should determine the probable taxable status of the investor for filing taxes or for analyzing investments. Regeneration expenses should be carried through to harvest and deducted as a cost of timber sold before taxable income can be determined (unless the owner elects to amortize up to $10,000 in reforestation expenses). Management-expense deductions can be entered as a return in the current year if they qualify; otherwise, they must be added to the cost basis, carried forward, and subtracted from harvest revenues.

If owners make intermediate harvests in a stand, they may subtract a portion of capitalized expenses from stumpage returns. The proportion of total merchantable volume removed to total merchantable volume of the stand determines the allowable expenses of sale. For example, if one-third of the merchantable volume were removed in a thinning at age 15 and the cost basis attributable to site preparation and planting was $180/acre, then the owner could deduct $60/acre for the cost of timber sale from the stumpage returns per acre. The unused or adjusted cost basis of $120/acre would be carried forward for recovery against revenue from future timber harvests.

The U.S. Congress Joint Committee on Taxation estimated that allowing the deduction of timber growing expenses after establishing a stand of trees, rather than capitalizing them, would reduce federal revenues by $1.9 billion from 1990 to 1994 (U.S. General Accounting Office 1990). This amounts to a cost of $380 million per year in forgone revenues, which is why the management expensing for passive owners was disallowed in the 1986 tax reform law.

Reforestation Investment Tax Incentive

In 1980 the reforestation tax incentive provision, or the Packwood Amendment, was enacted to allow forest landowners to receive a tax credit against their income taxes for timberland investments. To make passage of the law easier, the amendment was attached as a rider (Title III) to the Recreational Boating and Facilities Improvement Safety Act of 1980 (P.L. 96-451). Under this law, private landowners may receive both federal tax credits and deductions on their income tax for planting trees. For up to $10,000 per year of reforestation expenses, the legislation allows a 10 percent investment credit plus deduction of the expenses over an eight-year schedule, instead of waiting to deduct expenses at the time of harvest. If owners use this method, they cannot deduct the same reforestation costs from harvest sales, because they are capital expenditures and cannot be deducted twice. The method could be used by a forest industry firm as well as by individuals, but the $10,000 annual cap limits its application to about 50 to 100 acres per year, which may be too small an area for a company to bother with filing for the tax break.

The investment tax credit cannot exceed $1000 annually. The amortized deduction requires that one-fourteenth of the investment be deducted in the first year, one-seventh in the second through seventh years, and one-fourteenth the eighth year. If owners do take the full 10 percent investment credit (which is usually to their advantage if they have taxes due), they can deduct only 95 percent of the reforestation expenses. Reforestation tax incentives were retained in the 1986 Tax Reform Act—one of very few investment credits to survive tax reform.

The reforestation tax incentives program is widely used by nonindustrial private forest owners. In a sample of NIPF owners in nine southern states, Royer and Moulton (1987) reported that 59 percent of the landowners who planted trees claimed the tax incentives. The tax incentives also are easy to apply for and receive compared to financial incentives and cost-shares. One need only claim the credits and deduction on the tax return. Incentive payments depend on availability of funds and approval of a local Agricultural Stabilization and Conservation Service committee.

The U.S. General Accounting Office (1990) estimated that the amortization of reforestation expenses and the related income tax credit would reduce federal revenues by $400 million for the five-year period from 1990 through 1994, or about $80 million per year. As might be expected, the reforestation tax incentives have favorable impacts on timber investment returns made by nonindustrial private forest landowners (Dennis 1983). For landowners in the 40 percent tax bracket, average loblolly pine investment rates of return increased from 6.9 to 8.4 percent. Douglas-fir investments increased from 7.3 to 8.2 percent. Although income tax rates were reduced in the 1986 tax reform, the reforestation tax incentives still improve tree planting returns considerably.

PROPERTY TAXES

Property taxes are the principal source of funding for county, township, local, or city governments, as well as some state revenues. They provide the basis for schools, roads, police and fire protection, sanitation, parks, and other government services. Property taxes always have been a forest policy issue in the United States. In fact, the effects of property taxes were the first forest policies that received legislative attention. Property taxes are levied at the state or local level, so naturally, such tax legislation has been enacted by state, not federal, governments. Most state tax policies were designed to encourage reforestation and conservation of forests. Meeks (1982) concluded that tax legislation is the most extensive method used by the states to encourage management of nonindustrial private forests.

Ad valorem (according to value) taxes are levied on real and personal property, including land, timber, crops, houses, vehicles, livestock, buildings, and personal belongings. Various states exempt some of these items from taxation. For tax purposes, property usually is assessed at its fair market value, and then a percentage of the fair market value—such as 40 percent—is taxed. Local governments then add the totals for all property to determine the total taxable value of all their taxable property—termed the *grand list* in New England and the *tax digest* in the South.

To determine the tax rate, government agencies divide the total budget by the total taxable value of property to determine a *millage* rate. The millage rate is expressed as a dollar of tax due per $1000 of taxable value. For example, a millage rate of 25 mills (0.025) on timberland assessed at $500 per acre, at 40 percent of fair market value, would mean a tax of $5 per acre per year ($500 × 0.40 × 0.025 = $5).

Property taxes are a tax on total wealth, not on investment or employment income. They have provided the basis for local government funding since colonial days. As a wealth tax, they may at times cause problems for forest landowners. The tax occurs each year, but timber incomes occur only periodically. Furthermore, taxing standing timber as it grows gives older timber a higher assessed value than young timber, which may cause premature harvests to avoid higher taxes. Last, taxing forest land at its highest and best use in metropolitan fringe areas may lead to tax burdens that are greater than the income one can receive from growing timber, thus forcing land conversion to more developed uses. Problems such as these occur often with timberland taxes, especially as people demand better schools and local services but try to avoid higher taxes. Legislative debates, court challenges, and tax revolts about property taxes occur frequently throughout the United States.

Hickman (1982, p. 53) summarized the current status of forest property tax laws in the United States. First, he described the types of special forest property tax laws.

Special forest tax laws can be grouped into three classes: (1) exemptions and rebates, (2) yield taxes, and (3) modified property taxes. Statutes in the last group are themselves of three types— deferred payment laws, modified rate laws, and modified assessment laws. A fourth class of special forest tax—the severance tax—will not be considered because it is not a substitute for the general property tax, but is imposed in addition to it.

Exemption laws provide for removal of forest land and/or timber from the property tax rolls, either permanently or for some specified number of years. A timber exemption may apply to all standing timber, planted stands, immature stands, trees of a particular species, or trees retained for specific purposes, such as reforestation or windbreaks.

Rebate laws provide that landowners who engage in some approved activity, such as tree planting, may subsequently apply for abatement (i.e., refund) of a portion of the taxes levied on the value of their land, timber, or both. The rebates generally continue for only a limited period of time, and may be given as a direct cash payment or a reduction from the total amount of taxes owed.

Yield tax laws provide for a conceptual separation of land and timber values. Land values normally remain subject to the annual property tax, although sometimes in modified form. Timber values go untaxed until the time of harvest. At this juncture, a gross income tax equal to some percentage of the stumpage value of the products cut, is imposed.

Deferred payment laws provide that annual taxes on forest land and timber are to be determined as for other classes of property, but that some portion of each year's tax is to be postponed until the time of timber harvest.

Modified rate laws provide that forest land and timber are to be assessed like other forms of property, but that a different tax rate, lower than otherwise applicable, is to be used in computing the tax.

Finally, *modified assessment laws* provide that forest properties are to be valued differently from other forms of property. If the fair market value as highest and best use is retained as the basic valuation standard, forest assessments may be frozen or calculated using a reduced assessment ratio. Alternatively, fair market value may be abandoned in favor of another valuation standard such as current use value.

Exemption laws were the earliest form of tax relief enacted, beginning in the Great Plains (Nebraska, 1861) and spreading to the Northeast (1872–1878). During the 1940s, 15 states had such legislation. In 1982 only 10 states had such laws, partially because of their limited effectiveness (Williams 1961) and the equity consideration that all property owners should pay a fair share. Only two states enacted rebate laws (Pennsylvania in 1887 and New Hampshire in 1903). Beginning in 1910 exemptions and rebates began to be supplanted by yield tax laws. Yield taxes were designed to ensure local revenues, yet defer the taxes until the time that forest properties produced income. Modified property tax laws now are the most common form of special property taxes for forest and agricultural lands. Details of each state law are reported in Hickman (1982); only a brief summary is contained here.

Exemptions and Rebates

In 1982, 11 states offered a total of 10 exemption laws and one rebate law. About two-thirds are mandatory and one-third are optional. Exemption tax treatment varied from complete exemptions for all standing timber (Alabama, North Carolina, Tennessee), to exemption of planted timber or young growth, to exemptions for up to 15 to 30 years.

Yield Taxes

Counties and municipalities in most states levy annual ad valorem taxes on both forest land and standing timber in order to obtain revenue to support local schools, roads, and other services. In many states young growth timber is taxed at a lesser rate than mature timber. Two reasons make this a disincentive to long-term investments in timber growing. First, annual taxing of a timber crop that only generates yields at harvest favors short rotations in order to pay ad valorem taxes. Thus rotation lengths may be shorter than if timber were taxed only at the time of harvest as a yield tax. Second, taxing mature growth at rates greater than young growth discourages holding large or more valuable timber, such as pines in the West. Owners would clearly prefer to cut timber soon after it is classed as mature, despite biological and perhaps economic advantages in holding timber until it reaches larger size classes. For example, under a 1989 Georgia law, a mature pine stand with 10,000 board feet of sawtimber might be taxed at $16 per acre per year, a cut-over stand at $2 per acre per year. This is a clear incentive to cut timber, and indeed it caused extensive public debates about Georgia timberland property tax policy in 1989 and 1990.

Hickman's (1982) survey found that 10 states had yield tax laws and four had "severance" taxes that were actually yield taxes. These laws tax forest land on an annual basis and forest timber only at the time of harvest. Accordingly, when timber is sold, forest landowners must notify the local tax assessors and pay taxes on the value of the sale. This arrangement should not penalize landowners for holding timber as it matures. Timber owners in aggregate pay as much yield tax as they would pay general ad valorem tax. However, tax incidence (the amount of tax paid) varies among individual owners. Yield taxes favor those who do not cut timber (i.e., those who hold forest land for amenity values) and those who have a small ratio of cut to mature timber inventory. To avoid this problem, New Hampshire allows local assessors to tax the holders of mature timber on the market value of that timber whether they cut it or not. For any owner operating a fully regulated forest on a sustained-yield basis, it would make no difference whether an ad valorem tax or a yield tax is applied (Vaux 1983).

Modified Property Taxes

Ad valorem taxes have traditionally been assessed and levied on the basis of the highest and best use for a piece of property. This policy tends to force lands into their most commercially valuable uses in order to pay the tax burden. Taxing farm or forest land on the basis of subdivision values will force conversion, unless landowners are wealthy and are willing to pay high taxes. Because productive agricultural and forest lands are generally deemed desirable for society, the wisdom of forced conversion to urban uses has been questioned.

In response, most state legislatures enacted use-value taxation or preferential property tax assessment rate laws that allow nonindustrial agricultural and forest landowners to receive reduced property tax rates. A wide variety of interest groups, planners, and environmentalists promote use-valuation to prevent forced conversions to higher land uses and urban sprawl, as well as lower tax rates.

Under current use-value laws, qualifying landowners usually must agree to keep their land in agricultural or forest uses. Usually they must file with the local tax assessor to receive preferential treatment. If they meet state and local requirements, their land is taxed at its current use or at a reduced rate. All but a few of these laws have restrictions and penalties for landowners who withdraw from the programs or make conversions without notices—sometimes lasting up to 10 years or more after the year of the tax break. Otherwise, the programs could merely serve as a tax dodge, with no penalties for switching lands into higher-valued uses. Florida, for instance, offers "greenbelt" tax breaks but has no withdrawal penalties, so the law has not done much to prevent development. Although these laws do benefit rural landowners, it should be noted that they generally shift property taxes to other residential or commercial sectors, which is not without drawbacks and detractors. They also may shift taxes from small forest landowners to large forest landowners.

Hickman (1982) also surveyed such use-value (modified assessment) and modified rate laws in the United States. At that time 38 states had a total of 43 modified assessment and 5 modified rate statutes. Nearly one-third of the existing laws are mandatory and two-thirds are optional. States with optional laws impose a variety of eligibility constraints.

The most common, employed in 29 statutes, is based on tract size. The second most common, used in 10 statutes, pertains to the minimum number of years a property must have been in forest use before the owner can seek classification. Other constraints, in order of decreasing frequency of use, are based on: (1) income from past timber sales, (2) the existence of an approved timber management plan, (3) the question of whether or not an area has been "zoned" as forest land, (4) the level of stocking, and (5) the length of property ownership. (Hickman 1982, p. 60)

Payments in Lieu of Taxes

Public lands—federal, state, and local—are generally exempt from property taxes. In regions where public lands comprise a large share of the total land area, the tax base may be small. The loss of potential tax revenues created much of the early opposition to the national forests in the West and continues to create hard feelings in some Appalachian and TVA area counties.

Soon after the establishment of the National Forest System, Congress enacted the National Forest Revenue Act of 1908 and an additional act in 1911 to ensure that western counties would still receive some tax funds from national forests. These laws require that 25 percent of forest receipts taken in by the U.S. Treasury be distributed to county governments for public schools and roads. In fiscal year 1990 the 25 percent fund distributed $346 million to local governments (Knudsen and St. Clair 1991).

However, there were large differences in the revenues produced by different parcels of federal lands. In order to provide some type of minimum tax level for local governments, Congress enacted the Payments in Lieu of Taxes (PILT) program in 1979. The PILT program, which is administered by the BLM, generally guarantees counties a federal payment of at least $0.75 per acre each year.

The national forest 25 percent fund received about 90 percent of its funds from timber sales, with only about 10 percent generated by recreation, grazing, and land leasing fees. This places pressure on counties to support timber harvests, versus noncommodity types of management. In fact, counties with large national forest timber harvest levels often received more taxes per acre than from comparable private lands, while noncommodity counties received less.

To change these economic incentives for development, Knudsen and St. Clair (1991) suggested five alternatives. One would be for Congress to pay taxes equivalent to prevailing local rates, but this would be difficult to administer and would depend on yearly congressional funding. Other proposals have included a tax floor equal to the historic

25 percent levels (which would favor past timber-rich counties); making a temporary floor that would decrease as timber harvests did (a phased-in reduction); and developing a 50 percent fund to offset reduced timber sales (which might ameliorate or might magnify timber dependencies and would exacerbate problems with below-cost timber sales). Last, the authors suggested allowing the Forest Service to charge market prices for all resources, in order to increase their importance as management objectives. These national federal payment policies will continue to affect local services and affect forest resource management. Environmental groups favor policies that provide fewer incentives for timber harvest; forest industry prefers harvests; and local governments depend on the revenues. Thus, consensus on policies will be difficult.

FINANCIAL ASSISTANCE

Nonindustrial private forest landowners may receive a variety of direct financial incentives, again primarily for timber growing purposes. These range from federal and state cost-sharing programs to loans and low-cost seedlings. These laws began with seedling production assistance under the 1924 Clarke-McNary Act and gradually expanded as part of U.S. farm programs and separate forestry programs.

AGRICULTURAL CONSERVATION PROGRAM

As its name implies, the Agricultural Conservation Program (ACP) is a general farm program designed to promote resource-conserving practices on farms. ACP began as a federal policy response to the "dust bowl" problems in the 1930s. It was part of the Soil Conservation and Domestic Allotment Act of 1936 and has been continued in various forms to the present. ACP is designed to encourage farm conservation practices, including tree planting, timber stand improvement, and wildlife habitat improve-

ment. Landowners performing these or other conservation practices may receive partial reimbursements called cost-share payments through the county office of the Agricultural Conservation and Stabilization Service (ASCS). ACP was designed primarily to be a farm conservation program, and as such it differs from the timber-production orientation of most direct forestry programs.

Forestry funding and acreage treated under the ACP program has been rather limited. Table 17-2 summarizes ACP program accomplishments from 1960 through 1986. During this period, about 1 to 2 percent of the annual ACP funds were spent on planting trees and shrubs. ACP timber stand improvement funds decreased steadily from $2 million in 1960 to about $1.5 million in the 1970s and 1980s. Inflation reduced the value of the constant nominal dollar appropriations, so the acreage treated for both practices has declined significantly since the 1960s. Plantings made under ACP generally have been retained in trees (Kurtz, Alig, and Mills 1980).

FORESTRY INCENTIVES PROGRAM

ACP funds for tree planting and timber stand improvement dwindled in the 1960s because of increasing competition for the available funds and the reluctance of ASCS county boards oriented to farm management to approve forestry practices. Perceiving needs for a better funding base, forestry interest groups successfully lobbied Congress for a separate cost-share program for forestry practices. In 1973 Congress enacted the Forestry Incentives Program (FIP) attached as a rider (Title X) to the Agriculture and Consumer Protection Act of 1973. The use of a rider to another bill helped FIP to be enacted—as did the Packwood Amendment for reforestation tax incentives. This approach helped the rather small forestry interest groups get their modest laws through Congress as part of a larger package.

FIP is primarily a timber production program that authorizes cost-share payments for reforestation and timber stand improvement,

TABLE 17-2.   Funding of forestry practices through the Agricultural Conservation Program, 1960–1983

Year	Reforestation			Timber Stand Improvement		
	Nominal Dollars (millions)	Percent of Total ACP Funds	Acres (thousands)	Nominal Dollars (millions)	Percent of Total ACP Funds	Acres (thousands)
1960	3.9	2.0	339	2.0	1.0	256
1961	3.9	1.9	319	2.2	1.0	256
1963	3.0	1.6	203	1.7	0.9	183
1964	2.8	1.4	187	1.6	0.8	158
1966	2.7	1.4	181	1.6	0.8	210
1967	2.8	1.4	174	1.9	0.9	220
1968	2.5	1.4	148	1.5	0.8	169
1969	2.3	1.4	129	1.4	0.8	154
1970	2.4	1.4	133	1.4	0.9	132
1971	3.0	2.3	143	1.8	1.4	141
1972	6.8	3.6	227	n.a.[a]	n.a.	206
1973	2.3	1.1	62	n.a.	n.a.	62
1974	1.5	1.9	43	n.a.	n.a.	72
1975	1.5	1.1	37	n.a.	n.a.	52
1976	0.7	0.6	20	0.5	0.4	25
1977	1.9	0.8	33	0.9	0.6	43
1978	1.4	0.7	32	0.9	0.5	43
1979	2.1	0.9	47	1.2	0.5	66
1980	2.6	1.5	49	1.5	0.9	62
1981	3.3	1.8	53	1.7	0.9	75
1982	3.4	2.2	55	1.4	0.9	55
1983	3.8	2.2	66	1.2	0.7	38
1984	3.2	2.1	55	0.8	0.5	25
1985	4.8	2.9	87	1.0	0.6	34
1986	5.4	4.2	98	1.0	0.8	27

Source: Skok and Gregersen 1975; USDA Agricultural Stabilization and Conservation Service, Agricultural Conservation Program Fiscal Year Statistical Summaries; USDA Forest Service Internal Reports.

[a]n.a. = not available

site preparation for natural regeneration, and firebreak construction. ASCS is charged with program administration and the U.S. Forest Service is responsible for forestry technical assistance. State forestry agencies provide the assistance via cooperative agreements with the Forest Service. A state service forester must approve a landowners' forest management plan before practices can be performed and the county ASCS committee must decide which of the many applicants will receive funding. Service foresters also must approve performance of the practice before payment is made.

The federal cost-share rate is commonly 50 percent and has ranged up to 65 percent. The cost-share rate is determined by the state ASCS committee, which also allocates cost-share funds to counties in consultation with the state forester. In allocating funds, state committees follow criteria used by the U.S. Department of Agriculture in allocating funds to states. These include acreage of timberland and number of nonindustrial private forest landowners; potential productivity of timberland; and need for reforestation, timber stand improvement, and other practices. Consideration, however, also is given to the availability of vendor services for tree planting, site preparation and timber stand improvement work, historic use of cost-share funds, existence of forest landowner associations, and factors such as an adverse local timber growth–drain ratio (*Forest Farmer* 1985).

Nonindustrial private forest landowners are eligible for FIP cost-share funds, including individuals, groups, associations, or corporations whose stocks are not publicly traded. However, they cannot be primarily engaged in the business of manufacturing forest products or providing public utility services. Participants cannot own more than 1000 acres of forest land, but exceptions for ownerships of up to 5000 acres may be granted by the secretary of agriculture. In addition, tract sizes must be 10 acres or more to qualify. Minimum treatment size requirements were instituted after an early evaluation of the program, as was raising the maximum allowable forest land ownership size from 500 to 1000 acres. Land must be capable of growing 50 cubic feet of wood per acre per year. No landowner may receive more than $10,000 in total cost-share funds during one program year (Risbrudt, Kaiser, and Ellefson 1983).

Congress authorized $25 million per year for FIP. Appropriations have ranged from $10 to $15 million per year (Risbrudt et al. 1983). About 75 percent of the program funds are spent in the South. In the 1980s more than 200,000 acres were treated each year under FIP (Table 17-3). This is substantially more than the concurrent ACP treatment levels, but somewhat less than ACP in the early 1960s. The efficiency of FIP was reviewed in several evaluation studies (see Chapter 5).

By 1990 the FIP program had provided cost-share assistance to more than 110,000 participants on 3.7 million acres in 49 states and Puerto Rico, helping to provide broad political support for the program. Ten southern states accounted for more than 190,000 acres of FIP work each. Tree planting was the dominant practice, totaling 2.5 million acres. Timber stand improvement constituted 1.2 million acres of the total work accomplished, and site preparation for natural regeneration involved 22,000 acres (USDA Agricultural Stabilization and Conservation Service 1991).

Many advantages and disadvantages of state and federal cost-share programs have been noted, as discussed in Chapter 5. Royer and Moulton (1987) found that 48 percent of the

TABLE 17-3. FIP accomplishments and funding, 1974–1986

Year	Acres treated (thousands of acres)			Funding (millions of nominal dollars)	
	Total	Reforestation	TSI	Cost-shares paid	Cost-shares allocated
1974	293	168	125	9.1	10.0
1975–1976[a]	275	108	168	8.1	30.75
1977	307	153	155	10.3	13.5
1978	323	169	154	12.0	13.5
1979	329	212	117	14.5	13.5
1980	342	219	123	16.8	13.5
1981	314	211	103	17.8	11.25
1982	240	155	74	12.2	11.25
1983	205	143	58	10.2	11.25
1984	187	145	36	8.9	11.25
1985	207	167	37	10.0	11.23
1986	229	190	36	11.3	10.79

[a] Includes the short 1975 year when funds were received late, the full FY 1976, and the transition quarter when the beginning of the FY was changed from July to October.

Source: USDA Forest Service Internal Reports.

landowners contacted in a survey had used FIP, ACP, or one of the state cost-share programs when reforesting. Proponents stress the value of increases in long-run timber supplies and the corresponding decrease in wood prices. Incentive programs result in more wood being put on the market at any given price. In the long-run, consumers will pay a lower real price for wood products (Foster 1982, McKillop 1975). Other values supplied by incentive programs are water quality, recreation, wildlife, and aesthetics (Custard 1982). Opponents of cost-sharing point out that many NIPF landowners may delay reforestation when incentive money is not readily available (Wishart 1982), or that cost-sharing is being used by people who would have invested in reforestation anyway (Lee 1982). Additionally, some cronyism still exists on the rural ASCS committees, which often prefer that local farmers receive the cost-share payments, not absentee landowners, regardless of the site quality or needs for assistance.

Despite the criticisms and efforts by OMB to eliminate the program in the early 1980s, FIP survived and even prospered in the early 1990s. The American Forestry Association and other conservation organizations promoted FIP as a model public program that could be emulated to help plant trees to store carbon, thus ameliorating global climate change. The efforts were moderately successful and helped lead to the America the Beautiful tree planting program that was developed by the Bush administration to provide environmental benefits in urban and rural areas.

STEWARDSHIP INCENTIVE PROGRAM

In the 1990 farm bill, a new federal program—the Stewardship Incentive Program—was authorized to supersede FIP. The new farm bill—called the Food, Agriculture, Conservation and Trade Act of 1990—was signed into law by President Bush on November 18, 1990. Like prior farm bills, the 1990 law is massive and complex, containing 25 major titles. Title XII reauthorized or developed new authority for many forest Service State and Private Forestry programs. These programs fall under the general umbrella of President Bush's America the Beautiful (ATB) National Tree Planting Initiative.

Section 1216 of Title XII establishes a Stewardship Incentive Program (SIP), which will ultimately serve as the basis for all cost-share assistance for promoting protection, management, and reforestation of nonindustrial private forest lands, and it will replace FIP by December 31, 1995. The five-year transition period was provided to permit landowners and implementing agencies to become familiar with SIP. SIP is intended to provide cost-share assistance for a broader range of multiple-use forestry activities. The Stewardship Incentive Program was authorized to spend $100 million per year for fiscal years 1991 through 1995, but appropriations were less than $20 million annually in the first two years.

Nine SIP practices have been approved: management plan development; reforestation and afforestation; forest and agroforest improvement; establishment, maintenance, and renovation of windbreaks and hedgerows; protection and improvement of soil and water; protection and improvement of riparian areas and wetlands; fisheries habitat enhancement; wildlife habitat enhancement; and forest recreation enhancement. To qualify for payments, a landowner must have a stewardship management plan developed under the Forest Stewardship Program (FSP), established in 1989, or a plan developed through the SIP program.

At the state level, stewardship committees are being formed to develop statewide program policies. Membership on these committees will include representatives from local governments, consulting foresters, environmental and conservation groups, forest products industry, forest landowners, and land trust organizations. State foresters (or their designated representatives) will chair the committees. Each committee can adopt all or just some of the nine approved practices, depending upon the specific needs of each state, as well as establish flat rates of cost-share payments that will cover up to 75 percent of the actual costs of implementing SIP practices.

STATE INCENTIVE PROGRAMS

As of 1987, 14 states had some type of public or private state forestry incentive program (Table 17-4), and several others were considering programs (Bullard and Straka 1988, *Forest Farmer* 1985, Straka and Bullard 1987). In the South, Alabama, Mississippi, North and South Carolina, Texas, and Virginia all have significant programs that share the cost of

tree planting or timber stand improvement. In Florida, forest products firms provide free seedlings to landowners who plant pines. In the North and East, Illinois, Iowa, Maryland, Missouri, Minnesota, and New Jersey all provide cost-share funds for forestry practices. California is the only western state providing direct aid to nonindustrial private forest landowners.

Funds for these state programs are derived from a variety of sources, including severance taxes on timber, general state tax revenues, and voluntary forest industry contributions. Most state programs have acreage limits (min-

TABLE 17-4. Summary of State Forestry Incentive Programs, 1987

Alabama Resource Conservation Program (1985)—60 percent of the total costs for tree planting, site preparation, and timber stand improvement are reimbursed. Funded by trust fund from off-shore oil leases.

California Forest Improvement Program (1980)—75 percent for site preparation, reforestation, stand improvement, land conservation, planning, and fish and wildlife habitat improvements. Funded by revenues from timber sales on state-owned lands.

Florida Reforestation Incentives Program (1981)—Pine seedlings free of charge. Funded by forest industry through the Florida Forestry Association.

Illinois Forestry Development Program (1983)—60 percent through fiscal year 1986, 80 percent after July 1, 1987, for tree planting, site preparation, timber stand improvement, and fencing. Funded through a 4 percent harvest fee. Also, since 1987, seedlings provided without charge to landowners having an approved forest regeneration plan on record. Funded through general appropriations.

Iowa Woodland Fencing Program (1985)—50 percent for fencing of forest land subject to soil losses from grazing. Funded through general appropriations.

Maryland Woodland Incentives Program (1985)—50 percent for reforestation and timber stand improvement. Funded through a 4–5 percent tax on wooded lands transferred to nonagricultural use valuation for property taxes.

Minnesota Forestry Improvement Program (1985)—65 percent for woodlands fencing, firebreaks, and picket gopher control; 50 percent for road construction. Funded through general appropriations.

Mississippi Forest Resource Development Program (1974)—50 percent for tree planting or seeding, site preparation, timber stand improvement, and silvicultural burning. Funded through a timber severance tax.

Missouri Soil and Water Conservation Program (1985)—75 percent for tree planting and fencing. Funded by a 0.10 percent sales tax; purpose is to encourage conversion of marginal soils to woodland and to prevent erosion due to grazing.

New Jersey Farmland Preservation Program (1986)—50 percent for plantation establishment, site preparation, and timber stand improvement. Funded through a state bond fund.

North Carolina Forest Development Program (1977)—40 percent for tree planting or seeding, site preparation, silvicultural clear-cutting, and timber stand improvement. Funded through general appropriations and an assessment on primary forest products.

South Carolina Forest Renewal Program (1981)—50 percent for natural and artificial reforestation, timber stand improvement, and prescribed burning. Funded through general appropriations and an assessment on primary forest products.

Texas Reforestation Foundation (1981)—50 percent for approved reforestation practices. Funded through a voluntary assessment imposed by forest industry on harvested material.

Virginia Reforestation of Timberlands Program (1970)—50 percent for site preparation, tree planting, and pine release. Funded one-half by general state tax revenues and one-half from a forest products severance tax.

Source: Bullard and Straka 1988

imum and maximum ownership or treatment sizes) and require that a forest management plan be prepared for participating landowners. Flick and Horton (1981) did find that public investment returns from the Virginia plan were excellent, averaging over 9 percent per year. Few other state programs have had formal evaluations.

CONSERVATION RESERVE PROGRAMS

Soil Bank

The Conservation Reserve Program (CRP) of the 1950s—better known as the Soil Bank—was designed to encourage farmers to convert crop land to permanent grass or tree cover in order to reduce crop production and to remove excess farm land from production. The farm crop subsidy programs designed to stabilize farm income in the 1930s had become too successful by 1950, as farm production reached record levels, and crop payments ballooned. Because it was mostly a crop reduction program, both good and bad farm land was eligible for the Soil Bank. The program extended from 1956 to 1960 and paid for planting costs and made annual cash payments of $10 to $12 per acre per year to participating landowners for up to 10 years.

In the South, about 1,923,000 acres were planted with trees during the program, 700,000 acres in Georgia alone (Williston 1980). Nationally, the Soil Bank program financed planting of 2,154,428 acres of tree cover. Additionally, it helped establish 18.4 million acres of permanent vegetative (grass) cover, 14,000 acres of dams and ponds, 310,000 acres of wildlife cover, and 10,000 acres of managed marshlands. The program paid a total of $162 million in cost-share funds to establish these practices. Furthermore, Soil Bank rental payments amounted to $2.4 billion.

Returns to landowners under the CRP were excellent, but the program was a dismal failure at reducing farm production and surpluses, or stopping the mushrooming crop subsidy payments. Although millions of acres were taken out of production, intensive farming of other acres more than made up for this lost production.

The Soil Bank program made a significant contribution to timber inventory in the South. Most lands planted with trees remained out of agricultural crop production, even after cash payments to farmers were discontinued. Alig, Mills, and Shackelford (1980) found that 86 percent of the Soil Bank plantations in the South remained in trees, although some did need follow-up treatments such as thinning. With some stands approaching 25 years of age in 1976, more than 37 million cords of wood were standing on the plantations, and 11 million more had already been harvested.

An economic analysis of tree planting under the Soil Bank program in South Carolina found that the real social internal rate of return for the project was 6.3 percent (Marsinko and Nodine 1981). The analysts considered this to be a satisfactory return, particularly compared with other investments made during the 1950s.

Conservation Reserve

The 1985 farm bill—the Food Security Act—authorized a modern Conservation Reserve Program. The bill continued to grapple with problems of exploding crop subsidy payments—in excess of $20 billion per year in the early 1980s—and for the first time began to incorporate components that addressed environmental issues as well.

The 1985 Conservation Reserve Program was authorized for the crop years 1986 to 1990 and was intended to reserve not less than 40 million and not more than 45 million acres in the United States. At least one-eighth of this land, some 5 million acres, was to be planted in trees. Unlike the Soil Bank, the CRP was principally intended to be a soil conservation and wildlife habitat improvement program, not a crop reduction program. Thus only highly erodible lands were eligible. There was still some slight motivation to reduce crop payments, but by the 1980s policymakers realized that withdrawing marginally productive lands would not successfully affect production levels.

Owners or their agents could enter a contract with the secretary of agriculture and become CRP producers. Land ownership was not required. Applicants had to own or operate the land for at least three years, or since January 1, 1985, unless acquisition was by inheritance or succession, and they had to show that control of the land would be retained for the contract period. The land also had to be cultivated in three of the five preceding years.

Land enrolled in the CRP had to be placed in permanent grass or wildlife cover or trees. Most establishment costs, shared fifty-fifty by the government and the producer, were to be based on a flat rate for a particular practice. Annual rental payments to producers were to be made for 10 years under the conservation contracts to maintain the designated cover. Annual payments were determined through competitive bidding. All bids were placed in a countywide pool, and the lowest bids accepted first. Accepted initial bids ranged up to $90 per acre nationally, with an average of about $45 per acre—most tree planting bids were close to the average (Cubbage and Gunter 1987).

As of January 1990 a total of 33.9 million acres of land had been enrolled in the Conservation Reserve Program, with a total of 2.18 million acres in trees (Table 17-5). The South enrolled 1.99 million acres of forest land in the program. Georgia alone had 608,999 acres (28 percent of all tree planting in the United States), and Mississippi had 428,000 acres (20 percent of all tree planting). Other areas of the country had substantially smaller proportions of their Conservation Reserve Program enrollments planted in trees. The North had only 179,200 acres, or about 2 percent, of its total program acreage in trees. The Plains and Rockies had even less (about 4000 acres, or only 0.1 percent) of the total enrollment in trees. The Pacific Coast states also had very few acres enrolled in trees.

Although the Conservation Reserve Program retired substantial acreage from cropping, it should be noted that the program fell short of its goal of planting one-eighth of the acres reserved in trees. Only about 6 percent of the CRP has been planted in trees

as intended—not 12.5 percent. This suggests that developing public programs to establish even more tree plantations—such as those proposed to store carbon and reduce global warming—will require a more substantial effort and greater expenses to achieve higher enrollment rates.

The CRP established much more grass cover on erodible lands than tree cover (Table 17-5, 17-6). It provided cost-share payments of over $1 billion to establish about 32 million acres of grass and wildlife cover. These amounts far exceeded the $80 million paid to plant trees and the 2 million acres of resulting plantations. Planting of hybrid grasses was the dominant practice, involving almost 20 million acres and costing $750 million. There were also 8.1 million acres of native grasses planted, 1.9 million acres of wildlife plantings, 1.8 million acres already in grass or trees, and many windbreaks, water diversions and structures, and other soil conservation practices.

In total, the CRP expenditures were immense compared with traditional forestry or wildlife programs. CRP prompted the planting of as many trees in five years as FIP did in 16 years. Assuming the cash payments to keep land in the cover type cost $50 per acre per year, the total CRP payments for 10 years for all cover types would be $17 billion, in addition to the $1.3 billion of planting cost-shares. CRP tree planting annual payments and cost-shares alone will amount to more than $1 billion. Total cost-share payments for FIP since its inception through 1990 represent a comparatively small $167 million (USDA Agricultural Stabilization and Conservation Service 1991).

CRP expenditures were large for a natural resource program, but they were enabled by prevailing political realities. Retiring erodible farm lands proved to be good politics and reasonably good economics. The farmers who grew crops on these erodible lands received subsidy or support payments, and paying them to establish permanent cover was usually cheaper than the crop subsidy payments themselves. The farm interest groups generally supported the CRP proposal, because it

TABLE 17-5. Area Enrolled in Conservation Reserve Program as of January 1990

State	Total CRP (acres)	Grass and Other Cover (acres)	Tree Planting		
			Acres	Percent of State CRP	Percent of CRP Tree Total
Alabama	519,529	241,054	278,475	54	12.79
Alaska	25,375		0		0.00
Arizona	0	0	0	0	0.00
Arkansas	225,353	99,657	125,696	56	5.77
California	183,054	182,170	884	1	0.04
Colorado	1,953,042	1,952,400	642	0	0.03
Connecticut	10	0	10	100	0.00
Delaware	985	812	173	18	0.01
Florida	123,013	10,948	112,065	91	5.15
Georgia	663,156	55,109	608,047	92	27.93
Hawaii	85		0		0.00
Idaho	791,061	788,556	2,505	0	0.12
Illinois	633,580	611,019	22,561	4	1.04
Indiana	364,729	355,032	9,697	3	0.45
Iowa	1,970,159	1,959,232	10,927	1	0.50
Kansas	2,861,785	2,858,889	2,896	0	0.13
Kentucky	416,799	413,771	3,028	1	0.14
Louisiana	132,907	61,460	71,447	54	3.28
Maine	37,222	34,680	2,542	7	0.12
Maryland	16,058	14,735	1,323	8	0.06
Massachussetts	32	22	10	31	0.00
Michigan	196,304	187,279	9,025	5	0.41
Minnesota	1,830,672	1,787,673	42,999	2	1.97
Mississippi	726,897	298,782	428,115	59	19.66
Missouri	1,504,412	1,493,900	10,512	1	0.48
Montana	2,720,134	2,718,912	1,222	0	0.06
Nebraska	1,348,929	1,345,985	2,944	0	0.14
Nevada	3,124	3,124	0	0	0.00
New Hampshire	0	0	0	0	0.00
New Jersey	661	656	5	1	0.00
New Mexico	480,765	480,765	0	0	0.00
New York	54,605	51,808	2,797	5	0.13
North Carolinai	137,040	55,629	81,411	59	3.74
North Dakota	3,137,199	3,135,902	1,297	0	0.06
Ohio	254,129	244,906	9,223	4	0.42
Oklahoma	1,155,449	1,154,325	1,124	0	0.05
Oregon	517,150	513,959	3,191	1	0.15
Pennsylvania	92,646	90,337	2,127	2	0.10
Rhode Island	0	0	0	0	0.00
South Carolina	265,514	56,784	208,730	79	9.59
South Dakota	2,084,557	2,083,340	1,217	0	0.06
Tennessee	429,352	402,245	27,107	6	1.24
Texas	3,921,377	3,903,055	18,322	1	0.84
Utah	232,320	232,320	0	0	0.00
Vermont	187	187	0	0	0.00
Virginia	73,938	45,883	28,055	38	1.29
Washington	975,320	974,172	1,148	0	0.05
West Virginia	610	570	40	7	0.00
Wisconsin	604,060	560,265	43,795	7	2.01
Wyoming	257,022	257,014	8	0	0.00
States Total	22,922,125	31,719,323	2,177,342	6.4	100.00

Source: USDA Forest Service Internal Reports.

Note: Total for accepted contracts through the ninth CRP signup period.

TABLE 17-6. Conservation Reserve Program Accomplishments through February 1990

Practice	Acres	Cost-Share ($)	Cost Per Acre ($)
CP1 Tame Grass	19,818,043	740,958,422	37.39
CP2 Native Grass	8,121,510	365,093,838	44.95
CP3 Trees	2,012,805	79,860,581	39.68
CP4 Wildlife Plantings	1,946,915	73,403,865	37.70
CP5 Field Windbreaks	6,833	1,037,265	151.81
CP6 Diversions	83,472	808,217	9.68
CP7 Structures	38,017	1,871,487	49.23
CP8 Waterways	14,960	1,925,047	128.68
CP9 Wildlife Ponds	12,285	1,108,531	90.24
CP10 Already in Grass	1,767,440	42,230	0.02
CP11 Already in Trees	84,793	39,258	0.46
CP12 Wildlife Food Plots	14,953	0	0.00
CP13 Filter Strips	48,837	2,290,641	46.90
CP14 Wetland Trees	83,229	4,826,014	57.94
Total (Average)	34,054,092	1,273,265,396	37.39

offered income to remove marginal lands that were not very profitable even with crop subsidies. So did OMB and the Reagan administration. Forestry groups supported CRP for its tree planting components. Furthermore, retiring highly erodible lands was strongly supported by citizen conservation groups, who wanted to reduce water pollution and improve wildlife habitat on farms.

The preceding factors made CRP a political favorite. In fact, CRP and other conservation measures provided environmental protection groups with a strong carrot (incentive) that could be used to improve wildlife habitat on farms. They also were able to use the 1985 farm bill to help prevent loss of wildlife habitat by using the stick (regulation) to prevent plowing up wetlands (swampbuster) or arid soils (sodbuster) and force compliance (cross-compliance). These related measures, however, were less well received by farm groups, as discussed next.

The fears of supplanting people with pine trees prompted some political opposition to CRP, but these fears were overcome in the 1985 debates. Moulton et al. (1989) used the Forest Service IMPLAN model (Alward and Palmer 1985) to evaluate the economic effects of retiring erodible cropland in the CRP. Redmond, Cubbage, and Ullrich (1990) calculated the returns to tree planting under

the CRP program in southern Georgia and compared these with the returns to retaining lands in agricultural production, including the value of price supports for growing crops. Both studies found that the CRP offered excellent returns to landowners, as one would expect. They did find that removing crop land from production would have adverse effects on local communities for an initial period, due to reduced purchase of crop inputs. In later years, tree harvesting activity would exceed the earlier base-level farm activity.

The Department of Agriculture released regulations for implementing CRP that proved quite contentious. In implementing CRP, conservation groups lobbied that only highly erodible lands should qualify for government payments; they did not favor indiscriminate planting of any crop land in grass, or especially pine trees. Southern forestry interest groups lobbied continually for relaxed erodibility standards, so that greater areas could be planted. Indeed, from 1986 to 1989, the general standards for what was an erodible field and what percent of the field had to be erodible became more lenient. In 1988 drought throughout much of the Southeast and Midwest prompted the USDA to allow farmers to cut the hay on CRP reserve grasslands to feed livestock. This too created howls of protest from some wildlife groups, who pointed out that reserve lands were meant for wildlife, not domestic livestock.

The 1990 Revisions

The 1990 farm bill, which was the twenty-first such law enacted in the last 60 years, revised the CRP requirements. As mentioned in the discussion on SIP, the new bill is called the Food, Agriculture, Conservation and Trade Act (FACT ACT) of 1990. The conservation title in the 1990 law updated and broadened the CRP, creating a variety of new programs and acronyms. A broader Agricultural Resources Conservation Program (ARC) was established to address conservation of private farms and forests (Figure 17-1). The 1985 CRP and the new Wetland Reserve Program became parts of the Environmental Conservation Acreage Reserve Program (ECARP). Two other new programs were created as part of ARC—the Water Quality Improvement Program (WQIP) and the Environmental Easement Program (EEP).

Under the 1985 farm bill, about 34 million acres were enrolled in CRP. These became ECARP acres under the 1990 FACT ACT.

The 1990 bill authorized a total of 40 to 45 million acres in ECARP, including both CRP plus the Wetlands Reserve Program (WRP). The WRP component has a goal of 1 million acres by 1995, and 2 million acres were reserved as a safety net for farmers who will find it necessary to retire land in order to satisfy erosion control limitations under conservation compliance (see next section on cross-compliance).

The 1990 CRP continued the 1985 program with some modifications. To encourage planting of more hardwood trees CRP contracts may extend up to 15 years, as compared to only 10-year contracts for softwoods. Farmers also could elect and convert current CRP lands planted in grass to hardwood trees, and extend their contracts to a maximum of 15 years. Special CRP practices also were established for living snow fences (trees or bushes), permanent wildlife habitats, windbreaks, shelterbelts, filter strips, and sod waterways. All these practices that meet the basic eligibility requirements will be accepted without further competition and extended from 15 to 30 years, depending on the practice (Moulton 1991).

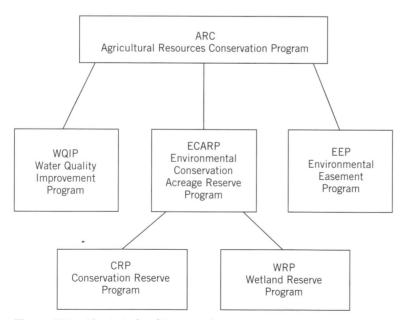

Figure 17-1. The Agricultural Resource Conservation Program

The Wetlands Reserve Program (WRP) is designed to provide cost-share payments for planting wetland trees. The EEP provides for perpetual easements for certain lands now in CRP and other critical areas such as riparian areas and critical wildlife habitats. Property owners would be paid for the value of the easement and receive up to 100 percent government cost-sharing. The Water Quality Improvement Program is designed to put 10 million acres under water quality plans by the end of 1995. Special targets of WQIP include critical croplands identified under state Section 319 nonpoint source pollution control plans, the protection of wellheads (water supply sources), areas with karst topography, and habitat for threatened and endangered plant and animal species. Payments under WQIP would be a 50 percent cost-share, with a $1500 limit, and direct payments of up to $3500 for additional costs or protection losses (Moulton 1991).

The 1985 farm bill and the subsequent 1990 bill represent classic examples of the modern issue network approach to making public policy. Farm interest groups, who have been very successful at obtaining government price supports and income guarantees, began their customary efforts to receive federal largesse in the farm bill. Wildlife interest groups also entered the fray, feeling that the best means of promoting wildlife conservation was through farm land habitat improvement or natural area retention. Several groups, especially the Sierra Club and the National Wildlife Federation, lobbied persistently to include the swampbuster, sodbuster, and cross-compliance provisions in the 1985 legislation. They also supported the Conservation Reserve Program in order to reduce soil erosion and wasteful crop production. Others interested in the CRP were forestry interest groups and legislators, particularly those in the South, who strongly supported the tree planting provisions of the bill. Farmers in other parts of the country also supported CRP, as long as they could plant permanent grass cover as well as trees.

SODBUSTER, SWAMPBUSTER, AND CROSS-COMPLIANCE

The impacts of the 1985 farm bill on improving wildlife habitat probably are greater than the substantial effect on future timber supplies. Taking erodible lands out of row crop production and placing them in either tree cover or permanent grass cover will obviously improve wildlife habitat. Another section of the 1985 farm bill contained a "sodbuster" provision designed to protect highly erodible land that has not been cultivated since 1980. Farmers who plow up such land can be disqualified from receiving any farm program commodity payments unless they follow an approved conservation plan. A companion "swampbuster" restriction applies to farmers who convert wetlands to croplands. The 1990 farm bill tightened the swampbuster requirements. Under the 1985 farm bill, no violation occurred, even if a wetland was drained, unless an agricultural commodity was actually planted on the site. The 1990 bill mandated that any action that made a wetland more suitable for crop production would be a violation. Highly erodible land used for crops between 1981 and 1985 was exempt from sodbuster penalties until 1990, but then it had to be farmed according to an approved conservation plan to be eligible for farm program benefits.

Conservation compliance under the 1985 and 1990 farm bills requires that farmers who crop highly erodible lands must apply conservation measures if they wish to participate in USDA farm programs. Farmers were to have conservation plans developed by January 1990 and fully implemented by 1995. These conservation requirements are termed cross-compliance—meaning that farmers must comply with all these conservation measures in order to receive other farm program benefits (Moulton 1991, Moulton and Dicks 1987).

The net effect of many interest groups working together produced the unique 1985 Food Security Act and the 1990 FACT ACT. One pundit noted that the farm bills actually did more *to* farmers than *for* farmers. Although both bills did continue to include crop subsidies, it also contained many conservation measures that would restrict farmers' actions. The CRP program has been a financial boon to many farmers, offering handsome returns on their enrollment in tree planting programs (Moulton and Dicks 1987). Sodbuster and swampbuster requirements have been received less favorably. The gradual tightening of the cross-compliance measures also has led to opposition by farmers.

The 1985 and 1990 farm bills have led to greater controls on farmers. Some critics view this federal intrusion as intolerable, but it seems to be part of the Faustian bargain one makes when accepting federal funds. College and universities that accept federal funds have had to meet federal guidelines for balance among women's and men's sports programs. Now landowners receiving crop subsidy or cost-share payments are being required to provide some balance between production and environmental protection. These tighter strings attached to federal cost-share/subsidy dollars could discourage landowners from enrolling in programs, and perhaps thus reduce program achievements.

It also is somewhat ironic that after years of seeking greater recognition, forestry interest groups succeeded by getting a title in the 1990 FACT ACT. The title includes both financial assistance and technical assistance programs. However, by being included in the farm bill, forest landowners who receive cost-share or technical assistance have since been interpreted to fall under the cross-compliance and farm management plan requirements. Several cases have occurred in which these strictures have been applied to regulate operations in wetlands. Thus inclusion in the 1990 farm bill has proven to be a mixed blessing for forest landowners.

OTHER DIRECT PAYMENTS

Landowners may receive direct financial support in the form of Farmers Home Administration or other subsidized loans. In addi-

tion, the cost of seedlings purchased from state nurseries for timber or wildlife plantings is subsidized with state and federal funds. These programs reduce direct costs for forest landowners and help improve their investment returns.

ILLUSTRATION: SEEDLING PRODUCTION AND PRIVATIZATION

Tree seedlings have been produced by the federal and state government for decades, but the programs have been threatened in recent years. State forestry technical assistance programs survived most budget cuts in the 1980s and 1990s. However, state seedling production capacities seemed most likely to be affected. These programs have used state and federal funds to subsidize growing costs and to ensure adequate growing stock for nonindustrial private forest landowners. The privatization arguments and politics have threatened these state programs in the 1990s.

The capacity of private firms to produce tree seedlings increased greatly during the 1980s. By 1990 forest industry nurseries produced a million seedlings; other industries 176,000; and states 560,000 seedlings. Except in the Midwest, where state nurseries dominated, private firms' tree nurseries far outproduced the state tree nurseries in all but a few states with a large forest industry sector (Mangold, Moulton, and Snellgrove 1991).

Critics questioned the quality of seedlings produced by state nurseries, both in terms of their genetic stock and quality control for lifting, planting, culling, and storing the trees. Seedlings from state nurseries also cost almost as much as those from private firms. Seedling production in some states perhaps represents the free marketeer's specter of a subsidized inefficient public program competing with efficient private firms.

The trends in nursery capacity, quality, and costs, coupled with the state budget deficits in the 1990s, threatened many state nurseries with closure. Effective private sector legislative pressures from large forest industries and small nursery owners, as well as the relentless need to cut state budgets, make state nurseries a prime target. And the alleged problems with seedling quality and almost comparable prices make nonindustrial private forest landowners and forest consultants reluctant to lobby actively to preserve the state programs. Thus it appears that many states will reduce their nursery operations and tree seedling sales as a result of the combination of technical, economic, and political factors.

TECHNICAL ASSISTANCE

Federal and state cooperation, not regulation, became the principal approach fostered by the Clarke-McNary Act of 1924. A variety of federal and state technical assistance programs stemmed from that act. They are designed to improve the conservation, management, and production of forest resources and include direct on-the-ground technical advice for landowners, extension programs, and education for loggers and timber processors. They also include a variety of wildlife programs that help private landowners improve wildlife habitat and populations. A large amount of private technical assistance is available now as well.

PUBLIC PROGRAMS

Cooperative efforts between the federal government and the states have officially provided technical on-the-ground forestry assistance to forest landowners since the Cooperative Farm Forestry Act of 1937 (Norris-Doxey Act). This act established a program of federal funding for technical assistance to farm woodland owners, which was actually provided by foresters employed by the states. The 1950 Cooperative Forest Management Act superseded the 1937 law and broadened the clientele served to include nonfarm private forest landowners, harvesters, and primary processors (Skok and Gregersen 1975). This was the first comprehensive program to provide substantial technical assistance to

nonindustrial private landowners. Under the programs, federal funds allocated to the states must be matched by state funds. Many private companies and consultants also provide forestry assistance to nonindustrial private forest landowners.

In 1978 the Cooperative Forestry Assistance Act consolidated all previous cooperative legislation. The act authorized the secretary of agriculture to provide financial and technical assistance to state foresters to produce seeds and seedlings; perform nonfederal forest planning; protect and improve watersheds; and provide technical and financial forestry assistance to private forest landowners, vendors, operators, wood processors, and public agencies. Funds provided by federal and state governments support state service foresters who perform the field work.

Every state in the nation has private forestry assistance programs. However, in the early 1980s large budget cuts were made in several state forestry budgets and federal appropriations for the U.S. Forest Service State and Private Forestry programs were declining (Borden 1982, Heinrichs 1983). Some states instituted a fee system for forest management assistance. Budget situations for most forestry agencies improved slightly in the late 1980s (Cubbage and Lickwar 1988), but the economic recession in 1990 through 1992 created new demands and budget cuts in almost all states, including for natural resource management agencies.

Current Status
Forestry technical assistance programs have evolved and changed their emphases over the years in order to continue and grow. The early programs provided mostly timber management assistance, including aid in timber marking. Foresters in many states now provide advice on how to comply with forest practice regulations. Pine regeneration was the focus of many state forestry assistance programs in the 1980s. Eastern state foresters in the 1990s have now become much more involved in multiple-use management and the forest stewardship program—designed to promote wildlife habitat and hardwood man-

agement. Forestry agencies in other states, such as Virginia, refocused their efforts to protect water quality by aggressively helping implement BMPs. These agency redirections have occurred in response to changing public opinions and helped maintain programs in the face of budget problems.

Title XII of the 1990 farm bill, the Forest Stewardship Act of 1990, amended the Cooperative Forestry Assistance Act of 1978, as mentioned before. The Forest Stewardship Program (Section 1215) established a forest stewardship program to encourage improved NIPF management. The stewardship program goal was to enroll 25 million acres of NIPF land by December 31, 1995. The expanded goals of technical assistance included a broader array of environmental protection benefits, such as protecting, maintaining, enhancing, restoring, and preserving forest lands and multiple values; protecting wildlife and fish species; producing alternative forest crops; managing the rural-urban land interface; protecting aesthetic values of forest lands; and protecting forests from fire, insects, and disease. The broader purposes in the 1990 legislation clearly reflected an increasing recognition of environmental values, as well as an effort by the State and Private Forestry (S&PF) division of the U.S. Forest Service and the state foresters to expand the clients and support for their programs.

The state foresters and State and Private Forestry cooperate in providing advice to loggers and sawmillers regarding harvesting, sawmilling, lumber drying, secondary processing, wood energy, and market and industrial development, as part of the Forest Product Utilization programs. Harvesting and marketing programs are available to landowners. In an evaluation of the Sawmill Improvement Program, Risbrudt and Kaiser (1982) found excellent returns to sawmillers and social returns to the program. The Forest Service and some states also offer urban forestry programs, which were authorized federally in 1972. The programs emphasize combatting insect and disease outbreaks and utiliz-

ing wood that would otherwise be lost from pests and land clearing.

Soil Conservation Service employees provide limited technical assistance to forest landowners when making SCS farm plans. In heavily forested counties and states, the SCS county soil conservationists provide considerable advice on multiple-use management and farm forest conservation practices. They often coordinate their farm plans with recommendations from state foresters or extension service personnel. Under the Farm Bill cross-compliance rules, SCS farm plans may be required by 1995 for all farms whose owners receive cost-share payments or crop subsidies, or are enrolled in the state Forest Stewardship Programs. The amount of expansion of the SCS role in forestry due to the 1990 farm bill is an unresolved issue.

Illustration: Program Evaluations
Forestry and forestry technical assistance programs were faced with significant budget cuts in the early 1980s. In order to respond to administration criticisms of their program, economists in State and Private Forestry initiated a host of studies designed to assess the benefits and costs of federal programs, such as the Forestry Incentives Program evaluations discussed in Chapter 5; forest fire, insect, and disease protection programs; and cooperative forestry and utilization assistance programs. Beginning in 1982 a series of studies of the effectiveness of technical assistance was funded by S&PF. Not too surprisingly, many (but not all) of these studies found that private forestry assistance programs improved forest management, and that the state/federal programs had positive benefit-cost ratios.

Boyd (1983, 1984) found that incentive programs encouraged investments in growing timber but not timber harvests. He computed that technical assistance was more likely to increase regeneration than were subsidy programs and that it was significant in increasing the probability of harvest.

A study in the Georgia Piedmont tried to determine if assistance from state service foresters had measurable impacts on the management practices of private forest landowners, on their returns on forest management, and on the social (governmental) returns. The study evaluated the effects of provision of technical assistance to assisted and nonassisted groups of landowners who made timber harvests (Cubbage 1983b, Cubbage, Skinner, and Risbrudt 1985, Cubbage, Risbrudt, and Skinner 1987). Harvest practices between the assisted and nonassisted landowner groups differed significantly. Landowners assisted by state foresters in the harvest of natural stands generally had less pine timber removed (1135 vs. 1485 cubic feet per acre), had more softwood volume left after harvest (810 vs. 226 cubic feet per acre), and had more pine seedlings (1602 vs. 803 per acre) after natural-stand harvests.

Harvest returns also differed significantly. Owners assisted by state foresters received an average price of $108 per thousand board feet of timber, while those making their own sales averaged only $66 per thousand board feet. A small amount of this difference could be explained by differing product distributions, but even in the most conservative case, assisted landowners received stumpage prices 58 percent greater than landowners making their sales without any forestry assistance. Greater returns for current sales and greater residual volumes also led to a greater total net present value per acre on lands whose owners received assistance ($1563), compared to the nonassisted group ($940), at a real discount rate of 4 percent.

Greater returns to landowners receiving assistance created large private, social, and program benefit-cost ratios. In fact, returns for sawtimber marking and harvesting assistance alone were enough to justify total cooperative forestry assistance program costs in most comparisons. Tax dollars that could be attributed to harvesting assistance exceeded costs for timber marking, but not entire program costs. Returns to the federal treasury would be greater than those to the state, and the federal share of program costs is less, so paybacks were greatest for the federal contribution.

In Montana, Jackson (1983) performed an economic evaluation of the Private Forestry Assistance (PFA) program by examining records of landowners who had sold timber. Holding other variables constant at their mean values, Jackson estimated that on the average, forestry assistance added $4205 per tract to the price of timber received by each landowner.

The favorable findings in Georgia and Montana prompted similar studies of state forestry programs in Florida, Minnesota, Washington, Mississippi, and Illinois. They generally found similar results. The study in Mississippi also found that landowners who received state forestry assistance often harvested less pine timber and had more residual volume than unassisted landowners (Bullard and Moulton 1988). Assisted landowners also received higher prices, although not as large as those in Georgia. The average pine pulpwood price for assisted landowners was $11.71 per cord; it was $10.55 per cord in unassisted cases. Pine sawtimber prices averaged 20 percent higher for assisted sales.

The Florida study developed regression equations to assess the effects of both market information—which was the only assistance provided by state foresters—and technical assistance available by private consulting foresters (Hubbard and Abt 1989). The provision of market information had a slight positive effect on prices received, but it was not statistically significant. The provision of consulting technical assistance varied by the value of the stands. For pulpwood stands, technical assistance actually resulted in a decrease in per unit stumpage price received. For sawtimber stands, technical assistance increased per unit stumpage prices. Technical assistance increased per unit stumpage prices for sawtimber stands. This suggests that the value of technical assistance is higher in sawtimber sales, where there is more price variability. Assisted landowners also were more likely than unassisted owners to reforest harvested stands.

The Minnesota study found a modest advantage for owners who sold aspen with the assistance of state foresters (Henly, Ellefson, and Baughman 1988). All assisted owners either contacted several buyers and negotiated for the best price or requested sealed bids; unassisted buyers simply accepted the first buyer's offer or selected buyers based on referrals from others.

Minnesota is one of a growing number of states that charge fees for technical assistance to landowners. Although the level of fees is nominal and not intended to fully recover costs, the state believes that owners who pay something for technical assistance are much more likely to employ management practices than owners who receive free services. Minnesota also has developed a computerized listing and referral service to help forest consultants contact landowners, and the state will provide timber harvesting assistance only after a certain waiting period.

The program evaluation study in Illinois examined the effects of technical assistance on harvest practices and returns in upland central hardwoods, where oak and hickory are the major overstory components (Budelsky et al. 1989). The study found that unassisted owners' stands had significantly more volume cut and less volume left per acre. Foresters marked mostly mature veneer-quality trees or inferior trees, leaving a much higher percentage of high-quality residual trees after the assisted sales. They also left the most desirable species, so the residual composition formed the nucleus of a highly desirable stand.

There were no statistically significant differences in logging site layout or use of best management practices between assisted and unassisted landowners. Less damage occurred in the residual stand in the forester-assisted sales, but the logger doing the work was the biggest factor influencing stand damage. The present value of future residual timber was more than 100 percent higher for assisted sales.

The state forestry assistance evaluation in Washington divided the state into two regions—the west and east sides of the Cascade Mountains (Salazar and Barton 1988). State foresters in Washington provide general timber management advice, including harvest planning and regeneration, but they do not actually mark timber before a sale.

The Washington study failed to find any statistically significant difference in timber sales attributable to forestry assistance. In western Washington, average harvest returns were moderately higher for landowners who received no assistance; in eastern Washington, they were slightly higher. Forest regeneration was slightly higher with assisted landowners, but not significantly so.

The researchers attributed the lack of detectable differences between assisted and unassisted owners to several factors. First, there are large differences among Washington timber types, causing large standard deviations of the sample population. Second, log quality is much more important here than it is in the South because it can be quite variable, but it is not measurable for cut trees. And finally, the wide variation in stand species composition probably had large effects on harvest returns.

In all of the state forestry evaluations, it was easiest to isolate the influence of foresters on timber sales in situations in which the foresters actually provided assistance, at least to the extent of determining sale volumes and marking the trees (or timber sale boundaries) to be sold. The studies also suggest that the type of service and the type of product influence the economic returns to harvesting assistance. More direct, intensive involvement, particularly in sawtimber harvests, could have considerable impact on harvest methods and returns. Mere provision of market information, or harvesting assistance in pulpwood harvests, does not produce such a significant difference. Perhaps the value of forestry assistance in pulpwood lies more in stand establishment than in harvesting a relatively homogeneous product.

The results from these studies of technical assistance programs were widely used by federal and state agency personnel to help justify their programs. The virtues of forestry technical assistance have been accepted by senior officials in the Forest Service and the Department of Agriculture. However, with the Reagan administration's preference for private markets rather than public programs, the officials tended to suggest that private forestry consultants should provide assistance and that federal cost-share funding with the states was unnecessary. In the end, S&PF and several states successfully used the favorable program evaluations to argue for stable or increased budgets for technical assistance programs; the less favorable findings received considerably less publicity.

The efficiency aspects of most of the evaluations proved satisfactory. Equity aspects also have continued to provide support for public technical assistance programs. Vertical equity favors providing public assistance to owners of small tracts, who might not be able to afford private consultants and still make profits growing timber or afford managing for wildlife. Equity also favors providing programs for nonindustrial private timber producers (landowners), so they are able to make informed management decisions and will not be at a disadvantage with timber buyers in sales transactions. Criteria that may tend to argue for reduced technical assistance support rest more on program costs, unproven program benefits in some regions, and availability of private consulting assistance in other regions.

These types of evaluations were common with other forestry programs in the 1980s. Forest research evaluations showed that forest products research paid handsome returns, but that forest management research was less lucrative; forest protection research determined the values that might be lost due to wildfire or forest pathogens. These research findings were often used by the Forest Service and state agencies to argue for greater program support.

By the 1990s, however, the free marketeers who arrived in Washington, DC, with President Reagan had largely been supplanted, and the need for and use of economic justifications of programs dwindled. Instead, successful support of private forestry programs seemed to revert to successfully motivating interest groups and constituents to lobby Congress members and executive officials.

PRIVATE ASSISTANCE

In addition to public programs, many private consultants and forest products firms provide technical forestry assistance. Consulting forestry services available to private landowners have increased greatly in the last 20 years. It has been estimated that there are more than 1900 consulting foresters in the United States; Georgia has the largest concentration with more than 100 known consultants (Field and Holt 1984). In addition, many forest products companies have formal management assistance or landowner assistance programs in areas around their mills. Companies also lease a large amount of forest land from private owners in the South.

Regional and national surveys have found a steadily increasing number of private forestry consultants through the 1970s and 1980s (Harou, Kronrad, and Mack 1981; Hodges and Cubbage 1986a,b; Kronrad and Albers 1984; Martin 1977; Myers and Goforth 1980; Pleasonton 1968, 1969). Forestry consultants provide services similar to state foresters for a fee. In addition, they can provide detailed assistance in timber marking, land surveying, timber and land sales negotiations, and many other forestry practices that are considered inappropriate for state foresters. Good estimates of the total area in the United States receiving consulting forestry assistance do not exist. Field and Holt (1984) performed a national survey of consulting services but had only a 12 percent response rate. Thus, total assistance levels could not be estimated.

A number of surveys have been performed to estimate the extent of private forestry assistance to NIPF landowners. Studies were begun at the Southern Forest Experiment Station (Pleasonton 1968, 1969; Siegel 1973; Siegel and Guttenberg 1968) and have been continued by others. Leasing programs began in the 1940s and 1950s. In these programs, a company leases NIPF land and generally manages it as if it were its own. The acreage under lease in the South seemed to peak at about 6.7 million acres in 1970 (Siegel 1973). Current surveys indicate that it declined to about 4,661,000 acres in 1982 (Meyer 1984, Meyer and Klemperer 1984). Average tract size under lease was 2078 acres.

Industrial forest management assistance programs also provide private forest landowners with forest regeneration, timber stand improvement, and harvesting assistance. Land management practices may be performed at cost for private landowners. Programs generally require that treated tracts meet minimum size and maximum distance criteria from the mill, and some require first refusal rights—the right to meet or exceed any other firm's bid—when participating landowners sell timber (Cleaves and O'Laughlin 1983, Cubbage and Skinner 1985, O'Laughlin, Cleaves, and Skove 1983). Land enrolled in formal industrial management assistance programs has increased steadily. Meyer and Klemperer (1984) found that total enrollment included 4.2 million acres in the South in 1982, with the largest programs being in the western Gulf states of Louisiana, Arkansas, Texas, and Oklahoma. Average tract size was 484 acres.

Public and Private Competition

If private forestry assistance is now available at reasonable costs, is public technical assistance necessary? Cubbage and Hodges (1986a,b) estimated the levels of assistance provided by all forestry sectors in Georgia in 1983 to examine that question. Results indicated that the total level of accomplishments and average tract size varied significantly among the industrial management assistance, private consulting, and state forestry programs. Consultants marked more timber than industry and state programs and generally provided many services and detailed management plans not offered by state foresters. This is not surprising because they are generally paid a percentage of timber sale revenues received by the landowner. Industry programs assisted considerably fewer owners, but they had very large average tract sizes (636 acres) associated with each ownership managed. Average tract size managed by state foresters was 131 acres; for consultants it was 376 acres. Georgia state foresters assisted the most landowners, but the bulk of the assistance consisted of brief plans that did not require intensive site examinations. The state also helped in marking less than 1 percent of the timber harvested in the state, compared with about 8 or 9 percent marked by consultants.

In a survey of foresters throughout the South, Hodges and Cubbage (1990) found similar results. Industry foresters managed larger tracts, state foresters the smaller tracts. Each sector generally managed nonindustrial private lands somewhat differently. Consultants used more natural regeneration, industry and state foresters more artificial regeneration. In total, all three sectors provided assistance on only about 5 percent of the NIPF land in the South in 1987. These findings also suggest that many opportunities exist for all three sectors to increase their clientele.

Overall, it seems that each of the three providers of technical assistance fulfills separate needs. Industry programs concentrated on owners of the largest forests, consultants focused on medium-size ownerships, and state foresters on the smallest ownerships. Many state forestry agencies have a yearly limit of about five person-days of assistance per owner per year, so they probably refer most large requests to private industry programs or forestry consultants. Public foresters may serve an equity function by providing assistance to smaller ownerships that might not be able to afford consultants or qualify for industrial programs; large owners are better able to pay for forestry services.

AMERICA THE BEAUTIFUL

As mentioned in the section on the Forestry Incentives Program, the America the Beautiful National Tree Planting Initiative (ATB) was enacted as part of Title XII of the 1990 FACT ACT (farm bill). The Stewardship Incentive Program is the rural tree planting cost-share component of America the Beautiful. The Forest Stewardship Program is the new technical assistance component that is incorporated into America the Beautiful for providing advice on multiple-use forest management to rural landowners. America the Beautiful also authorized an Urban and Community Forestry Assistance Program to offer technical assistance, education, and cooperation with communities and organizations. Under these urban/community forestry cooperative arrangements, the Forest Service would pay a percentage of the costs for tree planting programs.

The Forest Stewardship Program (FSP) is designed to help forest landowners manage their forests for multiple resources. It is intended to expand traditional state programs beyond their common timber focus. Implementation of FSP has proven more contentious than the old technical assistance programs, however. Some states drafted guidelines requiring FSP landowners to keep or plant some forest land in hardwoods, BMP use, recreation access, or wildlife food plots. Some discussions suggested that only participating FSP landowners would be allowed to receive cost-share funds. The stricter multiple-use guidelines and federal/state controls were prompted by efforts of recreation and wildlife groups to foster more diverse management (stewardship) on private lands. Many consultants and some forest products firms, however, opposed these strings being

attached to the federal and state funds, and even some state and federal agency personnel felt that the stricter conditions would harm program enrollment.

The ATB programs were developed to help President Bush achieve an environmental promise to plant 1 billion trees. Passage of the ATB programs was due to support from a wide group—environmentalists, who wanted to slow climate change; the American Forestry Association, National Association of State Foresters, and Forest Service State and Private Forestry, who wanted to revive dormant federal private forestry programs; the president, who wanted an environmental program; and members of Congress, who wanted to show that the United States was doing its part in responding to climate change threats (and satisfy their previously mentioned constituents).

EXTENSION PROGRAMS

The Smith-Lever Act of 1914 pioneered federal–state agriculture and forestry cooperation. The act provided for cooperative agricultural extension work between the U.S. Department of Agriculture and the state land grant colleges. The act is funded by the federal government, individual states, and local communities, with their total contributions totaling about $1 billion in 1985. In the mid-1980s, the federal government funded about 37 percent of the programs, local governments 7 to 11 percent, and the states the balance. Extension has proven to be quite powerful politically, with agents in each county providing services to influential farmers and their interest groups. This cooperation has been strongly supported and funded by state and federal legislators.

Extension includes a substantial forestry and wildlife component in most states. Separate congressional authority for forestry extension services was granted under the Renewable Resources Extension Act of 1978, but only modest additional funds have been appropriated. In the 1980s, annual forest management and utilization extension funds averaged about $4 million per year, and natural resources extension programs about $15 million.

State extension foresters provide information and education for private landowners, loggers, and forest products firms in the state, primarily by holding workshops, meetings, tours, and forestry demonstrations and by publishing forestry bulletins. Extension forestry specialists work closely with county agricultural extension agents in conducting local forestry education programs. In addition to public education, extension personnel have taken a leading role in disseminating research findings to public and private foresters, informing researchers of the concerns of forestry professionals and the public, and disseminating information on timber prices in their state.

By the 1990s many state extension programs had suffered from declining political support and weakened missions. Much of the new agricultural research and technology transfer work was performed by seed, fertilizer, chemical, and farm management companies. And the number of farm workers has dwindled to 2 percent of the total U.S. work force. In order to find new clients to use (and support) their services, extension programs tried to reorient some of their efforts toward urban planning or rural development. These efforts often foundered, though, because they antagonized the traditional farm interest groups. So extension programs in many states received significant budget cuts in the 1990 to 1992 recession. Nevertheless, these and other farm and forestry programs have not dwindled nearly as fast as have the numbers of farmers or residents in forested areas—indicating the difficulty in actually changing the status quo in federal and state legislatures.

The U.S. Forest Service branch of State and Private Forestry serves an extension and administrative role at the federal level. It helps administer federal funds given to the states for the cooperative forestry programs and provides technical expertise to the states in fire, pest management, and forest man-

agement programs. S&PF personnel assist in and coordinate state forest resource planning and provide advice in management of nontimber uses. The Reagan administration and OMB made concerted efforts to eliminate S&PF in the 1980s but were thwarted by the agency's supporting interest groups and Congress. However, S&PF budgets did dwindle significantly. In the 1990s S&PF revived, as President Bush and Congress looked to private landowners to plant 1 billion trees.

WILDLIFE MANAGEMENT ASSISTANCE

Most state wildlife agencies offer technical services to private forest landowners upon request. As of 1987, 40 of the 50 states provided some type of assistance. Most state assistance emphasized game species. Twenty-seven states provided landowners with wildlife management materials such as fencing and nest structures, 17 with planting materials, 13 with tree or bush seedlings, and 11 with herbaceous seeds. Eleven states offered landowners tax incentives for management habitat or permitting public access (Wigley and Melchiors 1987).

Teer, Burger, and Deknatel (1983) summarized state programs for habitat management and commercial hunting in the United States in detail (Table 17-7). In 1982, 42 states provided technical advice to private landowners. Nineteen provided some type of plant materials for wildlife habitat, and 12 provided wildlife management area signs. Fourteen states provided direct cost-sharing for wildlife management practices, and 14 also would make agreements with landowners to maintain wildlife management practices. Nine states would either buy conservation easements from private landowners to protect wildlife habitat or give private owners tax credits for wildlife protection.

Most of the habitat management programs occurred in the central United States, but others occurred throughout all regions of the country. State fisheries agencies provide direct assistance in farm pond management and stream improvement. Fish and wildlife

TABLE 17-7. Habitat management programs supported by state funds in 1982

Activity	States
Provision of technical advice	AL, AR, CA, CO, CN, FL, FA, HI, IA, ID, IL, IN, KS, KY, LA, ME, MD, MI, MN, MO, MS, MT, NE, NH, NJ, NM, NY, NC, ND, OH, OK, OR, PA, RI, SC, SD, TN, TX, VT, WA, WI, WY
Provision of plant materials	AR, CO, IA, IL, IN, KS, LA, NA, MD, MN, MO, NE, NC, OH, OR, PA, RI, TN, WI
Provision of signage	CO, IL, IN, KS, MD, NC, NE, OH, OR, PA, RI, SD
Conservation easements and tax credits	CO, HI, IA, IN, MD, MN, MT, NH, OR
Agreements made with landowner to maintain practices	CO, IA, IL, IN, LA, MN, NE, ND, OH, OR, PA, RI, SD, WI

Every state that reported some type of habitat management provided technical assistance to landowners by visits to the field. Some of these states had extension personnel whose main job was to work with landowners in wildlife management activities.

Source: Teer, Burger, and Deknatel 1983

agencies also conduct extensive information and education programs to promote resource conservation (Adams, Stoner, and Thomas 1988).

INDIRECT ASSISTANCE

FISH AND WILDLIFE AGENCIES

State fish and wildlife agencies provide indirect management assistance through game and nongame management programs, game law enforcement, and information and education programs. Massachusetts established the first fish and wildlife agency in 1865. By 1880 all states had enacted some type of fish and wildlife protection laws; by 1923 all had fully established fish and wildlife programs (Gottschalk 1978). These programs were described in Chapter 15.

All states undertake a variety of actions to maintain or increase important fish and wildlife populations. These actions include population surveys, establishment of hunting and fishing regulations, habitat acquisition and management, and information and education provision. Beginning in the 1980s and continuing into the 1990s, states have begun

to increase their focus on nongame and endangered species, particularly as nongame tax checkoff programs increase. However, hunting and fishing license fees still comprised 53 percent of state wildlife agency income in 1986, special programs such as nongame tax checkoffs only 13 percent (Williamson 1987).

PUBLICLY FUNDED RESEARCH

Forestry Programs
The USDA Forest Service and most land grant universities perform research that constitutes an indirect subsidy to nonindustrial and industrial forest landowners and wood processors. Forestry research and education programs have expanded in the United States since the early 1900s. Research in forest management concerns was formally initiated at the federal level when the USDA Forest Service established its research branch in 1915.

In 1928 the McSweeney-McNary Act was enacted, conferring legal status on regional experiment stations and reaffirming a policy of cooperation between the research units and their various clients. The act enlarged the responsibilities of Forest Service research, called for a nationwide forest survey to inventory all ownerships, and directed the forest experiment stations to determine

Methods of reforestation and timber growing, managing, and utilizing timber, forage, and other forest products.

Methods of maintaining quality water flow from forested areas.

Methods of protecting forests from fire, insects, and diseases.

Under the act research programs were to address economic considerations necessary for establishing sound forest policies.

The Forest Service experiment stations have since expanded to represent all regions of the United States, and they perform research on a wide variety of topics of interest to all forest landowners, including forest management, pest management, utilization, economics, and inventory. Funding for Forest Service research amounted to $165 million per year in 1990. This was a considerable increase over the early 1980s, when assistant secretary of agriculture John Crowell had led concerted administration efforts to reduce the annual Forest Service research budget to less than $100 million.

Beginning in the 1950s, most forestry schools began to develop active programs in forest research, in addition to their traditional teaching responsibilities. Since that time, most schools have had steadily increasing budgets and numbers of scientists devoted to research on forest management problems. They have been assisted by the 1962 federal McIntire-Stennis Act, which authorized the secretary of agriculture to cooperate with state colleges and universities in carrying out forest research, including the training of forest research workers. In 1985 McIntire-Stennis funds were about $12.5 million. Forestry school research budgets provided at least twice that amount from other sources such as state appropriations and external grants. In 1987 Senator Stennis from Mississippi, who chaired the Senate Appropriations Committee, successfully sponsored an increase in McIntire-Stennis funds to $17

million. The increase was essentially a parting present from Stennis to his long-time forestry interest group friends.

The 1990 Forest Stewardship Act reaffirmed the importance of the McIntire-Stennis Act and authorized several new forestry research programs or studies, including a Competitive Forestry, Natural Resources, and Environmental Grants Research Program. It also authorized special research on reforestation, urban forests, forest taxes, wood fiber recycling, and timber bridges. A number of different forestry research centers were authorized, as was a Commission on State and Private Forests.

Several state forestry agencies employ staff that perform research functions or fund cooperative research projects with universities and consultants. Forest industry companies perform research at several locations in the nation, and cooperate with forestry schools and USDA Forest Service experiment stations via individual contracts and numerous forest management cooperatives (Hodges and Harris 1988, Hodges, Jakes, and Cubbage 1988).

The public and private research efforts cover most areas of forest management, as well as forest products, recreation, and wildlife. The U.S. forest inventory programs and publications also are funded as part of the Forest Service research program. The state and federal research and education agencies also collect and publish general production and trade statistics, as well as perform supply and demand analyses. In fact, collection and dissemination of existing information is an increasingly important role of public forest research and education programs.

Research Evaluation

Tighter public budgets, increased scrutiny of public planning, and better analytical tools have led to several attempts to evaluate public research investments, led by the Forest Service. Forest Service research leaders perceived the need for greater economic justifications in the 1980s than had been used in prior years. A research work unit on research evaluation was established and has sponsored many studies. Reagan's appointees in OMB and in the Department of Agriculture indeed did seek more definite information on program costs and returns and used these in budget allocation decisions. Summaries of some of the key studies on returns to research follow.

Despite the difficulties of evaluating forest management research (Lundgren 1981, 1982), some economists have attempted to evaluate forestry programs (Hyde 1983). Several studies have evaluated the returns to investments in forest products research, and virtually all have found large benefit-cost ratios and rates of return. For example, Seldon (1985) reported rates of return of over 300 percent for southern pine softwood plywood research; Bengston (1984) reported excellent returns for structural particle board research; and Haygreen et al. (1986) reported annual rates of return of 18 percent for all U.S. forest products research.

Fewer studies have been made of the effects of forest management research, and the investment returns found have been considerably less. Westgate (1986) found excellent rates of return of at least 37 percent per year for containerized seedling research. In the only econometric study trying to measure timber supply shifts (increases in timber supplies) related to forestry research, Newman (1990) found aggregate productivity increases at annual rates of 0.5 to 1.0 percent for the South. If the benefits of these shifts were attributed to forest research, and the lags between implementation and timber harvest were considered, the resulting benefits of research investments could range from $1.2 to $12 million per year. Unfortunately, these benefits translated into very low to negative rates of returns on the forest management investments.

Fish and Wildlife Programs

In addition to forest management and forest products research, the federal government and the states sponsor extensive fish and wildlife research programs. The U.S. Forest Service conducts some research on these topics, but most such research is conducted by the Fish and Wildlife Service in the U.S. Department of the Interior. The FWS conducts a variety of research projects on game and nongame species, and has many cooperative research units located throughout the United States, usually in conjunction with university forestry schools or natural resource departments.

Like Forest Service research budgets, FWS research was threatened with drastic budget cuts, or even elimination, under the Reagan administration's proposals. However, it survived and budgets increased by the late 1980s. Unlike forestry, the FWS has relied less on formal economic evaluations of its research and more on emotional appeals and lobbying from interest groups to support its programs in Congress. This difference may reflect the fact that much of its research is nonmarket in nature. It also may reflect that noneconomic values and criteria are considered to be more important by fish and wildlife scientists and the many large environmental groups.

States also perform a substantial amount of fish and wildlife research, much of it funded via the Pittman-Robertson or Dingell-Johnson funds (see Chapter 15). Just as the Forest Service surveys timber inventory, growth, and removals, the state fish and game agencies continually inventory wildlife populations, hunter take, and animal food habits. Environmental and habitat studies and planning and user surveys also are common research topics. Little research to date has focused on nongame or endangered wildlife. Similarly, not much had focused on pollution, water quality or quantity research, or stream and lake improvement research.

FOREST PROTECTION PROGRAMS

Public forest protection programs for private lands have been considered necessary because fires, insects, and diseases spread with little regard to ownership boundaries and present risks to both economic and aesthetic values, as well as personal safety. The 1924 Clarke-McNary Act initiated the federal and state cooperative efforts to control forest fires.

Like the cooperative forest management programs, the states have assumed the brunt of funding and provide the personnel for fighting fires on NIPF and, in some cases, industry lands. Federal funds are now used primarily to defray some program costs, help train and equip local fire departments for forest protection measures, and coordinate U.S. Forest Service and state fire control efforts. Federal fire fighting crews usually fight fires only on public lands.

Fire control has without a doubt been the most important public program for protecting forests. In fact, fire control funds constitute the largest share of state forestry budgets, at about 60 percent (Cubbage and Lickwar 1988). Fire fighting is the most visible component of public forestry programs and is used to great advantage in promoting agency activities. Most state forestry agencies also fight fires in forested urban/suburban areas, such as in southern California or in the Northeast. They have used this part of their program to appeal to a broader political base than the traditional rural legislators.

The U.S. Forest Service gained much of its initial fame and credibility due to its excellent fire-fighting capabilities, and it still retains this image. Smokey the Bear remains the longest-running successful public relations tool ever developed by a natural resources agency. Critics charge that federal fire control efforts have succeeded too well, leading to problems with large fuel buildups and massive conflagrations that cannot be controlled.

The Forest Pest Management Act of 1947 instituted similar cooperative efforts and funding for pest control and diseases, regardless of land ownership. It authorized surveys to detect infestations and authorized federally performed or funded measures against incipient, potential, or emergency outbreaks. Substantial regional pest management control and research programs have been sponsored under this and other acts. Like forest fire programs, pest management funding often depends on large outbreaks to stimulate interest in research and control programs.

PRODUCTION AND MARKETING COOPERATIVES

In order to assist private forest owners in managing and marketing timber, some landowner cooperatives have been attempted to overcome diseconomies of size that are incurred by owners of small tracts (Cubbage 1983b). They also should be able to help owners bargain more successfully when selling timber to large forest products firms. However, the long time frames involved in growing timber and the rather short average tenure of most U.S. forest landowners have prevented the success of cooperatives. Forest owners only make sales periodically and tend to be very independent. McComb (1978) documents a few limited co-ops that have been successful in the South. These have employed only one part-time or full-time forester and relied heavily on the other public assistance programs.

PUTTING IT ALL TOGETHER: TOTAL STATE FOREST RESOURCE PROGRAMS

This chapter and the previous one discussed many means of providing public direction for management of private forest lands and wildlife habitat. Regulation may be used to control landowners' forest management activities, prevent pollution, compel regeneration, or limit the take of game and fish. Direct financial incentives may be used to encourage landowners to perform desirable practices, such as planting and growing trees. Federal and state agencies also influence management of private forest lands indirectly. They provide information and education, grow seedlings for planting and fish for stocking, provide stand and habitat management advice, inventory forest and wildlife resources, and perform research on forest resources and wildlife populations. Additionally, the states and federal government provide forestry and wildlife planning, which helps identify resource needs and desirable program alternatives.

A 1989 *State of the States* report summarizes much of the information on state forest resource programs and industry importance (Renew America Project 1989). Table 17-8 summarizes much of this information, including total forest land areas; state, federal, industry, and other private ownership shares; and timber industry importance. State forestry programs budgets are ranked; their regulatory and reforestation programs are noted; their forestry nonpoint source control programs are ranked; and state forestry agency programs for wildlife are itemized. The summaries of state participation in the Conservation Reserve Program can also be used to gauge direct conservation efforts in each state (see Table 17-5).

The Renew America project ranked the forest resource programs of the states, emphasizing personnel, budgets, regulatory laws, and forest resource planning. Washington, Idaho, California, Massachusetts, Oregon, Minnesota, Maryland, and Indiana were among the most highly ranked programs (see Table 17-8). Many mountain and southern states, however, ranked poorly—including Arizona, Utah, Texas, West Virginia, Alabama, Arkansas, Oklahoma, and Delaware. These poor rankings are based on small programs or perceived deficiencies in protecting the environment. Needless to say, not all state foresters were pleased with the *State of the States* report.

However, using the data in Tables 17-5 and 17-8 and different criteria for evaluation, one might arrive at quite different state rankings. Using the amount of forest land area and industry importance as criteria, many states would rank much higher. Alabama, Arkansas, Georgia, Idaho, Louisiana, Maine, Mississippi, Montana, Oregon, Vermont, Washington, and Wisconsin all had very important timber industry sectors. Many had good state programs as well. But these rankings of forest industry importance relative to other industries in each state are misleading from a national perspective. They can make a relatively small industry appear important, such as in Alaska or Vermont, or mask a large forest-based industry in a large and diverse state, such as Cali-

fornia, New York, or Texas. Figures 17-2 and 17-3 provide a more accurate picture of national rankings of forest industry by state.

If states were ranked according to the number of educational, technical assistance, tax incentive, and voluntary programs available for forestry and wildlife (without legal regulations), different conclusions might result. California, Delaware, Georgia, Idaho, Iowa, Kentucky, Michigan, Minnesota, and Missouri all have diverse state forestry programs. So do North Carolina, Ohio, South Carolina, and Wisconsin. Most of these states also have two or three different types of wildlife programs.

If states were ranked simply on participation in the CRP program, other orders might appear. At least 13 states enrolled more than 1 million acres in CRP—most of these were midwestern or mountain states that had large areas of qualified cropland. In terms of CRP tree planting, Georgia was the clear leader, with almost twice as many acres as the second state, Mississippi. Other southern states also planted many acres of trees; only a few other states outside the South had any significant amount of tree acreage planted under the CRP.

As the preceding summaries reveal, states use many means to implement forest policies. Ranking total state programs is difficult. States in the South are averse to planning and regulation and rely more on education and assistance programs to achieve forest policy goals. The good financial returns to subsidized tree planting also have prompted large participation in CRP. Forest industry in the South and West is very important in the economies of most forested states. States in the Midwest and Northeast offer a variety of programs and are more involved in forest resource planning. They also probably make more conscientious efforts to control pollution and protect nonmarket forest outputs than in the South. However, except for Maine, forest industries are generally less important in the Northeast than in other regions of the country. In the end, state forest resources, local social preferences, legislators' perceptions and actions, and other factors vary from state to

TABLE 17-8.   **Renew America Forest Management Matrix for the States**

	1	2	3	4	5	6	7
Alabama	21,725	67%	7%	1%	21%	74%	2nd/1st
Alaska	129,045	36%	55%	29%	7%	8%	2nd/3rd
Arizona	19,384	27%	79%	12%	0%	9%	9th/10th
Arkansas	16,987	51%	16%	2%	25%	57%	2nd/2nd
California	39,381	39%	50%	1%	12%	37%	9th/7th
Connecticut	1,815	59%	1%	11%	0%	86%	10th/10th
Delware	398	33%	14%	6%	8%	73%	3rd/3rd
Florida	16,549	48%	10%	5%	33%	50%	6th/6th
Georgia	23,907	65%	6%	<1%	21%	73%	3rd/4th
Hawaii	1,748	43%	1%	43%	31%	21%	5th/5th
Idaho	21,818	41%	77%	6%	6%	9%	2nd/2nd
Illinois	4,265	12%	7%	3%	<1%	89%	10th/10th
Indiana	4,439	19%	8%	7%	10%	76%	8th/10th
Iowa	1,562	4%	3%	3%	1%	92%	7th/9th
Kansas	1,358	3%	4%	1%	0%	95%	9th/9th
Kentucky	12,256	48%	8%	1%	2%	90%	9th/10th
Louisiana	13,883	49%	6%	2%	31%	60%	3rd/4th
Maine	17,713	90%	<1%	<1%	47%	49%	1st/1st
Maryland	2,632	42%	1%	7%	5%	85%	6th/9th
Massachusetts	3,097	62%	<1%	13%	2%	85%	9th/9th
Michigan	18,220	50%	14%	20%	11%	53%	8th/7th
Minnesota	16,583	33%	21%	22%	5%	35%	6th/3rd
Mississippi	16,693	55%	9%	2%	20%	65%	2nd/1st
Missouri	12,523	28%	10%	5%	2%	79%	9th/8th
Montana	21,910	24%	73%	3%	7%	16%	1st/2nd
Nebraska	722	1%	6%	6%	0%	88%	9th/11th
Nevada	8,928	13%	*45%	*4%	*6%	*45%	No Data
New Hampshire	5,021	88%	10%	3%	14%	72%	3rd/3rd
New Jersey	1,985	43%	2%	13%	1%	82%	9th/9th
New Mexico	18,526	24%	49%	5%	0%	46%	7th/8th
New York	18,775	62%	1%	21%	11%	66%	10th/11th
North Carolina	18,891	61%	10%	2%	13%	74%	5th/7th
North Dakota	460	1%	15%	6%	0%	78%	7th/7th
Ohio	7,397	28%	2%	3%	6%	87%	9th/10th
Oklahoma	8,971	20%	10%	2%	22%	66%	10th/10th
Oregon	28,055	46%	58%	3%	21%	16%	1st/1st
Pennsylvania	16,997	59%	3%	20%	6%	69%	8th/8th
Rhode Island	399	60%	0%	12%	0%	85%	9th/11th
South Carolina	12,257	64%	7%	1%	18%	73%	4th/3rd
Tennessee	13,258	50%	6%	2%	9%	81%	8th/6th
Texas	23,330	14%	6%	<1%	33%	60%	8th/8th
Utah	16,234	31%	69%	10%	0%	17%	9th/10th
Vermont	4,479	76%	7%	6%	8%	78%	2nd/2nd
Virginia	15,968	63%	11%	1%	12%	73%	3rd/6th
Washington	21,856	51%	*39%	*10%	*25%	*25%	2nd/2nd
West Virginia	11,942	78%	8%	2%	8%	82%	5th/7th
Wisconsin	15,319	44%	11%	5%	8%	60%	2nd/3rd
Wyoming	9,966	16%	86%	2%	1%	11%	No Data

TABLE 17-8. Renew America Forest Management Matrix for the States

8	9	10	11	12
5/15/20		ep, ta, fi	Local (2)	ep,ta
1/35/36	LAW	ir	State (2)	None
38/48/46		ep, ta	Local (2)	ep, ta
13/25/19		ta	Local (2)	ep, ta
2/2/	LAW	fi, ep, ta, vg, ir	Local (5)	ep, ta, vg, fi, ir
41/45/40		ep, ta	None (2)	ep, ta
50/50/50		ti, ta	None (0)	None
12/8/6		ep, ta, ti, fi	Local (2)	ep, ta, vg
4/4/12		ep, ta, vg, fl	Local (2)	exp, ta, vg
42/32/41	REG	fi, ta	None (0)	ta, ir
32/20/12	LAW	ep, ta, vg, ti, ir	State (4)	ep, ta, vg, ir
36/27/31		ta, ti, fi	Local (1)	ta, ti, fi
35/17/21		ep, ta, fi	Local (2)	ep, ta, ti, iir
44/38/41		ep, ta, ti, fi	None (0)	ep, ta, fi
45/44/49		ta, ep	None (0)	fi, ep, ta
21/28/28		ep, ta, ti, fi	Local (2)	ep, ta
18/33/30		ep, ti, fi	Local (0)	ep
7/29/9	REG	ep, ta	State (3)	ep, ta
39/23/28		ta, ti, fi, ir	Local (4)	ep, ta, fi, ti
37/14/37	LAW	ep, ta, ir	Local (4)	ep
10/13/15		ep, ta, ti, fi	Local (4)	ep, ta, fi, ti
17/7/5		ep, ta, ti, fi	Local (4)	ep, ta, fi, ti
11/10/08		ep, ta, fi	Local (0)	ep, ta, vg
23/16/21		ep, ta, vg, ti, fi	None (2)	ep, ta
31/24/17		ep, ta, ti, fi	Local (3)	ep, ta
46/41/43		ep, ta	None (0)	ep, ta, fi
26/47/43	LAW	ta, ir	Local (3)	vg, ta
33/34/38		ep, ta	Local (4)	ep, ta
40/37/23		ep, ta, fi	Local (3)	ta, ir
25/43/35	REG	ta, vg, ir	Local (2)	ta
6/11/10		ta, ti, fi	Local (2)	ta
8/9/13		ep, ta, vg, ti, fi	State (3)	ta
8/9/13		ep, ta, vg, ti,fi	None (1)	None
28/21/16		ep, ta, vg, ti	Local (2)	ep, ta, vg
27/39/32		ep, ta	Local (1)	ta
20/3/3	LAW	ir	State (3)	ta
9/5/7		ep, ta	Local (3)	ep, ta
48/36/34		ta	None (2)	ta
22/18/18		ep, ta, vg, fi	Local (1)	ep, ta, vg
19/26/26		ep, ta, h	Local (2)	ta
3/19/25	ep, ta, fi	— (0)	None	
30/49/45		ta, ti, fi	Local (1)	ta
34/49/45	ta, ti, fi	State (3)	None	
14/12/10	REG	ep, ta, fi	Local (2)	ep, ta, vg
16/1/1	LAW	ta, ir	State (4)	ta
24/31/23		ep, ta	Local (2)	ep, ta
15/6/4		ep, ta, ti, fi	Local (2)	ep, ta
43/42/48		ep, ta	Local (0)	ep, ta

Table 17-8. *(Continued)*

FOREST MANAGEMENT MATRIX NOTES

1. Total forest land: Thousands of acres (1987).
2. Land area covered by forests: As percent of state's total land area.
3-6. Forest land ownership: Percent of state's forest land owned by federal government (column 3), state government (column 4), timber industry (column 5), and other private landowners (column 6). Asterisk means that percentages are based on commercial forest acreage (land capable of producing commercial timber).
7. Timber industry rank: In terms of employment/dollar value. Ranking done in comparison with other manufacturing industries in each state (1985).
8. Forestry program budgets and staffs: Rank of state in amount of forest land under its jurisdiction/rank of state forestry program budget (excluding fire expenditures)/ and rank of program staff in number of managerial and professional employees (1987–1988).
9. Forestry laws: *Law* = states with comprehensive, modern forest practice laws; Reg = states with significant forest practice regulations (1986).
10. Reforestation policies: State response to survey on policies to promote reforestation on private forest land: ep = educational program; vg = voluntary guidelines; fi = financial incentive; ti = tax incentive; lr = legal regulation; ta = technical assistance (1985).
11. Water quality: State's responses to survey on water quality problems due to forest practices. State = more than 50% of state water degraded; Local = less than 50%, None = no significant degradation. In parentheses, evaluation of forest practice water quality protection policies (from 5 = highest score, to 0 = lowest).
12. Wildlife habitat: State's response to survey on policies to protect wildlife habitat on private forest land, (abbreviations same as column 10).

---

state. Accordingly, so do state forest resource management policies.

CONCLUSIONS

A variety of alternatives may be used to implement public policy for forest resources. In the broadest sense, a laissez-faire approach, government ownership, public regulation, or public incentives and education may produce socially desirable results. The appropriate mix of these programs at any given time depends on the goals of society and the current institutional structure. Successful policies must be designed to achieve a social objective or solve a perceived social problem. They must be socially acceptable and administratively and economically feasible. They also should consider other relevant policies that affect forest resources.

FORESTRY GOALS

Skok and Gregersen (1975) discuss four assumptions that underlie public expenditures for timber production on private lands. Three of these apply equally well as goals for any public involvement in forest resources. First, public programs assume more wood should be produced and that wood prices should not rise as much as in the past. Second, nonindustrial private forests should produce more forest outputs than they do and at costs less than the benefits produced. Third, divergent public (social) and private costs and benefits justify social involvement. Fourth, spending funds to assist private forests is more efficient than spending funds on public forests. Each of these assumptions is a mix of values and economic efficiency.

Free market advocates might question the wisdom of wood for wood's sake and of preventing rising real prices. In addition, they would not care if private (or public) forests could economically grow more wood. Eventually, markets would equilibrate available supply and demand by substituting other resources for scarce, expensive wood. However, the public and the forestry profession generally accept the values implicit in the goals of ensuring adequate timber supplies and preventing rising real prices. Duerr (1981) sug-

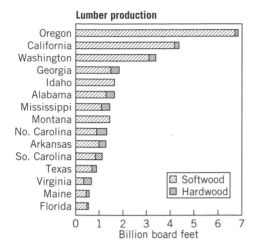

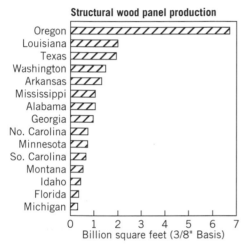

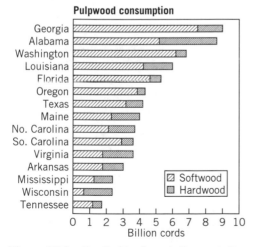

Figure 17-2.   Top Ranking States in Economic Contribution of Forest Products Manufacturing, Based on Value Added by Wood-Based Manufacturing.

Source: O'Laughlin and Williams 1988, from U.S. Department of Commerce, Bureau of Census reports.

gests that all we need to support public programs is the belief that wood has value and will prove useful in the future. Wildlife programs are based on such value judgments to an even greater degree. In practice, such beliefs are important in public policy, but not sufficient. Given limited public funds, public programs to improve natural or human resources must be based on clear economic benefits to society, but many programs are not supported on efficiency goals alone.

As discussed in Chapter 3, divergent private and public (social) costs suggest market failures are occurring, such as public goods (unpriced values), or externalities (nonmarket prices—over time or at present). Such problems seem likely in forestry, and public assistance programs or regulation are responses that have been used. In fact, even the establishment of the national forests was based largely on the perception that timber cutters were needlessly destroying wood and land needed by future generations.

The last assumption, that of investments in nonindustrial private forestry being more efficient than those in industrial or public forests, is debatable but academic. If the first three assumptions hold, the only realistic political alternative for increasing wood output is guidance and assistance to private forest landowners. National forest timber supplies are constrained by sustained-yield, multiple-use legislation and interest group pressures that will prohibit large incremental additions to supply. Additional public support for industrial forestry is unlikely. If additional timber and other forest resources are to be forthcoming, nonindustrial private forests are apt to be the source. Indeed, they are likely to be the source for enhanced wildlife management and recreational opportunities as well, despite the prevailing current focus on public recreation and wildlife management.

What, then, is the role for public policy? Although economic criteria for making resource policies may not dictate decisions, efficiency is important. Program evaluations can inform policymakers of the benefits and costs of alternative programs and the efficiency of existing programs within a particular institutional framework. By identifying the most ef-

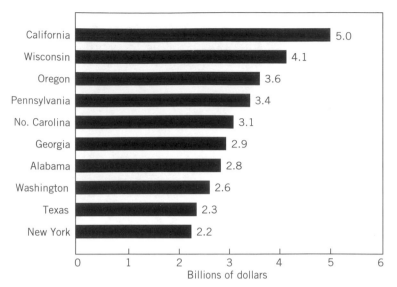

Figure 17-3. Top States in Lumber and Wood Panel Production and Pulpwood Consumption (a measure of paper pulp manufacturing importance).
Source: O'Laughlin and Williams 1988, from U.S. Department of Commerce and American Plywood Association reports.

ficient means of implementing public policy, the public could achieve the greatest returns for the dollars spent (Skok and Gregersen 1975). Wildlife and fish programs are less likely to rely on economic analyses of their effectiveness because of the nonmarket nature of the product. But programs still can be delivered in a cost-effective manner.

TIMBER PRODUCTION

Much of the discussion thus far has focused on the rationale for and the types of public programs available for increasing timber output from nonindustrial private forests (Royer and Risbrudt 1983). The views of the NIPF landowners and their objectives also are important. Royer (1979) reviewed the multitude of forest landowner studies that have been performed over the last 50 years. He concluded that landowner characteristics and attitudes have been thoroughly summarized, but the results still have not answered some very basic questions. In particular, the relationships between landowner behavior and increased timber supplies and the influence of markets and public programs still are unclear.

Some modern econometric regression models have helped explain landowner behavior. Binkley (1981) studied New Hampshire NIPF owners. He found that stumpage prices strongly influenced the probability of harvest; owners of large holdings were more apt than smaller ownerships to harvest; and the probability of timber harvest had an insignificant negative correlation with income. Farmers were nearly twice as responsive as nonfarmers to harvest prices. In North Carolina, Boyd (1983, 1984) found that harvest decisions were significantly and positively correlated with timber prices, size of forest holding, use of professional forestry assistance, and farm ownership. For planting and management practices, he found that education, professional forestry assistance, ownership size, and knowledge of cost-share programs influenced landowner decisions. Sawtimber prices had weak positive correlations and farmers and absentee owners had weak negative correlations with undertaking forest land improvements.

Royer (1987) used logistical regression and data from an earlier survey of nonindustrial private landowners in the South (Fecso et al. 1982) to examine the variables influencing reforestation decision made by NIPF owners.

Owner variables included tract size, part of farm, and the predominant local land use (urban, agricultural, mixed agriculture/forested, and forested). Personal characteristics examined included income, age, education, farming as a primary occupation, absentee ownership, and plans to sell harvested land. Indices of stumpage prices for sawtimber and pulpwood, an index of reforestation costs, and advice by industry or consulting foresters constituted the market factors analyzed. Financial (FIP) and technical (PFA) assistance were the relevant policy variables.

Ownership variables alone would correctly predict reforestation decisions only 17 percent of the time. Personal characteristics interacted with ownership variables, adding nothing to the model's explanation of reforestation probability. Economic (market) variables added 13 percentage points in explaining landowners' reforestation decisions. Public policy variables—the provision of FIP or public technical assistance—were most influential, explaining 60 percent of NIPF landowner reforestation decisions.

Royer then developed single-equation models that indicated that the asset positions (income or forest ownership size) of landowners had a strong positive influence on the probability of reforestation. Pulpwood (but not sawtimber) prices had a positive but only modestly significant effect on reforestation decisions. Technical assistance from both private and public foresters had large positive effects on reforestation, as did public cost sharing. Of the significant variables, increases in reforestation probability were greatest for the provision of public forestry assistance (about 66 percent greater), followed by FIP expenditures (+50 percent per dollar spent), and provisions of private forestry assistance (+44 percent). Other statistically significant factors were much less influential—size (+0.04 percent per acre); income (+0.05 percent per $100); farmer (−0.14 percent); and age (−0.6 percent per year). Plans to sell the land had a negative effect on the probability of reforestation (−21 percent), and pulpwood prices a slight positive effect (+1.3 percent).

Overall, these studies provide more information on the roles of owner characteristics, markets, and public policy. Virtually all the studies and evaluations have shown that public policy is crucial in the decisions made by nonindustrial private forest landowners. Markets may equilibrate timber supply and demand, but they are not particularly effective at eliciting increased supplies, even when significant real price increases occur. Most studies found that price was only moderately significant, at best, in increasing the probability of forestry investments. Ownership characteristics have only a small influence on forestry investment decisions. All public programs seem to be important in encouraging NIPF landowners to make forestry investments.

Almost all research evaluations have found that forestry technical assistance provided by the states is effective and has excellent private and social returns. Such assistance has helped inform unknowledgeable landowners, encouraged reforestation and harvest, and promoted investments in forestry. State and federal cost-sharing assistance has also encouraged reforestation. One evaluation indicated that some capital substitution may occur, but others did not. Either way, it seems that the probability of NIPF reforestation activity increases with all public programs. Thus, it seems likely that a mix of public programs is an effective approach to increasing NIPF timber supplies. Similar approaches and programs also may be used to accomplish other natural resource objectives, although little empirical research has been performed along these lines so far.

SUMMARY

Many public programs are designed to help private forest landowners produce various outputs. Public programs may be intended to protect forests in general, to produce timber, to promote wildlife management, or to protect nonmarket forest and environmental values.

Timber growing has been encouraged by preferential federal and state income tax provisions. Capital gains treatment of timber income, which lost its financial advantage in 1986, authorized substantially reduced tax rates for timber income. The 1990 tax revisions provided a slight advantage to capital gains use for high-income individuals. Reforestation investment credits are available for nonindustrial forest landowners. Ad valorem property taxes under the highest and best use concept may force forest land into higher-valued, more developed uses. In order to prevent unnecessary conversion, which may destroy timber stands and wildlife habitat, most states have current use-value property tax reductions for forest and farm landowners.

Many financial assistance programs are designed to help private landowners produce timber or protect wildlife. The federal Agricultural Conservation Program and Forestry Incentives Program pay landowners part of their costs for tree planting, timber stand improvement, and some wildlife habitat improvement practices. Some states offer similar programs. Between 1985 and 1990, the Conservation Reserve Program helped establish more than 30 million acres of permanent grass cover and 2 million acres of timberland.

Federal and state agencies provide a variety of direct technical assistance and indirect assistance programs to forest landowners. State foresters advise landowners on woodland management. Fish and wildlife personnel maintain wildlife populations through hunting regulations and habitat management. Government agencies inventory forest and wildlife resources and perform basic and applied research to improve production from and protection of forest resources. Public forest fire protection and insect and disease protection programs receive substantial amounts of funding—totaling more than all other state forestry programs.

The millions of private forest landowners are a diverse lot, with diverse objectives for the ownership and management of their forest resources. Because private owners hold more than 70 percent of our nation's forest resources, society does have a vested interest in how these lands are managed. The geographic scope and ownership diversity necessitate a variety of public programs for privately owned forest resources.

LITERATURE CITED

Adams, Clark E., Richard A. Stone, and John K. Thomas. 1988. Conservation education within information and education divisions of state natural resource agencies. *Wildlife Society Bulletin* 16:329–333.

Alig, Ralph J., Thomas J. Mills, and Robert L. Shackelford. 1980. Most soil bank plantings in the South have been retained; some need follow-up treatments. *Southern Journal of Applied Forestry* 4(1):60–64.

Alward, Greg, and C. Palmer. 1985. Implan User's Guide, Version 1.1. USDA Forest Service, Rocky Mountain Forest and Range Experiment Station. Fort Collins, CO.

Anderson, Walter C. 1975. Timber stand improvement—an entree to forestry for small-tract owners. *Journal of Forestry* 73(4):222–223.

Bengston, David H. 1984. Economic impacts of structural particleboard research. *Forest Science* (30)3:685–697.

Binkley, Clark S. 1981. Timber supply from nonindustrial private forests. Bulletin 92. Yale University School of Forestry and Environmental Studies. New Haven, CT. 97 pp.

Borden, Thomas B. 1982. Realizing our vision. *Journal of Forestry* 80(1):5.

Boyd, Roy. 1983. The effects of FIP and forester assistance on nonindustrial private forests. Pp. 89–107 in Nonindustrial Private Forests: A Review of Economic and Policy Studies. Duke University, School of Forestry and Environmental Studies. Durham, NC.

Boyd, Roy. 1984. Government support of nonindustrial production: The case of private forests. *Southern Economics Journal* 51(1):89–107.

Boyd, Roy, and David H. Newman. 1991. Tax reform and land- using sectors in the U.S. economy: A general equilibrium analysis. *American Journal of Agricultural Economics* 73:398–409.

Budelsky, Carl A., John H. Burde, Fan H. Kung, Dwight R. McCurdy, and Paul L. Roth. 1989. An Evaluation of State District Forester Timber Marking Assistance on Non-Industrial Private Forest Lands in Illinois. Southern Illinois University Department of Forestry. Carbondale. 93 pp.

Bullard, Steven H., and Robert J. Moulton. 1988. The economics of public assistance for nonindustrial private timber sales in Mississippi. Technical Bulletin 147. Mississippi Agricultural and Forestry Experiment Station. Mississippi State, MS. 9 pp.

Bullard, Steven H., and Thomas J. Straka. 1988. Structure and funding of state-level forestry cost-share programs. *Northern Journal of Applied Forestry* 5(2):132–135.

Clawson, Marion (ed.). 1974. Forest Policy for the Future: Conflict, Compromise, Consensus. Resources for the Future. Washington, DC. 360 pp.

Clawson, Marion. 1979. The economics of U.S. nonindustrial private forests. Research Paper R-14. Resources for the Future/Johns Hopkins Press. Washington, DC. 409 pp.

Cleaves, David A., and Jay O'Laughlin. 1983. Forest industry's management assistance programs for nonindustrial private forest landowners in Louisiana, 1980. *Southern Journal of Applied Forestry* 7(2):85–89.

Cubbage, Frederick W. 1983a. Economics of forest tract size: theory and literature. General Technical Report SO-41. USDA Forest Service, Southern Forest Experiment Station. New Orleans. 21 pp.

Cubbage, Frederick W. 1983b. Measuring the physical effects of technical advice from Service Foresters. Pp. 252–258 in Nonindustrial Private Forests: A Review of Economic and Policy Studies. Duke University, School of Forestry and Environmental Studies. Durham, NC.

Cubbage, Frederick W., and John E. Gunter. 1987. Conservation Reserves. *Journal of Forestry* 85(4):21–27.

Cubbage, Frederick W., John E. Gunter, and Jeffrey T. Olsen. 1991. Reforestation economics, law, and taxation. Chapter 2 (pp. 9–31) in Regeneration Manual for Southern Pines. Martinus Nijhoff Publishers. The Hague, Netherlands.

Cubbage, Frederick W., Christopher D. Risbrudt, and Thomas M. Skinner. 1987. Evaluating public forestry assistance programs: A case study in Georgia. *Evaluation Review* 11(1):33–49.

Cubbage, Frederick W., and Donald G. Hodges. 1986a. Professional advice leads in value. Pp. 385–389 in Proceedings, 1985 Society of American Foresters National Convention. Society of American Foresters. Bethesda, MD.

Cubbage, Frederick W., and Donald G. Hodges. 1986b. Public and private foresters. *Journal of Forestry* 84(12): 20–22.

Cubbage, Frederick W., and Peter M. Lickwar. 1988. Trends in funding state forestry programs. *Journal of Forestry* 86(12):19-25.

Cubbage, Frederick W., and Thomas M. Skinner. 1985. Industrial forest management and leasing: 1983 programs and accomplishments in Georgia. *Southern Journal of Applied Forestry* 9(4):217–222.

Cubbage, Frederick W., Thomas M. Skinner, and Christopher D. Risbrudt. 1985. An economic evaluation of the Georgia Rural Forestry Assistance program. Research Bulletin 322. University of Georgia College of Agriculture Experiment Stations. Athens. 59 pp.

Custard, William F. 1982. Tax-supported forestry incentive programs: the affirmative viewpoint. Pp. 70–71 in Proceedings, Forest Taxation Symposium II. Publication FWS-4-82. Virginia Polytechnic Institute and State University, School of Forestry and Wildlife Resources. Blacksburg.

Dennis, Donald F. 1983. Tax incentives for reforestation in Public Law 96–451. *Journal of Forestry* 81(5):293–295.

Duerr, William A. 1981. Productivity as a forestry theme. *Journal of Forestry* 79(8):519–522.

Fecso, R. S., H. F. Kaiser, J. P. Royer, and M. Weidenhamer. 1982. Management practices and reforestation decisions for harvested southern pinelands. SRS Staff Report Number AGES821230. USDA Statistical Reporting Service. Washington. DC. 74 pp.

Field, David B. 1986. Consulting foresters. *Journal of Forestry* 84(2):25–29.

Field, David B., and Stephen F. Holt. 1984. Consulting forestry services available to nonindustrial private forest landowners in the United States. Final Report, USDA Forest Service, Northeastern Area State and Private Forestry Grant No. 42-360. Mimeo. 115 pp.

Flick, Warren A., and Donald A. Horton. 1981. Virginia's reforestation of timberlands program: An economic analysis of the first six years. *Southern Journal of Applied Forestry* 5(4):195–200.

Forest Farmer. 1985. 25th Manual Edition. Forest Farmers Association. Atlanta. 144 pp.

Forest Industries Council. 1980. Forest Productivity Report. National Forest Products Association. Washington, DC. 66 pp.

Foster, Bennet. 1982. Taxpayer's gain from southern pine reforestation programs. *Southern Journal of Applied Forestry* 6(3):188–194.

Gottschalk, John S. 1978. The state–federal partnership in wildlife conservation. In Howard P. Brokaw (ed.), Wildlife and America. U.S. Government Printing Office. Washington, DC.

Gould, Ernest M., Jr. 1975. The search for parity. *Journal of Forestry* 73(4):217–221.

Gregersen, Hans M. 1977. Can we afford small woodland subsidies—it depends. Pp. 62–68 in Proceedings, 1976 Society of American Foresters National Convention, New Orleans.

Guertin, David S., and Douglas B. Rideout. 1987. 1986 Tax Reform Act and forest investment. *Journal of Forestry* 85(9):29–31.

Harou, Patrice A., Gary D. Kronrad, and Robert J. Mack. 1981. Massachusetts consulting foresters: A survey. *The Consultant* 26(1):23–25.

Haygreen, John, Hans Gregersen, Irv Holland, and Robert Stone. 1986. The economic impact of timber utilization research. *Forest Products Journal* 36(2):12–20.

Heinrichs, Jay. 1983. The sovereign state of confusion. *Journal of Forestry* 81(2): 78–91, 94.

Henly, Russell K., Paul V. Ellefson, and Melvin J. Baughman. 1990. Minnesota's private forest management assistance program: An evaluation of aspen timber sales assistance. *Northern Journal of Applied Forestry* 7: 31–34.

Hickman, Clifford A. 1982. Emerging patterns of forest property and yield taxes. Pp. 52–69 in Proceedings, Forest Taxation Symposium II. Publications FWS-4-82. Virginia Polytechnic Institute and State University, School of Forestry and Wildlife Resources. Blacksburg.

Hodges, Donald G., and Frederick W. Cubbage. 1986a. A survey of forestry consulting services provided to nonindustrial private forest landowners in Georgia. Research Report 490. University of Georgia College of Agriculture Experiment Stations. Athens. 41 pp.

Hodges, Donald G., and Frederick W. Cubbage. 1986b. Private forestry consultants: 1983 status and accomplishments in Georgia. *Southern Journal of Applied Forestry* 19(4):225–230.

Hodges, Donald C., and Frederick W. Cubbage. 1990. Nonindustrial private forest management in the South: Assistance foresters' activities and perceptions. *Southern Journal of Applied Forestry* 14(1):44–48.

Hodges, Donald G., and Thomas G. Harris, Jr. 1988. U.S. forest products research: Trends and outlook. *Forest Products Journal* 38(7,8):26–32.

Hodges, Donald G., Pamela J. Jakes, and Frederick W. Cubbage. 1988. The status of forest management research in the United States. General Technical Report NC-126. USDA Forest Service, North Central Forest Experiment Station. St. Paul, MN. 16 pp.

Hubbard, William G., and Robert C. Abt. 1989. The effect of timber sale assistance on returns of landowners. *Resource Management and Optimization* 6(3):225–234.

Hyde, William F. (ed.). 1983. Economic Evaluation of Investments in Forestry Research. The Acorn Press. Durham, NC. 106 pp.

Jackson, David H. 1983. The private forestry assistance program in the Division of Forestry on state lands. Missoula, MT. Mimeo. 37 pp.

Knudsen, Karen, and Jeffrey St. Clair. 1991. Reforming the 25 percent fund. *Forest Watch* 12(2): insert facing pages 14 & 15.

Kronrad, Gary D., and Catherine A. Albers. 1984. Consulting forestry services in North Carolina. *National Woodlands* 7(1):9–12.

Kurtz, William B., Ralph J. Alig, and Thomas J. Mills. 1980. Retention and condition of Agricultural Conservation Program conifer plantings. *Journal of Forestry* 78(5): 273–276.

Lee, Robert E., III. 1982. Tax-supported forestry cost sharing programs—the opposing viewpoint. Pp. 72–79 in Proceedings, Forest Taxation Symposium II, Publication FWS-4-82. Virginia Polytechnic Institute and State University, School of Forestry and Wildlife Resources, Blacksburg.

Lundgren, Allen L. 1981. Methods for evaluating forestry research: A problem analysis for Problem No. 3, Research Work Unit FS-NC-4252. USDA Forest Service, North Central Forest Experiment Station. St. Paul, MN. 52 pp.

Lundgren, Allen L. 1982. Research productivity from an economic viewpoint. Pp. 256–262 in Proceedings, 1981 Society of American Foresters. National Convention. Orlando, FL.

Mangold, Robert D., Robert J. Moulton, and Jeralyn D. Snellgrove. 1991. Tree planting in the United States 1990. USDA Forest Service, Cooperative Forestry. U.S. Government Printing Office. Washington, DC. 18 pp.

Marsinko, Alan P. C., and Steven K. Nodine. 1981. Tree planting under the soil bank program—an economic analysis. Forestry Bulletin Number 24. Clemson University, Department of Forestry. Clemson, SC. 5 pp.

Martin, James W. 1977. 1976 survey of forestry consultants. *The Consultant* 22(2):29–38.

McComb, William H. 1975. Mismanagement by the small landowner—fact or fiction? *Journal of Forestry* 73(4):224–225.

McComb, William H. 1978. Forest cooperatives—how successful? *Forest Farmer* 37(8):9, 14–18.

McKillop, William. 1975. Social benefits of forestry incentive programs. *Journal of Forestry* 73(4):214–216.

Meeks, Gordon, Jr. 1982. State incentives for nonindustrial private forestry. *Journal of Forestry* 80(1):18–22.

Meyer, Richard D. 1984. An analysis of long-term leasing and cutting contracts in the South. M.S. thesis. Virginia Polytechnic Institute and State University. School of Forestry and Wildlife Resources. Blacksburg. 159 pp.

Meyer, Richard D., and David W. Klemperer. 1984. Current status of long-term leasing and cutting contracts in the South. Pp. 125–130 in Proceedings, 1984 Southern Forest Economics Workshop. March 13–15. Memphis, TN.

Mills, Thomas J. 1975. Investment priorities for small-owner assistance programs. *Journal of Forestry* 73(4):210–213.

Moulton, Robert J. 1991. The Conservation Title of the 1990 Farm Bill. Pp. 159–167 in Proceedings, Southern Forest Economics Meeting, February 20–22. Washington, DC.

Moulton, Robert J., and Frederick W. Cubbage. 1991. Technical assistance programs for non-industrial private forest landowners. *Western Wildlands* 16(3):6–10.

Moulton, Robert J., and Michael R. Dicks. 1987. Implications of the 1985 Farm Act for forestry. Pp. 163–176 in Proceedings, 1987 Joint Meeting of the Southern Forest Economics Workers and the Mid-West Forest Economists. Asheville, NC.

Moulton, Robert J., Bengt Hyberg, Thomas Hebert, and Michael Dicks. 1989. Pp. 144–159. The timberland in Conservation Reserve Program and its effect on southern rural economies. Pp. 144–159 in Proceedings, Southern Forest Economics Meeting, March 3–5. San Antonio, TX.

Myers, J. K., and M. H. Goforth. 1980. Consulting foresters surveyed. *The Consultant* 25(3):68–78.

Newman, David H. 1990. Shifting southern softwood stumpage supply: Implications for welfare estimation from technical change. *Forest Science* 36(3):705–718.

O'Laughlin, Jay, David A. Cleaves, and David J. Skove. 1983. Forest industry programs for NIPFs: Management assistance and privately funded cost-sharing. Pp. 241–251 in Nonindustrial Private Forests: A Review of economic and Policy Studies. Duke University, School of Forestry and Environmental Studies. Durham, NC.

O'Laughlin, Jay, and Richard A. Williams. 1988. Forests and the Texas economy. Publication B-1596. Texas Agricultural Experiment Station. College Station. 65 pp.

Pleasonton, Alfred. 1968. Southern consulting firms, 1966. *The Consultant* 13(2):14–19.

Pleasonton, Alfred. 1969. Southern forestry consultants and their views. *Journal of Forestry* 67(9):658–660, 664, 666, 668–672.

Redmond, Clair H., Frederick W. Cubbage, and Richard D. Ullrich. 1990. An economic analysis of the conservation Reserve Program in South Georgia. *Southern Journal of Applied Forestry* 14(3):137–142.

Renew America Project. 1989. State of the States. Washington, DC. 48 pp.

Risbrudt, Christopher D., and H. Fred Kaiser. 1982. Economic analysis of the sawmill improvement program. *Forest Products Journal* 32(8):25–28.

Risbrudt, Christopher D., H. Fred Kaiser, and Paul V. Ellefson. 1983. Cost-effectiveness of

the 1979 Forestry Incentives Program. *Journal of Forestry* 81(5):298–301.

Royer, Jack P. 1979. Conclusions from a review of 50 years of landowner studies. In Proceedings, Southern Forest Economics Workshop, Chapel Hill, NC. 12 pp.

Royer, Jack P. 1987. Determinants of reforestation behavior among southern landowners. *Forest Science* 33(3):654–667.

Royer, Jack P., and Robert J. Moulton. 1987. Reforestation incentives: Tax incentives and cost sharing in the South. *Journal of Forestry* 85(8):45–47.

Royer, Jack P., and Christopher D. Risbrudt (eds.). 1983 Nonindustrial private forest landowners: A review of economic and policy studies, Symposium Proceedings. Duke University, School of Forestry and Environmental Studies. Durham, NC. 398 pp.

Salazar, Debra J., and Alan Barton. 1988. Measuring the value of technical forestry assistance: The Washington case. University of Washington, College of Forest Resources. Seattle. Mimeo. 31 pp.

Sedjo, Roger A., and David M. Ostermeier. 1978. Policy alternatives for nonindustrial private forests. Report of the Workshop on Policy Alternatives for Nonindustrial Private Forests. Society of American Foresters and Resources for the Future. Washington, DC. 64 pp.

Seldon, Barry J. 1985. A nonresidual approach to the measurement of social returns to research with application to the softwood plywood industry. Duke University, School of Forestry and Environmental Studies; Ph.D. dissertation. Durham, NC. 179 pp.

Siegel, William C. 1973. Long-term contracts for forest land and timber in the South. Research Paper SO-87. USDA Forest Service, Southern Forest Experiment Station. New Orleans. 14 pp.

Siegel, William C. 1978. Historical development of federal income tax treatment of timber. Pp. 17–25 in Proceedings, Forest Taxation Symposium Publication FWS 2–78.

Virginia Polytechnic Institute and State University, School of Forestry and Wildlife Resources. Blacksburg.

Siegel, William C. 1987. Implications of the 1986 federal tax reform act for forestry. Pp. 254–258 in Proceedings, 1986 Society of American Foresters National Convention. Bethesda, MD.

Siegel, William C., and Sam Guttenberg. 1968. Timber leases and long-term cutting contracts in the South. *Forest Industries* 95(4):62–64.

Singleton, William R. 1983. An empirical study of the effects of taxation on investment expenditures by selected firms in the forest products industry (abstract). Ph.D. dissertation. University of Hawaii. 246 pp.

Skok, Richard A., and Hans M. Gregersen. 1975. Motivating private forestry: An overview. *Journal of Forestry* 73(4): 202–205.

Straka, Thomas H., and Steven H. Bullard. 1987. State cost-share programs for nonindustrial private forestry investments. Pp. 262–266 in Proceedings, 1986 Society of American Foresters National Convention. Bethesda, MD.

Sunley, Emil M., Jr. 1976. Capital gains treatment of timber: Present law and proposed changes. *Journal of Forestry* 74(2):75–78.

Teer, James G., George V. Burger, and Charles Y. Deknatel. 1983. State-supported habitat management and commercial hunting on private lands in the United States: Pp. 445–455 in Transactions, Forty-eighth North American Wildlife and Natural Resources Conference. Wildlife Management Institute. Washington, DC.

USDA Agricultural Stabilization and Conservation Service. 1991. Forestry Incentives Program: From inception of program through September 30, 1990. U.S. Government Printing Office. Washington, DC. 34 pp.

U.S. General Accounting Office. 1990. Forest Service timber harvesting, planting, assistance programs and tax provisions. Report no. GAO/RECO-90-107BR. U.S. Government Printing Office. Washington, DC. 19 pp.

Vaux, Henry J. 1983. State intervention on private forests in California. Pp. 124–168 in Governmental Interventions, Social Needs, and the Management of U.S. Forests. Resources for the Future. Washington, DC.

Westgate, Robert A. 1986. The economics of containerized forest tree seedling research in the United States. *Canadian Journal of Forest Research* 16:1007–1012.

Wigley, T. Bentley, and M. Anthony Melchiors. 1987. State wildlife management programs for private lands. *Wildlife Society Bulletin* 15:580–584.

Williams, Ellis T. 1961. Trends in forest taxation. *National Tax Journal* 14(2):113–144.

Williamson, Lonnie L. 1987. State wildlife revenues increase. *Outdoor News Bulletin* 41(20):2–3.

Williston, Hamlin L. 1980. A statistical history of tree planting in the South, 1925–1979. Miscellaneous Report SA-MR 8. USDA Forest Service, Region 8. Atlanta. 36 pp.

Wishart, John E. 1982. Don't regulate—innovate? *Virginia Forests* 38(2):11–13.

Worrell, Albert C., and Lloyd C. Irland. 1975. Alternative means of motivating investment in private forestry. *Journal of Forestry* 73(4):206–209.

Chapter 18

Forest Resource Policy in a Global Context

Forest management poses acute policy issues, as industrialists, loggers, naturalists, hikers and hunters urge their conflicting interests, but the forest area is stable.

—Robert Repetto (Repetto and Gillis 1988)

In the developing countries the main pressures arise from the population explosion which leads both to the clearance of forests for food production and an increased demand for wood and more especially fuelwood and other wood for domestic use.... Changes in forest policy and practice can only delay catastrophe, they cannot avert it indefinitely.

—Fred Hummel and Adriaan van Maaren 1984

For decades, forestry has been the poor stepchild of development agendas emphasizing agricultural projects and capital-intensive energy schemes. Developing countries traditionally have undervalued forestry because national accounting methods often ignore the ecological and social benefits of forests.

—Sandra Postel and Lori Heise 1988

INTRODUCTION

International dependencies and relationships are escalating continuously. Realistic policy and action now require looking beyond national self-interest toward international exchanges of people, technologies, products, services, and ideas. There is no question that American forestry will be affected by the transformation of the world economy and social structure that is underway (Laarman 1988). An understanding of forest policy therefore requires a comprehension of the global situation. International forestry problems will require new forest policy objectives, new mechanisms to work toward those ends, and new institutional relationships.

Forest management requires knowledge and integration of forestry at the stand, forest, regional, and national level. Forest policy at the regional and national level requires an appreciation of the international context and a knowledge of world forest resources. International agencies, such as the Food and Agriculture Organization (FAO) of the United Nations, collect and disseminate such information (Peck 1984). Other organizations such as the World Resources Institute (1988) make this information available in comprehensive and highly readable summaries.

Understanding the forest resource policy of an individual government is basic, because it guides all forestry activities, including (1) conservation, protection, administration, management and utilization of forests; (2) environmental protection and preservation; and (3) forest industries and marketing of forest products, both domestically and abroad. In some countries activities related to wildlands, wildlife, and national parks also fall under forest resource policy. Ultimately, our public policies will determine how we use, manage, protect, and preserve forests, whether for the benefit of people today, future generations, or plants and animals alone.

Two brief examples illustrate why forest resource policy usually focuses on people, not trees. First, the establishment of fuelwood plantations is an important element of public policy designed to alleviate fuelwood shortages in developing countries. Experience has shown that such plantations will be successful only if villagers fully participate in such programs, so that the plantations become *their* plantations. This is an essential element of social or community forestry (Eckmullner and van Maaren 1984). Local villagers are needed to plant seedlings and, in many successful cases, produce the seedlings themselves. Villagers need to be allowed the flexibility to market as well as consume the results of their efforts (Gregersen 1988). Many poor rural villagers view trees as a source of wealth, in some cases, their only source of wealth. This has profound implications for forest resource policy, not the least of which is changing the bureaucratic attitude that the poor cannot be trusted to manage their trees (Chambers and Leach 1987).

As a second example, consider tropical moist forests. The best way to protect them is to reduce the pressure to harvest them. Legislation and enforcement measures, necessary elements of such a forest policy, can be effective only when the demand for land and lumber is not too great in the first place. Policy decisions for the future of tropical forests need to be viewed in the framework of a general land use policy. Many developing countries have a land policy that makes clearing of forest land a legal (and often encouraged) way to obtain title to agricultural land. One way to protect these forests is to promote good forestry and good agriculture on lands outside the tropical forest. Another might be to change land title policies so that they favor forest retention, not clearing. Environmental, social, and economic factors must be weighed, but long term ecological considerations should be considered. Eckmullner and van Maaren (1984) suggest the interests of local people should receive priority over those from distant urban areas. This same principle may favor local uses over global concerns, however, and indeed has been used as a justification for clearing rain forests and temperate forests.

Forest resource policy is the result of a process. It is dynamic, not static. Forest policies must be constantly reviewed and updated to meet the changing needs of society in a changing world. Recently, unprecedented changes in resource policy have taken place in many parts of the world, and more changes may be expected. The interdependence of forest policy and other national policies, especially those concerned with rural development and conservation of the environment, is widely recognized throughout the world. Demands for more goods and services are rapidly accelerating, affecting forests everywhere. Only by new policy initiatives can these demands possibly be met without irrevocable damage to the world's forest resources (Hummel and van Maaren 1984).

Government policies have intensified existing pressures and added new ones leading to wasteful use of forest resources, including government-owned forests. Changes in policy can substantially reduce resource waste. Emphasis on the policy dimension of forest resources is therefore worthwhile and necessary. The focus should include not only forestry policies, but also nonforestry policies such as agricultural programs, infrastructure projects, land tenure, and fiscal and monetary affairs (Repetto and Gillis 1988).

The conservation and careful use of the world's forests is a responsibility that transcends national interests. Perhaps more than anything else, what is needed is a clear understanding of basic worldwide forestry issues and a willingness to support other nations' attempts to resolve these issues. A brief list of the major global forestry issues would include the following (Peck 1984):

1. The fuelwood problem in the developing countries, especially in drier areas.

2. The conservation of as large an area as possible of the remaining natural forest, without endangering the livelihood of indigenous peoples (including habitat preservation, avoiding forest fragmentation, and retaining biological diversity).

3. Concentration of management efforts on the more productive forest sites.

4. The extension of tree plantations for fuelwood, industrial roundwood, and carbon storage.

5. The integration of policies for forestry and forest industries.

Our discussion of global forest resources addresses most of these issues and begins with forest resource management and protection in developing countries.

FORESTRY IN THE DEVELOPING WORLD

TROPICAL DEFORESTATION

Tropical deforestation has been the preeminent forestry issue of the 1980s and early 1990s. The media focused on the importance of the tropical forests in preventing soil loss, stopping habitat destruction, promoting biological diversity, and ameliorating global warming. In fact, the amount of literature is so vast and comprehensive that we will simply summarize a few salient concerns rather than thoroughly review them all. The World Resources Institute (1988), World Watch, Laarman and Sedjo (1992), the American Forestry Association, and others have published many books and articles on the subject.

In brief, tropical forestry issues center around the appropriate use of the forests. Developing countries—such as America was in the 1700s and 1800s—view the forests as a source of natural resource wealth, which they need to use to become more developed. Developing countries harvest valuable timber species for domestic consumption or for international export. They also harvest forests to provide sites for agriculture for their impoverished and rapidly increasing number of citizens. Many harvested lands provide for subsistence farming; some are for intensive agriculture; some are converted to tree plantations; and some degrade to infertile wastelands. America harvested much of its forests in the 1800s and 1900s for similar purposes (see Table 2-1).

The United States has been fortunate in that its temperate forests hold most nutrients in the soils and most of its forests have grown back if they were not converted to agriculture. Exploitation of tropical forests may not lead to such fortuitous results. Despite the denseness of the tropical jungles, they are among the most diverse and ecologically sensitive forest lands. Gradwohl and Greenberg (1988) list several reasons why tropical moist ecosystems are easily imperiled.

• Most nutrients in tropical forests are held in the standing biomass. Clearing and burning volatizes the nutrients or releases them into the poor soils. The nutrients are then leached out by warm tropical rains.

• Tropical forest regeneration is complex and most species cannot tolerate humidity or light conditions of open areas.

• Tropical forest seeds often are spread by a few species of animals, which must live in forests near cleared forest lands in order to be able to spread seed.

- Many forest plants have separate male and female plants, and they are often pollinated by animals; thus the plants and animals must live in close proximity.

- Both pollination and seed dispersal are made more difficult by the wide diversity of tropical species.

- Trees may require forest micorrhizae to grow on bare soils, and micorrhizae may be lost when forests are cleared.

- Tropical soils that are cleared of vegetation may not be conducive to long-term viability of forest plant seeds.

- Tough, browse, and fire-resistant grasses and shrubs take hold after long periods of burning and grazing, which can block forest regrowth.

Gradwohl and Greenberg (1988) further discuss many reasons that tropical moist forests are being converted to other uses. Fuelwood is needed for cooking, charcoal, iron smelters, and cement plants. Timber is used for construction and domestic items. Slash and burn agriculture is practiced to colonize the forest frontier and provide a means of subsistence living for native populations. Conversion to large-scale agriculture also contributes to deforestation. These problems are compounded by pervasive social problems such as population growth, debt crises, war, and wildfires.

The possible consequences of deforestation were listed by Gradwohl and Greenburg (1988). Indigenous people who live in tropical forests, and their knowledge, will be lost. Barren land and desertification will increase in drier regions and be exacerbated by regional decreases in rainfall. Global climate could also become warmer due to slash and burn agriculture, a loss of carbon storage, and a rise in atmospheric carbon. Many plant and animal species will become extinct, including potentially important food and medicinal plants. Soil erosion will increase; hydroelectric power potential will decrease.

And there will be an increasing downward cycle of rural poverty.

There are obviously no easy answers to the problems of tropical deforestation. The problems involve complex social, economic, and political dimensions. Surely developing countries need the capital that their natural resources provide. It may be that less destructive forest harvesting practices could occur. Rubber-tapping, agroforestry, harvest of native fruits, production of native crafts, and tourism have all been proposed as income alternatives to timber harvesting. But it is doubtful that these alone can supplant the income needs and land use policies that favor development. Even native people who promote alternatives to tropical deforestation are unpopular. Chico Mendez, who was a leader of the Brazilian rubber-tappers union, was murdered, probably for his active opposition to development and deforestation.

Another problem associated with deforestation is that the benefits of tropical forest protection are mostly nonmarket. Biological diversity, long-term productivity, and global climate are not goods allocated well or at all by market processes. Thus they must be protected or provided by some type of government intervention. Government policies must address basic social needs first—population pressures, poverty, land tenure, class structure, and so on—to help halt tropical deforestation. Various public policies of tropical countries and of developed northern countries can be used to help solve these problems, as will be discussed in the following sections of this chapter.

INTERNATIONAL DEVELOPMENT AND FOREIGN AID

Romm (1986) suggested that forest and development policies may be viewed by either of two models. Traditional forest policy has treated forest policy in isolation from the welfare of the nations in which they are located. An alternative historical model suggests that forest conditions are determined mostly by population growth and economic development. The traditional approach is obviously simplistic and the historical approach is fatalistic. Romm suggests that a synthesis of the two paradigms is more appropriate. Namely, social forces do indeed determine forest conditions, but government influences on these social forces can indeed provide means for implementing forest policy.

Countries and international development agencies and aid policies of developed countries can influence people and their actions. Most of the Western world and Japan spend large amounts of foreign aid that is designated to improve living conditions in developing countries. So do a number of international lending agencies such as the World Bank, the International Monetary Fund, and the Latin-American Development Bank. For example, the United States provides bilateral (two-country) development assistance through the Act for International Development of 1961 (Foreign Assistance Act), which has been amended many times. Several countries also may provide multilateral development aid.

The aid provided by the United States and by other countries is a political endeavor, serving a variety of purposes and interest groups. Critics question whether foreign aid and loans actually help developed countries or serve only to salve our conscience, to further Western trade interests, or to support aid-providing interest groups. Many developing countries have not developed according to plans and are not integrated into the world economy, unless one considers that they now owe an almost insurmountable debt to the developed world. Let us briefly examine how foreign aid works and its prospects for dealing with complex forest and social issues in developing countries.

Aid Agencies

The U.S. Agency for International Development (USAID) is the branch of the U.S. Department of State responsible for the disbursement of foreign aid or Official Development Assistance (ODA). ODA is disbursed according to current U.S. government policies and comes in two basic forms —development assistance (domestic pro-

grams) and security (military) assistance. Many other countries have agencies similar to USAID, such as Canada's CIDA, Germany's CTZ, Britain's ODA, Japan's JICA, and Sweden's SIDA. The United States is one of the largest donors of combined military and domestic aid, but a majority of the assistance is for military programs. Other countries, however, give a far larger proportion of their total gross national income for foreign aid.

The United States and many other countries participate in multinational development organizations. The United Nations oversees a number of development organizations such as the Food and Agriculture Organization (FAO), the UN Development Program (UNDP), the UN Education and Scientific Organization (UNESCO), and the World Health Organization (WHO). Consistent with the UN charter, each of these organizations implements programs and projects designed to benefit those countries with the greatest need.

The United States also participates in the Organization for Economic Cooperation and Development (OECD), a group of Western European and North American countries. OECD is intended to help growth and development in *member* countries and thus improve the world economy. The World Bank and the International Monetary Fund also provide large loans to developing countries. The World Bank has been joined by other banks working in these countries—the Inter-American Development Bank, the African Development Bank, and the Asian Development Bank. The international bank loans, like all loans, come with strings attached. The banks set conditions that must be met by the borrowing countries, including significant policy directives, such as reducing the countries' budget deficits or denationalizing some industries.

A large number of nongovernmental organizations (NGOs) also provide forestry assistance and funding. Examples include CARE International, the Pan American Development Foundation, the World Wildlife Fund, the International Union for Conservation of Nature and Natural Resources, and the International

Institute for Environment and Development. These and a host of other NGOs have become important in development assistance, as well as in environmental protection and farm and community forestry (Laarman and Sedjo 1992). Their expertise and funding often can be influential in developing countries where professional expertise and discretionary income for natural resource programs are scarce. The U.S. Peace Corps, a quasi-governmental organization, also has been a long-standing development assistance provider since the Kennedy presidency.

Aid Policy

Before 1980 U.S. foreign aid policy for economic development assistance focused heavily on social and community assistance. The Reagan administration redirected policy to focus more on military aid, bilateral assistance, and stimulation of private enterprise and market solutions. Most USAID forestry and related natural resource projects, however, still emphasize fuelwood and social forestry (Laarman 1987).

Loan conditionality, or policy-based lending, became more widespread in the 1980s. The United States and other donor countries give aid only because it is in their political, strategic, and economic interests to do so. Aid is given to reward countries we like or withheld to punish those we do not. The United States gives bilateral aid as a carrot to prompt favored government policies and has inveigled the World Bank and IMF to do so as well (Laarman 1987). Policy-based loans may require economic or social changes in countries, such as raising prices of agricultural commodities; devaluing local currencies, reducing civil service payrolls, raising taxes, or occasionally (especially in the Carter years) improving human rights.

The political ramifications of policy-based lending are substantial. Requiring economic reforms should improve the economy of debtor nations, and thus their ability to repay loans. But the cost in political relations may be enormous (Laarman 1987). Requests by the United States for reduced deforestation in South America certainly could seem self-serving and antagonize less affluent countries. As the largest users of energy and resources, it seems imperialistic for us to ask less developed countries to protect their trees to absorb the carbon dioxide we emit from driving cars and heating our homes.

Critics also have charged that the World Bank and the IMF, which have sponsored many of the largest development projects in the world, are the greatest cause of environmental destruction. Books and articles critical of the World Bank are common; environmental groups have picketed the bank's offices on many occasions. These charges and media attention have prompted the bank and other lending agencies to more actively seek means to protect the environment and wildlife, as well as promote development.

Given the politics of foreign aid, can it help deal with tropical deforestation and sustained development? Such a question depends mostly on one's values, not on empirical evidence. Given that development in the Third World and the forestry issues are crucial, perhaps the best one can hope for is that domestic development and foreign aid policies will be implemented efficiently, with benefits accruing to needy people, and that a high level of environmental protection will be maintained. Rural development programs should stress income production for the poor, avoid needless deforestation, and seek solutions that will foster long-term returns, not short-term gains that destroy the land's productive capabilities. Meeting these goals will be a challenge for developed and developing countries alike.

SOCIAL FORESTRY

As Romm (1986) and the preceding discussion on foreign aid suggest, forest policy in developing countries depends on economics and development. Thus forest policies often must be social in nature—that is, involved with local farm and community development. *Social* or *farm forestry* refers to a broad range of tree- or forest-related activities undertaken by rural landowners and community groups to provide products for their own use and for generating local income. Social forestry commonly makes use of agroforestry technologies, or the integration of trees with various forms of agricultural crops and livestock. Social forestry, agroforestry, and farm and community forestry are all related. Each directly or indirectly refers to growing and using trees to provide food, fuel, medicines, livestock fodder, building materials, and cash incomes via the active involvement of local people (Laarman and Sedjo 1992).

Social forestry also may include governments or other groups and organizations planting trees on public lands to meet local village needs. Social forestry can contribute both directly and indirectly to improving the environment, increasing food and energy security, and reducing unemployment. Two ingredients are common in successful social forestry programs: widespread local participation with government support, and locally acceptable, sustainable technologies (Gregersen 1988).

Gregersen (1988) describes the benefits and methods of implementing social forestry programs in detail. The basic issue in social forestry is how to change land use so that people get what they need on a sustainable basis from a fixed or shrinking land base. Program planning is important, but local participation and enthusiasm are essential. Programs must have adequate land and other resources, such as seedlings. They must include education about farm and forestry methods. Market incentives—good prices for the products—are important; so is a clear understanding about tenure rights for land and trees. In some cases, individuals may own land and the trees; in others the community may control the rights. Programs must consider these differences. Nonmarket incentives—such as free seedlings, tools, food, technical advice, land and capital—are crucial elements in most programs, but these must be tied to the right measure of program performance. Protection from fires, theft, or future government expropriation also is important. Various combinations of these approaches appropriate to local conditions can help develop viable, sustain-

able increases in productivity. These are the keys that will help improve living standards and forest resource protection over time.

SUSTAINABLE DEVELOPMENT

Population pressures and the associated needs for food, shelter, and clothing, along with political pressures, cause a large share of tropical deforestation. A primary challenge confronted by developing countries in the tropics and subtropics is attaining sustainable development and economic self-sufficiency. Developing countries aim to achieve economic growth in order to improve the quality of life for their citizens. They must balance this growth with conservation, so that they do not needlessly waste or pollute natural resources.

The need to balance economic growth with resource conservation has prompted calls for *sustainable development.* Many definitions exist, but the term may be considered as meaning development that involves changes in the production or distribution of desired goods and services that result in an increase in people's welfare that can be sustained over time. Sustainable development would include improving the production capacity of ecosystems and maintaining or improving environmental quality. It also would include maintaining or improving the well-being of people and enhancing their capacity to utilize resources effectively and efficiently over the long run to meet the needs of present and future generations. Thus sustainability could be considered to have both ecological and social welfare components (Gregersen and Lundgren 1990).

Sustainable development, or the integration of conservation and development, has become the focus of many international environmental and forestry policies. Debates of tropical (and temperate) deforestation and use have gained international agenda status. Forest exploitation, use, protection, and preservation are debated within and among all countries in the world. Developed countries implore developing countries such as

Brazil or Russia to protect their forests; developing countries chastise developed countries such as the United States for cutting its few remaining old-growth forests and using about 40 percent of the world's energy. These issues have made both the definition and practice of sustainable development a challenge.

PLANTATION FORESTRY

Social forestry and international development aid are two tools for improving the quality of life in many countries. Forest plantations are another means to improve social and forestry conditions in developing and developed countries. Some plantations in developing countries stemmed from social forestry/international aid programs, and some from domestic or market incentives to plant trees for industrial use.

Tree plantations have been planted in many countries for industrial wood and to a lesser extent, fuelwood. Large plantation programs were successful in Europe, Australia, New Zealand, Korea, and Brazil. When they were initiated, these plantations were seen as important means to produce wood fiber. In recent years, however, environmental groups have criticized many of the extensive plantings of monocultures and exotic species. Plantations still are seen as important means of providing wood fiber, but wide-scale plantings of exotics, especially after destruction of native forests, is less popular and pervasive. In addition, in some countries, such as Australia and New Zealand, cutting of native forests has been largely banned in response to the deemed excesses of plantation forestry in earlier years. Many foresters and development agencies still advocate large-scale, intensive, planting programs, stating that the fiber can help reduce deforestation or allow increased preservation of other forests. Plantation benefits often accrue to wealthier landowners, however, or may not be as great as promised by advocates. Thus, these public and private investments will be scrutinized closely in the future.

Postel and Hiese (1988) estimated the extent of industrial forest plantations in the world as of 1985 (Table 18-1). The former Soviet Union, China, the United States, and Western Europe had the greatest areas of plantations, at over 10 million hectares each, followed closely by Japan, with 9.5 million hectares. In South America, Brazil, Chile, and Argentina have substantial plantations. In Africa, South Africa and Nigeria are the leaders. Several countries in Southeast Asia and Oceania also have large areas in plantations, including India, Indonesia, New Zealand, Australia, and South Korea. These plantations provide a variety of products, from fuelwood

TABLE 18-1. Estimated Industrial Forest Plantations Worldwide, circa 1985[a]

Country/Region	Area (thousand hectare)
Soviet Union	21,900
China[b]	17,500
United States[c]	12,107
Japan	9,584
Brazil	3,500
India	1,960
Indonesia	1,800
Canada[d]	1,528
Chile	1,227
South Africa	1,115
New Zealand	1,089
Australia	838
Argentina	550
South Korea	400
Nigeria	270
Western Europe[e]	13,000
Other	3,335
Total	91,703

[a]Does not include areas that naturally regenerate after logging, a precess that occurs more readily in temperate countries than in tropical ones.

[b]Midpoint of estimated range of 15,000 to 20,000.

[c]Includes only industrial plantations in 12 southern states and in the Pacific Northwest, accounting for at least 90 percent of planting for timber.

[d]Includes only plantations established since 1975.

[e]Plantations as of 1975.

Source: Postel and Heise 1988.

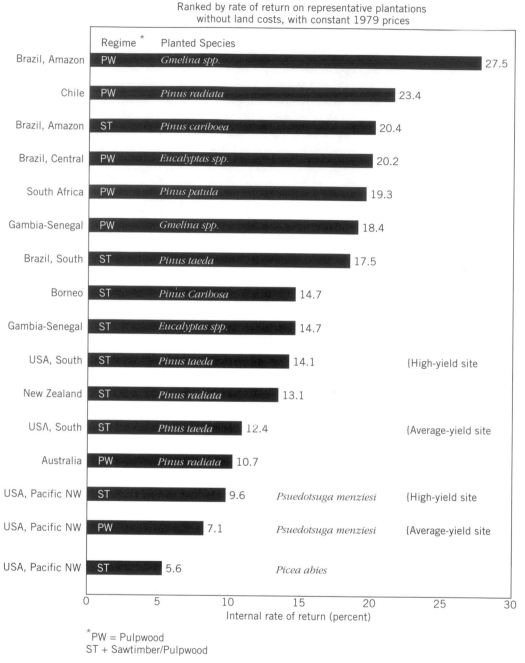

Figure 18-1. Worldwide Forestry Plantation Investment Returns
Source: Sedjo 1983

to pulpwood to sawtimber, depending on local markets and exporting policies.

Sedjo (1983) analyzed the investment returns from tree plantations in different parts of the world (Figure 18-1). The plantation internal rates of return (IRR) in South America and South Africa were excellent, ranging from 17.5 percent to 27.5 percent. Those in Southeast Asia were less, at 10 to 15 percent, but still quite good. Southern U.S. returns averaged around a 14 percent IRR, and Pacific Northwest returns were less, at about 8 percent. The average returns to investments in Scandinavia were the lowest, at only 5.6 percent per year.

Overall, the data in Figure 18-1 indicate that plantation forestry can generate attractive returns on investment for tropical countries if adequate land and capital are available to establish the plantations. Forest plantations can contribute to economic development, help improve standards of living, and decrease pressures for clearing tropical moist forests. They also can provide the base for greater industrial processing within a country and increase its domestic product for internal consumption or export markets. Planting trees without considering local uses or markets, however, can lead to problems. Some countries have established pine plantations in remote areas, where the timber cannot be harvested and transported economically, or even be used by local groups. Plantations can help provide domestic and industrial wood fiber, but local markets, tenure rights, equity, and environmental impacts need to be considered.

Illustration: UNCED: The Rumble in Rio

The June 1992 United Nations Conference on Environment and Development (UNCED) in Rio de Janiero, Brazil, clearly illustrates the international importance of environmental and natural resource policies. UNCED—also called the Earth Summit—was a milestone in international recognition of the importance of environmental protection, considering a host of specific proposals to reduce threatened plants and wildlife and protect forests, as well as means to reduce poverty and foster less destructive industrialization. UNCED was attended by negotiators and heads of state from 170 countries. Even President Bush capitulated and attended the conference after refusing to do so until the month before.

The basic issues prompting the UNCED conference were worldwide perceptions of environmental destruction, pollution, resource scarcity, and overpopulation, that would require global responses. The specters

of overpopulation, scarcity, and pollution had helped prompt much of the U.S. environmental movement in the 1970s; many of these issues were triggered by publication of Meadows et al.'s *Limits of Growth* in 1972. The authors wrote that population and growth would exceed the earth's ability to provide resources and absorb pollution. These dreary predictions were revered by environmentalists and attacked by economists, and they received international publicity. However, the economic growth of the late 1970s and early 1980s allayed fears of resource scarcity. These fears resurfaced in the late 1980s, as world population continued to soar, and environmental destruction increased. The perceived needs to provide economic growth so that developing countries could improve their quality of life and to protect the environment led to calls for sustainable development.

Treaties and Politics

A host of specific international treaties and declarations were considered at the Earth Summit. The Rio Declaration was a broad proclamation that outlined the environmental rights and responsibilities of nations. It discussed the principles for sustainable development, from eradicating poverty to making polluters pay for excesses. Agenda 21 was a 900-page action plan for sustainable development, including a blueprint of financial sources and methods to implement the Rio Declaration.

UNCED also included treaties on biodiversity and global warming, which were binding, and a statement of forestry principles, which was not. The forest principles consisted of 17 points outlining guidelines and means for protecting the world's forests. The biodiversity treaty is a binding pact to protect animal and plant species. The global warming treaty urges reduction in the emission of carbon dioxide and other "greenhouse gases" that are believed to cause global warming.

The Earth Summit proved to be politically controversial as well as popular, particularly for the United States. Although population clearly is a cause of poverty and environmental pressures, all statements about population control were kept off the agenda by the more populated countries and the Vatican. The Rio conference occurred a few months before the fall 1992 elections in the United States, so President Bush made the administration response to the UNCED proposals a national issue. After facing three years of slow growth in the economy, as well as considerable pressure from conservatives, Ross Perot, and the business sector, Bush entered the fray at Rio by steadfastly refusing to support the treaties or parts of treaties that he felt would reduce economic growth. The Bush administration took the stance that the United States was the leader in environmental protection, that the developing countries had wasted aid funds before, and that many Rio proposals would cost too much economic growth. The developing countries, in turn, thought that greater environmental protection measures should be instituted—but paid for by the northern industrialized countries. The international debate over who would pay for the Rio initiatives was perhaps the most fundamental question.

Agreements and Outcomes

The eventual policy statements of UNCED were concluded on June 14, 1992; the outcomes, actions, and policies implemented will evolve for years to come. The text of the nonbinding Rio Declaration principles to guide environmental policy was adopted by consensus of the attendees at the Earth Summit. The negotiators at UNCED created a new UN commission—the United Nations Commission on Sustainable Development—to monitor compliance with environmental treaties and to review progress toward the goals of the Earth Summit. The commission will provide a forum in which governments can be held accountable for their actions, and it will be a place to continue negotiations begun at the Earth Summit.

The Agenda 21 blueprint to protect the environment while encouraging development was also adopted. The agenda calls on the industrialized world to vastly increase its aid to the developing world, especially to protect the environment. The Agenda 21 costs could exceed $100 billion if fully funded.

Developing countries wanted the Agenda 21 funds to be controlled directly by them in a "Green Fund." Developed countries wanted the funds channeled through the World Bank, in order to prevent control or waste by corrupt leaders and to retain conditions on the funds. A compromise in the final hours brought agreement between the 12-nation European Community and a coalition of 77 Third World countries on funding Agenda 21. European countries did agree to boost development funding but refused to set a deadline, and retained control over their own contributions. On the other hand, the Europeans agreed to let the newly created U.N. Sustainable Development Commission review their foreign aid donations each year.

To help implement Agenda 21, President Bush pledged a $1.4 billion long-term fund for research on climate change and $150 million to help preserve the world's forests. However, hours after Bush declared that the United States is the world's environmental leader, Japan announced a five-year, $7 billion environmental aid initiative. This would mean that every year for the next five years, Japan would spend nearly twice as much as the United States in environmental aid. Japan's total foreign aid expenditures are $10 billion per year (still mostly domestic programs), compared to the $11 billion of the United States (mostly military programs). European countries also pledged far greater levels of foreign environmental/development aid, including $4 billion in new funds, and significant increases in foreign aid as a share of gross national product.

The statement of forestry principles also was approved, albeit not without some contention. Industrialized countries focused on protection of tropical rain forests, and developing countries sought better regeneration of temperate forests. The issue of financial control of donations also proved difficult. The United States did not want to commit itself to providing aid in exchange for protecting forests; Malaysia sought to make that link explicit in the forestry statement. The developing countries also opposed infringements on their rights to use their own forests.

The binding climate change and biodiversity treaties were agreed upon by most major nations, although the Bush administration opposed parts of both. The Global Warming Convention recommended curbing emissions of carbon dioxide and other gases that cause global warming. The treaty was weaker than most countries wanted, but the Bush administration argued against strict regulations and limits on emissions because no one has definitely proven that carbon dioxide and other greenhouse gases are warming the globe. The climate treaty instead modestly suggested that emissions targets should aim to return emissions to 1990 levels by the year 2000, but it did not provide specific enforcement measures. U.S. industry representatives preferred the looser treaty as adopted; all other major nations and environmental groups preferred a stricter treaty mandating emission outputs at 1990 levels.

The Biodiversity Convention to protect rare and endangered plants also was signed by most nations at Rio—the United States was the only major power that refused to agree. President Bush refused to sign because he believed that the treaty would hurt U.S. industry, especially by weakening patent protections for biotechnology companies. Furthermore, he believed the treaty would cause the loss of U.S. jobs. The biotech industry opposed the biodiversity agreement; many other scientists did not.

Overall, the rumble in Rio will be a milestone in international environmental policy. The conference was the first major gathering of the leaders throughout the world in decades, and it catapulted the environment onto the world's agenda. In order to protect the environment and promote development, the developing countries sought greater aid and assistance from the developed northern countries. All major nations except the United States responded by agreeing to the UNCED principles, signing the treaties, pledging large amounts of new aid, and stating they would exceed the climate change accord requirements. Over $6 billion a year in new funds were pledged for "green projects" in developing nations, a sevenfold increase over the pool of money the World Bank Global Environmental Facility now dedicates to environmental programs. The $6 billion still fell far short of the $125 billion sought by conference organizers and the southern developing countries. The treaties, the UN Sustainable Development Commission, and new aid funds will serve as a basis for ongoing efforts in international cooperation in development and environmental protection.

The Bush administration supported some, but not all, of the Rio treaties. (Recall that the U.S. president, not Congress, has authority to negotiate treaties.) Bush opposed strict climate controls and the endangered species treaty because he believed the costs for U.S. business and reduced economic growth were excessive. Perhaps he also thought that the expenses of foreign aid, the left-wing ideology, and prior government mismanagement in developing countries were not compatible with the administration's need to strengthen its conservative constituency and domestic program focus in the 1992 presidential elections. In any case, the Bush administration often found itself alone in opposing much of the outcome of the summit. Whether this will prove good for sustainable development, environmental protection, or presidential politics will be determined over time.

INTERNATIONAL TRADE OF FOREST PRODUCTS

Less than 5 percent of the wood used in the world is traded internationally (FAO 1985). Because forests are widespread over the planet and wood has a low value relative to its bulk, most wood is consumed locally. Nevertheless, world trade in wood products exceeded $50 billion in 1985, making it the third most valuable primary commodity in world trade, after petroleum and natural gas. Developed countries dominate world trade in wood products, with more than 85 percent of the exports (World Resources Institute 1988).

World trade in forest products is a particularly important international issue because it is influenced directly by policies of the more developed, temperate countries. Developed countries often have been accused of exploiting the forest resources of developing countries, thus exacerbating local forestry or fuelwood problems. Use of destructive logging practices or clearing of tropical forests may be caused by demands from developing countries for wood product imports. Increased prices, environmental constraints, or export/import restrictions imposed by governments could help prevent such problems. Forest products trade has led to many disputes and policy debates among developed countries. Ongoing debates about Canadian lumber exports to the United States are a primary example.

Forest products trade occurs for a number of reasons. First, trading countries buy wood and paper products that they do not grow or manufacture themselves. The demand for wood products in some developed countries, such as Japan and the United Kingdom, far exceeds the supplies available from their own forests. Some developing countries, such as Saudi Arabia and Egypt, have few forest resources and import most of their wood needs (World Resources Institute 1988).

A healthy international trading environment is important for strong economic growth in developing countries, most of which have small domestic markets, making them highly dependent on trade. Proceeds from exports are needed to pay for imports of manufactured goods, which are vital for continuing industrialization and technological progress (World Bank 1988).

Every country will try to export finished or semifinished goods and to import, if necessary and possible, raw material (roundwood or wood chips) that will maximize export earnings, minimize the cost of imports, and provide employment for its own people. This holds especially for developing countries with surplus labor and limited export possibilities. The assistance that developed countries can provide to help developing countries establish forest-based industries is one of the most effective forms of aid there is (Eckmullner and Madas 1984).

However, the establishment of forest products industries can create ecological problems as forests are exploited in the attempt to solve economic problems. Repetto (1988b) describes several such problems, but he is optimistic that with well-designed policies, developing countries can harvest their forests on a sustainable basis. Postel (1988b) points out that the principal cause of tropical deforestation is the combined action of land clearing for crop production, fuelwood gathering, and cattle ranching. World trade in forest products is probably a lesser factor in the deforestation problems facing the world today, but it is one that can be directly influenced by policies or prices in developed countries.

WORLD PRODUCTION AND MARKETS

Fuelwood

Recall from Chapter 1 (Figure 1-5) that approximately half of the wood harvested in the world is used for fuelwood and charcoal, predominantly in the developing world. In terms of volume and perhaps economic value, fuelwood and charcoal are important forest products in many countries (Gray 1983).

It is not economically feasible to ship fuelwood and charcoal long distances because they are heavy and bulky. Thus these products are not very important items in world trade. Nor does wood burned as fuel represent a significant source of revenue for the governments of producing countries (Gray 1983), although burning local wood may substitute for the costs of paying for imported oil. FAO (1985) data indicate that less than 1 percent of all fuelwood and charcoal produced is exported to other countries.

Industrial Roundwood

The other half of the world's wood harvest is used for industrial purposes, predominantly in the developed world. Many of the forest policy concerns in the developed world thus tend to focus on industrial roundwood and products manufactured from it. Although trade between the developing and developed world in forest products is important—most of it in tropical hardwoods—the majority of international trade in forest products is from one developed nation to another.

FAO (1985) statistics indicate that harvest of tropical hardwoods is a relatively small contributor to tropical deforestation. Fully 85 percent of the hardwoods harvested in developing countries are for domestic fuelwood and charcoal. Of the remaining 15 percent harvested as industrial roundwood in the developing world, only 18 percent is exported as either logs or lumber. The rest is used domestically for building products or paper. World trade in tropical hardwoods thus represents less than 3 percent of the harvest of tropical hardwoods in the developing world. On a local level, however, commercial harvest of hardwoods may be a significant forest policy problem.

Japan imports almost half of the world trade in hardwood logs and lumber and is therefore directly responsible for, at most, 1.5 percent of the harvest of hardwood forests in the developing world. No other nation comes even close to importing this amount of tropical hardwood products. Although the percentage seems small, the quantity of wood is not, and local areas can be severely affected by commercial harvest. The Rainforest Action Network Newsletter (1989) describes problems resulting from Japanese timber concessions in the Malaysian states of Sarawak and Sabah, including denuded lands, massive erosion, and inadequate or no regeneration.

Logging in tropical moist forests is not usually a direct cause of deforestation. Only a few of the thousands of tropical tree species are commercially valuable, and these are usually harvested selectively rather than by clearcutting. Even though selective logging usually removes 2 to 10 trees per hectare and between 3 to 30 percent of the total timber volume, the forest structure is altered. The forest canopy is disturbed, residual trees are damaged by the felling and extracting of their neighbors, and the forest ecosystem is modified to varying degrees. Logging roads provide shifting cultivators access to new areas, which then may be cleared and burned. So the indirect effects of logging for tropical hardwoods are indeed a contributing factor to deforestation.

Manufactured Wood Products

As Figure 18-2 indicates, the large, temperate zone forest countries in the northern hemisphere (the United States, Canada, and the former USSR) dominate in both the produc-

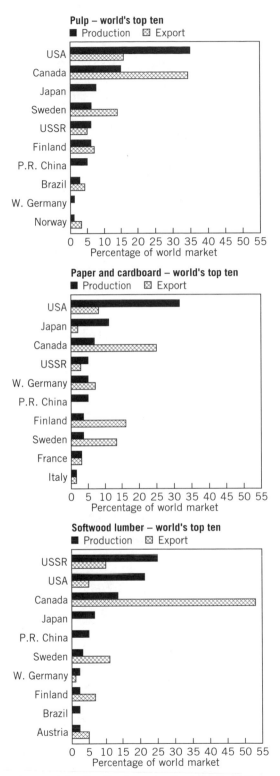

Figure 18-2.   Top Ten Countries, Production and Export of Forest Products, 1985
Source: FAO 1988a.

tion of the major groups of forest products (pulp, paper and cardboard, and softwood lumber) and the export of these products. Canada clearly is the largest exporter of these forest products.

Japan, a leading producer in all three product sectors, also is a leading consumer, exporting only a small fraction of its paper production, and none of its pulp or lumber (Figure 18-2). Indeed, wood plays a special role in Japanese culture; the Japanese are wood aesthetes. Almost half of the tropical hardwood timber exported from developing countries ends up in Japan. According to Eckmullner and Madas (1984), approximately 90 percent of the dwellings in Japan are wood, compared to 60 percent in Norway. Vast quantities of unprocessed softwood logs exported from the U.S. Pacific Northwest and semiprocessed logs from Southeast Alaska end up in Japanese sawmills, and then Japanese homes.

Sweden and Finland also are prominent in world export markets. They depend heavily on international forest products trade. Sweden, in particular, has designed a set of forest policies to ensure its future in world forest products trade. Three-fourths of Sweden's forests are privately owned. The major feature of Swedish forest policy is a set of forest practice regulations that require management plans on every private forest holding. Harvesting and other silvicultural practices to ensure timber production and environmental protection are strictly prescribed (O'Laughlin and Messina 1988).

TRENDS

Again recall from Chapter 1 (Figure 1-5) that the world's total roundwood production increased by 67 percent between 1963 and 1983. The driving force behind the increased harvest of wood in the world is fuelwood and charcoal needs in the developing nations. The use of wood for fuel almost doubled in the same 20-year period. In the developed world, the harvest of industrial roundwood leveled off between 1973 to 1983, while industrial roundwood harvests in the

developing world rose by 40 percent during the same period. Only 10 percent of the industrial roundwood harvested in the developing world is exported in unprocessed form. The remainder is manufactured locally into wood products that are either consumed domestically or exported.

There are now 33 developing countries that are net exporters of some $7 billion worth of forest products. By the turn of the century, fewer than 10 countries are expected to be net exporters, at a reduced level of $2 billion (Repetto and Gillis 1988). Another source says there will be 20 such countries (Postel and Heise 1988). A third source expects tropical hardwood exports to double by 2000 (World Resources Institute 1988). Whatever the situation turns out to be, there can be little doubt that historic and current levels of tropical forest exploitation are not sustainable.

In 1986 worldwide consumption of wood was 3.26 billion cubic meters; 51.5 percent was for fuelwood, 48.5 percent was industrial roundwood. By the turn of the century, FAO (1988a) forecasts indicate a total increase in consumption of 26 7 percent, to a level of 4.13 billion cubic meters. Fuelwood is projected to increase by 22 percent, to 2.05 billion cubic meters. Industrial roundwood is projected to increase 31.6 percent to a total of 2.08 billion cubic meters.

As indicated in Figure 18-3, the developing market economies of the world are the countries in which both fuelwood and industrial wood demands will increase the most. The developed market economies and centrally planned economies—formerly the USSR and still the People's Republic of China—will require substantial increases in industrial roundwood, but only modest increases in fuelwood.

How accurate are these projections of future wood needs? Only time will tell. Two other projections of industrial roundwood uses fall short of the previously cited FAO forecast of 2.08 billion cubic meters. One study—the Global Trade Model developed by the International Institute for Applied Systems Analysis (IIASA) in Austria—projects a

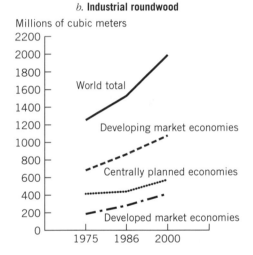

a. Fuelwood and charcoal

Millions of cubic meters

World total

Developing market economies

Centrally planned economies

Developed market economies

1975   1986   2000

b. Industrial roundwood

Millions of cubic meters

World total

Developing market economies

Centrally planned economies

Developed market economies

1975   1986   2000

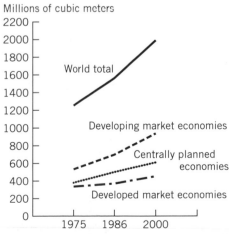

c. Total roundwood consumption

Millions of cubic meters

World total

Developing market economies

Centrally planned economies

Developed market economies

1975   1986   2000

Figure 18-3 World Wood Consumption Trends, 1976 to 1985, with Projections to 2000
Source: FAO 1988a.

range of growth assumptions, projecting industrial roundwood removals of 1.6 to 1.9 billion cubic meters by the end of the century. This same study forecasts wood scarcities and steep increases in log prices. Another study of global timber supply by Resources for the Future, a Washington, DC, nonprofit research organization, projects 1.8 billion cubic meters of annual wood removals by the year 2000. This is slightly higher than the IIASA model's base scenario of 1.7 billion, but lower than the FAO projection of 2.08 billion cubic meters. The Resources for the Future study projects what are essentially constant real timber prices—in contradiction to the IIASA study (World Resources Institute 1988).

Timber supply and demand forecasting at the global level is extremely complex. It should not be surprising that different forecasters produce different results. The message is basically the same. The world will require more industrial wood in the future than it does today. Where will the wood come from? That depends on a multitude of forest policies and their interaction with a variety of other policies.

TRADE POLICY

Trade policy, like any policy, consists of a course of action taken over time by an actor (in this case a country) to achieve a public purpose or goal (usually a favorable balance of trade). Like most goods and services, international trade in wood and wood products is regulated by means of tariff and nontariff measures. Governments may pursue various objectives with their tariff and nontariff trade restrictions. Most try to promote viable native forest products industries, the manufacture of goods within the country, rather than export of logs or other fiber. Industries within a country produce goods for domestic consumption or for export. Both are important to creating favorable trade balances and to earning (or to avoid paying) foreign exchange. Domestic industries provide employment and earnings for a country's citizens. For these reasons, most countries try to discourage imports of goods that can be produced domestically, including forest products. Many countries, including Canada and the United States, export large volumes of logs and lumber but would prefer to increase domestic manufacturing. Similarly, some countries levy an export tax to encourage domestic processing or to glean revenues from raw material exports. Despite their avowed preference for free markets, all developed and developing countries have extensive government controls in exports and imports.

Olechewski (1987) discusses the barriers to trade in wood and wood products. He notes that tariffs on wood products tend to be consistently high in developed, market economy countries. These tariffs are levied as an ad valorem tax on imported products. The tariffs tend to increase with the level of fabrication, which is called tariff escalation, and discourages import of processed forest products. For developed market economies, Olechewski (1987) found that tariff duties on secondary wood products (e.g., furniture) are about 225 percent higher than those on primary products (e.g., lumber), and over 680 percent higher than wood in the rough.

Olechewski (1987) also describes many direct nontariff means to limit imports in the developed market countries. These include quantitative import restrictions—such as outright prohibitions or limited import authorizations—and "voluntary" export restraints between exporting and importing countries. Different governments also may agree on setting prices, such as the minimum price that a good can be sold for by an exporter. They also may have increasing tariff levies at different levels, depending on the volume of a product imported. Countries also use other import management measures, such as antidumping rules that prohibit selling below cost or countervailing duties that levy a tax on goods sold below cost. Developing countries employ nontariff measures even more frequently than developed countries, in part because of their higher degree of government involvement in economic activities, and in part because of the need to tightly regulate the allocation of scarce foreign exchange.

ILLUSTRATION: U.S. TRADE WITH CANADA AND JAPAN

U.S. trade with Canada and Japan illustrates the sensitivity of these issues. Canada has exported large amounts of lumber and newsprint into the United States for decades. In the 1980s lumber imports, primarily from British Columbia, increased to one-third of the U.S. market. This rise in Canadian imports from the more common one-fifth to one-fourth of the U.S. market prompted protests and political action by U.S. lumber manufacturers. They charged the Canadians with selling below cost, because the stumpage prices on the prevalent Crown lands in the province of British Columbia (less than $25 per thousand board feet-MBF) were much less than those on private or Forest Service lands in the United States (more than $150 per MBF). These protests by U.S. forest industry trade associations and by individuals prompted administrative negotiations between the countries.

After considerable congressional debate and executive office negotiations, in 1986 the U.S. Department of Commerce found Canada in violation of antidumping laws and levied a 15 percent countervailing duty on Canadian lumber bound for the United States. However, the duty was never implemented. Instead the United States and Canada negotiated an eleventh-hour agreement that established an alternative arrangement for collecting the fee. Unlike most trade sanctions, this agreement, referred to as the 1986 Memorandum of Understanding, allowed the exporter (Canada) rather than the importer (the United States) to collect the duty in the form of an export tax.

In effect, the export tax was designed to force Canadian lumber producers to compensate the government for the alleged timber subsidy received from the government. Subsequent amendments to the 1986 Memorandum of Understanding allowed provincial governments to raise their stumpage fees rather than assess the full tax. Provincial governments therefore could correct the alleged subsidy by either of these methods. Most major lumber-producing provinces, including British Columbia, adopted this approach. In either case the policy was designed to increase the price of Canadian lumber in U.S. markets and thereby reduce any Canadian competitive advantage arising from a timber subsidy (Wear and Lee 1991).

The Memorandum of Understanding took effect at the beginning of 1987 and was not popular in Canada. The export tax–stumpage fee assessment was seen as coercive control of Canada's resource use and management by the United States, and the existence of the subsidy was contested. Canadians argued that the economic comparisons of stumpage prices were flawed by not accounting for important differences in quality and in harvesting and transportation costs for logs.

In an analysis of the effect of the export tax, Wear and Lee (1991) found that Canadian imports had indeed declined during the period that the tax was implemented, and that U.S. producers had captured much of the reduction in Canadian softwood imports. This gain to U.S. producers, however, came at a net cost of greater lumber prices and reduced lumber supply, which was borne by U.S. consumers. In September 1991 Canada unilaterally announced that it would withdraw the export tax and the debates over the appropriate U.S. response began anew. The announcement prompted protests by some U.S. interest groups, despite the fact that the Canadian stumpage price increases were not scheduled for reduction. President Bush also was facing challenges to his trade policies by conservative Republicans during the 1992 presidential campaign. In 1992 the Department of Commerce found that the Canadians were still subsidizing lumber exports, so it placed an actual import tax on the Canadian product.

United States exports of primary forest products (i.e., lumber and plywood) illustrate the other side of the exporting issue. Trade issues over exports from Japan to the United States are well known. We buy tremendous quantities of Japanese vehicles and electronic goods, creating large trade deficits. We borrow Japanese cash to finance our federal budget deficit. In fact, in three years in the 1980s, we went from being the world's largest creditor (lender) nation to the world's largest debtor (borrowing) nation, most of it financed with Japanese or European funds. This trade and finance imbalance prompted calls to remove Japan's tariff and bureaucratic barriers to a range of U.S. imports, including forest products.

Throughout the 1980s, U.S. forest products trade associations and the Reagan administration lobbied for no less than the complete elimination of all Japanese tariffs on processed forest products as being "fair." The unrelenting pressure from Washington prompted Japan to announce reduced tariffs in a range of 20 percent to 67 percent, taking effect in 1987–1988. This was the first definitive Japanese action on the matter after years of vagueness and inertia. However, many U.S. forest products sectors, especially plywood, still felt the action was inadequate (Laarman 1987).

The dispute over Japanese explicit tariffs and their difficult system of technical standards continued to prompt acrimony in 1989 and 1990. The Bush administration made import restrictions on U.S. forest products one of its three high-priority industrial sector problems in trade negotiations with Japan. Sen. Max Baucus of Montana still charged that Japanese trade restrictions were robbing American mill workers of jobs. Furthermore, he threatened that if Japan could not negotiate reduced direct and indirect tariffs, he had legislation drafted to retaliate (NFPA 1989). Given U.S. desires to export raw and manufactured products, and Japanese direct and indirect resistance, these trade issues will remain on the public agenda.

Another factor in these trade debates has been the export of raw logs or cants to Japan. The Japanese prefer to import logs and saw them to their specifications—providing jobs and "Japanese" quality. Log exports from national forests in the West have been legislatively banned for decades, in response to pressure from timber buyers who disliked increased prices caused by Japanese competition. However, private landowners in the state of Washington and several large forestry corporations still sell large amounts of logs to Japanese buyers. Local mills must then rely on federal timber to supply their wood needs when private or state logs are exported.

The log export business grew substantially in the late 1980s and prompted many charges by environmental groups that the United States was cutting down its ancient forests to sell to Japan. (This could happen only indirectly because old-growth forests occur mostly on federal lands, which cannot be cut for export markets.) Opponents believe the harvests cause environmental destruction, species extinction, and global warming and consider log sales to Japan a good symbol to use to expand environmental issues. The media became involved. A one-hour "McGyver" network television show in 1990 focused on a nefarious lumber manufacturer who was leveling old-growth forests and smuggling the logs to a Japanese racketeer for a large profit. In fact, the Japanese are willing to pay several times more for logs than prevailing U.S. market prices. This issue will continue because of employment and environmental implications.

COMPARATIVE FOREST POLICIES IN THE DEVELOPED WORLD

A country with bountiful forest resources geared to timber production—such as the United States or Canada—presents different forest management problems than does a densely populated industrialized country with few forests—such as the United Kingdom or Denmark—that are needed as green belts or recreation areas (Hummel and van Maaren 1984). Yet many heavily populated regions of countries well endowed with forest resources face problems similar to those of smaller countries with less abundant forests. Any country can benefit by understanding how other countries both in different places and at different times have used policy to approach forest resource management problems.

Unlike other scientific fields of forestry research, knowledge concerning forest policy is generally found within a framework of individual country case studies. Relatively few comparative studies have been done. But there is much to be gained from understanding how forest policy problems have been dealt with beyond one's own national boundaries. Global forestry issues—forest decline or "Waldsterben" in Europe is one—are obvious examples of the need for such comparative analysis (Krott 1986).

Compilations of case studies are a good starting point for shedding light on how government policies can influence forest resource use. There are several examples of such work that will be duly noted in this section. But three things are evident: (1) A comprehensive approach to comparative forest policy analysis has yet to be undertaken; (2) case study compilations have tended to focus on the developing world; and (3) comparisons seem to lack any systematic analytical framework (Krott 1986). Understanding the complex nature of forest policy in any one country is a daunting task. To try to unravel such complexity at international levels is even more intimidating. But that is not to say it should not be attempted. Part of the reason for this chapter and this book is to provide the groundwork for analyzing complicated forest policy issues—which occur and change over time and across domestic and international political boundaries.

In this chapter, we provide a brief overview of selected forest policies in other countries. These policies can be classified and examined in various ways, but we use those already discussed in this book, which are similar to those by Hummell and van Maaren (1984)—forest ownership, legislation, taxation, incentives, education and training, research, organization, and personnel. To further simplify the discussion, we focus mostly on the policies of the countries of Western Europe. Because these countries are further along in the resource development and protection stages of development (see Table 2-1), they may provide the most insights regarding paths American forest policy may follow.

Obviously, no single reference can summarize forest policies of all countries in the world. A recent FAO (1988b) publication does provide information on forest policies of all European countries, including Scandinavia and Eastern and Western Europe, as well as the former USSR, Turkey, and Israel.

FOREST OWNERSHIP

The importance of forest ownership was emphasized in Chapter 1. Forest owners decide what is to be done with a forest, and how it is to be done. Throughout the world, forests are owned by either public or private entities. About three- fourths of the world's forests are publicly owned (Laarman and Sedjo 1992). Virtually all countries with forests have placed some in public ownership. Many countries, even those with centrally planned economies, have privately owned forests.

Figure 18-4 depicts forest land and ownership in 11 selected countries, chosen because information on private and public forest ownership was available. Several of these countries have a high percentage of land covered by forests: Brazil, Japan, Sweden, and Finland all have more than 60 percent of the country forested. Almost half of Canada is forested. The United States, France, New Zealand, Norway, and Germany range between 27 and 37 percent forested. Australia and the United Kingdom have a small portion of their land in forest cover. Sweden, Finland, France, the United Kingdom, Japan, Brazil, and the United States all have more private than public forest land. Canada, Australia, New Zealand, Norway, and Germany are the opposite. Canada is the extreme, with only 6 percent of its forests privately owned.

For the most part, forests in the developing countries are publicly owned. In centrally planned economies, by definition government ownership is the norm. The former USSR alone has 27 percent of the entire world's closed forests, an amount exceeding that of either North or South America. Much of this, however, is not accessible with the existing infrastructure and equipment. The forests have been looked to as a primary source of foreign currency for Russia, particularly after the political freedoms won in 1991. Import of Siberian logs was proposed as one means of making up for reduced harvest of old-growth forests in the western United States. But imports were temporarily halted in 1991 to assess whether the logs could bring fatal pests or diseases that could infect U.S. forests. Similar bans have been considered on New Zealand radiata pine. These bans contain elements of true fears about disease and infection, and politically-motivated elements to prevent foreign competition.

REGULATION

Few, if any, comparative studies of forest regulation in different countries have been performed. Thus one must rely on piecemeal or anecdotal information to compare forest regulation among countries. For illustration purposes, we briefly discuss some relevant legislation in selected European countries. It is worth noting that most regulation in Western Europe stemmed from wood shortages occurring throughout medieval to modern times. As such, most laws governing forestry in Europe are designed to ensure continuous tree cover and harvests to provide timber products and to a lesser extent, environmental protection. This can be contrasted with modern state forest practice acts, federal environmental laws, and local regulation in the United States, which have focused much more on environmental protection and restriction of logging and forestry in environmentally sensitive areas than on timber production per se.

Regulation of forestry has existed in Europe for centuries. For example, the 1876 Forest Policy Law of Switzerland classed forests into protective and nonprotective zones; all mountain areas now fall in the protected class (Price 1988). The law stated that the total forest area could not be decreased without consent of the local canton (government body) and required a permit for felling in these forests. Additionally, all cleared and logged areas must be reforested; alternately, a nearby corresponding area must be afforested. Manage-

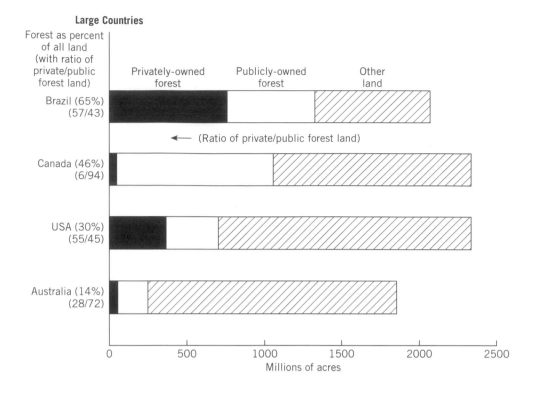

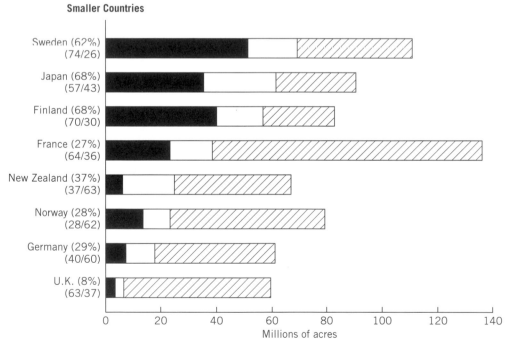

Figure 18-4.   Forest Land, Ownership, and Total Land Area in Selected Countries
Source: Arthur Andersen & Co. 1985

ment plans were required for forests, and harvests were not to exceed sustained yields without permission of the local canton. The cantonal government also could require afforestation of bare land. The 1876 law was strengthened by a 1902 law that provided further federal financial assistance and required individual cantons to bring their forestry legislation into agreement with federal legislation (Price 1988).

The 1902 Swiss law has remained in effect through the 1980s. Proposals have been made to broaden the country's forest policy to encompass a wider range of services, cultural landscape values, and environmental protections. This new legislation would ensure the minimal level of management forests need to fulfill a broad range of functions in the long term and would provide assistance so that forest owners do not suffer financial hardship by undertaking activities that are in the common interest (Price 1988).

Denmark, too, has a long history of public involvement and regulation of forestry (Plum and Honore 1988). Efforts to halt deforestation began in the seventeenth century and included a number of royal edicts between 1670 and 1781. These proved ineffective, so in 1805 an edict was issued that provided better protection. It began with enclosure of the forest commons, with assignment of divided rights in property. (Note the similarity of this action to that recently proposed for U.S. public lands by free market economists and for lands in developing countries.) The edict further mandated fencing of forests, prohibited grazing, and required public inspection of private forests. The 1805 Danish edict was updated periodically and was replaced by the present forest act of 1935 (Plum and Honore 1988). The purpose of the 1935 act is to ensure "a great and valuable wood production." The act requires "good forestry"—the maintenance of forest areas with a tree cover of a kind, quality, quantity such that it forms a closed high forest or will be able to do so in a reasonable period of time. Forested areas cannot be converted to other uses without permission. Such permission is almost always given only on the condition of afforesting another area.

Like Switzerland, Denmark has considered new legislation designed to broaden forest policy and uses (Plum and Honore 1988). The law now includes the existing "great and valuable wood production" as one of its goals, but it adds the maintenance of environmental protection and production of recreational benefits. More attention is to be given to management and growth of broadleaved trees and bushes. A new forest council representing forestry organizations, recreation associations, and a nature conservation association also was proposed. Public foresters were to assume more of an advisory role and have less direct control over private forest lands than in the past—perhaps indicating that even in Europe, the long-established profession of forestry is losing some of its influence to landowners and environmentalists.

The Federal Republic of Germany (formerly West Germany) has a federal forest law of 1975 supplemented by state forest laws. These laws also now apply to the former East Germany since the 1990 reunification. The laws' purpose is "to preserve and protect the forests, when needed to improve them and to safeguard their orderly regulated/prescribed use" (Sundberg 1989, p. 35). Forests may be converted to another land use only by permit, and the law prescribes standards that forest owners must use in managing their forests. Clear-fellings are only permitted if the soil fertility is not damaged, if water use is not influenced greatly, and if other protected and recreational uses are only influenced minimally (Sundberg 1989).

Other Western and Eastern European countries also have stringent laws regulating timber harvest, environmental protection, and forest conversion. The United Kingdom has extremely strict laws that regulate the growing and harvesting of native and planted forests for amenity values as well as for wood production (Griffin and Watkins 1988). The Scandinavian countries of Sweden, Norway, and Finland also require management, harvest, and regeneration of their public and private forest lands. In Scandinavia, forestry is one of the main contributors to the economy and is regulated and subsidized to a great extent in order to protect its vital contribution.

The types of regulations also vary considerably among countries. For example, many policies directly regulate clear-cutting, an activity that arouses public concern everywhere. In Sweden, clear-cutting is the only acceptable harvesting method (O'Laughlin and Messina 1988). In Switzerland, clear-cutting is prohibited. In Austria, clear-cuts are limited to a maximum of 2 hectares; any clear-cut exceeding 0.5 hectares requires permission from the forest authority (Eckmullner and Madas 1984). Most other European countries strictly limit the size of clear-cuts (Harou 1986).

INCENTIVES

Harou (1986) summarizes the prevalent forms of forestry incentives and educational programs in Europe (Table 18-2). Extension programs provide owners with technical forestry advice, prices and other market news, and details about aid programs. Often extension is targeted toward creating owner cooperatives and enterprises that contract for the harvest or management of woodlands. Indirect financial incentives also may be provided. Property tax rates may be reduced or forgiven entirely for a period of time, as in Belgium. Many countries grant favorable tax treatment of timber income.

Harou notes that European countries also provide many direct financial incentives, including direct cash grants, cash loans with interest rebates or deferred payments, and similar cash loans to contract for state services. These financial incentives serve mainly to increase timber production through afforestation of marginally productive agricultural and waste land; to fund reforestation after disaster; and to encourage conversion, improvement, and enrichment of low-yield stands. A second use of direct subsidies is to provide access and maintenance. These measures support construction of forest roads and trails and protection against fire and disease. A third principal incentive helps the formation of

forestry associations to increase timber production on small and medium-sized holdings. All these government subsidies help promote the forest policies of timber production and environmental protection.

Comparisons among incentives and regulation in the United States, Canada, and Europe are interesting. The European countries regulate all land use strictly, including forest management, especially to encourage timber production. However, most European private lands are open by law to public access. Furthermore, European countries grant many more types of subsidies to encourage conversion to forest lands or for protection and management of forest lands.

Public forest policies in the United States and Canada differ from those in Europe and from each other. Almost all forest land in Canada is owned by the provincial governments. About one-fifth of the total forest land in the United States is owned by the federal government, and states and counties own about 6 percent. The United States manages its national forest lands under the RPA/NFMA, as discussed in Chapter 13. This includes multiple-use and sustained-yield mandates and allows individual sales to timber purchasers. Canada's provincial governments, in contrast, lease vast tracts of Crown lands to forest products firms, which then harvest and manage them as they deem best. Regeneration requirements and environmental standards on U.S. national forest lands are strict, on provincial lands rather lax. Environmental groups and nontimber users have substantial input and influence on U.S. national forest management; timber lessees and forestry unions have dominated decision making on Crown forest lands in Canadian provinces (Leman 1988). Timber pricing policies between countries are also quite different and helped lead to charges of subsidized Canadian lumber imports into the United States in the 1980s (see prior illustration on United States trade).

On private lands, government policy has been more influential on forest harvesting and regeneration in the United States than in Canada. The United States provides a number

TABLE 18-2. Systems of Aid for Nonstate-Owned Forests in the European Community

Purpose	France	Federal Republic of Germany	Italy	Denmark	Belgium	U.K.	Netherlands	Luxembourg	Ireland
Increase of timber production									
First afforestation	S-D-L	S	S-D-L	S	S	S	S	S	S
Conversion or improvement	S-D-L	S	S-D-L	S	S			S	
Reafforestation after disasters	S-D-L	S	S-D-L		S			S	
Normal reafforestation	S-D-L	S			(S)	S	S	(S)	S
Planting outside forest areas	S-D-L	S	(S-D)		S	S	S	S	S
Soil preparation, clearance of vegetation	(S-D-L)		(S-D-L)	S-D					S
Opening up and maintaining existing forest areas									
Construction of roads and tracks	S-D-L	S-D	S-D	(S)	S		(S)	S	
Fire protection	S-D-L	S	S-D	(S)	S			(S)	
Protection (insects, diseases, game)	S	S	S	S					
Assisting forestry associations									
Aid in forming associations	S	S	(S)						
Supplying special equipment	D	S	(S)						
Other measures									
Recreational forest		S	D		S	S	S		
Drawing up economic plans	S-D	S	S		S				
Aid after disasters		S		S		S	S		
Owners retention of forests, land purchase	D	S-D	D						
Fire insurance		S							
Day-to-day expenditures	(S-D-L)	(S)				(S)	(S)		
Improvement of forest- or meadowland			S						
Conferences, research, and other projects	S	S	S	S		S			

S = nonrepayable grant; D = cash loan; L = loan in form of service contracts; ( ) = contingent and not an aid measure on its own.

Source: Harou 1986

of income and property tax advantages for private forest owners, as well as financial incentives such as FIP, ACP, and CRP. Many states and localities regulate logging to some extent. Canadian private landowners also enjoy various federal tax concessions, but most are general rather than specific to forestry, and they do not seem as large as those found in the United States (Leman 1988).

TAXATION

A rebellion against unjust taxation was one cause of the American revolution in the late eighteenth century. At that time, Benjamin Franklin coined many of our most enduring popular phrases, including, "But in this world nothing can be said to be certain, except death and taxes." For most people, taxes are almost as foreboding and distasteful as death. Yet taxation remains a primary instrument of government policy, and one worthy of attention in the context of international forest policy.

Forest policy should stimulate good forest management and stewardship. Undue bureaucracy that stifles goodwill and initiative is to be avoided. A bad taxation system also may paralyze forestry activity and forest re-

source development. A good taxation system may promote good forestry and simultaneously discourage undesirable practices (Eckmullner and Madas 1984).

With an eye toward maintaining favorable provisions in the U.S. timber income tax system prior to the sweeping Tax Reform Act of 1986, the Forest Industries Committee on Timber Valuation and Taxation commissioned a comparative study of forest and timber taxes in 11 selected countries (Arthur Andersen & Co. 1985). All but one, Brazil, are developed countries. The results of the study are summarized in Tables 18-3 and 18-4. In the countries studied—the United States has been added for this book—timber and forest land often receive favorable tax treatment to further national policy. Tax incentives and benefits, supplemented by a variety of nontax programs such as special grants and financing programs, play a crucial role in achieving national goals. The primary goals appear to be to provide for the development of new forests and the regeneration of old ones, to keep timber and forest land productive, and to retain family ownership of timber and forest land (Arthur Andersen & Co. 1985).

Taxation is also of major concern in the developing world. The World Bank's (1988) Development Report contains a chapter de-

TABLE 18-3. Selected Income Tax Features Benefiting Timber and Forest Land

Income Tax	Australia	Brazil	Canada	Finland
Lower tax rate applies		X		
"Demand" income favorably defined by formula				X
Special deduction based on income		X		
Special deduction or credit allowed in addition to actual costs			X	X
Forest management costs treated as period cost (expensed)	X	X	X	N/A
Special loss carryforward or income averaging rules	X			
Timberland/forest sales qualify for capital gain treatment	N/A	N/A	X	X

Note: N/A signifies that the country does not have the indicated tax at all; therefore, the benefit is "Not Applicable."

[a]Reforestation costs not included in this category. Only certain landowners "active in the timber trade or business" qualify for this benefit

[b]Since 1987 capital gains are taxed at the same rate as ordinary income.

Source: Arthur Andersen & Co. 1985

scribing the importance of taxation and tax reform in developing countries.

FORESTS AND GLOBAL CLIMATE

Global climate change has become an increasingly important domestic and international issue. The biological and political problems intertwined in the global climate change issue make this an interesting case with which to end this book. A variety of scientific debates, international groups and governments, and market and government factors will influence climate change policies.

Although scientific consensus does not exist, considerable evidence suggests that mean global air temperatures are increasing measurably. Accelerated global climate change is believed to occur primarily because the burning of fossil fuels and biomass releases stored carbon into the atmosphere at a rate greater than that experienced in the past (Blake and Rowland 1988, Harrington 1987, Ramanathan 1988). Atmospheric CO_2 levels were estimated to have been at 280 parts per million in 1860; by 1987 they were measured at 348 parts per million. Since 1958, when scientists began to routinely monitor CO_2 levels, they have risen 10 percent (Postel 1988a).

Biomass combustion also releases methane, whereas deforestation releases nitrous oxides (MacDonald 1988). This buildup of CO_2 and other small-molecule gases traps long-wave infrared radiation in the atmosphere, thereby warming the earth and raising global temperatures by the "greenhouse effect."

Release of excess carbon through fossil fuel combustion is only part of the problem. Through the carbon cycle, forests contribute significantly to determining how much CO_2 is converted to other carbon compounds. Although forest clearing and burning is a major contributing source of trace gases in the atmosphere, forests also are one of the principal mechanisms available to store carbon—serving as a sink via the carbon cycle. Limiting fossil fuel combustion and retaining or replanting more forests may help reduce this increase in atmospheric CO_2 greatly, thus delaying significant climate changes for more than a century (Postel 1986).

Principal concerns about climate change are based on fears that such rapid changes will have drastic effects on the earth's ecosystems and society's abilities to deal with these changes. Global warming would shift temperature and rainfall patterns. Some key food-producing regions would become more vulnerable to heat waves, drought, and the loss

TABLE 18-3. *Continued*

France	Germany	Japan	New Zealand	Norway	Sweden	United Kingdom	United States
	X						
X						X	
	X	X			X		
X	X	X	X	X	X	X	X[a]
	X	X	X	X	X		
X	X	X	N/A	X	N/A	X	X[b]

TABLE 18-4. Selected Other Tax Law Features Benefiting Timber and Forest Land

	Australia	Brazil	Canada	Finland
Inheritance and transfer taxes				
Favorable valuation	N/A	N/A		X
Lower rates for transfers to family/relatives	N/A	N/A		X
Capital (wealth) tax				
Exemption for timber	N/A	N/A		
Favorable valuation	N/A	N/A		X
Property or land taxes				
Favorable valuation		X		N/A
Exemption for timber	X			N/A
Value added/sales tax				
Exemption from one or both	X		N/A	X
Lower rates applied			N/A	

Note: N/A signifies that the country does not have the indicated tax at all; therefore, the benefit is "Not Applicable."

[1]Reforestation costs not included in this category. Only certain landowners "active in the timber trade or business" qualify for this benefit

[2]Since 1987 capital gains are taxed at the same rate as ordinary income.

Source: Arthur Andersen & Co. 1985

of irrigation water. Cooler regions could benefit from extended growing seasons, and some countries may benefit from wetter weather. Increased carbon dioxide levels do increase plant growth in greenhouse environments and might help trees grow much faster, if water or nutrients are not limited. Warmer temperatures would reduce the polar icecaps, thus raising sea levels. This potential rise could be disastrous, affecting a significant portion of the current population and industrial base of all countries (Postel 1988a). Such shifts also would have immense effects on agriculture, forestry, and wildlife.

Changes in global climate could have substantial effects on the distribution of forests in the world. Warmer temperatures would generally move the range of boreal, temperate, and tropical forests more toward the poles of the planet. This tendency would depend on climates in broad regions, which are difficult to project. Shifts in the range of tree species will occur slowly. The number of endangered and extinct plant and animal species would undoubtedly increase as the climate changes. This occurs naturally as ecosystems change and will be exacerbated by climate changes. This process of natural selection will tend to favor insects and annual plants rather than mammals and woody plants.

Wetland habitats will change greatly as climate changes and the sea levels rise. For example, much of southern Louisiana may be covered by the ocean; freshwater wetlands in many coastal areas are likely to be inundated and become saltwater wetlands. Whether this will improve or harm biological diversity and commercial productivity is unclear. But the rising sea levels are likely to result in more open water, destroying wetlands and wildlife habitats. Some new wetlands may be created as hydrological conditions change. Likely changes in rainfall patterns and higher temperatures may convert much of Oklahoma and eastern Arkansas into grasslands rather than sites for pine forests. Other regions of the country, and indeed the world, may experience substantial shifts in cover types.

A variety of primary and secondary economic effects may result from changes in tree distribution, growth rates, and wood quality. These changes could result from differences in timber yields, forest products yields, product quality, industrial structure, or regional employment (Cubbage, Hodges, and Regens 1987, Hodges, Regens, and Cubbage

TABLE 18-4 *Continued*

France	Germany	Japan	New Zealand	Norway	Sweden	United Kingdom	United States
X	X	X				X	X
	X			X	X		
X		N/A	N/A				N/A
	X	N/A	N/A	X			N/A
	X	X				N/A	X
X		X		X		N/A	
X		X	X				N/A
	X					N/A	

1988). In the United States, aggregate loblolly pine yields would probably decline, causing substantial primary and secondary economic losses. Douglas-fir yields might increase slightly, but management costs would probably increase with the shift to higher elevations.

Increased plant growth due to carbon dioxide enrichment might offset these productivity changes, but the changing climate and forest distribution would create adaptation difficulties in all countries. Broad shifts in wildlife ecology also could be expected in other parts of the world if the climate changes rapidly. Climate change would have substantial impacts on market and nonmarket goods.

CONTRIBUTION OF FORESTS

Proposals to reduce the rate of temperature increase must focus on two principal components of the carbon cycle: burning less fossil and biomass fuels and recapturing more carbon in forests. Use of fossil fuels and forestry-related activities can be modified in order to reduce climate change. The real question is how effective these efforts can be. Some rough estimates of the problems of deforestation and potentials of afforestation illustrate the magnitude of the problem.

The earth's total carbon pool is distributed among organic and inorganic forms. Fossil fuel reserves account for 20.5 percent of the total pool. The oceans contain about 74 percent of the world's carbon, mostly in the form of carbonate and bicarbonate ions. An additional 3 percent is held in the soil, 1 percent by vegetation. The remaining carbon, approximately 1.5 percent, is held in the atmosphere, circulated, and used in photosynthesis (Houghton and Woodwell 1989, Joyce, Fosberg, and Comanor 1990).

The earth's trees, shrubs, and soils hold about 2.3 trillion metric tons of carbon, about triple that stored in the atmosphere (Joyce et al. 1990, Woodwell 1983). When vegetation is cleared or burned, or just left to decay, the carbon and nitrogen it contains, along with some in the underlying soil, are released into the atmosphere. Each year, about 11 million hectares (28 million acres) of tropical forests are destroyed through the combined actions of land clearing for crop production, fuelwood gathering, and cattle ranching (Postel 1988a). Commercial timber harvesting occurs on an additional 4.3 million hectares, but these areas remain in forests. Houghton et al. (1987) estimated that the net release of carbon to the atmosphere from tropical deforestation is about 1.5 to 2.0 billion metric tons per year. Because 4.5 to 5.0 billion metric tons are emitted each year by fossil fuel burning, about one-quarter of the total annual incremental atmospheric carbon buildup could be attributed to deforestation (Postel 1988b).

Improved retention of tropical forests and better growth of existing forests could reduce much of this net carbon loss from forest lands. Trees use and produce CO_2. When photosynthesis occurs at a rapid rate, trees will use much more CO_2 than they emit, storing the carbon in other forms such as wood in the tree and tissue in the leaves. When photosynthesis takes place at slow rates, trees will emit more CO_2 through respiration into the atmosphere than they use in photosynthesis.

How much carbon do forests retain? A productive southern pine or Douglas-fir forest can produce 15 cubic meters of wood per hectare per year. Assuming that 15 cubic meters of wood are associated with 24 cubic meters of biomass, and that 1 cubic meter of biomass contains 0.26 tons of carbon, 1 hectare of forest could sequester 5.67 metric tons of carbon each year (Sedjo 1989, Sedjo and Solomon 1989).

Reduced carbon emissions and increased carbon storage in trees could help ameliorate global warming substantially. Postel (1988a) estimated that successfully planting and maintaining an additional 121 million hectares in trees by the year 2000 would create forests that would absorb roughly 710 million metric tons of carbon every year until the trees reach maturity. That would cut net carbon releases from tropical forests almost in half. The American Forestry Association (AFA) also supports planting trees on 9.3 million hectares of marginal cropland in the South. Given the productivity of these lands and the density with which trees could be planted, this would provide a net annual reduction of about 54 million metric tons of carbon, representing about 3 percent of the estimated losses

to tropical deforestation—a small but significant improvement in global CO_2 balances.

The AFA also proposes planting trees in urban U.S. environments to absorb carbon and provide shade-cooling effects. The association estimates that 100 million trees could be planted in cities, yielding a net reduction of 5900 metric tons of carbon per year in the United States. Globally, this is insignificant for carbon storage. But locally, the cooling effects of the shade could be important in reducing energy consumption. Reforestation programs offer other advantages. In urban environments, trees help reduce ambient temperatures and provide more pleasant surroundings.

Reforestation would help reverse the loss of valuable forest ecosystems, resulting in improved habitat for wildlife and better water quality. Forests are a renewable resource, and tree plantations could provide fuelwood for vast regions of the world that depend almost exclusively on forest fuels. Excessive reliance on this option as an energy resource would, however, cause local air pollution and increase methane emissions, which would contribute some to warming.

Slowing the destruction of existing forests is important for reducing CO_2 buildup. Reducing by one-fourth the destruction due to tropical deforestation would reduce their net carbon releases by 350 million metric tons per year. This would amount to a 6 percent net reduction in incremental atmospheric carbon emissions annually.

EVALUATION OF FOREST POLICY RESPONSES

What policies should we follow to reduce the rate of increase of atmospheric carbon? What should we do to ameliorate the adverse impacts of any climate changes on forests themselves? Are they worth the costs given the unproven threat of climate change? These are crucial questions. The possible policy options at the international level harken back to the debate concerning market versus government that was discussed in Chapter 3, as well as to the public programs discussed in Chapters 12 through 17.

Market Processes

Can markets help reduce deforestation and prevent CO_2 buildup? Perhaps. For instance, much of the rapid deforestation in developing countries can be attributed to their timber pricing policies. Timber is often priced cheaply, much below prevailing world market prices, in order to encourage development and to open new areas for settlement. These incentives encourage more forest destruction to occur than would be the case without favorable government concessions. One "market" solution that would promote forest retention would simply be extracting higher prices for timber concessions, thus encouraging greater utilization on existing harvests and less pervasive destruction and waste (Repetto 1988a,b).

Markets foster technological changes that will help countries adapt to changing resource bases. High product prices will attract producers; high input costs such as timber prices will force marginal firms out of business. Another advantage of market mechanisms is their relative efficiency in reallocating production among countries, based on their comparative advantages. Most predictions of global climate change are very general in nature, and the ability to predict long-range weather patterns decreases greatly at regional levels. Thus it may be folly to implement large- scale government regulation programs based on limited knowledge of localized biophysical impacts. Perhaps it would be much better to let these changes occur naturally, and let the market sort out the winners and losers from climate change effects.

Markets also may prompt increased tree planting in urban environments, rural regions, and developing countries. Maybe trees will reduce heat so much that they will pay for themselves in cities. Maybe timber prices will increase enough to make wide-scale planting programs economically attractive. And maybe environmental protection, agroforestry, or other conservation rationales

will become compelling in the Third World. Increased afforestation due to these market-based signals could reduce atmospheric carbon buildup. But we doubt it. Long-term benefits of forest retention will not be convincing to someone who is desperate for food or for fuelwood, *now.*

Public Intervention

Although market mechanisms may be used effectively to help prevent deforestation in developing countries, it is doubtful that they alone will be adequate. By definition, much of the benefits of forest protection—such as improved global climate, preservation of rare and endangered species, protection of soil productivity and water quality—are derived from common-pool, collective, non-market goods. Markets simply will not provide socially desirable levels of production or protection for such goods, because they fail to capture their full value. Thus, government intervention usually is required.

Many government policies can be used to encourage conservation. First, unplanned or subsidized deforestation should be eliminated to the extent possible. Settlement programs often fail to yield long-lasting, desirable outcomes. Land is often cleared, burned, and farmed until it is degraded and abandoned, often in an unproductive state. Government funds supporting such short-term development programs would be better invested in long-term solutions such as agroforestry systems on productive agricultural lands.

Second, social reforms must be implemented to assist in eliminating the need for unnecessary development. This will be difficult but should be pursued. Third, international agencies should implement their programs and loans in ways that are designed to protect tropical forests. Fourth, creative new mechanisms, such as debt for equity swaps, should be developed to protect valuable tropical forests. Last, perhaps governments should buy and manage tropical forests in order to prevent their liquidation. This may be ineffective, however. In Nepal and several West

African countries, government acquisition of traditionally community managed forests has accelerated deforestation.

In addition to government involvement to protect forest resources, there also should be government involvement to plant forests. The pressing needs of fuelwood, subsistence farming, and fast economic returns are more important to individuals in Third World countries than are global benefits, or even future local benefits, of forests. Even in developed countries, the extent of forests has been reduced greatly due to population, development, and commercial market forces. Major government programs will be required to enhance reforestation of cutover tracts or afforestation of denuded areas.

Policies encouraging these reforestation efforts vary considerably. Most countries have relied largely on specific government programs and financial subsidies to plant trees. Korea's massive afforestation efforts were partially funded by international lending agencies to develop sources of fuelwood. Plantations in the Philippines were designed only to grow fiber for domestic market pulp production (Gregersen and Contreras 1979). Extensive tree planting in New Zealand was funded by the government, on government-owned lands, and until 1986 the government also paid 45 percent of the cost of planting on private lands and allowed landowners to expense the remaining 55 percent against income. In the United States, various combinations of financial subsidies, tax breaks, forest protection programs, and educational policies have been used to promote reforestation and afforestation. The choice of which strategies might be best will depend on the country, its forests, its economy, and its political situation.

SUMMARY

This book has focused mostly on U.S. forest policy. But the forest resource principles and policy tools employed in the United States are not dissimilar to those considered and used by other countries. Furthermore, U.S. forest policy is affected by policies of other nations, and we can also learn much from their policies. This chapter has outlined the role of forest resource policy in a global context.

Forestry issues in the developing world have often focused on tropical deforestation. Deforestation results from population pressures, low standards of living, capital needs, and development practices, as well as other factors. Reducing the amount of tropical deforestation will require improved economies, social programs, international aid, and forestry programs. All these factors must be used together and administered well to improve living standards and lessen pressures on tropical forest and wildlife resources. Plantation forestry also offers a means to reduce pressures on tropical forests, at attractive rates of return. Forest policies in the rest of the developed world are similar to those employed in the United States. However, most European countries provide more financial incentives to grow forests, regulate their harvest much more strictly, and allow public access to a much greater degree.

Trade in international forest products is substantial but still consists of less than 5 percent of the total volume of harvest. Nevertheless, trade policies in forest products have been quite contentious. Cutting timber for export has caused considerable environmental damage in some developing countries. Most countries levy tariffs on imports of forest products, which increase with the level of processing. These levels of tax and internal subsidies are subjects of continuing debates throughout the world.

Forests are often looked to as a means to ameliorate possible global warming. To the extent that we can reduce deforestation, or supplant natural forests with planted forests, forests may ameliorate the buildup of carbon in the atmosphere. A variety of government policies may be used to encourage such massive tree planting or preservation programs.

LITERATURE CITED

Arthur Andersen & Co. 1985. Taxation of timber and forest land in selected countries with important timber resources. Paper prepared for the Forest Industries Committee on Timber Valuation and Taxation. Washington, DC. Mimeo. 99 pp.

Bourke, I. J. 1988. Trade in forest products: A study of the barriers faced by the developing countries. FAO Forestry Paper 83, Food and Agriculture Organization of the United Nations. Rome, Italy. 140 pp.

Blake, Donald R., and F. Sherwood Rowland. 1988. Continuing worldwide increase in tropospheric methane, 1978 to 1987. *Science* 239:1129–1131.

Chambers, Robert, and Melissa Leach. 1987. Trees to meet contingencies: Savings and security for the rural poor. Institute of Development Studies Discussion Paper 228. University of Sussex. Brighton, U.K. 22 pp.

Cubbage, Frederick W., Donald G. Hodges, and James L. Regens. 1987. Economic implications of climate change impacts in the South. Pp. 266–279 in Mark Meo (ed.), Proceedings, Symposium on Climate Change in the Southern United States. University of Oklahoma, Science and Public Policy Program. Norman.

Eckmullner, Otto, and Andras Madas. 1984. The production functions. Pp. 161–212 in Fred C. Hummel (ed.), Forest Policy: A Contribution to Resource Development. Martinus Nijhoff/Dr W. Junk Publishers. The Hague, Netherlands.

Eckmullner, Otto and Adriaan van Maaren. 1984. Some special topics. Pp. 161–212 in Fred C. Hummel (ed.), Forest Policy: A Contribution to Resource Development. Martinus Nijhoff/Dr W. Junk Publishers. The Hague, Netherlands. 310 pp.

FAO. 1985. Yearbook of Forest Products, 1972–1983. Food and Agriculture Organization of the United Nations. Rome, Italy. 408 pp.

FAO. 1988a. Forest Products: World Outlook Projections. FAO Forestry Paper 84. Food and Agriculture Organization of the United Nations. Rome, Italy. 350 pp.

FAO. 1988b. Forestry Policies in Europe. FAO Forestry Paper 86. Food and Agriculture Organization of the United Nations. Rome. 283 pp.

Gradwohl, Judith, and Russell Greenberg. 1988. Saving the Tropical Forests. Island Press. Covelo, CA. 214 pp.

Gray, John W. 1983. Forest Revenue Systems in Developing Countries: Their Role in Income Generation and Forest Management Strategies. FAO Forestry Paper 43. Food and Agriculture Organization of the United Nations. Rome, Italy. 261 pp.

Gregersen, Hans M. 1988. People, trees, and rural development: The role of social forestry. *Journal of Forestry* 86(10):22–30.

Gregersen, Hans M., and Arnoldo H. Contreras. 1979. Economic Analysis of Forestry Projects. FAO Forestry Paper No. 17. Food and Agriculture Organization of the United Nations. Rome, Italy. 193 pp.

Gregerson, Hans M., and Alan L. Lundgren. 1990. Forestry for sustainable development: Concepts and a framework for action. Forestry For Sustainable Development Working Paper 1. University of Minnesota, College of Natural Resources. St. Paul.

Griffin, Neil, and Charles Watkins. 1988. The control of tree felling: Recent developments in statutes and case law. *Quarterly Journal of Forestry* 82(1):26–33.

Harou, P. A. 1986. The EC context for private forestry incentive evaluation. *Silva Fennica* 29(4):366–375.

Harrington, J. B. 1987. Climatic change: A review of causes. *Canadian Journal of Forestry Research* 17:1313–1339.

Hodges, Donald G., James L. Regens, and Frederick W. Cubbage. 1988. Evaluating potential economic impacts of global climate change on forestry in the southern United States. *Resource Management and Optimization* 6(3):235–251.

Houghton, R. A., R. D. Boone, J. R. Fruci, J. E. Hobbie, J. M. Melillo, C. A. Palm, B. J. Peterson, G. R. Shaver, and G. M. Woodwell. 1987. The flux of carbon from terrestrial ecosystems to the atmosphere in 1980 due to changes in land use: Geographic distribution of the global flux. Tellus, Series B: *Chemical and Physical Meteorology* 39B(1–2):122–139.

Houghton, Richard A., and George M. Woodwell. 1989. Global climate change. *Scientific American* 260(4):36–44.

Hummel, Fred C., and Adriaan van Maaren. 1984. Policy formation. Pp. 283–303 in Fred C. Hummel (ed.), Forest Policy: A Contribution to Resource Development. Martinus Nijhoff/Dr W. Junk Publishers. The Hague, Netherlands.

Joyce, Linda A., Michael A. Fosberg, and Joan M. Comanor. 1990. Climate change and America's forests. USDA Forest Service General Technical Report RM-187. Rocky Mountain Forest and Range Experiment Station. Fort Collins, CO. 12 pp.

Krott, Max. 1986. The politics of forest bureaucracy as a subject of comparative studies. Pp. 252–256 in Division 4 Proceedings, 18th IUFRO World Congress. Llubjana, Yugoslavia.

Laarman, Jan G. 1987. Forest policy and foreign policy: The politics of trade and aid in a sensitive world. Pp. 51–55 in Proceedings, 1986 Society of American Foresters National Convention. Bethesda, MD.

Laarman, Jan G. 1988. Preparing U.S. forestry for its international future. *Journal of Forestry* 86(7):27–30.

Laarman, Jan G., and Roger A. Sedjo. 1992. Global Forests: Issues for Six Billion People. McGraw-Hill. New York. 337 pp.

Leman, Christopher K. 1988. A forest of institutions: Patterns of choice on North American timberlands. Pp. 149–200 in Elliot J. Feldman and Michael A. Goldberg (eds.), Land Rites and Wrongs: The Management, Regulation and Use of Land in Canada and the United States. Lincoln Institute of Land Policy.

MacDonald, Gordon J. 1988. Scientific basis for the greenhouse effect. *Journal of Policy Analysis and Management* 7(3):425–444.

Meadows, Donella H., Dennis L. Meadows, Jorgen Randers, and William Behrens III. 1972. The Limits to Growth. Signet Publishing/New American Library. New York. 207 pp.

NFPA. 1989. NFPA in Focus. National Forest Products Association. Newsletter, December 1989–January 1990. 12 pp.

O'Laughlin, Jay, and Michael G. Messina. 1988. Swedish forestry and forest policy. *Journal of Forestry* 86(7):17-22.

Olechewski, A. 1987. Barriers to trade on wood and wood products. Pp. 371–390 in Markka Dallio, Dennis P. Dykstra, and Clark S. Binkley (eds.), The Global Forest Sector, An Analytical Perspective. Wiley. New York.

Peck, Tim. 1984. The world perspective. Pp. 21–66 in Fred C. Hummel, (ed.), Forest Policy: A Contribution to Resource Development. Martinus Nijhoff/Dr W. Junk Publishers. The Hague, Netherlands.

Plum, Peter Munk, and Brigit Honore. 1988. Forest policy and forest legislation in Denmark. Pp. 141–152 in Franz Schmithusen, (ed.), Forestry Legislation, Number 6. Report of the IUFRO Working Party S4.08-03. Zurich.

Postel, Sandra. 1986. Atmospheric warmup. *Environmental Science and Technology* 20(12):1208–1209.

Postel, Sandra. 1988a. A green fix to the global warm-up. *World Watch* 1(5):29–36.

Postel, Sandra. 1988b. Global view of a tropical disaster. *American Forests* 94(11/12):25–29.

Postel, Sandra, and Lori Heise. 1988. Reforesting the Earth. Worldwatch Paper 83. Worldwatch Institute, Washington, DC. 66 pp. Summarized as Chapter 5 in State of the World 1988: A Worldwatch Institute Report on Progress toward a Sustainable Society. W. W. Norton. New York. 237 pp.

Price, Martin F. 1988. A review of the development of legislation for Swiss mountain forests. Pp. 153–170 in Franz Schmithusen (ed.), Forestry Legislation, Number 6. Report of the IUFRO Working Party S4.08-03. Zurich.

Rainforest Action Network. 1989. The Japanese logging cartel: Behind the monopoly on Borneo's rainforests. Rainforest Action Network Action Alert #37. San Francisco. 2 pp.

Ramanathan, V. 1988. The greenhouse theory of climate change; a test by an inadvertent global experiment. *Science* 240:293–299.

Repetto, Robert. 1988a. Needed: New policy goals. *American Forests* 94(11/12):58, 82–86.

Repetto, Robert. 1988b. The Forest for the Trees? Government Policies and the Misuse of Forest Resources. World Resources Institute. Washington, DC. 105 pp.

Repetto, Robert, and Malcolm Gillis (eds.). 1988. Public policies and the misuse of forest resources. Cambridge University Press. Cambridge, U.K./New York. 432 pp.

Romm, Jeff. 1986. Forest policy and development policy. *Journal of World Forest Resource Management* 2:85–103.

SAF. 1988. Briefings on federal forest policy. Society of American Foresters, Bethesda, MD. 36 pp.

Sedjo, Roger A. 1983. The comparative economics of plantation forestry: A global assessment. Research Paper 0-8018-3107-5. Resources for the Future. Washington, DC. 191 pp.

Sedjo, Roger A. 1989. Forests to offset the greenhouse effect. *Journal of Forestry* 87(6):12–15.

Sedjo, Roger A., and Allen M. Solomon. 1989. Climate and forests. Pp. 105–120 in N. J. Rosenburg et al. (eds.), Proceedings, Greenhouse Warming: Abatement and Adaptation. Resources for the Future. Washington, DC.

Sundberg, Ulf. 1989. How Europeans control environmental impacts of logging operations. Pp. 31–37 in O. F. Hall and R. L. McElwee (eds.), Proceedings, Nineteenth Forestry Forum. Virginia Cooperative Extension Service and Virginia Polytechnic Institute and State University. Blacksburg.

Wear, David N., and Karen J. Lee. 1991. U.S. policy and Canadian lumber: The effects of the 1986 Memorandum of Understanding. Southeastern Forest Experiment Station. Research Triangle Park, NC. Mimeo.

Woodwell, G. M. 1983. Biotic effects on the concentration of atmospheric carbon dioxide: A review and projection. Pp. 216–241 in Changing Climate. National Research Council. Washington, DC.

World Bank. 1988. World Development Report 1988. Oxford University Press. New York. 307 pp.

World Resources Institute. 1988. World Resources 1988–89. Basic Books. New York. 372 pp.

Appendix A

Principal Federal Laws Relating to Forestry, Wildlife and Fisheries, Range, and Recreation

This appendix contains a selection of the principal laws relating to forest resources, including legal citations and a summary of their main provisions. Where it is unclear, a description of the law's relevance to forest resources is included.

Agriculture and Consumer Protection Act of 1973—Title X: Forestry Incentives Program

16 U.S.C. 1503, 1504, 1510.

P.L. 91-524, Title X, Section 1003, as added P.L. 93-86, Section 1(28), August 10, 1973, 87 Stat. 242. As amended.

This act authorizes the secretary of agriculture to contract with landowners for conservation of soil and water resources. If the landowner implements an approved conservation plan and meets other statutory requirements, the secretary will make payments for the use of the land maintained for conservation purposes. It also includes special provisions for the protection of wetlands. The secretary is authorized to provided "conservation materials" to the landowner. The incentive contracts are intended to supplement other federal programs. The act forms the basis for federal cost-share assistance to landowners who plant trees, perform timber stand or wildlife habitat improvement, or engage in other conservation practices.

Alaska National Interest Lands Conservation Act (1980)

16 U.S.C. 410hh, 410hh to 410hh-5, 431 notes, 460mm to 460mm-4, 539 to 539e, 668dd note, 1132 notes, 1274, 1276, 1279, 1280, 1285b, 3101 to 3103, 3111 to 3126, 3141 to 3145, 3146 to 3151, 3161 to 3173, 3181 to 3182, 3191 to 3215, 3231 to 3233.

P.L. 96-487, Section 101, December 2, 1980, 94 Stat. 2374.

This act was intended to obviate the need for additional legislation to protect the scenic, natural, cultural, and environmental values of public lands in Alaska. It also provides opportunities for the satisfaction of the economic and social needs of local residents. The act codifies the policy of conserving fish and wildlife populations with a minimum impact on the "subsistence uses" of the public lands. Local participation in the administration of public lands is designed to implement this policy. Special provisions are included to protect wilderness areas from unregulated oil, gas, and mineral exploitation. Similar provisions for regulations of transportation routes and access to public lands are specified. The coordination of federal and state regulation is the responsibility of the Alaska Land Use Council, whose primary function is to study resource conservation and "subsistence use" by native populations and make recommendations to state and federal officials. Extensive provisions for the protection of wilderness, national park and monument sites, natural preserves, and other public lands are balanced with the interests of local residents.

Bankhead-Jones Farm Tenant Act (1937)

7 U.S.C. 1000 (1001 to 1005d, 1006, 1006c to 1006e, 1007, 1008, 1009) notes, 1010, 1011, 1012, 1013 note, 1013a, (1014 to 1029) notes.

Act of July 22, 1937, chapter 517, Section 31, 50 Stat. 525. As amended.

This act authorizes the secretary of agriculture to develop a program of land conservation and utilization to correct maladjustments in land use. The objectives of this program include controlling soil erosion, reforestation, preserving natural resources, protecting fish and wildlife, and developing recreational opportunities and other activities in the public interest, but it excludes the construction of private industrial or commercial enterprises. The secretary is authorized to provide technical and other assistance to rural communities concerning water storage and waste treatment facilities. Millions of acres of abandoned farm land were purchased by the government under this act for rehabilitation, and many have since been transferred to the National Forest System.

Clarke-McNary Reforestation Act (1924)

16 U.S.C. 471 note, 499, 500, 515, 564, 565, 567 notes, 568, 569, 570.

Act of June 7, 1924, chapter 348, Section 9, 43 Stat. 655. As amended.

This act authorizes the secretary of agriculture to (a) cooperate with land grant colleges and universities and state agencies to aid farmers and small forest landowners in the production and distribution of seeds and seedlings for the creation, maintenance, and utilization of woodlots, shelterbelts, windbreaks, and other forest growth; (b) identify

and purchase lands valuable for stream-flow protection or timber production for inclusion in the national forest system; and (c) accept title to donated lands. This act marks the origin of federal–state cooperation in forestry and authorized the purchase of national forest lands in the foothills and plains of eastern states for the purpose of timber production. Sections 1 through 4 of the act, which have been superseded, authorized cooperation between the secretary of agriculture and state officials to protect timber lands from fire, to study the effects of tax laws on conservation and timber production, and to cooperate with state universities and other agencies in providing information to farmers regarding the use and management of farm woodlots.

Clean Air Act (1955)

42 U.S.C. 7401 et seq.

Act of July 14, 1955, chapter 360, Section 1, 69 Stat. 159. As amended and renumbered, in 1970 and 1990.

This act recognizes air pollution as a threat to human health and requires the surgeon general to promote research to reduce pollution. The 1970 amendments authorize the administrator of the Environmental Protection Agency to promulgate emission standards for industries, including pulp and paper mills and timber processing industries. The act regulates ambient air quality, including particulate matter and thus indirectly constrains silvicultural activity such as prescribed burning.

(Includes the Clean Air Act Amendments of 1970, P.L. 91-604, Sec. 1, December 31, 1970, 84 Stat. 1676, and Clean Air Act Amendments of 1977, 42 U.S.C. 4362 et seq., and Clean Air Act Amendments of 1990, P.L. 101–549, November 15, 1990.)

Cooperative Forestry Assistance Act of 1978

16 U.S.C. 565 note, 566 note, 567 note, 568c to 568e notes, 594-1 to 594-5 notes, 594a note, 1509 note, 1510, 1606, 2101 to 2111.

P.L. 95-313, Section 2, July 1, 1978, 92 Stat. 365.

This act repeals the Forest Pest Control Act, Cooperative Forest Management Act, and sections 1 through 4 of the Clarke- McNary Reforestation Act. It recognizes the role of private, state, and locally owned forest land in providing the nation with renewable resources. To facilitate management and protection of forest resources, the secretary of agriculture is authorized to cooperate with state officials in implementing federal programs affecting nonfederal forest lands. Such assistance includes (a) financial, technical, and related assistance to promote both urban and rural forestry; (b) a forestry incentives program; and (c) cooperation in control of disease and insects.

Creative Act of 1891

16 U.S.C. 471.
Act of March 3, 1891, chapter 561, Section 24, 26 Stat. 1103. Repealed.

This act authorized the president to reserve public lands covered wholly or in part with timber or undergrowth as forest reserves.

Economic Recovery Tax Act of 1981

26 U.S.C. 2032A(c)(2)(E) and 2032A(c)(13) are the only sections considered.
P.L. 97-34, Title IV, Section 421, August 13, 1981, 95 Stat. 307. As amended.

This act establishes special estate tax provisions for persons inheriting qualified woodland. If a qualified heir disposes of (or severs) any standing timber on qualified woodland, then (a) such disposition shall in law be treated as a disposition of a portion of the interest of the qualified heir in the property, and (b) the amount of additional tax imposed with regard to the disposition of timber shall be the lesser of (1) the amount realized on disposition (or the fair market value of the portion of the interest disposed) or (2) the amount of additional tax imposed if the *entire* interest of the qualified heir had been disposed of, *less* the sum of additional tax imposed with respect to all prior transactions involving the qualified woodland.

Endangered Species Act of 1973

16 U.S.C. 460k-1, 4601-9, 668aa to 668cc-6 notes, 668dd, 715i, 715s, 1362, 1371, 1372, 1402, 1531 to 1543.
P.L. 93-205, Section 2, December 28, 1978, 87 Stat. 884. As amended.

This act provides a program for the conservation of endangered species and the ecosystems upon which they depend for survival. This program includes provisions for (a) determining whether any species is endangered or threatened, (b) acquiring land for habitat protection, and (c) facilitating cooperation among states, federal agencies, and foreign nations. The secretary of the Department of the Interior, in consultation with the Fish and Wildlife Service, prepares official lists of threatened and endangered species eligible for protection under federal law. The act lists exceptions and penalties relating to the regulations promulgated by the secretary of the interior. The secretary of the Smithsonian Institution is authorized to review endangered plant species and propose methods for their conservation.

(Includes Endangered Species Act Amendments of 1978, 16 U.S.C. 1531 note, 1532 to 1536, 1538 to 1540, 1542, and Endangered Species Act Amendments of 1982, 16 U.S.C. 1531 note, 1531 to 1533, 1533 note, 1535, 1536, 1537a to 1539, 1540, 1542; and 1988 reauthorization amendments.)

Federal Aid in Fish Restoration Act (1950) or Dingell-Johnson Sport Fish Restoration Act (with Wallop-Breaux funds)

16 U.S.C. 777 to 777i, 777k.
Act of August 9, 1950, chapter 658, Section 2, 64 Stat. 431. As amended.

The secretary of the interior is authorized to cooperate with state fish and game departments in "fish restoration and management projects." These projects are funded by an excise tax on fishing equipment. Part of the Aquatic Resources Trust Fund is used to finance conservation programs and research on marine and freshwater migratory fish. The remainder of the fund is apportioned among state governments based upon land area and the number of fishing licenses sold. The Wallop-Breaux Trust Fund expands the funding for sport fish restoration by including import duties on pleasure boats and yachts and motorboat fuel taxes. A state desiring to avail itself of these funds must submit an acceptable fish and wildlife management plan to the secretary. Expenditure of restoration funds is restricted by the statute to construction, maintenance, and personnel costs incurred in administering the act.

(Includes Federal Aid in Fish Restoration Act Amendments of 1970, 16 U.S.C. 777c, 777e, 777g, 777k.)

Federal Aid in Wildlife Restoration Act (1937) or Pitman-Robertson Wildlife Restoration Act

16 U.S.C. 669 to 669b, 669c to 669i.
Act of September 2, 1937, chapter 889, Section 2, 50 Stat. 917. As amended.

The secretary of the interior is authorized to cooperate with state fish and game departments in "wildlife restoration projects." Such projects are funded by an excise tax on sales of arms and ammunition. A portion of these funds is used to administer the Migratory Bird Conservation Act. The remainder is apportioned among state fish and game departments based upon land area and the number of hunting licenses sold. A state desiring to avail itself of these funds must submit an acceptable plan for fish and wildlife management to the secretary. Expenditure of restoration funds is restricted by the statute to construction, maintenance, and personnel costs incurred in administering the act.

(Includes Federal Aid in Wildlife Restoration Act Amendments of 1970, 16 U.S.C. 669b, 669c to 669g-l.)

Federal Insecticide, Rodenticide, and Fungicide Act (1947)

7 U.S.C. 135 to 135k, 136 to 136y.
Act of June 25, 1947, chapter 125, Section 2 to 13, 61 Stat. 163 to 172. As amended, in 1972, 1978, and 1988.

This act prohibits the distribution, sale, or transfer of any unregistered pesticide, unless allowed by statute. It requires states to regulate the use of pesticides through certification procedures designed to supervise the use of registered pesticides. The act contains provisions for strict control of pesticide use, including registration and inspection of retail establishments, import/export restrictions, penalties for violations, administrative and judicial review procedures, and specifications for "unlawful acts."

(Includes Federal Environmental Pesticide Control Act of 1972, 7 U.S.C. 136 to 136y, and Federal Pesticide Act of 1978, 7 U.S.C. 136 to 136f, 136h, 136j, 136l, 136o, 136q, 136r, 136u, 136u to 136w, 136x, 136y; and 1988 reauthorization amendments.)

Federal Land Policy and Management Act of 1976

43 U.S.C. 270-12 note, 315b, 315c, 315i, 661, 664, 665, 687b-2, 869, 869-1, 913c, 934 to 939, 942-1 to 942-9, 943, 944, 946 to 958, 959, 961 to 970, 1701, 1702, 1711, 1722, 1731 to 1748, 1753, 1761 to 1771, 1781, 1782.
P.L. 94-579, Section 102, October 21, 1976, 90 Stat. 2744.

This act authorizes the secretary of the interior to prepare and maintain an inventory of all public lands and their resource (including recreational and aesthetic) values, giving priority to areas of critical environmental concern. It establishes (a) the organization of the Bureau of Land Management and Grazing Advisory Boards, (b) management guidelines for public lands, (c) right-of-way, boundary, and access guidelines for public lands, and (d) wilderness review procedures for Bureau of Land Management roadless areas.

Federal Water Pollution Control Act Amendments of 1972

33 U.S.C. 1251, 1252, 1253 to 1257, 1258 to 1263, 1264 note, 1265, 1281, 1282 to 1283, 1294 to 1299, 1311 to 1313, 1314 to 1326, 1327 note, 1341 to 1345, 1361 to 1376.
P.L. 92-500, Section 1, October 18, 1972, 86 Stat. 816. As amended, in 1977 and 1987.

This act authorizes the administrator of the Environmental Protection Agency to issue to federal and state agencies information including (a) guidelines for identifying and evaluating the nature and extent of nonpoint sources of pollutants, and (b) processes, procedures, and methods to control pollution resulting from nonpoint sources, including silvicultural activities. Each state must submit a biennial report to the administrator that includes a description of the nature and extent of nonpoint sources of pollutants, as well as recommendations of programs that must be undertaken to control each category of such sources. The administrator must establish a national "standard of performance" for categories of effluent sources, including pulp and paper mills, paperboard, builders paper and board mills, and timber products processing industries. Section 208 of the act requires areawide planning to prevent nonpoint source pollution, including forestry activities. These planning efforts have led to the development of voluntary or regulatory state best management practices to control pollution from forestry activities. Section 404 of the act also requires landowners to obtain permission for dredge and fill operations in the nation's waters and wetlands. This review and permit process has evolved into an extensive wetland protections program. Section 319 of the 1987 amendments to the 1972 act authorizes additional nonpoint pollution control planning, including explicit consideration of regulatory and nonregulatory control methods.

(Includes Clean Water Act of 1977 amending 16 U.S.C. 1251, 1252, 1254 to 1256, 1259, 1262, 1263, 1281, 1282 to 1288, 1291, 1292, 1311, 1314, 1315, 1317 to 1319, 1321 to 1324, 1328, 1341, 1342, 1344, 1345, 1362, 1375, 1376, and 1987 amendments of 33 U.S.C. 1251 et. seq.)

Fish and Wildlife Coordination Act (1934)

16 U.S.C. 661 to 666c.
Act of March 10, 1934, chapter 55, Section 1, 48 Stat. 401. As amended.

This act authorizes the secretary of the interior to assist and coordinate federal, state,

and private efforts concerning the development, protection, rearing, and stocking of wildlife species and their habitat. With exceptions for small water impoundments and the Tennessee Valley Authority, any federal agency proposing to impound, divert, or modify any stream or body of water must first consult with the U.S. Fish and Wildlife Service. All such activities must include the conservation of wildlife in their general plans. The secretary is authorized to investigate the impact of domestic and industrial waste and sewage on wildlife.

Food Security Act of 1985

16 U.S.C. 3801, 3811 to 3813, 3821 to 3823, 3831 to 3836, 3841 to 3845.
P.L. 99-198, Section 1201, December 23, 1985, 99 Stat. 1504. As amended in 1990.

The 1985 farm bill contains at least four provisions with substantial specific impacts on forestry and wildlife. The Conservation Reserve Program authorizes the secretary of agriculture to retire land from crop production to conserve and improve the soil and water resources of farms and ranches. Land was to be placed in permanent grass or trees, and landowners would receive payments for stand establishment and maintenance. A sodbuster section protects highly erodible land that has not been cultivated since 1980. Farmers who plow up such land are disqualified from receiving any farm commodity program payments unless they follow an approved conservation plan. A companion swampbuster restriction applies to farmers who convert wetlands to cropland. Highly erodible land used for crops between 1981 and 1985 is exempt from sodbuster penalties until 1990. Then it too will have to be farmed according to an approved conservation plan to be eligible for farm program benefits. The 1990 amendments reauthorized the 1985 farm bill provisions. They also enacted a new part, Title XII, authorizing the Stewardship Incentives Program and other forestry components.

Forest and Rangeland Renewable Resources Planning Act of 1974

16 U.S.C. 1600 note, 1600 to 1606, 1607 to 1614.

P.L. 93-378, Section 2, August 17, 1974, 88 Stat. 476. As amended.

This act authorizes the secretary of agriculture to prepare a decennial assessment document to facilitate long-term planning for the national forests. The minimum content of the assessment includes (a) an analysis of present and anticipated demand and supply of renewable resources, (b) an inventory of present and potential renewable resources, (c) a description of Forest Service programs and responsibilities, and (d) a discussion of policy considerations, laws, and regulations affecting forest management. As part of the assessment, the secretary must develop and maintain on a continuing basis a comprehensive inventory of renewable resources. In addition, a five-year program document that includes alternatives for the protection, management, and development of the national forest system must be prepared and submitted to the President. The assessment and program documents, together with a detailed statement of policy, are intended to be used in framing presidential budget requests for Forest Service activities.

Forest and Rangeland Renewable Resources Research Act of 1978

16 U.S.C. 581 to 581i notes, 1600 note, 1641 to 1647.
P.L. 95-307, Section 1, June 30, 1978, 92 Stat. 353.

This act repeals the McSweeney-McNary Act and authorizes the secretary of agriculture to implement a comprehensive program of forest and rangeland resources research and dissemination of the findings of this research. It authorizes the maintenance of experiment stations, research laboratories, and other forest and rangeland research facilities and authorizes research funds for cooperators and grantees. The secretary is charged with (a) encouraging cooperators and grantees to seek the proper mix of short- and long-term, basic and applied research, (b) avoiding unnecessary duplication among federal agencies, and (c) encouraging the training of scientists and other specialists.

Knutson-Vandenberg Act (1930)

16 U.S.C. 567 to 567b.
Act of June 9, 1930, chapter 416, Section 1, 46 Stat. 527, as amended.

This act authorizes the secretary of agriculture to establish and maintain forest tree nurseries in preparation for planting or seeding national forests and provides for the protection, maintenance, and improvement of the resulting forest. The secretary may require a purchaser of national forest timber to deposit money sufficient to cover the cost of undertaking certain reforestation, silvicultural, and wildlife habitat improvement activities on harvested areas in national forests.

Lacey Act (1900)

16 U.S.C. 667e.
Act of May 25, 1900, chapter 553, Section 5, 31 Stat. 188. As amended.

This act declares illegal the import, export, transport, sale, or any commercial transaction concerning fish, wildlife, or plant taken or possessed in violation of any law, treaty, or regulation of the United States. It describes provisions for the administration and enforcement of the statute, as well as penalties for violations.

(Includes Lacey Act Amendments of 1981, 16 U.S.C. 667e, (851 to 856) notes, 1540, 3371 to 3378.)

Land and Water Conservation Fund Act of 1965

16 U.S.C. 460d, 4601-4, 4601-5, 4601-6, 4601-6a, 4601-7 to 4601-11.
P.L. 88-578, Section 2a, September 3, 1964, 78 Stat. 899. As amended.

This act authorizes the chief of engineers, under the secretary of the army, to develop and maintain outdoor recreational facilities at water resource development projects. Proceeds from the sale of certain surplus property, the motorboat fuels tax, and appropriated funds are collected into the land and water conservation fund. These funds are available to assist states in developing recreational facilities and to assist federal land acquisition and development. Admission fees are to be charged only at designated units of the National Park System.

Marine Mammal Protection Act of 1972

16 U.S.C. 1361, 1362, 1371 to 1383, 1384 note, 1401 to 1406, 1407 note.

P.L. 92-522, Section 1, October 21, 1972, 86 Stat. 1027, including 1988 reauthorization amendments.

This act establishes a moratorium on taking and importing marine animals and marine mammal products, with specific exceptions. It authorizes regulation and permit programs for the taking of marine mammals and establishes guidelines for enforcement and penalties for violations. It authorizes the transfer of management authority from the federal government to individual states, as well as research grants and research programs for the development of commercial fishing equipment to reduce incidental taking of marine mammals.

McSweeney-McNary Act (1928)

16 U.S.C. 581, 581a, 581b to 581i.

Act of May 22, 1928, chapter 678, Section 1, 45 Stat. 699. Repealed.

This act authorized the secretary of agriculture to establish forest experiment stations for cooperative research on reforestation and forest products development. It was replaced by the Forest and Rangeland Renewable Resources Research Act of 1978.

Migratory Bird Conservation Act (1929)

16 U.S.C. 715 to 715d, 715e, 715f to 715k, 715n, 715r.

Act of February 18, 1929, chapter 257, Section 1, 45 Stat. 1222. As amended.

This act authorizes the creation of the Migratory Bird Conservation Commission to pass upon lands recommended for purchase or lease by the secretary of the interior for migratory bird conservation. The secretary may purchase or rent land and water areas approved by the commission for use as inviolate sanctuaries or management areas for migratory birds. Areas acquired under the statute must be administered in accordance with treaty obligations.

Migratory Bird Hunting Stamp Act (1934) or Duck Stamp Act

16 U.S.C. 718 to 718b, 718c to 718h, 718j.

Act of March 16, 1934, chapter 71, Section 9, 48 Stat. 452. As amended.

In conjunction with the Migratory Bird Treaty Act and Migratory Bird Conservation Act, "no person over 16 years of age shall take any migratory waterfowl unless he or she carries on his or her person a valid federal migratory bird hunting and conservation stamp." However, a resident owner, sharecropper, tenant, or federal official may under prescribed circumstances take migratory waterfowl without a stamp. Proceeds from annual stamp sales are deposited in the migratory bird conservation fund. The secretary of the interior is authorized to use these funds to acquire wetland and pothole areas (designated as "waterfowl production areas"), or other lands suitable for migratory bird refuges.

Migratory Bird Treaty Act (1918)

16 U.S.C. 703 to 708, 709a to 711.

Act of July 3, 1918, chapter 128, Section 2, 40 Stat. 755.

This act establishes by treaty with Great Britain (on behalf of Canada), Mexico, and Japan provisions for the protection of migratory birds. It authorizes the secretary of the interior to determine when and how such birds may be taken, killed, or possessed. It declares illegal the transportation of migratory birds, nests, or eggs possessed in violation of the statute.

McIntire-Stennis Act of 1962

16 U.S.C. 582a to 582a-7.

P.L. 87-788, Section 1, October 10, 1962, 76 Stat. 806. As amended.

This act recognizes the importance of forestry research in promoting technological advances necessary to efficiently utilize and protect forest and range resources. To promote forestry research, the secretary of agriculture is authorized to cooperate with state colleges and universities and provide technical assistance and financial support.

Multiple-Use Sustained-Yield Act of 1960

16 U.S.C. 528 to 531.

P.L. 86-517, Section 1, June 12, 1960, 74 Stat. 215.

This act codifies the policy that "national forests are established and shall be administered for outdoor recreation, range, timber, watershed, and wildlife and fish purposes." The act was intended to supplement the policy established in the Organic Administration Act of 1897. The secretary of agriculture is directed to "develop and administer the renewable surface resources of the national forests for multiple use and sustained yield." A utilitarian definition of *multiple use* is given: "The management of all of the various renewable surface resources of the national forests so that they are utilized in the combination that will best meet the needs of the American people." Similarly, *sustained yield* is defined as "the achievement and maintenance in perpetuity of a high-level annual or regulated output of the various renewable resources of the national forests without impairment of the productivity of the land."

National Environmental Policy Act of 1969

42 U.S.C. 4321, 4331 to 4335, 4341 to 4347.

P.L. 91-190, Section 2, January 1, 1970, 83 Stat. 852.

This act codifies the national policy of encouraging harmony between humans and the environment by promoting efforts to prevent or eliminate damage to the environment, thereby enriching our understanding of ecological systems and natural resources. It declares the federal government to be responsible for (a) coordinating programs and plans regarding environmental protection, (b) using an interdisciplinary approach to decision making, (c) developing methods to ensure that nonquantifiable amenity values are in-

cluded in economic analyses, and (d) including in every recommendation, report on proposals for legislation, or other major federal actions significantly affecting the quality of the environment a detailed Environmental Impact Statement. It authorizes the creation of the Council on Environmental Quality to advise the president on environmental issues. It triggered policy efforts for the creation of the Environmental Protection Agency to consolidate federal efforts to control air, water, and land pollution, especially water and air quality standards and pesticide controls.

National Forest Management Act of 1976

16 U.S.C. 472a, 476 notes, 500, 513 notes, 514 note, 515, 516, 518, 528 note, 576b, 1600, 1601, 1602, 1604, 1606, 1608 to 1614.

P.L. 94-588, Section 14, October 22, 1976, 90 Stat. 2949. As amended.

This act amends the Forest and Rangeland Renewable Resource Planning Act of 1974 and the Organic Administration Act of 1897 by requiring land and resource management planning for units within the national forest system and additional regulation of timber harvesting on national forests. The major provisions of the act require (a) public participation in the planning process, (b) regulations for the preparation and revisions of the management plans, (c) resource management guidelines for controversial management activities such as clear-cutting, and (d) economic analysis of management alternatives.

National Park Service Organic Act (1916)

16 U.S.C. 1, 2 to 4, 22, 43.

Act of August 25, 1916, chapter 408, Section 1, 39 Stat. 535. As amended.

This act created the National Park Service within the Department of the Interior, which is responsible for the promotion and regulation of national parks, monuments, and reservations, except those under military jurisdiction. The purpose of these sites is to conserve and protect the scenery, wildlife, and natural and historic objects so that they may be enjoyed unimpaired by future generations. It establishes the authority of the director of the Park Service to manage, supervise, control, and promulgate rules and regulations necessary for the proper use of the park system. It authorizes the secretary of the interior to regulate the timber, mineral, wildlife, fisheries, and other natural resources, with special reference to protection of Yellowstone and Sequoia National Parks.

National Trails System Act (1968)

16 U.S.C. 1241 to 1251.
    P.L. 90-543, Section 2, October 2, 1968, 82 Stat. 919. As amended.

This act establishes a system of trails along historic travel routes and within scenic areas to promote public outdoor recreational opportunities. The initial components of the trail system included the Appalachian and Pacific Crest Trails. The act describes provisions for the administration and development of scenic, historic, and recreational trails, including volunteer assistance in the planning, development, maintenance, and management of these trails.

National Wildlife Refuge System Administration Act of 1966

16 U.S.C. 668dd, 668ee.
    P.L. 89-669, Section 4, October 15, 1966, 80 Stat. 927. As amended.

This act consolidates the authority of federal agencies for conservation of fish and wildlife by creating the National Wildlife Refuge System administered by the U.S. Fish and Wildlife Service. It describes provisions for the acquisition and administration of refuges. It strictly regulates activities permitted on the refuges and specifies enforcement and penalties for violations. It also distributes a portion of the funds collected from the sale or disposition of timber, minerals, or other resources to local governments.

(Includes National Wildlife Refuge System Administration Act Amendments of 1974, 16 U.S.C. 668dd, 668ee, 715s.)

Organic Administration Act of 1897

16 U.S.C. 473 to 475, 477 to 482, 551.
    Act of June 4, 1897, chapter 2, Section 1, 30 Stat. 34, 36. As amended.

This act establishes custodial management direction for the Forest Service by mandating that no forest be established except to improve and protect the forest within boundaries designated by the president. The purpose of the forest reserves is to (a) secure favorable conditions of water flow and (b) furnish a continuous supply of timber by preserving living and growing timber and promoting young growth on the national forests. The secretary of agriculture is authorized to sell (for not less than an appraised value) dead, matured, or large growth trees found in national forests. Before being sold, such trees must be marked, cut, and removed under the supervision of the secretary. National forest lands found to be better adapted for mining or agricultural purposes than for forest usage may be returned to the public domain.

Recreational Boating Safety and Facilities Improvement Act of 1980, Title III or Reforestation Tax Incentives, or Packwood Amendment

26 U.S.C. 194 (tax provision is the only section considered).
    P.L. 96-451, Section 101, October 14, 1980, 94 Stat. 1983.

This act allows a taxpayer with "qualified timber property" to elect a deduction with respect to the amortization of the amortizable basis of the property based on a period of 84 months. The *amortizable basis* of the property is defined as that portion of the basis that is attributable to specific "reforestation expenses." The act establishes a Reforestation Trust Fund to finance national forest reforestation requirements. This section allows forest landowners to receive a tax credit and tax deductions on their income tax.

Renewable Resources Extension Act of 1978

16 U.S.C. 1600 note, 1671 to 1676.
    P.L. 95-306, Section 1, June 20, 1978, 92 Stat. 349.

This act recognizes the importance of forestry extension apart from general agricultural extension services. The statute facilitates the creation of educational programs to assist in renewable resource problem analysis and technological transfer and dissemination of research results. Special attention is given to the problems of small forest landowners and range, fish, and wildlife management. The secretary of agriculture is authorized to prepare a five-year plan for implementing forestry extension and guidelines for state forestry extension directors. The act requires that state directors and the extension administrators of colleges and universities develop, by mutual agreement, a comprehensive and coordinated renewable resource extension program.

Revenue Act of 1943 (capital gain tax treatment of timber)

26 U.S.C. 117.
As amended by P.L. 78-127, February 25, 1944, 58 Stat. (46 is the only section considered here).

This wartime statute was the genesis of capital gain tax treatment of timber. A taxpayer may elect to have the proceeds of timber harvests recognized for tax purposes as an amount equal to the difference between the adjusted basis for depletions of the timber and its fair market value. Such an election will apply to all timber owned by the taxpayer. Favorable tax treatment was reduced in the Tax Reform Act of 1986. Current tax treatment of timber and other natural resources is codified at 16 U.S.C. 631 (P.L. 99-514, Title III, Section 311(b)(3), October 22, 1986, 100 Stat. 2219).

Sikes Act (1960)

16 U.S.C. 670a to 670f, 670g to 670m, 670n note to 670o.
P.L. 86-797, Sections 1 to 5, September 15, 1960, 74 Stat. 1052, 1053. As amended.

This act authorizes the secretary of defense to conduct a program for the coordination of wildlife, fish, and game conservation and rehabilitation of military reservations. A cooperative plan mutually agreed upon by the secretaries of defense and the interior and the relevant state agencies must be developed. The act requires cooperation between the secretaries of agriculture and the interior in the conservation and rehabilitation of public lands, including the development of comprehensive plans for the protection of wildlife and fishery resources. A public land management area stamp is required for persons hunting, trapping, or fishing on public lands included in the conservation and rehabilitation programs.

(Includes Sikes Act Amendments of 1974, 16 U.S.C. 670a to 670f, 670g to 670m, 670n note, 670o, and Sikes Act Amendments of 1978, 16 U.S.C. 670a note, 670f, 670o, and Sikes Act Amendments of 1982, 670a, 670f, 670g, 670o.)

Soil Bank Act of 1956

7 U.S.C. 1801 to 1816 (repealed), 1821 to 1824 (repealed), 1831 (repealed), 1831a, 1832 to 1837 (repealed).
Act of May 28, 1956, chapter 327, Title I, section 107, 70 Stat. 191. As amended.

This act was designed to withdraw land from agricultural production for conservation use. From 1957 to 1959, the U.S. Department of Agriculture paid landowners part of the establishment cost and annual payments for a specified contract period to maintain crop land in permanent cover. Section 1831a specifies contract restrictions on payments for conservation practices.

Taylor Grazing Act (1934)

43 U.S.C. 315 to 315f, 315g note, 315h to 315m, 315n, 315o note, 315o-l, 1171 note.
Act of June 28, 1934, chapter 865, Section 1, 48 Stat. 1269. As amended.

This act authorizes the secretary of the interior to establish grazing districts in the unreserved public domain and to promulgate regulations concerning their protection, administration, and improvement. A public hearing is required before the creation of any district. The act authorizes the secretary to issue trading permits to allow access to settlers, residents, and stock owners to the districts created under the statute. In the promulgation of grazing regulations, the secretary must provide for cooperation with local associations of stock owners and state officials concerned with wildlife conservation. The secretary is empowered to accept contributions toward the administration, protection, and improvement of the land. Funds received from the permit program are disbursed to the states. Unappropriated public lands lying within watersheds forming a part of a national forest may be reserved by proclamation of the president under the national forest system, provided such reservations do not interfere with legal rights acquired under any public land laws.

Weeks Law (1911)

16 U.S.C. 515 to 519, 521, 552, 563.
   Act of March 1, 1911, chapter 186, Section 6, 36 Stat. 962. As amended.

This law authorizes the secretary of agriculture to purchase forested, cutover, or denuded lands within the watersheds of navigable streams to regulate their flow. This law was amended by the Clarke-McNary Act (1924) to include the production of timber. It provides for the acquisition of privately held land within national forest boundaries through exchange for other national forest land in the same state. It authorizes states to enter into agreements for conserving water resources and protecting watersheds of navigable rivers. This act led to the purchase of national forest lands in the mountainous areas of eastern states. The 1924 amendments authorized purchases in the piedmont and coastal plains.

Wild and Scenic Rivers Act (1968)

16 U.S.C. 1271 to 1287.
   P.L. 90-542, Section 1b, October 1, 1968, 82 Stat. 906. As amended.

This act codifies the policy that certain rivers and their immediate environments possess outstanding scenic, recreational, geo-logic, fish, wildlife, historic, cultural, or similar values and thus must be preserved in free-flowing condition. It prescribes methods by which the quality of scenic rivers will be protected and maintained, and the standards under which additional rivers may be added to the system. Provisions for land aquisition and restrictions on water resource projects and mining are specified. The management of public lands adjacent to designated rivers must comply with the management policies and regulations promulgated by the statute.

Wilderness Act (1964)

16 U.S.C. 1131 to 1136.
   P.L. 88-577, Section 2, September 3, 1964, 78 Stat. 890. As amended.

This act establishes the National Wilderness Preservation System composed of federally owned areas designated by Congress as "wilderness areas" for the purpose of preserving these areas in their natural condition. A *wilderness area* is defined as "an area where the earth and its community of life are untrammeled by man, where man himself is a visitor and does not remain." This definition includes "undeveloped Federal land retaining its primeval character and influence, without permanent improvements of human habitation, which is protected and managed so as to preserve its natural conditions." A review process for evaluation of potential wilderness areas, including five predominate characteristics of wilderness, is described. Amendments include special provisions for the creation of eastern wilderness areas. The act limits the use of public land designated as wilderness and specifies the rights of state and private landowners whose land is surrounded by wilderness.

(Includes Eastern Wilderness Act, 16 U.S.C. 1132 note.)

Youth Conservation Corps Act of 1970

16 U.S.C. 1701 to 1706.
   P.L. 91-378, Section 1, August 13, 1970, 84 Stat. 704. As amended.

This act recognizes that all segments of society are benefited by a program providing "gainful employment in the healthful out-door atmosphere of the national park system, the national forest system, [and] other public land and water areas." It authorizes the secre-taries of the interior and agriculture to estab-lish equal employment opportunity programs to provide short-term (90-day) employment for persons between the ages of 15 and 19.

Appendix B

An Introduction to Legal Research and Citation

INTRODUCTION

The purpose of this appendix is to introduce nonlawyers to the fundamentals of legal research. This discussion is not intended to be exhaustive; for a comprehensive treatment of the subject consult the references listed in the following discussion.

Before beginning legal research, one must understand two important legal principles, *stare decisis* and the *ratio decidendi* of a judicial decision. The doctrine of *stare decisis* means that precedent should be followed. The doctrine is based upon fairness: People similarly situated should be treated the same. Legal research is a search for a precedent that applies to a legal problem. Specifically, legal research is a search for primary resources such as the *ratio decidendi* or "holding" of judicial decisions. The *ratio decidendi* of a decision is the guiding legal principle applied by the court to resolve the legal issues. Other conclusions reached by the court are *obiter dictum,* that is, something "said by the way."

From these legal principles one may deduce that not all legal materials are equally persuasive. The primary resources of judicial decisions or "cases" and statutory law have the greatest authority because they form the basis of precedent. Secondary materials such as treatises and legal periodicals do not have equal authority. Instead, secondary sources function as a guide to finding and understanding the legal principles of primary resources.

PRELIMINARY LEGAL RESEARCH

There are countless methods of finding primary resource materials. With experience, the researcher usually develops a personalized research method. A good way for the novice to begin is by reading nonlegal research materials such as books and journal articles. The purpose of such preliminary work is to acquaint the researcher with the various perspectives on a particular legal problem. After this preliminary work, the researcher should succinctly summarize the research problem and list key words and phrases associated with the topic. A thorough understanding of the problem *before* entering the law library greatly enhances the efficiency of legal research.

PRIMARY LEGAL RESOURCES

JUDICIAL DECISIONS

The goal of legal research is to identify precedent (cases and statutes) relating to the research problem. To find cases, the researcher uses key words and phrases (developed in the preliminary research) to access case digests.

West Publishing Company (hereafter "West") compiles decennial digests of all cases appearing in its digests over a 10-year period. This digest provides a broad view of all cases relating to a subject. Other West case digests are organized by jurisdiction, for example, U.S. Supreme Court digests and federal, regional, and state digests. Key words lead the researcher through the Descriptive Word Index and into the volumes of the digest in which cases are listed by subject area. The subject areas of West's digests are organized by key numbers. The same key number is used to identify similar subject matter in other West legal references. Thus, key numbers are "road signs" directing the researcher to additional legal references. In summary, the primary method of locating cases is by using the Descriptive Word Index of a case digest to transform key words into cases organized under the key number system.

The annotated reporters, for example, *American Law Reports* (A.L.R.), combine the text of a leading decision on given legal topic with an annotation discussing related cases. A "Quick Index" organizes the annotations by subject area. It is used to trace key words to cases relating to a given subject. Annotation revisions are found by using the History Table, which lists superseded annotations, and the pocket-part listing of supplemental case decisions. The method of citing leading cases reported in the A.L.R. is described in Table B-1. The annotations (a secondary legal resource) may be cited as

Annotation, *Construction and Applications of Wilderness (16 U.S.C. sections 1131 et seq.) Providing for National Wilderness Preservation System,* 14 A.L.R. Fed 508 (1973).

This citation indicates that annotation for the leading case of *Parker* v. *United States* 448 F.2d 793 (10th Cir. 1971) may be found in volume number 14 of the *American Law Reports-Federal* at page number 508. The annotation was compiled in 1973.

Both case digests and A.L.R. list cases by citations to legal reporters. Legal reporters or-

TABLE B-1   Case Citation Examples

Federal Court Reporter Citations

Kleppe v. Sierra Club, 427 U.S. 390 (1976). A U. S. Supreme Court case found in volume number 427 of the official reporter of the court, *United States Reports,* at page number 390, decided in 1976.

Atlanta Coalition of Transportation Crisis, Inc. v. Atlanta Regional Commission, 559 F.2d 1333 (5th Cir. 1979). A case from the U. S. Court of Appeals, Fifth Circuit, found in volume number 599, at page number 1333 of the second series of West's *Federal Reporter,* decided in 1979.[a]

Chesapeake Bay Foundation v. Virginia State Water Control Board, 453 F. Supp. 122 (E.D. Va. 1978). A case from the U. S. District Court, the Eastern District of Virginia, found in volume number 453, at page 122 of West's *Federal Supplement,* decided in 1978.

Adams v. North Carolina, 295 N.C. 683, 249 S.E.2d 402 (1978). A case from the supreme court of North Carolina, volume number 295, page number 683, decided in 1978. Also found in West's South Eastern (second series) regional case reporter at volume number 249, page number 402.

Baker v. Fortney, 299 S.W.2d 563 (Mo. Ct. App. 1957). A Missouri Court of Appeals case reported *only* in West's South Western regional case reporter at volume 299, page number 563, decided in 1957. There was no official state reporter published after 1952, so there is not parallel citation.

[a]For state court citations, a "parallel" citation is given, listing West's regional case reporter and the official state court reporter. Some states, however, do not publish an official reporter. In these states only the West regional case reporter is cited.

ganize published judicial decisions using the jurisdiction system of the case digests. Cases are cited by using a reporter volume and page number, as shown in Table B-1.

West's case reporters publish the text of each judicial decision and other information such as a case syllabus and headnotes. The syllabus is a summary of the decision. Headnotes denote specific issues or legal conclusions reached in the case. They are a guide through the case based upon the key numbers and descriptive words of the case digests. Headnotes also assist the researcher in using the case citators.

The final step in locating cases involves the use of Shepard's case citations to identify subsequent decisions. Shepard's citators are organized by jurisdictional "units." For example, federal decisions are found in the *Federal Citations,* U.S. Supreme Court decisions in the *United States Citations,* and so forth. A separate unit is published for each state. Within each of these units, Shepard's lists "cited" cases by volume and page number. For each cited case, Shepard's lists subsequent citing cases that mention the cited decision. Headnotes are used to focus the research on specific legal issues. The mechanics of "shepardizing" are described in *How to Use Shepard's Citations,* an instructional pamphlet available at any law library.

Comprehensive shepardizing is essential to good legal research. By shepardizing a case, the researcher can ascertain if it has been reversed by the same court or overruled by a higher court. If a case has been reversed or overruled, it loses its precendential value.

STATUTES

The other primary legal resource, statutory law, is accessed through the use of codes. A code is similar to a case digest in that it summarizes current statutes using a subject index. As before, key words are applied to a descriptive word index to locate statutes pertaining to the research problem. Alternatively, statutes may be located by using a "popular name" table that lists the citation for popular statutes organized under official names.

Federal Statutes

The text of various legislative acts is published in a series: slip law, session laws, code, and annotated code. Slip laws contain the text of a single act published under a "public law number" (Table B-2). Session laws publish slip laws in a chronological sequence. A code preserves the original language of the session laws but rearranges the session laws into subject categories called "titles." Federal statutes are arranged into 50 general title categories within the official *United States Code.* An an-

TABLE B-2   Statutory Citation Examples

Federal Statutes

I. *Slip law or Session Laws*

National Environmental Policy Act of 1969, P.L. No. 91-190, 83 Stat. 852 (1970). This citation identifies NEPA as being located at Public Law Number 91-190, volume number 83, page number 852 of the Statutes at Large, effective date 1970.

II. *Official Code*

National Environmental Policy Act of 1969, 42 U.S.C. Section 4331 (1982). This citation identifies NEPA as being located in Title 42, Section 4331 of the 1982 edition of the official *United States Code.*

III. *Unofficial Annotated Code*

National Environmental Policy Act of 1969, 42 U.S.C.A. Section 4331 (West 1977). This citation identifies NEPA as being located in Title 42, Section 4331 of the 1977 edition of the unofficial *United States Code Annotated.*

State Statutes

Official Code Ga. Ann. secs. 12-5-230 to 12-5-246 (1988). This citation identifies the Shore Assistance Act of 1979 which is located in Title 12, chapter 5, sections 230 to 246 of the *Official Code of Georgia Annotated* 1988 edition.

notated code retains the official code's text and subject arrangement, but it adds an annotation after each statutory section. Annotations describe the relationship between judicial decisions and statutes. In West's *United States Code Annotated* (an unofficial annotated code), the key number format is used to relate case annotations to other West legal references.

State Statutes

The pattern of publication for state statutes is similar to that of federal statutes. All states have either an official state code or state code annotated. State codes may be accessed through descriptive work indexes or popular name tables.

Statute Citators

Once the relevant statutory section has been identified, the researcher uses the pocket-part of the code and Shepard's statute citator to be certain that the statute has not been amended or repealed. Also, Shepard's statute citators may be used to identify subsequent judicial decisions that construe, apply, or interpret the statute. The mechanics of Shepard's statute citators is described in *How to Use Shepard's Citations.*

CONSTITUTIONS

Constitutions are a special category of legal research. A constitution is an organic document that embodies the fundamental law and organization of a political entity. Thus, legal research concerning constitutional law is commonly a search for the authority and limits of government actions. The large body of secondary legal resource materials is especially important to constitutional law research (Table B-3).

Federal Constitution

Research on topics under the United States Constitution is similar to that previously de-

TABLE B-3 Constitution Citation Examples

Federal Constitution[a]

U.S. Const. art. I, sec. 9, cl. 2.

This citation identifies the second clause of the ninth section in the first article of the U.S. Constitution.

U.S. Const. amend. XIX (1919, repealed 1933).

This citation refers to the nineteenth amendment to the U.S. Constitution, enacted in 1919 and repealed in 1933.

State Constitutions

Ark. Const. of 1868, art. III, sec. 2 (1873).

This citation gives the date of adoption of the state constitution, 1868, and the date that article III, section 2 was enacted, 1873.

[a] Note that the word constitution is only capitalized in legal writing when naming any constitution in full or when referring to the U.S. Constitution. The parts of the constitution (e.g., amendments, sections, articles) are not capitalized.

scribed for locating judicial decisions and statutes. Two unofficial annotated editions of the U.S. Constitution are available. In addition, cases interpreting the U.S. Constitution are organized by case digests. West's *United States Supreme Court Digest* classifies constitutional decisions by key number and descriptive words.

State Constitutions

State constitutions frequently correspond to provisions of the U.S. Constitution. The annotated editions of the U.S. Constitution include citations to state constitutions. In addition, state constitution decisions may be found under the Descriptive Word heading of "Constitutional Law" in the West's case digest system.

SECONDARY LEGAL RESOURCES

Secondary legal research materials assist the researcher in finding and understanding primary legal resources. The use of major secondary legal resources and their citation forms are discussed in this section, and examples are shown in Table B-4.

Legal Periodicals

Legal periodicals include academic law reviews, bar association periodicals, commercially published journals, and legal newspapers. An index, the *Index to Legal Periodicals* (ILP), is used to locate articles. The ILP provides four methods of locating periodicals: (1) a subject–author index, (2) a table of cases commented upon, (3) a table of statutes commented upon, and (4) an index of book reviews. A second index, the *Current Law Index*, is similar, except that it includes full subject and author bibliographic information. Cases citing legal periodicals also may be located by using *Shepard's Law Review Citations.*

Legislative History

Legislative history ranges from congressional bills and hearings to House and Senate reports. This information is used by the courts

TABLE B-4   Secondary Legal Resource Citation Examples

I. *Legal Periodicals*

Sagoff, *On Preserving the Natural Environment,* 84 Yale L.J. 205 (1974).

This citation refers to Professor Sagoff's law review article entitled *On Preserving the Natural Environment,* located in volume number 84 of the Yale Law Journal beginning at page 205. The article was published in 1974.

II. *Legislative History*

Forest and Rangeland Renewable Resources Planning Act of 1974, S. Rep. No. 686, 93rd Cong., 2d Sess., *reprinted in* 1974 U.S. Code Cong. & Admin. News 4060.

This citation indicates that Senate Report number 686 of the 93rd Congress concerning the Forest and Rangeland Renewable Resources Planning Act of 1974 is located in the 1974 edition of USCCAN at page 4060.

III. *Administrative and Executive Publications*

36 C.F.R. 211, 219 (1987).

This citation refers to title 36 of the 1987 Code of Federal Regulations, sections 211 and 219, concerning administrative appeals of National Forest Land Management Plans.

36 C.F.R. 251 *as proposed in* Fed. Reg. May 16, 1988 at 17315.

This citation refers to a proposed change in the administrative appeals process of National Forest Land Management Plans, to be located at title number 36 of the code of Federal Regulations, section 251. The proposed change was published in the Federal Register of May 16, 1988, at page 17315.

IV. *Looseleaf Services*

McCloskey and Desautels, *A Primer on Wilderness Law and Policy,* 13 Envtl. L. Rep. (Envtl. L. Inst.) 10278 (Sept. 1983).

This citation refers to McCloskey and Desautels's article entitled *A Primer on Wilderness Law and Policy* located in volume number 13 of the Environmental Law Reporter (published by the Environmental Law Institute) at page 10278. The article was published in September 1983.

Northwest Indian Cemetery Protective Association v. Peterson, 17 Envtl. L. Rep. (Envtl. L. Inst.) 20021 (Jan. 1987).

This citation refers to the case of Northwest Indian Cemetery Protective Association versus Peterson, as located in volume number 17 of the Environmental Law Reporter at page 20021. The case was published in January 1987.

V. *Legal Encyclopedia*

35 Am. Jur. 2d *Fish and Game* sec. 43 (1967).

This citation refers to section 43 concerning water pollution regulation of fish habitat as located in volume 35 of the 1967 edition of American Jurisprudence, a national legal encyclopedia.

29 Encyclopedia of Georgia Law VII, *Water Conservation* sec. 19 (1980 Rev.).

This citation refers to section 19 of Title VII concerning water conservation committees as located in volume 29 of the 1980 revision of the Encyclopedia of Georgia Law.

VI. *Treatises and Restatements*

N. Williams, Jr. and J. Taylor, American Land Planning Law sec. 9.20 at 306 (1988 Rev.).

This citation refers to page 306 of section 9.20 concerning "open space" regulation in zoning law as located in the 1988 revision of the treatise entitled American Land Planning Law by Williams and Taylor.

C. Wilkinson and H. Michael Anderson, Land and Resource Planning in the National Forests sec. 2 at 46 (1987).

This citation refers to section 2 of Wilkinson and Anderson's treatise on national forest planning, page 46. The treatise was published in 1987.

VII. *Legal Textbooks and Commercial Study Aids*

T. Schoenbaum, *Environmental Policy Law,* 41-45 (1982).

This citation refers to Professor Schoenbaum's casebook entitled Environmental Policy Law, pages 41 to 45. The book was published in 1982.

R. Wright and S. Webber, *Land Use,* 19–25 (1984).

This citation refers to West's "nutshell edition" entitled Land Use, pages 19 to 25. The "nutshell" was published in 1984.

to understand the congressional intent underlying statutes. These materials may be accessed through many research aids. The *Congressional Record* provides both a daily digest and a biweekly table, *The History of Bills and Resolutions,* for tracking bills through Congress. The *CCH Congressional Index* offers an index of all public general bills and a status table of actions taken on bills and resolutions. Finally, the *United States Code Congressional & Administrative News* (USCCAN) publishes the House and Conference Committee Reports for important legislative proposals.

Administrative and Executive Publications

The growth in the administrative state has resulted in an explosion of administrative regulations having the effect of statutory law. To understand these regulations, a researcher must start with the enabling legislation authorizing an agency to develop administrative rules. Agency regulations first appear in the *Federal Register.* Some enabling statutes (e.g., the National Forest Management Act) require solicitation of public comment before the proposed regulation is incorporated into the *Code of Federal Regulations.* Eventually, a regulation may be codified in the *United States Code* and attain the status of statutory law. Administrative materials are located by using subject indexes and the *United States Code Annotated.*

Looseleaf Services

A "looseleaf" service is a set of law books that is continuously updated by regular insertion of new pages and removal of superceded materials. A looseleaf collection is essentially a minilibrary on a specialized topic. For example, the Bureau of National Affairs' *Environmental Reporter* includes cases, statutes, and administrative regulations concerning environmental issues in one set of books. Primary legal resources may be located in a looseleaf collection by using subject indexes and the table of cases or statutes.

Legal Encyclopedias

Legal encyclopedias are useful for case-finding and introductory research but are seldom cited as independent authorities. The two national encyclopedias, *Corpus Juris Secundum* (West) and *American Jurisprudence 2d,* offer general descriptions on legal issues and citations to related statutes and cases. State encyclopedias are similar, except that they focus on the cases in a particular state. Key words and subject indexes are used to locate legal topics within the encyclopedias.

Treatises and Restatements

A treatise is a narrative text that discusses the central topics of a legal subject area in a logical sequence. Treatises cite primary legal resources to support the principles stated. Encyclopedic treatises comprehensively cover an area of the law. Hornbooks are a form of treatise used as a supplement to casebook study. Hornbooks are designed to succinctly introduce the terminology and fundamental principles of an area of the law. Restatements of the law are prepared under the direction common law developed by judicial decision and interpretation of statutory law. As the product of scholarly effort, restatements are often criticized as stating what the law *ought* to be rather than what the current law *is.* Treatises and restatements are located by using the card catalog.

Words and Phrases

Words and Phrases is a specialized digest that organizes judicial decisions by the legal terms of act used by courts. Case abstracts are classified by special words and phrases that they define, interpret, or construe. This digest is particularly important when the resolution of a legal issue depends upon the meaning of a statutory phrase.

Legal Casebooks and Commercial Study Aids

Legal casebooks are an excellent source for the historical and leading cases relating to a specific legal subject. Casebooks are designed to provoke questions to facilitate self-study in a particular area of the law. Thus, they provide little explanation or discussion to assist the nonlawyer's research. "Nutshell" summaries (West) are an example of the numerous commercial legal aids available to supplement the law in an attempt to distill "legal truths" from complex cases and statutes. Legal texts and study aids are located by using the card catalog.

REFERENCES

Cohen, M., and R. Berring. 1984. Finding the Law, 8th ed. West Publishing Company.

How to Use Shepard's Citations. 1987. McGraw-Hill, New York.

Legal Research Primer. (undated). Lawyers Co-operative Publishing Company.

A Uniform System of Citation, 14th ed. (1986). Harvard Law Review Association. Boston.

Appendix C

Forest Resource Policy Acronyms

AAAS	American Association for the Advancement of Science	ASCS	Agricultural Stabilization and Conservation Service
ACE	Allowable cut effect	ASQ	Allowable Sale Quantity (of national forest timber)
ACP	Agricultural Conservation Program	ATB	America The Beautiful
AFA	American Forestry Association	BLM	Bureau of Land Management
AFS	American Fisheries Society	BOR	Bureau of Outdoor Recreation (see HCRS)
AFRA	American Forest Resource Alliance	CBO	Congressional Budget Office
AFC	American Forest Council, formerly AFI	CCC	Civilian Conservation Corps
AFI	American Forest Institute	CEQ	Council on Environmental Quality
AFRA	American Forest Resource Alliance	CERCLA	Comprehensive Environmental Response, Compensation, and Liability Act of 1980 (Hazardous Waste)
ANILCA	Alaska National Interest Lands Conservation Act of 1980		
APA	American Pulpwood (or Plywood) Association	CFA	Cooperative Forestry Assistance Act
API	American Paper Institute	CFM	Cooperative Farm Management Program
ARC	Agricultural Resources Conservation Program	COE	Corps of Engineers
		CRP	Conservation Reserve Program

*Adapted from Dana and Fairfax 1980.

CWA	Clean Water Act	FORPLAN	Forest Planning model, used by the USDA Forest Service
DEIS	Draft Environmental Impact Statement		
"DJ funds"	Money for state fisheries programs under Dingell-Johnson Act	FPRS	Forest Products Research Society
		FWPCA	Federal Water Pollution Control Act
DNR	Department of Natural Resources	FWS	Fish and Wildlife Service, or USFWS
EA	Environmental Assessment		
ECARP	Environmental Conservation Acreage Reserve Program	GAO	General Accounting Office
		GLO	General Land Office
		HCRS	Heritage and Conservation Resources Service (formerly BOR)
EDF	Environmental Defense Fund		
EEP	Environmental Easement Program	HEW	Health, Education and Welfare, Department of; now Health and Human Services
EIS	Environmental Impact Statement		
EPA	Environmental Protection Agency	"K-V"	Programs and funding under the Knutson-Vandenberg Act
ERTA	Economic Recovery Tax Act of 1981		
		LMP	Land Management Plan (for a national forest)
ESA	Endangered Species Act		
FACT ACT	Food, Agriculture, Conservation, and Trade Act of 1990 (farm bill)	LRMP	Land and Resource Management Plan (for a national forest)
FAO	Food and Agricultural Organization of the United Nations	LWCF	Land and Water Conservation Fund
		MBF	Thousand Board Feet
FEIS	Final Environmental Impact Statement	MMPA	Marine Mammal Protection Act
FEPCA	Federal Environmental Pesticide Control Act	MU-SY	Multiple-Use Sustained-Yield Act
FICTVT	Forest Industries Committee on Timber Valuation and Taxation	NASF	National Association of State Foresters
		NDEF	Nondeclining even flow, a sustained yield goal
FIFRA	Federal Insecticide, Fungicide and Rodenticide Act	NEPA	National Environmental Policy Act of 1969
FIP	Forestry Incentives Program	NFMA	National Forest Management Act of 1976
FLPMA	Federal Land Policy Management Act	NFPA	National Forest Products Association

NFS	National Forest System division of the USFS	PILT	Payments in Lieu of Taxes Act
NGO	Nongovernment Organizations	PLLRC	Public Land Law Review Commission (1970)
NIPF	Nonindustrial private forest (also PNIF)	PNIF	see NIPF
NIPFL	Nonindustrial private forest landowner	"PR funds"	Money for state wildlife programs under Pittman-Robertson Act
NIRA	National Industrial Recovery Act	PRIA	Public Rangeland Improvement Act of 1978
NMFS	National Marine Fisheries Service	RARE II	Roadless Area Review Evaluation II
NOAA	National Oceanic and Atmospheric Administration	RCRA	Resource Conservation and Recovery Act of 1976 (solid waste disposal)
NPDES	National Pollution Discharge Elimination System	REA	Rural Electrification Administration
NPS	National Park Service	REAP	Rural Environmental Assistance Program
NRDC	National Resources Defense Council	RPA	Forest and Rangelands Renewable Resources Planning Act of 1974
NRPA	National Recreation and Parks Association		
NWPS	National Wilderness Preservation System	SAF	Society of American Foresters
O&C	Oregon & California lands	SCORP	State Comprehensive Outdoor Recreation Plans
OCS	Outer Continental Shelf		
OMB	Office of Management and Budget	SCS	Soil Conservation Service
ORRRC	Outdoor Recreation Resources Review Commission (1960)	SEA	Science and Education Administration
		Section 404	Wetland Dredge & Fill Permit Process of FWPCA
OSHA	Occupational Safety and Health Administration		
OTA	Office of Technology Assessment, U.S. Congress	Sections 208, 319	Nonpoint Source Pollution Control Process of FWPCA
PAPTE	President's Advisory Panel on Timber and the Environment (1972)	SES	Soil Erosion Service
		SFI	Southern Forest Institute or Sport Fishing Institute
PCAO	President's Commission on Americans Outdoors	SFPA	Southern Forest Products Association
PETA	People for the Ethical Treatment of Animals	SIP	Stewardship Incentives Program

SRM	Society for Range Management	USDI	United States Department of the Interior
S&PF	State and Private Forestry division of USFS	USFS	United States Forest Service; or USDA Forest Service
TAPPI	Technical Association of the Pulp and Paper Industry	USFWS	United States Fish and Wildlife Service
TGA	Taylor Grazing Act	USGS	United States Geological Survey
TSI	Timber Stand Improvement	WMI	Wildlife Management Institute
TWS	The Wildlife Society		
TVA	Tennessee Valley Authority	WQIP	Water Quality Improvement Program
USAID	U.S. Agency for International Development	WRP	Wetlands Reserve Program
		WWPA	Western Wood Products Association
USC	United States Code		
USCA	United States Code Annotated	YACC	Young Adult Conservation Corps
USDA	United States Department of Agriculture	YCC	Youth Conservation Corps

Index

Abbey, Edward, 210
Acid rain, 377
Administrative appeal, 338, 342
Advertising, 258, 268
Ad-valorem taxes, 190, 453
Agencies, 164, 167, 292
Agenda:
    formal, 80
    systemic, 80
Agenda 21, 504
Agenda setting, 78, 88, 275
Agendas, 80
Agnew, Spiro, 84
Agricultural Conservation and Stabilization
    Service, 457
Agricultural Conservation Program, 457
Agroforestry, 500
Air Quality Control Regions (AQCRs), 376
Alaska National Interest Lands Conservation
    Act, 313, 528
Alaska National Lands, 313
Alaska Native Claim Settlement Act of 1971,
    314
Albright, Horace M., 295
Allowable sale quantity (ASQ), 335
Alternative dispute resolution, 93
Amenity values, 50
America the Beautiful (ATB), 475
American Association for the Advancement
    of Science, 214, 228
American Economic Association, 229
American Farm Bureau Federation, 208

American Fisheries Society, 214
American Forest Council, 212
American Forest Resource Alliance, 212, 317
American Forestry Association, 208, 228
American Forests, 208
American Society for the Prevention of
    Cruelty to Animals, 404
American values, 44
Anadromous Fish Conservation Act, 399
Ancient forests, 316
Andrus, Cecil, 154
Animal Damage Control Act, 396
Animal rights, 272
Animal unit month, 300
Anthropocentrism, 237
Antitrust laws, 127
Anti-hunting groups, 272
Anti-hunting issue, 404
Appellate courts, 186
Appropriations, 130, 134
Arbitrary and capricious action, 193
Arctic National Wildlife Refuge (ANWR), 315
Army Corps of Engineers, 170, 307, 366
Arnold, Ron, 233
Articles of Confederation, 285
Association of Forest Service Employees for
    Environmental Ethics, 173, 318
Attention groups, 82
Attentive public, 82
Authorizations, budget, 134
Avoyelles Sportmen's League v. Alexander,
    184

Bald Eagle Act of 1940, 398
Bankhead-Jones Farm Tenant Act, 529
Bayou Marcus Livestock v. *Army Corps of Engineers, 369*
Behan, Richard, 341
Below-cost timber sales, 307
Berglund, Bob, 154
Best Available Pollution Control Technology (BACT), 377
Best Management Practices (BMPs), 47, 112, 356, 378
Big Green, 235
Bill of Rights, 139
Biocentrism, 237
Biodiversity, National Forest Management Act, 407
Biodiversity Convention, 505
Biological diversity, 101, 407, 414
Bitterroot National Forest, 34
Black, Hugo, 201
Block, John, 154
Bolle Report, 34
Books, 264
British conservation, 284
Broad arrow policy, 307, 353
Brower, David, 311
Brown movement, 233
Budget:
   development, 156
   presidential, 156
Budget and Accounting Act of 1921, 156
Budget Reform Act of 1974, 156
Bureau of Biological Survey, 303
Bureau of Fisheries, 303
Bureau of Forestry, 160
Bureau of Indian Affairs, 292, 303
Bureau of Land Management, 116, 170, 289, 299
Bureau of Reclamation, 170, 299
Bureau of the Budget, 156
Bureaucracy, 158
   power, 170
   problems, 171
Burford, Ann, 154
Bush, George, 155, 158, 360
Business regulation, 436

Campaign contributions, 219
   PACS, 219
Canadian lumber, 510

Capital gains timber tax treatment, 450, 537
Capital substitution, 109
Capitalism, 65
Capture, agency, 171
Carbon storage, 522
Carpenter, Farrington, 29
Carter, Jimmy, 45, 154, 308
Case studies, 24
Central planning, 65
Certification:
   fisheries biologist, 244
   foresters, 243
   loggers, 425
   wildlife biologists, 244
Certiorari denied, 188
Circuit courts, 186
Citizen interest groups, 206
Civil law, 126
Civil suits, 178
Civilian Conservation Corps, 293, 356
Claims courts, 189, 361
Clapp, Earle H., 355
Clarke-McNary Act of 1924, 291, 354, 447, 529
Clawson, Marion, 299
Clean Air Act, 375, 529
   1990 amendments, 377
   air pollutants, 375
   control methods, 375
   forest practices, 377
Clean Water Act, 363, 531
Clear-cutting, 33–37, 187, 304, 335, 338, 402
Cleveland, Grover, 290
Climate change, 519
Closed forest, 11
Coastal Management Zone Act of 1972, 378
Coastal zone management, 374, 378
Code of Ethics:
   Society of American Foresters, 244
   The Wildlife Society, 246
Collective goods, 46, 283
Colonial America, 353
Commerce clause, 126
Committee for the Application of Forestry, 64, 354
Common property, 16
Common-pool goods, 46, 283
Community, 45
Competition, market, 52
Compton, Wilson, 49
Conference committees, 143

Conflict resolution, 344
Congressional Budget and Impoundment
    Control Act of 1974, 136, 156
Congressional Budget Office, 158
Congressional Research Service, 139
Congressional staff, 146
Conservation, 67, 226
Conservation compliance, 467
Conservation ethics, 236
Conservation Foundation, 214
Conservation Movement, 228
Conservation Reserve Program (CRP), 462
Constitution, 126, 543
Consulting foresters, 473
Coolidge, Calvin, 153
Cooperative Farm Forestry Act of 1937, 469
Cooperative Forest Management Act, 469
Cooperative Forestry Assistance Act, 469, 529
Cooperative Wildlife Research Unit Program,
    303
Cooperatives, 480
Corps of Engineers, 170, 307, 366
Costle, Douglas, 154
Cost-share rate, 458
Cost-sharing, 458, 487
Council of Economic Advisors, 163
Council on Competitiveness, 360, 371
Council on Environmental Quality, 163, 181,
    363
Court of customs and patent appeals, 189
Court packing, 158
Courts, 183, 193, 194
    appellate, 186
    circuit, 186
    district, 184
    public policy, 193
    state, 189
    tax, 189
    trial, 184
    supreme, 188
Cousteau Society, 208
Creative Act of 1891, 33, 530
Criminal cases, 177
Criminal law, 127
Criteria, 60, 68, 99
Critical habitat, 411
Critical zone, 100
Cross compliance, 465, 467
Crowell, John, 154
Cultural acceptability, 106
Cumberland Island National Seashore, 6

Current-use value laws, property tax, 455
Customs courts, 189
Cutler, Rupert, 154, 312

Darling, Jay N. "Ding," 82, 260, 303
Decision Notice, 339
Deep ecology, 237
Defenders of Wildlife, 208
Deferred payment laws, 454
Deficit, budget, 137
Deforestation, 496
Delegates, 150
Democrats, 205
Department of Defense, 307
Department of the Interior, 292
Depression, 293, 320
Desert Land Sales Act of 1877, 287
Developed countries, policies, 13, 512
Developing countries, 13, 496
Development assistance, 498
Devoto, Bernard, 288
Diminution of value, 358
Dingell-Johnson Sport Fish Restoration Act,
    398, 530
Discounted cash flow, 103
Dispute resolution, 93
Distribution, 59
District courts, 184
Diversity, animal/plant, 335, 336
Doctrine of waste, 357
Douglas, Justice William O., 188
Dred Scott v. *Sanford,* 182
Duck Stamp Act, 395, 534
Ducks Unlimited, 209
Duerr, William, 66, 234

Earth First!, 6, 208, 268
Earth Summit, 269, 503
Echo Park, 311
Ecocentrism, 238
Ecological criteria, 100
Ecological management, 318
Ecological Society of America, 214
Ecology, 237
Economic criteria, 102
Economic efficiency, 51, 102, 108
Economic Recovery Tax Act of 1981, 530
Economic systems, 65
Ecophilosophers, 212

Ecosystem management, 403
Educational films, 268
Efficient market requirements, 51
Eisenhower, Dwight, 153
Electronic broadcasting media, 265
Eminent domain, 357
Endangered species, protection, 409
Endangered Species Act:
    critical habitat, 409
    economics, 413
    listing, 409
    reauthorization, 415
    Section 7, 411
Endangered Species Act of 1973, 196, 332,
    400, 408, 412, 530
Endangered Species Committee, 413
Ends and means hierarchy, 30
Entropy, agency, 171
Environmental, values, 233
Environmental action, 208
Environmental Assessment (EA), 5, 8, 81,
    338, 339
Environmental Conservation Acreage
    Reserve Program, 466
Environmental Defense Fund, 184, 207, 369
Environmental Easement Program, 466
Environmental ethics, 238
Environmental groups, 206, 209
Environmental Impact Statement (EIS), 8,
    81, 332, 338, 362
Environmental Law Institute, 214
Environmental Leadership Conference, 206
Environmental movement, 231, 331
    business, 234
Environmental protection, local, 430
Environmental Protection Agency, 363, 379
Environmentalism, 226, 231
    critics, 232
Environmentalist, definition, 230
Equity, 45, 58, 105, 109
Equity remedy, 192
Ethics, 236
    professional, 242
Executive branch, 153
Executive Office of the President, 161
Executive supervision, 155, 159
Exemption laws, property tax, 455
Expansion strategy, 82
Expenditures, government, 131, 134
Exports, 510–512

Extension programs, 475
Externalities, 55
Exxon Valdez oil spill, 315

Fair market value, 190, 454
Fairfax, Sally, 340
Farm Bill, 374, 460, 462, 466, 475, 532
Farm Bureau, 208
Federal Aid in Fish Restoration Act, 530
Federal Aid in Wildlife Restoration Act of
    1937, 397, 531
Federal Environmental Pesticide Control Act,
    378, 379, 531
Federal Insecticide, Rodenticide, and
    Fungicide Act, 378, 379, 531
Federal land area, 292
Federal Land Policy and Management Act of
    1976, 117, 300, 342, 531
Federal regulation, 354
Federal Water Pollution Control Act
    Amendments of 1972, 363, 531
Fernow, Bernhard E., 229, 270
Financial assistance, 457
Finding of No Significant Impact (FONSI), 8,
    181, 339
Fire control, 480
Fish and wildlife agencies, 479
Fish and Wildlife Coordination Act, 396, 401,
    532
Fish and Wildlife Service, 170, 302, 394, 406,
    409
Fish Restoration and Management Act of
    1950, 398
Fishery Conservation and Management Act
    of 1976, 401
Food Security Act of 1985, 462, 532
Food, Agriculture, Conservation, and Trade
    Act of 1990 (Farm Bill), 460, 462, 466,
    475
Ford, Gerald R., 333
Foreign aid, 498
Foreign aid agencies, 498
Foreign policy, 157, 498
Foreign trade, 505–512
Forest and Rangeland Renewable Resources
    Planning Act of 1974, 327, 332, 532
Forest and Rangeland Renewable Resources
    Research Act, 533
Forest area, 10

Forest conservation movement, 159
Forest Farmers Association, 167, 213
Forest fires, 291
Forest Pest Management Act of 1947, 480
Forest policy:
  analysis, 31
  approaches, 23
  definition, 18
  elements, 17
  formulation, 87
  history, 23
  institutional, 25
  instruments, 18
  objectives, 28, 30
  process, 28
  statements, 19
Forest practice law, 355
Forest product companies, 20
Forest Products Research Society, 214
Forest protection programs, 479
Forest Reform Network, 197, 318
Forest Research, 28
Forest Reserve Act (1891), 33, 530
Forest Reserve Organic Administration Act,
  19, 33, 290, 350, 536
Forest reserves, 159–161, 290
Forest Service, 159, 167, 170, 187, 196, 304,
  311, 317, 354, 387, 478
  bureaucracy, 171
  ideology, 172
  International Forestry, 28
  issue identification, 79
  organization, 33–37
  planning, 327
Forest Service experiment stations, 478
Forest Stewardship Act, 470, 478
Forest Stewardship Program, 475
Forest Wildlife Refuge Act of 1934, 397
Forestland preservation, local, 432
Forestry development, 24–28
Forestry Incentives Program, 108, 457, 528
Forestry roundtable, 95
Formulation, policy, 87
FORPLAN, 334, 338
Four Notch, 5
Franklin, Jerry, 318
Freedom, 105
Friends of Animals, 208, 272
Friends of the Earth, 207
Fritz, Edward G. "Ned," 197, 318

Fuelwood, 13, 495, 506
Fund for Animals, 208

Gaia, 237
Game management, 388
Gang of Ten, 206
Gatekeepers, 81
General Accounting Office, 117, 138, 139
General Land Office, 288, 292
General public, 82
General Revision Act of 1891, 290
Giltmeier, James, 341
Global Tomorrow Commission, 209
Global Warming Convention, 505
Goals:
  forestry, 30
  public, 484
  wildlife, 386
God Committee, 413
Golden fleece award, 108
Gorsuch, Anne, 154
Government advocates, 64, 70
Gramm-Rudman-Hollings Act of 1985, 137
Grant, Ulysses S., 153
Grazing policy, 116
Grazing Service, 298
Greatest good, 160
Green Movement, 212
Greenhouse effect, 519
Greenpeace USA, 208
Group theory, 202

Habitat management, 392
Habitat protection, 432
Hardwood, 13
Harper Cliffs Timber Sale, 338
Harrison, William H., 286
Hearings, 143, 219
Hearst, William Randolph, 258
Herbicides, 254
Hetch Hetchy Valley, 294
Hierarchy, environmental needs, 234
Hierarchy, human needs, 234
Historical approach, 23
Hollywood, 267
Holmes, Oliver Wendell, 358
Homestead Act, 288
Hoover Dam, 298

Hough, Franklin B., 228
Humane groups, 405
Humphrey, Hubert H., 36, 311, 332
Hunting and fishing licenses, 391
Hunting rights, 406

Ickes, Harold, 298
Identification groups, 82
Imperfect competition, 58
Imperfect knowledge, 57
Incentive programs:
　Europe, 516
　federal, 448
　state, 461
Income tax, 449
　capitalizing expenses, 450, 451
　management cost deductions, 451
Incrementalism, 90
Indians, *see* Native Americans
Individualism, 44
Industrial plantation, 501
Industrial roundwood, 13, 505
Insects and disease, 480
Interest group, 20, 81, 167
　decision-making, 215
　definition, 201
　development, 215
　free-rider problem, 222
　operating budgets, 222
　problems, 221
　process, 216
　strategies, 217
　structure, 216
　tactics, 218
　tax-exempt status, 222
　types, 206
International development, 497
International Forestry, 28, 494
International trade, 505
　Canada, 510
　Japan, 510
Inter-agency relationships, 169
Inverse condemnation, 361
Investment tax credit, 452
Iron triangle, 166, 171, 203
Issue:
　characteristics, 83
　creation, 77
　definition, 77

expansion, 80–83
global, 496
types, 79
Issue networks, 203
Izaak Walton League of America, 207
Izaak Walton League v. *Butz,* 187

Jefferson, Thomas, 285
Jeopardize:
　definition, 411
　wildlife, 414
Johnson, Lyndon B., 92
Johnstown flood, 291
Judicial decisions, 540
Judicial review, 182
Judiciary, 176, 183
　actions, 191
　decision processes, 191
　powers, 182
　remedies, 192
　structure, 183

King George III of England, 158
Knutson-Vandenburg (KV) Act of 1930, 131,
　307, 344

Lacey Act of 1900, 355, 394, 533
Lacey, John, 302
Lake Mead, 298
Land acquisitions, 285, 319
Land and Water Conservation Fund Act, 319,
　398, 533
Land ethic, 67, 240, 242, 389
Land Ordinance of 1785, 287
Land reservations, 309
Land use regulation, 189
Law, 126, 176, 178
　administrative, 179
　definition, 178
　fish and game, 390
　forest practice, 355
　legislative, 179
　sources, 179
　statutory, 179
　types, 178
　wildlife, 354
Law enforcement, wildlife, 391

Laws:
  civil, 126
  criminal, 127
  environmental, 127
  environmental protection, 431
  local, 429
  public safety, 429
  urban/suburban, 430
Le Master, Dennis, 341
Leasing programs, 474
Legal citations, 176
Legal research, 540
Legislators:
  delegates, 150
  influences, 147
  issue selection, 148
  philosophy, 149
  trustees, 150
Legislature, 125
  committees, 144
  limitations, 139
  natural resource committees, 145
  organization, 142
  powers, 125
  process, 140
Leopold, Aldo, 3, 67, 240, 310, 356, 387,
  390
Licenses:
  forester, 243
  hunting and fishing, 391
  logging, 425
Limits to Growth, 503
Line-item veto, 156
Listing species, 409
Loan conditionality, 499
Lobbying, 202
Lobbyist, 212
Local regulation, 429
  causes, 433
  types, 429
Log exports, 511
Louisiana Purchase, 285
Lujan, Manuel Jr., 155, 414
Luther, Martin, 44

Madigan, James, 155
Magazines, 261
Maine Forest Practice Law, 439
Man and Nature, 289

Management:
  ecosystem, 403
  wildlife, 386
Marbury v. *Madison*, 182
Marine Mammal Protection Act, 534
Marine Mammal Protection Act, 400, 534
Market:
  failure, 55
  goods, 46
  information, 25
  political, 71
  private, 71
  proponents, 61–69
Market processes, 523
Marshall, Alfred, 51
Marshall, Robert, 310, 356, 389
Marsh, George Perkins, 289
Marx, Karl, 59
Maslow, Abraham, 234
Mass communication, 253
Mass media, 253
Mather, Stephen T., 295
McGee, W. T., 293
McGuire, John, 341
McIntire-Stennis Act of 1962, 478, 534
McKinley, William, 159, 290
McSweeney-McNary Act of 1928, 477, 534
Mean annual increment, 99
Media, 9, 275
  education, 259
  entertainment, 259
  roles, 256
  types, 260
  effectiveness, 275
  influence, 276
Mediation and negotiation, 93
Mendez, Chico, 497
Micro-politics, 33
Migratory Bird Conservation Act, 395, 534
Migratory Bird Hunting Stamp Act, 534
Migratory Bird Treaty Act, 176, 395, 534
Millage rate, 454
Mining Law of 1872, 288
Mixed economy, 66
Mixed scanning, 93
Modified assessment laws, property tax, 455
Monkeywrenchers, 210, 237
Monongahela Decision (1975), 36
Monongahela National Forest, 34, 187
Montreal Protocol, 158

Moseley, James, 155
Motion pictures, 267
Muddling through, 90
Muir, John, 229, 294
Multiple demands, 331
Multiple use, 338
Multiple-use planning, 327
Multiple-Use Sustained-Yield Act of 1960, 19, 327, 330, 535
Music, 266

National Ambient Air Quality Standards (NAAQS), 376
National Association of State Foresters, 167
National Audubon Society, 207
National Environmental Policy Act of 1969, 8, 179, 332, 361, 535
National Forest Management Act of 1976, 20, 36, 90, 327, 334, 535
  diversity requirements, 402
  planning, 335, 337, 343
National Forest Products Association, 212, 317
National Forest System (NFS), 15, 28, 291, 304–306
National Geographic Society, 208
National Marine Fisheries Service, 409
National Park Service, 293, 294
  park land types, 295
National Park Service Organic Act, 19, 535
National Park System, 149, 294
National Parks and Conservation Association, 207
National Pollutant Discharge Elimination System, 364
National Recovery Administration (NRA) Codes, 355
National Rifle Association, 208
National Trails System Act, 313, 536
National Wild and Scenic Rivers Act, 312
National Wilderness Preservation System, 5, 312
National Wildlife Federation, 207, 303, 356
National Wildlife Refuge System Administration Act, 399, 536
National Wildlife Refuges, 303, 402
Native Americans, 286, 303
Natural resource agencies, 167
Natural Resources Council of America, 209
Natural Resources Defense Council, 207, 339

Nature Conservancy, 209
Negotiation, 345
Neoclassical economic theory, 51
New forestry, 318
New perspectives, 37, 318
New Zealand, 54
Newell, Frederick H., 159, 293
News:
  interpretation, 256
  reporting, 256
Newspapers, 260
Nixon, Richard, 153, 156, 333
Nongame wildlife, 390
Nongovernmental organizations (NGOs), 498
Nonindustrial private forests (NIPFs), 15, 153, 156, 446, 459, 485
Nonmarket:
  costs and benefits, 55
  failure, 53
  goods, 46
Normal silviculture, 185
Northern spotted owl, 316, 414
Notification, forest practices, 424
Nuisance, legal definition, 354, 356

Office of Management and Budget, 156, 161
Office of Technology Assessment, 139
Old growth, 306, 316
Olmstead, Frederick Law, 309
Open forest, 11
Option value, 101
Oregon Forest Practice Act, 426
Organic Administration Act of 1897, 19, 33, 290, 330, 536
Osceola, 286
Outdoor recreation programs, 296
Outdoor Recreation Resources Review Committee (ORRRC), 88, 296, 320
Oversight powers, 138
Ownership:
  forest land, 15, 513
  wildlife, 385
Ozone depletion, 377
O'Toole, Randall, 344

Pacific Northwest Planning Act, 401
Packwood Amendment, 452, 536
Patent appeals, 189

Payments in Lieu of Taxes, 131, 456
People for the Ethical Treatment of Animals
    (PETA), 272
Permits:
    wetland Section 404, 367
    logging and forest practices, 424
Peshtigo fire, 56
Pigou, Alfred, 56
Pinchot, Gifford, 3, 159–161, 172, 229, 271,
    291, 328
Pine beetle, 5
Pittman-Robertson Wildlife Restoration Act,
    397, 531
Planning, 332
Planning/appeal process, 337, 343
Plantation forestry, 501
Pocket veto, 155
Police power, 126, 356, 359
Policy, 16
    acronyms, 547
    adoption, 89
    advocacy, 98
    analysis, 98
    courts, 193
    definition, 16
    foreign aid, 499
    formulation, 87, 164
    implementation, 164
    importance, 10
    international trade, 509
    law, 178
    participants, 88
    tax, 447
    wildlife management, 390
Policy process, 76
Policy process model, 31
    applications, 37
    limitations, 37
Political action committee (PAC), 202, 219
Political cartoons, 260
Political parties, 205
Politics:
    criteria, 107
    initial realities, 39
Pollution:
    air, 375
    water, 363
Pork-barrel, 149
Powell, John Wesley, 292, 297
Practicality criteria, 106
Predator control, 396

Preservation, 229
Preservationists, 316
Presidency, 153
Presidential powers, 154
    appointment, 154
    budget, 156
    foreign policy, 157
    legislation, 155
    limitations, 158
    supervision, 155
Presidential/congressional relations, 161
President's Commission on Americans
    Outdoors (PCAO), 297
Prevention of Significant Deterioration
    (PSDs), 377
Print media, 260
Private goods, 46, 283
Private property rights groups, 319
Privatization, 53, 54, 468
Problem, definition, 77
Procedural approach, 28
Procedural law/failings, 192
Procedural rules, 181
Professions:
    associations, 212
    definition, 243
    ethics, 243
    professionalism, 243
    professionals, 273
Program evaluation, 116
Program implementation, 110
    committment, 113
    cost/benefits, 115
    direct federal involvement, 116
    enforcement, 113
    monitoring, 112
    quantitative standards, 112
    specific goals, 111
Progressive conservation movement, 161,
    404
Property rights, 52, 385
Property tax, 189, 453
Public choice theory, 53
Public domain, looting, 288
Public image, 272
Public interest, 358
Public intervention, 523
Public involvement, 106
Public Land Law Review Commission, 88,
    299
Public lands, disposition, 287

Public opinion:
   environment, 227
   influencing, 258
   Texas, 5
Public ownership, 283, 289
Public participation, 335
Public relations, 221, 255, 258, 269
Pure enterprise, 66

Radio, 265
Range, 48
   ecological indicators, 300
   rangeland, 299
Range Inventory Standardization Committee,
   301
Rationalism, 89
Reagan, Ronald, 154
Reasonably Available Control Measures
   (RACM), 378
Rebate laws, 454
Recreation, 49, 388
Red-cockaded woodpecker (RCW), 195
Reforestation Tax Incentives, 452, 536
Registration:
   forester, 243, 425
   logger, 425
Regulation:
   alternatives, 438
   business, 436
   constitutionality, 357–361
   Europe, 513
   local, 429
   powers, 359
   state forest practices, 420
   water quality, 436
   wildlife, 385
Reilly, William, 155
Renew America, 481
Renewable Natural Resources Foundation,
   215
Renewable Resources Extension Act of 1978,
   475, 536
Renewable Resources Planning Act, 532
Republicans, 205
Research, 477, 479
   evaluation, 471
   Forest Service, 28
   groups, 213
   wildlife and fish, 479

Reserved powers, 126
Resource managers, 238, 272
Resources for the Future, 213
Revenue Act of 1943, 537
Revenues, 130
Rio Declaration, 503
Rio Earth Summit, 268, 503
Roadless Area Review II, 312
Road-building, 307
Robertson, Dale, 342
Roosevelt, Franklin Delano, 153, 158, 293
Roosevelt, Theodore, 153, 159–161, 228,
   291, 294, 302
Rotation ages, 336
Ruckelshaus, William, 41
Rutledge, Richard, 299

Sand County Almanac, 240, 389
Schumacher, E. F., 67
Schurz, Carl, 290
Section 208 of Clean Water Act, 364
Section 319 of Clean Water Act, 364
Section 402 of Clean Water Act, 364
Section 404 of Clean Water Act, 366
Section 631 of IRS Code, 450
Section 7 of Endangered Species Act, 411
Seed tree laws, 355, 421
Seedling production, 468
Shrubland, 11
Sierra Club, 5, 34, 207
Sikes Act, 398, 537
Silvicultural exemptions, wetlands, 367
Smith, Adam, 51
Smith-Lever Act of 1914, 475
Smokey Bear, 84
Snail darter, 412
Social criteria, 104
Social discount rate, 57
Social forestry, 499
Society of American Foresters, 214, 244,
   354
Society of Range Management, 214
Sodbuster, 465, 467
Softwood, 13
Soil and Water Conservation Society,
   215
Soil Bank Act of 1956, 537
Soil Bank Program, 462
Soil Conservation Service, 170, 470

Soil Erosion Service, 356
Sound bites, 265
Special courts, 189
Species:
    endangered, 409, 410
    reintroduction, 6
    taking, 411
    threatened, 410
Sport Fishing Institute, 215
Spotted owl, 316, 414
Staff:
    committee, 146
    personal, 146
Standing committees, 143
Standing to sue, 188
State and local land, 308
State and Private Forestry, 28, 167, 470,
    476
State budgets, 133
State Comprehensive Outdoor Recreation
    Plan, 321
State forest practice laws, 420, 423
    administration, 423
    applicability, 425
    modern laws, 423
    practices regulated, 426
    purposes, 423
    violations/penalties, 425
State incentive programs, 461
State of the Union address, 155
State v. *Dexter*, 359
States:
    budgets, 133
    courts, 189
Statute citators, 542
Statutes, 126
Statutory law, 179
Stewardship Incentive Program, 460
Strategic Lawsuit Against Public Participation
    (SLAPP), 232
Streamside Management Zones (SMZs),
    378
Substantive law, 181
Subsystem politics, 33
Supreme Court, 188
Sustainable development, 104, 500
Sustainable Forestry Roundtable, 95
Sustained yield, 99
Swampbuster, 465, 467
Symbols, 83, 273

Taft, William, 169
Taking:
    private property, 356
    wildlife, 414
Tax deductions, 451
Taxation, 447
    income, 449
    Europe, 516
    property, 189, 453
Taylor, Edward, 298
Taylor Grazing Act of 1934, 117, 294,
    397, 537
Technical assistance, 469, 487
    consulting foresters, 474
    industrial, 474
    private, 473
    program evaluations, 470
    wildlife management, 476
Technocentrism, 238
Tecumseh, 286
Television, 266
Tellico Dam, 412
Tennessee Valley Authority (TVA),
    294
Tenure rights, 500
Texas Committee on Natural Resources
    (TCONR), 6, 197
Think tanks, 89, 212
Threatened species, 317, 410
Timber Culture Act of 1873, 287
Timber and Stone Act of 1878, 287
Timber production, 47, 486
Timber salvage, 5
Timber supply, 109
Timberland, 11
Timber/Fish/Wildlife agreement,
    94
Tocqueville, Alexis de, 45
Toll goods, 46
Tongass National Forest, 314
Trade associations, 212
Transaction costs, 52
Transfer Act of 1905, 19, 160, 291
Tree Farm Program, 84
Trial courts, 184
Trickle-down theory, 105
Tropical deforestation, 496
Tropical forests, 495
Trout Unlimited, 209
Twenty-five percent fund, 456

United Nations Commission on Sustainable
    Development, 504
United Nations Conference on Environment
    and Development (UNCED), 269, 503
Urban and Community Forestry Assistance
    Program, 475
Use-value taxation, 455
Usufructuary rights, 357
Utilitarian, 229
U.S. Agency for International Development
    (USAID), 498

Valdez oil spill, 315
Valdez Principles, 234
Values, 44, 234
Veto, 155, 156
Voting records, 221

Wallop-Breaux Funds, 530
Washington State Wilderness Act of 1984,
    127
Water Quality Act, 365, 531, 532
Water Quality Improvement Program,
    466
Water Quality Standards, 112, 365
Water resources, 48, 160
Watt, James, 84, 154
Weeks Law, 291, 538
Weeks-McClean Act, 355
Wetland:
    area, 371
    definition, 370
    mitigation, 373
    protection, 366
    recapture, 368
Wetlands Delineation Manual, 370
Wetlands Reserve Program, 466
Wild and Scenic Rivers Act, 538
Wild Free-Roaming Horses and Burros
    Protection Act, 399
Wilderness, 49, 127, 309, 389
    release, 128
    Washington state, 127

Wilderness Act of 1964, 20, 311, 538
Wilderness Society, 207, 356, 389
Wildlife, 48
    conservation, 209
    definition, 384
    federal lands, 401
    goals, 386
    habitat, 386
    law, 391
    law enforcement, 390
    management objectives, 386
    ownership, 385
    public opinion, 405
    regulation, 385
    take, 390
    water pollution, 400
Wildlife management, 386
Wildlife management assistance, 476
Wildlife Management Institute, 215
Wildlife refuges, 160
Wildlife Society, 214, 246
Wilson, Jim, 160
Wilson, Woodrow, 294
Wise use movement, 233
Woodland, 11
World Bank, 498
World Resources Institute, 215
World War II, 329
World Wildlife Fund, 209
WorldWatch Institute, 215

Yellowstone, 309
Yeutter, Clayton, 155
Yield taxes, 455
Yosemite, 309
Youth Conservation Corps Act, 538

Zahniser, Howard, 311
Z'berg-Nejedly Forest Practice Act of 1973,
    435